John the Blind Audelay

POEMS AND CAROLS

(Oxford, Bodleian Library MS Douce 302)

John the Blind Audelay

POEMS AND CAROLS

(Oxford, Bodleian Library MS Douce 302)

Edited by
Susanna Fein

TEAMS • Middle English Texts Series

MEDIEVAL INSTITUTE PUBLICATIONS
Western Michigan University
Kalamazoo

Library of Congress Cataloging-in-Publication Data

Audelay, John, fl. 1426.
  Poems and carols : (Oxford, Bodleian Library MS Douce 302) / John the Blind Audelay
; edited by Susanna Fein.
      p. cm. -- (Middle English texts series)
  Text in Middle English; critical material in English.
  Includes bibliographical references and index.
  ISBN 978-1-58044-131-5 (pbk. : alk. paper)
  1. Christian poetry, English (Middle) I. Fein, Susanna Greer. II. Bodleian Library.
Manuscript. Douce 302. III. Title.
  PR1818.A93 2009
  821'.2--dc22
                          2008047893

ISBN 978-1-58044-131-5

Printed in the United States of America

P 5 4 3 2 1

CONTENTS

☙ ACKNOWLEDGMENTS

This edition, the first to present John Audelay's book in its entirety, owes its existence to the support and encouragement of many colleagues. My first debt is to Russell Peck and Derek Pearsall, who urged me to undertake it. Familiar as I was with Audelay, it had not occurred to me to edit his book until I was told it had to be done. Eventually I saw that they were right.

Audelay's opus is both rich and complex, and I find it necessary to sort these acknowledgments in accordance with the chaplain's own varied design. I have benefited often from the wisdom of those who know individual texts well, and I remain deeply grateful to have had ready access to the generosity and profound learning that typifies the community of medievalists. Concerning the fascinating *Piers*-type poem *Marcolf and Solomon*, I have had several rewarding discussions with Richard Firth Green, Derek Pearsall, and James Simpson, and I am grateful to Fiona Somerset, Emily Steiner, and Lawrence Warner for the welcome my work received at the 2007 *Piers Plowman* Conference in Philadelphia. More broadly, regarding the multiple contents of *The Counsel of Conscience*, my knowledge was enhanced by conversations and correspondences with Ann Astell, Robert Easting, Robert Meyer-Lee, Ann Nichols, Veronica O'Mara, Oliver Pickering, Sue Powell, and Martha Rust. In working on Audelay's salutations section, I received valuable feedback from Martha Driver, Sr. Mary Clemente Davlin, Ann Hutchinson, Melissa Jones, Miri Rubin, and Christina von Nolcken, and I was honored to present portions of my findings at the Devotion before Print Conference, University of Chicago, in April 2006. For Audelay's carol collection, I have gained much in conversations with Julia Boffey and John Hirsh. For the devotional prose, I am indebted most of all to Ian Doyle, who generously answered my first letters to him about the Audelay manuscript and its scribes more than a decade ago. Regarding *Three Dead Kings* and its companion *Paternoster*, my debts are more widespread than can be recounted here, but they include support and advice from Larry Benson, the late Morton Bloomfield, Hoyt Duggan, Ruth Kennedy, Ashby Kinch, Sophie Oosterwijk, Ad Putter, Eric Stanley, Thorlac Turville-Petre, and Kathryn Vulic. In sharing with me a desire to see Audelay situated in his times, I must mention Michael Bennett, whose historical investigations have given literary scholars a better sense of where to begin.

Other medievalists who have made a difference in my thinking about Audelay include Tony Edwards, Alan Fletcher, Maureen Jurkowski, Michael Kuczynski, Linne Mooney, Glending Olson, Helen Phillips, and Edward Wheatley, as well as several others with whom I work in near proximity at Kent State University: Radd Ehrman, Elizabeth Howard, Kristen Figg, John Block Friedman, Catherine Rock, and Isolde Thyret. To Radd I owe special gratitude and respect as a resourceful, ever-cheerful comrade in securing accurate translations and sources of Audelay's Latin. It is his translation of *Cur mundus militat* that appears in this edition, and his learning graces the Latin translations throughout; any errors that remain are wholly my own responsibility. I also thank my student Daryl Green.

I have been blessed with generous institutional support for this project. The Kent State Research Council has granted me research release time as well as funds for travel to libraries in the United Kingdom. The Institute for Bibliography and Editing along with the English Department have given me moral and material support. The Middle English Texts Series staff in Rochester — particularly John H. Chandler, Valerie Johnson, Michael Livingston, and Russell Peck — have offered expert assistance and advice at every turn. I am also indebted to Alan Lupack, who served as another editorial reader. I thank the helpful librarians at the Bodleian Library (particularly Greg Colley and Tricia Buckingham), British Library, Kent State University Library, Oberlin College Library (particularly Ed Vermue), Ohio State University Library, and Stonyhurst College Library. I am grateful, too, to the National Endowment for the Humanities for its generous support of the TEAMS editions, and to editor Patricia Hollahan and the staff of Medieval Institute Publications, who are always a pleasure to work with.

A personal note of gratitude goes to my family: to Carolyn, who typed carols into the computer at an early phase of the project; to Elizabeth, who provided me with visuals for an Audelay presentation on short notice; to Jonathan, who likes to suggest that the chaplain-poet's surname is oddly apt; and a profound thank you, as ever, to David.

# INTRODUCTION

The book is finished. Praise and glory be to Christ. The book is called The Counsel of Conscience, thus is it named, or The Ladder of Heaven and the Life of Eternal Salvation. This book was composed by John Audelay, chaplain, who was blind and deaf in his affliction, to the honor of our Lord Jesus Christ and to serve as a model for others in the monastery of Haughmond. In the year 1426 A.D. May God be propitious to his soul. (Finito libro *colophon; MS Douce 302, fol. 22vb; translated from Latin.)*

Whose end is good, is himself entirely good. The book is finished. Praise and glory be to Christ. No man remove this book, nor cut out any leaf, for I tell you, sirs, it would be a sacrilege! Be accursed in this deed, truly! If you wish to have any copy, ask permission, and you shall have [it], to pray for him especially who made it to save your souls, John the Blind Audelay. He was the first priest of Lord Lestrange [assigned] to this chantry, here in this place, who made this book by God's grace — deaf, sick, blind, as he lay. *May God be propitious to his soul.* (*Audelay's Conclusion*, lines 40–52, MS Douce 302, fol. 34ra–b; translated from Latin and Middle English.)

Almost everything known about John the Blind Audelay, *capellanus*, is contained in the medieval book edited here, Oxford, Bodleian Library MS Douce 302. The passages quoted above conclude two of its sections. They highlight a prominent feature of the book, that is, how often it is stamped with the name of Audelay, as if to preserve his worldly memory and ensure prayers for his soul's salvation. But such recurrent passages, taken as contemporary comments, are not without ambiguity. Does the closing benediction — "Cuius anime propicietur Deus" (May God be propitious to his soul) — indicate that Audelay was already dead when the scribe wrote it? Or is Audelay himself directing the scribe's actions and overseeing this commemorative performance on his own behalf? The answer would seem to be the latter, that Audelay is still alive and close at hand, because the Middle English portion of the second passage (rendered above in roman font) is composed in Audelay's favored 13-line stanza and dotted with his distinctive tags of moral admonition ("I tell you, sirs, . . . truly!"). At the same time, the portrait of John the Blind Audelay drawn in this stanza is set eerily in past tense, as if the poet were imagining himself as already a dead man lying supine on his deathbed ("He *was* . . . he *lay*").

The persistent naming of John the Blind Audelay in MS Douce 302 works overall to make the book identifiable as an anthology of the collected works of an early fifteenth-century poet. Poets in medieval England were virtually never broadcast by name in the way seen here. This aspect of the Audelay manuscript represents something different and novel, and it begs for an explanation, especially since most poetry of the period comes wrapped in blank papers, that is, without any degree of scribal attribution or authorial self-naming. The creator of the Audelay manuscript clearly relishes self-ascription. Audelay's name appears sixteen times on thirty-five vellum leaves, fourteen of those instances in Middle English verse and

1

two in Latin prose (in the colophon cited at the head of this introduction and the incipit of
a poem honoring Saint Bridget). The instances in Latin might have been provided by a
scribe, but, considering the general manner of the book, we may safely assume that they too
belong with the poet's overt agenda of declaring his name from the leaves of a book.

The development of what has been called "the author collection" is a subject of some
interest as literary scholars seek to know how the sense of an "author" as an entity of author-
ized authority — that is, as a named writer whose works would merit an anthology — grad-
ually came into being in England sometime during the late fourteenth or early fifteenth cen-
tury. The evidence varies, of course, as one examines the various manuscripts containing
the attributed and nonattributed works of different writers — Chaucer, Hoccleve, Lydgate,
Gower, Langland, the anonymous works of Cotton Nero A.x. — and it differs according to
the criteria one chooses. One may, for example, examine an author's own statements. When
in the lyric "Adam Scriveyn" Chaucer puts a curse upon the scribe who would miswrite his
words, he asserts as an author that his precise words *do* matter.[1] In *Troilus and Criseyde* Chau-
cer pens another plea that his words not be altered:

> And for ther is so gret diversite
> In Englissh and in writyng of oure tonge,
> So prey I God that non myswrite the,
> Ne the mysmetre for defaute of tonge. (V.1793–96)

Ralph Hanna calls Chaucer's "awareness of the ways he might be misunderstood" both "fas-
tidious" and "prescient,"[2] for it little agrees with the way medieval texts were typically repro-
duced with some indifference to textual variation.

The question of ascription may also be approached from the other end; that is, instead
of thinking about authorial authentication before the accidents of production, one may ex-
amine manuscripts for clues as to how an "anthologizing" impulse came to be exhibited by
compilers or scribes, with works variously attached to the names of their creators. From this
angle, the concept of Chaucer as an author to be named and collected in one place was not
as transparently simple as one might think. In the first decades after Chaucer's death, the
idea does not seem, in A. S. G. Edwards's wry phrase, "to have commended itself readily to
posterity."[3] Given the scarcity of direct attributions to Chaucer and the frequent mixing in
of Chaucerian and non-Chaucerian texts, Edwards concludes that "closed authorial collec-
tions of Chaucer's works seem atypical: the more general anthologizing tendency was to

---

[1] See especially Hanna's chapter "Presenting Chaucer as Author," pp. 174–94, in *Pursuing History*.
For other statements on medieval authorship and authority, see Minnis, *Medieval Theory of Authorship*;
and Machan's chapter "Authority," pp. 93–135, in *Textual Criticism*. Our view of Chaucer's relation
to his scribe — perhaps identifiable as Adam Pinkhurst — is now much more historically nuanced as
a result of the exacting paleographical research of Mooney, "Chaucer's Scribe."

[2] Hanna, *Pursuing History*, p. 175.

[3] Edwards, "Fifteenth-Century Middle English Verse Author Collections," p. 102; for Edwards'
discussion of Audelay, see p. 105. Attention has been paid in recent years to clarifying how medieval
anthologies differ from miscellanies. On this question, see, e.g., S. Nichols and Wenzel, *Whole Book*;
Lerer, "Medieval English Literature and the Idea of the Anthology"; and Fein, *Studies in the Harley
Manuscript*.

mingle his own works with those of the emergent Chaucerian tradition, linking him with Hoccleve, Clanvowe, Ros, and particularly Lydgate."[4]

Against the backdrop of an emergent English literary tradition, the contents of MS Douce 302, the Audelay manuscript, might seem inconsequential. Yet, in assessing how literary authorship was perceived and how books contributed to a budding culture of vernacular canonicity, one must acknowledge the exceptional status that MS Douce 302 holds among author collections of its day. Produced at a time when the authority of English writers was still in flux, the Audelay manuscript stands at counterpoint to the prevailing trend to treat attributions casually. As a book that ascribes texts with insistence to a contemporary English author, it becomes a living account of what authority and authorship meant in a localized, datable setting in medieval England.

There are, moreover, many other reasons for scholars of medieval English poetry to read John Audelay's book. His idiosyncratic devotional tastes, interesting personal life history, and declared political affiliations — loyalty to king, upholder of estates, anxiety over heresy — make him worthy of careful study beside his better-known contemporaries, for example, John Lydgate, Thomas Hoccleve, and Margery Kempe, all of whom are objects of recent renewed attention.[5] Of particular note: MS Douce 302 preserves Audelay's own alliterative *Marcolf and Solomon*, a poem thought to be descended from Langland's *Piers Plowman*, though the nature of that relationship still requires better definition and better historical-geographical situating. The Audelay manuscript also contains unique copies of other alliterative poems of the ornate style seen in *Sir Gawain and the Green Knight* and *The Pistel of Swete Susan*. These pieces are *Paternoster* and *Three Dead Kings*, both set at the end of the book. Whether or not they are Audelay's own compositions, they seem certain to be his own selections, arranged in his anthology at a deliberate point for a decisive purpose, that is, a sober meditation upon endings and death. Furthermore, to judge from the range of verse styles in his book, Audelay was an aficionado of metrical variety and musical form. In this regard, Audelay deserves keener recognition for his ordered collection of twenty-five carols — not only because a sequence of this kind is rare but also because several individual carols rank high among all medieval verse of this type. Audelay displays a persistent habit of sequencing materials in generic and devotionally affective ways. His is a pious sensibility delicately honed by reverence for liturgy and by an awe of God (and his saints) worshipped by ritual. This aesthetic is perhaps most evident in Audelay's salutations sequence, where he is working in a genre little recognized for its artistic capabilities, and never before noted for its sequential possibilities. That Audelay's poetry can awaken us to new poetic sensitivities in medieval devotional verse is reason enough to bring him into the ambit of canonical fifteenth-century English poets.

The autobiographical element in many MS Douce 302 items is most poignantly featured in the important poems *Audelay's Epilogue to The Counsel of Conscience* and *Audelay's Conclusion*. These works provide revealing hints of a contrition-wracked soul moved to make open declarations of himself as penitent chaplain, instructor of *soulehele*, and divinely inspired

---

[4] Edwards, "Fifteenth-Century Middle English Verse Author Collections," p. 103.

[5] See Fein, "John Audelay and His Book."

author. In signing his verse, Audelay patents a trademark stanza that blends penitential modesty with egotistical assertion.[6] A typical version appears in *Our Lord's Epistle on Sunday*:

> Mervel ye noght of this makyng —
> Fore *I me excuse, hit is not I.*   *excuse myself*
> *Fore this of Godis oun wrytyng*   *this [work is created] by; own*
> That he send doun fro heven on hye,
> Fore I couth never bot he foly.   *high folly*
> He hath me chastist for my levyng;   *chastised; living*
> I thonke my God, my Grace, treuly,
> Of his gracious vesetyng.   *visiting [with affliction]*
>   Beware, serys, I you pray,   *sirs*
>   Fore *I mad this* with good entent,
>   Fore hit is Cristis comawndment;
>   Prays for me that beth present —   *Pray*
>   *My name hit is the Blynd Awdlay.* (lines 196–208; italics added)

In this stanza Audelay denies that he is the true maker of the content. It is instead derived from an inspired source — God, or (in other versions) Anselm, Paul, or the Holy Spirit. Nonetheless, the stanza always ends with an emphasis upon the poetic maker's name, "the Blynd Awdlay," after a statement that he, Audelay (with an emphatic "I"), did make the verse with "good entent."

The passages naming John the Blind Audelay are copied by both of Audelay's two scribes, indicating that they were knowledgeable accomplices in a program to preserve the chaplain-poet's name for posterity. Taking close notice of their shared labor helps to elucidate another ambiguity that hovers about the book's biographical passages. How can it be that Audelay "made" this book if he was, as he often attests, deaf and blind? Scholars agree that this book, MS Douce 302, is the very codex referred to by Audelay when he writes that he "made this bok by Goddus grace, / Deeff, sick, blynd" (*Audelay's Conclusion*, line 51). Thus the book itself serves as witness to the conditions of authorial production, and it may even betray signs of the writing process itself. Although Audelay tells readers repeatedly that he suffers disabilities of hearing and sight, it is inconceivable that he was both wholly blind and wholly deaf during the process of making the book. He would have been, however, very much dependent on his two scribes, and completion of the project probably required a blended process of copying from exemplars, reading aloud, and correcting both by dictation and by reference to written papers. Ultimately, then, the codicological side of the Audelay manuscript is about observing the joint operations of three men who transformed Audelay's collected works into a physical book. They are:

> First, Audelay himself, a secular chaplain retired to a chantry priesthood at Haughmond Abbey in Shropshire, who planned and directed production of an anthology consisting of texts he had authored in the broadest medieval sense of authorship — that is, created from

---

[6] He follows this template five times in *The Counsel of Conscience*. The other instances are *The Remedy of Nine Virtues*, lines 77–89, *Visiting the Sick and Consoling the Needy*, lines 378–90, *The Vision of Saint Paul*, lines 353–65, and *Audelay's Epilogue to The Counsel of Conscience*, lines 495–507, and he crafts variations of it elsewhere.

scratch, or translated, or paraphrased, or borrowed, or recombined in pastiche, or arranged in meaningful sequences.

Second, Scribe A, probably a monk at Haughmond, who executed Audelay's basic plan, copying all but the last two texts in Audelay's prescribed order, but leaving spaces for most of the titles (incipits) and endings (explicits), and occasionally leaving gaps where his copy was defective. Scribe A copied virtually all the signatures that occur within Audelay's verse compositions, so we know that he had direct access to Audelay's conceptual plan (that is, the living poet) and Audelay's papers.

Third, Scribe B, probably another monk at Haughmond, who had the subsequent oversight task of putting in the finishing touches. He added — in red ink — incipits, explicits, textual pointers, small initials, and instructional couplets composed in tones that sound exactly like Audelay. He also added — in blue and red ink — large initials and top-of-column numerals, providing a visual *ordinatio*. Scribe B completed several texts left in a tentative state by Scribe A, proofread and corrected the entire book, and extended the length of the book by adding the two final items. He redacted the biographical passages cited above and put in other passages featuring Audelay's name. Thus Scribe B also had direct access to Audelay and his papers.[7]

In overall design, MS Douce 302 consists of four genre-based mini-anthologies, each with its own internal arrangement in planned sequence. Somewhere between a quarter and a third of the original book does not survive. The greatest loss occurs at the front, where up to nineteen folios are gone.[8] Noting how insistently are recorded John the Blind Audelay's authorship, mission, and moral example in MS Douce 302, we may safely guess that the lost portions held yet more ascriptions to Audelay. While it is fruitless to speculate about the genres or texts that might have figured among Audelay's lost writings, it does seem likely that the original book included a table of contents keyed to Scribe B's numerals and a preface (or opening rubric) meant to emphasize the prevailing presence of Blind Audelay as pastoral author. An influential contemporary book may have been John Mirk's *Instructions for Parish Priests*, written a bit earlier at neighboring Lilleshall Abbey, also an Augustinian house, and no doubt circulating actively among clerical communities in Shropshire when Audelay's book was made. Mirk's verse *Instructions for Parish Priests* opens in the following manner: "God says himself, as we find written, that when the blind lead the blind, into the ditch they both fall, for they do not see where to go; so now do priests go by day."[9] Audelay adopts the stance of the blind man leading the blind, but rightly led by God's illuminating light, while he continues in the manner of Mirk to correct the priesthood, as well as chastise lapses among the other eccesiastical orders and the laity. In stating his own mission, Audelay deploys the theological figure of the Book as the Word. In the last poem of the manuscript, *Audelay's Conclusion*, the poet asserts that the now-complete book conveys "my wyl and my wrytyng" (line 33) while it bears spiritual similitude to "the bok of lyfe in hevun blys" (line 19).

---

[7] For delineation of the division of scribal labor, see the explanatory notes on each text.

[8] Fein, "Good Ends," p. 98n3.

[9] Lines 1–5, my translation. See Peacock, *Instructions for Parish Priests by John Myrc*, p. 1.

Ending upon another note evocative of Mirk's *Instructions for Parish Priests*, the poet then asks for prayers on his behalf and bequeaths the book to future readers for their spiritual benefit.[10]

Almost all of what we know about John the Blind Audelay is contained within the boards of MS Douce 302. We are fortunate, though, to have one life-record for Audelay that is external to the manuscript. A court document from London, dated April 1417, enumerates the members of Lord Richard Lestrange's retinue and includes the name of his chaplain, John Audelay.[11] This detail matches the information found in *Audelay's Conclusion*. From the circumstances of this record, we gain a glimpse of Audelay's earlier life as a secular cleric who traveled routinely to the capital in company with his patron. In this instance, the London stay had a tragic outcome, with Lestrange committing and being arraigned for a high crime: inciting a violent brawl in a London parish church, St. Dunstan's-in-the-East, on Easter Sunday, with a knight severely wounded and an innocent parishioner killed. For this violation of God's house on its most sacred day, Lestrange was jailed in the Tower and then ordered to do penance in the streets of London, walking barefoot and in a plain shift with his wife beside him, and followed by his retinue — including, presumably, his chaplain — from St. Dunstan's to St. Paul's Cathedral. The notoriety and shame of this public spectacle certainly dealt a blow to Lestrange, whose reputation in posterity rests on little else, and it must also have set an indelible blot upon the conscience of John Audelay, Lestrange's spiritual advisor. Since the discovery in 1982 of Audelay's part in this well-known scandal, most scholars accept that Audelay's penitential cast bears the scars of this episode of spiritual and social trauma. Its effect on Audelay seems evident in his incessant expressions of contrition and penance, as well as in his oft-repeated conviction that his ailments are visitations from God, signs of divine punishment now and hoped-for mercy later.

The known facts about the life of John the Blind Audelay may be set out in brief space. In the 1410s and 1420s he was chaplain to Lord Lestrange of Knockin, Shropshire, and after a secular career in service to his patron, dishonorably marked by the shame of 1417, he was appointed priest of the family chantry at nearby Haughmond Abbey, an Augustinian house. Audelay calls himself the "furst prest" of the chantry, so his appointment would seem to have been part of its initial endowment by Lestrange. Audelay need not have taken orders as a monk to have been made one of the Haughmond community. His residence there would have been a means by which Lestrange could provide him with a secure retirement after years of active service. At the same time, Lestrange was purchasing the ongoing strength of the chaplain's prayers for the welfare of his own soul and those of family members, living and deceased. Audelay's role as chantry priest would have been to pray a specified number of times for certain individuals, by name, on an ongoing quotidian basis. In this regard, the preoccupation with naming that occurs in the Audelay manuscript is exceptionally pertinent to Audelay's daily existence.[12]

The making of the Audelay manuscript occurred during this period of Audelay's life, but parts of its contents, perhaps whole sections, were probably composed years before, when Audelay's vocation was as the master of religious instruction and devout entertainment (that is, the singing of pious songs) within a secular household. One can see such materials in each of its four parts — the quasi-liturgical sequences of prayers and indulgences in the

[10] Peacock, *Instructions for Parish Priests by John Myrc*, pp. 59–60.

[11] Bennett, "John Audley: Some New Evidence" and "John Audelay: Life Records."

[12] See Meyer-Lee, "Vatic Penitent."

acephalous penitential *The Counsel of Conscience*; the veneration of female saints and an interest in their *vitae* in the *Salutations*; the convivial *Carols*, some of which are directed to women and seem meant for singing in a hall; and the *Meditative Close*, the part most congruent with the codicological project of making a multi-section book that ends well, which is comprised of narrative, instructional, and allegorical texts that seem to target those in secular life. Even as we may perceive the shades of this original audience, the book that survives declares another group of readers. The *Finito libro* colophon asserts that the first section was compiled "to serve as a model for others in the monastery of Haughmond." So to understand the reception of Audelay's works, we must imagine different audiences in different phases of Audelay's life: the secular nobles of Audelay's active career with Lord Lestrange; the monks who surround him in his later life, when he devotes himself to the anthologizing project; and perhaps, too, an ongoing reception by laity (such as Lestrange) who visit the chantry and know about Audelay by past association, present reputation, or both.[13]

The year 1426, the only exact date found written in the folios of MS Douce 302, appears in the *Finito libro* colophon, at a point two-thirds of the way into the manuscript, and it refers only to *The Counsel of Conscience*. The date does not necessarily designate, therefore, the year of the making of the whole manuscript or its textual elements. The copying of texts into MS Douce 302, during which *The Counsel of Conscience* was teamed with other works, could have occurred later than 1426. For example, it is plausible that Audelay's *King Henry VI* was written after 1426; if it was composed in celebration of the young king's coronation, as Rossell Hope Robbins assumes, then its date would be 1429 or 1431.[14] On the other hand, *Marcolf and Solomon* (the second work found in the manuscript) is usually ascribed a much earlier date, that is, probably before 1414, because it seems to reflect the political climate prior to the Oldcastle uprising.[15] Numerous poems by Audelay, especially the carols, contain borrowings from *True Living* (the first piece in MS Douce 302), so it may be that this item is the oldest work in the book, and that the lost works copied before it were older still.[16] The internal dating questions are thus complex, and the best we may do at this point in our knowledge is assign an approximate range for the manuscript itself, c. 1426–31, because the colophon date tells us neither the date of the book's creation nor the year of Audelay's death. There is, moreover, evidence that the process for ending the book was a drawn-out one, occurring three separate times: first, when Scribe A finished his copy; then later, when Scribe B appended a Latin moral poem; and finally, when Scribe B inscribed the last poem — the poet's address to the reader. This sequence of endings suggests a poet who, living beyond the book's original conception, takes a continuing interest in its closing formulation.[17]

---

[13] It is impossible to say how far Audelay's influence or fame extended beyond the abbey walls. Evidence in the book suggests that Audelay cultivated a persona as blind prophet and public penitent. See Fein, "Good Ends," pp. 101–03.

[14] Robbins, *Historical Poems of the XIVth and XVth Centuries*, p. 108. See also the explanatory note for *King Henry VI*, lines 63–64. A later date for this carol would also pertain to the entire carol collection, for it is a composed set.

[15] See explanatory notes to *Marcolf and Solomon*, lines 242, 501, and 503.

[16] This possibility is suggested by Pickering in "Make-Up," pp. 120, 131–32.

[17] Fein, "Death and the Colophon in the Audelay Manuscript."

THE COUNSEL OF CONSCIENCE

The long colophon on fol. 22v gives the first section of Audelay's anthology a dual title: *The Counsel of Conscience* or *The Ladder of Heaven and the Life of Eternal Salvation.* These two titles suggest the purpose of this first Audelay "book." The chaplain Audelay urges readers to cleanse their souls through contrition and confession, to submit humbly to priestly counsel based in the teachings of Holy Church, and to advance steadily toward heaven through a well-governed life of good deeds. The two titles (the second one abridged to *The Ladder of Heaven*) also appear in the last work of *The Counsel of Conscience, Audelay's Epilogue to The Counsel of Conscience* (lines 417–18). While we thus know exactly where *The Counsel of Conscience* ends, we cannot be sure, as Oliver Pickering has pointed out, just where it begins.[18] The dual title does, however, characterize all the contents that survive before the colophon, with an explicit theme of *soulehele* being raised as early as *Marcolf and Solomon* (lines 526, 798) and mentioned again in *Audelay's Epilogue to The Counsel of Conscience* (line 105).[19]

The Counsel of Conscience seems a miscellaneous mix of texts because the genres contained in it vary a good deal: prayer and Passion meditation, instructions on the mass and tenets of the faith, salutation, pious exhortation, truth-telling voiced by God himself, and even a semi-satiric admonition of the ecclesiastical orders. The poem of the last type is Audelay's *Marcolf and Solomon,* which is famously written in an alliterative style evocative of *Piers Plowman.* Yet all works found in *The Counsel of Conscience* commonly preach with insistence about penance, and they deliver this message in Audelay's distinctive tones. Many texts are based on models (Latin or English) that exist elsewhere, but still they are transmuted into Audelay's idiosyncratic voice. Taken together, the works in *The Counsel of Conscience* provide a representative sampling of the variety of texts of popular devotion promulgated for lay use in fifteenth-century England, and they are far too centered on the veneration of saints, belief in indulgences, and orthodox pastoral practice to invite any sustainable charge of Lollardy, which Audelay nonetheless earnestly denies.[20]

Audelay's *Counsel of Conscience* contains, furthermore, several internal symmetries and recurrent interests, which are evident particularly in its frequent evocations of Passion imagery to be paired with thoughts of reverent things grouped by mystical number, especially the number seven: seven bleedings, seven words on the cross, seven hours of the cross, often to be blended penitentially with thoughts of the seven deadly sins, seven works of mercy, and so on. Many prayers and devotions are grouped in quasi-liturgical sequences, with Audelay poised as the chaplain who leads a congregation or an individual congregant. Study of the many analogues and sources, as well as manuscript indicators, show that he ranged un-self-consciously among a variety of compositional methods: translation from Latin to foster lay understanding; free borrowings from other works and free elaborations; imaginative metrical restylings, with a real preference for a distinctive 13-line stanza; knowledge of many literary types, such as refrain poems and dream visions; original sequencings that mix

---

[18] Pickering, "Make-Up," p. 114.

[19] See also *Virtues of the Mass,* line 3 (and explanatory note). "Sawlehele" is the title applied to the Vernon MS by its compiler; see explanatory note to *Audelay's Epilogue to The Counsel of Conscience,* line 105.

[20] See explanatory notes to *Marcolf and Solomon,* lines 131–43, 501, 678–88, and to *Audelay's Epilogue to The Counsel of Conscience,* lines 248–60; and Fein, "Good Ends," p. 100n9.

old hymns and devotions with fresh instructions and prayers; authorial signposts and marginal asides to readers; and so on.[21]

The unity of *The Counsel of Conscience* rests in its persistent method of instruction on how to gain indulgence for one's sin. The book is in essence a handbook for the remission of sins, with sinfulness understood as a specific quantity of willfully evil deeds and thoughts counted against one's soul. Thus, penitential acts are needed to reduce the tally, which will come to account when God affixes to each soul its final judgment. Audelay offers ways to avoid hell, where there is no respite from pain other than the mercy offered on Sundays, as explained in *The Vision of Saint Paul*. Hopeful that his readers will heed his warning and escape hell's tortures, Audelay offers additional advice on how, in this life, one may reduce one's term of agony in purgatory and thus hasten the way to heaven. Audelay's guidelines are literal and detailed, and they are based not only on Church teaching but on the authority of exemplary churchmen who have offered such counsel through pious writings or specific prayers that would smooth the way. Thus Audelay's emphasis upon *words* and *authority* comes about not for the same reason that Chaucer asks readers and scribes to respect his exact text, but because one is to pray certain words in certain ways in order to receive a specific quantity of remission. Sometimes the instructions are general, sometimes particularized, but they are ever-present in the collected texts of *The Counsel of Conscience*, and always the goal is clear and literal. In the first two works — the acephalous *True Living* (line 122) and the alliterative *Marcolf and Solomon* (line 39) — we are told to please God and to keep his commandments (i.e., follow his Word) to receive remission of sins.[22] Then in the third work, *The Remedy of Nine Virtues*, the ventriloquized voice of Christ counsels us to use our free will wisely and to depend upon the assembled saints of heaven to pray for us:

> Yif thou fall, aryse anon,
> And call to me with contricion;
> Then my moder and sayntis uchon
> Wil fore thee pray. (lines 34–37)

Mary and the heavenly body of saints live in Audelay's poem, and they await the call to pray effectively to save souls.

The remaining texts of *The Counsel of Conscience* assert by authority of a named holy presence that such-and-such action or prayer will grant him who is truly penitent an indulgence, which is said to be offered by ultimate authority of God. The first is a prayer on Christ's blood, requesting remission of sins: the reader is told to say this prayer every day and worship every wound of Christ in order to gain a place in heaven; should he teach it to another, his salvation will be secure (*Seven Bleedings of Christ*, lines 110–39). Next is the *Prayer on Christ's Passion*; he who says this prayer every day will gain remission of sins (lines

---

[21] Two other manuscripts that appear to contain pastoral agendas similar to Audelay's *The Counsel of Conscience* are London, British Library MS Harley 3954 and Cambridge University Library MS Ii.4.9.

[22] The interesting poem *Marcolf and Solomon* has often been seen as belonging to the *Piers Plowman* tradition because of, for example, the appearance of Mede the Maiden and some apparent verbal echoes; see the explanatory notes to *Marcolf and Solomon*, lines 490–95, 705, and 937–43. On the Langland and Audelay connection, see especially Green, "Marcolf the Fool and Blind John Audelay"; Simpson, "Saving Satire after Arundel's *Constitutions*"; Pearsall, "Audelay's *Marcolf and Solomon* and the Langlandian Tradition"; and Green, "Langland and Audelay."

37–42). Then appears *The Psalter of the Passion*, a sequence of Latin prayers with English instructions that explain how its recitation brings remission of sins. The first of these prayers, the Latin hymn *Anima Christi sanctifica me*, was indulgenced at Avignon in 1330 by Pope John XXII.[23] The pious reader is told to follow this petition with another prayer, then an Ave, and then a third prayer recited with one's rosary beads, followed by the Creed and a last prayer in Latin prose provided by Audelay.

After the prayer sequence Audelay asks a devout reader to commemorate the seven words uttered by Christ on the cross, which serve mystically to allow the seven deadly sins to be remitted (*Seven Words of Christ on the Cross*, lines 1–12). Each holy utterance becomes the focal point for a two-stanza meditation, in which, after it is cited, it is then appended to a petition on behalf of the reader. For example, Christ's words "Father, forgive them, for they know not what they do" (Luke 23:34) lead to a petition that God forgive the petitioner's enemies (lines 13–24). Finally, in order to worship properly these seven words, the petitioner is to say seven Paternosters and seven Aves (lines 99–100). And, just as Christ granted remission to his tormentors, Audelay tells us, "Well is he who will worship devoutly these words every day, for *he* shall have plain remission" (lines 109–14).

Audelay's overriding concern for remission of sins based in God's authoritative grace continues to dictate the next sequence, *Devotions at the Levation of Christ's Body*, which contains instructions, a salutation, and prayers in English and Latin. This text prepares a worshipper to venerate appropriately, in mind and gesture, the moment at which the host is raised in the mass. Upon the enactment of this holy event, an early reader (not one of the scribes) highlights the word "assencion" by drawing in the right margin a sleeved hand pointing upward at the word, which also marks the center of Audelay's poem (*Salutation to Christ's Body*, line 26). The next of Audelay's texts is a verse sermon, *Virtues of the Mass*, which follows logically the Levation sequence. In *Virtues of the Mass* Audelay names Saints Bernard, Bede, Augustine, and Gregory as authorities on the mass, and he offers an amusing, well-disseminated exemplum — here told as an anecdote of Augustine and Gregory — on the evils of gossip during the holy service (lines 298–342). To this lengthy poem on the benefits of the mass, which is also found in variant form in the Vernon Manuscript, Audelay adds his own ending, in which he tells the reader how to gain protection throughout the work week by praying during the service in a specific manner: pray for oneself, for one's parents and kin, for the weather, and for peace; then say three Paternosters to Christ, five to God, and seven to the Holy Ghost for one's seven deadly sins; then say ten more for the breaking of the Ten Commandments; and, finally, for having heard this sermon, the reader will gain, according to Saint Gregory, one hundred days of pardon (lines 352–414).

From this point on in *The Counsel of Conscience*, the ascriptions to the authority of holy men multiply. In the prayer sequence *For Remission of Sins*, Audelay prefaces the *Prayer of General Confession* (given in English) with an explanation of how it is part of an indulgence granted by Saint Gregory, for which one is granted 14,000 years of pardon, with more years added by other bishops (*Saint Gregory's Indulgence*, lines 1–10). Here Audelay instructs one to say five Paternosters and five Aves, and then to say the prayer kneeling where it is painted on the wall. The next work, *Visiting the Sick and Consoling the Needy*, which Audelay attributes to Saint Anselm as he renders it in his own idiomatic 13-line stanza, is a consolation for those afflicted by God for their sins, preaching that Peter, Mary Magdalene, and Thomas

---

[23] Ker, *Facsimile of British Museum MS. Harley 2253*, p. x.

are exemplars of God's mercy extended to sinners. Its basic message is to prepare for "soden deth" (line 395). Next comes a sequence that Audelay calls, interestingly, *Blind Audelay's English Passion*, in which the central work is *Pope John's Passion of Our Lord*, which offers three hundred days of remission (line 5). According to Audelay, Pope John made this meditation three days before he died. After reading it devoutly, one should say five Paternosters in worship of the Passion, then five Aves kneeling in reverence of the five wounds, and finally the Creed, to order to obtain the promised remission (line 119). After meditation upon the Passion comes (as with *Seven Words of Christ on the Cross* following *The Psalter of the Passion*) a meditation on a mnemonic seven holy things. This time the focus is upon the *Seven Hours of the Cross*, which offers a prayer that the reader's sins be remitted should he keep this text devoutly in mind (lines 77–90).

The next two works, *Our Lord's Epistle on Sunday* and *The Vision of Saint Paul*, are translations by Audelay of Latin texts that are frequently paired in other manuscripts. Audelay also juxtaposes them purposefully, rendering both in his favored 13-line stanza. In a rubric supplied by Scribe A, *Our Lord's Epistle on Sunday* is said to be originally transmitted through Saint Peter, bishop of Gaza. The Sunday Letter reveals a truth sworn to by all the saints, written as it was by Christ's own fingers, and it grants remission (line 172). This item connects readily to the one that follows it, *The Vision of Saint Paul*, where the opening lines declare that it was on a Sunday that Paul and the Archangel Michael traveled together to view the pains of souls in hell (lines 1–6). Although Christ declares that there is no remission in hell, this dictum will be mercifully alleviated after the visit of Saint Paul: the souls of hell are now to be offered relief on Sundays (lines 296–300). This highly visual narrative poem, which paints starkly the sufferings of sinners in hell as viewed by an astonished Paul, closes with one of Audelay's many signature stanzas. Here Audelay attributes authorship of the poem to God, through the witness of Paul:

> Mervel ye not of this makyng —
> Y me excuse, hit is not I.
> Thus Mychael lad Powle, be Goddis bedyng,
> To se in hel the turmentré,
> Fore I couth never bot hy foly.
> God hath me chastyst fore my levyng;   *chastised*
> . . . .
>   Thus counsels youe the Blynd Audlay.   (lines 353–58, 365)

And now comes the closing movement of *The Counsel of Conscience*. Audelay ends this long book at the front of MS Douce 302 with a last sequence of two poems and a colophon, to which his second scribe assigns the heading *The Lord's Mercy* ("*De misericordia Domini*"). The topic of God's grace allows a smooth transition out of the visionary climax featured in the last poem, closing the book with the hoped-for *soulehele*. The first poem in this final sequence, *God's Address to Sinful Men*, returns the authorial voice to God, as in *The Remedy of Nine Virtues* and *Our Lord's Epistle on Sunday*. In 8-line stanzas with a Latin refrain,[24] God

---

[24] "*Nolo mortem peccatoris*" ("I desire not the death of the wicked," Ezechiel 33:11). On Audelay's frequent use of this biblical passage, compare *True Living*, line 128; *Marcolf and Solomon*, line 790; *Our Lord's Epistle on Sunday*, line 115; and the explicit to *The Vision of Saint Paul*. It may hold a contemporary resonance in regard to correction of Lollards, for it occurs in a confession of heresy made by a Suffolk

issues stern warnings to mankind while continuously offering remission in return for heartfelt contrition. The next poem, *Audelay's Epilogue to The Counsel of Conscience*, makes the subject personal. The chaplain composes this work in his own voice, with a first-person, prophetic-sounding "I," and in his own trademark 13-line stanza. The poem even bears a hint of dream-vision framing in the third stanza

> Fore as I lay seke, in my dremyng,   *sick*
> Methoght a mon to me con say: *It seemed to me; did say*
> "Let be thi slouth and thi slomeryng!   *slumbering*
> Have mynd on God both nyght and day!" (lines 27–30)

paired with the penultimate stanza (lines 482–94), which begins "As I lay seke in my langure."

In *Audelay's Epilogue to The Counsel of Conscience* Audelay betrays a personal hope that his visitation from God — that is, his being struck with blindness — is something that may associate him with Saint Paul,[25] give him license to speak truth, and ultimately lead to his redemption:

> And take record of the apostil Poule   *heed*
> That Crist callid to grace and his mercé,
> Fore so I hope he hath done me
> And geven me wil, wit, tyme, and space,
> Throgh the Holé Gost, blynd, def to be,
> And say this wordis throgh his gret grace. (lines 16-21)   *these*

Audelay harbors a belief that his words may acquire an authoritative power akin to those of the apostle. Finally, this last poem in *The Counsel of Conscience* closes with another signature stanza, this one attributing the written words to the Holy Ghost:

> Mervel ye not of this makyng,   *Marvel*
> Fore I me excuse — hit is not I;   *excuse myself*
> This was the Holé Gost wercheng,   *Holy Ghost's making*
> That sayd these wordis so faythfully,
> Fore I quoth never bot hye foly.   *I [myself] say; high folly*
> . . . .
>   Beware, seris, I youe pray,
>   Fore I mad this with good entent,
>   In the reverens of God Omnipotent.
>   Prays fore me that beth present —   *[those] who are*
>   My name is Jon the Blynd Awdlay. (lines 495–99, 503–07)

Audelay closes the book by attributing, again, the primary creative act to a higher authority — either the Deity or one with sainted proximity to the Deity — while he then turns around and claims the secondary act as his own. Audelay's modest form of "makyng," we might

---

priest in 1429, as cited in Shinners and Dohar, *Pastors and the Care of Souls in Medieval England*, p. 280.

[25] This is one of many instances where Audelay makes spiritual reference to blindness; see Fein, "Good Ends," p. 101n11.

glean, refers mainly to actions of translating and metering, and seldom in his mind to any claim of original content.

SALUTATIONS

The salutation section directs the worship of Audelay and his pious readers toward five holy figures: the Virgin Mary, three women saints (Bridget, Winifred, and Anne), and eventually God himself, whose image is mediated by the agency of another woman, Saint Veronica. The final approach to God is by means of an image of the Holy Face as preserved upon the Vernicle. These salutations provide the words by which to honor and invoke saints, summoning them by name, as in the first one to Mary:

> Hayle, Maré, to thee I say,
> Hayle, ful of grace, God is with thee.
> Hale, blessid mot thou be, thou swete may.   *may; virgin*
> (*Salutation to Jesus for Mary's Love*, lines 1–3)

The poems in this section seem sometimes to be directed at a faithful congregation, as when Scribe A inserts the word "*Oremus*" (Let us pray) and Scribe B adds "*collecte*" (together) before each of the three prayers in Latin prose. Yet the drawing of God's face upon the Veronica Shroud that occurs at the end of the salutations is expressly bookish in constructing a meditative site for a person practicing his quiet devotions. The act of reading piously and privately, as figured by a book of devotional verse, and the coherent religious logic of the sequence itself, punctuated with clerical instructions, suggest that Audelay envisions his salutations as bringing comfort and spiritual well-being to individual users.

The salutations devoted to the worship of Mary lead off the section in a way that suggests that the mother of God is to be seen as the primary intercessory figure for the whole section. The word by which to hail her, "Ave," is essentially synonymous with the genre itself, and Gabriel's utterance of this word to the Virgin — in the Annunciation — is the prototypical salutation, the word that prefaced incarnation of the Word. Interestingly, this section becomes a kind of dialogue with the Virgin. The first incipit invites this dialogue by asking the reader not to pass by, but to pause and say "Ave." Then (in the same incipit) the Virgin herself speaks to the reader, pronouncing, with a delicate pun on *ave* (hail) and *a ve* (without woe), the rewards that accrue to those who salute her: "May they always be without woe who to me say 'Ave.'" The Marian section then moves from salutation and prayer into a healing meditation upon the Virgin's five joys, then another salutation to Mary, a delicate lyric translation of the Latin hymn *Angelus ad Virginem* (voiced by Gabriel), and finally, continuing the biblical reference to Luke 1, a version of the *Song of the Magnificat* (voiced, of course, by Mary) in refrain stanzas. Thus the Marian salutations operate as a chorus of modulated voices in praise of Mary, with even Mary herself participating, as if in conversation with the medieval person who says "Ave."

The first of the salutations to Mary has an astonishing structure by which it encloses an embedded salutation to Jesus as Redeemer. The poem assumes a form in imitation of Mary's pregnancy, as if it were a statue of the Virgin that can be opened to reveal the Blessed Child within. This first salutation, which begins in seeming address to Mary alone, reveals itself to be actually an address to Jesus *through* Mary and her five joys, and it movingly dramatizes the impossibility for an Englishman of orthodox faith to approach God without a mediating presence (a stance much challenged by Lollards). In this *internal* salutation to Mary's Son, the verse reiterates the name of Jesus for some seventy lines: "O Jhesu, fore these Joys Fyve, / O Jhesu, thi moder had of thee" (*Salutation to Jesus for Mary's Love*, lines 91–92), and so on. Moreover, during this worship in direct address to Jesus, Audelay's professed hope for the sight of God's face at Doomsday (lines 150–51) anticipates the way he will close his salutations section.

After this well-integrated cluster of Marian salutations come the poems dedicated to Saints Bridget, Winifred, and Anne, female saints who are each venerated for the miraculous healing powers associated with their sanctity. Bridget of Sweden was canonized as saint in 1391. Audelay's salutation to her bears significant historical witness to the founding of the Bridgettine order in England, which resulted in the establishment of Syon Abbey by Henry V's royal decree in 1415. In the poem Audelay compliments "gracious Kyng Herré" for this noble promotion of the faith in England (lines 136–48), and elsewhere, in his carol *King Henry VI*, there also surfaces the chaplain's patriotic desire to praise the reigning Lancastrian monarchy. The *Salutation to Saint Bridget* narrates the saint's *vita* at some length, and it stands alone without accompanying apparatus, while the salutations to Winifred and Anne are set within devotional sequences that include prayers to the saintly women.

The Winifred devotion is actually a double salutation for there are two poems to honor her, one in carol form (the only carol outside the carols section of the manuscript) and one in a 9-line stanza that is identical to that used by Audelay in his lengthy *Salutation to Saint Bridget*.[26] Two Latin prayers, one in verse, one in prose, conclude the devotion. While Winifred's *vita* is set in seventh-century Wales, Audelay and the residents of Haughmond Abbey would have viewed her as a local saint because her relics rested in Shrewsbury, four miles to the north, having been translated there in 1138. Moreover, Winifred's popularity had widened when her feast day was made binding throughout England in 1415. An effigy of Winifred stands among those carved in the outside arches of the abbey chapter house, where her foot rests upon the head of Prince Caradoc, an iconographic gesture that ironically reverses the most famous moment in her *vita*: when the prince found he could not deflower her, he decapitated her in a furious rage, but her uncle restored her head to her body, and Winifred lived thereafter with a thin white thread of scar adorning her neck as a necklace. One of Audelay's prayers to Winifred emphasizes the saint's miraculous restoration to bodily wholeness, which pertains to her power to heal others, such as himself.

Womanly healing in the form of miraculous fertility, leading to the birth of the Savior, forms the focus of the devotion to Saint Anne, mother of the Virgin Mary. This sweetly graceful worship service possesses two parts: an English verse salutation and a Latin prose prayer. Audelay emphasizes in both elements the miracle of Anne's fruitful womb, which gave birth to Mary after a long period of barrenness. As with Winifred, Audelay composed two poems in honor of Anne — an anaphoric salutation and a carol — but he situates *Saint Anne Mother of Mary* in the next section of carols, where it is located, significantly, in a series given to the topic of chaste female fecundity. The wondrous quality of Anne's unexpected fertility, leading to the birth of Mary and later Christ, contributes to the conceptual theme of miraculous healing that runs through the salutations.

---

[26] It may be that Audelay planned or executed a series of salutations for female saints in this meter, and that these two poems are the only remaining vestige of that plan. The meter resembles that used for *Marcolf and Solomon*; see explanatory notes to *Salutation to Saint Winifred*.

In the last devotional sequence, dedicated to the Holy Face, God's image is venerated by means of a salutation and a drawing — the only non-marginal illustration to occur in MS Douce 302. The sequence opens with Latin prose instructions that identify the English salutation (with drawing) as an indulgence from Rome granted by Pope Boniface IV, which should be said twenty days in a row. The drawing of Christ's face on the Veronica Shroud follows these instructions and forms a visual meditative site. It resembles one of a series commonly found on indulgence rolls that venerate the *Arma Christi*, a tradition also occurring in Audelay's *Seven Bleedings of Christ* (lines 67–72). When Scribe A came to this point in the manuscript, that is, the end of the salutations, he left space for the drawing and inscribed the verbal exercise *Salutation to the Holy Face* and the final Latin prose prayer below that space. The drawing appears to have been inserted later by Scribe B. Thus the image and the English salutation support vernacular devotion, but it is mediated through a clerical frame of Latin prose instruction and prayer.

It appears that Audelay has designed the series of salutations so that a meditant is deliberately brought to this climactic image and textual moment, which rehearses the much-anticipated sight of God's Holy Face on Doomsday, to which the opening *Salutation to Jesus for Mary's Love* referred. Viewed as a unified set, Audelay's salutations develop aesthetic wholeness from sacred logic, progressing from God in Mary's womb, in the *Salutation to Jesus for Mary's Love*, to God upon the sudary of Veronica, in the *Salutation to the Holy Face*. In each, God is imaged in human form and made accessible by the mediation of female sanctity and clerical guidance. *Soulehele* as conceived of in this section arrives by means of holy women.

CAROLS

Twenty-five in number, Audelay's carols are a thoughtfully arranged collection, the first known grouping of its kind. They are arranged by topic: articles of faith; feasts of the Church; support of king and social order; honor to the holy family; praise of virginity, chastity, and love of God; a holy fear of death; and, last of all, honor to Saint Francis, promoter of vernacular Christian song. The Audelay manuscript eventually fell into the hands of a minstrel, late in the fifteenth century, and one reason for this may be that the minstrel, William Wyatt of Coventry, wanted copies of these carols.[27] Their character is more religious than secular, and while the manuscript does not contain music, they were likely meant to be sung: as the headnote proclaims, "Syng these caroles in Cristemas." It may be that some of the longer ones were designed more for reading; these include the ceremonial carols dedicated to Henry VI and Saint Francis. Another long carol, dedicated to Saint Winifred, is copied in the salutations section, where it fits into a longer devotion to that saint. The fact of its existence, and the nicety of the number twenty-five, would seem to suggest that Audelay might have composed, during the course of his chaplaincy, other carols that are now lost, and that this well-planned sequence results from a process of selection mixed with a process of new composition directed purposefully toward the making of this anthology.

Determining when and for what occasions Audelay originally composed these carols is complicated by several factors. Because six of the carols appear in similar or variant forms in other manuscripts, it would seem that Audelay may have borrowed them from other

---

[27] Fein, "John Audelay and His Book," pp. 4, 12–13.

sources. In most cases where duplicates exist elsewhere, scholars have tended to question Audelay's role in the composition process,[28] but it is also possible that some of these songs were indeed Audelay's own and that the other copies indicate a multi-regional dispersal of Audelay's works, his carols especially. There are certain carols that bear sophisticated lyrical or metrical charms that seem to soar beyond Audelay's normal poetic range. Examples include *Day of the Lord's Circumcision*, *Day of Epiphany*, *Jesus Flower of Jesse's Tree*, and *Joys of Mary*, all of which appear in other manuscripts. Moreover, scribal actions sometimes tell us that copies were sought by unusual means. When Scribe A redacted *Day of the Lord's Circumcision*, it appears that he lacked it in complete form, and Scribe B later located and supplied it. What this initial tentativeness may indicate about authorship is, however, uncertain.[29] The carols most definitely Audelay's own are those composed in either of the two dominant metrical modes — a 7-line stanza and a 6-line stanza — for which there were surely tunes that were familiar. Audelay's own idiom, however, is ever-present, and the *idea* of the sequence and its execution are certainly Audelay's own creations.

The unity of the collection can be conceived of, roughly, as five groups of five carols, set in thematic order. The first five carols, Carols 1 to 5, form a group centered on basic articles of faith: Ten Commandments, Seven Deadly Sins, Seven Works of Mercy, Five Wits, and Seven Gifts of the Holy Ghost. All are composed in Audelay's 7-line carol stanza (the fifth line is a tag, the sixth and seventh are the burden). All are similar in length: the first four have five stanzas; the fifth has six. In a pedagogical manner, all address standard topics of doctrine that priests were enjoined to impart to the laity. These topics are treated elsewhere in Audelay's verse, and sometimes the chaplain has drawn from earlier works to construct carols almost verbatim. For example, portions of *True Living* (the first poem in the manuscript) crop up in five different carols.[30] Comparative study of the carols with the rest of Audelay's oeuvre can therefore tell us much about the chaplain's compositional methods and his sense of meter matched to genre.

Carols 6 through 10 constitute another internal group, all written in 6-line stanzas. The topics of these carols follow the Church calendar of observance for December 25 to 29. First comes a song of convivial Yuletide joy and welcome, in which Audelay names the saints honored in the next songs:

Welcum be ye, Steven and Jone,	*Stephen and John [the Evangelist]*
Welcum, childern everechone,	*children (i.e., Holy Innocents)*
Wellcum, Thomas marter, alle on —	*Thomas martyr, all together*
(*Day of the Nativity*, lines 13–15)	

Here Audelay invokes the feast days that immediately follow Christmas Day, which his next four carols honor: Saint Stephen's Day, Saint John's Day, Holy Innocents Day, and Saint Thomas à Becket of Canterbury's Day. In *The Golden Legend*, Jacobus de Voragine explains

---

[28] Greene, *Early English Carols*. See explanatory notes to *Seven Deadly Sins*, *Day of the Nativity*, *Day of the Lord's Circumcision*, *Day of Epiphany*, *Jesus Flower of Jesse's Tree*, and *Joys of Mary*.

[29] There are signs of similar circumstances in the copying of *Chastity for Mary's Love* and *Gabriel's Salutation to the Virgin*. See the explanatory notes for each poem.

[30] The carols that show signs of construction from stanzas in *True Living* are: *Ten Commandments*, *Seven Works of Mercy*, *Seven Gifts of the Holy Ghost*, *Four Estates*, and *Chastity of Wives*. See the explanatory notes to these carols.

that the martyrdoms of Stephen, John, and the Innocents, all associated with Christ's birth, exemplify "all the different classes of martyrs . . . the first is willed and endured, the second willed but not endured, the third endured without being willed. Saint Stephen is an example of the first, Saint John of the second, the Holy Innocents of the third."[31] John the Evangelist was, moreover, the patron saint of Haughmond Abbey, and his statue appears among others in the columns outside the chapter house. An effigy of Saint Thomas of Canterbury, with mitre and archbishop's cross-staff, also stands there. Following the orthodoxy of the English Church, Audelay cites Thomas's martyrdom in *Marcolf and Solomon* (line 342), reminding readers how the archbishop courageously defended the Church against pressure from secular powers.

The sequential logic of the next five carols, Carols 11 to 15, seems to work by an association of ideas about the Christ Child, kingship, the boy king Henry VI, social order, and childhood innocence. Carol 11 commemorates the feast day of the Lord's Circumcision, January 1, honoring the newborn King and carrying forward the chronology found in the last internal group (Carols 6 to 10). Although Audelay's version of this lovely carol is the best of the variant texts, scholars have doubted that Audelay wrote its innovative lyrics, which appear to mix parts for a soloist and a chorus, allowing a joyous dialogue to develop between a company and a "messenger." Nonetheless, a modern musical adaptation of this Christmas choral work ascribes it to Audelay, and that is how it has been recorded in recent years.[32] The carol dedicated to King Henry VI occurs in the twelfth position, and it appears that Audelay wanted this spot to be understood as the center of the whole carol sequence, for Scribe B highlights it with a prominent leaf-point drawn in the foliage of the ornamental initial *A*. Audelay's loyalty to the monarch has emerged earlier in the manuscript, in the *Salutation to Saint Bridget*. The next carol, with borrowings from *True Living*, expresses Audelay's conservative attitude that those of each estate should serve in it properly and not seek to do other than their own calling. The fourteenth carol, *Childhood*, covers a topic quite unusual in lyrics of Audelay's time, and it is especially interesting to see how Audelay gives the general theme found in this group of carols a personal turn.[33] The grouping ends with a return to the theme of Christ the Child King and the Christmas season, in a commemoration of the Visit of the Magi and the feast day of Epiphany, January 6 (Carol 15).

The fourth internal set of five carols, Carols 16 to 20, takes a genealogical turn, encouraged by the preceding theme of Christ's birth, with a steady focus on Marian devotion. Carol 16 celebrates Saint Anne, mother of Mary, and one can see that Audelay wanted it placed here for thematic reasons, rather than beside the *Salutation to Saint Anne* that appeared with the other salutations. Rosemary Woolf praises this carol as "a Marian variation of the Tree of Jesse,"[34] and by introducing this theme, Audelay pairs it explicitly with the next carol, *Jesus*

---

[31] Jacobus de Voragine, *Golden Legend*, 1:49–50.

[32] The modern choral adaptations may be found in: Stevens, *Mediaeval Carols*, pp. 8–9 (no. 11) and p. 20 (no. 27); and Hoddinott (composer), "Carols, op. 38," in Audelay, "What Tidings?" Other arrangements appear in the British Library catalogue, but I have not examined them: Oldroyd, "The Flower of Jesse"; Rutter, "There Is a Flower"; and Lloyd, "The Fairest Flower." I am aware of the following three sound recordings: The Elizabethan Singers, *Carols of Today*; New York Pro Musica Antiqua, *English Medieval Carols and Christmas Music*; and Oxford Camerata, *Medieval Carols*.

[33] Salter praises this carol for its "warmth of feeling for the innocence of a child — an emotion more unusual in [Audelay's] age than we might think possible" (*Fourteenth-Century English Poetry*, p. 17).

[34] Woolf, *English Religious Lyric*, p. 297.

Flower of Jesse's Tree. With *Saint Anne Mother of Mary* using the Tree of Jesse to describe Mary's conception, this one brings the image to full bloom: the branch is Mary, the flower Christ.[35] The next two carols celebrate the Virgin Mary directly: Carol 18 is about her five joys, recalling Audelay's handling of the subject in the *Salutation to Jesus for Mary's Love*; Carol 19 salutes her with an "Ave" (that is, "Heyle") and centers all feminine beauty and floral fecundity in her person, "Heyle, of wymmen flour of alle, / Thou herst us when we to thee calle!" (burden). The last carol of this grouping declares how the male speaker (a monk or a cleric) has chosen chastity for the love of Mary.

After these twenty carols, Audelay finishes the carol sequence in an eloquent manner. Carols 21 and 22 redirect the message about chastity, which was drawn from the holy example of Mary, so that it is now aimed at secular women. The first of these carols speaks to single maidens, preaching that they have a moral duty to preserve virginity before marriage. The next focuses on the moral and social mandate that wives be chaste, with Audelay betraying his disgust for ladies who "wil take a page" (line 36) for lust or fashion. The seventh stanza declares that England is in decline as the result of such wanton behavior (lines 43–47), which not only disgraces the upper classes, but also creates unlawful heirs and causes English nobility to waste away. So Audelay continues to develop the genealogical theme, moving it from the biblical and spiritual realm (the Tree of Jesse) to the current social realm (the nobility of England). Finally, he addresses chastity's highest purpose: love of God (Carol 23). In this austere yet touching carol, the word *love* suffuses every line, with its different meanings devotionally intertwined, to create, in the words of John Hirsh, "a gentle reflection . . . upon what [Audelay] and many of his contemporaries would have regarded as the greatest of medieval themes, the love which exists between God and all of humankind."[36]

After this enraptured moment, and as Audelay nears the end of the carol sequence, the chaplain turns to a natural closing topic in his *Dread of Death*, the best-known and most-praised carol of the collection. Its tone is direct and sincere, personal and moving:

As I lay seke in my langure,	*sick; languishing*
With sorow of hert and teere of ye,	*tear of eye*
This caral I made with gret doloure —	*sadness*
Passio Christi conforta me.	
Ladé, helpe! Jhesu, mercé!	
Timor mortis conturbat me. (Saint Francis, lines 43–48)	

Woolf ranks this poem beside the verse of George Herbert and observes that "for perhaps the first time in an English lyric poem, the poet truly speaks in his own voice."[37] Audelay signs this poem, asking his reader to "Lerne this lesson of Blynd Awdlay" (line 61). He also signs the last carol, which honors Saint Francis. One cannot be certain why it is that Audelay concludes by honoring this saint, but the purpose seems both religious and literary: Audelay has praise for friars elsewhere, and credit went to Francis as the originator of popular reli-

---

[35] In the art-edition of this poem created by Loyd Haberly in 1926, the artist develops a visual theme of Mary and Jesus as the conjoined flower of salvation progressively unfurled in Christian narrative (*Alia Cantalena de Sancta Maria by John Awdlay*).

[36] Hirsh, *Medieval Lyric*, p. 193.

[37] Woolf, *English Religious Lyric*, p. 335; see also pp. 7, 387–88.

gious song. The full sequence ends with a petition to gentlemen-readers that they be reverent receivers of this carol:

> I pray youe, seris, pur charyté,   *for*
> Redis this caral reverently,
> Fore I mad hit with wepyng eye,
> Your broder Jon the Blynd Awdlay. (*Saint Francis*, lines 73–76)

Viewed in their totality, the carols create a narrative of faith. To judge them in terms of how Audelay responds to authority, one may note that they are much like the salutations in how they honor the saints and avow fealty for the monarch. There are liturgical carols celebrating Stephen, John the Evangelist, the Holy Innocents, and Thomas of Canterbury. Female saintliness is honored in carols to Saint Anne and the Blessed Virgin Mary, and chastity is lauded in the name of the virgin saints Katherine, Margaret, and Winifred (*Chastity for Mary's Love*, line 19). The series ends in celebration of Saint Francis. Thus Audelay makes prominent among his aims the naming of saints and the invocation of their beneficence. Before any of these saints were invoked in specific carols, the sixth carol, *Day of the Nativity*, seemed to enfold all the company of saints as a prelude to what is to come. With the burden "Welcum, Yole, in good aray, / In worchip of the holeday!" this carol sings a welcome by name to Mary and Christ Child, to Stephen, to John and Thomas, and lastly to the present company:

> Welcum be ye, lord and lady,
> Welcum be ye, al this cumpané,
> Fore Yolis love, now makis meré —
>   Welcum, Yole, foreever and ay! (lines 25–28)

After enumerating the doctrines of faith in Carols 1–5, Audelay summons the community of saints, with himself playing a kind of cosmic host who draws together a grand assemblage of living and convivial carolers with the saints and martyrs of heaven.

MEDITATIVE CLOSE

The final section of the Audelay manuscript provides texts for private meditation, which are, again, in meaningful sequence. Its focus is on endings — the end of the book, the end of one's life, for the reader and for Audelay. It begins with two short treatises in English prose, one by Richard Rolle (but not attributed to any author) and another by an anonymous writer. These two items are prefaced by an instructional pair of couplets from Audelay, written by Scribe B:

> Rede thys offt, butt rede hit sofft,
> And whatt thou redust, forgeete hit noght,   *read*
> For here the soth thou maght se   *truth*
> What fruyte cometh of thy body. (*Instructions for Reading 4*, lines 1–4)   *fruit*

The verse asks a meditative reader to absorb these items tenderly and often as a way to think upon the spiritual rewards ("fruyte") that may follow one's bodily life. They seem to preface the prose alone, but it is possible that they refer to the whole closing movement redacted by Scribe A during the first stage of the manuscript's making. In this movement, which I will term "Phase 1," there are two prose texts followed by two poems in alliterative stanzas. The successive phases for ending the manuscript appear to be three in number.

Phase 1 texts are in the hand of Scribe A, with Scribe B performing his normal oversight duties of correcting errors and adding incipits and explicits. The first of the prose texts is an excerpt from Rolle's *Form of Living*, the Yorkshire hermit's last work, written in 1348–49 for the instruction of a young female recluse. Drawn from this popular treatise's sixth chapter, Audelay's extract, *The Sins of the Heart*, catalogues moral transgressions according to a threefold scheme of bodily origin in the heart, mouth, or hand. Rolle's exposition offers a fine preaching text to someone of Audelay's vocation. Intriguingly, one finds embedded in Rolle's prose an alliterative stanza matching the type found in *Marcolf and Solomon*. This little bit of verse, *Over-Hippers and Skippers*, concerns the abuse of prayer. It would seem that here is another remnant of Audelay's professional method of composition. Drawing material together for effective sermonizing, Audelay borrows a pertinent snippet from Rolle and interjects a lively verse exemplum. We may thus imagine this item not only as a private meditation but also as a likely vestige of pastoral performance. And, again, when matter derived from elsewhere appears in the Audelay manuscript, it is subsumed and transformed "according to" Audelay. The next prose piece, an allegory of the soul, also bears the chaplain's creative sensibility in how it works in juxtaposition with *The Sins of the Heart*. Comparable in manner to the *Abbey of the Holy Ghost*, *An Honest Bed* allegorizes the penitent soul as a bed made ready for Christ. Set in tandem with the Rolle extract, this fine piece of soul-cleansing enacts a process of penance and calm readiness for death and union with Christ.

Audelay then shifts from pastoral prose to dignified verse: alliterative stanzas deliver a solemn prayer and an exemplum on death. These texts are the last ones redacted by Scribe A. They advance the book to the point of human death, squarely confronted, humbly acknowledged. The prayer-poem *Paternoster* creates an important moment in which the Lord's Prayer is enunciated in English. As Audelay asserts in *Marcolf and Solomon*, the Paternoster will protect one's soul from damnation: "Fore better is a Paternoster with repentyng / To send hem, to the mercé of God, to purgatoré" (lines 927–28). Its ruminative recitation here, in stanzas that articulate its seven points, touches the chords of faith. In its "seven-ness," moreover, *Paternoster* seems to summon, cumulatively, all the theological sevens previously enumerated to Audelay's reader for penitential contemplation: *Seven Words of Christ on the Cross*, *Seven Bleedings of Christ*, *Seven Hours of the Cross*, and so on. This poem, a specimen of alliterative high style, bears formal affinity — and almost certainly a shared exemplar — with the next item, *Three Dead Kings*. Although Audelay's authorship of these two pieces remains in doubt, he deserves credit for the way they effectively close his book and produce a sobering devotion. Numerous efforts to correct wordings show that the two scribes found the language and metrical exactitude of the verses to be challenging and foreign, yet both poems receive the scribes' care and, indeed, reverence. *Three Dead Kings* narrates a classic ghost-story motif, the Three Living and Three Dead, in a *tour de force* of dense alliteration and rhyme. This popular theme of *memento mori* brings three kings face to face with unsettling mirrors of themselves in future time, when they meet the Three Dead, that is, the walking, speaking corpses of their fathers.

These works complete Audelay's plan for the book as first conceived.[38] Read as a textual sequence, *The Sins of the Heart*, *An Honest Bed*, *Paternoster*, and *Three Dead Kings* capture the mystery, awe, and dread of death. The last-place positioning of *Three Dead Kings* invites a reader to look in the book as if in a mirror that brings dead author and living reader into a reciprocal relationship.[39] The third figure of the Dead issues a warning to the Living that reaches out to the reader: "Makis your merour be me!" (line 120). The message implicit in the vernacular icon suits Audelay's own daily office of singing trentals, that is, the living have a double responsibility to offer prayers for the dead (to alleviate their purgatorial sentences) and to continually ponder their own dying. As the first ending of the Audelay manuscript, the point where Scribe A's work ends (Phase 1), this ending is austere and magnificent in its simple, stark appeal.

But the Audelay manuscript does not quite stop here. Judging by the scribal work, Audelay twice expanded its manner of closure by adding new texts, and for each operation he relied upon Scribe B (with Scribe A now absent). An interval must have fallen between Phases 1 and 2 because the verse text inserted after *Three Dead Kings* — *Cur mundus militat sub vana gloria* — was apparently put there after Scribe B had completed his extensive work of correcting, decorating, and numbering the texts redacted by Scribe A. Phase 2 takes the book into Latin, as if the language of the Church helps to solemnize and sanctify the process toward death. Using a formal hand rarely seen elsewhere in the book, Scribe B adds this commonplace poem on the vanity of life, an aphoristic piece that surfaces often in English and Continental manuscripts. It dates from at least the thirteenth century and has been ascribed to various authors, Bernard of Clairvaux and Robert Grosseteste among them. The Latin poet declares that one should "put more trust in letters written on ice than in the empty deceit of the fragile world" (lines 5–6), and in two stanzas of *ubi sunt*, he uses the passings of Solomon, Samson, Absalom, Jonathan, Caesar, Dives, Tullius, and Aristotle to illustrate this sad, transitory life (lines 13–20). Near the end, the poet chastises the flesh and exhorts good works: "O food for worms, O pile of dust, O dew, O vanity, why are you so extolled? You have absolutely no idea whether you will be alive tomorrow, [and so] do good to all for as long as you are able" (lines 29–32). And he offers trust in God as his final advice: "Think on heavenly things; may your heart be in heaven. Happy is the one who will be able to despise the world" (lines 39–40). The insertion of this familiar piece proceeds from the same clerical logic by which several of Audelay's works conclude with Latin prayers. *Cur mundus* moralizes poetically upon the world's transitoriness in the professional manner of Audelay the chaplain.

The final phase of completing the Audelay manuscript probably occurred not too long after the addition of the Latin poem, for Audelay, though gravely ill, was still acutely engaged with the bookmaking endeavor, and he still had the services of Scribe B. Phase 3 returns the book to Audelay's own distinctive voice. The chaplain-poet lays authorial claim here to its composition and compilation, even as he returns to his typical formula of

---

[38] Even though Audelay seems here to be acting more as a cleric who culls disparate materials than as a writer of new compositions, these four items are a fully integrated part of his well-ordered anthology. It is therefore regrettable that Audelay's Early English Text Society editor, Ella Keats Whiting, passed over the prose works entirely (*Poems of John Audelay*). Their omission from the only prior edition of Audelay's works purporting to be complete has left Audelay's crucial closing pattern entirely obscured from view until now.

[39] Fein, "Life and Death, Reader and Page."

modestly ascribing true authorship to God, saying that he "made this bok by Goddus grace" (*Audelay's Conclusion*, line 51). *Audelay's Conclusion* is an original poem in 13-line stanzas with Latin headings, which the ailing chantry priest composed especially for the occasion here. Its four stanzas are, in their autobiographical manner, much like *Audelay's Epilogue to The Counsel of Conscience* at the end of *The Counsel of Conscience*.[40] In it, Audelay signs off with a bold flourish of retrospective finality, proclaiming his purpose consummated, in implicit likeness to God's act of the creating the world by a word (lines 1–8). He also invokes, by means of the physical manuscript, the heavenly book recording the names of the saved (line 19). Following these audacious similitudes comes another vigorous assertion of authorship: the claim that this book displays Audelay's own "wyl" and "wrytyng" (line 33). As he departs for the last time, the poet makes a penitential, pious appeal for prayers for "Jon the Blynde Awdelay" (line 48) and draws a portrait of himself situated in the abbey, serving as chantry priest for Lord Lestrange, but now lying close to death (lines 45–52). Thus does a fine aesthetic sensibility unify the three-phase process of closure. Like the third Dead in *Three Dead Kings*, Audelay holds *himself* up in *Audelay's Conclusion* as a mirror of mortality for all readers who come after him and behold this image.[41] And one of his Latin epigrams directly recalls the last line of *Cur mundus*: "*Hic vir despiciens mundum*" (This man despising the world) (*Audelay's Conclusion*, heading to line 27).

The Audelay signature found at the end of this last poem is the only signing to appear in the meditative close, but it is typical for the book as a whole. Nine signatures occur in *The Counsel of Conscience*, and the salutations and carols sections each contain two or three more. When one absorbs the reading experience offered by MS Douce 302, one quickly comes to know the identity of its central creative agent, for his name, John the Blind Audelay, is much recorded, usually in the verse itself though occasionally in a colophon or incipit. Both scribes partake in this grand goal of naming Audelay. Authorial identity — indeed celebrity — thus becomes blended with the verse experience, and, in fact, Audelay's distinctive style — exhortative, preacherly, admonitive, insistently repeating the pronoun "I" — works strenuously to imprint the author's convictions on piety and contrition within the mind and heart of a reader or auditor.

AUDELAY, AUTHORSHIP, AND AUTHORITY

The salutations had culminated in a devotion consisting of prayers, a drawing, and an address to the Holy Face, in which God is called the mirror of holy men (*Salutation to the Holy Face*, line 7). Ultimately, the climactic approach to God's Holy Face offers a meaning that supersedes Audelay's human agency, in a manner analogous to Audelay's own declarations of modesty in his signature stanzas. It is God who is the *author* of all things. Audelay's acts of working or making verse look to God and his word for guidance. The core of this idea surfaces in the last poem, Audelay's farewell to the reader:

---

[40] The two poems appear to be related compositions, and some of the Latin headings in *Audelay's Conclusion* repeat exact phrases found in the *Finito libro* colophon; see the translations that open this Introduction.

[41] Fein, "Good Ends," pp. 101–09.

Only in God ys all comforde.   *comfort*
For ther nys noon odur Loorde   *is no other*
That can do as he can.
All thyng he made here with a worde. (*Audelay's Conclusion*, lines 4-7)

God — Creator of the world, Font of the word — grounds the devotional spirit of this signed poem. Set where it is, *Audelay's Conclusion* operates like the salutations' climactic face of God, that is, as a final mirror in which sinners may view themselves and assess their contrite readiness before God's judging countenance. All we may bring to the judgment are our deeds, our words, our will, and our thoughts, as Audelay counsels in his *Dread of Death* (lines 31–33). So Audelay's final affirmation of his own modest "makyng" — here and in all the signature stanzas — is enclosed within a context of God's higher Word. The words inscribed in MS Douce 302 represent the pious acts that Audelay will offer when he is to be judged.

How Audelay himself would have perceived authorial authority emerges, therefore, from the folios of MS Douce 302 in a way apparent only if one looks past the *self*-namings and examines other namings in the book. In order to comprehend what rationale exists for Audelay's obsessive recording of his own name, one has to understand the joyful reverence he reserves for uttering other *auctoritee* — naming the names, that is, of those held to be most holy and saintly. Therefore, the reasonable modern classification of MS Douce 302 as an "author collection" has to be qualified by an understanding of just what "authorship," "authority," and even "canonicity" would have meant in around 1426 to the Shropshire chaplain who obsessively inserts his name into the book. His name is there beside those of the holy fathers and saints, to whose authority he defers, and it is there in humble, blissful, awed, and fearsome expectation of facing the holy countenance in judgment, where he will discover his deeds, words, and thoughts recorded in a roll. Bringing sinners out of pain constitutes the most beneficent deeds of the saints, and this is the role the chaplain carves for himself, in humble likeness to God, Christ, Mary, and their heavenly followers:

These halowne — al the sayntis in heven,   *These [ones sing] praise*
Angelis, patrearchis, and prophet,
The postilis al, with marters steven,   *martyrs' voices*
The confessours, with vergyns swete —
. . . .
Ther bodé and soule in fere schal met.   *Where; together; meet*
When Jhesu schal schew his wondis wete,   *wet*
Maré, thou be our mayne-paroure,   *legal surety*
With these sayntis to have a sete. (*Salutation to Mary*, lines 109–12, 116–19)

The attribution of the Audelay manuscript to the poet John the Blind Audelay thus occurs because Audelay situates himself as a holy man whose role is to mediate between two worlds. His words apprehend and animate the lively host of saints in heaven, and his book is designed to set these virgins, martyrs, prophets, and apostles in prayerful, redemptive conversation with an audience of those who dwell in sin on earth.

Note on the Presentation of Texts

The texts are printed in the modern alphabet and follow the conventions of the Middle English Texts Series. I list here a few details of presentation that require special notice.

Transcription. Final *l* or final *k* with a medial horizontal line is rendered as *le* or *ke*. Following the practice of past editors (and especially Halliwell and Whiting), the abbreviation *p* with a horizontal line through the descender is rendered variably as *per* or *par* in Middle English, and as *per* in Latin. Other editors' variant readings of these forms are listed in the textual notes. When scribal *þe* denotes the pronoun, it is rendered *thee*.

Abbreviations. Roman numerals appearing in texts (not as title numbers) are normally treated like other abbreviations and are silently expanded to the scribes' usual Middle English forms; for example, scribal *v.* is rendered as *fyve*.

Foliation. Material from the manuscript is cited by folio number, recto or verso ("r" or "v"), and column ("a" or "b").

Titles. The titles of works in MS Douce 302 usually derive from the Latin incipits. Works assigned a roman numeral by Scribe B have titles rendered in all capital letters.

Ordinatio. Signs of authorial and/or scribal arrangement of matter are reproduced so far as is practical. Roman numerals attached to titles replicate those inserted by Scribe B in red and blue ink at the tops of columns, where they denote the beginning of texts. Underlining replicates the original underlining of textual lines in red ink. Where Scribe B provides marginal indicators, they are reproduced in this edition by the insertion of a typographical hand sign. In the manuscript these indicators take different visual forms: a hand with extended forefinger (twice), a horn, and pointing leaf foliage.

Stanza forms. Stanzas are presented in forms that respect scribal indicators of stanza length and rhyme schemes. Different interpretations of stanza lengths and line breaks in previous editions are discussed in the explanatory notes.

Carols and burdens. In the manuscript each carol opens with its burden (i.e., refrain), followed by the verses. The burden was sung after each verse, and the scribes assume an audience that knows the pattern. In just three of the carols (Carols 11, 13, 18), one of the scribes writes "*ut supra*" to indicate a portion of the repetitions. In this edition the carols are printed in their full sung form: opening burden and then its repetition after each verse stanza. The carols are copied in the manuscript by Scribe A (burden and verses) with Scribe B supplying the titles.

Cross-references to the Whiting edition. Numbers prefixed with "W" refer to Ella Keats Whiting's editorial system of numbers assigned to the verse contents of MS Douce 302. Other previous editors are cited in the explanatory and textual notes.

[X.] TRUE LIVING [W1]

. . . .

	In hel ne purgatoré non other plase,	*nor; nor any other place*
	Thes synnes wold make you schamyd and schent,	*ashamed; disgraced*
	And lese your worchyp in erth and grace.	*lose your honor on earth*
	Al day, with ene, sene thou has	*eyes, you have seen*
5	Hou men bene slayne fore dedlé synne	
	And han vengans fore here trespace;	*receive retribution; their*
	Both lyve and goodes thay lesyn then,	*life; lose*
	Bi londys law.	*law of the land*
	Yif thai had kept Cristis comaundment,	
10	Thai schuld never be schamyd ne chent,	*disgraced*
	Ne lost here lyfe ne lond ne rent,	*income*
	Nouther hongud ne draw.	*Nor be hanged nor drawn (executed)*
	Hel is not ordent fore ryghtwyse mon,	*ordained; righteous man*
	Bot fore hom that here serven the Fynd;	*them; Devil*
15	No more ys a preson of lyme and ston	*prison; limestone*
	Bot to hom that the lauys thai done offend,	*Only for them; laws*
	Fore wyckyd dedys makys thevys ischent,	*thieves disgraced*
	Hye on galouys fore to heng.	*gallows*
	Ther rightwyse men thai han god end,	*These; have a good end*
20	Fore thay bene treue in here levyng —	
	Trust wel therto!	
	He that levys here ryghtwysly,	*lives here righteously*
	On what deth that ever he dy,	
	His soul never schal ponyschyd be,	*punished*
25	Ne never wyt of wo.	*experience woe*
	The syn of sodom, into heven	*sodomy*
	Hit crys ever on God Almyght!	*cries*
	And monslaght, with a rewful steven	*manslaughter; rueful voice*
	Hit askys vengans day and nyght!	
30	Extorcyons agayns the ryght,	
	And huyrus that with wrong holdon be:	*payments*
	Damnacion to ham hit is ydyght	*them; ordained*

That usyn these, and avowteré —   *adultery*
    Everychon!
35   These synnys a mon thai done blynde,   *These sins do blind a man*
    Fore thai be don agayns kynde,   *against nature*
    And bene the werkys of the Fynde
        Of damnacion.

Thre synns princypaly a man doth mare —   *ruin*
40   Murthyr, theuft, and avoutré —   *Murder; theft; adultery*
    Thai wyl you schend ore ye be ware!   *disgrace you before you know [it]*
    Be thai done never so prevely,   *privately*
    The Fynd wyl schew ham hopunly,   *them openly*
    That al the word schal have wyttyng,   *world; knowledge*
45   Fore thai bene cursyd in heven on hye.
    Ale that usus that cursid doyng,   *use; doing*
        Thai wyl be schent.
    Fore morther, Cayme cursud of God was he,   *Cain [Genesis 4:11]*
    And fore theft, thevys al day hongud thay be;
50   Fore avoutré, vengans had Kyng Davé   *adultery; David received punishment*
        Fore brekyng of the sacrement.

Avowtré ne lechory, men set not by   *men fear not*
To breke the bond of the sacrement;
Thay schul aby ful sekyrly,   *be punished most certainly*
55   Bot thai have spase ham to repent.   *Unless; space themselves*
    Herefore, ye curatis, ye wyl be schent,   *curates; disgraced*
    And prestis that bene lewyd in here levyng,   *unchaste*
    Fore to this syn ye done asent
    With evyl ensampyl to other yeveng!   *giving*
60   And wretyn hit ys:
        Ye were choson to chastyté,
    To kepe your holy order and your degré   *profession*
    In parfyt love and charité,
        And mend ale other that done amys.   *correct*

65   Kepe youre wedloke, ye weddid men!
    In paradyse God furst hit mad
    Betwene Adam and Eve, with trew love then,   *[Genesis 2:21–24]*
    Both mon and womon therwith to glad;
    Therwith he is both plesud and payd   *satisfied*
70   Yif hit be kept laufully.
    Hymselfe was borne of a mayde   *[God] himself*
    To fulfyl that sacrement princypaly;
        Into herth he come   *earth*
    To make ther eyrus of heven blys;   *their (Adam and Eve's) heirs [gain]*
75   That Lucefyr lost and al hys,   *What Lucifer and all his [company] lost*

Monkynd schal hit agayne encrese　　　　　　　　*replenish*
　　Or the Day of Dome.　　　　　　　　　　　　*Before*

Nou yif a woman maryd schal be,　　　　　　　　*married*
Anoon sche schal be boght and sold;　　　　　　*Soon*
80　Hit is fore no love of hert, treuly,
Bot fore covetyse of lond or gold.
This is Goddis wyle, and his lau wolde:　　　*This [instead]; law's command*
Evan of blood, evan good, evan of age,　　　　*Equal*
Fore love togeder thus cum thai schalde,　*For thus shall they come together for love*
85　Fore thes makus metely maryage　　　*these [equal conditions] suitably make*
　　　　Here in al wyse.　　　　　　　　　　　*in every way*
　　Thai schal have ayres ham betwene,　　　　*heirs*
　　That schal have grace to thryve and thene;　*prosper*
　　Ther other schul have turment and tene　*These others; trouble*
90　　　Fore covetyse.

Ther is no cryatour, as wreton Y fynde,　　　　*creature*
Save only mon that doth outrage;　　　　　　*perverts nature*
Thai chesun here makus of here houne kynd,　*[Animals] choose their mates; own*
With treu love makun here mareage.　　　　　*make*
95　Nou a ladé wyl take a page
Fore no love bot fore fleschely lust,
And al here blood dysparage;　　　　　*disparage by marrying low*
Thes lordys and lordchips, thay ben ilost
　　　In moné a place!　　　　　　　　　　*many*
100　　Lordys and lorchypus, thay wastyn away,
　　That makys false ayris, hit is no nay,　*[By those] who; heirs*
　　And wele and worchyp, foreever and ay,　*weal*
　　　　Onour and grace.　　　　　　　　　*Honor*

Now yif that a man he wed a wyfe
105　And hym thynke sche plese hym noght,
Anon ther rysis care and stryfe;　　　　　　*arises*
He wold here selle that he had boght,
And schenchypus here that he hath soght,　*embarrasses*
And takys to hym a lotoby.　　　　　　　*paramour*
110　These bargeyn wyle be dere aboght　*This bargain; dearly bought*
Here ore henns he schal aby!　　　　　*or later he will pay*
　　　He is foresworne:　　　　　　　*has broken his oath*
　　When he as chosyn hyr to his make,　*has; mate*
　　And plyght here trowth to here ytake,　*plighted his troth to marry her*
115　Hy schulde never here foresake,
　　　Even ne morne.　　　　　　　　　*Evening or morn*

Agayns ale this, remedy I fynde:
Foresake youre syn, Y you pray!

To God and mon loke ye be kynde
120   (To heven ther is nother way),   *no other*
       And make amendis wyle that ye may!   *while*
       Yif ye wyl have remyssyon,
       God ye most both plese and pay   *please and satisfy*
       (Or ellus have damnacion)   *else*
125   ·   Wyle ye han space.
       Thus graciously says the Kyng of Blys,
       "Yeff ye wyl mend that ye do mysse,   *If; amend; amiss*
       Nolo mortem peccatoris,[1]
            Ye schul have grace."

130   In what order or what degré   *religious order or estate*
       Holé Cherche hath bound thee to,
       Kepe hit wel, I counsel thee;   *Uphold*
       Dyssyre thou never to go therfro,
       Fore thou art boundon, go were thou goo.   *wherever you go*
135   When thou hast ressayvd the sacrament,   *received*
       Ther is no mon may hit undoo,
       Bot he be cursid, verament.   *Unless he be damned, truly*
            In the Gospel thou sist   *see*
            That God be law byndus yfyre,   *That what God by law binds together*
140   Ther is no mon that hath pouere   *power*
       Hit to undo in no manere,
            Bot he be curst.

       Love your God over al thyng,   *above*
       Youre neghbore as yourselfe, as I you saye.   [Matthew 19:19]
145   Let be youre othis, youre false sweryng.   *Forsake; oaths*
       In clannes kepe youre haleday.   *sinlessness; holy day*
       Youre fader, youre moder, worchip ay.   *always*
       Sle no mon fore wordlé thyng.   *Slay; worldly*
       Bakbyte no mon, nyght ne day,   *Gossip about*
150   Ne say no word to hym sklaunderyng;   *slanderous*
       False wytnes, loke thou non bere.   *Look that you do not bear false witness*
       Dysseyte ne theft, loke thou do non,   *Deceit*
       And lechory, thou most foreswere;
       Here beth the comaundmentis, everychon —   *every one* [Exodus 20:1–17]
155   ·   Loke ye kepe hem wele!

----

[1] *I desire not the death of a sinner.* Compare Ezechiel 33:11 (*dicit Dominus Deus nolo mortem impii sed ut revertatur impius a via sua, et vivat,* "saith the Lord God, I desire not the death of the wicked, but that the wicked turn from his way, and live"), Ezechiel 18:32 (*quia nolo mortem morientis dicit Dominus Deus revertimini et vivite,* "For I desire not the death of him that dieth, saith the Lord God, return ye and live"), and Ezechiel 18:23. This Latin line serves as the refrain in *God's Address to Sinful Men.* Compare also *Marcolf and Solomon,* lines 790–92; *Our Lord's Epistle on Sunday,* line 115 (see explanatory note to lines 114–17); and *The Vision of Saint Paul,* explicit.

I rede ye serven Heven Kyng,   *counsel*
Fore ané loust or lykyng,   *any desire or pleasure*
Have mynd apon youre endyng,   *Be mindful of*
    Of the payns of helle.

160   Another remedé yet ther is —
    Gentyl seres, herkens to me! —
    The Seven Werkys of Mercé, so have I blys,
    I wyl declare ham oponlé.   *openly*
    Thai schul be schewed ful petuysly   *shown; pitiably*
165   At Domysday, at Cristis cumyng,
    Ther God and mon present schal be,
    And al the world on fuyre brennyng,   *fire burning*
        A reuful aray!   *pitiful*
      Then wele is hym, and wele schal be,
170   That doth these werkys with peté;   *compassion*
      He schal have grace and mercé
        On Domysday.

    The hungré, gif mete; the thorsté, gif dryng.   *food; thirsty; drink*
    Cleth the nakyd, as I thee say.   *Clothe*
175   Vysyte the seke in preson lying,   *Visit; sick*
    And beré the ded, as I thee pray.   *bury*
    And herbere the pore that goth be the way,   *shelter*
    And teche the unwyse of thi cunnyng.[1]   *ignorant; knowledge*
    Do these werkys both nyght and day
180   To Goddis worchip and his plesyng —
        This is his wylle! —
      Ever have this in thi mynd:
      To the pore, loke thou be kynd,
      Then in heven thou schalt hit fynd
185   Thou schalt never spyle.   *be destroyed*

    Thi Fyve Wyttis thou most know —
    Thonke thi God that land ham thee! —   *lent them*
    Thi heryng, thi seyng (as I thee schewe   *call*
    Thi syght), thi smellyng, here be thre;
190   Thi touchyng, thi tastyng, here fyve ther be,
    To reule thee withyn thi levyng.   *rule; existence*
    God hath thee graundid ham graciously,   *granted*
    Hym to love over al thyng.   *[So that you might] love him*
        His wyl hit is.
195   Yif thi fyve wittis here bynn welle spend,   *are; spent*

---

[1] The seven works of mercy; compare Matthew 25:31–46. Audelay treats the subject elsewhere: *God's Address to Sinful Men*, lines 164–71, and *Seven Works of Mercy*.

Thi God thou schalt noght afend,   *offend*
Bot bryng thiselfe to good end
    Into heven blys.

Ellys a mon, he were unablle   *Suppose; incapable [of reason]*
200   As a best ys of kynd;   *beast; by nature*
Bott mon ys made resnabyle,   *able to reason*
Good and evyl to have in his mynd,
And has fre choys, as we fynde,   *free choice*
Weder he wyl do good or ylle,   *Whether; evil*
205   Owther ysavyd or ellys yschent.   *Either to be saved or else ruined*
Owther have heven or ellus have helle,
    Thou hast fre choys!   *free choice*
    Then, I red, foresake the Fynd!   *advise*
    To God and mon, loke thou be kynd,
210   And have his Passyon in thi mynd,
    That dyed on cros.

Thou most have Fayth, Hope, and Charyté.
This is the ground of thi beleve,
Ellys isavyd thou maght not be.
215   Thus Poul, in his pystyl, he doth preve.   *epistle* [1 Corinthians 13:13]*; attest*
Then God and mon thou schalt never greve;   *grieve*
This is the ground of good levyng.
Then Charyté, he is chif;   *chief*
Herfore he lovys God over al thyng.
220   This wyl I preve:
    Lok in thi merour —   *mirror*
    Yif thou love thi neghtboure,   [Matthew 19:19]
    Then thou lovyst thi Savyoure;
    Thou art trew in thi beleve!

225   Thi beleve is the Fayth of Holé Cherche.
Soule, in Hope God hath ordynd thee   *ordained*
Ever good werkys that thou schuld werche   *Always*
And be rewarded therfore in heven on hye.
Then Charyté chif callid is hee,
230   Fore he counselys uche mon that is levyng
To do as thou woldest me dud by thee,   *one* [Matthew 7:12]
And bryng thi lyf to good endyng,
    Here and hen.   *hence*
    Do fore youreself ore ye gone,   *before; go*
235   Or mede of God get ye none,   *reward*
    Bot sone be foregetone   *[you will be] forgotten*
    Of kyth and of kyn.   *people and kinsmen*

	Ever have peté of the pore	*Always; compassion*
	Of the goodus that God thee sende.	*By [sharing] the goods*
240	Thou hast non other here tresoure	*treasure here*
	Agayns the Day of Jugyment,	
	Or ellys thou schalt be schamyd and chent	
	When thou art callid to thi rekynyng.	*reckoning*
	Ther God and mon schal be present,	
245	And al the world on fuyre brenyng,	*fire burning*
	Thee to afray!	*frighten*
	Yif thou have partyd with the pore,	*shared*
	God wyl thonke thee therfore,	
	And in his kyngdom thee restore	
250	The lyf that lastyth ay.	

	The pore schul be made domysmen	*judges*
	Apon the ryche at Domysday;	
	Let se houe thai cun onswere then	*how*
	For al here ryal, reverent aray!	*royal, dignified array*
255	In hunger, in cold, in thurst — weleway! —	*alas!*
	Afftyr here almes ay waytyng:	*always waiting*
	"Thay wold not vysete us, nyght ne day!"	
	Thus wyl thai playn ham to Heven Kyng,	*complain*
	That is above:	
260	"Thus we dydon myschyvysly;	*suffered*
	Fore hungyr and thurst, ful petuysly	*piteously*
	Thai nold not on us have no peté,	*would not*
	Ny for thai love."	*Nor; thy*

. . . .

INSTRUCTIONS FOR READING 1   [NOT IN W]

The Day of Dome shuld come in here;	
Ver the defawte of the wrytere;	*On account of the writer's mistake*
At the thirtenth leef afore hyt ys;	*before [this folio]*
Seche hyt there, thou shalt nott mys.	*Search for*

XI. MARCOLF AND SOLOMON   [W2]

[Lines 1–65: Introduction]

De concordia inter rectores fratres et rectores ecclesie.[1]

God hath grauntyd grace unto oure lernyng
Al that we fyndon fayfully wrytyn in Holé Wryt,
That be our pacyens, princypaly, and holy wrytyng,   *by; patience*
We schuld have consolacion and comford — byleve truly in hyt!
5   I schal say you the soth, that wele schul ye wyt,   *truth; know*
Hit is Godys Word and his werke and his worchyng.   *It (i.e., Holy Writ); making*
Be the grace of the Holé Gost, togedyr hit is yknyt,   *By; composed*
Redlé us to remembyr in oure redyng,   *For us to recall easily*
          And hold hit in mynde:
10   Ther is no mon that saved may be,
              But he have Faythe, Hope, and Charité,   *[1 Corinthians 13:13]*
              And do as thou woldust me dud by thee,   *[See Matthew 7:12]*
                  To God and men, be kynde.   *courteous (as nature demands)*

Hec est fides catholyca.[2]

This foreward furst we mad at the fontston,   *agreement; baptismal font*
15   Tofore owre fader faythfely, that folowed us in fay,   *Before our father; sought; faith*
To forsake Syr Sathanas — his werkus everychon —   *every one of his deeds*
And become Criston men to byleve in God veray,   *truly*
And kepe his comawndmentis kyndly, nyght and day.   *by natural instinct*
Ther we were croysid in a crysum, with a carful krye;   *crossed; chrism; anxious cry*
20   To this covenant was callud to wytnes, Y say,
Oure godfars, oure godmoders, to stond ther us by.   *godfathers*
              When we myght not speke,
              Ther thai answerd fore us
              In the name of Jhesus,
25   Al thre with one woys.   *voice*
                  This bond we schuld noght breke!

Time Dominum, et mandata serva.[3]

Hwoso brekys this bond, bare thai bene of blys —   *Whoso; barren; are*
Bot thai ben salvyd of here syn or thai hense passe,   *Unless; absolved; before*
Thai schuln wytt of wo, Y warne youe ywys!   *shall know woe; indeed*

---

[1] *Concerning a loveday [i.e., accord] between friars and secular priests.*

[2] *This is the catholic faith.* From the Athanasian Creed.

[3] *Fear the Lord, and keep his commandments.* Compare Ecclesiastes 12:13.

30   Hit schale be ponyschid here, ore hennus evere trespasse;[1]
        Men have not this in mynd, nowther more ne lasse.   *nor less*
        Thai most obey obedyans that thai be boundon to,   *rules*
        And mend here here mysdedys, and here matens and masse,[2]
        And kepe the comawndmentis of Crist. This deuté most thai doo   *duty*
35   With devocion,
            Fore thai beth ayres of heven blis!   *are heirs*
            The Fader of Heven hath grauntud ham this,   *has granted them this*
            Yif thai wyle mend that thai do mys   *amend what they do amiss*
                To have remyssyon.

        Sapiencia huius mundi stulticia est aput Dominum.[3]

40   "Alas, al the wyt of this word fallus to foly!"   *wisdom; world*
        Thus sayth Sapyens, forsoth, in the Boke of Lyfe.   *(i.e., Solomon, in Ecclesiastes)*
        He has wysdam and wyt, I tel yow trewly,
        That can beware or he be wo and leve in clene lyve.   *Who; before; woeful*
        Who mai kepe hym unkyt fro a kene knyfe   *himself uncut*
45   Yif he boldly that blad touche in his tene?   *blade [should] touch wrongfully*
        No more may a mon here, maydon, ne wyfe   *here a man, maiden, nor wife*
        Plese God unto his pay bot his consyans be clene.   *Satisfy; debt; unless; conscience*
                Ensaumpil I make:
                Who may here serve a lorde?
50   Bot yif he hold hym forwarde,   *abides by an agreement*
                He getys never reward,
                    Y dare undertake!

        Si quis diligit me sermonem meum servabit.[4]

        He that sayth he lovys his Lord — on hym take good eme —   *heed*
        And kepus not his comawndmentis as a Cristyn mon,
55   Leve he is a lyere! His dedis thai done hym deme,   *Believe; liar; will him judge*
        Fore he schuld walke the same wayes his Lord had igone.
        Ellys, lely, hit is like that treu love ys ther non,   *[Or] else, truly*
        Fore he schuld sew his Soferayns and his Saveour.   *follow*
        This may ye kyndlé know. Hit is treu as ané ston!   *instinctively; any*
60   He lese ale his lyve-days and his labour,   *[shall] lose; life-days*
                And stondis in gret drede.
            He that is untreu to his Lorde,
            Outher in dede or in word,   *Either*

---

[1] *It shall be punished here, or afterwards always work evil*

[2] *And mend here their misdeeds, and hear matins and mass*

[3] *For the wisdom of this world is foolishness with the Lord.* Compare 1 Corinthians 3:19. Compare also *Audelay's Conclusion, incipit.*

[4] *If anyone love me, he will keep my word.* John 14:23; compare John 14:15.

	The law wyl hym rewarde —	
65	Deth to his mede.	*Death [is] his reward*

[Lines 66–169: Criticism of those who neglect souls]

Vox populi vox Dei.[1]

	I, Marcol, the more fole mon, on my mad wyse,	*Marcolf; more fool; way*
	I send thee, broder Salamon, to say, as I here,	*enjoin; brother Solomon; hear*
	Hou homlé hosbondusmen, here hertis thai aryse,	*humble husbandmen, their*
	Thai woldon thai wroghton wysely, that schuld ham lede and lere.[2]	
70	Do thi message mekely to pryst and to frere;	*Take; priest; friar*
	Thai are the lanternys of lyf, the leud men to lyght,	*illiterate*
	Bot thai be caght with covetyse, with consians unclere,	*Unless; are entangled in avarice*
	Ageyns the lauys of here Lord, reson and ryght.	*laws*
	Hit is noght unknow.	*(i.e., It is well known)*
75	Comawnd hem in al wyse —	
	Never onother thai dar dyspyse! —	*(i.e., They will listen only to you!)*
	Fore here cursid covetyse,	*their*
	Here horne is eblaw.	*horn (i.e., judgment); blown; (see note)*

Ubi est tesaurus tuus, ibi et cor tuum erit.[3]

	Counsel ham fro Covetyse. Cursid mot he be!	*them [to turn away] from*
80	He wyl hem lede to here lost and lyke to be lore;	*loss and likely damnation*
	Yif thai foluyn his fare, thai fallyn to foly.	*follow; path; fall*
	He wyl ham gyde gylfully and goo hem before;	*guide guilefully*
	Have thai never so mekyl mok, he wyl have more;	*much muck (i.e., property)*
	With wylis and with wrongus, he wyl hit ay wyn.	*always acquire [more]*
85	He is unkynd and uncurtes. He kepis not to restore	*unnatural; uncourteous*
	That he takys amys, to no maner mon,	*What; wrongfully*
	Hent his endyng.	*Until*
	Then is he a traytour	
	Fore he trustys to his secatour;	*executor*
90	He schuld his soule socour	*succor*
	Here in his levyng.	*Here in his life*

Averte oculos tuos, ne vidiant vanitatem.[4]

---

[1] *The voice of the people [is] the voice of God.* Compare Isaias 66:6.

[2] *They want those who should lead and teach them to act wisely.*

[3] *Where thy treasure is, there is thy heart also.* Compare Matthew 6:21, Luke 12:34.

[4] *Avert thy eyes, so that they may not see vanity.* Compare Psalm 118:37, which has *meos*, "mine," instead of *tuos*, "thy."

	Dispise thou no pristhod, broder, I thee pray,	*priesthood*
	Bot Veynglory, and here vysis and here vanité;	*Vainglory; their vices; their vanity*
	Bed ham mend that thay do mys — spare not to say! —	*Bid them amend*
95	Fore her dedus wyl hem deme, yif thai be gylté.	*guilty*
	Thai schuld rader repreve the synnys that thai se	*rather; reprove*
	Rennyng and reynyng in the reume al aboute,	*Running and flourishing; realm*
	And clanse here consyans clene, and kepe charité;	*cleanse*
	Then myght thai say a sad soth, and stond out of doute	*sober truth; guiltless*
100	In al mens syght.	
	Therof the pepul wold be fayne	*pleased*
	Fore to cum home agayne,	
	That hath goon gatis ungayne	*[on] unpleasant roads*
	For defaute of lyght.	*lack*

Quod natura didit nemo tollere poterit.[1]

105	Uche best that ys blest, togeder thai wyl draw	*beast; blessed*
	Be kynd to the cuntré that thai come fro,	*By nature; region*
	Yet thai ben unleryd, unwyse in the law,	*Though; unlearned*
	Bot as nature has ham noryschid, hit nedus no noder to do.	*Nourished; other*
	We were put in paradise to have wele withoutyn woo,	*happiness*
110	Hent we had, unblest, brokyn the comaundmentis of our Kyng,	*Until*
	That is Lord of ale lordys. Hwere bene oné moo	*Where is [there] any other*
	That mai us salve of oure sore, oure botyng to us bryng?	*Who; heal; health*
	That Lord, be he blest!	
	I rede, ye draun to your Kyng,	*draw*
115	Fore oné lust or lykyng!	*By a [natural] desire*
	Pray hem with here prechyng	*Bid them (i.e., priests)*
	To set mon soule in rest.	

Filius non portabit iniquitatem patris, etc., set unusquisque onus suum portabit.[2]

	What was Abel the worse, thagh Kayme his borne broder[3]	
	Were cursid for his covetyse and his creuel dede?	*[Genesis 4:11]*
120	No more ys a good prest the worse fore another,	
	That wyle love his Lord God, hym serve and drede.	*Who*
	Make moche of a good mon! On hym, take good hede!	
	Loke ye bete not Bayard for bryd ne fore brend!	*beat; rashness nor for passion*
	Ale a seté may be savyd and schal the better spede	*city; prosper*
125	Throgh the prayere of a good prest, an holé and an hynd,	*a holy one and a servant*

---

[1] *What nature has given, no one will be able to take away.* Proverb.

[2] *The son will not bear the iniquity of the father [and the father will not bear the iniquity of the son: the justice of the just shall be upon him, and the wickedness of the wicked shall be upon him], but everyone shall bear his own burden.* Compare Ezechiel 18:20; Galatians 6:5.

[3] *How was Abel any the worse, though Cain his born brother*

That kepys his ordore.	*Who upholds his sworn duties*
He whot never hou sone	*knows; soon*
God wyl here his bone,	*request*
And ale that here wele done,	*do well*
130 Heryd ys here prayoure.	*Heard is their*

Declinate a me, malingni, etc.[1]

Yif ther be a pore prest, and spirituale in spiryt,	*humble*
And be devoute with devocion, his servyse syng and say,	
Thay lekon hym to a Lollere and to an epocryte.	*Lollard; hypocrite*
Yif he be besé in his bedus, the Prince of Heven to pay,	*busy; prayers; satisfy*
135 And holde hym in Holé Cherche, dulé uche day,	*conforms to; duly*
Oute of the curse of cumpané, and kepe his concyans clene,	*course; company*
He ys a nythyng, a noght, a negard, thai say.	*niggard*
Bot yif he folou his felows, his chekys mai be ful lene —	*Unless; cheeks*
On hym, men han no mynde.	
140 A holy prest men set not by!	
Therfor ther bene bot feu, truly!	*few*
Thai kepe not of here cumpany —	
To hom, men beth unkynde.	*are discourteous*

Increpasti superbos. Maledicti qui declinant a mandatis tuis.[2]

Oure gentyl Ser Jone — joy hym mot betyde! —	*noble Sir John; may come to him*
145 He is a meré mon of mouth among cumpané.	*merry*
He con harpe! He con syng! His orglus ben herd ful wyd!	*instruments are (see note)*
He wyl noght spare his purse to spend his selaré —	*salary*
Alas, he ner a parsun or a vecory!	*he seems not; vicar*
Be Jhesu, he is a gentyl mon, and jolylé arayd —	*By; jollily*
150 His gurdlis harneschit with selver, his baslard hongus bye —[3]	
Apon his perte pautener, uch mon ys apayd,	*open purse*
Both maydyn and wyfe.	
Ifayth, he schale noght from us gon,	
Fore oure myrth, hit were edon,	*For [then] our mirth would be over*
155 Fore he con glad us everychon!	*gladden*
Y pray God hold his lyve!	*shield his life*

Vanitas vanitatum et omnia vanitas.[4]

---

[1] *Depart from me, ye malignant: [and I will search the commandments of my God].* Psalm 118:115.

[2] *Thou hast rebuked the proud. They are cursed who decline from thy commandments.* Compare Psalm 118:21.

[3] *His girdles equipped with silver, his dagger hangs by*

[4] *Vanity of vanities, and all is vanity.* Ecclesiastes 1:2; compare Ecclesiastes 12:8.

	Thus this wyckyd world is plesid with vanité,	*vanity*
	And wrathyn God wyttyngly, unwysely evermore;	*[it] angers; knowingly, foolishly*
	God, of his gret grace, graunt hem that beth gulté	*guilty*
160	Here mysse and here mysdedus, to mend here therfore;	*sins; misdeeds; repent*
	And let hem never fore here lust, Lord, be forelore,	*desires; damned*
	Bot send soreue in here hert, here synnus to slake;	*contrition*
	Into thi curte and thi kyngdam, Lord, hem restore;	*court*
	From ale temtacion and tene, the Treneté us take,	*trouble; Trinity*
165	His hestis to fulfyle.	*commands*
	Here schul ye here anon	
	Of men of relegyon —	
	What lyfe thay leedon,	*lead*
	Goddus heest to fulfyl.	*commandment*

[Lines 170–390: On monks]

Relegio munda et inmaculata. Hoc est preceptum meum: ut diligatis invicem.[1]

170	I move these mater to monkys in a meke maner,	*address this subject*
	And to al relegyous that beth iblest by Goddis ordynans.	*ordinance*
	Forst Saynt Benet hom enformyd to kepe her cloyster,	*First Benedict informed them*
	In povert and in prayerys, in prevé penawns;	*private penance*
	And to abeyde abstinens, and foresake abundans,	*endure*
175	To sle the lust of hore lycam and hore lykyng;	*slay; body; pleasure*
	And obey obedyans, and kepe observans;	*monastic rule*
	Both in cloystyr and in quere, holdyth sylens fore ané thyng.	*choir; silence*
	And to God and mon, be kynde,	*naturally harmonious*
	And ryse at mydnyght out of here ryst,	*sleep*
180	And pray fore here good-doers, as breder iblest,	*their; brethren blessed*
	And depart here almys, lest hit be lest,	*disperse; lost*
	Fore the founders that hem fynd.	*On behalf of the donors*

	Fore in the rewle of relygyous, ther may ye rede	*rule*
	Hou the graceous goodys of God schuld be spend;	*spent*
185	Uche person schuld have his part after that he had ned,[2]	
	And cast hit al in comyn, the goodys that God ham send,	*common*
	And leve not lyke leud men fore schame, lest ye be schent,	*Live; ignorant*
	That storon stryf and wrath because of covetyng.	*stir strife*
	Ye schuld have no propurté; on the pore hit schuld be spend!	
190	And hold up youre houshold and youre housyng,	*(i.e., maintain your standards)*
	And let hem not adoune,	

---

[1] *Religion pure and unspotted* [James 1:27]. *This is my commandment: that you love one another* [John 15:12]. For the phrase *ut diligatis invicem*, see also John 13:34, 15:17; 1 Thessalonians 4:9. Audelay repeats the phrase at *Marcolf and Solomon*, line 268.

[2] *Each person should have his share according to his need*

	And herbore the pore, pur charyté,	*shelter; for*
	And yef mete and dreng to the nedé,	*give food; drink*
	And cumford hom that woful be —	*comfort; miserable*
195	Ellis be ye no relegyon!	*Or else you are no [man of] religion*

Servite Domino in timore, et exultate ei cum tremore.[1]

	Both in cloyster and in quere, when that thai syng and rede	*choir*
	Aperte et distincte,[2] han mynd for hom thay pray,	*whom*
	And kepun her pausus and her poyntis — ellus myght thai gete no mede! —[3]	
	Fore thus sayth here Sovereyns, sothly to say:	
200	"Mi pepyl praysy me with here lyppus; here hertis ben far away,[4]	
	Fore thai be caght with covetyse, that schal ham cast in care.	
	To the worchip of this world, thai wryn fro me away;	*turn*
	Thai han no lykyng ne no lust to lerne apon my lare.	*teaching*
	To me, thai beth unkynd —	
205	Agayns my gret goodnes,	
	Thai chewyn me unbuxumnes,	*show; disobedience*
	And I graunt ham foregifnes —	
	Thai have not this in mynd."	

. . . rat in vanum . . . t

	Thus he prevys youre prayers and your spiritualté,	*assesses*
210	For when ye prayyn to your God, ye spekyn with hym in spyrit,	
	And yif ye redon in Holé Wryt, he speke agayn with thee.	*read; speaks*
	Remembyr you redely when ye red — ther may ye wyle wyt! —	*readily; well learn*
	Take knoulache at youre consians, fore ther hit is yknyt;[5]	
	Thus sayth Marke, sothely, Mathou, Louke, and Jon.	
215	No mon mese in this mater ny in Holy Wryt,	*No one [may] dispute; nor*
	For ale the four doctors acordon ale in hon,	*(i.e., Gospels) accord entirely in unity*
	And clerkys of deveneté,	*divinity*
	Thai conferme the same,	*confirm*
	And comawndoun in Cristis name:	
220	Holé Wryt no mon blame;	
	Hit is Goddis preveté.	*divine mystery*

---

[1] *Serve ye the Lord with fear: and rejoice unto Him with trembling.* Compare Psalm 2:11.

[2] *[And they read in the book of the law of God] distinctly and plainly [to be understood: and they understood when it was read].* 2 Esdras 8:8.

[3] *And keep their pauses and their periods — else might they get no reward*

[4] Compare Isaias 29:13; Matthew 15:8.

[5] *Take knowledge from your conscience, for there it is joined*

Beatus qui intellegit super egenum et pauperem.[1]

	Fayne mai be the fadyrs and al the fonders	*Pleased; fathers; founders (lay patrons)*
	That sustyne or sokeron relygious in oné way,	*sustain; support; men of religion*
	And so mai be, sothli, ale here good-doars,	*truly; their good-doers*
225	That prayn for hom besyly, both nyght and day.	*For whom [those monks] pray busily*
	When your caren is yclunggun and cast into clay,	*flesh; withered*
	Hore matyns, here masse, fore ham, thai red and syng.[2]	
	When ale the welth of this word is went from hem away,	
	Then the bedis of Holé Cherche, thai beth abydyng	*prayers; are permanent*
230	Foreever and for ay.	
	And do you dredles out of drede:	*(i.e., And do believe this)*
	Thai schal have heven to here mede,	
	That socures relegyous at nede,	*[They] who help*
	Her in ané way.	*Here*

Da tua dum tua sunt; post mortem tunc tua non sunt.[3]

235	Lokys, lordus, to youre lyffe and to your levyng —	
	For I am touchid upon the tong, the soth for to say! —	*tongue; truth*
	Thagh ye be leders of the lond, gete you lovyng,	*leaders; acquire [Christian] loving*
	And cale the clargé to your counsel, that beryn Cristis kay,[4]	
	And holdist up Holé Cherche, the Prinse of Heven to pay.	*support; satisfy*
240	Y dred lest dedlé sun this reeme wyl dystry,	*sin; realm; destroy*
	Fore the lauys of this lond ben lad a wrong way,	*are led*
	Both temperale and spirituale, Y tel you treuly,	*temporal*
	Even up-so-doune!	*upside down*
	Yif Goddes lawys ye dystry,	*destroy*
245	And Holy Cherche set not by,	
	Then, farewelle, the clergy!	
	Hit is your damnacion.	

	Takys fayre ensampyle be your faders that were you before,	
	Hou thai worchypd Holé Cherche hyly to Godys honore:	*piously*
250	Therfore thai blessun her burth and the bodys that ham bare,	
	For thai knouyn wel in her consians hit was her tresoure;	
	For al har lordchip and here londys, hit farys as a floure —[5]	
	This day hit ys fresche, tomorow hit is fadyng!	
	A sad ensampyl, forsoth, your soule to socour,	*somber example*

---

[1] Compare Psalm 40:2, *Blessed is he who understands above all the needy and the poor.*

[2] *Their matins, their mass, for them (the patrons), they read and sing*

[3] *Give your things while they are yours; after death then they are not yours*

[4] *And call the clergy to your counsel, who bear Christ's key.* Compare Matthew 16:19.

[5] Lines 250–52: *Therefore they bless their birth and the bodies that bore them / For they know well in their conscience it (i.e., their lives) was their treasure; / For all their lordship and their lands, it passes as a flower*

255   And do as youre faders ded before, here in here levyng.   *did; their*
            Hit is fore the best —
            Do fore youreself or ye gone;   *before; go*
            Trust not to another mon
            (Ellus med of God get ye non!),   *reward*
260   Bot then ye be eblest.   *blessed*

Qui perceveraverit usque in finem, hic salvus erit.[1]

      Redelé these relegyos men schul have hygh reward   *Certainly*
      Yif thai kepyn her cloyster and here comawndment.   *maintain; monastic rule*
      Fore oné fondyng of the Fynd, fulfyl your forward,   *Against any temptation; agreement*
      And castis awai covetyse, that is cause of cumberment,   *encumberment*
265   And kepe youe clene in chastyté. To chareté ale asent.   *wholly assent*
      What sayd your Soveren to his dyssiplis, when he dyd wasche hem,   [John 13:5]
      And knelud louly apon his knen tofore his blessid covent,[2]
      And betoke hom this tokyn, *diligatis invicem?*[3]   *gave them*
            "As I have lovyd yow,
270   Then joyful schal ye be,
            For in my kyngdom ye schul me se,
            And sit apon my dome with me.
            My counsel schale ye knoue."

Honora Deum tuum de tuis substanciis.[4]

      Withdraw ye not fro Holé Cherche your faderes han yeven before[5]
275   To the prelatis and the prystis, fore hom fore to pray;   *them (i.e., your fathers)*
      Bot ye han grace of God hit to restore,   *Unless*
      Ye schul yild a carful counte on dredful Domysday.   *yield an accurate account*
      Y rede ye mend your mysdedus here wyle ye may,   *advise; repent*
      And let no cursid counsel cast you in care,   *wicked*
280   Fore ale the worchyp of this word, hit wyl wype sone away —   *world*
      Hit falls and fadys forth, so doth a cheré fayre!   *cherry fair*
            Thenke wel on this:
            Thai bene acursid be Goddis law,   *by*
            The goodys of Holé Cherche that withdrawe,[6]
285   That other han geven in holdon daw   *What others have given in former days*
            To mayntyn Godys servyse.

---

[1] *The one who perseveres to the end will be saved.* Compare Matthew 10:22.

[2] *And knelt humbly upon his knees before his blessed band of apostles*

[3] *[That] you love one another.* John 13:34, 1 Thessalonians 4:9; see *Marcolf and Solomon,* line 169a.

[4] *Honor your Lord with your substance.* Compare Proverbs 3:9.

[5] *Do you not withdraw from Holy Church [the alms] your fathers have given before*

[6] *Who withdraw [from] the goods of Holy Church*

Quid prodest homini, si universum mundum lucretur?[1]

Thus have I cumford you, covens, and counsel you fro care![2]

I rede ye obey obedyens that ye bene bowndon to.   *rules*

Then schul ye bles your byrth and the bodys that youe bare,   *bodies that bore you*

290   For ye forsake this wyckyd word, to have wele without woo. *For [then] you [shall]; joy*

This may ye know kyndlé, yfayth, both frynd and fo.   *instinctively, in faith*

Remember you of the ryche mon, and redlé on his end,   *actively [think] upon*

What is reches, his reverans, his ryot broght hym to: *his riches; dignity; extravagance*

Sodenlé was send to hele with moné a foul fynde[3]

295   To serve Ser Satanas,

     Fore to his God he was unkynd;

     The lazar he had not in his mynd,   *poor man*

     Fore worldys worchip, hit con hym blynd,

     Therfore he syngys, "Alas!"[4]

Humilitas est radix omnium virtutum.   *Humility is the root of all the virtues.*

300   Eever have mekenes in your mynd, relegyouse, I you rede,   *humility; advise*

And use vertuys, and leve visis ale vayne, and vaneté;   *practice; abandon vices; vanity*

For yif ye love your Lord God his lauys, thai wyle yow leede   *laws*

Into his court and his coindam, were ys no vangloré —   *kingdom, where; vainglory*

That unfyttyng sun, forsothe, al verteus hit duystry! *unfitting sin (i.e., Pride); destroys*

305   Hit lad Lusyfer to his los, that was an angel clere —   *fall; pure*

God had claryfyud hym so clene of his cortesy,   *purified; courtesy*

He sygh the Trinyté apere within his body clere;   *saw*

     Then enterd in hym envy —

     Whan he hade seyne this gloryis syght,   *glorious*

310   He wolde arast hym his myght;   *wrest from*

     Anoon he fel downe ryght

     Into hel sodenly.

Qui se exaltat umeliabitur.[5]

A sad ensampyl, forsoth, to ale relygyous men   *somber*

That bene caght with covetyse, to be sit in hye astate: *seated; high*

---

[1] *What good does it do a person if he gains the whole world as his profit?* Compare Matthew 16:26, Luke 9:25. The passage also appears in *Marcolf and Solomon*, line 364a.

[2] *Thus have I comforted you, fellows, and counseled you from care*

[3] *Suddenly was [he] sent to hell with many a foul fiend*

[4] The reference is to Jesus' parable of the rich man and the poor man Lazarus, Luke 16:19–25, to which Audelay also alludes in *Marcolf and Solomon*, lines 536–39, and *God's Address to Sinful Men*, lines 241–46.

[5] *The one who exalts himself will be humbled.* Compare Luke 14:11, Luke 18:14.

315	Thai most hem ground furst in grace, hemselve know and ken,[1]	
	Ellys the worchip of this world, hit wyle sone abate.	*soon*
	Ye most have mekenes and mercé, hyghnes of hert hate,	*[and] hate pride of heart*
	And werche not hafter wylsumnes, bot wysdam to youe cale.	*after willfulness; call*
	After chec fore the roke, ware fore the mate,	*check; rook; beware; checkmate*
320	For yif the fondment be false, the werke most nede falle	*foundation*
	Withyn a lytyl stounde.	*time*
	No mon make a covernour	*No man can be a governor*
	Bot yif hit be to Godys honour;	*Unless*
	His worchip wyl fare as floure,	*pass as a flower*
325	Anon gurd to grounde!	*fall*

Non honor sed honus accepere nomen honoris.[2]

	Ther is no worchyp wyt hit, bot a gret charche,	*with it (i.e., high office); responsibility*
	To take the name of astate and of hye honour,	*[high] estate*
	Fore both to God and to mon, thou most ned be large,	*generous*
	Fore thou are choson fore chif and made here covernour;[3]	
330	Then loke thou grounde thee in God and drede thi Saveoure	
	That wyle cale thee to thi countus and to thi rekynyng —	*call; accounts*
	Hou thou hast done thi deuté and, treuly, thi devour,	*duty; obligation*
	And spend his goodys princypaly to His plesyng —	*spent*
	Fore this most thou nede.	
335	Yif thou hast spend more fore the worde	*world*
	Then fore love of thi Lord,	
	The law wyl thee reward —	
	Deth to thi mede!	

Concilium meum non est cum impiis.[4]

	A foul defaute, feythfuly, in Holé Cherche we fynde:	*flaw*
340	To let lordis or leud men make election;	*ignorant; election [of prelates]*
	Thai schul not know your consel. Hit is agayn kynde!	*against nature*
	Fore this cause Saynt Thomas soferd deth and passyon.	*suffered*
	Your chapytre schuld be Cownsel and Confession,	*chapter [of religious order]*
	And now boldly theryn, thay mon thee both halle!	*they both shall haul you in*
345	Thus these preletus, of her prevelache, thay deprevon;[5]	
	There Holy Chirche was fre, now they make hit thrale,	*Where; [once] free; enslaved*

---

[1] *They must ground themselves first in grace, make themselves known*

[2] *It is not an honor but a burden to receive the name of honor.* Perhaps influenced by Ovid, *Heroides* 9.31, *non honor est sed onus* (punning on *honor* and *onus*). The tag also heads *Cur mundus*, copied at the end of the manuscript by Scribe B.

[3] *For you are chosen for chief (i.e., high office) and made here governor*

[4] *My council is not with the wicked.* Written by Scribe B.

[5] *Thus these prelates, by the lords' privilege, deprive [Holy Church]*

lessen

And leson worchip and grace.

To let lord or leud men

Know of youre corexeon,   *correction*

350   Ye men of relegyon   🖎

Beth cursid in that case.

Leges meas custodite, dicit Dominus.[1]

Ye schuld rather sofyr deth, payn, and passyon,   *suffer; torment*

Then lese the love of youre Lord and let down his laue.

Corsid covetyse, hit is the cause, prid, presomseon.   *presumption*

355   Ye beth ungroundid in grace; your God ye con not knowe;

Your dedus demeys youe, dredles! Devocion hit is withdraw.   *deeds judge you, indeed*

Ye han chasid away charyté and the reule of relegyon;

Al gestlé grace and holénes, hit is layd fule lowe.   *spiritual; holiness*

Thus have ye pot Holé Cherche to gret confusion,   *put*

360   And made yourselfe thral!

Godys lauys ye han suspend,

Herefore ye wyl be schamyd and chend;   *disgraced*

Bot ye han grace you to amend,   *Unless*

Ful dere aby ye schal!   *dearly buy [it]*

Quid prodest homini si universum mundum lucretur?[2]

365   Thenke on the cursid covetyse mon that to hymself gon say:

"Ete and drenke and make thee meré; this word is at thi wyle!"[3]

A voyse onswerd hym anon: "Tomorw or hit be day,   *before*

Thi soule sodenly schal be send into the fouyre of hele,   *fire*

Fore thou trustis more to thi tresoure and to thi catele   *property*

370   Then in the love of thi Lord, that ale thi wele hath wroght."   *fortune*

Thou carful caytyf, the curst, hit is treu that I thee telle: *wretched caitiff*

Thou schuldyst thonke thi Lord God that with his blod thee boght —

To hym, thou art unkynd;

Therfore damnyd schalt thou be

375   Into hele perpetualy,

Withoutyn grace and mercy,

World withoutyn end.

---

[1] *Keep my laws, says the Lord.* Written by Scribe B. Compare Leviticus 18:5, 19:19, and 20:22.

[2] *What good does it do a person if he gains the whole world as his profit?* Written by Scribe B. Compare Matthew 16:26, Luke 9:25. The passage also appears in *Marcolf and Solomon*, line 286a.

[3] Lines 365–66: *Think on the cursed covetous man that to himself did say: / "Eat and drink and make merry; the world is at your will!"* Ecclesiastes 8:15.

Qui vult venire post me abneget semetipsum.[1]

	Bot he that wyl come after Crist, and kyndlé bere his cros,	*kindly*
	And crucyfé his caren with love and charyté,	*mortify; flesh*
380	Leve thou me that his love schal not turne to losse;	*Believe*
	Both fore his meryd and his mede, rewardyd schal he be.	*merit; award*
	Ther is no tong that con tele, hert thenke, ne ye se	*tongue; heart conceive, nor eye see*
	That joye, that jocundnes, that Jhesus wyle joyn hym to,	*joyousness*
	Ne the melodé, ne the myry minstrasye!	*merry minstrelsy*
385	Hit is without comparisoun, wele withouton woo,	*joy*
	And love that lastis ay!	
	That joy hit schal never sesse,	*cease*
	Bot ever endoyre and ey ever encresse;	*endure; always increase*
	Thus with rest and with pesse,	*peace*
390	I make a loveday.	*day of accord*

[Lines 391–546: On friars]

Pacem et veritatem diligite ait Dominus omnipotens.[2]

	My blessid broder, Salamon, spesialy I thee pray,	
	Meve this mater maysterfully to prest and to frere;	*Stress this subject*
	Spare not to say the soth, and make a loveday.	
	Loke thou coré not favele ne be no flaterer.	*curry not duplicity nor*
395	I am hevy in my hert, and chaunget al my chere,	*changed entirely in my countenance*
	To wyt leud men, unleryd, lagh ham to scorne.	*teach ignorant; unlearned, [and] laugh*
	Thai were better unborne and broght on a bere,	*bier*
	Bot yif thai mend here mysdede — Y lykyn hem be lorne! —	*Unless they repent*
	And kepe charyté.	*practice charity*
400	Fore mon soule thai schuld save;	
	No spot of sun thai schuld have;	*sin*
	Alas, I trou that thai rave!	*believe*
	Lord, benedyceté!	*Lord, your blessing!*
	Fore schryfte and fore trentale, thai scorne ale this stryf;	*Despite shrift; strife*
405	Yif hit be cause of covetyse, cursud then thai be!	*on account of avarice; doomed*
	Yif thai loven more here lucour then the soule lyve,	*lucre; than; soul's immortality*
	Lytul deynteth of here doctrine and of here dyngnité.	*[They] think little; dignity*
	Fore thai were chosun to be chast and kepe charyté,	
	And cast away covetys, is cause of cumberment,	*sinning*
410	And be clene kalender, the sekelers on to see,	*[a] pure example, for the laity to view*

---

[1] *If any man will come after me, let him deny himself[, and take up his cross, and follow me].* Matthew 16:24; compare Luke 9:23.

[2] *Love peace and truth, says the Lord Almighty.* Compare Zacharias 8:19–20: "only love ye truth and peace. Thus saith the Lord of hosts."

Ellys with chenchip and with chame, thai wyle be echent.   *disgrace; shame; ruined*
    Thai stond in gret drede!
    Pray ham ale, for charyté,
    To save mon soule, spesialy,
415   Ellys woful schale thay be
      Fore her falshede.

Si linguis hominum loquar et angelorum caritatem autem non habeam.[1]

I say thee, broder Salamon, tel in thi talkyng
Furst of the frerys; thus meve thou may   *friars; talk about*
Of here prevelache and of here prayrys and here prechyng,   *privilege*
420 And of here clergé and clannes and onest aray.   *learning; honest garment*
Yif thou say not the soth, then may won say   *one*
That thou art leud and unlerd, and letter canste thou non.[2]
Yif thou touche the treuth, truly thou hem pray   *you [may] bid them*
Fore to holde thee excusid, evereche mon,   *To excuse you, every man*
425   Yif hit be here wyle.   *will*
    I hold hit bot a leude thyng   *corrupt*
    Fore to make a lesyng —   *lie*
    To God hit his displesyng,   *is*
      Outher loud or style.   *Either aloud or silent*

Vos amici mei estis si feceritis quae precepio vobis.[3]

430 The furst founders of the freres and of the four oordyrs   *orders (see note)*
Weron four bernes iblest of oure Saveour, I say,   *men blessed by*
And betokyn here bokys and baggus to be beggers,   *[who] carried; in the way of beggars*
To preche the pepul apert the Prince of Heven to pay,   *[to] the people openly; please*
To borou, to beg, to put schame bothe away,   *borrow*
435 To by and to bylde with here beggyng,   *buy; build*
And pray fore here good-doerys both nyght and day,   *good-doers (i.e., benefactors)*
That sendus ham here sustynans and here levyng   *sustenance; living*
    Here in this worlde —
    Nyght and day, contynualy,
440   Fore hom thai prayn spesealy,
    In matyns, messe, and memoré,
      To here lovely Lord.   *loving*

Petite et accipietis.   *Ask, and you shall receive* [John 16:24]

---

[1] *If I speak with the tongues of men, and of angels, and have not charity[, I am become as sounding brass, or a tinkling cymbal].* 1 Corinthians 13:1.

[2] *That you are foolish and unlearned, and you cannot read*

[3] *You are my friends if you do what I command you.* Compare John 15:14.

	Whosoever sparys fore to speke, sparys for to spede,	*fails to speak; prosper*
	And he that spekys and spedys noght, he spellys the wynd;	*spills the wind*
445	I do youe clene out of dout and dredles out of drede,	
	Better is to speke and sped then hold hit in mynd,	*than*
	Fore moné hanne moné maners, and moné beth unkynd,	*many; unnatural*
	Unclene in here consyans because of covetyse.	*conscience*
	Spek and have, Y thee hete; seche and thou schalt fynd,[1]	
450	Ellys may thou fal in myschif and fare ale amysse;	
	Nyk not this with nay.	*Deny*
	Asay thi frynd or thou have nede,	*friend (confessor or God) before*
	And of his answere take good hede;	
	Thou getyst no good, withoutyn drede,	*certainly*
455	Bot yif thou byd or pray.	*Unless; ask*

Querite et invenietis.   *Seek and you will find* [see Matthew 7:7]

	Yif ye wyle yef ham of your good without beggyng,	
	Thai wold nowther begge ne borou, thus dare I say;	
	And fynd hem here houshold and here housyng,	
	Nouther by ne byld — I red ye asay![2]	
460	Behold, syrus, apon here chyrche, now I you pray,	
	Apon here bellys, on here bokys, and here byldyng,	
	Apon here prechyng, here prayes, her reverent aray;	*prayers*
	Thai pase ale other men in here governyng —	*surpass; governance*
	I whot hit is no nay!	*know it is undeniable*
465	Thai play not the fole,	*fool (i.e., honest truth-teller)*
	Contenualy thai gon to scole;	*school*
	Lordys worchip han thai wole,	*Lords' worship they wish to have*
	And poton folys away.	*put foolishness*

Dingnus est mercenareus mercede sua. Ego autem mendicus sum et pauper.[3]

	Sum men sayn these selé frerys thai han no consyans —[4]	
470	A mon to take seven salerys, ten trentale, yif thai may,	*salaries; trentals*
	And cast ham in a hogpoch togedur fore to daunce —	*[these pluralities]; hodgepodge*
	Hit ys no ferly thagh the folke in hom thai han no fay!	*wonder; faith*
	I lekyn ham to Judas that Crist he con betray —	

---

[1] *Speak and have [reward], I promise you; seek and you shall find.* Compare Matthew 7:7.

[2] Lines 456–59: *If you [good Christians] were to give them money without making them beg [for it], / They would neither beg nor borrow, thus I dare wager; / And [if you were to] provide for them their household and housing, / [They would] neither buy nor build — I advise you to try [this]!*

[3] *The hired worker is worthy of his wages. But I am a beggar and poor.* The first sentence echoes Luke 10:7 (*dignus enim est operarius mercede sua*, "the labourer is worthy of his hire"), and also 1 Timothy 5:18. The second sentence is the beginning of Psalm 39:18, used again in *Marcolf and Solomon*, line 481a.

[4] *Some men speak about these innocent [ironic] friars that have no conscience*

	Because of his covetyse, he sold his Soferayn —	
475	So to begyle the selé pepul and greve God — weleaway! —[1]	
	Redelé thai ben ravenourys and non relegyous men,	*Certainly; plunderers*
	That schal han reuful sore.	*Who shall have miserable pain*
	Hit is agayns Godys ordenans	
	To covet more then youre sustynans;	*sustenance*
480	This makys debat and dystans —	*dispute and disagreement*
	And mend you, syrus, herefore!	*repent*

Ego autem mendicus sum et pauper.[2]

	Sothly, hit is wel beset, at my wetyng,	*by my understanding*
	The grace and the goodnes that men done hem here;	*that people grant friars here*
	Hit prevys wel apert by here levyng	*It shows quite openly in their way of life*
485	To pot hom to povert in soche a manere.	*put themselves in poverty*
	Yet thai makyn moné men ful mekusly chere	*In addition; meek countenance*
	With the grace and the goodys that God here hom sende;	
	Wyselé and wyttlé the leud thai wyle lere	*knowingly; laity; teach*
	Here mys and here mysdedis her to amende;	*sins*
490	Why schuld men be wroth,	
	Sethyn God sendys hom of His sond —	*Since; gifts*
	Withoutyn plogh or londe	
	Ore saleré of kovenande —	*salary of covenant (i.e., employment)*
	Mete and drenke and cloth?	

Fratres, nolumus vos ignorare veretatem.[3]

495	I wyl not faver youe, frerys, with no flateryng;	*curry your favor*
	Ye were better unborne then fore to be to bolde!	*brazenly corrupt*
	Passe not youre prevelege because of covetyng,	*Neglect; greediness*
	Fore this tale treulé apon youe hit is told.	
	Of soche that knouen hom gulté, agayns me thai hold,[4]	
500	And I repreve no presthod bot here leud levyng;	*reprove; except for their lewd behavior*
	Fore to stond at a stake, bren ther Y wolde	*burn*
	Yif I say falslé at my wyttyng —	*by my understanding*
	Blynd as Y am,	
	To me hit were a slawnder	
505	To lye apon my broder;	*lie*

---

[1] *So to beguile the innocent people and insult God — alas! —*

[2] *But I am a beggar and poor[: the Lord is careful for me. Thou art my helper and my protector: O my God, be not slack].* Psalm 39:18. Compare *Marcolf and Solomon*, line 468a.

[3] *Brethren, we would not have you ignorant of the truth.* Compare 2 Corinthians 1:8, which omits *veritatem*: *non enim volumus ignorare vos fratres.* The phrase echoes a standard exhortation used by Paul; compare also Romans 1:13, 11:25; 1 Corinthians 10:1, 12:1; 1 Thessalonians 4:12.

[4] *Of such who recognize their own guilt, against me they cast [accusations]*

I wold han fayn forther,
    Bot *sonn gelo cuiuscam.*[1]

Attendete a falsis prophetis.[2]

	Beth faythful, ye frerys, in your fay. Let be your flateryng.	*Cease*
	Preche the pepul pryncypaly the Prince of Heven to pay.	*please*
510	Pil not the pore pepule with your prechyng,	*Pillage*
	Bot begge at abundand and at ryche aray.	*from the wealthy and richly dressed*
	Ye may mete moné men ye walkyn be the way,	*[as] you walk*
	That bene nedé and nedful and woful begoon,	*woebegone*
	That ave a peny in here purse — thagh ye beg and pray,	*have [barely]*
515	Agayns twenty of yours, Y trou, thai have not hone.	*I believe; one*
	This is no charyté!	
	Fore to beg at the pore,	
	Ye schuld haven here socoure	*Whom you should aid*
	Of that ye potyn in tresoure,	*With what you put*
520	On ham have peté.	*compassion*

Estote micerecordes, sicut Pater vester miserecors est.[3]

	Thus ye techyn truly to ale maner men	
	Fore to part with the pore — on ham have peté!	*share*
	As ye counsel other, Y counsel you then,	
	To solans ham, to socour ham in here fyrmeté —	*solace; infirmity*
525	Ellys, lelé, hit is lyke ye have no chareté.	*truly*
	Ye schul schew good ensampyl to the soulehele;	*soul's health*
	Men waytyn apon your werkys, Y tele you wytterly.	*observe; surely*
	As ye techen other to do, ye don never a dele!	*at all*
	Beth seche as ye seme.	*such*
530	A prechur schuld lyve parfytly,	
	And do as he techys truly,	
	Ellys hit is ypocresy —	*hypocrisy*
	Your dedus, thai doth you deme.	

Nulli malum pro malo reddentes.[4]

---

[1] *I would like to say more, / But [they] are jealous of a certain one (Audelay himself?).* The odd phrase of line 507 mixes French and Latin: *sont jaloux cuiusquam.* Compare *Marcolf and Solomon*, line 701.

[2] *Beware of false prophets[, who come to you in the clothing of sheep, but inwardly they are ravening wolves].* Matthew 7:15.

[3] *Be ye [therefore] merciful, as your Father [also] is merciful.* Compare Luke 6:36.

[4] *To no man rendering evil for evil[. Providing good things, not only in the sight of God, but also in the sight of all men].* Romans 12:17; compare 1 Thessalonians 5:15, 1 Peter 3:9.

	He that wyle not forther these frerus wyllun hom no harme;	*support; wishes them*
535	Wyle thai loven her Lord God, thai mow not fare amys.	*While; may*
	Thenk on the leyth Lazar was borne into Abraamus barme;[1]	
	With ys povert and his payne, he boght hym heven blys,	*his*
	Fore the ryche mon hym refusid, he faryth ale amys,	*While the rich man refused him*
	And lyus law with Lucefyr, leghyst in hele![2]	*lies low; most deceitful*
540	Parte with these pore frerus — your Fader wyle hit his! —	*Share; Father's will; is*
	Last the case on youe fal that on hym befelle.	*Lest; fate*
	Ye schuld fynde hit fore the best.	
	Do as thou woldus me dud be thee;	*one [Matthew 7:12]*
	Apon thi broder thou have peté;	*brother (i.e., a friar)*
545	Depart with hym and he with thee,	*Share*
	Then be thai both yblest.	

[Lines 547–857: On secular clergy]

Ingnorancia non excusat saserdotem.   *Ignorance does not excuse a priest* [see Hebrews 9:7]

	Moné men of Holé Cherche thai ben ale to lewd;	*too unlearned*
	I lekyn ham to a bred is pynud in a cage.	*bird; confined*
	When he hath shertly hymselfe ale bescherewd,	*quickly; befouled*
550	Then he begynys to daunse, to harpe, and to rage,	*rave*
	Fore he is leud and understond not his oune langwage;	*poorly literate*
	Therfore he settys therby bot a lytyl prise,	*value*
	Fore he lerd hit in his youthe and in his yenge age,	*learned*
	And castis hym never to lerne more att here oune devyse.	*on his own*
555	I say you forewhy —	
	Thus leud men thai can say,	*Thus do common men say*
	He is an honest prest in good faye,	
	Yif his goune be pynchit gay,	*pleated stylishly*
	He getis a salary.	*[And] he*

Legere et non intellegere est quasi neclegere.[3]

560	Now yif a pore mon set hys son to Oxford to scole,	
	Both the fader and the moder hynderyd thay schal be;	*financially deprived*
	And yif ther falle a benefyse, hit schal be gif a fole,	*Yet if; benefice; given to a fool*
	To a clerke of a kechyn, ore into the chauncheré.[4]	
	This makys the worchip of clerkys wrong fore to wry,	*honor; turn*
565	Seth sekeler men schul have mon soulys in kepyng,	*Since laymen*

---

[1] *Think on the loathsome Lazarus, [who] was taken into Abraham's bosom*

[2] The reference is to the story of Lazarus, Luke 16:19–25; compare Audelay's *Marcolf and Solomon*, lines 292–99, and *God's Address to Sinful Men*, lines 241–46.

[3] *To read and not understand is as to be neglectful* (punning on *legere* and *intellegere*).

[4] *To a kitchen clerk (i.e., a lord's servant), or into the chancery*

And pytton here personache to ferme to a baylé,[1]
And caston doune here howsold and here housyng,   *neglect; household*
    Here paryschun dystroy.   *[And thus] their parish*
    Clerkys that han cunyng   *knowledge*
570   Schuld have monys soule in kepyng,
    Bot thai mai get no vaunsyng   *advancement*
      Without symony!   *ecclesiastical bribery*

Qui intrat in ovile nisi per hostium, . . . ille fur est et latro.[2]

Symony is a sun forbedun be the laue   *sin forbidden by the law*
Hyly in Holy Cherche — no mon hit use!   *Sacredly; [may] no one*
575 And fro that dredful dede ye schul you withdraw,
Ellus the lauys of God ye doth not bot dyspyse.[3]
Curatis that beth unkunyng, hem ye schuld refuse,   *are untrained*
And aspy pore prevyd clerkys among the clergy,   *notice; trustworthy scholars*
And gef hem awaunsment and a benefyse   *advancement; benefice*
580 To save synful soulys with here feleceté.   *blessedness*
    Goddys wyl hit ys:
    Curatus resident thai schul be,   *Curates should be in residence*
    And ald houshold oponly,   *hold*
    And part with the pore that beth nedé,   *share; are in need*
585   And mend that ye do mys.   *amend what you do amiss*

In tres partes dividite rerum ecclesie substanciam.[4]

The furst princypale parte lungus to your levyng;   *share; belongs; benefice*
The secund part to Holé Cherche, to hold his honesté;   *maintain its honor*
The third part to your parechyngs that ale to youe bryng, *parishioners*
To hom that faylun the fode and fallun in poverté.   *lack food*
590 Thus the goodys of Holé Cherch schuld be spend specyaly; *spent specifically*
Both your meryt and your mede in heven schul ye have.
Al Cristyn men on Crist wold thai crye,
Fore the bodé and the soule bothe do ye save
    Here in this word;   *world*
595   That susteyne ham both nyght and day,   *You (honest curates) who*
    And techyn to heven the redé way,   *direct [them]; straight*
    Pryncepal fore youe thai wold pray   *Principally*
      To here gracious Lord.

[1] *And assign the farming of their [Church-granted] property to a bailiff*

[2] *The one who enters into the sheepfold except through the door, he is a thief and robber.* Written by Scribe B. Compare John 10:1.

[3] *Or [it will be clear that] you entirely despise the laws of God*

[4] *Divide [your] wealth into three parts for the Church.* Written by Scribe B.

Aprehendite disciplinam, ne quando irascatur.[1]

     Trulé, I trow this rewme where chamyd and chent   *believe; realm is shamed; disgraced*
600 Nere the foretheryng of the frerys and here prechyng,[2]
     Fore the seculars prestis take non entent   *pay no attention*
     Bot to here leudnes and her lust and here lykyng;   *To anything other than; stupidity*
     Thai beth nothyng covetese to lerne no conyng,   *not at all willing to learn any doctrine*
     The laus of here Lord God to know and to ken.   *laws; understand*
605 Hit demys wele be here dedys thay have no lovyng,
     Nowther to God, ne goodnes, ne non to odyr men.[3]
         This is a gret peté!
     Here holé order when that thai toke,   *ordination*
     Thai where exampnyd apon a boke,   *were examined*
610 Godys lauys to lerne and to loke,
         And kepe charyté.

Accipite jugum castitatis.   *Accept the yoke of chastity*

     Clerkys were choson to be chast and kepe charyté,
     With alle here wyt and here wyle and here worchyng,   *knowledge; will; work*
     And be a clene calender, the leud men on to se,   *pure example; laity*
615 And not to stere stryf and wrath fore here covetyng.   *stir strife; avarice*
     Hit is a schenchyp and a schame and a sclawnderyng   *disgrace; slandering*
     Agayns the order of Holé Cherch and Goddys ordenawns,
     Prestis fore to covet ale, the frerys to han nothyng!   *have*
     This dole is undeulé dalt. Hit maketh dystans,   *portion is unduly dealt; discord*
620   And al thai beth breder.   *brethren*
     And sethen thai serven won Lord,   *since; one*
     Thai schuld never be at dyscord,
     Nouther in ded nor in word,
         Bot ychon part with othyr.   *each one [should] share*

Erant illis omnia communia.   *All things were common to them [see Acts of the Apostles 4:32]*

625 *In Actibus Apostolorum* ther may ye rede   *Acts of the Apostles*
     Hou the goodys of Holé Cherche sumtyme were isempde;   *collected*
     Uche postyl had his part, ryght as he had nede;   *Each apostle*
     Thai cast hit ale in comyn, the goodys that God hym sende.
     Curst Covetyse, foresoth, the clergé hath yblynd,   *Cursed Covetousness; blinded*
630 That schuld be lanterns lyght in Holé Cherche to bren,   *burn*

---

[1] *Embrace discipline, lest at any time [the Lord] be angry[, and you perish from the just way].* Written by Scribe B. Psalm 2:12.

[2] *Were it not for giving support to the friars and their preaching*

[3] Lines 605–06: *Their deeds demonstrate clearly that they feel no love / Or goodness toward either God or other men*

	And chasud away Charyté! Therfore thai wyl be chent,	*disgraced*
	And turne hemself fro the treuth and marrun other men.	*mar*
	More arme is!	*harm*
	Thai pottyn hamselfe in gret parel,	*put; peril*
635	Fore treuly the pepul thai schuld tele,	*preach [to]*
	And warne ham of the payns of hele,	
	And mend that thai do mys.	*[to] repent; amiss*

Ecce quam bonum et quam jocundum.   *Behold, how good and how pleasant* [Psalm 132:1]

	Take tent to this tyxt, prestis, I you pray.	*Pay attention*
640	*Habitare semper fratres in unum,*[1]	
	Thus Davit in the Sauter, sothlé con he say.	*David; Psalter truly did*
	Crist of his curtessé to curatis tak his kay,	*courtesy; bestowed; key*
	Mon soul with mekenes to have in kepyng,	
	With the treuth of here toung to teche hem the way,	*tongue (i.e., preaching)*
645	Throgh the seven sacramentis here soule to blis bryng.	
	God grantyth hem his pouere	*power*
	To asoyle that wyl repent,	*absolve [them]*
	And schryve hem clene with good entent,	
	And do here penans verament,	*truly*
650	Wyle that thei ben here.	*While*

Ego sum pastor bonus.   *I am the good shepherd* [John 10:11; see John 10:14]

	The ground of al goodnes, curatis schuld be the cause,	
	And knyt hem kyndly togeder, ale the clergé,	*bring together naturally*
	And leve here leudnes and here lust and lern Godys laues,	*forsake; stupidity*
	With hare conyng and clannes, dedlé synnus dystory,	*knowledge; purity; destroy*
655	Both the flesche and the Fynd, false covetys defye,	*[and] false avarice*
	With mercé and with mekenes, the treuth for to teche,	
	The comawndmentis of Crist to kepe kyndly	
	Tofore the pepul apart. Thus schuld he preche!	*Before; plainly*
	Fore ye ben schepardys ale one.	
660	Then Crist to Peter, what sayd he?	
	"My keyis I betake to thee;	*give* [Matthew 16:19]
	Kepe my schepe fore love of me,	*sheep*
	That thai peresche never on."	*perish; one*

	The prophecy of the prophetus, ale nowe hit doth apere,	*is now wholly fulfilled*
665	That sumtyme was sayd be the clergy:	*concerning*
	That leud men, the laue of God that schuld love and lere,	
	Fore curatis fore here covetyse, wold count noght therby,	
	Bot to talke of here teythys, Y tel you treuly.	

---

[1] *It is for brethren always to dwell together in unity.* Compare Psalm 132:1, which omits *semper*: *habitare fratres in unum.*

	And yif the secular say a soth, anon thai bene eschent,	
670	And lyen apon the leud men and sayn, "Hit is Lollere!"[1]	
	Thus the pepul and the prestis beth of one asent;	*assent*
	Thai dare no noder do,	*do nothing else*
	Fore dred of the clergé,	
	Wold dampnen hem unlaufully	*[Who] would accuse them of heresy*
675	To preche apon the peleré,	*preach (ironic); pillory*
	And bren hem after too.	*burn*

Ve vobis qui dicitis malum bonum et bonum malum.[2]

	Lef thou me, a Loller his dedis thai wyl hem deme.[3]	
	Yif he withdraue his deutes fro Holé Cherche away,	*duties*
	And wyl not worchip the cros, on hym take good eme,	*heed*
680	And here his matyns and his masse apon the haleday,	*hear; holy day*
	And belevys not in the sacrement, that hit is God veray,	*true*
	And wyl not schryve him to a prest on what deth he dye,	*confess; when he dies*
	And settis noght be the sacrementus, sothly to say,	*cares nothing about*
	Take him fore a Loller, Y tel you treuly,	
685	And false in his fay!	*faith*
	. . . .	
	Deme hym after his saw;	*Judge him according to his words*
	Bot he wyl hym withdraw,	*Unless; recant*
	Never fore hym pray.	

Corripite inquietos, quod nolunt intelligere ut bene facerent.[4]

	Thagh the pepyl be never so leud in here levyng,	*wanton; behavior*
690	And brekun the comawndementis of Crist, and wykud werk worch,	*do wicked work*
	Thay may go mery ale the yere for ané reprevyng	*without any reproof*
	Outher of parsun or of prest or men of Holé Cherche;	*From either*
	Bot yif thai fayle slus or schof, anon therwith thai groche,	
	Comawnd in Cristis name here tethyng to hem bryng,	
695	Ellis a letter of sentens thai wyle on hem sorche;	

---

[1] Lines 666–70: *That common people, who should love and learn the law of God, / Shall be wholly disregarded by curates, who, on account of their avarice, / Preach only about their tithes, I tell you truly. / And if the laity speak the truth (i.e., in criticism of the clergy), they are disgraced straightway, / And [the clergy] lie to the common people and say, "It is Lollardy!"*

[2] *Woe to you who say that evil is good and good is evil.* Compare Isaias 5:20.

[3] *Believe me, a [true] Lollard will be exposed by his deeds*

[4] *Rebuke the unquiet, because they would not understand that they might do good.* The first part is found in 1 Thessalonians 5:14, and the rest paraphrases Psalm 35:4.

Hit cemys that to the celé soule thai have no lovyng.[1]
    Thus may ye wel knowe!
Y pray, serys, that ye aspye   ☙
Houe contenuys Lechoré —   *continues*
700   Have he cordit with the consteré,   *(How) he has accorded; consistory*
    Vola veredé voo?[2]

Videte, rectores ecclesie, ne propter lucrum dampnatis animas Christianas.[3]

Alas, that thes offecers of Holé Cherchis laue   *law*
Lettyth these leud men lye in here syn,   *Allow; lay folk [to] remain*
That dredun nothyng here domus hem to withdrawe,[4]
705   Fore Mede the maydyn mantens hem therin,   *maintains them (i.e., the clergy)*
Because of Ser Covetys, is neyre of here kyn,   *near*
May do with mon of Holé Cherche hollé his entent;   *wholly*
The wyf and the hosbond he mai part atwyn;   *allow to divorce (i.e., for payment)*
Thagh thai be boundon togeder be the sacrement,
710   He wyle dessever hem two,   *divorce*
And yet the Gospel hom dos lere,   *does teach them*
That God juins togeder yfere,   *What; in companionship*
Ther is no mon that hath pouere   *power*
That sacrement undoo.

Episcopus debet esse sine crimene, et corrigere rectores ecclesie. Sicut vult respondere coram summo Judice.[5]

715   Thus oure blessud byschop, dene offecialle,   *dean*
Sofers thes sekelers in here syght to sun opynly,   *Allows; laity; sin*
Thagh thai to here constri, hom to here court calle,
Thai mercyn hem with moné and med prevely.[6]
Thai schuld put hom to prayers and to penans opunly,
720   Fore "opun syn, opun penans," this is Godys laue —
Yif ye wyl serche the soth, here is remedé!   *assess*

---

[1] Lines 693–96: *Yet if they [the parishioners] fail or refuse to pay bribes (lit. shillings), immediately forthwith [the clergy] complain, / [And] command them to bring their tithing in Christ's name, / Or else they will serve them a letter of judgment (i.e., a formal accusation of heresy or excommunication); / It seems to the innocent soul that they [the clergy] have no charitable love*

[2] *Do you wish [to know] the truth? This odd phrase must be French: Voulez vérité vous? Compare* Marcolf and Solomon, *line 507.*

[3] *See to it, leaders of the church, that you do not damn Christian souls for the sake of profit*

[4] *Without any fear to amend their dooms*

[5] *A bishop must be without blame* [compare 1 Timothy 3:2, Titus 1:7], *and he must correct the leaders of the church. Just so will he answer in the presence of the highest Judge.*

[6] Lines 717–18: *Although the bishops call the laity to [account in] their consistory court, / They grant clemency (literally mercy) to them for money and bribes*

Then wold thai dred your domys and sone hom withdraw,   *judgments*
    And kepe Godys laus.
  Curatis the soth thai dar not say,
725   Fore thai be worse levers then thai,   *miscreants*
  And leven in syn fro day to day,   *live*
    So thai beth the cause.

Inclina cor meum, Deus, in testimonia tua, et non in avariciam.[1]

Ye curatis, fore your covetys ye castun in the new fayre   *(i.e., barter and trade)*
The churches that ye byn chosun to, be Godus ordenauns,   *by*
730 And callun hit "permetacion," cuntreys about to kayre,[2]
Bot yif ye han pluralytis, hit is not plesans.   *two or more benefices held at once; proper*
I preve the pope principaly ys worthy to have penaunce   *declare; is suited for penance*
That grauntus ané seche grace because of covetyng;   *Who*
Hit dous dysese in Holé Cherch, and makys bot dystauns —[3]
735 A mon to have four benefyse, anoder no lyvyng.   *another*
    This is not Godys wyle!   *will*
  The furst benefyce ye ben bound to —
  Ye schuld not desyre to go therfro,
  And take a levyng and no mo,   *But take one benefice and no more*
740   Lest ye your soulis spyle.   *destroy*

Nemo potest duobus dominis servire.[4]

Ye schul make no marketys ne no marchandyse,   *markets; merchandise*
Nouther for to by ne sel for lucur, I say;   *buy or sell for lucre*
Hit chasis away charyté, your covetyse,   *chases*
Alle your goostly grace hit wypis clene away.   *wipes*
745 Who may serve two lordis, and bothe to here pay —[5]
That is, this wyckyd word and God — to plesyng?   *world*
Yit ye serve not your God! The Fynd wyl you fray   *Thus; confront*
When ye ben callud to your countys and to your rekynyng,   *are called; accounts*
    That most ye nede.
750 Yif ye have servyd the worlde,
  And be untreue to your Lorde,
  The laue wyle youe rewarde:
    Deth to your end!

---

[1] *Incline my heart to your testimonies, God, and not to covetousness.* Compare Psalm 118:36.

[2] *And call it "permutation," to disturb the surrounding regions*

[3] *It causes unrest in Holy Church, and makes only discord*

[4] *No man can serve two masters.* Matthew 6:24; compare Luke 16:13. See also line 745.

[5] *Who may serve two lords, and both to their satisfaction*

Hoc quocienscunque feceritis, in meum memoriam faciatis. Qui vero propter lucrum quodlibet temperale officium Dominicum presumit celebrare prossus quidem simulis proditore Jude qui Christum Judeis propter denarios XXXta, non dubitavit vendere. Qui ergo hoc modo accedit ad corpus Dominicum indigne vere sibi id ipsum accipit et sanguinem Dominicum non ad salutem sed ad judicium et juste. Nullus itaque propter lucrum hoc agat ne Jude proditore sociis in penis fiat.[1]

	A foule defaute, faythfully, I fynd in Holy Cherche,	*fault*
755	Prestis to syng twyse a day fore here leucur,	*twice; payment*
	Yef thai schuld fore Cristis sake, anon then thay groche,[2]	
	And thus thai sellyn here Soverayn and here Saveour;	
	I lekyn hem to Judas that was a traytoure —	
	Because of his covetyse, his Soveren he solde.	
760	Boldlé the byschop is to blame that doth ham favour,	
	Fore this tale, treuly, on hem hit is tolde.	*truth-telling tale*
	This is a gret schame.	
	And yet the laue hit doth hem lere	*teach*
	Thai schuld syng bot twyse a yere,	
765	At Crystymas and Astere,	*Easter*
	Ellys thai beth to blame.	

Sicut aqua extinguit ignem, ita elemosina extinguit peccatum.[3]

	Prestis, ye schul preve yourselfe and princypalé in dede:	*in good action*
	Ever depart with the pore. On hem have peté.	*Always share*
	Cownsel ham and cumford ham, and cloth hem at here nede,	
770	In presun and in poverté and infyrmety.	*prison; infirmity*
	Thus ye prechyn the pepul in the pylpit opynlé	*pulpit; plainly*
	The seven werkys of mercé mekelé to fulfyl,	*meekly*
	And to ressayve here reward, remissyon redelé	*receive; remission straightaway*
	At the dredful Dai of Dome, fore this is Godis wyle,	
775	Ore ellus schul thai rew!	*rue*
	As ye techon other to do,	
	Do yourselve also,	
	Ore ellis men wyl part youe fro,	
	And say ye bene untrew.	

[1] *Whenever you do this, do it in memory of me. The one who dares to celebrate the Lord's office (i.e., the eucharist) for the sake of temporal profit of any kind, is indeed like the traitor Judas who did not hesitate to sell Christ to the Jews for 30 denarii. Therefore, the one who approaches the Lord's body like this, in an unworthy way, receives it and the Lord's blood not for salvation, but for judgment — and rightly so. And so let no one do this for the sake of profit lest in his punishment he become like the traitor Judas to his friends.* Written by Scribe B. Compare 1 Corinthians 11:24–29, with Judas' treason inserted (see Matthew 26:14–16, 27:3, 27:9). Compare also *Marcolf and Solomon*, line 831a.

[2] *If they should [sing] for Christ's sake, immediately then they complain [for payment]*

[3] *Just as water quencheth a fire, so do alms extinguish sins.* Compare Ecclesiasticus 3:33.

Nota. De confescione et de sacramento altaris.[1]

Subjecti estote omnis humane creature propter Dominum.[2]

780	I counsel youe, ale Cristun men, and comawnd in Cristis name	
	That ye obey your curatis that ye ben boundon to;	
	Yif oné be fallyn be frelté in ané febel fame,	*frailty; poor repute*
	God graunt hem of his grace no more so to do;	
	And beth in ful charyté with frynd and with foo,	*friend*
785	Fore that is the grownd of al goodnes, with contricion,	
	And serve that Lord of al lordys. Where ben ané mo	*[may] be any others*
	That may soyle youe of your sunne and graunt you remyssyon?	*absolve; sin*
	In fayth, no mo bot hee.	*[there is] no other but he*
	Of al lordis, be he blest!	
790	He wold no mon where elost	*wants; to be lost* [see Ezechiel 33:11 and note]
	That wyl in his mercé trust,	
	And in his benyngneté.	*benignity*

	Yif your curatis comaund you to kepe Cristis lawus,	
	Then do aftyr here doctrine, and ye bene out of drede,	*you are secure*
795	Fore, serys, thai may save your soule throgh here soth sauus,	*their true sayings*
	Then in heven schale ye have your meryd and your mede;	*merit; reward*
	Bot do not as thai doun — therof take good hede! —	
	Bot yif thai schowe youe good ensampil to the soulehele,[3]	
	Fore God in the Gospel, thus he forebed.	*forbade*
800	After here werkus, worche ye never a dele,	
	Ellus schul ye reue!	*regret [it]*
	Fore as thai techyn you to do,	
	Bot yif thai don hamselve also;	
	Ellus Y rede ye gon hem fro,	
805	And say thay bene untreu.[4]	

Quodcumque ligaveris super terram.[5]

	Fore God hath graunt of his grace to curatis his pouere —	*power*
	Thagh thai ben synful men — to asoyle youe of your synne,	*absolve*

---

[1] *Observe: concerning confession and the sacrament of the altar.* Written by Scribe B.

[2] *Be subject to all human creatures for the Lord's sake.* Compare 1 Peter 2:13. Written by Scribe A.

[3] *Unless they show you a good example to the soul's health*

[4] Lines 802–05: *For [do] as they teach you to do, / If they themselves also do it; / If not, I advise you to go [separately] from them, / And declare them untrue*

[5] *[And I will give to thee the keys of the kingdom of heaven. And] whatsoever thou shalt bind upon earth, [it shall be bound also in heaven: and whatsoever thou shalt loose on earth, it shall be loosed also in heaven].* Matthew 16:19; compare Matthew 18:18. See also *Marcolf and Solomon*, lines 238, 961a, and *Visiting the Sick and Consoling the Needy*, line 199.

Thorgh vertu of the sacrementte, sothlé I yowe enseure;   *assure*
No mon mese in this matere yif he wyl savyd bene.   *[should] dispute*
810   Everé prest he hath pouere to asoyle you then,
And to here confession in your nesescyté;   *hear; necessity*
Yif to your curatis ye mai not cum, that beth your soveren,   *sovereign (confessor)*
Thai may do youe ryghtus, Y telle youe treuly.[1]
        Thai have this pouere,
815   To asoyle that wyl repent,   *[those] who*
        And schryve ham clene with good entent,
        Be vertu of the sacrement,
                Both prest and frere.

*Nota secundum decretalis et constitucionis ecclesie quod omnis homo utriusque sexus tenetur
confitere suo proprio saserdoti semel in anno ad minus, nisi habeat licenciam vel dispen-
sacionem, vel prevelegium a superiori.*[2]

Bot ye most come to your curaturus be the comen laue,   *common law*
820   And schryve youe sothely of your synne at the lest enns a yere;   *once a year*
Ye stonden in doute and in dred yif ye you withdraw   *(i.e., neglect confession)*
Without lysens or leve, outher to prest or frere.   *license; permission either from*
Thai most your counsel knoue, that schal youe led and lere,   *guide and teach*
That have the charche of youre soule in here kepyng;   *charge*
825   Ye byth princypaly under here pouere —
Go not ungoodly away without here wytyng,   *knowledge*
        And know your entent: *understand your duty*
        Thai may not answere fore youe
        Your consel bot thai know;   *Unless they know your counsel*
830   Thai beth excusid be the laue,
                And ye schul be schent.   *doomed*

Quicumque enim manducaverit . . . vel biberit calecem Domini indigne.[3]

Yif the prest unworthelé presume to syng his mas,   *unworthily presumes*
Serus, Y say the sacrement enpayrd hit may not be,   *impaired*
Bot his owne deth and his dome he ressayvs — alas! —   *receives*
835   Yif in his consians he knaw that he be gulté.   *knows; is guilty*
Thagh he syng and say his mas, the prest, unworthelé,
Both your meret and your mede in heven ye schul have,   *merit; reward*
Fore God hath grauntyd of his grace, be his auuctoreté,   *his (the priest's) authority*

---

[1] *They [other clergy] may administer your holy rites, I tell you truly*

[2] *Observe that, according to the decrees and constitution of the church, every person of either sex is obliged
to make confession to his own priest once a year at least, unless he has permission or a dispensation, or a privilege
from his superior*

[3] *Whoever will have eaten . . . or drunk of the cup of the Lord unworthily.* Compare 1 Corinthians 11:27,
and see *Marcolf and Solomon,* line 753a.

	Be he never so synful, youre soulys may he save.	*he (the priest)*
840	Have this in thoght:	
	The masse is of so hye degré	*sacred*
	Apayryd, forsoth, hit mai not be,	*Impaired*
	Ne no mon mend hit may,	*improve*
	Theron doctours han soght.	*learned men have inquired*

Nichil imposebele apud Deum.[1]

845	Take ensampil by the sunne ye syne here with syght.	*sun; see*
	Wha may depreve hym of his pouere and let his lyghtyng,[2]	
	That schenus apon a synful man as wele as on a ryght?	*shines; righteous*
	Alse wele on fouele as on fayre, without defouteryng?	*foul; fair; faltering*
	Alse wel apon a knave as apon a kyng?	
850	A sad saumpil, foresoth, her may ye se:	*serious example; here*
	Hit is Godys Word and his werke and his worchyng.	
	The sacrement of the autere defoulyd mai not be,	*altar; desecrated*
	I do youe out of drede.	*assure you*
	His Godhed may not be sayne	
855	With no fleschlé eyne,	*eyes*
	Bot in the sacrement ye may hit sene	*see*
	In fegure and fourme of bred.	*figure; form; bread*

[Lines 858–1013: Exhortations to adhere to the faith: the Trinity, the sacraments, and penance]

	I se, sothlé, in the sune knyt thre maner kynde,	*sun [are] joined three types of nature*
	His clerté and his clerenes, what clerke can declare;	*clarity; brightness, as*
860	Bohold the hete in thi hert, and have hit in mynd;	*heat; heart*
	The conselacion and the comford, thai thre what thai are.	*consolation; comfort*
	Fore al that levys in this lond, ful evyl schul hit fare	*lives; evil shall it go*
	Nere that gloreus Gleme that fro the heven glydis;	*Were it not for; glides*
	Ho that servyth not that Soverayn, his hert may be ful sare,	*Whoever; unhappy*
865	That lenus of his love seche a lyght that ale this word gladis	*Who lends by; gladdens*
	In everych a place.	*every*
	A, synful mon! Have this in mynde!	
	To that Lord, be not unkynde,	
	Fore he may both louse and bynde,	*loosen [see Matthew 16:19, 18:18]*
870	Graunt mercé and grace.	
	I declare the clerté to the Fader of myghtis most;	*assign; clarity*
	The heete hylé therof to his onlé Sunne;	*heat spiritually; only*
	The consolacion and the comford to the Holé Gost;	*Holy Ghost*

[1] *Nothing is impossible with God.* Compare Matthew 19:26, Mark 10:27, Luke 1:37, 18:27.

[2] *Who may deprive it of its power and stop its light*

Kyndly yknyt togeder, without devesioun.   *Intrinsically joined; division*
875 The Fader, the Son, the Holé Gost, al thai beth bot hone —   *are but one*
Thre persons prevyd in the Treneté —   *proved; Trinity*
That never had begynyng, ende have thai none,
That now is, and ever was, and ever schal be,
     Lord of myghtys most!   *might*
880 Thus the Fader oure lyght us broght;
With the hete of his blod, his Son us boght;
Consolacion and cumford thus have thai wroght
     Throgh the grace of the Holé Gost.

Fides non habet meretum.[1]

Ryght as ye se all this world is glorefyd with one sunne,   *glorified; sun*
885 Serrs, so is mons soule with the sacrement:
Als moné men at a mas as ye acount con,   *many; mass; count*
Uche person has his part that is ther present,   *Each; share*
And ale hit is bot hone Good — beleve this verament! —   *one; truly*
That is sacyrd on the autere betwen the prestis honde,   *consecrated; altar*
890 That schal you deme at Domysday at his Jugement,   *judge*
After your dedis, dredles, thus schul ye understonde.   *doubtless*
     Thagh ye have done amys,   *Though*
     Yif fore your synnus ye be soré,   *sorry*
     Then ye resseyven hem worthelé,   *receive him worthily*
895 And schul have grace and mercy
     And joy in heven bliss.

Estote fortes in bello.   *Be valiant in war* [see Wisdom 8:15, Hebrews 11:34]

Dredles, uche dedly sunne Y declare a wounde,   *Indeed, each; sin; [to be] a wound*
That when the Fynd hath foght with youe, and hath the maystré,   *Fiend; mastery*
Then most ye seche a surgoun yif ye wyl be save and sound,   *seek a surgeon; safe*
900 That con sothlé serche your sore and make youe hole.   *truly search your wound; whole*
Confession and contresion, thi salve schal hit be,   *contrition; remedy*
The penans of thi penetawnsere, thi satisfaccion;   *priest appointed to assign penance*
Then feghtust with the Fynd agayne, and hast the maystré,
And dost hym schenchip and schame, foreever confucyon,[2]
905   Thi soule fore to save!
     Thus thi wondis helyd schul be,   *healed*
     With gret worchip to thee —

---

[1] *Faith has no reward.* The phrase derives from a homily by Gregory the Great, cited by Peter Lombard: *Fides non habet meritum cui humana racio prebet experimentum,* "Faith has no reward for which human reason offers proof" (*Homil. 26 in Evang.*).

[2] Lines 903–04: *Then [you shall] fight with the Fiend again, and have the victory / And do him disgrace and shame, [and] forever confusion*

        Because of thi victoré,
            Reward schalt thou have.

Misere mei, Deus, quia infirmus sum.[1]

910	I lekyn uche a synful soule to a seke mon	*liken; each; sick*
	That is yschakyd and schent with the aksis;	*shaken; harmed; aches*
	Ther is no dayntet edyght that pay hym thai con,	*dainty [thing] prepared; satisfy*
	Bot al that is agayns hym that wyl hym pleese.[2]	
	So hit farus by a mon that ys recheles,	*reckless*
915	That is seke in his soule — the soth he nel not here,	*will not hear*
	Bot wrys away fro Godys Word to his wyckydnes.	*turns*
	Here may ye know kyndlé yif your consians be clere,	*by nature; conscience; clear*
	The soth verament.	*truly*
	Cristyn men yif that ye be,	
920	Then loke ye done cristynlé,	*christianly*
	Ellus ye berun that nome in veyne, treuly;	*Or else; bear; name in vain*
	Ye wyl be shamed and yshent!	*ruined*

	I counsel ale youe, ale curators, that wyselé you wayt,	*curates; wisely; take heed*
	That han the cure of mons soule in youre kepyng,	*care*
925	Engeyne ye not to yeesy penans, ne to strayt alegat,[3]	
	Lest ye slene both bodé and soule with youre ponyschyng,	*slay; punishing*
	Fore better is a Paternoster with repentyng	
	To send hem, to the mercé of God, to purgatoré,	*by*
	Fore Crist enjoynd no nother penans in his levyng,	*other penance; life*
930	Bot *vade in pace, amplius noly peccare.*[4]	
	Fore as possebel hit were	*possible it is*
	Here, with a tere of thyn nye,	*tear of your eye*
	To qwensche the foyre of purgatoré,	*quench the fire*
	As al the water in the se,	*sea*
935	To qwench a blase of foyre.	*blaze*

	Ye that be chosun to ben chif and sittyng in Cristis place,	*chief [officials]; [are] sitting*
	Ye most have Treuth and Ryghtwysnes in your demyng;	*Righteousness; judgment*
	Then let Treuth dele and tok hym both Mercé and grace,	*allow; deal and give*
	And Ryghtwysnes rest Pes, fore dred of perechyng.	*Justice rest [with] Peace; perishing*
940	These four sistyrs made acord betwene Heven Kyng	*[Psalm 84:11]*
	And Manse Soule, that was forjuggyd to damnacion,	*destined for*
	Fore Pes agayns Ryghtwysnesche was ever pletyng,	*pleading [her case]*

---

[1] *Have mercy on me, God, because I am weak.* Compare Psalm 6:3.

[2] *But he opposes all that is [prepared] to please him*

[3] *Impose not too easy penance, nor too strict in any case*

[4] *Go in peace, sin no more.* Compare Mark 5:34, Luke 7:50, Luke 8:48 for *vade in pace*, John 8:11 for *vade . . . amplius noli peccare* (which omits *in pace*).

Hwyle Mercé with his mekenes turrne Treth to remyssioun.[1]

945
    Herewith God plesid was,   *pleased*
    And send doune his Son from heven an hye   *down*
    To leght in the vergyn mayde Mary,   *alight*
    In herth to be boren of here body,   *earth; born*
    To graunt mercé and grace.

Qui praemunitur non falletur.[2]

    I hold hym wyse that wyl beware whan he has warnyng —
950
    Have this mater in your hert, and hoolde hit in mynd!   *subject; heart*
    Bot never honé whyl beware in here levyng,   *[they who are] never any while*
    Bot al blustyrne furth unblest, as Bayard the blynd.[3]
    Agayns the goodnes of God, men bene unkynde.
    Frerys fekul and freel and false in here fay,   *fickle; frail; faith*
955
    Amonke the men of Holé Cherche, feu ther I fynd   *Among; few*
    That worchyn wysly hemselfe to wyse men the way.   *apply themselves wisely to show*
    This is a carful case.   *sad*
    To curatis sayth Saynt Gregoré,
    That thai schal answere, trewlé,   *be called to account*
960
    Fore mon soul specyalé   *especially*
    Tofore Goddis face.   *Before*

Verbi gratia, qui sicut dicit papa episcopo, episcopus rectoribus eclesie qui resipiunt potestatem ligandi atque solvendi et curam animarum: fratres in Christo, habet, trado vobis curam animarum parachanorum vestrorum ut respondiatis pro me et pro nobis coram summo Judice in die judicii.[4]

    I meve this mater mekelé fore murmur of men,   *broach this subject; grumbling*
    Wherefore I pray you spesyaly that ye wyl aspye   *notice*
    At clerkus that have conyng, that can this know and ken,   *understand*
965
    Houe thus Treuth is he touchid, wherefore and hwy.   *How; affected; why*
    I red ye, rede hit aryght. Remembyr you redlé.   *counsel; correctly; readily*
    Fore the love of our Lord, nouther lagh ne gren.   *neither laugh nor grin*
    As God, of my mysdedis, He have mercé,
    I meve this to amend me and ale other men,   *broach*

---

[1] *While Mercy with his meekness turns Truth to remission*

[2] *The one who is forearmed will not be deceived.* Compare *Audelay's Epilogue to The Counsel of Conscience,* line 182a.

[3] *But entirely bluster forth unblessed, as Bayard the blind (a horse)*

[4] *The grace of the Word, which, just as the pope says to a bishop, the bishop says to the secular priests who receive the power of binding and of loosening and have the care of souls: "Brothers in Christ, I hand to you the care of the souls of your parishes (dioceses) so that you may respond on my behalf and on our behalf before the highest Judge on the Day of Judgment."* Compare Matthew 16:19, 18:18. See also *Marcolf and Solomon,* lines 238, 805a, and *Visiting the Sick and Consoling the Needy,* line 199.

970	My God to plese and pay.	*satisfy*
	No mon deney this	*deny*
	Yif that he thynke to have blys;	
	Betwene prestis and frerys, ywys,	*indeed*
	I make this loveday.	*day of accord*

Misericordia et veretas obbeaverunt sibi; pax et justecia osculati sunt.[1]

975	Thus sayth David, foresoth, in the Sautere,	*Psalter*
	And verefyus in a verse the love of our Lord:	*verifies*
	Misericordia et Verytas han thai met efere	*Mercy and Truth have met together*
	That long tyme before had bene at dyscord;	
	Ther was faythfolé made a feneal corde,	*faithfully; final accord*
980	Fore *Justicia et Pax* mad ham to kus,	*Justice and Peace; kiss* [Psalm 84:11]
	Fro that day furth to fulfyl that forward,	*compact*
	Never that mater to have in mynd, tofore was amys.	*[which] before*
	So I you pray,	
	Fore Godis wyl, forsoth, hit is,	
985	That ye amend ye han do mys,	*what you have done amiss*
	And hoch on other here ye cusse,	*each other; kiss*
	Forever and for ay.	

Cuius finis bonum, ipsum totum bonum.[2]

	Thus Salamon hath sayd the soth, verement,	*truth, truly*
	As Marcol, the more fole, warned hym, I wene;	*Marcolf, the very fool; believe*
990	Bot yif this draght be draun wel, thai goun wil be schent,[3]	
	And schal turne treulé to turment and to tene.	*truly; torment; trouble*
	Have mynd on this mater; ye wot what I mene.	*Pay attention to; know; mean*
	Blust not furth unblest, as Bayard the blynd,	
	Bot cal agayne charyté with consians clene,	*call again [for]; conscience*
995	And wry not fro Godis word, as the wroth wynd —	*turn; like the angry [who] twist away*
	Herkyns hit as the hynd.	*good servant*
	Apon your levyng, take good eme,	*behavior; heed*
	And beth seche as ye schul seme,	*such*
	Fore be your dedis men wyl you deme.	*deeds; judge*
1000	Here I make an end.	

---

[1] *Mercy and truth have given blessing to themselves; peace and justice have kissed.* Compare Psalm 84:11, and see *Marcolf and Solomon*, line 940, and *God's Address to Sinful Men*, lines 144a–51.

[2] *Whose end is good, is himself entirely good.* Peter Lombard cites this aphorism: *Cuius finis bonus est, ipsum quoque bonum est*, "Whose end is good, is itself also good" (Boethius, *II. De Differentiis topicis*). Audelay uses his version as a proverbial tag, repeating it at *Audelay's Conclusion*, line 39a.

[3] *But if this draught is drawn well, your gown will be ruined*

Si veretatem dico, quare non creditis mihi? Qui ex Deo est, verba Dei audit. Ideo non auditis quia ex Deo non estis.[1]

	Fore I have towchid the trouth, I trow I schal be schent,	*Because; disgraced*
	And said sadlé the soth without flateryng;	*seriously*
	Hald me fore no parté that beth heere present;	*Assign me to no faction*
	I have ne lykyng ne lust to make no lesyng.	*liking nor pleasure; any lies*
1005	Fore Favel with his fayre wordis and his flateryng,	*Flattery (i.e., one who curries favor)*
	He wyl preche the pepul apert hem for to pay;	*openly to please them*
	I nel not wrath my God at my wetyng,	*will not anger; with my knowledge*
	As God have mercé on me, Syr Jon Audlay,	
	At my most ned.	
1010	I reche never who hit here,	*care; hears*
	Weder prest or frere,	*Whether*
	For at a fole ye ma lere,	*from a fool you may learn*
	Yif ye wil take hede.	

. . . .

[XV.] THE REMEDY OF NINE VIRTUES   **[W3]**

. . . .

	"To thi neghbour fore love of me,	
	To make debate ny dyscorde,	*nor*
	And thou dust me more cumford,	*give; comfort*
	Then thagh thou wentust barefote in the strete,	*Than if; walked*
5	For love of me that ys thi Lorde,	
	That stremus of blood folewed thi fete.	
	I sai forwi:	*explain why*
	A wekid worde a mon may schame,	
	To lese his godes and hys good name;	*lose; goods*
10	Whoso falsly duth men fame	*defame*
	Beth curst truly.	
	"The seventh vertu ys good conselyng;	
	Entyse not thi neghbour to wekednes,	*Entice; wickedness*
	Ny say no worde to hym ni sklanderyng,	*nor slander*
15	But consel hym to al goodenes,	
	And this thou myght me more plese	
	Then thagh thou stydest ones a day	*ascend (i.e., meditate) once*
	Into heven, thi sowle to sese	*Than if; establish*
	Into that joy that lastus ay,	*forever*

---

[1] *If I speak the truth, why do you not believe me? The one who is from God hears the words of God. Therefore you do not hear because you are not from God.* Compare John 8:46–47.

20   Withowten drede!   *Assuredly*
    For bi this goodenes and this consele,
    Thou may pytte thi neghbour fro gret perele,   *remove; from*
    And save hym fro the peynes of hele,
      And encrese thi mede.   *reward*

25   "The eighth vertu is holé prayere
    Dyssyre, and aske of me ryghtwesly.   *correctly*
    Thiselfe thou schalt be messangere,
    And do thi message dewoutly;
    And thou plesust me more speciali,
30   Then thagh my moder and sayntis alle   *Than if*
    Praydyn in heven on hy fore thee —
    For thou ast fre choyse to ryse or falle,   *hast*
      Both thou may.
    Yif thou fall, aryse anon,
35   And call to me with contricion;
    Then my moder and sayntis uchon
      Wil fore thee pray.

   "The ninth vertu is thou schalt only
    Love me in hert over al thyng,
40   Then gold or selver, or lond or fee,   *[More] than*
    Or wyf or child, or wordlé thyng;
    And thou dost me then more plesyng
    Then thagh thou styedust upon hygh peleré *Than if; ascended; pillory*
    Folle of rayssors kene stekyng   *Full of spikes sharply protruding*
45   Fore my love, thi flesche to tere.   *tear*
      Bileve wyl this!   *well*
    Love plesis me over al thyng,
    Fore Chareté with hym is ever dwellyng;
    Mon soule to joy hit doth hit bryng
50   Into my blis.

   "These nine vertus son soth thou schalt fynd — *soon true*
    Lerne this lesson now, I thee pray.
    To God and mon, loke thou be kynd,
    And make amendis wyle thou may,
55   For to heven ther ys noon oder way,   *no other*
    Yyf thou wolt have salvasyon;
    Me thou most nede plese and pay,
    Or ellus have damnacyon.
      Hit ys for the best.
60   Do as thou woldust me dud by thee,   *one [Matthew 7:12]*
    Ucheon of oder ye have pyté,   *Of one another have compassion*
    And leves in love, in charyté —   *live*
      Then be ye blest.

"Sum men ther ben that stelon heven   *obtain*
65   With penans, prayers, and poverté,   *penance*
And sum goon to hele ful even   *very directly*
For lust and lykyng of here body.   *desire and pleasure*
Here twey wayes, my sone, ther be;   *two*
Thou hast fre choyse wedur to passe.
70   Chese the better, Y consel thee,
Lest thou syng the sung 'alasse'   *song*
            Forever and ay.
        I rede thou serve Heven Kyng —   *advise*
        For any lust or lykyng,
75   Have mynde apon thi endyng,
                And dredeful Domusday!"

Mervel ye not of this makyng;
I me excuse, hit ys not Y.   *excuse myself*
Hit ys Goddus worde and his techyng,
80   That he taght a salutary,   *remedy*
For Y kowthe never but hye foly.   *know nothing but high folly*
God hath me chastest for my levyng.   *chastised*
I thonk my God, my Grace, trewly,
Of his gracyouse visetyng,   *visiting (i.e., affliction)*
85   Ellus were Y lore.   *lost*
        Ever that Lorde, be he blest!
        Al that he duth ys for the best,   *doth*
        Ellus were ye lyke to be lost,   *likely*
            And better unbore.   *unborn*

90   Upon your lyfe take good eme;   *heed*
Bewar lest God that ye offende.   *lest ye offend God*
As he fyndes yow, he wil you deme,   *finds; judge*
Owther be saved, or ellus be schent.   *Either; else*
For soden deth, loke ye amende,   *For [fear of]*
95   And settus no trist where noon ys,   *trust*
For al ys good that hath good ende
When ye han mended ye han do mys —   *amended [what]; amiss*
            This ys no nay!   *cannot be denied*
        Y made this wit good entent,   *with*
100   In hope the rather ye wolde repent.
        Prayes for me that beth present —   *Pray; (you) who are*
            My name hyt ys the Blynde Awdelay.

Explicit de salutare.   *[Here] ends the remedy.*

XVI. Seven Bleedings of Christ   [W4]

De effusione sanguinis Christi in remissione peccatorum.[1]

	An holy prayer here bygynnes	
	In remedy of seven dedly synnes.	
	Seven blodes, Crist he bled,	
	The fyrst in his *Circumsycyoun*;	*Circumcision*
5	The secund in holé *Oresown*,	*Orison (i.e., Paternoster)*
	The deth when that he dred.	*dreaded*

	The thred in his *Flagellacion*;	*third*
	The fourth in his *Coronacion*;	
	The fyfth in his *Hondis* also;	
10	The sixth in his holé *Fete*;	
	The seventh blood ran out of his *Hert* wete	*wet*
	To wasche us out of our wo.	

	With moné another enstrement,	*many other instruments*
	He suffyrd tene and turmentyng	*trouble*
15	In his Monheed;	*Manhood*
	In tyme of his Passion,	
	Here fore oure redemcion,	*redemption*
	His blesful blod he bled.	

	O Jhesu, fore the blod thou bledyst,	
20	And in the furst tyme thou cheddust	*shed [blood]*
	In thi Circumcecion,	
	That I have synnyd in *Lechoré*,	*[When] that; lechery*
	That stynkyng syn, foreyif thou me,	*forgive*
	And my delectacion.	*pleasure*

25	O Jhesu, at the Mount of Olefete,	*Mount of Olives*
	There blod and water thou con swete,	*sweat*
	To thi Fader when thou dydist pray	
	So, Fader, yif thi wyl hit be,	*(i.e., the Paternoster)*
	Put *Envy* away from me,	
30	And temtacions nyght and day.	

	O Jhesu, thi payns were ful strong,	
	When the skorgis both scharp and long,	*scourges*
	Mad thi body to bled;	
	To thee, Lord, mercé I cry,	

---

[1] *Concerning the pouring out of Christ's blood for the forgiveness of sins*

35   Thou kepe me out of *Glotoné*,   *Gluttony*
            And helpe me at my ned.

        O Jhesu, fore thi scharp croune,
        That mad the blod to ren adoune
            About thi fayre face,
40   Ther *Proud in Hert* I have be,
        Lord, unbuxum to thee,   *disobedient*
            Grawnt mercé and grace.

        O Jhesu, as I understond,
        Thou ched blod at both thi hond   *shed*
45   When thai were naylid;
        Thou cast me out of *Covetyse*,   *avarice*
        And graunt me grace sone to aryse
            Of syn when I am seyled.   *From; assailed*

        O Jhesu, thou bledyst more blod
50   Wen thou wast nayld apon the rood
            Throgh thi fete with naylis;
        Let me never in *Slouth* stynke,   *sloth*
        Bot grawnt me grace fore to swynke   *labor*
            Thyng me avaylis.   *[For] what profits me*

55   O Jhesu, blessid be thi bones,
        Fore blod and water thou chedist at ones   *shed simultaneously*
            Out of thi pressious hert;   *precious*
        Out of *Wrath* kepe thou me,
        And grawnd me love and charyté,   *grant*
60   Fore thi woundis smert.

        O Jhesu, for the *Peler* strong,   *Pillar (i.e., for the Flagellation)*
        Thi bodi was bound therto with wrong,
            Ybuffet and yblend;   *Buffeted and made blind*
        That Holé Cherche as bound me to,   *What; has*
65   Grawnt me grace that fore to do,   *to do that*
            Lest I be chamyd and schent.   *shamed and ruined*

        O Jhesu, fore thi blesful *Face*,
        Thou betoke Veroneca bi grace
            Upon here sudaré;   *shroud*
70   That Face be me consolacion,
        And to the Fynd confusion,   *Fiend*
            That day when I schal dye.

        O Jhesu, fore thi holé *Cros*,
        Thi body sprad theron was   *spread*

75   Fore our syn sake;
      That Cros be my proteccion,
      Agayns myn enmys everychon,   *enemies*
          Weder I slepe or wake.   .   *Whether*

      O Jhesu, fore thi *Naylis* thre,
80   That persid thee to the rod-tre,   *pierced*
          Ydrevyn with gret distres;   *Driven; pain*
      Thou grawnt me repentawns,
      Fore my syns to do penans,
          My payns to relesse.

85   O Jhesu, fore the *Vessel* also,
      That aysel and gal thai broght thee to,   *vinegar; gall*
          That drenke, hit was unsete;   *foul-tasting*
      That I have synd in gloteney,   *sinned*
      That stynkyng syn, foreyif thou me,
90   That me hath thoght ful swete.   *has seemed to me*

      O Jhesu, fore the charp *Spere*,
      That throgh thyn hert Longyus can bere,   *Longinus [John 19:34]*
          That was a blynd knyght,
      Thou perse me hert with contricion   *pierce my*
95   Fore the syns I have edone,   *done*
          As thou yif him his syght.   *gave*

      O Jhesu, fore the lovelé *Ladder*,
      And fore the *Tongis* and fore *Hamyr*,   *Tongs; Hammer*
          That laust thee fro the tre,   *released*
100   Thou graunt me contemplacion,
      To thong thee for thi Passion,   *thank*
          That thou soferest fore me.

      O Jhesu, as Josep of Haramathé[1]
      Beryd thee ful onestlé   *Buried; honestly*
105   In his monument,
      Fore thi gloryous Resurexion,
      And thi marvelis Assencion,
      Thou grawnt me remyssion
          Tofore thi Jugement.   *Before; (i.e., Doomsday)*

110   In worchip of thi holé Passion
      And of my syns remyssion,
          Fiftene Paternoster Y say,

---

[1] *Joseph of Arimathea.* See Matthew 27:57–60, Mark 15:43–45, Luke 23:50–53, John 19:38–42.

	And fiftene Aves to our Lady,	
	Fore heo is the wel of al pyté,	*well of all compassion*
115	That heo wil fore me pray.	*she*

	He that says this prayere	
	Everé day in the yere,	
	He worchips everé wonde	
	That Crist sofyrd fore his sake,	
120	Fore his syns amendis to make;	
	Iblessid be that stounde!	*time*

	Wherefore Y pray youe specialy	
	That ye say hit dewoutly —	
	Youre souls ye may save;	
125	Fore Crist hath grawndtid seche a grace;	*granted such*
	In heven he schal have a plasse,	*place*
	That other schal noght have.	

	That fulfyld not this prayere,	*Those who have not fulfilled*
	And worchipd not his Passion wyle thai bene here,	
130	With devocion,	
	Thes that to him be unkynd,	
	He wil not have ham in mynd	
	In here trebulacion.	*tribulation*

	He that techis another mon this,	
135	He schal be sekyr of heven blis —	*assured*
	Thus wretyn I fynde —	
	Fore thai be blessud of our Lord,	*they shall be*
	That heren and don after Godis word,	
	And holdyn hit in mynd.	

Explicit de sanguine Christi.   *[Here] ends the blood of Christ.*

XVII. PRAYER ON CHRIST'S PASSION   [W5]

Quomodo Jhesu fuit reprobatus a Judeis.   *How Jesus was tortured by the Jews*

	O God, the wyche thou woldust, Lorde,	*because you willed, Lord*
	Fore the redempcion of the worlde	
	Of Jewis to be reprevyd,	*reproved*
	And to be betrayd of Judas,	
5	Of that traytur with a cos,	*kiss* [Matthew 26:48–49]
	Strayt boundyn and dispilid.	*Tightly; despoiled*

And as a lomb and ennosent,	*innocent*
To be lad to sacrefyce tofore present	*led; before [those]*
Of Ann and Kayface,	*Annas; Caiaphas [John 18:13–14]*
10 Of Pilate, Erod, and moné mo,	*Herod; many*
Unsemelé to be offyrd up so,	*Unseemly*
That never didist trespace.	

And to be acusid of false witnes,	
Reprevyd and scorgid with creuelnes,	*Reproved; scourged; cruelty*
15 And to be crownd with thorns,	
And to be spit in the face,	*[Matthew 27:30, Mark 15:19]*
And to be bofet and blyndfuld — alas! —	*blindfold*
With moné schamful skorns.	*taunts*

And to be throullid hond and food	*pierced; foot*
20 With charp naylus to the rod,	*sharp; cross*
And to be lift up in the cros,	
Betwene two thevys for to hyng;	*hang [Luke 23:33]*
Of aysel and gal thai propherd thee drynke;	*vinegar; proffered [John 19:29]*
With a spere thi hert persid was.	*[John 19:34]*

25 Be these most holé payns, Lord,	
Fore me, synful, that thou soffyrd,	
I worchip with hert and wylle;	
Also, fore the holé cros,	
Delyver my soule, Lord, fro losse,	
30 Fro the payns of helle.	

And led me, Lord, graciously,	
Synful wreche and onworthé,	*unworthy*
Into that some plasse	*same place*
Thou ladist the thefe hongyng thee by,	*led*
35 And grauntust him grace and thi mercy;	*[Luke 23:42–43]*
Foregif me my trespace.	

Wele is him that wil and may	*wishes to and can*
Say this oreson everé day	
Of Cristis Passion;	
40 Out of this word or that he wynd;	*world before he departs*
Of al his synnus, as wretyn I fynd,	
Schal have remyssion.	*[He] shall*

XVIII. THE PSALTER OF THE PASSION   [W6]

De psalterio passionis.   *Concerning the Psalter of the Passion*

INSTRUCTIONS FOR PRAYER 1   [W6]

<u>Wele is him that wele can</u>   *(see note)*
<u>Sai the Sauter of the Passion;</u>   *Psalter*
<u>Here thus thou schalt begyn</u>
<u>In the remission of thi synne.</u>

LATIN VERSE PRAYER *ANIMA CHRISTI SANCTIFICA ME*   [W6]

	Anima Christi sanctifica me,	*Spirit of Christ, sanctify me,*
	Corpus Christi salva me,	*Body of Christ, save me,*
	Sanguis Christi inebrea me,	*Blood of Christ, inebriate me,*
	Aqua latris Christi lava me,	*Water from the side of Christ, bathe me,*
5	*Passio Christi conforta me.*[1]	*Passion of Christ, fortify me.*
	O bone Jhesu exaudi me,	*O good Jesus, hear me,*
	Et ne permittas me seperare a te.	*And do not let me be separated from you.*
	Ab osti maligno defende.	*Defend me from the wicked enemy.*
	In hora mortis voca me,	*In the hour of death call me,*
10	*Et pone me juxta te*	*And place me next to you*
	Ut cum angelis tuis laudem te	*So that with angels I may praise you*
	In saecula saeculorum. Amen, pur chareté.	*Forever and ever. Amen, for charity.*

INSTRUCTIONS FOR PRAYER 2   [W6]

Instid of thi Paternoster, this thou take,
And this thi Ave, fore Cristis sake.

LATIN VERSE PRAYER *O PENDENS DUDUM*   [W6]

O pendens dudum	*O long hanging*
In hara crucis nudum	*On the altar of the cross naked*
Pro nostro scelere,	*For our sin,*
Jhesu, nostri miserere. Amen.	*Jesus, have mercy on us. Amen.*

---

[1] Audelay uses this line elsewhere as a refrain; see *God's Address to Sinful Men* and *Dread of Death*.

INSTRUCTIONS FOR PRAYER 3   **[W6]**

<table>
<tr><td></td><td>And say on thi bedis in this manere</td><td>rosary beads</td></tr>
<tr><td></td><td>As thou didist our Ladé Sautere;</td><td>Lady's Psalter (i.e., Hours of the Virgin)</td></tr>
<tr><td></td><td>When the Sauter hit is edone,</td><td></td></tr>
<tr><td></td><td>Then say thi Crede with hit anon;</td><td></td></tr>
<tr><td>5</td><td>Then in the worchip of Cristis Passion,</td><td></td></tr>
<tr><td></td><td>Say this holé oresoune.</td><td></td></tr>
</table>

LATIN VERSE PRAYER *O DEUS QUI VOLUISTI*   **[W6]**

<table>
<tr><td></td><td>O Deus qui voluisti</td><td>O God, you who were willing</td></tr>
<tr><td></td><td>Pro redemcionem mundi</td><td>For the sake of the salvation of the world</td></tr>
<tr><td></td><td>A Judeis reprobare,</td><td>To be condemned by the Jews,</td></tr>
<tr><td></td><td>A Juda traditory</td><td>By the traitor Judas</td></tr>
<tr><td>5</td><td>Osculo dare,</td><td>To be given a kiss,</td></tr>
<tr><td></td><td>Vinculis aligary,</td><td>To be bound in chains,</td></tr>
<tr><td></td><td>Et sicut agnus innocens ad victimam, eia!</td><td>And to be led as an innocent lamb to sacri-
fice, ah!</td></tr>
<tr><td></td><td>Ante conspectum Anne, Cayfe, Pilate, et Herodis,</td><td>In the sight of Annas, Caiaphas, Pilate,
and Herod,</td></tr>
<tr><td></td><td>Indecenter offerri,</td><td>To be profanely offered up,</td></tr>
<tr><td>10</td><td>Falsis testibus accusary,</td><td>To be accused with false witnesses,</td></tr>
<tr><td></td><td>Flagellis et oprobryis vexare,</td><td>To be tormented with whips and abuse,</td></tr>
<tr><td></td><td>Spinis coronare,</td><td>To be crowned with thorns,</td></tr>
<tr><td></td><td>Cholafiis cedi,</td><td>To be struck with blows,</td></tr>
<tr><td></td><td>Clavis aculeys perforari.</td><td>To be pierced with points of nail.</td></tr>
<tr><td>15</td><td>O Deus qui voluisti</td><td>O God, you who were willing</td></tr>
<tr><td></td><td>Pro redemcionem mundi</td><td>For the salvation of the world</td></tr>
<tr><td></td><td>A Judeys reprobari,</td><td>To be condemned by the Jews,</td></tr>
<tr><td></td><td>A Juda traditory,</td><td>(And) by the traitor Judas,</td></tr>
<tr><td></td><td>Et sicut angnus innocens ad victimam duci,</td><td>And to be led as an innocent lamb to the
sacrifice</td></tr>
<tr><td>20</td><td>Ante conspectum Anni, Cayfe, et Pilati,</td><td>In the sight of Annas, Caiaphas, and Pilate,</td></tr>
<tr><td></td><td>Et Erodes, indecenter offerre,</td><td>And Herod, to be profanely offered up,</td></tr>
<tr><td></td><td>A falsis testibus acusare,</td><td>And to be accused by false witnesses,</td></tr>
<tr><td></td><td>Flagellis et oprobryis vexari,</td><td>And to be tormented with whips and abuse,</td></tr>
<tr><td></td><td>Spinis coronari,</td><td>To be crowned with thorns,</td></tr>
<tr><td>25</td><td>Sputis conspui,</td><td>To be spat upon,</td></tr>
<tr><td></td><td>Colaphiis aculeys perforari,</td><td>To be pierced with blows and points (of
nails),</td></tr>
<tr><td></td><td>In cruce levari,</td><td>To be raised onto the cross,</td></tr>
<tr><td></td><td>Inter latrones deputare,</td><td>To be accounted among thieves</td></tr>
<tr><td></td><td>Felle et aceto potare,</td><td>To drink gall and vinegar,</td></tr>
<tr><td>30</td><td>Lance vulnerare.</td><td>To be wounded with the spear.</td></tr>
</table>

LATIN PROSE PRAYER *TU DOMINE PER HAS SANCTISSIMAS PENAS TUAS*   [W6]

Tu Domine per has sanctissimas penas tuas, quas ego indignis etiam recolo, et per sanctum crucem tuam, libera me de penis inferne et perducere me digneris, indignum, quo perduxisti latronem tecum crucifixum, Qui vivis et regnas.[1]

XIX. SEVEN WORDS OF CHRIST ON THE CROSS   [W7]

De septem verbis Jhesu Christi pendentis in cruce.[2]

	O Jhesu Crist, hongyng on cros,	
	Seven wordis thou saydest with myld voys	
	Unto the Fader of Heven.	
	Be the vertu of tho wordis, foregif thou me	*power*
5	That I have trespast here to thee	*What*
	In the dedlé syns seven.	
	In Pride, in Wrath, and in Envy,	
	In Lechory, in Glotony,	
	With gret unkyndnes,	
10	In Slouth, Lord, in thi servyse,	
	And in this wordis Covetyse,	*world's Avarice*
	Graunt me foregifnes.	
	O Jhesu, this word furst ye sayde:	
	"Fader, I am elé apayd;	*ill paid*
15	Graunt ham remission	
	That don me al this turmentré,	*torment*
	On ham, Fader, have peté,	*compassion*
	That wot not what thai done."	*know* [Luke 23:34]
	O Jhesu, so I thee beseche,	
20	Ryght with herfulli speche,	*heartfelt*
	Thou graunt myn enmes grace;	*enemies*
	Here mysdedis here to mende	
	Out of this word or thai wynde,	
	Fader, thou gif ham space.	

---

[1] *Thou, Lord, by these thy most blessed torments, which I am unworthy even to recall, and by thy holy cross, free me from the torments of hell and deign to lead me, unworthy though I am, whither thou brought the thief crucified with thee, thou who live and reign.* Audelay alludes elsewhere to the thief redeemed by Christ (Luke 23:42-43); see *Prayer on Christ's Passion*, lines 31–35, and *Seven Words of Christ on the Cross*, lines 25–30.

[2] *Concerning the seven words of Christ hanging on the cross*

25   O Jhesu, the theff to thee con say: *thief*
      "Have mynd on me, Lord, I thee pray,
            When thou cumyst to thi kyngdam."   *come*
      "Amen, I say thou schalt be
      This day in paradyse with me,
30   Without syn and schame."   [Luke 23:42–43]

      O Jhesu, my Soveren and my Lord,
      Have mynd on me with that word
            In that same wyse;
      When my soule schal wynd away,   *pass*
35   Graunt me part, I thee pray,
            Of the joys of paradyse.

      O Jhesu, thi moder had gret peté   *compassion*
      When heo se the turment on rod-tre;   *she saw*
            To here thus con thou say:
40   "Womon, lo, here thi sune,
      Take here to thi moder, Jon,   *her*
            And kepe here now, I thee pray."   *her* [John 19:26–27]

      O Jhesu, for thi moder love,
      That is cround in heven with thee above,
45   And Jon, thi dere derlyng,
      Fore the love thai hadyn to thee,
      Uppon my soule thou have peté,
            And graunt me good endyng.

      O Jhesu, thou saydyst ful petuysly,
50   *"Eloy lama zabatani?"*[1]
            With a rewful voyse —
      "My God, my God," hit is to say,
      "Wy foresakis thou me this day?" —   *Why*
            Hongyng apon the croyse.   *cross*

55   O Jhesu Lord, I thee pray,
      Graunt me grace that I may say
            In tyme of temptacion,
      "Fader, thou have mercé on me,
      As thou chadist thi blood on rod-tre   *shed*
60   Fore my redempcion."

---

[1] *Eloi, lamma sabacthani?* [My God, why hast thou forsaken me?] Mark 15:34; compare Matthew 27:46.

O Jhesu, thou saydist *"Citio"*;   *"I thirst"* [John 19:28]
Eysel and gal thai propherd thee to;   *Vinegar; gall; proffered* [John 19:29]
    Thou foresoke that bittere drynke.   *forsook*
Hit were the soulis that were in payn,
65   To delyver ham, thou wast ful fayne,
    Out of that darke dwellyng.

O Jhesu, graunt me grace to thorst   *thirst [for]*
The water of lyve that ever schal last,   *life*
    The wel that is ever lyghtyng,   *shining*
70   With al the dessire of my hert
To foresake my synns with terys smert   *painful tears*
    Here in my levyng.

O Jhesu, thou saydist ful spiritualy:
"*In manus tuas, Domine,*
75   *Comendo spiritum meum.*"[1]
Out of this word when I schal wynd,   *world; depart*
My soule to thee I recomend;
    Fader, to thee I cum.

O Jhesu, my Lord and my Soveren,
80   When bodé and soule schal part antwyn,   *in two*
    My speryt I comende
In manus tuas, Domine,   *Into your hands, Lord*
In thi blis with thee to be,
    Word without ende.

85   O Jhesu, thou saydist, "Al endyd is."   [See John 19:30]
Labors, sorowys wooful, iwys,   *sorrows woeful, indeed*
    Thou sofyrd fore synful men.   *suffered*
To us, Lord, thou wast ful kynd;
Graunt us grace to have in mynd,
90   To thonke thee here and hen.   *hence*

And make me worthé, Fader dere,
Thi swete voyse that I may here   *voice*
    In the oure of my partyng —   *hour*
"Cum to me, my chosun blest" —   *chosen [one]*
95   And have the blis that ever schal last,
    Word without endyng.

In the worchip of these wordis seven,
Devoutlé to the Fader of Heven,

---

[1] Lines 74–75: *Into your hands, Lord, / I commend my spirit.* Compare Luke 23:46.

	Seven Paternosters ye say,	
100	And seven Aves to our Lady,	
	Fore sche is the wel of al peté,	*compassion*
	That heo wyl fore me pray.	*she*

      And graunt me trew confession,

      And very contrecion,   *true contrition*

105   Hens ore I wynd,   *Before I depart hence*

      That Cristis holé Passion

      May be my satisfaccion,

        And schenchip to the Fynd.   *disgrace*

      Welle is him that wil and may   *wishes to and can*

110   Worchip these wordis everé day

        With devocion.

      Ful secur then may he be,   *assured*

      Yif he be in love and charyté,

        Hath playn remyssion.   *full remission*

Explicit septem verba Domini nostri Jhesu Christi.[1]

XX. DEVOTIONS AT THE LEVATION OF CHRIST'S BODY   [W8]

De salutacione corporis Christi Jhesu.   *Concerning a salutation to the body of Jesus Christ*

INSTRUCTIONS FOR PRAYER 4   [W8]

      When thou seyst the sacrement,   *see*

      Worchip hit with good entent.

        Thus thou schalt begyn:

      Knele on thi kneys; then mekely

5   Bececke him, of grace and mercy,

        Foregifnes of thi synne.

SALUTATION TO CHRIST'S BODY   [W8]

      Hayle, gracious Lord in thi Godhede,

      Hayle, faythful Fygur in forme of bred,   *Figure*

      Hayle, matryal Mater in thi Monhede,   *maternal Matter*

        Worchip mot thou be.

5   Hayle, Fader and Son and Holé Gost,

---

[1] *[Here] ends the seven words of our Lord Jesus Christ*

Hayle, Maker of medylerd of myghtis most,   *middle-earth (i.e., earth)*
Hayle, Halnere of this holé Host,   *Alms-Giver; eucharistic Host*
    Thre Persons in Trenité.

Hayle, thi gloryous Godhede, hit may not be sene,
10   Hayle, with no freelté of flesly yene.   *frailty; fleshly eyes*
Hayle, I beleve truly in this bred that ye bene
    Verey God and Mon.
Hayle, of a maydyn ye were borne
To save thi pepul that was forelorne.
15   A, seche another was never beforne   *such*
    In thi Carnacion!   *thy Incarnation*

Hayle, I beleve lelé in that lady ye lyght.   *loyally [that] you alighted in that lady*
Hayle, I beleve ye were conseyvyd in here body bryght.   *conceived in her*
Hayle, throgh the grace of the Holé Gost and thi Fader myght,
20   Borne of hyre thou was.
Hayle, thou sofyrdst ther payne and passion   *suffered*
Here fore our redempcion,
And graunt us now remissione
    Fore our trespase.

25   Hayle, I beleve in thi gloryous resureccion.
Hayle, I beleve in thy mervelus assencion.
Hayle, I beleve the Holé Gost thou sendist here adowne
    Among the postillis alle.   *apostles*
Hayle, he enspyrus everé spirite,   *breathes life into*
30   And gewes hem wysdam and wit   *gives*
That wille reule ham affter hit,   *rule them[selves] by these gifts*
    And to his grace calle.   *calls [them] to his grace*

Hayle, I beleve faythfulé ye beth Fader Omnipotent.
Hayle, I beleve thou schalt me deme at thi Jugement.   *judge*
35   Hayle, I beleve body and soule schal be ther present
    Tofore thi gloryouse face.
Hayle, I beleve savyd to be,   *[myself] saved*
And al Cristyn men, treuly,
That fore here syns here beth soré.   *their; sorry*
40   Thou grawntis mercé and grace.

Hayle, pereles Prince withowton any pere,   *peerless*
Hayle, blesful Blood and Flesche both yfere,   *sacred; together*
Hayle, thus I worchip youe with al my pouere,   *power*
    With hert and good entent.
45   Hayle, graunt me grace goostely   *spiritually*
To ressayve thi blessid body   *receive*

In parfyte love and charité,
    That is here present.

Hayle, Ground ai of my goodnes and my Governowre,   *Foundation always*
50 Hayle, Sustenans to my soule and my Saveour,   *Sustenance*
Hayle, Cumforder of the seke and al here socour   *succor*
    In the Lord hit is.
Hayle, Solans to hom that beth sory,   *Solace to those*
Hayle, Help to hom that beth gulté,   *guilty*
55 Hayle, Hope of grace and of mercy,
    Thou grawnt us al thy blys.

INSTRUCTIONS FOR PRAYER 5   **[W8]**

He that wyl say this oreson   *prayer*
With good hert and dewocion   *devotion*
Afftyr the Levacion
    Of that sacrement,
5 He schal have this pardon
Of his synns, remyssione;
Thus I fynd ewretyn
    Of Pope Enocent.   *Innocent*

PRAYER FOR PARDON AFTER THE LEVATION   **[W8]**

O Lord Jhesu Crist, fore thi holé flesche most worthi,
And thi presious blood thou toke of the vergyn Mari,   *Virgin Mary*
    And that same blod be grace
Thou chidist out of thi presious syde,   *shed*
5 Hongyng on cros with wondis wyde,
    Fore our hele hit was.   *health*

And in that same flesche thou rose fro deth to lyve,   *from; life*
And stydist up to heven with joyis, with joyful ryve;   *ascended; abundance*
    For thens thou art to cum   *thence; come*
10 To deme the pepul both quyk and dede,   *judge; quick*
In that same flesche, withoutyn drede,   *certainly*
    At the Dai of Dome.

Lord, delyver me, both gracious and good —
Fore thi holé flesche and blod
15   Is sacred in this autere —   *altar*
From alle unclenes of bodé and soule,
And payns and perellis both seke and hole,   *perils; sick; whole*
    And graunt me my prayere.

LATIN PROSE PRAYER *ADORAMUS TE CHRISTE ET BENEDICIMUS*   [W8]

Adoramus te Christe et benedecimus tibi quia per sanctam crucem tuam.[1]

Ecce Angnus Dei. Ecce qui tollis peccata mundi. Ecce Deus noster, ecce Deus justus. Ecce Deus vivorum et mortuorum. Ecce vita vivencium, spes moriencium, salus omnium in te credentium quem adoramus, quem gloreficamus, cui benedicamus. Dominum omnipotentem Patrem et Filium cum Sancto Spiritu laudemus et superexaltemus eum in secula. Adiutor et protector et defensor sis, Judice benignissime et gloriosissime. Amen.[2]

LATIN VERSE PRAYER *LAUDES DEO DICAM PER SECULA*   [W8]

	Laudes Deo dicam per secula,	*Let me speak praises to God forever,*
	Qui me plassmavit manu dextera,	*The One who formed me with his right hand,*
	Atque redemit cruci	*And redeemed me by the cross*
	Propria sanguine nati.	*With his Son's own blood.*
5	*Spiritus Sancti assit nobis gracia,*	*May the grace of the Holy Spirit be with us,*
	Soli Deo remanet honor virtus et gloria.	*May honor, power, and glory be for God alone.*
	A. M. E. N.	*Amen.*

Explicit salutacio.   *[Here] ends the salutation*

XXI. VIRTUES OF THE MASS   [W9]

De meritis misse, quomodo debemus audire missam.[3]

	Lordis, yif ye wil lythe	*if; listen*
	Of a thyng I wil you kythe,	*show*
	Is helth to al monkynd,	
	Of the medis of the masse,	*rewards*
5	Hou everé mon, more and lasse,	
	Schuld have hem in mynd.	
	How ye schul your servyse say,	
	Your prayers prevelé to pray	*privately*
	To hym that mai unbynd,	

[1] *We worship thee, Christ, and we bless thee because of thy holy cross*

[2] *Behold the Lamb of God. Behold the One who takes away the sins of the world. Behold our God, behold the righteous God. Behold God of the living and the dead. Behold the life of the living, the hope of the dying, the salvation of all believing in thee, whom we adore, whom we glorify, whom we bless. Let us praise the Lord Almighty, Father and Son with the Holy Spirit, and let us exalt him above forever. Be [our] helper and protector and defender, O Judge most kind and glorious. Amen*

[3] *Concerning the virtues of the mass, [and] how we are to hear mass*

10	In salvyng of your synis seven,
	To Jhesu Godis Son in heven,
	Oure Fader that we schul fynd.

10 In salvyng of your synis seven,   *spiritual healing*
    To Jhesu Godis Son in heven,
         Oure Fader that we schul fynd.

    Your faythful Fader he schal be fond
    To everé mon that is ebonde   *bound*
15   In syn, fore to say;
    Be hys soferens we may se   *sufferance*
    How he provys thee and me,   *tests*
         And letys us wyle he may.   *hinders us while*

    Fore he is boune our bale to bete   *prepared; relieve*
20 Yef we wyl of our syn lete   *If; desist*
         Into our deth-day;
    And yif we wyl leve our synne,
    He wyl wys us fore to wyne   *instruct*
         To heven the redé way.   *direct*

25 What mon long Y wold sofir to se,   *I would endure a long time to see*
    Fore hys syn himselfe to sle,   *[Who would] for his sin slay himself*
         Yif he myght lif agayne;   *live*
    Fore yif he were fore traytre take,   *taken for a traitor*
    Then he most amendis make,
30   Or ellis to be slayne.

    Ryght, serus, soo most we   *In the same manner, sirs*
    In our hertis soré be   *sorry*
         Fore our synys sake,
    And to the prest schryve thee,   *confess*
35 And do thi penans devoutly,
         And this amendis make.

    Holeer thyng may no mon here,   *Holier; hear*
    Ne lyghtyr thyng fore to lere,   *Nor more delightful; learn*
         To lerne men of lore,   *learned*
40 To teche mon in what wyse   *[Than] to teach*
    Hou thay schal say here servyse
         In chorche, when thai be thore.   *there*

    Yif thou to the cherche go,
    Toward, froward, or ellis cum fro,   *away from*
45   To here masse, yif thou may,
    Al the way that thou gase   *go*
    An angel payntus thi face   *adorns*
         The Prynce of Heven to pay.   *satisfy*

So in that oure thou lest noght   *So that in that hour you do not fail to*
50   That thou hast ther in thi thoght,   *[Remember] what*
          In thi prayers fore to praye;
     Blynd that day thou schalt noght be,
     The sacrement yif thou may se,
          Sothlé, as I thee say.

55   And seche grace God hath thee yeve,   *such; given*
     Yif thou be clene of syne schreve   *shriven*
          When thou his bodé ast yseyne,   *have seen*
     Yif thou dey that ilke day,   *same*
     Thou schalt be found in the fay   *faith*
60   As thou houseld hadust bene.   *purified*

     And both thi mete and thi drynke   *food*
     Thou schalt wyn with lasse swynke,   *labor*
          Without travayle or tene,   *travail; trouble*
     And yif thou stond in oné drede,   *any*
65   Alle day thou schalt the bettyr spede   *speed*
          To kever thi cars kene.   *relieve; sharp cares*

     Saynt Austyne comawndis youe spesialy   *specifically*
     That ye beleve truly
          In that sacrement:
70   That he is ther, God veray,   *true*
     That schal you deme at Domysday,
          At his Jugement.

     That sofyrd payn and passione   *He*
     Here fore your redempcion
75   Apon the rod-tre,
     And grawntis you remission
     Yif ye have contresion,   *contrition*
          When schrevyn that ye be.   *shriven*

     When that thai knele to the sacreyng,   *consecration*
80   Knelis adoune fore oné thyng,
          And hold up your hond,
     And thonk that Lord of his grace,
     That al thyng land you he has,   *loaned [to] you*
          Throgh his swet sond.   *gift*

85   Then glad mai ye be
     Your Saveour so to se,
          Tent and ye wold take,   *If you would take heed*
     Fore hit is the same brede

<pre>
          That he dalt or he was dede,   before
90   Fore his discipilis sake,   disciples'

          And lafft hit with hem in memoré,   left
          And to ale other prestis truly,
                To have hit in mynd,
          Yevery day of the yere,   Every
95   To ofur hit upon his autere   offer; altar
                In salvacion of al monkynd.

          And he that ressayvs hit worthely,   receives
          At that day wen he schal dye,
                Hit is his salvacion;
100   And he that is in dedlé syn,
          Anon as hit enters him withyn,   As soon as
                Hit is his dampnacion.

          Take ensampil be Judas: by
          At Cristis soper, Y wot, he was,   supper; know
105   And ete of that blessid bred,   ate [Matthew 26:23–25]
          Bot fore he was in didlé syn,   deadly
          The Fynd entyrd anon him yn,
                Fore his Lord he had betrayd.

          Therfore loke that ye be
110   In parfite love and charyté,
                And out of dedlé syn.
          Loke what bone that ye crave;   boon
          Aske God and ye may have,
                And heven blis to wyn.

115   Youre Paternostere, loke ye con,
          And your Ave, everé mon,   every
                And spesialy youre Crede,   especially
          Ellis esavyd ye may not be;   saved
          Bot ye con your beleve, truly,   Unless; know
120   Ye stond in gret dred.

          For al that ever nedis to thee,   is needful
          And to thi nyghtbore, truly,
                In the Paternoster hit is.
          Seven petecions ther be in,   petitions
125   That getis you foregifnes of your syn,   get [for] you
                And bryngis your soule to blis.

          Fyve worchipis thou dost to our Lady,   honors
          When that thou sayst thyn Ave —
</pre>

             Blessid mot heo be!   *she*
130   Thus angel Gabreel, he con say:
      "Hayle! Ful of grace, thou swet may,   *maiden* [Luke 1:28]
             God he is with thee."

      Twelve arteklus of thi beleve —   *articles; belief*
      Thus clerkis thai don ham preve —   *have proven them*
135   That beth in this Crede,
      That getyn thee salvacion,
      And of thi syns remission,
             And heven to thi mede.

      Your Ten Comawndmentis ye most con,   *must know*
140   And kepe hem wel, everé mon,
             Thus Crist he bede;   *commanded*
      Thi gostlé Fader schal teche ham thee,   *spiritual*
      Or ellis ful woful schal ye be;   *else*
             Thai stond in gret dred.   *awe*

145   The seven dedlé synns ye most know,
      Wyche thai bene I wyl you schew,
             Ryght here anon —
      Pride, covetyse, wrath, envy,   *avarice*
      Lechoré, slouth, and glotoné —
150   Here thai bene echon.

      Yif any of these that ye in falle,   *commit (fall into)*
      Anon on Crist loke that ye calle
             With contricion;
      Anon schryve you of your syn
155   Be frelté, yif ye fal theryn,   *By frailty*
             And ye schal have remission.

      Then in the cherche ye knele adowne,
      With good hert and devocion,
             Hold up your hondis then;
160   Furst fore yourselfe ye schul pray,
      Sethen fore fader and moder, as I thee say,
             And then fore al thi kyn,

      And fore thi frynd and fore thi foo,
      And fore thi good-doeres also,
165   Alse moné as thou mai myn,   *As many; mention*
      And fore the prest that syngis masse,
      That God forgif him his trespasse,
             And al the cherche beth in.   *all who are in the church*

Yif that the prest the masse doth syng
170 Be not at thi lykyng,   *In a manner not pleasing to you*
    Therfore let thou noght,   *be not apprehensive*
For thee, his masse is as good to here   *hear*
As ané monkis ore ané frere;   *As [that] of any monk or any friar*
    Have this in thi thoght.

175 Bot his prayers and his bone   *Even if; petition*
Be not hard half so sone   *heard; soon*
    As the mon that wele hath wroght,   *well has performed [the service]*
Y do you out of dispaire —   *I do [counsel]*
The sacrement no mon may mend ne payre;   *improve; impair*
180   Theron doctors han soght.   *theologians; confirmed*

Both Saynt Barnard and Saynt Bede
Sayne the masse is of so gret mede   *Say; benefit*
    That no mon mend hit may;   *improve*
Weder that he were wold or yong,   *Whether; old*
185 He myght tel with no tung,   *express [it]; tongue*
    Thagh he myght leve fore ay,   *live forever*

Ne expone hit opres,   *Nor expound it exactly*
Half the medis of the masse,   *rewards*
    Into his last day;
190 Were he never so wyse of art,
He schuld fayle the fifth part   *fifth*
    Of the soth to say!

I pray yo, serrys, more and lasse,   *you, sirs*
When ye stond at your masse,
195   Sum good word ye say
Fore as moné as ye prayn fore —   *many; pray*
Securly fore moné a score   *Certainly*
    At masse myn ye may.   *remember*

All thyng, thagh ye myn noght,   *though; mention*
200 Hold ham stil in your thoght,
    Hom that ye fore pray;
I do you clene out of dout   *advise you full assuredly*
Ther is non the masse without   *[who is] without the mass*
    Bot he be in hel for ay.   *forever*

205 Fore alse moné as ye may myn   *as many; mention*
When ye beth the cherche withyn,
    Ther is non a masse without,   *none [of them] without a mass*
Bot yif he be in dedlé syn,   *Unless*

	And thynke to contenu theryn,	*continue*
210	Then he stondis en dowte.	*doubt*

	When that ye bene in the kerke,	*church*
	Thenke theron, and thenke not erke,	*with annoyance*
	Hent to the last endyng.	*Until*
	Then have no dout of thi doole —	*portion*
215	Thou hast a masse, thiselfe, al hole;	*a whole mass to yourself*
	Hit is so hy a thyng!	*sacred*

	Saynt Austyn sayth, fore soulis here	
	A thousand and thou woldist, here,	
	Do a masse fore to syng,	
220	Hit is nouther more ny lasse,	
	Bot everé soule he hath a masse;	
	Hit is to Godis plesyng.[1]	

	In that houre thou herst thi masse,	*hear*
	Soules hit doth gret solas,	
225	That byth in payns bidyng;	*are in pains abiding*
	Of that oure thai beth ful fayne,	*hour; glad*
	Fore hit delyvers hem of here payne;	*[out] of*
	This is a gracious thyng.	

	Fore his love that you dere boght,	
230	Have mynd of this. Foregete hit noght!	
	Ye not when ye schul passe.	*know not; die*
	Yif ye will be sekyr and sere,	*secure and sure*
	Everé day in the yere,	
	Loke thou here thi masse.	

235	Yif thou may not thi masse here,	
	Then this lesson Y rede thou lere:	*advise you [to] learn*
	When thai to masse do knyle,	*kneel*
	Pray God, of his gret grace,	
	To send thee part of that masse,	
240	Yif hit be his wylle.	

	I do thee clene out of dout	*I do advise you full assuredly*
	Thou art not that masse without,	
	Seche grace is gif to thee;	*Such; given*
	Fore thi hert dissiryng,	*heart's desiring*

---

[1] Lines 217–22: *Saint Augustine says [that] for souls here / If you were to hear a thousand [masses], / [Or] have sung a [single] mass, / It is neither more nor less, / For every soul receives a mass; / It pleases God that this be so.* On the sense of this stanza, compare *Visiting the Sick and Consoling the Needy*, lines 92–94.

245	Thou hast part of beedis and masse syngyng,	*prayers*
	Where that ever thou be.	*Wherever*
	Fore the prest that syngis the masse	
	For al astatus, more and lasse,	*ranks*
	That is here levyng;	*their vocation*
250	He takis hem in his memoré,	
	And soulis that beth in purgatoré,	
	That God to blis hem bryng.	
	Herefore, serys, more and lasse,	*Therefore, sirs*
	Everé day here your masse,	
255	On morowe, yif ye may.	*morning*
	And yif ye mai not on morwe,	
	Loke ye do be undorne,	*by undern (9 a.m.)*
	Or ellis be mydday.	
	Sertenly, without fayle,	*Certainly*
260	Lese thou schalt not of thi travayle	*Lose; travail*
	Half a fote of thi way;	*foot*
	Al dai thou schalt be the lyghtur,	*lighter [of sin]*
	And have grace to do thee better,	
	Foresoth, as I thee say.	
265	Yet Saynt Austyn bedth take tent	*Augustine bids [you]; heed*
	That ye hold no parlement	*conversation*
	With no levyng mon,	
	Fro tyme the cherche ye ben within,	
	And the prest he doth begyn	
270	His vestmentus to take on.	*vestments*
	Fore wyckid gostis, thai wyl hit wyt,	*wicked spirits; note*
	And your wordis thay wil ham wryte	
	In here bokis, everechon.	*every word*
	That witnes wele Saynt Austyne,	*witnessed well*
275	That furst in Englond with his gyn	*followers*
	The treuth to preche began.	
	Tofore that Awstyn in Englond come,	*Before*
	With Saynt Gregoré in gret Rome	
	Ful derelé con he dwel,	*reverently did*
280	Hent on a day of gret dernes,	*Until; reverence*
	Saynt Gregoré wold syng his masse,	
	So fayre as him befelle.	*So fairly as befell to him*
	To the Austyn, he mad a syne	*sign*
	Fore to be his dekyn dene	*presiding deacon*

285   To red his Cospel,   *read; Gospel*
       And as he red, he sau sit   *saw sitting*
       Thre fyendys, as ye may wit,   *fiends; understand*
           And talis con thai telle.   *gossip did they tell*

       What thai sayd, he herd hit alle
290   Throgh a wyndow of the walle,
          No fer fro his face.   *far*
       He se a fynd sit witin,   *saw; within*
       With pen and enke and parchemen,   *ink; parchment*
          As God gif him grace.   *gave*

295   He wrot so lung that he ded want,   *wrote; long; want [more room]*
       And his parchement wex scant —   *became*
          To speke, thai had space —   *had space (i.e., they gabbed on)*
       With is teth he con hit tug,   *his teeth; did*
       And as Rofyn begon to rug,   *Ruffin (the devil's name); pull*
300   His rolle began to rase.   *tear*

       So hard Rofyn rogud his rolle,   *pulled*
       That he smot with his choule   *struck; jowl*
          Agayns the marbys stone;   *marble*
       Of that dynt, thai had gret doute —   *blow; were startled*
305   Al that setyn ther aboute —   *sat*
          Fore thai herd hit echon.   *For each of them heard it*

       When the fynd so hard drou,   *fiend; fell down*
       Saynt Austyn stod and low.   *laughed*
          Saynt Gregoré then con grone;   *did groan [with dismay]*
310   Neverthelees, fore grame he get.   *Furthermore, he became irritated*
       Sone after masse the Austyn he met,
          And myldelé mad his mone.   *mildly; complaint*

       He sayd to him with myld mode: *demeanor*
       "What aylid thee, thou wytles woode,   *ailed; foolish madman*
315   Todai to do this dede?
       Seche a dede was never done."
       Then he answerd him ful sone,
          Fore of him he had gret drede:

       "Sere, greve ye noght or ye wyt,   *before you know*
320   Fore yonder I se a satanas sit —   *saw; demon*
          Hit semyd his hed did blede —   *seemed*
       What he wrot tofore he brayd,   *before he cried out*
       That thre wyvys seton and sayde,   *[All] that three wives sat*
          As I stode to rede.   *stood to read [the Gospel]*

325	"I was adevyd of that dynt;	*deafened; noise*
	Hit stoned me and mad me stont,	*astonished; stupified*
	Styl out of my steven!	*Speechless; voice*
	I schal you tel what I se,	*saw*
	And word therof I wyl noght lye;	*not lie*
330	Be Godis Son in heven,	

	"Syr, ye may wyl trow."	*well believe*
	He lad him to the wyndow.	*led*
	"Cum nere, syr, and sene!"	*see*
	Tho Saynt Gregoré was adred,	*Then; afraid*
335	Fore blak blood he se espred	*spread out*
	Apon the aschelere even.	*ashlar directly*

	Then this good mon grevyd him lasse,	*was less aggrieved*
	And comawndit at everé masse	
	Of this mater to myn.	*remember*
340	Kepe you out of Godis wreke,	*vengeance*
	Fore ther is no word that ye speke,	*speak [in church]*
	Bot ye don syn!	

	Therfore, serys, with good wyl,	
	Loke that ye hold you styl	*be quiet*
345	The cherche when ye bene in;	*When you are in church*
	A prest, to stone in his masse,	*A priest, to astonish*
	Al a lond may fare the worse,	*[Can mean that] an entire land*
	Out of wo to wyn.	*[Rather than] be won out of woe*

	The chorche is a house of prayere;	
350	Hold hilé to Godis honoure,	*reverently*
	To worchip hym therin.	
	What ryghtful bone that ye crave,	*prayer*
	Aske God and ye schul have,	
	And be foregevyn of your syn.	

355	Hit were hard, to oure behove,	*properly speaking*
	Uche proferbe fore to prove,	*Each maxim to demonstrate*
	Of our awntros alle;	*mysteries*
	Here schortlé I wyl chew hit,	*briefly; explain*
	Lewd men to know hit,	*Laymen*
360	Crist on fore to calle.	

	In the cherche thou knele adown,
	With good hert and devocion;
	Hold up thi hondis then —
	Fore thiself, furst thou pray,

365   Fore fader and moder, as I thee say,
          And sethyn fore al thi kyn,   *then*

       And fore the weder, and fore the pes,   *weather; peace*
       And fore men and wemen, mo and lees,
          That Cristyndam an han tane.   *Who have accepted Christianity*
370   In the name of the Treneté,
       Then Paternoster say thou thre —
          Say furst in Cristis name.   *the first one*

       Then fyve Paternoster thou schalt say,
       To pray him that best may
375   To gyf thee wit and grace,   *give; understanding*
       Thi fyve wyttis so to spende,
       Thi synful soule here to amend,
          To heven to folou the trasse.   *path*

       Sethin seven to the Holé Gost   *Afterwards [say] seven [prayers]*
380   To kepe thee out of werkis wast,   *wasteful deeds*
          And out of dedlé syn.
       Ten Paternoster say thou then
       Fore brekyng of thi Hestis Ten;   *Ten Commandments*
          And thus thou schalt begyn.

385   On the werkeday yif that thou be   *workday*
       About thi labor, treuly,
          In word, as thou most nede,   *the world*
       On the haleday thou fulfyl   *holy day*
       Ryght as I have sayd thee tyll,   *Just; to you*
390   And thou art out of drede.   *safe*

       And oche a day thi masse thou here,   *each; hear*
       And take halé bred and halé watere   *holy*
          Out of the prestis hond;
       Seche grace God hath gif thee,   *Such; given*
395   Yif that thou dey sodenly,   *die suddenly*
          Fore thi housil hit schal thee stond.   *received eucharist; protect*

       Fore suche power that blessyng hit has,
       That God blessud the bred in wildernes,
          And two fyschis also,
400   And fedd therwith fyve thosand men,[1]
       Twelve lepus of relef laft affter then;   *baskets of relief (were) left over*
          Soche lordis ther be no moo.

---

[1] Matthew 14:17–21, Mark 6:38–44, Luke 9:13–17.

And also loke that ye be
In parfyte love and charyté
405   And out of dedlé syn;
What ryghtful bone that ye crave,   *proper boon*
Aske God and ye schul have,
        And heven blis to wyn.

Alle that han herd this sermon,
410   A hundred days of pardon,
        Saynt Gregoré grauntis you this.
Out of this word wen ye schal wynd,   *world when; depart*
Jhesu save you from the Fynd,
        And bryng your soule to blis!

Explicit meritis misse.   *[Here] ends the virtues of the mass*

XXII. FOR REMISSION OF SINS   [W10]

SAINT GREGORY'S INDULGENCE   [W10]

Quomodo Dominus Jhesus Christus apparuit Sancto Gregorio in tale effugie.[1]

Apon a day Saynt Gregoré
Song his mas at Rome, truly;
Crist to him he con apere   *did appear*
In the fegure of his autere;   *In the painted image on his altar*
5   Then Gregoré had conpassion,
And grawntis fourtene thousand yere of pardon,
And other bischops, moné mo,   *many more*
Grawntyd more pardon therto;
The nowmbur hit is of al efere   *in total*
10   Twenty thousand and six days and thirty-six yere.

Say fyve Paternoster and fyve Ave
In reverens of this holé peté   *indulgence*
With good herd and devocion,   *heart*
In worchip of his Passion,
15   Knelyng down apon your kne,
Askyng grace of this peté.
Yif ye be out of dedlé syn,
Then this pardon may ye wyn,
In what plase hit payntid is,   *painted*
20   The same pardon therto ther is.

---

[1] *How the Lord Jesus Christ appeared to Saint Gregory in such an image*

INSTRUCTIONS FOR PRAYER 6   **[W10]**

<u>Then loke thou say anon
Dewowtlé this confession.</u>   *Devoutly*

PRAYER OF GENERAL CONFESSION   **[W10]**

De confesione generali.   *Concerning general confession*

Swete Jhesu Crist, to thee,
Coubabil wreche, Y yild me;   *A culpable wretch, I yield myself*
Of al the syns I have edo   *done*
In al my lyve hederto,   *hitherto*
5   In Pride, in Wrath, and in Envy,
In Lechoré and in Glotony,
In Slouth, Lord, in thi servyce,
And in thi worldis Covetyse,   *avarice*
To oft I have in my lyve   *Too often*
10   Isynnud with my wyttis fyve —   *Sinned*
With eren her, with eyne syght,   *ears' hearing, eyes' sight*
Wyth synful speche, day and nyght,
With clepyng and with cussyng bo,   *embracing; kissing both*
With hond ehandild, with fete ego,   *hands' having handled; feet's having gone*
15   With hert synfulli I have thoght,
With al my bodi mys ewroght —   *having misdone*
Here, of al my foly,
Lord, mercé to thee I cry!
Ale thagh I have synyd ever,
20   Lord, I foresoke thee never;
No nother god toke I non,
Fader of Heven, bot thee alone;
Herefore, Fader, I thee beseche,   *Therefore*
Ryght with hertful speche,   *heartfelt*
25   That thou gif me no mede   *give; reward*
After my synful dede,   *Accordant to my sinfulness*
Bot, Lord, fore thi gret mercy,   *But rather*
Have reuth and peté apon me,   *compassion; pity*
And send me hereof, er Y dye,   *here (i.e., to confession); before*
30   Sorou of hert with tere of ye,   *Sorrow of heart*
And let me never heft begyn   *again*
Fore to do no dedlé syn,
So at myn endyng day,
Clene of syn dey I may,   *Clean; die*
35   With schryft and housil at myn end,   *penance and Holy Communion*
So that my soule mai wynd   *go*

Into that blis withoutyn pere,   *equal*
Ther ye dwel, Lord and Syre. Amen.   *There [where]*

INSTRUCTIONS FOR PRAYER 7   **[W10]**

Loke ye say this oresoun   *prayer*
Dewoutlé with devocion.   *Devoutly*

PRAYER FOR FORGIVENESS   **[W10]**

Quomodo Jhesus in cruce rogabat Patrem pro inimicis. Oracio.[1]

O Lord Jhesu Crist, hongyng on cros —
Fore our syn I wot hit was —   *know*
Ther thou praydist thi Fader alhone   *prayed [to]; alone*
To foregif thyn enmys everechon;
5   I beseche thee, fore that holé word,
Foregif myn enmys, Y pray thee, Lorde,
That han trespassid here to me,
And grawnt ham love and charyté.
I pray thee, Lord, that hit so be
10   And that ye wil foregif me.

Amen.

XXIII. VISITING THE SICK AND CONSOLING THE NEEDY   **[W11]**

De visitacione infirmorum et consolacione miserorum.[2]

Saynt Ancelyne, that holé bischop,   *Anselm*
He med this tretys be Godis grace,   *made*
Hou ye schul set in God your hope,   *How*
Out of this word wen ye schul passe,   *world when; pass (die)*
5   And to foresake al that thou has —
Wyfe and child, al wordlé thyng —   *worldly*
And to dissyre to have that plas   *desire; place*
Were joy and blis is ay bydyng,   *Where; ever abiding*
        And have this in thi mynd —
10   Fore that joy schal never sese,   *cease*
Bot ever endure, and ever encres,   *increase*

---
[1] *How Jesus on the cross prayed to the Father for his enemies. A prayer*

[2] *Concerning the visitation of the sick and consolation of the wretched*

And ever in love, rest, and pesse,   *peace*
        In joy and blis, without end!

Thus to thi God, thou schalt thee yild,   *yield yourself*
15 And knowleche to him al thi trespas —   *acknowledge*
    His comawndmentis not fulfillid;   *[how you have] not*
    Thi fyve wittis myspend thou has —   *misspent*
    And aske him mercy loulé and grace.   *humbly*
    The werkis of mercy thou hast not don —
20 Vesid the pore in evereche plase;   *every place*
    Ne done the seke consolacion.   *Nor given the sick consolation*
            Then thus schal thou say:
        "I knowleche me, Lord, gilté,   *guilty*
        In pride, covetys, wrath, envy,   *avarice*
25   In lechoré, slouth, and glotony.
            I have esynyd both nyght and day."   *sinned*

    Thus alle men he doth cumford,   *does comfort*
    And cowncelis you, pur charité,   *counsels; for*
    Settis noght be the joy of this word —   *by; world*
30 Hit is bot vayn and vaneté! —   *vanity*
    Fore youre namys wretyn thay be   *are*
    In the boke of lyve in heven blis,   *book of life in heaven's bliss*
    To have joy ther perpetualy!
    Al erthlé joy hit schal vanysche
35   Within a lytil stound,   *while*
    Fore ale this wordlé honor
    Schal fal and fade as doth a floure.   *flower*
    Pope, kyng, duke, emperoure —
            Al schul thai go to grounde.

40 Behold a charnel ful of boonys —   *burial place; bones*
    What clerke con therowte a boone   *recognizes there*
    Of lord ore ladys, schete al at ones?   *enclosed all together*
    Of ryche, of pore, of gentilmon?   *nobleman*
    So bredern and sisterne we beth echone;   *brothers; sisters; each one*
45 And he that doth best in his levyng   *living actions*
    Schal have most mede when he is goon,   *reward*
    And most thonk of his Fader Heven Kyng.   *most esteem from*
            Uche mon in his degré,   *Each; rank*
        As he hath kept his oune astate,   *position*
50   To Godis worchip, erlé and late,   *early*
        He schal have reward algate —   *in any case*
            Bale or blis — wedersoever hit be.   *whatsoever*

Allas, that we con not beleve
That we felyn and sen with syght!   *What; feel and see*

55	How lytil a thyng mon may greve	*may grieve a man*
	When eny syknes is on him dyght!	*any sickness; ordained*
	Anon he has lost al his myght;	
	Then hard on Crist he wyl crye!	*loudly*
	Fore payn of deth, he is afryght,	*afraid*
60	That al wordlé joy he settis not by.	*values not*
	Then comford is ther non.	*comfort*
	A, synful mon! Have this in mynd —	
	Thi mysdedis betyme amend,	*misdeeds in time*
	And serve thi God; forsake the Fynd.	*Fiend*
65	Then schal thou have remyssion.	
	Fore cursid be he that trustis in mon	
	And doth not affter Cristis wil,	*acts not according to*
	More then he doth in God alone,	
	That bodé and soule may save and spil;	*Who; or destroy*
70	Fore Cristis bidyng we schuld fulfil,	
	And do fore ourself or we passe hen,	*act on our own behalf before; hence*
	And pot oure soulis out of parelle,	*put; peril*
	And trust not ale to other men.	*other men*
	Fore thou getyst no more with thee	*shall bring*
75	Save thi good dydis, withoutyn drede,	*Other than; deeds, doubtless*
	Holé prayers, masse, and almusdede.	*almsdeeds*
	After thi meryd and thi mede	*According to*
	Rewardid schal thou be.	
	Fore Cristis love, doth almesdede —	
80	In thi good lyve, gif a pené	*living, give a penny*
	To the pore that hath gret nede,	
	Or mete, drynk, clothis, or herbar fre —	*food; clothes; lodging*
	And thou plecyst God more specyaly	*please; significantly*
	Then a thowsond hillis of gold, as I thee say,	*thousand hills*
85	Were made in mynt and in money	
	To dele after thi deth day.	*distribute*
	Fore mede getis thou none	*reward*
	Bot yif thiselfe thi soule sokoure,	
	Ellis may not thi cecatoure.[1]	
90	Hit is the wordis — alle thi tresoure —	*It belongs to the world*
	When thou art goon.	
	More med is a mas here in thi lyve	*More meed [accrues from] a mass*
	Then to have a thausand after thi day;	*thousand [said for your soul]*
	Yif to the prest thou wylt thee schryve,	*confess*
95	And do thi penans here wyl thou maye,	*while*

---

[1] Lines 88–89: *Unless you yourself succor your soul, / Your executor may not [do this for you]*

Thus thou myght God plese and pay,   *please and requite*
Yif that thou wold thi soule socour
Or thi caren be cast in clay,   *Before; body; earth*
And trost not to thi secatoure.   *trust; executor*
100   Gregoré thus con he say:
        "Better hit is now fore thee
        To wenche the fuyre of purgatoré —   *quench the fire*
        Therin cast or that thou be —   *before*
              Thiselfe here wyle thou may."   *[To save] yourself here while*

105   Thus Seynt Ancellyne to youe he sayd: *Anselm*
        "Dissyre ye not agayns Godis wile,   *Desire not against*
        Bot ever ald you wel apayd,   *hold yourself well paid*
        What vesetacion he send you tylle,   *Whatever visitation he sends to you*
        Fore his mercé in you he wil fulfil
110   When tyme is cum at his lykyng;
        Fore wom he lovys, he chastest wele,   *whomever; chastises well* [Hebrews 12:6]
        And save his soule fro perescheng   *saves; perishing*
              Fro the payns of helle —
        Fore his grace and his goodnes,
115   His benyngnyté and his blessidnes,   *mildness*
        His hye mercé and his mekenes,   *great*
              Con no tung here telle!"   *tongue*

        "Thus clepth agen yusterday,"   *"Thus think upon yesterday"*
        Saynt Ancellyne, he cownsellis thee,   *Anselm*
120   "And mesure thi wynde, Y thee pray,   *be careful what you say*
        And wy the foyre of purgatoré!"   *weigh; fire*
        These thre wordis declared schal be
        What thai beth to understond;   *As they are to be understood*
        Lerne this lesson, pur chareté,   *for*
125   And thonke thi God of his swet sond —   *message*
              Fore hit is fore the best
        To have thi payne, thi purgatorye,
        Out of this word or that thou dye,   *before*
        Fore God ponysche not twyse, truly!   *punishes; twice*
130   Take hede mekelé; then art thu bleste.

        Thus yistyrday thou clepe agayne,   *think upon*
        And take knoulesche of thi consians —   *knowledge; conscience*
        Hou thou hast spend thi lyve in vayn,   *spent*
        Agen Godis wil and his plesans.   *Against; liking*
135   Then mesoure thi wynd with repentans,   *speak carefully*
        And schryve thee clene of alle thi synne.
        Then wey the fouyre with trew balans —   *weigh the fire; balance*
        What purgatoré thou schuldist have then.
              Fore this is Godis oune wyll,

140	That everé good dede rewardid schal be	*every*
	In erth or ellis in heven on he,	*high*
	And uche syn eponyst, truly,	*punished*
	In erth, in purgatoré, or ellis in helle.	

	Bot above his warkis is his mercy.	
145	Thenke what did Maré Mawdleyn,	*Mary Magdalene*
	And Peter, that foresoke him thry,	*thrice*
	Fore the ways of twey wemen,	*two* [Matthew 26:69–75]
	And Thomas of Ynd, that mysbelevyd then —	*doubted* [John 20:25]
	Al thai had mercy and grace.	
150	And so schul have al Cristyn men	
	That wil repent wyle thai han space.	*while; time*
	Fore as possibil hit were	
	With watere of thi ne	*your eye*
	To wenche the fuyre of purgatory,	*quench; fire*
155	As al the water in the se	*As [it would be]*
	To wenche a gnost of fuyre.	*spark*

	Fore more joye in heven ther is	
	Of a mon that foresakis his syn,	
	And wil amende he dothe amys,	*amend [what]*
160	And do his penans is enjunyd then,	*[as he] is enjoined*
	Then of four score of ryghtwys men —	*Than [there is]* [see Luke 15:7]
	In the Gospel wretyn hit is —	
	Fore hom ned is heren oune medsyn,	*For whom need is their own medicine*
	Bot thai that beth seke in soule, iwys.	*Unless; sick; indeed*
165	Cryst sayth thus, graciously:	
	"I come not to clepe ryghtwyse men,	*call*
	Bot tho that in erth synful bene;	*those who*
	Hom I cal to penans then	*Them*
	To graunt hom grace and my mercy."[1]	

170	For he that wil himselve here loue,	*bow down [in humility]*
	And forsake his syn and be soré,	*sorry*
	And to the prest him schryve and chewe,	*shows [his sins]*
	And do his penans dewoutly,	*devoutly*
	He never rehersid schal be	*mentioned*
175	When he is callid to his rekynyng,	
	Fore Crist hath foregifne him throgh His mercy,	
	Here in erth in his levyng,	
	Throgh his specyale grace.	
	Yif thou wilt sekyr savyd be,	*securely*

---

[1] Compare Matthew 9:13, Mark 2:17, Luke 5:32, and also Audelay's *God's Address to Sinful Men*, line 24a.

180   Foresake thi syn or hit do thee,   *before it forsakes you*
       Ellis thai schul be cheuyd opynlé,   *shown openly*
              At Domysday before Cristis face.

       Fore Peter wept ever aftur moore   *evermore afterwards*
       When he herd eny koke crowe;   *any cock* [Matthew 26:69–75]
185   And Maré Mawdlyan, wepeng ful sore,
       Askid grace of Crist with hert so low;   *humble* [see John 20:11–18]
       And Thomas of Ynd mad us to know
       Hou false he was in his beleve,   [John 20:25]
       Fore Crist his wondis to him con shew —   *did show*
190   The soth himselve he mad him preve: *prove*
              "Thomas, to thee I say,
              Blessid be thai that never seyn,   *witness [the wounds]*
              And trewlé in my werkis belevyn,
              Fore thai schul have the blis of heven,
195   And my blissyng, nyght and day."   [John 20:29]

       Affter Crist made Peter of paradyse porter,   *gatekeeper*
       And betoke him the kyis of heven gate,   *keys*
       And yif him fullé his pouere   *gave; power*
       To louce and bynd, erlé and late,[1]   *loose; bind, early*
200   And bede him thynke on his astate —   *bid; estate*
       How freel he was, and eth to falle —   *frail; susceptible*
       And he him graunt mercé, allegate,   *in any case*
       To al that in erth his grace wyl calle,
              With sorow of ert and confession: *heart*
205   "Peter, as I geve thee mercy,
              So on other thou have peté;   *compassion*
       That foresakis his synus and beth sory,   *Whoever*
              Thou graunt hem ale remission."

       Thus we ben bleste of Godis mouth!
210   Al that beleven in him truly —
       Est and west, north and south —
       Thai schal have grace and mercy,
       And no nother sekyrly.   *assuredly*
       Dampnacion to hom al is dight   *prepared*
215   That wol witt how and wy   *wish to understand*
       That al thyng Crist do he myght.
              Ensampil ale day we se,
              Fro the heven, on he token —   *a high token*
              The lyght, the thonder, and ster, mone, and son —

---

[1] Matthew 16:19; compare Matthew 18:18.

220	That he is Almyghté God alhon,	*alone*
	And no nother Lord bot he!	
	Fore Holé Cherche prays fore no mo	*only for*
	Bot tho that belevyn and dye in Crist;	*Those who believe*
	Al other to penans thai schal goo,	
225	That to his mercé and grace wil not trost,	
	Bot leven after here flesschelé lust	*live by their fleshly desire*
	As bestis don, unresnabelé;	*beasts; unreasonably*
	Hur lyve days thai han elost;	*days of life; lost*
	Here dedis schul deme hem openly	
230	At Cristis Jugement.	
	Fore Cristyn men callid thagh ye be,	
	Bot yif ye done Cristynly,	*Unless*
	Ye bere that name in wayn, truly —	*vain*
	Ye wil be schamyd and schent!	*shamed; disgraced*
235	Herefore, beleve in Crist truly,	*Therefore*
	And foresake youre lust and your lykyng,	
	And set your trust in him, truly,	
	To have that joy that is everlastyng;	
	And let this be al thi wylnyng,	*entirely your intent*
240	Yif that thou turne to lyve agayn,	
	And to amend thi myslevyng,	*misbehavior*
	And him to serve be glad and fayn —	*eager*
	And have this in thi mynd! —	
	And aske him grace and his mercy,	
245	Fore his moder love, maydyn Maré,	*For love of his mother*
	And al the sayntis in heven on hye,	
	To graunt thee grace to make good end.	
	Thus in thi God thou cumford thee,	
	And thenk apon his Passion —	
250	That fore thi love here wold he dey	*die*
	With cros, spere, nayle, and croune —	
	Fore in him is al consolacion,	
	And may thee hele of thi sekenes,	*heal; sickness*
	And grawnt thee here now remission,	
255	And of thi syns foregifnes.	
	Loke thou beleve wel this!	
	Thagh thou have grevyd Crist here before,	*Although*
	His mercé is mekil more,	*much*
	Fore he hath salve fore everé sore,	*remedy*
260	And may amend thou dost mys.	*amend [what]; amiss*
	Thi baptim and thi confyrmacion,	*baptism*
	Thes be his salvys, verament;	*remedies*

And holé order, and matremon,   *matrimony*
And schreft, and housil that sacrement;   *penance; Holy Communion*
265   Then the last anelyng with good entent,   *extreme unction*
Hit may thee clens, both out and yn.   *cleanse*
The prest hath pouere that is present   *power*
To asoyle thee of al thi syn —   *absolve*
          Of God he hath pouere,
270   Thorghe vertu of the sacrement,
To asoyle al that wil repent,
And chryve him clene, verament,   *shrive; truly*
          And do here penans wyle thay beth here.

Fore this is Godis ordenans,   *ordinance*
275   Thes sacrements to save monkynd,
Fore in hom is al sofecians,   *sufficiency*
Both fore to loos and fore to bynd.   *release*
Then to that Lord, be never unkynd,
That hath grawnt his spesial grace;
280   Thow we al day him offend,   *Although*
Remedé thus ordend he has.   *ordained*
          Thow we han don amys,
          Yif fore our syns we beth sory,
          And ressayve his pressious body,   *receive; precious*
285   We schul have grace and mercy,
          And part of heven blis.

Then aske thi sacrements, pur charyté,   *request; for*
And when thou ressayvst that sacrement,   *receive*
Beleve in hert, truly,
290   That he is that Lord Omnipotent,
And Crist is God Son, verament,   *truly*
That with his blod thee dere hath boght,   *dearly*
That schal thee save at his Jugement.
Have this in mynde — foreget hit noght!
295   And beware, uche Cristin mon,   *each*
          Fore heretekis and renegatis that uncriston be,   *heretics; renegades*
          That beleve not in that sacrement, treuly —
          That Crist was not borne of the vergyn Mari —
          Of hom is no redemcion!   *For them*

300   Herefore beleve in Crist, treuly,
That thorghe the Holé Gost conseyvd he was,   *conceived*
And borne of the vergyn Mari,
And sofyrd payn and passion, crucifid on cros,
Ded and beryd fore oure trespace.   *buried; sin*
305   Into hel he dissendid, with myght and mayn,   *descended; strength*
And toke Adam and Eve out of here place;   *their*

	The thrid day he ros to lyve agayn;	*third*
	Into heven he stid up then,	*ascended*
	And syttus there on his Fadur ryght honde.	
310	Fro thens he is to cum, thus understond,	*thence*
	To deme his pepil, ded or lewand,	*judge; dead or living*
	After here dedis, al maner men.	*According to their deeds, all kinds of men*

	Also beleve in the Holé Gost,	
	As Holé Cherche hath informed thee,	
315	And in the Fader and Sone of myghtis most,	
	Thre Persons in Treneté,	
	And in comenecacions with sayntis to be,	*communications*
	And to have foregifnes of thi syn,	
	And the uprysyng of thi flesche, treuly,	*resurrection; body*
320	And to have everlastyng lyve. Amen.[1]	
	Here is the conclucion.	
	These beth the artecelis of thi beleve;	*articles*
	Kepe hem wele without repreve,	*reproof*
	And thou schalt never have myschife.	*misfortune*
325	Hit is the wel of salvacion!	

	And beleve and hope and trust also	
	As thy gostlé faders cownsels thee;	*spiritual fathers*
	Loke thou never go herefro	
	Thagh thou have fal throgh thi freelté,	*fallen; frailty*
330	Bot aske God grace and his mercé,	
	And foregifnes of al other men,	
	And foregif thou, pur charyté,	*give forgiveness yourself for*
	And thou art savyd, my soule fore thyn,	
	And stondis clene out of dred,	*fully; doubt*
335	Fore Crist he says thus to thee:	
	"Yif thou foregif fore love of me,	
	Then foregifne schalt thou be	*forgiven*
	Of al thi mysdede."[2]	

	And let make thi testment and thi last wil.	*testament*
340	Furst pay thi dettis alle treuly,	*debts; honestly*
	And remembir thee, fore that is skil,	*appropriate*
	What thou hou and other to thee;	*owe*
	Then let hit be selid opynlé,	*settled openly*
	And make thi soule a sekyr way,	*secure*
345	Lest thi sekatours don not treuly.	*executors act dishonestly*

---

[1] Lines 300–20 paraphrase the Apostles' Creed. Compare *Salutation to Christ's Body*, lines 17–36.

[2] Lines 336–38: Compare Luke 6:37, also used in *God's Address to Sinful Men*, line 160a, and *Audelay's Epilogue to The Counsel of Conscience*, line 442a.

Ensampil be other, se thou may: *you may see*
    Beware, ye sekators —   *[of the] executors*
The dedis wil loke that ye done,   *dead will see what*
Out of the word when thai bene gon,   *world*
350   That setyn here trust in youe alone,
    Ellis to God and mon ye be traytours.

Yif ye do trewly your devor,   *duty*
Ful wele rewardid schal ye be,
Of Jhesu that is your Saveour,   *By*
355   At that day when ye schul dee;   *die*
Fore hit is a dede of charité   *deed*
To do treuly unto the dede,   *dead*
That lyen in the paynes of purgatori,   *Who lie*
After your help, ther to abyde.   *[Seeking] after*
360   No nother sokyr thai han, treuly,   *succor*
    Save holy prayers, mas, and almesdede,
    That qwenchyn here synus and here mysdede   *quench; sins*
    As water doth foyre, without drede,   *fire; assuredly*
    And al the payns of purgatory.

365   Ye that wepe for childer and frynd   *weep; children; friends*
Wen thai schul dey, have this in mynd: *When; die*
Hyly ye ofend swet Jhesus,   *Greatly; offend*
As childer uncurtes and unkynd;   *uncourteous*
In Holé Wret thus wretyn I fynd
370   That joyful and glad schal ye be
When your Fader wold after youe send —
Ever to him make youe redy   *to [dwell with]*
    As blessid childer then.
    Fore when fader and moder has you foresake,   *forsaken*
375   Then Jhesus oure soulus to him wil take,
    Bot they him grete cause sorou to make,   *cause him to make great sorrow*
    That dyen in det and dedlé syn.   *die; debt*

Mervel ye not of this makyng,   *Marvel*
Fore I me excuse — hit is not I;   *excuse myself*
380   This was Seynt Ancelme cownselyng,   *Anselm's*
That was a bischop ful holy.
Fore I couth never bot hye foly;   *could never [make anything] but great folly*
Crist has me chastist fore my levyng.   *chastised*
I thonke me God, my Grace, trewly,
385   Of hys graciouse visetyng.   *visiting [of affliction]*
    Ye curatis here, I you pray,
    That han mon soule in your kepyng,
    Let red this treté fore oné thyng   *Let [them] read this treatise*

190   To the seke at here endyng.
390   Thus counsels you the Blynd Audley.

  And of your lyve, take good eme.   *heed*
  Beware lest God ye offend,
  Fore as he fyndis youe, he wil you deme,   *judge*
  Other be savyd or ellis be schent;   *Either; else; destroyed*
395 Fore soden deth, lok ye amend,   *For [fear of]*
  And set not your trust were non is,   *where*
  Fore al is good that good end,   *that [has a] good end*
  When ye amend it ye han do mys.   *what; amiss*
   This is my cownselyng —
400   How Godis wesitacion ye schuld take, *adversity (visitation)*
   Fore your mysdedis and your syns sake,
   And howe ye schul amendis make,
    To have that joy that is everlastyng. Amen.

Explicit visitacio infirmorum et consolacio miserorum.[1]

BLIND AUDELAY'S ENGLISH PASSION   **[W12–W14]**

INSTRUCTIONS FOR READING 2   **[W12]**

I pray you, serys, pur charyté,   *for*
When ye han red this, treuly,
Then redis this Passion,
What Cryst sofyrd fore synful mon.

5 Here schul ye here a treu lessoun
  Hou fayth and charyté away is gon.

ON THE WORLD'S FOLLY   **[W12]**

Multis diebus iam peractis, When many days have already passed,
Nulla fides est in pactis.   There is no reliance in agreements.
 Videte.   See.
Mel in ore verbis lactis, Honey in the mouth with words of milk,
5 *Fel in corde, fraus in factis.* Gall in the heart, deceit in deeds.
 Cavete.   Beware.

Moné days now agone
Fayth ne covenant is ther non —

---

[1] *[Here] ends the visitation of the sick and the consolation of the wretched*

Behold and se!

10   In mouth is honé swet wordis uchon;   *honey sweet words each one*
In hert is galle, in dede, tresoun.   *deed, treason*
Ware now be!   *Beware now*

Godis laus beth turnyd up-so-doun,   *are*
In Holé Cherche devocion,
15   And fore chareté.
Fore trew corexion is ther non,   *correction*
Fore love of Mede, that swet maydyn,   *Material Reward*
In non degré.   *To no degree*

Fore ale that clerkis now prechon,   *preach*
20   Of holé Cristis Passion,
Is no peté,   *Is not heartfelt*
To make here satisfaccion,
With wrong that men here geten
With sotelté.   *subtlety*

25   Ye schul acownt everechon   *account every bit*
Fore your goodis, when ye bene gone,
Ful sekyrlé,   *certainly*
Yif ye have dissayvyd oné mon,   *deceived any*
Bot ye make satisfaccion   *[Take care that] you*
30   Or that ye dye.   *Before*

Here may ye se an he tokyn   *see a great token*
That God he is wroth with mon,
In heven on hye:
Now werris then don awakyn,   *wars; do arise*
35   The erth we fele quakyn,
Honger hathe be.

Pestlens we sen raynen,   *Pestilence we see raining [down]*
Men al day thai dyen,
Sum sodenlé!
40   Fore al that trew tokyn,
Oure wittis yet we wantyn   *wits; lack*
To make us redy.

Nou excusacion hath we non   *excuse*
Out of this word when that we gon —   *world*
45   Leve ye me!   *Believe*
Godis bedyng bot we done,   *Unless we do God's bidding*
We schul have confucion,
Ful ryghtwysly.   *Full assuredly*

Fore men wil not beleven
50   That heven nor hel ther is non,   *That there is [any] heaven or hell*
            Ne turmentré.   *Or [eternal] torments*
     And sekyr thou schalt have thet on —   *certainly; one of them*
     Joy or ellis dampnacion —   *[Either] joy or else damnation*
            Perpetualy!

55   I red that nowe we amend   *urge*
     To God and mon, that we offend,
            Here specialy;
     And do fore oreselve or we goon,   *ourselves before*
     And trust not to another mon —
60   Hit is foly!

     Fore other cownsel nede ye non,
     Yif ye wil have salvacion
            Or that ye dee: *Before you die*
     Schryve youe clene with contrition,   *Confess yourself*
65   And make treu satisfaccion —
            Then blessid ye be!

     I mad this with good entent,
     In hope the rather ye wold repent,   *sooner*
            The soth to say,
70   Fore I say soth, I am eschent.   *Were I not to speak truth; disgraced*
     Prays fore me, that beth present,   *Pray*
            The Blynd Audlay.

XXIIII. POPE JOHN'S PASSION OF OUR LORD   [W13]

De passione Domini nostri Jhesu Christi et de horis canonicis.[1]

Pope Jon the XXII at Avyon was.   *Avignon*
Ther, in the worchip of Cristis Passion,
He made this gospel, be Godis grace,   *by*
And gaf therto a gret pardoun —   *gave*
5   Thre hundred days of remyssion —
The thred day before or he schuld dye,   *third*
To al that sayd or herd hit with dewocion,
And on Cristis Passion had peté.   *compassion*

---

[1] *Concerning the passion of our Lord Jesus Christ and concerning the canonical hours*

	Passio Christe conforta me[1]	
10	Out of this word when I schal wynd;	*depart*
	A, synful mon! Make memory:	
	Of Cristis Passion have in thi mynd.	
	To that Lord, be never unkynd,	
	That after his fegur he formyd thee,	*image*
15	And bond himselve thee to unbynd,	
	And al hit was fore love of thee.	

	This is the Gospel of Jon truly —	
	To this passion take good entent!	
	Pilat, Jhesu, fore gret envy,	
20	Toke that Lord Omnipotent,	
	And scorgid him nakud in his present,	*scourged; presence* [John 19:1]
	Fro top to too with turmentry,	*toe; torture*
	That skyn and flesche, hit was torent,	*torn to pieces*
	And al hit was fore love of thee.	

25	His knyghtis mad a croun of thorne	*[Pilate's] knights*
	And set on his hede — hit persid his brayn! —	*pierced*
	And clothid him in purpul with chamful scornns:	*purple; shameful* [John 19:2]
	"Hayle, Kyng of Jewys," to him con sayn.	*[they] did say* [John 19:3]
	To boffet him, thai were ful fayn,	*glad*
30	And spit in his face welansly,	*villainously* [Matthew 27:30; Mark 15:19]
	And smot him on his hed with a rodde agayn,	*rods*
	And al hit was fore love of thee.	

	When thai hed don him this turmentry,	
	The knyghtis tokon swete Jhesus	*took*
35	And drou him to the Mownt of Calvaré,	*drew*
	Apon his schulder beryng a cros.	*bearing* [John 19:17]
	Both hondis and fete naylid on ther was,	*were nailed on there*
	Betwene two thevys hongud to be,	*to be hung* [John 19:18]
	That were damnyd fore here trespace,	
40	And al hit was fore love of thee.	

	Then up thai lyft that hevé tre,	*heavy tree*
	And gurdid into a mortes of stone;	*fastened [it] into a mortise*
	That grevys Jhesus more grevesly	*caused Jesus to suffer; grievously*
	Then al the turment thai had him done,	
45	Fore vayns and seneus, hit brast, and bone,	*veins; sinews; burst*
	That everé joynt men myght ese —	*every joint; might have seen*

---

[1] *Passion of Christ, fortify me.* This is the fifth line of the familiar prayer *Anima Christi sanctifica me*, which is copied earlier in MS Douce 302 (fol. 9r). It is also used as a refrain in *Dread of Death.*

He was most lyke a leperus mon,   *leprous*
And al hit was fore love of thee.

Then Jhesus wyst after what was cummyng   *knew what came next*
50   And sayd, "Now I thorst ful sore."   *thirst* [John 19:28]
Of aysel and gal thai geven him drynk,   *vinegar; gall*
And put hit in a sponge his mouth before;   [John 19:29]
When he hit tastid, he wold no more,
And sayd, "Al endid is now treuly,"
55   And bowd doun his hed with sekyng sore,   *bowed; grievous sighing*
And gif up his spiryt fore love of thee.   *gave* [John 19:30]

Then the herth anon con quake,   *earth soon did*
And also the sun, he lost his lyght;   *it; its*
The stons of the tempil, on pesis thai brake,   *into pieces; broke*
60   The vayle therof, atwyn was twyght;[1]
Gravys thai opend, anon ther ryght   *Graves; immediately*
Ther ros up moné a ded body   *many a dead*
Of men and wemen, were seyn with syght,   *seen* [Matthew 27:51–53]
And al hit was fore love of thee.

65   When sentoreo this syght had sene,   *centurion*
He sayd, "This is verey Godis Son."   *true* [Matthew 27:54, Mark 15:39]
A blynd knyght with a spere ful even   *sharp*
Smot Jhesus into the hert anon.   *Struck*
Blod and water out ther ron;   *ran out there* [John 19:34]
70   A drop therof fel in his hee.   *eye*
He had his syght, this synful mon,
Fore on Crystis Passion he had peté.

He that al this sorous se,   *He who sees all these sorrows*
He bers treu witnes hereon,   *bears*
75   That was keper to mayd Mary,
The holé evangelyst, swete Saynt Jon;
And bedis you beleve this everechon   *commands*
Yif that ye wil savyd be,
That Crist sofyrd this for synful mon   *suffered*
80   Apon his Passion to have peté.

A, synful mon! Have this in mynd,
Weder that thou slepe or wake:
To that Lord, be never unkynd,
That sofyrd these sorous for thi syn sake.
85   Hou schalt thou amendis make?

---

[1] *The veil thereof, was torn in two*. Compare Matthew 27:51, Luke 23:44–45.

What sofyrd thou fore him? Onswere me!   *Answer*
Into his mercé, loke thou thee take,   *look that you entrust*
And say this prayour with gret peté.

O, Jhesu, that bothe thi holy hond   *hands*
90   And thi blessid fyet, also,   *feet*
And al thi body, I understonde,
Fore me, synful, on cros was do,   *done (i.e., nailed)*
And cround of the Jewis with thornes, thi fo,[1]
In dispite of thi holy body —
95   Apon thi hed, thou sofyrd gret wo,
And alle hit was fore love of me!

With fyve captel wondis fore me, synful,   *capital*
Thou were ipaynd apon the cros,   *put in pain*
Me to agayn by, Lord merceful,   *to buy again*
100 With thi precyous blood, throgh thi gret grace.
Of repentans thou gif me spase   *By means of; give me space*
To foresake my synnus and be sory,
And foregif hem here trespase,   *forgive them*
That on thi Passion han peté.

105 And grawnt me, Lord, that I may
Everé day do sum penans,
With sobirnes thee plese and pay,   *soberness; please and requite*
And kepe me chast with abstenans,   *abstinence*
And gif me wit and wisdam with perseverans
110 To kepe my state and my degré,   *estate (i.e., social place)*
Thee to serve to thi plesans,   *liking*
And on thi Passion to have peté.

Fyve Paternoster nou thou schalt say
In the worchip of Cristis Passion,
115 And grete our Lady nou, I thee pray,   *greet*
With fyve Aves knelyng adoune;
In reverens of his fyve wondis alon,
Spesialy, thou say thi Crede,
That Crist graunt thee remission,   *[So] that Christ [may] grant*
120 That fore thi synnus, thi blod con schede.   *did shed*

---

[1] *And crowned with thorns by the Jews, thy foe*

AUDELAY'S PRAYER EXPLICIT TO *POPE JOHN'S PASSION*   [W13]

Amen, Jhesu, now I thee pray,
Have mynd and mercé on Blynd Audlay,
That mad in Englesche this Passion,
Fore synful men to have mynd theron.

SEVEN HOURS OF THE CROSS   [W14]

Hic incepiunt hore canonice passionis Jhesu Christe.[1]

	Crist, that was crucifyd on cros for our synnus sake,	
	Lord, on our mysdede no vengans thou take,	*vengeance*
	Bot send sorou into our hert, our synus fore to slake,	*sorrow*
	And let thi mercy be medysyn, our mendis for to make —	*medicine; amends*
5	Lord, we thee pray.	
	Here schul ye here anon,	*hear*
	What hard payn and passion,	
	That Crist sofyrd fore synful mon —	*suffered*
	Gret dole here ye may!	

Patris sapeencia, veritas divina.[2]

10	The wysdam of the Fader above ben the treuth of his Godede;	*Godhead*
	God and Mon, he was ytakun in the oure of morotyde,	*hour; morning*
	His fryndis and his dyspilis sun him had elevyde;	*disciples soon; left*
	When he was takyn of the Jewys, to deth he was betrayde —	*from*
	Judas had him sold.	
15	Fore thyrty pens of lytil pryce,	*worth*
	With Jewys he mad his marchandyce,	*merchandise*
	Because of cursid covetyse,	*covetousness*
	As a traytur bold!	[Matthew 26:14–16]

Hora prima ductus est Jhesus ad Pilatum.   *In the first hour, Jesus was brought to Pilate*

	At prime Jhesus out thai lad; to Pilat thai cun him draw.[3]	
20	Moné was the false wetnes thai saydyn in here saue;	*Many; witness; said; sayings*
	Thai blynfeld him, thai buffet him, and bond him agen law,	
	And spit in his fayre face — his chere myght no mon know! —	
	And spulid him al nakyd,	

---

[1] *Here begin the canonical hours of the passion of Jesus Christ*

[2] *Wisdom of the Father, divine Truth.* From the hymn *Patris sapiencia* (see explanatory note).

[3] *At prime (6 a.m.) they led Jesus out; to Pilate they did bring him*

And cast loot fore his cote anon,[1]

25 And bondon him to a peler of ston,   *bound; pillar*

And betin him with scorgis fro top to ton.   *beat; scourges; toe*

    The red blod fro him strakid!   *flowed*

"Crucifige" clamatant hora terciarum.[2]

At undor thai droun him to his deth; loud cun thai cri: *undern (9 a.m.); drew; did*

"Crucifi him on the cros. Dispoyle we him in hye!"   *despoil*

30 Thai cround him with a croun of thornes; the blood ran in his ye.   *eye*

He bere his cros on his chulder to the Mount of Calveré,   *shoulder; Calvary*

    That his Monhod lost his myght.   *manhood*

    Thai drown him forth with ropis then;   *drew*

    Tho wept the wyfis of Jerusalem;   *Then; women*

35 His moder, and Jon, Maré Maudlene,   *John [the Evangelist]; Mary Magdalene*

    Thai swonyd ther in his syght!   *swooned*

Hora sexta est cruce conclavatus.   *At sext he was nailed to the cross*

At mydday thai nayld him on the cros, and crucifid Heven Kyng,

And lift him up apon the tre betwen two thevus to hyng.   *thieves; hang*

Because of turment he thurstid; then of aysel thai gif him dryng.[3]

40 Thus the Lombe he did away our synn, his Godhed gloryfyyng,   *removed*

    Hongyng apon the cros.

    To his moder, he sayd anon:

    "A, womon, lo! Here thi sun;

    Take here to thi moder, Jon."[4]

45   He swonyd before his face!   *They swooned*

Hora nona Dominus Jhesus experavit.   *At none Lord Jesus breathed his last*

At the heour of non Jhesus gif up the gost.   *none (3 p.m.); spirit*

His spyrit cryd "*Eloy*" to the Fader of myghtis most.

A blynd knight with a scharpe spere, to the hert him throst.

---

[1] Lines 21–24: *They blindfolded him, they buffeted him, and bound him against the law / And spit in his fair face — his countenance might no man know! / And stripped him all naked, / And cast lots for his coat soon.* Compare Matthew 27:30, Mark 15:19 (line 22), Matthew 27:28 (line 23), and Matthew 27:35, Mark 15:24, Luke 23:34, and John 19:23 (line 24).

[2] *"Crucify!" they kept shouting at the hour of terce.* Compare Matthew 27:22, Mark 15:14, John 19:6.

[3] *Because of the torment he was thirsty; then they gave him vinegar to drink.* Compare John 19:28–29.

[4] Lines 43–44: *"Ah, woman, lo! Here [is John] your son; / Take her [Mary] as your mother, John."* Compare John 19:26–27.

The stons tobreke, the erth con quake, the son his lyght had lost.[1]

50   Then senterio con he say: *centurion did*

         "This is veray Godis Sun,   *true* [Matthew 27:54, Mark 15:39]

         To deth that ye han here don,   *have here brought*

         Was borne of a maydyn,

            Schal deme you at Domysday!"   *judge*

De cruce deponetur hora vespertina.   *At vespers he is taken down from the cross*

55   At the oure of evensong of the cros thai toke him doun.   *off; took*

     The strenkth of his Godhed, in him was hit alleone.   *strength; alone*

     Seche a deth he sofyrd then, of our syn to be medysyn.   *medicine*

     Alas, that the croun of joy was cast up-so-doun!   *upside down*

         Thai toke him of the tre —   *off*

60   Necodeme, he was thet one,   *Nicodemus*

         And Josep of Barmathé, that holé mone —   *Arimathea* [see John 19:38–42]

         Thai beren him to his tombe of stone,   *bore*

            Therin beryd to be.   *buried*

Hora completore datur sepulteure.   *At compline he is given to the tomb*

     At the hore of cumplyn in grave thai cun him bryng —.   *compline; did*

65   Then was the nobil body of Crist, our hope of lyfe comyng.   *noble; future life*

     Thai beryd hym with blessid bamus, the prophcy fullyng.   *buried; balms; fulfilling*

     Ever have we his delful deth in our hertis mynyng.   *doleful; hearts' remembrance*

         Hereof we schul be fayne!   *glad*

         When he had fulfillid the prophesé,   *prophecy*

70   That was sayd of hym, trewly,   *truly*

         The thyrd day he ros with gret maystry,   *strength*

            Fro deth to lyve agayn.   *life*

Has hororas canonicas cum devocione.   *[Remember] these canonical hours with devotion*

     These holé hours have we in mynd with devocion,

     And worchip we Jhesu Crist with these meke oresoun,   *humble prayers*

75   That fore our sak, with brenyng love, sofyrd payn and passioun.   *burning; suffered*

     In the hour of our deth, be he our solacion!   *consolation*

         Lord Omnipotent,

         Fore thi holé Passion,

         That thou sofyrd fore synful mon,

80   Thou graunt us alle remyssion   *remission [of sin]*

            Tofore thi Jugement.   *Before*

---

[1] Lines 47–49: *His spirit cried "Eloy [my God]" to the Father of most might. / A blind knight [Longinus] with a sharp spear thrust him to the heart. / The stones broke to pieces, the earth did quake, the sun its light had lost.* Compare Matthew 27:46, Mark 15:34 (line 47), John 19:34 (line 48), and Matthew 27:51 (line 49).

He that these ours wil say with devocion,   *hours; say*
In reverens and worchip of Crist Passion,
And schryve him clen to a prest with contricion,   *confess*
85   God he grauntis him, of his grace, ful remyssion
Of al his trespace.
Then joyful may ye be
Agens the day that ye schul dye,   *Against*
To have grace and mercé,
90   In heven foreever a place!   *[And] in heaven forever*

XXV. OUR LORD'S EPISTLE ON SUNDAY   [W15]

De epistola Domini nostri Jhesu Christi de die Dominica.[1]

Audite hec, omnes gentes: hanc epistolam scripsit Dominus Jhesus Christus manibus suis et misit in sivitatem Gazon ubi ego Petrus primum episcopatum accepi.[2]

Now here this pistil, I you pray,   *hear; epistle*
Fore Crist hit wrot with his oun hond —   *wrote; own*
Hou ye schul halou the Sonday,   *hallow*
Al Cristin men in everé lond —   *every*
5   And send hit to Petir, thorogh his swete sond,   *message*
To preche the pepul with good entent,
And do ale curatours to understond   *curates*
That hit is Cristis comawndment —
Beleve this, everechon!   *everyone*
10   He that belevys this treuly   *who believes*
Schal have grace and mercy,
And no nother, securly,   *anyone else, indeed*
He is the child of perdecion.   *perdition*

Fore ye con not of God this holeday   *If you do not know how to*
15   Kepe clene out of dedlé syn,   *cleanly*
Therfore his wrath, syrus, Y yow say,   *sirs*
Schal fal on youe, false Cristyn men!
Your enmys and aleans schal over you ren,   *enemies; strangers; overrun*
And lede youe to thraldam foreever and ay,   *servitude*
20   Both ryful, rob, sle, and bren.   *plunder; slay; burn*
Bot yif ye kepyn that holeday,   *Unless; keep*
Herefore ye wil be chent!   *Therefore; ruined*
Raveners sodenly schal fal on you,   *plunderers*

----

[1] *Concerning the epistle of our Lord Jesus Christ regarding the Lord's day.* Written by Scribe B.

[2] *Hear these things, all peoples: the Lord Jesus Christ wrote this letter with his own hands and sent it to the city of Gaza where I, Peter, accepted the first episcopate.* Written by Scribe A.

And wyckid terantis cast you ful loue,   *tyrants; low*
25   Fore gracyous God ye wyl not know,
        Ne kyndlé kepe his comawndment.   *kindly*

        "Herefore fro you I wil turne my face,   *[away] from*
        And betake you into your enemyse hond,
        And withdraw fro you mercé and grace,
30   And blynd you both with schame and schond,   *with both; disgrace*
        And drown you within a lytyl stownd —   *while*
        As I did Sodom and Comor,   *Gomorrah*
        That the erthe swolewd to hel ground   *swallowed*
        Sodenly or thai were ware!   *Suddenly before they*
35   Have mend, seris, here apon,   *Think, sirs, upon this*
        Beware betyme, or ye be schend!   *in time before; ruined*
        And your mysdedis, loke ye amend,
        And serve your God. Foresake the Fynd!
            Then schul ye have remyssion.

40   "Hwosoever wil go, seris, truly,   *Whosoever*
        Into ony other plase, I say,   *place*
        Bot to Holé Cherche, specialy,   *Than; specifically*
        In the fest of that holeday,   *On the feast*
        Or on pilgremage, seyntis to pray,   *saints*
45   Or vesid the seke that woful be,   *visit*
        Ore make acord and treu loveday   *day for the settlement of difference*
        To bryng mon into charyté,
            And serve your Saveour —
        Ellis I schal bete youe with scorgis sore,   *beat*
50   And send into your place, herefore,
        Sorou and sekenes foreevermore,   *Sorrow; sickness*
            Swerd, pestlens, hongir with gret dolour! *War, pestilence, hunger*

        "He that on any erand wil ryd or goo
        In the fest of that holeday
55   Fore oné cause he hath to do,   *any reason*
        Or schave heerus of heed or berde away,   *shave hair from [his] head or beard*
        Bot go to the cherche, yif that ye may,   *Rather than*
        And hold him ther in his prayere —
        Al evylis Y wil send him, soth to say,   *evils*
60   And chortyn his days he schuld have here!   *shorten*
            Beware, serys, I you pray,
        Or he that waschis clothis or hed,   *Before; washes clothes or head*
        On Sunday breuys or bakus bred,   *brews; bakes*
        Y schul him blynd with carful red,   *blind; sore punishment*
65   Nother have my blessyng, nyght ne day.   *Never [to] have*

"Bot my curse have he schal:
Y wyl send sekenes and sorous sore   *grievous sorrows*
Apon you, and your childer alle,   *children*
That ye schul curse that ye were bore!   *born*
70   Ye unbelevyd pepul, herkyns more,   *unbelieving; listen*
And schreud generacions that nyl beleve,   *wicked; will not*
Your days schal be ful schort therfore,
Fore ye set noght by your God to greve.
I am among you, ever-present,
75   And synful men I wyl abyde,   *await*
Yif thay wil turne in oné tyde,   *convert at any time*
Foresake cursid covetyse, envy, and pride,
And here mysdedis betyme repent.   *in time*

"In six days, al thyng I made;
80   On the Sunday, Y rest of my werkis ale.
The same do ye. Then schul ye glad   *be glad*
Of your labors both gret and smale!
Non other thyng do ye schal
Bot go to the cherche, to Godis servyse,   *God's service (i.e., the mass)*
85   Alse wel your servandis that beth youe thral;   *As well [as should]; who are to you bound*
Non other warkis loke that thai use.   *labor*
Then ful joyful schul ye be —
Your corns, your vynes, and creaturs alle   *grains*
Schul bryng forth froyt, both gret and smale —   *fruit*
90   That nothyng to Cristyn men wont hit schale   *want*
Bot pese and rest in uche contré!   *peace; country*

"Bot yif ye kepyn this holeday   *Unless*
Fro Setterday at non, Y say you then,   *Saturday at noon*
Into the furst our of Monday,   *hour*
95   In reverens and worchip of your Soveren,   *Sovereign*
I schal curse youe tofore my Fader in heven;   *before*
Ye schul have no part therin with me,
Ne with my angelys that with me bene
In the word of wordis perpetualy.   *forever and ever*
100   Bot Y wyl send youe herefore
Gret fuyrus and leytis, youe fore to bren,   *fires; lightnings; burn*
Al evelys to perysche your lobors then —   *evils; destroy; labors*
Your cornes, your froytis, your vynus, your tren —   *grains; fruits; vines; trees*
And never rayn schal fal on you more.   *rain*

105 "Your tethis, your offryngis, yevyn treuly   *tithes; offerings give*
To my prestis, I you pray,
That serven me in Holé Cherche spesialy,
And prayn fore you both nyght and day.
Hwosoever his tethys defraudys away,   *defrauds*

110	His froyttis in erth defraudid schuld bene,	*fruits*
	And never se lyght bot derkenes ay,	
	Ne never have your lastyng lyve hen,	*eternal life henceforth*
	Bot hungyr in erthe among Cristin schal be.	*hunger on earth among Christians*
	Fore I kepe my dome fro unbelevyd men,	*withhold my reward from unbelieving*
115	And yet I nold dampne hem then,	*wish not to damn them*
	My comawndmentis to kepe and ken,	*[But rather I want them] my; learn*
	And foresake here synus, and aske mercy.	*sins [see Ezechiel 33:11]*

	"Treulé, yif ye wil haloue this holeday,	*hallow*
	The rakkis of heven I wil opyn	*paths*
120	And multyplé you in me foreever and ay,	
	Yif ye wil do after my tokyn,	*sign*
	And knouth wel that I am God alone,	*know*
	And non other ther is save Y	*except*
	That may you grawnt remyssion,	
125	And gif you grace and mercy.	*give*
	Loke ye leven truely this!	*Believe*
	Amen, foresoth, to you I say,	
	Yif ye wil halou this haleday,	
	Al evelis fro you, Y wyl do away —	*evils*
130	Then schul ye never fare amys!	*go amiss*

	"What prest this pistil nyl not teche	*will not*
	To my pepil, as I ham pray —	*people; them*
	In cetis, in tounus, in cherche hem preche	*cities; towns*
	How thai schal halow the holeday,	
135	To have hit in memory foreever and ay —	
	My domys apon my prestis schal passe!	*judgments*
	I schal ham ponys treuly, in fay,	*punish; indeed*
	Both without mercy and grace.	
	Bot yif thai techen this pistil, treuly,	*Unless*
140	And make men to haloue this holeday,	
	I schal ham curse in herth, I say,	*earth*
	And in the word of wordis that lastyth ay	*through all eternity*
	And in myn oun trone in heven on hye."	*throne*

	This pistil then our Lord Jhesu Crist	
145	Send into the seté of Gason,	*city of Gaza*
	Ther Y, Petur, was made bischop furst	
	In the present yere tofore agoone —	*year before gone by*
	That hit be trewe and leosyng non,	*lying not*
	Y, Peter, swere be Goddus pouere,	*swear; power*
150	And be Jhesu Crist, his honlé Sone,	*only*
	And be the Holé Treneté, in fere,	*together*
	And be the four evaungelistis, this is no nay,	*lie*
	And be the patryarchis and prophetus and postlius holy,	*apostles*

And be angelis and archangelis and Mary,
155   And be al the holy seyntis in heven ther be,
       That hit is soth that I you say.

Ryght as the sun hath more clerté   *splendor*
Then ané ster of the fyrmant,   *any; firmament*
So the Sunday is worthear of dyngneté   *worthier of reverence*
160   Then ané day in the wike present: *week*
That day mad angeles omnipotent,   *angels were made*
The nine orders in heven on hye;
That day Noys flod sesud, verament —   *ended truly*
His schip toke rest of the hil of Armony. *came to rest on; Armenia*
165   I swere to youe that beth present,
       This pistil was never ordent of erthlé mon, *created by*
       Bot transelat out of heven trone — *was translated; heaven's*
       Crist wrot hit with his fyngers alon   *alone*
           To warne his pepel lest thay were chent. *ruined*

170   Fore he callis you to his grace echon: *each one of you*
"Cum to me fore giftis, I you pray,   *gifts*
Fore I grawnt you remission,
And joy and blis foreever and ay."
No hert may thenke, tung tel hit may, *conceive, [no] tongue may it tell*
175   The lest joy Jhesus wil joyne you to;   *least; bring to you*
Yif ye halou the Sunday,   *keep holy*
Ye schul have wel without wo!   *weal*
       A, synful mon! Hereof have mynde:
       That joy, hit schal never sees,   *cease*
180   Bot ever endeuer and ever encrese,   *endure; increase*
       And ever in love, rest, and pes,   *peace*
           In joy and blis withouton ende!

To that blis, Crist he us bryng —
Was crucefyd on cros and croned with thorne — *crowned*
185   And foregif us oure myslevyng,   *misbelief*
That we han offendid here beforne,
And let us never, Lord, be forlorne,   *utterly lost*
Bot graunt us grace that we may —
As ye were of a maydyn borne —
190   In clannes to halou the Sounonday.   *cleanness; hallow Sunday*
       Lord Omnipotent,
       Fore thi Passion, thou have peté
       Apon our soulis when we schul dey,   *die*
       And grawnt us thi grace and thi mercy,
195   Fadur, tofore thi Jugement.   *before*

Mervel ye noght of this makyng —
Fore I me excuse, hit is not I.   *excuse myself*
Fore this of Godis oun wrytyng   *this [work is created] by; own*
That he send doun fro heven on hye,
200   Fore I couth never bot he foly.   *high folly*
He hath me chastist for my levyng;   *chastised; living*
I thonke my God, my Grace, treuly,
Of his gracious vesetyng.   *visitation (i.e., affliction)*
        Beware, serys, I you pray,   *sirs*
205   Fore I mad this with good entent,
        Fore hit is Cristis comawndment;
        Prays for me that beth present —
            My name hit is the Blynd Awdlay.

XXVI. THE VISION OF SAINT PAUL   [W16]

Incipit narracio quo Michel duxit Paulum ad infernum. Interogandum est quis primus rogavit ut anime haberent requiem in infernum, i.e., Paulus apostolus et Michael archangelus. Dies Dominicus est dies electus.[1]

The Sononday is Godis oun chosyn day,   *Sunday*
The wyche angelis in heven, thai worchipyn thore.   *On which; there*
Gret sorow and dole here ye may,
Hou Mychael and Poule thay went in fere   *together*
5   To se what payns in hel were ther,
And ther thay se a sorouful syght!   *saw*
Herkyns to me! Now moy ye here   *may you hear*
What payns to synful mon be dyght
        Because men nel not beleve.   *will not*
10   Therefore, hit was Godis oune wyl
        That Mekel schuld led Poule to hel   *[archangel] Michael*
        To se the payns, the gret parel,   *peril*
            The soth himselve he myght hit preve.   *[So that] the truth; witness and relate*

Tofore hel-gatis furst thai se then   *Before hell-gates*
15   Moné an orebil brenyng tre   *horrible burning tree*
Hengyng ful of wemen and men —
That was a sorouful syght to se!
Sum be the hed, sum be the tungus, treuly,   *head; tongues*
Sum be the fyt, sum be the hond,   *feet*
20   Sum be the membirs of here body,
That thai han sunnyd within herthe levand.   *sinned; earth [when] alive*
        The angel to Poule, he sayd then:

---

[1] *[Here] begins the narration in which Michael led Paul to hell. It must be inquired who first asked that souls have rest in hell, i.e., the apostle Paul and the archangel Michael. The day of the Lord is the chosen day*

"These grevyn God ful grevously   *grieve*
With al the lymys of here body,
25   In lechory, slouth, and glotoné,
       And dyed in det and dedlé syn."   *debt*

Withyn the gatis wen thay were passid,
A mervelis fournes ther thai se: *marvelous furnace*
Moné a synful soule were therin cast —
30   Four flamys o foyre stod on a lye,   *fire were ablaze*
Of dyvers colours wonderfully!
About that fournes, seven sorous ther were: *furnace*
Gret snow, gret yse, gret cold greslé,   *grisly*
Gret eddyrs, gret stenche, gret leyte, gret foyre.   *adders; light*
35   Then the angel sayd to Poule, treuly,
       "These were proud men, raveners echon,   *robbers each one*
Extorcioners, monslers, robbid moné one;   *manslayers*
Satisfaccion in erth thai wold do non,
       And deseredyn treu ayrs unryghtfully.   *disinherited; heirs*

40   "Here thai schal have here payns, therfore.
Fore al the synns thai han don cursidly,
Sum wepin, sum waylin, sum gron ful sore,   *weep; wail; groan*
Sum broudun, sum brennen, dissyryn to dye —   *writhe; burn; desire*
Hou dredful is hel, here may ye se!
45   In the whyche is hevenes without gladnes;   *heaviness*
In the wyche is sorou of hert contenualy;
In the wych of wepyng is gret plenteuesnes;   *plenitude*
       In the wych ther is a brenyng wel —   *burning well*
       A thosand tymys an our about doth ren,   *hour around [it]; run*
50   Uche day an angel, foresmytis him then,   *[who] strikes them to pieces*
A thousand soulis therin thai bren."
       "Alas!" sayd Poule, "Here is gret deel!"   *dole*

Affter, Poule se an orebbil flood   *Next; saw; horrible sea*
In the wyche moné develis bestis were in fuyre: *many devils' beasts*
55   As feschis in the se, about thai yod,   *fish; swam*
Devowreng soulis as hit chep were.   *Devouring; as if they were sheep*
A brygge was over that gret water,   *bridge*
That soulis passud over after here meryt;   *according to their*
Moné an evyl mancion was ordent ther   *dwelling spot in hell; ordained*
60   As Crist in the Gospel reherse het:
"*Lygate faceculus ad comburandum similis cum similibus*"[1] —
       Bynd bundels togeder to be ibrent;

---

[1] *Bind bundles together to be burnt, like with like.* The beginning of this sentence derives from Matthew 13:30 (and is discussed by Easting, "'Choose yourselves,'" p. 174). This line expands the stanza from thirteen lines to fourteen.

	Bynd spouse-brekers with awouters,	*adulterers*
	And ranegates with raveners,	*renegades; robbers*
65	And cursid levers with here cumpers,	*sinners with their companions*
	And cast ham in the fuyre without end.	*fire*

Ther Poule, moné soulis he se — *saw*
That were dround in that watere — *drowned*
Sum stod up to the kne,
70 And sum to the armes, a lytil layghere, *lower*
And sum to the lippis, moche deppere, *deeper*
And sum to the brouys oche day were paynd! *brows; pained*
Then Poule sykud and wept with gret douloure, *sighed*
And at the angel anon he fraynd: *asked*
75 "What soulis ben these, bene drownyd here?"
"Tho that stodyn up to the kne
Bakbidit here neghtbore fore envy, *Backbit*
And sklaundird hem in erth ful falseley —
That loston here goodis, hir lyvus yfere. *They; goods; together*

80 "And tho that stodin up to the armus
Weron spouse-brekers and levyd in lechory. *adulterers*
And tho that stod up to the leppis, *lips*
Be the servys of God, thai set noght by, *service (i.e., mass)*
And did no reverens to Cristis body,
85 In Holé Cherche were ever changilyng, *jangling*
And sayd here prayers undevoutly, *impiously*
And let other men of mas hereng — *prevented; from hearing mass*
Herefore thai have passyng payn! *surpassing*
And tho that stod up to the elbow,
90 At here neghtbors harmes thay low — *laughed*
Yif thai ferd wel, her hertis hit slow, *fared; slew*
And of here losse, were glad and fayne." *delighted*

Holé Cherche is a house of prayere —
The gat of heven, Crist doth hit calle — *gate*
95 To worchip therin our Saveour.
Whatever thou askis ther, have thou schal
Yif that ye bene in chareté alle,
And serve your God in love and dred.
No myschif on them hit schal falle; *It shall not go badly for them*
100 In al your werkis, wel schul ye spede!
A, synful mon! Hereof have mynd:
In Holé Cherche, nothyng thou say, *[if] you refrain from speaking*
Bot with holé prayers to God ye pray,
He grawnt youe grace, both nyght and day,
105 Him to serve, that al you send. *who gives you all*

	Then Poule wept and sayd in good sothnes:	*honest sincerity*
	"Wo is him to these payns ben ordent!"	*ordained*
	Then he se a plase of gret darknes	*saw; place*
	In the wyche men and wemen wern in gret turment,	*were; great torment*
110	That etyn here tongis, here torent!	*They ate their tongues, here torn to pieces*
	Then the angel sayd to Poule, treuly:	
	"These were makers of moné with cursid entent,	*makers of money (i.e., counterfeiters)*
	With wrong mokerers, false mesurs, and useré;	*hoarders; measures; usury*
	Ther, fore wo, thai etin here tung,	*Therefore*
115	Fore thai foreswere ham wettanly	*forswore; knowingly*
	On Cristis Passion, have no peté	*[and] had no compassion*
	To part with the pore that were nedé,	*share*
	Bot holdun hit fast thai geten with wrong."	*kept what they stole wrongfully*
	Then after, Poule a plase he se	*place; saw*
120	In the wyche were moné damselse blake,	*damsels black*
	Iclothid in blake al cresly,	*grisly*
	In pych and brymston, fuyre and smoke;	*pitch and brimstone*
	About here nekis were nedirs and snake,	*necks; adders and snakes*
	Fore wickid angelus reprevyd hem ther,	*punished*
125	With horns of fyre, here heedus to schake,	*heads*
	And went about hom with hedus bere,	*hideous noise*
	And saydon to hom with carful cry:	
	"Cnow ye now the Sun of God	*Know*
	That agayn boght the word,	*redeemed the world*
130	That ye han grevyd in dede and word,	*Whom; sinned against*
	And slayn his creatours, your childer distrye?"	*slay; children destroy*
	Then Poule he askid: "What ben these?"	*Who are*
	The angel onswerd without tareyng:	*answered; delay*
	"Hylé God these con displese,	*Supremely did these displease God*
135	And kept hem not chast to here wedyng,	
	And slowyn here childer in burth-beryng,	*slew; at birth*
	And cast ham to houndis in prevé place,	*hidden*
	In watirs, in pittis, about drounyng,	*in order to drown [them]*
	And never wold shryve hem of that trespase,	*confess*
140	Fore dred of sklawnder and penans doyng.	*doing of penance*
	So the Fynd, he con hem blynd	*did blind them*
	With disperacion — hem schame and schend! —	*desperation; ruin*
	Lest here mysdedis thai wold amend,	
	And broght hem ta evyl endyng."	*to an evil end*
145	Then after, Poule he se moche more:	*next*
	Men and wemen on kamels rydyng —	*camel*
	Moch froyt ther was here face before;	*fruit; before their faces*
	To ete therof was here lykyng;	*desire*
	Thai myght not hit touche, fore no thyng!	

150	Then the angel to Poule con say:	
	"These brekyn the tymys of here fastyng,	*broke the times*
	And wold not fast the Good Fryday	
	That Crist sofyrd deth apon,	
	Bot wastin here goodis in glotoné	*gluttony*
155	Fore fleschelé lust of here body.	
	Fore thai wold not parte with the pore nedy,	*Because; share*
	Thai schil have hongir and thrust wereever thai gon."	*thirst wherever*

Then after, Poule in plase he se
A sorouful syght: a horé hold mon   *white-haired old*
160 Betwene four fyndis, in turmentré —
And gryd and wept with ful gret mon!   *[he] cried out; moan*
Then Poule he askid the angel anon
What maner of mon hit myght be.
The angel answerd him ful sone:
165 "A neclygent mon, foresoth, was he,   *rule*
And kept not obedyans he was bound to,
Ne levyd not chast in his bodé,   *body*
In word, in dede, in thoght, treuly,
Bot covetis, prude, ever out of charyté —   *[in] avarice [and] pride*
170 To al payne ent Domysday, he schal go."   *until*

Then Poule he weppid with hevé chere.   *wept*
The angel sayd: "Why wepis thou soo?
Thou sest not the gret payn that beth here!   *see; greatest*
Come, on with me now thou schal goo."
175 He lad him to the blak pit tho,   *led; then*
With seven selys was selid treuly;   *seals; sealed*
Therin was care, sorow, and wo,
Stenche, and al maner turmentry!   *all types of torment*
"Stond uttir, Poule," quod the angel then.   *Stand back*
180 Anon he unselid the pit thore —
With a stynche, gurd out a rore —   *stench, a roar rose [from there]*
Al the payns hit passid before!   *It surpassed all the pains [seen] before*
Hit wold have slayn al Crystin men!

Then Poule he askid the angel in hye:
185 "What pepul in this pit ben don?"
"These belevid not in vergyn Mary,
Ne treuly in Cristis Carnacione.   *Incarnation*
Thai beth uncristynd, everechon,   *unbaptized*
And never resayvyd Cristis body.   *received*
190 Al tho, into that pet thay gon —   *pit*
Of hem, schal never be memory   *They shall be forgotten*
On him in heven, tofore Godis Son,   *By those*
Fore hit is Godis wil, specialy,

	Of eretekis schal be no memoré,	*heretics*
195	Ne false Cristin men — renegatis that dyed curstly,	*renegades; accursed*
	Of hom is no redempcion!	

	Then after, Poule, forsoth, he se	
	In a wonderful depe plase —	*deep place*
	As fro the erth to heven on hy —	
200	Uche soule on other couchid ther was;	*laid*
	For fader and moder thai had dispisid, alas,	
	Orebil wormys devouryd hem there!	*Horrible worms*
	Then Poul he herd a dolful noyse —	
	As layte or thonder that hit were —	*lightning*
205	Then was he ware of a soule anon:	
	Between four fendes, borne he was.	
	He rored and cryd, "Alas! Alas!" —	
	That ever his bodé con forth passe	
	Without shrift, housil, contricion!	*confession, eucharist*

210	The angelis of God agayns him criud:	
	"Alas, wrechid soule, what hast thou done	
	In erth?" The fyndis them verefyd:	*The fiends verified them [his earthly sins]*
	"Dispisid Godis laus, everechon."	*[He] despised; laws*
	Tofore him, thai red his dedis anon,	*Before; read his deeds*
215	And cast him into derkens, deppist of alle.	*darkness, deepest*
	Quod angel to Poule: "Beleve uche mon,	*Believe that each man*
	As ye do in erthe, so have ye schal.	
	He hath fre choys to do good or elle,	*ill*
	Fore uche good dede rewardid schal be	
220	In erth, or ellis on even on hei,	*in heaven on high*
	And uche cursid dede ponyschid, truly,	*[shall be] punished*
	In erth, in purgatoré, or ellis in hel.	

	"For this schal be here ponyschyng:	
	Pride, covetyse, wrat, envy —	*[For] pride*
225	These be the brondis in hel brenyng! —	*brands burning in hell*
	Lechoré, slouth, and glotery,	
	Then disperacion of Godis mercy.	*desperation for*
	Of al the payns in hel, hit is most,	
	Fore thai soght no grace, ne no mercy,	
230	Bot synnud agayns the Holé Gost.	*sinned against*
	That sin schal never foregeven be.	
	To God, hit is most hye trespace	
	To mystrost his mercy and grace —	*mistrust*
	So ded that traytur false Judas	*did; traitor*
235	And dampned himself perpetualy."	

Anon, Poule a joyful syght gon se:
A ryghtful soule angelis beryng —
That oure was ravyschid fro his body —   *[same] hour [in which he]*
Up taward heven thai con him bryng.   *toward*
240   Then Poule herd a voyse — a hevenlé thyng! —
A thousand anglis, togeder holy,   *wholly*
That said and song in his heryng: *sung*
"Be glad, blesful soule, perpetualy,
     Fore the wil of thi God thou hast edon!"   *done*
245   Thai beryn hym up before oure Lord.   *bore*
     Then Mychael let him to gret cumford,   *led; comfort*
     In joy and blis to have reward.
       "*Laudes Deo!*" thai song, ucheon!   *"Praise God!"*

Then sayd Poule with gret gladnes:
250   "Wele is ham to even may go!"   *heaven*
The angel answerd in good sothnes:
"Thai schul have wele without wo!   *weal*
No tong con tel, hert thynke therto,   *[no] heart may conceive*
The lest joy that is in paradyse!   *least*
255   In heven bene a thousand underde mo —   *hundred more*
Was never clerke couth ham devyse   *able to devise them*
     The lest joy to mon God hath ordend!   *ordained*
     Fore tho joys schul never sese,   *those; cease*
     Bot ever enduyre and ever encres,   *increase*
260   And ever leve in rest and pese —   *remain; peace*
     That joy and blis schal never have ende!"

Then al the sorouful soulus in hel
That were ther in turmentyng,
Thai crydyn: "Holé archangel Mechael,
265   Have mercy on us, in payne bydyng!   *[who are] abiding in pain*
And thou, Poul, belovyd with Heven Kyng,
To that Lord for us thou pray!"
Then sayd the angel: "Loke!" — with sore wepyng —
"Prays with Poule yif that ye may   *Pray*
270   Gete you grace of oné mercé."   *any*
     When he had sayd this word, anon
     Thay wept and cryd out, everechon:
     "A, the Sun of David, in heven trone,
       Have mercé on us, fore thi gret peté!"

275   A voyse fro heven answerd agayn:
"What good dedes have ye nou done?
Ye did me to deth with passion and payn —
Hwy aske ye me now remyssioun?   *Why*
I was crucifid on cros fore you alon;

280   With spere and nayles, Y sched my blood.
       Of aysel and gal, ye yeven me drenkyn   *vinegar; gall; gave* [John 19:29]
       When I was on therst, hongyng on the rode,   *afflicted with thirst*
              And I put myself to the deth fore yow,
       That ye schul ever have levyd with me.   *abided*
285   Bot ye were proud, covetyse, ful of envy,   *avaricious*
       And wold do no good dede, bot cursid, treuly,   *accursed [deed]*
              And false lyers in your lyve, as wel ye cnow."   *[were] false liars; lives; know*

       Then, sore wepyng, Poul knelid adowne,
       And al the angelis in heven ther,
290   And prayd hylé to Godis oune Sun   *reverently*
       Fore the soulis in hel, sum ryst have ther.   *rest*
       Oure Lorde he made hem this honswere: *answer*
       "Throgh the besechyng of myn angelis alle,
       And of Poule, myn apostil, leve and dere,   *beloved and dear*
295   This special grace graunt ham, I schal,
              Fro Setterday at non, Y say treuly,   *Saturday*
              And al the fest of the Sununday   *feast; Sunday*
              Into the fyrst our of Monday,   *hour*
              In reverens that ye here fore ham pray,
300   Thai schal have rou and rest perpetualy."   *peace*

       Then al the soulis in hel with one steven,   *voice*
       Thai cryd and sayd with gret gladnes:
       "The Sun of God on hi in heven,   *high*
       We bles thi grace and thi goodnes,
305   That thou woldist, of thi worthenes,
       Graunt us thi grace and thi mercy,
       Oure gret payns fore to reles
       Uche Sunday perpetualy!
              Herefore, we thonke the Lord of al!"
310   Wosoever wil halou this Sununday
              Wele and worchipful, as I youe say,
              With angelis of God in heven, fore ay,
                     Joy and blis ther have ye schale!

       Then Poule askid the angel anon
315   Houe moné payns in hel ther be.   *many*
       The angel answerd him ful sone:
       "Four thousand a hundred and fourté.   *4,140 [for 144,000]* [Apocalypse 7:4]
       And hunder men thagh ther were truly   *[a] hundred*
       Fro the bekynyng of world ay spekyng,   *beginning; always speaking*
320   And uche a hundred tungis had, sothly,   *tongues*
       Thai myght not tel the payns in hel duryng,   *enduring in hell*
              For thai may not be noumbyrd, treuly."
       Herefore, dere breder that beth present,   *brethren*

	That heren these payns, these gret turment,	*Who hear [about]*
325	Torne you to God Omnipotent	
	That we mow reyng with him in heven perpetualy.	*flourish*

	Alas, that ever oné Cristyn mon	*any*
	Wil not have that mater in mynd!	*subject*
	What schame and chenchip, confucion,	*torment*
330	Thai schal have that serven the Fynd!	
	That here mysdedis thai nyl not mend,	*[They] that*
	And foresake here synnus and be sory,	
	And sen al day what chamful end	*see; shameful*
	Thay have, that levyn here unryghtwysly —	*live here unrighteously*
335	To God this is a he trespas!	*supreme*
	That never on be other ware wil be,	*never will one beware of another*
	And wrath here God wetyngly,	*[will] anger their; knowingly*
	That dyud fore hom on rod-tre —	*Who died for them*
	Thai bene acursid, syrs, in thys case!	*damned*

340	Fore hel is not ordend fore ryghtwyse mon,	*ordained*
	Bot fore hom that serven the Fynd,	*Except for them*
	No more than is a preson of lyme and stone	*prison; limestone*
	Bot fore hom the lawis offend.	*them that break the laws*
	Cursid dedis makis men al day eschend	*ruined*
345	And theffys on galous on hye to hyng.	*thieves; gallows*
	Ther ryghtwys men, thai han good end,	
	That servyn here God in here levyng.	*their lives*
	Y pray you, seris! Trest wele hereto!	*trust*
	Fore he that levys here ryghtwysly,	*lives; righteously*
350	On what deth ever he dey,	
	His soule never paynd schal be,	
	Ne never after wit of wo.	*experience*

	Mervel ye not of this makyng —	
	Y me excuse, hit is not I.	
355	Thus Mychael lad Powle, be Goddis bedyng,	
	To se in hel the turmentré,	
	Fore I couth never bot hy foly.	
	God hath me chastyst fore my levyng;	*chastised*
	I thonke my God, my Grace, treuly,	
360	Of his gracious vesityng.	*visitation*
	Beware, serys, I you pray,	
	And your mysdedis loke ye amend	
	Betyme, lest ye be chamyd and schend!	
	Fore al is good that hath good end.	
365	Thus counsels youe the Blynd Audlay.	

Hec dicit Dominus Deus convertimini ad me et salvi eritis. Nolo mortem peccatoris set ut magis convertatur et vivat. Quia Cananeum et puplicanum vocavit ad penitenciam et peccatum lacrimantem. Ita et vos venite et audite incredoli quod timorem Domini docebit vos.[1]

XXVII. THE LORD'S MERCY   [W17–W18]

De misericordia Domini.[2]

GOD'S ADDRESS TO SINFUL MEN   [W17]

Alle Cristyn men, Y bid you cum —	*come*
Ye unbelevyd, cum wyle ye may,	*unbelievers; while*
And thenkis apon my dredful dome!	*judgment*
Hit schal you teche — hit is no nay! —	*I shall teach it to you*
5	Hou dredful then is Domysday,	
In the wyche nowther grace ne mercé is.	*[there is] neither*
Ther is no saynt may fore youe pray.	

Nolo mortem peccatoris.[3]

Ego sum Deus judex et justus, et do uniquique secundum opera sua.[4]

Thenke that I am God ryghtwyse,	*Know; righteous*
10 And yif uche mon after his wark:	*give each; accord to his labor*
To my blissid, I have orden blis,	*blessed [ones]; ordained*
And to the cursid, dampnacion darke.	
Leud and lerd, prest and clerke,	*Ignorant and learned*
Thai schal be rewardid, ywis,	
15 Affter here dedis — this word ye mark!	

Nolo mortem peccatoris.

The valey of wepyng, this word I cal,	*weeping; world*
I say you, serys, foresoth, forehwy:	*tell; the reason why*
Fore al day in myschif of syn ye fal	
20 And greven me, ful grevosly!	
Ucheon for other may be sory,	*Each; another*

---

[1] *These things says the Lord God: "Return to me, for I have redeemed thee. I do not wish the death of a sinner, but rather that he turn and live." For he called the Canaanite and the publican to repentance, and also the one who wept for [her] sin. And so you also, unbelievers, come and hear, because I will teach you the fear of the Lord* (see explanatory note). Written by Scribe A.

[2] *Concerning the Lord's mercy.* Written by Scribe B.

[3] *I desire not the death of a sinner.* Compare Ezechiel 33:11.

[4] *I am God, judge and just, and I give to each one according to his deeds.* Compare Psalm 7:12, Psalm 61:13, Proverbs 24:29, Romans 2:5–6.

Fore anon ye lesin heven blis,   *lose*
Savyng my grace and mercy.   *Unless [you have]*
Nolo mortem peccatoris.

Non veni vocare justos, sed peccatores ad penitenciam.[1]

25   I come not to cal ryghtwys men   *call*
      To penans, as I you say,   *penance*
      Bot thos that in erth synful bene —   *are*
      Hem I clepe, both nyght and day! —   *call*
      With disese and sekenes, yif that I may
30   Make ham to mend thai done amys.   *[what] they have done amiss*
      Cum to me now, I you pray!
      Nolo mortem peccatoris.

Magis gaudium est in celo super unum.[2]

      For ther is more joy, iwys,   *indeed*
      Of a synner that foresakis his syn,
35   And wil mend he doth amys,
      Then four score and twenty of ryghtwys men —   *(i.e., one hundred)*
      Fore hom nedis no medesyne.   *medicine*
      Bot he that in soule seke he is,   *that is sick in soul*
      Hom I clepe to my grace then!
40   *Nolo mortem peccatoris.*

Tradide me ipsum pro vobis ad mortem ut mecum . . .[3]

      Fourté days fore you I fast   *Forty; fasted*
      To fulfil my Fader law.
      Fore my deth I was agast;
      I wist ryght wel I schuld be slaw —   *slain*
45   And al hit was fore love of yow
      Lest that ye schuld fare amys.   *wander astray*
      My grace, my goodnes, now ye schul know!
      Nolo mortem peccatoris.

Sic oportet vos jejunare propter peccata vestra et pro amore passionis Jhesu Christe.[4]

---

[1] *I came not to call the just, but sinners to penance.* Compare Luke 5:32, Matthew 9:13, Mark 2:17. Compare also *Visiting the Sick and Consoling the Needy*, lines 166–69.

[2] *There is more joy in heaven over one [sinner that doth penance, than upon ninety-nine just, who need not penance].* Compare Luke 15:7, 15:10.

[3] *Hand me over to death for your sakes so that with me . . .*

[4] *Thus you need to fast for your sins and for the love of the passion of Jesus Christ*

So fourté days ye schul fast
50   Fore love of my Passion, I you pray,
        In the tyme that holé Lentyn last,
        Save onlé apon the Sunnday;
        In the clensyng days, hom fast ye may,   *them (i.e., in those days)*
        The fourté days to fulfil hit is;
55   This is my comawndmentis, hit is no nay.   *commandment*
        Nolo mortem peccatoris.

        Save wemen with child, and sekelou men,   *Except [for]; unhealthy*
        And laborers that worchyn both nyght and day,   *work*
        And pilgrems and palmers, and yong childer then,
60   Al other schuld fast, as I you say.
        Yif a resnabil mele have thai may,   *If they should have a moderate meal*
        Relegeus, prestis, and seculers,   *Men of religion; secular clergy*
        Non excusacion have thai may!   *excuse*
        Nolo mortem peccatoris.

        Qui cum jejuneo visia comprimis mentem elevas, etc.[1]

65   Fore, serys, I say that bodélé fast   *bodily*
        Lifftis up your mynd to heven on hye,
        And visis and synnus adown doth cast,   *vices*
        And getis youe vertus and mede with me,   *reward*
        And putis away the Fyndis pousté,   *power*
70   And distroys your thre enmys,
        Curst Pride, false Covetis, and Glotoné,   *avarice*
        And bryngis you into heven blis.

        On Aske Wenesday ye schul come   *Ash Wednesday*
        To Holé Cherche, serus, I you pray,
75   And takis askis, al and sum,   *ashes, everyone*
        Fore thus the prest to youe wil say:
        "Umthynk thee, mon, thou are pouder of clay,   *Remember; powder*
        And in to askis schal turne, iwis."   *indeed*
        Have mynd hereon both nyght and day,   *Be mindful of this*
80   *Nolo mortem peccatoris.*

        Fore clansyng days I do hom calle,   *cleansing*
        In hom to clanse your concians   *In which to clean your conscience*
        Of al your synnus, both gret and smal,
        And schryve youe clene with repentans,   *confess yourself clean*
85   And with good wil, do youre penans
        Fore al the yere ye han don amys;   *amiss*

---

[1] *When you fast, you repress your sins and raise your mind, etc.* Preface for the Third Sunday in Lent. Written by Scribe B.

Then I wil withdraw my venchance.   *vengeance*
Nolo mortem peccatoris.

90   Fore ye most nede do your penans   *need*
     In the tyme of holé Lentyn,   *holy Lent*
     And shryve youe clene of repentans   *confess yourself*
     In the clansyng days, yif that ye mouen,   *may*
     To make a syth satisfaccion   *true*
     Fore al the yere ye han don mys,
95   Fore then I grawnt remyssion.
     Nolo mortem peccatoris.

     Now ye schul schryve youe, I wil youe telle: *Now [how]*
     Mekelé to the prest, ye knele adoune;   *Humbly*
     Hele no thyng, bot truly spel   *Hide; recount*
100 Hou and were that ye han done,   *where what*
     Hwen, to hwom, outher God or mon;   *When; whom, either*
     Tellis forth treuly, ryght as hit is,   *truthfully*
     Then this is treue confession.
     Nolo mortem peccatoris.

105 Thre thyngys longis to confession —   *pertain*
     Beware, seris, now I you pray! —
     Tru schryft of mowth, contricion,
     And then satisfaccion, hit is no nay!
     Never on without other be ther may,   *one*
110 Yif ye wil bryng your soule to blis —
     To heven ther is no nother way.
     Nolo mortem peccatoris.

     Trust ye not to esy penans   *too easy penance*
     That the prest injoyns you to;
115 Bot yif ye have veré repentans,   *Unless; true repentance*
     And thynke never more so to do,
     And make satisfaccion also —
     Ellis the pop asoylis no mon, iwys —   *Or else; pope; absolves*
     To purgatoré or to hel ye most nede go.
120 *Nolo mortem peccatoris.*

Penetentes penitentes et non irritentes, si estis penitentes imitate mores corigite vitam et convertemini ad Dominum secundum Augustinum.[1]

     Bot ye have very contricion,   *Unless; true contrition*
     To me hit is a he scornyng: *strong repudiation*

---

[1] *Penitents, being penitent and not being scoffers, if you are penitent, imitate [good] morals, correct your life, and turn to the Lord, according to Augustine.* Augustine, *Sermo* 393 (*PL* 39.1713–15).

	Your schryft is bot confusion!	*confession*
	Ye schul have schame at your endyng;	*damnation*
125	Bot yf ye change your maners, your cursid levyng,	*Unless; cursed way of life*
	And clanse your consians of al malis,	*conscience; malice*
	To evel end hit wel you bryng.	
	Nolo mortem peccatoris.	

	Ye that foregete me in your levyng,	
130	And on my Passion hath no peté,	*compassion*
	I wil foregete youe in your dyyng,	
	And withdraw my grace and my mercy,	
	And your good angel fro you schal fle	*flee*
	And betake yow into the honde of your enmys;	*abandon*
135	Then ful woful schul ye be,	
	That nyl not mend that thai do mys.	*will not amend what; amiss*

Quia numquam peccatum diluatur nisi satisfaccio operis restituatur.[1]

	Ye curatours, wysely ye wayt,	*curates; take heed*
	That han mon soule in your kepyng;	*have*
	Enjoyne ye not penance to strayt,	*too rigorous*
140	Lest ye slen mon soule with ponyschyng!	*slay; punishment*
	A Paternoster with repentyng	*repentance*
	To send ham to purgatoré, better hit is,	
	And save bodé and soule fro peryschyng.	*perishing*
	Nolo mortem peccatoris.	

Misericordia et veritas obviaverunt sibi; justicia et pax osculate.[2]

	Ye that sittyn here, in my place,	
145	Ye most have treuth and ryghtwysnes.	
	Then let Treuth, Mercy, and Grace,	
	And Ryghwysnes take rest and pese;	*bring about; peace*
	These four sistyrs mad me pese	*appeased [Psalm 84:11]*
150	Of my vengans and my males,	*From; vengeance; malice*
	Fore mercé and grace hit you mo ples.	*may*
	Nolo mortem peccatorys.	

Qui sola contricion deluit peccatum.   *Because only contrition washes away a sin*

	Fore as possebil, foresoth, hit is,	
	With a tere of thyn ye,	

---

[1] *Because a sin could never be atoned for unless satisfaction for the deed is rendered*

[2] *Mercy and truth have met each other; justice and peace kiss.* Compare Psalm 84:11, and compare also *Marcolf and Solomon*, line 974a.

155	To quenche al the synns thou hast do mys,	*done amiss*
	Yif fore thi synns thou be sory,	
	As al the water is in the se	*sea*
	To qwenche a gnost of fuyre, iwys,	*spark of fire, indeed*
	Fore to hom I grawnt mercy.	
160	*Nolo mortem peccatoris.*	

Dimittite et demittetur vobis.[1]

	And loke ye bene in charyté,	
	And foregif ucheon other then,	*forgive each other*
	And quetis your det, treuly;	*repay your debt*
	Then brekis your bred to my pore men,	*break your bread [with]*
165	And gif ham drynk that thorsté bene,	*thirsty are*
	And clethe nakid, that nedé is,	*clothe*
	And harbare the pore, that woful ye syn.	*whom you see are woeful*
	Nolo mortem peccatoris.	

Date elemosenam et omnia nobis munda.[2]

	And vysette the seke that in preson be,	*visit; prison*
170	And beré the dede, I you pray,	*bury*
	And cownsel the unwyse, pur charyté,[3]	*for*
	And here my Word when that ye may,	*hear*
	And do therafter, both nyght and day,	*accordingly*
	Fore this wil bryng you to my blis;	
175	To heven hit is the hyewaye.	*highway*
	Nolo mortem peccatoris.	

Convertimini ad me in toto corde vestro.   *Be converted to me with all your heart* [Joel 2:12]

	And turne you to me fore oné thyng	*before anything [else]*
	In al your hartis, with myght and mayn,	*hearts*
	In fastyng, in wepyng, with sorowyng,	
180	Yif ye have gon mys, cum home agayn!	*amiss*
	Then of youe I wil be fayne.	*attentive*
	And kuttus your hertus with contrecion hit is,	*pierce; hearts*
	Bot kutt not your clothis, let hem be playne.	*clothes; unadorned*
	Nolo mortem peccatoris.	

---

[1] *Forgive and it will be forgiven you.* Compare Luke 6:37, and compare also *Visiting the Sick and Consoling the Needy,* lines 336–38, and *Audelay's Epilogue to The Counsel of Conscience,* line 442a.

[2] *Give alms and everything [will be] clean for us.* Compare Luke 11:41.

[3] Lines 164–71 refer to the seven works of mercy; compare Matthew 25:31–46, and also *True Living,* lines 173–85, and *Seven Works of Mercy.*

Anima que peccaverit, ipsa moreatur.[1]

185 A soule hit doth a dedlé syn,
  He schal dye in good sothnes,
  Bot the fader of the child then
  Schal not bere his synns, his wyckidnes;
  Be the Fader of the Sun,

  ....

  ....

190 That for my love han forsakyn this word,   *[They] who; world*
  That nyght and day knelis on knen,   *Who; kneels; knees*
  Thai pray for you to me your Lord;
  Then loke that ye han here cumford,   *comfort*
  And wit ye han not fare amys,   *be certain [that]*
195 Fore in heven I wil you rewarde.
  Nolo mortem peccatoris.

  And ever depart with the pore   *share*
  Of the gracis and goodis that God you send;   *gifts*
  Ye have non other sycur tresoure   *secure*
200 Agayns the Day of Jugement;
  Ellis wil ye be chamyd and chent   *shamed and disgraced*
  When I cal youe to your cowntys, iwys,   *accounts, indeed*
  How wordlé goodis ye han spend.   *worldly*
  Nolo mortem peccatoris.

205 Meche be ye aldyn to the pore   *You are much beholden*
  That ye geven here oné thyng,   *any*
  Fore that is your trew trusté tresoure,   *assured*
  Ye gif hit to me is Heven Kyng;   *as*
  Fore thai get no more bot here levyng,   *their living [sustenance]*
210 And ye schul have therfore heven blis,
  And that lyve that is everlastyng.   *life*
  Nolo mortem peccatoris.

  Fore the pore schal be mad domysman   *made judges*
  Apon the ryche on Domysday;   *rich*
215 Let se how thai con answere then   *they (i.e., the rich)*
  Fore al here reverent ryal aray,   *dignified royal array*
  In hungere, in thorst, in gold — welay! —   *cold; alas*
  Affter here almes ay waytyng: *alms always waiting*
  "Thai wold not us vesit, nyght ne day!"
220 Thus wil thai playn to me, Heven Kyng.

---

[1] *The soul that sinneth, the same shall die.* Compare Ezechiel 18:4 and 18:20.

Date et dabetur vobis *Give and it shall be given to you [Luke 6:38]*
To my pore that leven in payne; *who live*
Dimitte, et dimittetur vobis, *Forgive, and you shall be forgiven [Luke 6:37]*
And then foregifyn schul ye ben; *forgiven*
225 *Querite, et invenietis,* *Seek, and you shall find [Matthew 7:7, Luke 11:9]*
Taré not to long bot cum betyme, *Tarry not too long; in time*
Pulsate, et aperietur vobis, *Knock, and it shall be opened to you [Matthew 7:7, Luke 11:9]*
Or I me gatis for you tyne, *I will myself close [heaven's] gates to you*
Yif ye wil oné thyng that is myne, *wish for any*
230 *Petete, et accepietis;* *Ask, and you shall receive [John 16:24]*
Here may ye know wel and sene, *soon*
Nolo mortem peccatoris.

Take ensampil be Saint Martyne: *example; Martin*
The nakid he clothid with gret peté —
235 With his swerd he swapt atwyn *sword; cut in two*
His mantil, and said, "This gif I thee." *cloak; give*
Anon in heven, he con hit se —
Myselve therin was clothyd, iwys, *clothed, indeed*
And sayd: "Martyne, this gif thou me."
240 *Nolo mortem peccatoris.*

Thenke on the ryche mon, had no peté
On the lazare lying on the gate, *leper*
And ther he dyed myschifusly; *died miserably*
The ryche mon sterve in his astate, *died; estate*
245 Hes soule, to hel hit toke the gate; *His; made its way*
The lazar was borne to heven blis!¹
Have mynd on this, erlé and late.
Nolo mortem peccatoris.

Thus I cal youe to my grace, ucheon — *each one [of you]*
250 Cum to me for giftis, I you pray,
And I wil gif you remissiown,
And joy and blis foreever and ay! *always*
No hert con thonke, ne tung tel hit may *conceive*
The lest joy in heven ye schul have, iwys, *least*
255 Yif ye wil do as I you say!
Nolo mortem peccatoris.

Joy be to the Fader and to the Sun,
And to the Holé Gost, al thre efere, *together*
That in the word of wordis togeder thai were, *forever and ever*
260 That now is, and was, schal be ever!

---

¹ Lines 241–46 refer to the parable of the rich man and Lazarus, Luke 16:19–25. Compare *Marcolf and Solomon*, lines 292–99, 536–39.

To that perles Prince without pere   *peerless; peer*
Be worchip and joy in heven blis,
That says to us with so good chere,
Nolo mortem peccatoris!

AUDELAY'S EPILOGUE TO THE COUNSEL OF CONSCIENCE   **[W18]**

Here I conclud al my makyng,
In the mercé of God, I have sayd before;
God grawnt ham grace of good endyng
That done theraftir, both lasse and more,
5   And let ham never, Lord, be forelore,   *forlorn*
That prayn for Jon the Blynd Audlay.   *pray*
Into the kyngdam thou ham restore,
Unto that blis that lasteth fore ay,
        In word without end!   *world*
10   Fore blessid be thai that heren the Word   *hear*
And don therafter here in this word,
Fore in heven thou wilt hem reward,
        That here mysdedis here wil amende.   *their misdeeds*

Fore al that is nedful to bodé and soule
15   Here in this boke then may ye se,
And take record of the apostil Poule   *heed*
That Crist callid to grace and his mercé,
Fore so I hope he hath done me
And geven me wil, wit, tyme, and space,
20   Throgh the Holé Gost, blynd, def to be,
And say this wordis throgh his gret grace.   *these*
        So synful a wreche, unworthély,
        Y pray you, seris, fore Cristis sake,
        Ensampil at me that ye wil take,
25   And amendis betime ye make   *amends in good time*
        Wile ye han space here specialy.

Fore as I lay seke, in my dremyng,   *sick*
Methoght a mon to me con say: *It seemed to me; did say*
"Let be thi slouth and thi slomeryng!   *slumbering*
30   Have mynd on God both nyght and day!
Bohold and se a reuful aray —   *sorrowful sight*
Al the word on foyre brenyng!   *world; fire burning*
Warne the pepul now, I thee pray —
Thai lovyn here God overe al thyng.   *They [who]*
35   Aryse anon, and awake!
        Fore thus God wil take venchans on thee,   *vengeance*
        Apon his pepil sodenly,

Fore pride, covetyse, wrath, envy,
    Fore God is wroth fore here syne sake!"   *their sins'*

40   Herewith I woke of my dremyng,   *from*
    And al fore fryght I was afrayd.
    Anon I barst on wepyng;   *burst out*
    With soroue of hert, to Crist I prayd:
    "Take no venchanche, Lord!" I sayd,
45   "Bot send the pepul sum warnyng,
    As thou was borne al of a mayde,
    And withdraw thi wenchanse that is comyng,   *vengeance*
        And grawnt me, Lord, throgh thi gret grace,
        Sum good word that I may say
50   To thi worchip, Lord, I thee pray,
    To help mon soule, that hit may,   *as it may*
        That hit heren in honé plase!"   *Who it hears in any place*

    I pray youe al, in Cristis name —
    Beware, seris, ye han warnyng!
55   Fore I say soth. No mon me blame.
    God hath me grawntid myn askeng.
    He hath youe send a hye tokenyng,   *powerful sign*
    And erthquake the last day,   *recently*
    That Domysday is nygh cumyng,   *coming nigh*
60   Fore to his dissiplis, thus con He say:
        "I pray you, seris, tent herto take —   *take heed hereto*
    Tofore my dome this tokyn schal fal: *Before; sign*
    Vengans fore syn my pepil se chal —   *shall see*
    Werrs and pestelens, hungir with ale,   *Wars*
65   That, fore drede, the erth schul quake."

    A, thenke on, mon! Thou art made of erth;   *Consider*
    In thi hert, fore, thou may quake!   *therefore*
    Moche payn and penans thou art wele worthe *you thoroughly deserve*
    To greve thi God so, fore thi syn sake;   *[Because you] grieve*
70   Herefore, wo hit wil awake   *woe*
    Fore the brekyng of Cristis comawndment
    Betyme, amendis bot ye make   *Soon, unless you make amends*
    And seche grace tofore His Jugement,
        Wile ye han tyme and spase.   *While*
75   Of al lordis be He blessid!
    He wold not mon were lost,   *does no desire that a man be lost*
    That wil in His mercé trost,
        And foresake His syn and soche His grace.   *seek*

    Alas, in my hert sore I drede
80   Lest men beleve not faythfully,

Fore to prechyng and techyng, thai take non hede!
Here dedis, hom demys ful opynly —   *They are judged by their deeds*
To bye and sel thay be besy,   *buy*
Bot feu to purches heven blis;   *few [work] to purchase*
85 Thai have no trest therin, treuly,
Ellis wold thai mend that thay do mys.   *repent what they do amiss*
        Bot, seris, ther is cause: *a reason*
        Curatis the soth thai dare not say —   *Curates dare not say the truth*
        The soth yourselve, se ye may —
90   How thai lye in syn fro day to day   *they (i.e., the curates)*
        And been the furst that breken Cristis laws!

Fore and curatis lyved spirytualy,   *For if curates*
Ful evel durst ané mon offend   *Very evilly (fearfully) would anyone dare*
The laws of God in oné degré;   *any manner*
95 Anon therfore thai schul be chent!   *damned*
Alas, our bischopis thai ben yblynd   *are made blind*
That to this myschif thai cun not se!
Fore few ther be that wile amend
Fore oné corexion now trewly   *By means of any reprimand*
100   Of Holé Cherche, I say.   *From*
        I pray you, seris, that ye aspie   *take note*
        Howe contenwes Lechoré —   *Lechery continues*
        Have he cordid with Constery —   *He has joined with Consistory [courts]*
        Leve forth in syn thai may.   *They may live forth in sin*

105 Few ther bene that sechen soulehele —   *soul's health*
Herefore ye ston in gret drede! —   *stand*
Bot moné ther ay sechen ryches and wele,   *always seek; wealth*
That schal youe fayle here at your nede.
Y pra youe, seris, that ye take hede: *pray*
110 Ye schul acownt ful securly   *certainly*
Fore al your goodus, withoutyn dred,
How ye han getin and spend, treuly;   *gotten and spent [it]*
        Foresoth, acownt ye schul   *shall [make]*
        Tofore that Lord that you dere boght —
115   Fore word, fore wil, fore dede, fore thoght,
        Your synys loke excuse ye noght;
        That greveth God most of alle.

Now ye callyn pride honesté.
Whrath, envy, hardénes.   *[You call] wrath [and] envy hardiness*
120 False covetys, wisdam callid his he.   *is*
Lecheouré, a lover of lustenes.   *lustiness (i.e., high spirits)*
Glotoné, a felaw of gentilnes.   *companion of nobility*
Slouth, ye callyn onest levyng.   *honest living*
Thus have ye cullord your wickidnes   *colored*

125	Agayns Godis hest and his bedyng!	*command and bidding*
	I say you, seris, forewy:	*therefore*
	Thus the Fynd he hath you blynd	*blinded*
	Lest your mysdedis ye schuld amend —	
	With pride, wrath, covetyse, envy, you schend,	*you are damned*
130	With lechoré, slowth, and glotoné!	
	Thenke to the Fynd, when ye were boren,	*Consider*
	Ther ye foresokyn the werkis of the Fynd,	*At that time you forsook*
	Ellis I lekyn you to be forelorne,	*Or else I depict you as*
	Bot your mysdedis that ye amend.	*Unless*
135	Thus Adam, your fader, furst con affend,	*did offend (i.e., sinned)*
	And excusid him of the appil etyng,	
	And sayd Eve, his wyf, so had him kend,	*advised*
	And soght no grace of Heven Kyng,	
	Herefore God was wroth hylé.	*highly enraged*
140	An angel with a swerd brenyng bryght	
	Drof him out of paradyse anon ryght,	*immediately*
	Fore he had synyd in Godis syght	
	With pride, covetyse, and glotoné.	
	Your synus, loke excuse ye noght —	*Look not to excuse your sins*
145	He is above that knowis ale,	
	Your werd, your wil, your dede, your thoght.	*word*
	Ye wot never whent he wil on you calle,	*know; when*
	Fore at his bar, stond ye schal;	*bar (i.e., court)*
	Your consians schal cuse youere cursid levyng	*conscience; excuse*
150	And al your dedis, both gret and smale;	
	Ther schul ye here a hard rekenyng!	*judgment*
	Beware, seris, hereby!	
	Anon schryve youe of your syn	*confess*
	Be frelté, yif ye fal therin,	*frailty*
155	Fore the Fynd he takis youe in his gren	*Before; snare*
	With pride, covetys, and glotony.	
	Fore he that wil himself here lowe,	*be humble*
	And foresake his syn, and be sory,	
	And to the prest him schryve and chewe,	*confess and show [sin]*
160	And do his penans dewoutly,	
	He never reprevyd schal be	*reproved*
	When he is callid to his rekenyng,	*reckoning*
	Fore God hath foregeven him throght his mercé,	*forgiven; through*
	Here in herth in his levyng,	*on earth*
165	Throgh his special grace.	
	He wil not ponyche youe twice then —	
	Yif ye han don your penans fore your syn,	

Ye schul never have penans hen,   *hence (i.e., later)*
   When God hath foregifyn you your trespace.

Non est verior probacio quam oculorum demonstracio.[1]

170   Thus Experiens treulé me tolde,
    That walkis amongis youe ever spyyng,   *Who; spying*
    What ye deth, both yong and hold,   *do; old*
    And al the maner of your levyng;
    He bede me, in the name of Heven Kyng,   *bid*
175   I schuld not spare the soth to say,
    Ne faver youe with no false flateryng —
    That nygh hand is Domysday,   *near at hand*
       Fore al the tokens beth efalle!   *signs have happened*
    Thus sayth Luke in his Gospele, truly,
180   That Domysday schal cum sodenly
    When men in erth ben most besi,
       That never onother help thai schal.   *[When] they shall never help another*

Qui praemunitur non fallitur.[2]

Reght as in the tyme of Noyé   *Just as; Noah*
Sodenly al the word was drownd,
185   And as Sodom and Gomor, that gret ceté,   *city*
    Sodenlé was sonkyn to hel grownde,   *to the ground of hell*
    So within a lytil stownd,   *while*
    Domsday schal fal, treuly!   *befall*
    In Lukis Gospel thus I fond —
190   Seche hit, serys, and ye may se.   *[Luke 17:24–30]*
       Herefore, beth redé nyght and day!   *ready*
    Alas, ye dred not God to greve!
    Alas, ye bene false in your beleve!
    Alas, your dedis thay don youe preve!   *become your test*
195   Alas, alas, and waylaway!

Alas, swerde and pestelens al day doth falle!
Beware lest froytis withdrawn be!   *fruits (i.e., rewards)*
Alas, erthquake is comen with al!
Alas, amende yow, pur charyté!   *for*
200   These takyns fro the heven ye se
    That God sendis youe in fayre war.   *warning*
    Alas, bot fewe ware . . .
    Alas, for . . .

---

[1] *There is no surer evidence than the demonstration of the eyes*

[2] *The one who is forearmed is not deceived.* Compare *Marcolf and Solomon*, line 974a.

	Alas! Thus sayth the profecé:	*prophecy*
205	Was never more better purchesyng	*Nothing was ever better purchased*
	Then schal be agayns Cristis cumyng,	*Than [safeguards taken] against*
	Ne never alf so cursid levyng;	*Nor [against] half so cursed a living*
	Herefor this word God wil distroye.	*Soon; world*

	Alas, that ye con not beleve	
210	That ye felyn and se with syght!	*What*
	Hou lytil a thyng a mon may greve	*How little a thing may grieve a person*
	When oné sekenes is on him light!	*fallen*
	Anon he has lost al his myght —	
	Then ard on Crist wil he cry,	*hard*
215	Fore payne and deth he is afryght.	
	Al wordlé good he settis noght by.	*worldly; gauges as nothing*
	A, thynke on this, thou synful mon!	
	In wele beware, or thou be wo,	*before you grow woeful*
	And thynk weder that thou wilt go —	*which way*
220	To hel or heven, on of tho —	*one of those*
	Fore other joyse is ther non.	*choice*

	Fore to lye I have no lust,	
	Fore yif I did, I schuld hit rew;	*regret*
	Bot to this tale, treulé ye tryst,	*trust*
225	Fore wil I wot that is trew.	*well; know*
	The soth I wold, seris, that ye knewe —	
	At your concians take knowlescheng!	*In your conscience acknowledge*
	Among Cristyn men ther be to fewe	*too*
	That lovyn here God over al thyng,	
230	And as amselve here trew neghtboure,	*themselves*
	Fore al the lawys of our Lord,	
	In this two comawndmentis hengus uche worde;	*hang in each word*
	Herefore, al the wo of this worde	*Therefore; world*
	Is fore we kepe not the wyl of your Savyour.	*[Occurs] because*

235	Al Cristin men, Y cownsel youe	
	That ye wil do as Y youe say,	
	Then in yore conseans ye schul wele know	
	That schal youe deme at Domysday —	*What shall be your verdict*
	Weder hit be soth, ore ellis nay.	*or else not [true]*
240	Yif hit be trew, at your wittyng,	*by your understanding*
	Then doth therafter, I youe pray,	
	And lovys your God over al thyng —	
	Y hwolde hit for the best.	*hold (i.e., declare)*
	I rede ye loven Heven Kyng,	
245	And your neghtbore fore oné thyng,	*before*
	Fore oné lost ore lykyng.	*Despite any desire or pleasure*
	Then, seris, al ye beth eblest.	*all of you are blessed*

	I wot ryght wel I schal be chent	*destroyed*
	Of Godis enmys — hit is no nay! —	*By God's enemies*
250	Fore to the treuth thai take no tent;	*pay no heed*
	The soth fore hem, Y dar not say;	*on account of them*
	Herefore the Fynd he wil hem fray,	*frighten*
	Fore thay cal trew Cristyn men Lollard,	*Lollards*
	That kepyn Cristis comawndmentis nyght and day,	*Who*
255	And don Godis wil in dede and worde.	
	Agayns ham, I take Crist to wytnes;	*witness*
	Here is non error ne Lollardré,	*heresy; Lollardy*
	Bot pistill and gospel, the Sauter, treuly;	*epistle; Psalter*
	I take witnes of the treue clargy	
260	That han Godis lauys fore to redres.	*Whose duty it is to redress God's laws*

	Yet I wil say more yif I bere grame —	*righteous anger*
	Fore wele I wot that hit is trewe —	
	Fore Holé Wryt ye may not blame,	
	Nowther the Hold Lawe ne the Newe;	*Old*
265	God gif you grace your synnys excuse;	*to excuse*
	The treuth to preche, men may be bold,	
	Ore ellis, ye curatis, ye schul sore rew,	*regret*
	That han the kepyng of Christis folde	*flock*
	In Holé Cherche, in heveré place —	*every*
270	Fore to curatis, sayth Saynt Gregory,	
	Thai schul onswere treuly	*answer (i.e., be held to account)*
	Fore mons soule specialy,	*man's soul*
	At Domusday tofore Crystis face.	

	Of al the createurs that ever God mad,	
275	Mon soule was most pressious —	*precious*
	A prynt of the Treneté that never schal fade,	*Trinity*
	Partener and eyre of even blis!	*Partner; heir; heaven's*
	Al erthelé thyng hit schal vanysche.	
	Into the erth we schul be broght.	
280	Thou getist no more with thee, iwys,	
	Save good werd, good wil, good dede, good thoght;	
	Fore these four, specialy,	
	In heven thou shalt have joy and blis,	
	After thi merit have mede, iwis;	*reward, indeed*
285	Beware, seris, fore nede hit is,	*needful*
	Lest bodé and soule ye distroy!	

	Fore God, mon soule he hath betake	*For God has committed man's soul*
	To curaturs in ilke lond,	*curates; every*
	To kepe hem wel fore his love sake.	
290	He wil hem seche out of here hond	*He will seek them from the curates' hand*
	Fore to his face thai schal stond,	*[When] before*

	And yild ther a hard rekynyng	*pay*
	Fore everé soule, both fre and bond,	
	Yif oné be peryschid throgh here kepyng.	*their (i.e., the curates')*
295	Fore God hath grawnt youe his pouere,	*power*
	Be the vertu of the sacrement,	
	To asoyle al that wil repent,	*absolve*
	And chryve ham clene with good entent,	*shrive*
	And do here penans wyle thai bene here.	

300	Then yif ané fal throgh here frelté	*frailty*
	In ané maner dedlé syn,	
	What maner man that ever hit be,	*Whatever sort of person he is*
	Anon corect im as law wil then,	*him; decrees*
	And take no mede of no maner men.	*reward; no man whatsoever*
305	Fore opyn syn, gif opin penans.	*open penance*
	In the decretals, ther ye may sene,	
	Hit is Godis law, his ordenans,	*ordinance*
	That ye schul bryng mon soule to blis —	
	Fore treuly the pepil ye schuld telle,	
310	And warne ham of the payne of helle,	
	And to put hem out of the parel,	*peril*
	And make ame amend that thai don mys.	*them; what they do amiss*

	Fore a holé curate, he schal have	
	In heven coronacion	
315	Fore everé soule that he doth save	
	And bryngis ham to salvacion;	
	And other schul have confucion,	*others*
	Under fyndis of hel turmentré,	*fiends; hell's torments*
	That bryngth mon soule to dampnacion	*Who*
320	Throgh evyl ensampil in prestis thay se.	
	Thus Jon Belet, he gon you tele	*Beleth; he did tell you*
	How mon soule that ye schuld save —	
	No spot of syn ye schuld have.	
	Alas, I trow now that ye rave,	
325	Fore ye dred nowther heven ne hel!	

	Ye prestis, I pray youe take good kepe,	*pay close attention*
	That mas ne matens nyl say ne syng:	*neither mass nor matins will not*
	Ye deprevyn the Treneté of his worchip,	*deprive*
	And al sayntis in heven with him dwellyng,	
330	And al Cristin soulis in payne bydyng	
	Affter your prayors in purgatory,	
	And al your god-doers of here helpyng.	*good-doers; their share [of salvation]*
	Alas, this is a gret peté —	
	To God and mon a hye trespace! —	
335	To take your hoyre, your salaré,	*hire; salary*

Bot yif ye levyn spyretwaly,   *Unless you live spiritually*
And sayne your servyse dewoutly!   *say*
    Ye ben Godis traytors in this case!

Dissyre ye nowther wyke ne dede;   *Desire neither living nor dead*
340 Beth holé prestis in your levyng;
     In trust ther schuld be no falsode;   *falsehood*
     Men in your prayours, thai bene hopyng,   *expectant (i.e., trusting)*
     Ellis schuld ye yild ard rekenyng,   *receive a hard judgment*
     Fore your hoyre, your selaré.
345 Mon soule to blis bot ye hit bryng
     With your prayors specialy,
         Fore God hath geven thee pouere   *power*
     To be mens betwene God and mon,   *means (i.e., mediator)*
     That al day agayns his laus thai don,
350 To get ham grace, remyssion,
         Throgh here halmys and your prayere.   *alms*

     Fore oche day ye spekyn with Crist asyt   *in privacy*
     When ye dewotlé to him pray,   *devoutly*
     And yif ye reden in Holé Wryt,   *if you read in the Bible*
355 He spekis to youe, hit is no nay;
     Remembyr, youe prestis, I you pray,
     And say your servys dewoutly;   *service (i.e., mass)*
     Then the sothe ther se ye may.
     Yif that ye wil not then leve me,   *believe*
360   Thys ensampul Y pray yow leve: *example; believe*
         Yif ye schuld do omache to a kyng,   *homage*
     Ye most with reverens, adown knelyng,
         Say your mesache without faylyng,   *message*
             Ellis that lord wil youe repreve.   *reprove*

365 Fore wyle hert worchipis noght,   *while*
     The tong foresoth lebors in vayne;   *labors*
     Have mynd on him that youe dere boght,
     That sofyrd both passion and payne —
     Fore him to plese ye schuld be fayne,   *eager*
370 And in your prayers, specialy,
     Have mend on hom fore hom ye prayne,   *Be mindful of them for whom*
     I pray youe, seris, fore charyté!
         I say you, breder, in Cristis name,
         To me hit were a hy slawnder
375   To lye apon my blessid breder;
         Y wold youe fayne here forther,   *I would gladly advance you here*
             Bot your wyckid dedus thay don you fame.   *defame you*

	A sad ensampil her may ye se;	
	I pray youe, breder, have hit in mynd.	
380	Thagh I say soth, blamys not me —	
	I blustur forth as Bayard blynd.	*bluster*
	Fore to Crist, ye bene unkynd,	
	Freris, and freel, false in your fay;	*frail; faith*
	Among men of Holé Cherche, fewe men fynd	
385	That worchyn wysely to wyse men the way	*instruct*
	Into the courte of heven blis —	
	Fore as ye techyn other to do,	
	Yourselfe ye gon clen therfro!	*fully away from there*
	Thus be ye wercher of al our wo	*maker*
390	Hent ye wil mend that ye do mys.	*Until; amend; amiss*
	Beware hereby, bothe frynd and foo,	*friend*
	A sad soth I wil youe say —	*serious*
	This is the cause of al our woo:	
	We beleve not treuly in Cristis fay,	*faith*
395	Ellis wold we dred God both nyght and day,	
	And kepe the comawndment of our Kyng,	
	That wot never how sone we schul wynd away,	*Who know (referring to "we")*
	To hel or even at our endyng,	*heaven*
	Fore ther is non other joyse;	*choice*
400	And yet wil ye serve the Fynd,	
	To God and mon both, be unkynd;	
	Ye have not his Passion in your mynd,	
	That dyid fore youe apon the cros.	
	I pray you al, pur charyté,	*for*
405	That heryn or redin in this boke,	
	Doth therafter specialy;	*Follow its counsel specifically*
	Cownsel therat I wold ye toke,	*I want you to take*
	Fore here is nowther wyle ne croke.	*wile nor trick*
	I faver you noght with no flateryng;	*compliment*
410	The hyeway to heven I wold ye toke,	
	To joy and blis without endyng,	
	Fore other cownsel nedis you non.	
	Doth therafter then, I youe pray,	
	Fore to heven ther is no nother way.	
415	Then meré in hert be ye may	*merry*
	To go to the way of salvacion.	
	The Cownsel of Conseans this boke I calle,	*Counsel of Conscience*
	Or *The Ladder of Heven*, I say, forewy:	*because*
	Ther is no mon may clym up a walle	*climb*
420	Without a ladder, sekyrly;	*certainly*
	No more may we to heven on hye	*may we [climb]*

Without treu cownsel of consians.
Clyme up this ladder — then may ye se
What ye schul do to Godis plesans,   *delight*
425   And weder ye wil have wele or wo.   *whether; weal*
Clyme up this ladder — then may ye se
What joys in heven that ther be,
And what payns in hel and turmentré.   *torments*
Then chese yourselve weder to go.   *choose*

430   Al Cristyn men, I cownsel yow
No mon deme other specially,   *judge*
Fore oche mon schuld himselve here know,   *each; should [know]*
And deme himselve whatever he be,
Fore a lytil mote ye con sone se
435   In another mons ye then,   *eye*
Bot in your owne ye con not se,
Thagh ther be fallyn in nine or ten.   *nine or ten [motes]*[Matthew 7:1–5]
Alas, thus bene ye blynd!
Lest he be gilté in the same,
440   No mon be to bold to blame,   *ought to be too eager to blame*
Bot uche mon mend hymselve fore chame.   *each; ought to amend; shame*
Yif ye deme mys, ye wil be chent!   *amiss; ruined*

Nolite judicare et non judicabimini. . . . Eadem messure qua messi fueritis messietur vobis.[1]

Fore Crist sayth, the same mesere
That ye metin to other men,   *mete out*
445   The same ye schul have to your hoyre —   *hire*
Outher joy or fuyre that ever schal bren.   *fire*
Ye wot never what day ne wen   *know; when*
Ye schul be callid to your rekenyng;
Ryght as ye demon other men,   *judge*
450   Ye schul be dampnyd at your endyng.   *judged*
In the Gospel thus wretyn hit is;
To this ensampil takys good yeme: *heed*
Uche mon his dedis, thai schul him deme,
Then be seche as ye schuld deme,   *such*
455   And deme ye never onother amys.

Takis no venchans, this Crist forebede: *vengeance*
"Your venjans ye schul yif to me,

---

[1] *Judge not, and you shall not be judged: [condemn not, and you shall not be condemned. Forgive, and you shall be forgiven. Give, and it shall be given to you: good measure, and pressed down, and shaken together, and running over, shall they give into your bosom. For] with the same measure that you shall measure, it shall be measured to you.* Compare Luke 6:37–38. Audelay refers to this passage elsewhere: *Visiting the Sick and Consoling the Needy*, lines 336–38, *God's Address to Sinful Men*, line 160a.

Fore I wil elde uche mon after his mede."   *requite; deserved reward*
In everé state whatever he be,   *rank*
460 What cyté or rem devidid ye se,   *realm divided*
Hit schal be distroyd, wretyn hit is;
Bot yif ye leve in charyté   *Unless; believe*
And foregif uche onother, ye don amys.   *forgive one another*
     Thus in this Gospel wretyn I fynd,
465   He that lovys here rust and pese,   *rest; peace*
    He is Godis child without lese,   *lie*
    And he that sterys debate with his males,   *stirs discord; evil intentions*
     Thai be the chylder of the Fynd.   *children*

To the Treneté I me recomend,   *commend myself*
470 That al this word at his wil wroght,   *created*
That myght and grace he hath me send,
And to Crist his Sun that me dere boght,
And to the Holé Gost foregete I noght,   *forget*
Fore him I thonke specialy,   *in particular*
475 That wit and wysdam to me hath broght
To foresake my syn and my foly.
    In this word here levyng,   *[I pray that] in this world*
    To have my payne, my purgatory,
    Out of this word or that I dy,   *before I die out of this world*
480   A, gracyus God, gramarsy,   *grant mercy*
     To grawnt me grace of good endyng!

As I lay seke in my langure,   *illness*
In an abbay here be west,
This boke I made with gret dolour   *grief*
485 When I myght not slep ne have no rest.
Offt with my prayers I me blest,   *blessed myself*
And sayd hilé to Heven Kyng: *reverently*
"I knowlache, Lord, hit is the best   *acknowledge*
Mekelé to take thi vesetyng,   *meekly; visitation*
490   Ellis wot I wil that I were lorne."   *know I well; lost*
    Of al lordis be he blest!
    Fore al that ye done is fore the best,
    Fore in thi defawte was never mon lost,   *misdeed*
     That is here of womon borne.

495 Mervel ye not of this makyng,   *Marvel*
Fore I me excuse — hit is not I;   *excuse myself*
This was the Holé Gost wercheng,   *Holy Ghost's making*
That sayd these wordis so faythfully,
Fore I quoth never bot hye foly.   *say; high folly*
500 God hath me chastyst fore my levyng;   *chastised*
I thong my God, my Grace, treuly,   *thank*

Fore his gracious vesityng.   *visiting (i.e., by affliction)*
    Beware, seris, I youe pray,
Fore I mad this with good entent,
505   In the reverens of God Omnipotent.
Prays fore me that beth present —   *[those] who are*
    My name is Jon the Blynd Awdlay.

LATIN PROSE COLOPHON *FINITO LIBRO*   **[W18]**

Finito libro. Sit laus et gloria Christo. Liber vocatur Concilium conciencie, sic nominatur, aut Scala celi et vita salutis eterni. Iste liber fuit compositus per Johannem Awdelay, capellanum, qui fuit secus et surdus in sua visitacione, ad honorem Domini nostri Jhesu Christi et ad exemplum aliorum in monasterio de Haghmon. Anno Domini millesimo cccc visecimo vj. Cuius anime propicietur Deus.[1]

Amen.

---

[1] *The book is finished. Praise and glory be to Christ. The book is called The Counsel of Conscience, thus is it named, or The Ladder of Heaven and the Life of Eternal Salvation. This book was composed by John Audelay, chaplain, who was blind and deaf in his affliction, to the honor of our Lord Jesus Christ and to serve as a model for others in the monastery of Haughmond. In the year 1426 A.D. May God be propitious to his soul.* Compare *Audelay's Conclusion*, lines 39a and 52a.

XXVIII. DEVOTIONS TO JESUS AND MARY HIS MOTHER [W19]

Hic incipiunt salutaciones beate Marie virginis. Hic transire cave nisi primo dicis ave.[1]

"Sint semper sine ve qui michi dicit ave."[2]

SALUTATION TO JESUS FOR MARY'S LOVE [W19]

	Hayle, Maré, to thee I say,	
	Hayle, ful of grace, God is with thee.	
	Hale, blessid mot thou be, thou swete may,	*may; virgin*
	Hayle, among al wemen, so mot hit be.	
5	Hayle, blessid be the froyt of thi body.	*fruit*
	Hayle, the Holé Gost thee lyght withyn.	*alighted within thee*
	Hayle, the moder of Crist thou art trewly.	
	Hayle, thou bare swet Jhesus. Amen.	
	Hayle, mayd! Hayle, moder! Hayle, vergyn swete!	
10	*Hayle, grawnt ham the grace that thus con thee grete.*	*them; who*
	Hayle, mayd merceful. Hayle, fayryst of face.	*fairest*
	Hayle, ale our hope of help al hone.	*all one (i.e., whole)*
	Hayle, meke. Hayle, myld, myghtfulst of grace.	*mightiest*
	Hayle, solans and socur to synful mon.	*solace; help*
15	Hayle, vergyn. Hayle, moder to Crist Godis Son.	
	Hayle, ye dysservydyn, I say, honly,	*you alone deserve*
	To be a moder unknowyn to mon,	*unknown to man (i.e., a virgin)*
	Hayle, and to gef thi Sun sowke so mervesly.	*suck; marvelously*
	Hayle, mayd! Hayle, moder! Hayle, vergyn swete!	
20	*Hayle, grawnt ham thi grace that thus can thee grete.*	

---

[1] *Here begin salutations to the blessed virgin Mary. Take care not to pass by here without first saying "ave"*

[2] *"May they always be without woe who to me say 'ave.'"* This sentence contains a pun upon *sine ve* "without woe" and *ave/a ve* "hail"/"without woe."

Hayle, quene and empers of angelis ale.   *empress*
Hayle, cumfordor of wreschis, ywis.   *comforter; wretches, indeed*
Hayle, cumford me yif I in sorow fale,   *fall*
Hayle, fore my synns that styyng is.   *on account of my growing sins*
25   Hayle, socore me in al synnys.
Hayle, gif not thi worchip fro me away.   *take not thy esteem from me*
Haile, moder of mercé. Hayl, makeles.   *matchless [one]*
Hayle, quene of heven, I thee pray.
Hayle, maid and moder! Hayle, vergyn swete!
30   *Hayle, grawnt ham thi grace that thus gan thee grete.*

Hayle, gracyous lady. Excuse ye me
To Crist, thi Sune, thou swete may.
Hayle, I drede his wrath in hert hylé.   *greatly*
Hayle, I trembil fore fere both nyght and day.
35   Hayle, I have synyd to him, I say.
Hayle, vergyn Mary, wil not ye
Be wroth with me foreever and ay?   *angry*
Hayle, ful of hevenlé grace and of peté.   *compassion*
Hayle, mayd! Hayle, moder! Hayle, vergyn swete!
40   *Hayle, grawnt ham thi grace that thus con thee grete.*

Hayle, be ye keper of hert myn.   *heart*
Hayle, with dred of God marke ye me.
Hayle, gif me lyve of consians clene   *[a] life of clean conscience*
And ale moner of onesté.   *all manner of honesty*
45   Hayle, grawnt me grace my synnus to fle,
Hayle, fore to love al ryghtwysnes.   *righteousness*
Hayle, vergen swete, blest mot ye be.
Hayle, seche another was never, ne is.   *nor*
Hayle, maid! Hayle, moder! Hayle, vergyn swete!
50   *Hayle, grawnt ham thi grace that thus con thee grete.*

Hayle, among al wemen that ever were bore,
Hayle, thi Sun, Maker of al thyng,
Hayle, he ches thee his moder hom before.   *before them (i.e., all other women)*
Hayle, that Maré Mawdlen, that synful thyng,   *Mary Magdalene*
55   Hayle, he clansid here clene of here giltyng.   *cleansed; guilt*
Hayle, he me, throgh your prayere,   *he [may do so for] me*
He wype away al my synyng,
Hayle, fore love of thee, his moder dere.
Hayle, mayde! Haile, moder! Hayle, vergyn swete!
60   *Hayle, grawnt ham thi grace that thus con thee grete.*

Hayle, the rose without thorne.   *(i.e., either Mary or Christ)*
Hayle, medicyn of al our syne.
Hayle, pray the Sun of thee was borne,   *[who] of thee*

Hayle, he me save fro temptacion then.	
65 Hayle, of this word that wyckid ben	*world*
That steren me both nyght and day,	*steer*
Hayle, everé our to dedlé syn,	*hour*
Hayle, save me fro the Fyndis fray.	*Fiend's*
Hayle, mayd! Hayle, moder! Hayle, vergyn swete!	
70 *Hayle, grawnt ham thi grace that thus con thee grete.*	
Hayle, yif I fal throgh my frelté,	*frailty*
Haile, grawnt me grace to ryse anon.	
Haile, lest the Fynd, is myn enmy,	*[who] is*
Hayle, bryng me into disperacion.	*despair*
75 Hayle, grawnt me trew confession,	
Hayle, and veré repentans,	*true repentance*
Hayle, and ful satisfaccion,	
Hayle, and fore my synys to do penans.	
Haile, mayd! Haile, moder! Haile, vergyn swete!	
80 *Haile, grawnt ham thi grace that thus can thee grete.*	
Haile, lady, for thi Fyve Joys swete,	
Haile, thou hadist of thi dere Sune,	
Haile, when Gabryel con thee grete,	*did (i.e., Annunciation)*
Haile, and of his blisful burth ale one,	*birth all whole (i.e., Nativity)*
85 Haile, and of gloreus Resureccion,	
Haile, and of his Assencion mervely,	*miraculously*
Haile, and of the joyful Assumsioun,	*Assumption*
When angelis thee bere to heven on hie.	
Hayle, moder! Haile, maide! Haile, vergyn swete!	
90 *Haile, grawnt ham thi grace that thus can thee grete.*	
O Jhesu, fore these Joys Fyve,	
O Jhesu, thi moder had of thee,	
O Jhesu, that was both mayd and wyfe.	
O Jhesu, so was no mo bot che.	*none was so [honored] more than she*
95 O Jhesu, with al laudabeleté,	*laudability*
Thou crownd here quene, that blisful floure,	
O Jhesu, with alle onorabeleté,	*honorableness*
Within thi tabernakil in heven toure.	*tabernacle; heaven's tower*
O Jhesu, thi grace and thi mercy,	
100 *O Jhesu, fore thi moder love, mayde Mary!*	
O Jhesu, the Sun of the Fader on hye,	
O Jhesu, fore the love of thi moder,	
O Jhesu, that bere thee of here body,	*who bore*
O Jhesu, and fed thee with gret onour,	*honor*
105 O Jhesu, bere that blesful floure.	*flower (i.e., Mary)*
O Jhesu, our help to us ye be,	

O Jhesu, both solans and socour,   *solace*
O Jhesu, to the soulis in purgatori.
O Jhesu, thi grace and thi mercy,
110   *O Jhesu, fore thi moder love, mayde Mary!*

Thagh I be gilté, Lord, I thee pray,
O Jhesu, thou have mercé on me.
O Jhesu of mercé, have mercé I say.
O Jhesu, a Rewere foresoth bene ye.   *Dispenser of Mercy*
115   O Jhesu, my synys away do ye.
O Jhesu, clanse my hert within.
O Jhesu Crist of al peté,
O the Sun of God, have mercé then.
O Jhesu, thi grace and thi mercy,
120   *O Jhesu, fore the love of mayd Mari!*

And grawnt me stidfast hope and trew beleve,
O Jhesu, and parfid charité,   *perfect*
O Jhesu, and good endyng without repreve.   *disgrace*
O Jhesu, of al gifftis blest these be.
125   O Jhesu, yet more grawnt ye me
Fore the love of thi moder:
O Jhesu, in oure when we schul dye.   *hour*
O Jhesu, my soule that ye sokore.   *[may] succor*
O Jhesu, thi grace and thi mercy,
130   *O Jhesu, fore the love of thi moder Mari!*

O Jhesu, then clanse my herte within,
O Jhesu, my soule thou take to thee,
O Jhesu, that I may worthlé then,   *worthily*
O Jhesu, ressayve thi blessid body.   *receive*
135   O Jhesu, thi wrath greve hit not me.   *grieve me not with thy wrath*
O Jhesu, thi blod wasche me withyn,   *[with] thy blood*
Both bodé and soule, fore thi mercé,
O Jhesu, fro the fulthe of dedlé syn.   *filth*
O Jhesu, thi grace and thi mercé,
140   *O Jhesu, fore thi moder love, mayde Mary!*

O Jhesu, in that our that I schal dye,   *hour*
O Jhesu, my good angel to me cum.   *[let] my good angel*
O Jhesu, make him my keper be,
O Jhesu, to lede me to thi kyngdam.
145   O Jhesu, when deth my body hath slayne,
O Jhesu, the secounde deth toche not me,   *second death (i.e., damnation)*
When flesche and bons in erth rotyn.   *rot*
O Jhesu, my soule hit ryst with thee.   *[let] it rest*
O Jhesu, thi grace and thi mercé!

150   O Jhesu, when I schal ryse up thee to se,
         O Jhesu, at dredful Domysday,
         O Jhesu, me grawnt perpetualy
         Joy and blys foreever and ay!

         O thou moder of God, quene of heven, I say,
155   O thou lady of the word, of hele empers,   *world; empress of hell*
         O thou moder of mercé, I thee pray,
         Thou grawnt me part of paradyse!
         Hayle, maydyn! Haile, moder! Haile, vergyn swete!
         Hayle, grawnt ham the grace that thus con thee grete.

PRAYER RUBRIC   [W19]

         I pray thee, Fadur Omnipotent,
         Graunt mercy tofore thy Jugement,
         And alle that don yow here servyse,   *who give you their worship*
         Thou graunt hom part of paradyse.   *them*

PRAYER ON THE JOYS OF THE VIRGIN   [W19]

         O allmyghty God everlastynglé,   *everlastingly*
         For holy Gabryel salutacion,
         And for thy blesful Nativité,
         And for thy gloryouse Resurexcion,
5   And for thy merveles Ascencion,
         And for the Assumpcion of oure Ladye,
         And for thes Joyes and Coronacion
         That Mary, thy modur, heo had of thee,   *she*
         For heere love to us, graunt ye   *her*
10   To have forgevenes of oure syn,
         And from alle sorowes delyvered to be,
         And to have everlastyng joyes. Amen.

INSTRUCTIONS FOR PRAYER 8   [W19]

         Wel ys hym that wil and may
         Say this prayere every day.

XXIX. OTHER DEVOTIONS TO MARY   **[W20–W21]**

SALUTATION TO MARY   **[W20]**

Alia oracio de Sancta Maria virgine.   *Another prayer concerning the Blessed Virgin Mary*

	Haile, the fayrst ther ever God fond.	*created*
	Haile, maid and moder. Haile, mayd fre.	
	Hayle, the floure of Josep wand.	
	Hayle, the froyte of Jesse.	
5	Hayle, blossum that our bale unbonde.	
	Haile, mans bot was borne of thee.	*remedy*
	Haile, our beleve in thee can stonde	
	Whan Crist was raght on rode-tre.	*stretched out*
	Hayle, rose on ryse. Haile, lellé.	*branch; lily*
10	Hayle, swet, swettist of savore.	
	Hayle, hygh princes of peté.	*princess*
	Haile, blessid froyt! Haile, swet floure!	

	Haile, tabirnakil the Trewth con tyelde.	*did build*
	Haile, garden ther grace gan spryng.	*where; did*
15	Haile, scheltyrne schours to schyelde.	*shelter to shield [one] from showers*
	Hayle, bryghtnes ever-chynyng.	*ever-shining*
	Haile, yonketh that never schal yilde.	*youth; yield (i.e., grow old)*
	Haile, beuté ever-duryng.	*beauty everlasting*
	Haile, thi Barne in blis thi boure cun bilde.	*Child; bower did build*
20	Haile, grace and goodnes ever-growyng.	
	Haile, fresche and no fadyng.	
	Haile, of Charité the paramour.	
	Haile, Love. Haile, Leche. Haile, hie Kyng.	
	Haile, blessid froyt! Haile, swet flour!	

25	Haile, prayerys of the postilis alle.	*prayers; apostles*
	Haile, the martyrs gladenes.	
	Hayle, comford confessours on to calle.	*comfort [of]; upon [which we can] call*
	Haile, of vergyns the clennes.	*cleanness*
	Haile, the Sun that ever chyne schale.	*shine*
30	Haile, maide of worchip makeles.	*matchless*
	Haile, of worthénes the walle.	*worthiness*
	Haile, perseverens of holénes.	
	Haile, moder to the norcheles.	*unnurtured*
	Haile, to the synful mon socore.	*succor*
35	Haile, moder to the helples.	
	Haile, blest froyt! Ayle, swete flour!	

	Haile, quene of hevenryche blis.	*blissful kingdom of heaven*
	Haile, ladé of this worde wide.	*world*

Haile, of hel the hy emperes.   *high empress*
40   Haile, fallere of the Fyndis pryde.   *conqueror*
Haile, the joy of paradise,
Thi wil schal never be denyed.
Haile, angelis done thee servyse.   *do worship thee*
Haile, perré patrearkis to gyde.   *jewel to guide patriarchs*
45   Haile, dissire prestis to abyde.   *awaited desire of priests*
Haile, silour of our Saveour.   *shelter*
Haile, pardun throgh whom our pes is criud.   *peace; declared*
Haile, blessid froyt! Haile, swete flour!

Haile, solans to ham that bene sory.   *solace to those who are penitent*
50   Haile, to ertekes — a, waiful wyght! —   *heretics; ah, woeful creature*
Haile, help to hom that ben gulté.   *them*
Haile, hope to thayme that grace is dyght.   *for [whom] grace is prepared*
Hale, wel of worchip and mercé.   *well*
Haile, thi peté on us thou pyght.   *[have] set*
55   Haile, thou bildist ful beselé   *nurture; busily*
To al that leven here in thi myght.   *believe*
Haile, bussche. Hayl, blase brenyng bryght,   *bush; blaze burning*
Yet was not blemyschid thi colour.   *blemished*
Haile, berel the blynd to lyght.   *beryl; illuminate*
60   *Haile, blest froyte! Haile, swete flour!*

Ryght as the lelé is freschist in hew,   *lily; freshest*
Haile, beuté passeth, as maydyns clene,   *beauty [that] surpasses [all], as [do] pure virgins*
Haile, so, vergyn, vertu and trew.   *virtuous*
Thou worchipist alle that ever han bene.   *honor (i.e., fulfill)*
65   Haile, the Olde Law and the New
Opon thiselve hit was sene —
Was never bot ye that monkynd knew   *Mankind never knew anyone but you*
Too bere a child, and maide clene!   *[remain] clean*
Haile, deystere. Haile, saver chene.   *daystar; lovely savor*
70   Haile, diamand delycious of odour.
Haile, ryal rebé. Haile, crownyd quene.   *ruby*
Haile, blessid froyt! Haile, swete floure!

Haile, onex. Haile, olif. Haile, vyne vertuys.   *onyx; olive; virtuous vine*
Haile, the rose without thorne.
75   Haile, gresse on growND most gloreous.   *grass (or herb)*
Haile, bryghtter then sun on somyr morowe.   *summer morning*
Haile, gude gladlé. Haile, gracious.   *[one who is] gladly good*
Haile, hert that with a swerd was chorne.   *cut [see Luke 2:35]*
Haile, Joseps wyf. Haile, Joseps spous.   *Joseph's*
80   Haile, thi Breder thou hast eborene.   *Brother; borne*
Was never non seche beforen,
Moder and maid us to honour.   *[for] us*

Haile, helpe to hom that were forelorne.
Haile, blist froyt! Haile, swet floure!

85   Haile, chif chosyn charbokil stone.   *choicest carbuncle*
      Haile, ryal rygal, thi reme to lyght.   *royal regal [one]; realm*
      Haile, athamond that God and Mon   *adamant (i.e., diamond)*
      Thou drew into thi blessid bodé bryght.
      Haile, lyghter of lymbo, were never sun chone,   *illuminator; where; shone*
90   Bot darker then the myrke mydnyght.   *darker (referring to limbo); murky*
      Haile, glader of Adam and moné mo   *gladdening source for*
      That to damnacion thai were dyght —   *set*
      Fyve thousand yere thai se never syght,   *saw*
      Lyyng in longyng in here langure —   *languishing*
95   Abydyng, in grace, thi mekil myght.   *Awaiting*
      Haile, blest froyt! Haile, swet flour!

      Thus, haile to thee, thi Sun to send,
      With haile, myghtfulst of grace.   *most mightily full*
      This word hit may not comprehend,   *world*
100 Fore of thi body borne he was!
      Haile, medycyne that ale may mend.
      Haile, kever in everé case.   *shelter*
      Haile, tapere that ever is tent.   *taper; tended to*
      Haile, lamp lyghtand in everé place.
105 Hayle, most fayryst of fygure and face.
      Haile, tabyrnakil of heven toure.   *tabernacle*
      Hayle, moder of mercé withouton manse.   *abode*
      Hayle, blessid froyt! Hayl, swete floure!

      These halowne — al the sayntis in heven,   *These [ones sing] praise*
110 Angelis, patrearchis, and prophet,
      The postilis al, with marters steven,   *martyrs' voices*
      The confessours, with vergyns swete —
      Al that was made in days seven!   *(i.e., all of creation)*
      Us aght thee love, love of Grete.   *We should love thee, beloved [one] of Great [God]*
115 When hellis and dalis thai schal be even,   *hills; dales*
      Ther bodé and soule in fere schal met.   *Where; together; meet*
      When Jhesu schal schew his wondis wete,   *bloody*
      Maré, thou be our mayne-paroure,   *legal surety*
      With these sayntis to have a sete.
120 *Her haile, blest froyt! Haile, swete flour!*

      Explicitur.   *The end*

GABRIEL'S SALUTATION TO THE VIRGIN   **[W21]**

Hec salutacio composuit angelus Gabrielus.   *The angel Gabriel composed this salutation*

     The angel to the vergyn said,
       Entreng into here boure,   *bower*
     Fore drede of quakyng of this mayd,   *trembling*
       He said, "Haile," with gret honour.   [see Luke 1:28]
5   "Haile be thou, quene of maidyns mo.
          Lord of heven and erth also
            Consayve thou schal,
            And bere withale
              The Lord of myght,
10   Hele of al monkyn.   *Health; mankind*
        He wil make thee the gate of heven bryght,
          Medesyne of al our syn."   *Medicine*

     "How schuld I consayve and gete?   *get [with child]*
       No syn never I knew.   [see Luke 1:34]
15   How schuld I breke that I have forehete   *break what I have contracted*
       Of thought stedfast and trewe?"
         "The grace al of the Holé Gost   *entirely* [see Luke 1:35]
         Schal bryng ale forth, without boost.
           Ne drede thou take,
20   Bot joy thou make,
              Serten and sere.   *Certain and sure*
       This message he send to thee,
       To dwel withyn thee ful pere   *pure*
         Throgh myght of his Fader fre."   *generous*

25   The angel went this ladé fro.   *departed from this lady*
       This womons wombe with wele   *happily*
    Hit wax gret, as odur do,   *others*
       This blessid burthe of hele.   *health (i.e., salvation)*
       He was in here wome, I wene,   *think*
30   The nombur ful of monethis nene.   *nine months*
         Hent he outyed,   *Until he emerged*
         Batelis bede   *[And] battles commanded*
           To al the floke,   *flock [of followers]*
       Beryng on his chulderis bloo   *shoulders [black and] blue*
35   The holé cros that kene a knok   *gave a keen knock*
         Unto oure dedly Foo.

     Thys may bare Chyelde with mylde chere;   *maiden bore; sweet demeanor*
       This Chylde bede kepe hyer chaast.   *promised to keep her chaste*
     Goddus Sone heo broght us forthe and bere,   *she brought forth [for] us and bore*
40   Geffing hym wombe and waast.   *Giving; waist*

Then he blessud here sydus sere,   *womb affording safety*
And so he ded here pappus dere,   *dear breasts*
    For thay ber that
    Thay nyst nott hwat
45   In law, as we fyende.
And so he ded here pappus dere,
How these werkus wroght arne,
Hit was agaynes al monkynde —
    A maydon to ber a barne!

Make joy, modir of oure Lorde,
50   That Cryst concevedust cleene;   *Who; chastely*
Angelus, men, and al this worlde,
   God, pes and rest us leene!   *loan*
    Mary, thy Son thou for us pray,   *[to] thy Son*
    As ye beth ful of mercy ay,
55   And send us to,
      And soo to do
       Away oure syn,
   And gef us helpe of thee,
   Heven blys we may dwel in
60   Afftur thys owtlary.   *outlawry (i.e., life outside God's law)*

Explicitur.   *The end*

XXX. SONG OF THE MAGNIFICAT   [W22]

Hic incipit psalmus de Magnificat.[1]

"My soule, my Lorde hit mangnefyth,"
Our lady thus to here Sun con say.   *her Son did say*
"Fore he me here gloryfyd,
To be his moder, vergyn and may;
5 He hath me chosyn — hit is no nay —
To lyver his pepil fro thraldam.   *deliver; servitude*
Mangneficat, herefore I say,
Anima mea Dominum.   *My soul doth magnify the Lord* [Luke 1:46]

"My speryt hit joys in my God;   *rejoices*
10 He is my hele, my sustynans,   *health; sustenance*
That is so graceous and so good;
He hath me prevelid to his plesans,   *prevailed upon; liking*
Fore to make delyverans
Of al that before our fader Adam

---

[1] *Here begins the song of Magnificat.* This poem paraphrases and expands Luke 1:46–55.

15 Had cast into cumbyrrans.   *debt*
  Mangnificat anima mea Dominum.

  "Fore the makenes of his mayd he hath behold: *meekness; beheld (and said)*
  'Lo, herefore, forsoth I say,
  Me schul worchip you, yong and hold,   *Men shall honor; old*
20 Al generacons in uche cuntré,
  That I was boren, hit is no nay,
  Into this word that I come.'   *world*
  Now '*mangefygat*,' syng thai mai.
  Anima mea Dominum.

25 "Fore he hath made me gret throgh his pouere — *pregnant; power*
  Forewy al myght in him hit is —   *Because*
  And his holé name, when I him bere
  To bryng his pepul unto his blis.
  With his precious blod, iwys,
30 He hath here payd heere rawnson,   *their ransom*
  Fore to amend the ded mys.   *misdeed*
  Mangneficat anima mea Dominum.

  "For now his mercé is knowyn ful wyde
  Throgh generacions in uche cuntré —   *every country*
35 To al that dreden hym, on uche a syde,
  And sechen his grace and his mercé,   *seek*
  And kepe here stat and here degré,   *estate*
  And to his lauys thay bene buxum,   *laws; obedient*
  The ayrs of heven, foresoth, thay be!   *heirs*
40 *Mangneficat anima mea Dominum.*

  "His myght has made, in his pouere,
  Proud men to sparpil from his face   *scatter*
  With the mynd of his hert, fere and nere;
  That nyl not seche mercé and grace,   *[They] that will not seek*
45 Ne hem amend wile thai han space,   *Nor amend themselves*
  Thai schul be cast fro his kyngdam,
  And have no part within that place.
  Magnificat anima mea Dominum.

  "Thenke on Kyng Robart Sesel: *Robert of Sicily*
50 He went no lord had be bot he,   *thought; [ever] existed*
  Yet sodenlé downe he felle
  And was put into a folis degré!   *fool's position*
  An angel was set apon his se,   *throne*
  Fore he had these verse in his scornyng — *had scorned this verse*

55   *Deposuit potentis de sede*[1] —
            And sayd in heven ther was no Kyng.

            "Thus myghté men God pittis ful loue,   *puts very low*
            And meke men he liftis ful hye,   *meek*
            That his grace and his goodnes here wil knowe,
60   And seche his grace and his mercé,
            And no nother sekyrly —   *no other certainly*
            At the dredful Day of Dome,
            Here dedis schal deme ham hopynly.   *openly*
            Mangneficat anima mea Dominum.

65   "The pore and hongré he had fulfillid
            With his grace and his goodnes,
            And ryche men, he am revylid,   *reviled them*
            And let ham ly in here lewdnes,   *them lie; ignorant ways*
            That trustyn al in hor reches   *riches*
70   And not in the joy that is to cum —
            Thai schal have seche here as thai ches.   *choose*
            Mangneficat anima mea Dominum.

            "Fore he hath takyn up Yrael,   *Israel*
            That is child of ryghtwysnes;   *righteousness*
75   In recordacion he had everé dele,   *he remembered [them] in every way*
            His grace, is mercé, and his goodnes,   *[With] his*
            Fore thagh he fel throgh freelnes,   *they; frailty*
            He hath foregifyn ham, al and sum,
            And schal have that blis that is endles.   *[they] shall*
80   *Mangneficat anima mea Dominum.*

            "Ryght as our fader Abraam   *Abraham*
            Had spokyn to our Fader beforne,
            And to al the sede that com fro ham,   *seed*
            To multepli ham foreevermore,
85   Fore was never mon yet here forelorne
            In his defawte in Cresendam;   *lack; Christianity*
            Into his kyndam he wyl ham restore.   *kingdom*
            Mangnificat anima mea Dominum.

            "Now joy be to the Fader and to the Sun
90   And to the Holé Gost, al thre efere,   *together*
            That in the word of wordis togeder thai won,   *forever and ever; dwell*
            That is now and was and schal be ever,
            In wom hit is now al pouere,   *whom it; power*
            Mercé, grace, al wit, wysdam,

---

[1] *He hath put down the mighty from their seat.* Luke 1:52.

95   That is that Prynce without pere.
        Mangneficat anima mea Dominum."

        "Mangneficat," our ladi thus can say
        To here Sun both leve and dere;   *beloved and dear*
        Blessid mot heo be, that swete may,   *may she*
100   And that berthe when heo him bere!   *birth*
        Heo graunt us grace in our prayoure
        Here to worshyp with hert gladsum,   *gladsome*
        With *"mangnifycat,"* wen we ben here,   *when*
        "Anima mea Dominum."

        Explicitur.   *The end*

XXXI. SALUTATION TO SAINT BRIDGET   [W23]

Hic incipit salutacio Sancte Brigitte virginis et quomodo Dominus Jhesu Christus apparuit illi corporaliter et dedit illi suam benedictionem quod Awdelay.[1]

        Hayle, maydyn and wyfe, hayle, wedow Brygytt,   *widow*
        Hayle, thou chese to be chast and kepe charyté.   *chose*
        Hayle, thi special spouse kyndlé to thee knyt,   *joined*
        Hayle, he consentyd to the same by concel of thee   *counsel*
5   To be relegyous.
           Hayle, fore the love of Jhesus Crist,
           Ye foresake your fleschelé lust —
           Therfore be ye both eblest
              In the name of swete Jhesus!

10   Haile, the moder of God to thee con apere.   *did appear*
        Haile, he told thee of his Passion and of his spetus payne.   *she; cruel*
        Haile, ye wepit fore wo togeder when ye were,
        Haile, for his dolful deth that so was eslayne.   *who; slain*
           Our Ladé to thee gan say:
15   "Hayle, blessid Bregit, let be the tere,   *cease crying*
           And thonke my Sun fore his deth dere,
           That has egeven thee powere   *given*
             To be wyfe, wedow, and may."   *maiden*

        Haile, seche a kyndlé coupil can no mon herekyn.   *natural; hear of*
20   Hayle, ye foresoke reches and ryal aray.
        Hayle, ye hopid hilé in your hert then,   *hoped fervently*
        Hayle, al the worchip of this word wol sone wynd away *world; pass*

---

[1] *Here begins a salutation to Saint Bridget, virgin, and how the Lord Jesus Christ appeared to her physically and gave her his blessing, says Audelay*

Within a lytil stownd.   *while*
Haile, this wordlé honour,
25   Hit fallis and fadis as a flour;
Today is fresche in his colour;   *[he who] is*
Tomorow he gyrdis to grownd.   *dashes to ground*

Hayle, ye betoke your tresour to the Trineté,   *took*
Fore he is trusté and trew without treynyng.   *trustworthy; deceit*
30   Hayle, he dissayvyd never no soule with no sotelté,   *deceived; trickery*
Hayle, faythfullé, that ye fond at your endyng,   *you were found faithful until death*
The sothe fore to say!   *truth*
Hayle, other tresoure have we noght,
Out of this word when we be broght,   *world*
35   Bot good word, wil, dede, and thoght,
When we schuld wynd away.   *shall*

Hayle, with these four feythfully ye boght youe heven blis,
With good word, wil, dede, and thoght, to obey Godis bidyng.
Hayle, with the werkis of mercé ye geten you mede, iwis.[1]
40   Haile, ye foresoken flesschelé lust, the Fend, false covetyng,
That were your thre enmys.
Haile, thai settyn al here sotelté
Houe mons soule thai mow dystré,   *destroy*
With pride, lechory, and glotonye,
45   And cursid covetyse.   *avarice*

Haile, blessid Bregid fore thi benyngneté,   *mildness*
Haile, the perles Prynce to thee con apere.   *peerless; did appear*
Haile, he grownded thee in grace in thi vergeneté.   *virginity*
Haile, spesialy he speke with thee oft in thi prayere.
50   Haile, to the pope he thee send
Fore to grawnt thee his special grace,   *grace*
And to al that vesid thi holy plase,   *visit*
To assoyle ham of here trespas,   *absolve*
That here mysdedis wol amend.   *their misdeeds*

55   Haile, he bed thee bild a plas o relygion,   *bid you to build a place of*
Haile, blessid Bregid, fere fro oné plase: *far*
"Haile, to Pope Urban, to Rome, thou shalt goon,   *Pope Urban [V]*
That is my veker in erth to grawnt thee his grace,   *vicar*
To have the same pardon
60   That is in Peters Cherche at Rome,
To al the pilgrems that to thee cum,
That vesid thee in Cristis name,
To have playn remyssion."   *complete remission*

---

[1] *Hail, with the works of mercy you obtained reward [for] yourself, surely*

Haile, he said: "Yif that pope wil grawnt thee no grace

65   Without moné or mede, becawse of covetys,   *money or fee*

Haile, the Fader of Heven schal prevelege thi place.   *sanctify*

Haile, I schal conferme thi bul that above him is,[1]

      That schal he yknow.

Haile, my moder my sele schal be,   *my mother shall be my seal*

70   My witnes al the sayntis of heven on hye,

My blessyng the Holé Gost I betake to thee.

      The pope schal lout ful low."   *bow*

Haile, to that perles prelat, to the pope when thou come,   *peerless prelate*

Haile, thou mendist thi mesage in a meke manere.   *mentioned*

75   Haile, faythfulli that fader ful reverenly at Rome,

Haile, he welcumd thee worthelé with a wonder chere   *worthily; wondrous demeanor*

      Into that holé place.

"Haile," he said with myld steven,   *voice*

"Welcum be ye fro the Kyng of Heven;

80   Now blessid be thai that in thee leven,   *believe*

      That ever thou borne was.

"Haile, mervelus maide ful of mekenes.

Haile, helé the Holé Gost is lyght thee within.   *miraculously; alighted*

Haile, God hath grouned thee gemfulli in his goodnes.   *crowned you with gems*

85   Haile, to be saver of soulis and seser of syn,   *destroyer*

      Be his ordenans.   *ordinance*

Haile, I grawnt to al remyssioun

That chryven hem clene with contrichon,   *Who confess (shrive) themselves*

And wil do here satisfaccion;

90   I reles here penans.   *release [them from] their penance*

"Haile, to al that worthely vesetyn the holé place.

Haile, that sechen thi socor, schal have salvacion.   *seek the succor*

Haile, fore sake of that Sofren that thee to me send had.   *Sovereign*

Haile, in reverens of that Lord I grawnt hem remyssion

95   Of al here trespace.

Haile, to thi pilgrems perpetualy

That worchipen thi place graciously

With prayers, selver, gold, lond of fe,   *land rents*

      I grawnt ham this special grace."

100   "Now, gramarcé, gracious fader, of your blessyng I you pray."   *grant mercy*

"Mi blessid suster Bregit, my blessyng gif I thee;   *sister; give*

Here I graunt thee this grace, specialy I say,

Withowton moné or mede, I make hit to thee fre,   *freely*

      This special pardoun:

---

[1] *Hail, I shall confirm your status by bull that supersedes the pope's*

105	To al the pilgrems fer and nere	*far and near*
	That vesityn thi place in good manere,	*visit*
	To here gostelé fader I grawnt pouere	*spiritual father (i.e., priest); power*
	To asoyle ham, everechon.	*absolve them, every one*

	"Haile, to that pereles Prynce, Bregit, fore me pray,	
110	That hath groundid thee in grace and is thi Governoure.	*Governor*
	Haile, my blessid doghter, thi blessidnes hit may	
	At the day of my deth my soule then socour;	
	And gif me wil and wit	
	Mi mysdedis here to amend,	
115	Out of this word or that I wynd.	*depart*
	To the Treneté I thee recomend.	
	Farewel, blessid Breget."	

Thus the pope prevelegd here place and haloud hit to Cristis entent.[1]

	Anon hure holé husband a covennt to him con take,	*her devout; convent*
120	And Bregit mad here of maydyns another blest covent,[2]	
	That foresoke here fleschlé lust fore Jhesu Cristis sake,	
	In the name of the Treneté.	
	Thus thai disceverd hem to —	*separated themselves*
	Hure husbond to his bredern con go,	
125	And to hure susteres heo whent him fro	*she went*
	To leve in chastité.	*live*

	Haile, thus this perles prelat fro thee passid away,	*peerless prelate (i.e., Pope Urban)*
	When he with his benyngneté had geven thee his blessyng.	*holy manner*
	Haile, at the day of our deth that settis no day,	*happens on no determined day*
130	Haile, then, blessid Bregit, our soulis to blis bryng,	
	And graunt us thi special grace	
	In erth that we mowe werchip thee;	
	After in heven we may thee se,	
	In joi and blis perpetualy,	
135	Within that blisful place.	

	Beside the Chene, sothly, seven myle fro Lundun,	*Sheen (now Richmond, in Surrey)*
	Our gracious Kyng Herré the V wes founder of that place.	*Henry V*
	Haile, he let prevelege that holé place and callid hit Bregit Sion.	
	The pope conferme therto to his bul throgh his special grace,[3]	
140	In the worchip of Saint Bregit,	
	To al here pilgrems an Lammes Day,	*(August 1)*

---

[1] *Thus the pope sanctified her place and hallowed it to Christ's purpose*

[2] *And Bridgit made herself of nuns another blessed convent*

[3] Lines 138–39: *Hail, he granted royal dispensation to that holy place and called it Bridget Syon (i.e., Syon Abbey). / The pope confirmed that by papal bull through his special grace*

And also Myd-Lentyn Sunday,
This pardon to last foreyever and ay.
   God graunt us part of hit.

145 Mekil is al Ynglan ihold to pray for Kyng Herré,[1]
That so worthelé our worchip in everoche place,   *worthily [deserves]*
Both in Fraunce and in Breten and in Normandy,   *Brittainy*
That our faders had lost before he get agayn be grace;
   And, moreover, speciali,
150 To make soche a house of relegioun,   *such*
And to preveleche therto that gracious pardon,   *privilege [it]; [by] that*
Al Ynglond to have remyssioune.   *[So that] all England [might] have*
   Now Crist on his soule have mercé.

Was never a holeer order preveleged in no plas   *holier; place*
155 Fore to red al the rollis of relegyown,   *read; rolls of religioun*
Fore thai schal never schew no chappe ny fygure of face,[2]
Ne without lycence or leve, speche speke thai non,   *permission; speech speak*
   Bot the warden be present.   *Unless*
Nother fader ne moder, ne no mon levyng,
160 Schal speke to hom no erthlé thyng,   *any earthly thing*
Without the warden be ther hereng,   *there [within] hearing*
   And know both here entent.   *their*

Redlé thei rysun with gret reverens onethus out of hure rest,[3]
Devoutelé with devocion here servys to syng and say,   *Devoutly*
165 And crucefyen here caren and slen here fleschelé lust,   *mortify their flesh; slay; desire*
With prevé prayers and penans the Prynce of Heven to pay,   *private; satisfy*
   Devotlé day and nyght.
Thai prayn to God specialy
Fore al that thai here levyng be,   *all who live here [on earth]*
170 In masse, in matyns, in memoré,
   To that Lord of myght.

Fore hit fars noght be gostelé goodis as doth be temperale —
The men that han part therof so lasse is uche dole,[4]
Bot he that delis gostlé goodis, hit is so spiritual,   *But when he (i.e., God) doles out*
175 That uche mon that hath his part hath fullé the hole.   *each; has fully the whole*
   Ensampil chul ye se: *Example shall*
Alse moné men as may here a mas,   *many; mass*

---

[1] *All England is much obliged to pray for King Henry [V's soul]*

[2] *For they shall never show nor depict an image of a face*

[3] *Readily they arise with great reverence scarcely out of their sleep*

[4] Lines 172–73: *For it fares not by spiritual goods as [it] does by temporal — / [As when] men possess a part of it, each portion is less*

	Uche mon his parte holé he has,	*wholly*
	And yet the masse is never the lasce,	*less*
180	Bot so more of dyngneté.	*But [instead is] so much greater in dignity*

	Pray we to God specialy to save that spiritual plas,	*place (i.e., Syon Abbey)*
	That thai obey obedyans that thay be bound to;	*religious vows*
	Fore thay may throgh here precious prayoure purches here our grace,	*purchase*
	Have we never in this word wroght so moche wo —	*created so much woe*
185	Thai han that pouere —	*power*
	Fore al that here wele done,	*[have] done well*
	Crist wil graunt hem here bone,	*request*
	Thai wot never hou sone	*know; soon*
	He hers here prayere.	*hears*

	Crist that was crucefid on cros, and cround with thorne,	
190	And ched his blesful blod fore oure syns sake,	*shed; blessed*
	Let never this worthé lond, Lord, be forelorne,	
	Bot puttis doune here pouere that werris wil awake,[1]	
	And sese al males.	*cease all malice*
195	Fore yong Kyng Herré now we pray,	*Henry VI*
	That Crist him kepe both nyght and day,	
	And let never traytor him betray,	
	And send us rest and pes.	

	Al that redis reverenly this remyssioune,	*read*
200	Prays to blisful Bregit, that merceful may,	*Pray*
	Fore hom that mad this mater with dewocion,	*him who made*
	That is both blynd and def, the synful Audelay.	
	I pray youe, specialy,	
	Fore I mad this with good entent,	
205	In the reverens of this vergyn, verement,	*truly*
	Heo graunt youe grace, that beth present,	*She*
	To have joy and blis perpetualy. Amen.	

XXXII. Devotions to Saint Winifred   [W24–W25]

Saint Winifred Carol   [W24]

| | *Wenefrede, thou swete may,* | *maiden* |
| | *Thow pray for us bothe nyght and day.* | |

| | As thou were marter and mayd clene, | *martyr; virgin* |
| | Therfor thou hadist turment and tene; | *trouble* |

---

[1] *But remove here the power of those who wars will awake*

A princes love thou myghtis have bene,   *prince's*
   A lady of ryal aray.   *royal*
5   Wenefrede, thou swete may,
   Thow pray for us bothe nyght and day.

Bot to that syn thou woldist noght sent;   *assent*
To kepe thee chast was thyn entent,
Therfore of Cradoc thou wast echent;   *by Caradoc; disgraced*
10   Anon he thoght thee to betray.
    Wenefrede, thou swete may,
   Thow pray for us bothe nyght and day.

He was ful cursid and cruel,
And dred not God ne no parel;   *peril*
15 Smot of thi hede; thou knelist ful stil;   *Smote off your head; quietly*
    Hit ran into a dry valay.   *It rolled; valley*
    Wenefrede, thou swete may,
   Thow pray for us bothe nyght and day.

Then Bewnou, thin unkul, with gret peté,   *Beuno; uncle; compassion*
20 Set thi hede to thi body;   *Reconnected*
Thou levedust after merwesly   *lived afterwards miraculously*
    Fiftene yere — hit is no nay!
    Wenefrede, thou swete may,
   Thow pray for us bothe nyght and day.

25 About thi nek hit was esene,
The stroke of the swerd that was so kene,   *keen*
A thred of perle as hit had bene,   *thread of pearl*
    Hit besemyd thee wel, sothlé to say.   *complemented; truly*
    Wenefrede, thou swete may,
30   Thow pray for us bothe nyght and day.

When Cradoc han don this cursid dede,
The erth him swoloud in that stede;   *swallowed; place*
The foyre of hel hit was his mede,   *fire; reward*
    Therin to be foreever and ay!
35   Wenefrede, thou swete may,
   Thow pray for us bothe nyght and day.

A wonderful wel ther sprong anon —   *fountain*
Seche on se never Cristyn mon! —   *Such a one saw*
Thi blod was sparpild on everé stone;   *spattered*
40   No water myght wasche hit away.   *might wash*
    Wenefrede, thou swete may,
   Thow pray for us bothe nyght and day.

Ther ben mesis at that wel,   *mosses*

That bene swete and sote of smel,   *fragrant*

45   And yet ther is a more marvel —   *a greater marvel*

    Hevenlé bryddis in numerus aray!   *Heavenly birds in immense numbers*

    Wenefrede, thou swete may,

    Thow pray for us bothe nyght and day.

Be the streme of that fayre wel   *By*

50   Ther went a myl-wele, as I you tel;   *mill wheel*

Hit bere down a child with gret parel;   *bore down a child [who fell in]; peril*

    The wele stod stil, might not away.   *mill wheel stood still*

    Wenefrede, thou swete may,

    Thow pray for us bothe nyght and day.

55   Then the moder cryd out and yeld: *yelled*

"Alas, my child! He is spillid!"   *killed*

Be the ladlis he him huld,   *floatboards of the waterwheel; held*

    And logh and mad gomun and play.   *laughed and made [it a] game*

    Wenefrede, thou swete may,

60   Thow pray for us bothe nyght and day.

A mon, a grote downe he felle   *groat (i.e., a coin); dropped*

Out of his hond into the well;

He se hit then al other wel;   *[in] another well*

    Thai myght not tak the grote away.

65   Wenefrede, thou swete may,

    Thow pray for us bothe nyght and day.

Also ther was a gret marvel;

Wyne was couchid in here chapel;   *stored; her (i.e., Winifred's)*

The wel stod styl, ran never a del;   *fountain*

70   Hit trobild as hit had bene with clay.   *grew muddy*

    Wenefrede, thou swete may,

    Thow pray for us bothe nyght and day.

Ther was no fuyre, treulé to tele,   *fire*

Myght hete the water of the wel,   *heat*

75   To seth ne dyght no vetel,   *boil nor prepare any food*

    Wile that wyne in that chapil lay.   *While*

    Wenefrede, thou swete may,

    Thow pray for us bothe nyght and day.

Then thai west wel afyne   *knew; finally*

80   Of Wynfryd hit was a syne;   *sign*

Anon thai hurled out the wyne

    Into the stret, on dele way.   *every bit away*

    Wenefrede, thou swete may,
    Thow pray for us bothe nyght and day.

85   Anon a merekel fel in that plas;   *miracle; place*
    A mon of that wyne enpoysund was,
    That was savyd throgh Godis grace,
        And Wynfryd, that holé may.
    Wenefrede, thou swete may,
90   Thow pray for us bothe nyght and day.

    Anon this wel began to clere;   *clear*
    The streme ran forth as hit dede ere;   *did before*
    The plumys thai mad a hedus bere,   *plumes; head's gesture*
        When thai began to play.   *operate*
95   Wenefrede, thou swete may,
    Thow pray for us bothe nyght and day.

    Fore ye chuld make no marchandyse   *should; business transaction*
    In Holé Cherche in no wyse;
    God himselve he ded dispyse,
100   And drof hom forth in here aray.   *drove them (i.e., the moneylenders) out*
    Wenefrede, thou swete may,
    Thow pray for us bothe nyght and day.

    Fore hit is a house of prayore,   [see Mark 11:15–17]
    Hold hilé to Godis honour,   *Conducted reverently*
105   To worchip therin our Saveour
        With mas, matens, nyght and day.   *mass, matins*
    Wenefrede, thou swete may,
    Thow pray for us bothe nyght and day.

    Ther hath be botynd moné a mon,   *have been healed*
110   Blynd and crokid, that myght not gon,   *lame*
    Seke and sorouful, moné hone,   *many a one*
        Ther at that wel there hur heed lay.   *where her head*
    Wenefrede, thou swete may,
    Thow pray for us bothe nyght and day.

115   Then Wynfred anon chorun che was,   *soon chosen she*
    Echosun fore chefe to be abbas,   *Chosen as leader; abbess*
    Fol of vertu and of grace,   *Full*
        And servyd God both nyght and day.
    Wenefrede, thou swete may,
120   Thow pray for us bothe nyght and day.

    Then Bewnow toke his leve anon,   *took his leave*
    And betoke here this tokyn: *gave her*

"Over the se schal swem a stone   *sea; swim*
    To bryng vestementus — ther ys noo nay!"   *holy vestments*
125   Wenefrede, thou swete may,
    Thow pray for us bothe nyght and day.

"Yif that stone abyde with thee,   *remains*
Then wit wel that I schal dye;   *know well*
God of my soule he have mercy;
130   Have mynde on me then, I thee pray."   *thee (i.e., Winifred)*
    Wenefrede, thou swete may,
    Thow pray for us bothe nyght and day.

Then Wenfred heo knelid adowne,   *she*
And toke mekelé his benesoune;   *received meekly; blessing*
135   This monke he toke his way anon
    Over the se to his abbay.
    Wenefrede, thou swete may,
    Thow pray for us bothe nyght and day.

When that Bewnew he was dede,
140   The ston styl with here hit levyd;   *remained*
Then anon heo prayud,
    He schul pas on his chornay.   *[That] he; journey*
    Wenefrede, thou swete may,
    Thow pray for us bothe nyght and day.

145   Son after Wenefred heo dyid then,
At Shrosberé men dedon here schryne;   *Shrewsbury; established her shrine*
Moné a merakil ther hath be syne,   *miracle; seen*
    Of dyvers pepul in fer cuntré.   *By diverse people from many countries*
    Wenefrede, thou swete may,
150   Thow pray for us bothe nyght and day.

Moné a merakil heo hath edo,   *she has done*
Presonars feters ibroke atwo,   *Prisoners' fetters broke in two*
Blynd and crokid helid moné mo,   *lame healed*
    That were in rewful aray.   *a pitiful state*
155   Wenefrede, thou swete may,
    Thow pray for us bothe nyght and day.

Glad mai be al Schrosberé
To do reverens to that lady;
Thai seche here grace and here mercy
160   On pilgrymage ther everé Fryday.
    Wenefrede, thou swete may,
    Thow pray for us bothe nyght and day.

Wynfrede, we thee beseche,
Now ryght with herfilly speche,   *heartfelt speech*
165   That thou wilt be our soulis leche,   *physician*
        Thee to serve, both plese and pay.
      Wenefrede, thou swete may,
      Thow pray for us bothe nyght and day.

We prayn thee, al that beth present,   *thee (i.e., Winifred)*
170   Save thyn abbay and thi covent,
      That thai be never chamyd ne chent   *shamed nor ruined*
        With wykkid mon ne Fyndis pray.   *By; prey*
      Wenefrede, thou swete may,
      Thow pray for us bothe nyght and day.

175   I pray youe al, pur charyté,   *for*
      Redis this carol reverently,
      Fore I hit mad with wepyng ye.   *eye*
        Mi name hit is the Blynd Awdlay.
      Wenefrede, thou swete may,
180   Thow pray for us bothe nyght and day.

Salutation to Saint Winifred   **[W25]**

Hic incipit salutacio Sancte Wenefrede virginis.[1]

Hayle, Wenefryd, that worchipful with thi vergeneté.   *virginity*
Hayl, mervelus marter and merceful may.   *martyr*
Haile, meror of meraclys, our medecyne to be.   *mirror of miracles*
Haile, solans to the seke, here soker, I say,   *solace; their succor*
5   Treuly in trouth!
      Thi grace, thi goodnes, I con not telle,
      Thi merakels and thi gret mervell,
        Bot woso wil go to thi welle,   *whoso*
          Ther may thai se the soth.   *see the truth*

10   Haile, thou chese to be chast and kepe charité.   *chosen*
      Haile, Cadoc the curst cast thee in care.   *Caradoc (Winifred's betrayer) the accursed*
      Haile, he smot of thi hede without peté.   *off; pity*
      Haile, fallere of his foly fore alle his false fare.   *conqueror; folly; actions*
        Fore sodenlé he felle   *suddenly*
15   Fore love and lust of lechoré,   *lecherous desire*
        To have payne perpetualy,

---

[1] *Here begins a salutation to Saint Winifred, virgin*

With sorow and care and turmentré,   *torments*
    Into the fuyre of helle.   *fire*

Haile, the blessyng of Bewnow, thi botynyng was be grace.[1]
20 Haile, that merceful munke savyd thee mercefully,   *monk*
    Haile, when thi hed fro thi halse, hent away hit was;   *head; neck, cut*
    Haile, set hit save and sound to thi body,   *[Beuno] set it safe; [back] on*
        The soth fore to sayn!
    Ther was moné a wepyng ye   *many*
25 Of men and wemen that hit se;   *saw*
    When Bewnow blessid thee gracyously,
        Thou ros to lyfe agayne.

Haile, our Lord lenketh thi lyfe fiftene yere,   *lengthened*
    Haile, after thi holé hede hent of hit was.   *cut off*
30 Haile, Bewnow the blest, anon he thee chere.   *cheered*
    Haile, thou were chosun to be chef, to be here abbas.   *chief; their abbess*
        With hert and good entent
    Thou servys thi God in that place;   *served*
    Ful of vertuys and of grace,
35 A good ensampil thou was
        To al thi covent.

Haile, lover of that Lord with laudabeleté.   *praiseworthiness*
    Haile, preysere of his Passion, with peté nyght and day.   *One who praises*
    Haile, servand to that Soveren, I sai thee sothly.   *servant*
40 Haile, he hath joynd thee to joy in heven fore ay.   *forever*
        Thre giftis geven thee has: *[He] has given you three gifts*
    A ston to eswem over the se;   *stone; swim; sea*
    The stonus in the wel, blodé to be;   *bloody*
    And al that seche sokor to thee   *seek succor from*
45   To have mercé and grace.

Haile, the kyngdam of this word, thou hit refusust.   *world; refuse*
    Haile, reverens and reches and ryal aray.   *honor; riches; royal attire*
    Haile, fore the love of Jhesus Crist, hit thou dispisist,   *despise*
    Haile, him to love. Haile, hym to plese and pay
50   Herefore with gret reverens.
    Fore thou foresoke this wickid word
    Fore the love of thi Lord,
    In heven thou hast thi reward,
        Icrownd in his presens.   *crowned; presence*

---

[1] *Hail, the blessing of Beuno (Winifred's uncle), thy healing was by grace*

55	Haile, to that perles Prynce for us now thee pray.	*peerless*
	Haile, he was Grownder of thi grace and thi Governour.	*Originator*
	Haile, Wenefryd, thi worthenes, I wot wele hit may,	
	At the dai of our deth our soulis then socour,	
	And put us out of drede.	
60	Out of this word or that we wynd,	*before we pass*
	Our mysdedis that we mow mend,	*may amend*
	That we be never chamyd ne chend,	*shamed or disgraced*
	We pray thee, Wenefryde.	

Explicitur salutacio. — *[Here] ends the salutation*

LATIN VERSE PRAYER *VIRGO PIA WYNFRYDA* [W25]

Hic incipit oracio. — *Here begins a prayer*

Virgo pia Wynfryda, pollens in myraculis,
Tua presentia nos emunda a peccatorum maculis,
Et cuntis parvis vite defende peryculis.
Ora pro nobis, beata Wenefryda,
5 *Quia per te est nobis gracia data.*[1]

LATIN PROSE PRAYER *DEUS QUI BEATAM VIRGINEM TUAM WENFRYDAM* [W25]

Oremus collecte. — *Let us pray together*

Deus qui beatam vergenem tuam Wenfredam post capitis absisionem tua potencia reddevivam fyere precepis et fac nos quaesimus ea interveneente presente vite et future conveneente ad ipsissem per Christum Dominum nostrum. A. M. E. N.[2]

XXXIII. DEVOTIONS TO SAINT ANNE [W26]

SALUTATION TO SAINT ANNE [W26]

Quicumque hanc salutacionem in honore Sancte Anne matris Marie cotidie devote dixerit sine dubio mala morte non morietur.[3]

---

[1] *Pious virgin Winifred, mighty in miracles, / Cleanse us by your presence from the stain of sins, / And defend us from all the little hazards of life. / Pray for us, blessed Winifred, / Because through you grace is given to us*

[2] *God, who commanded that by thy might the blessed virgin Winifred be brought back to life after the cutting off of her head, make us also [whole], we pray, by her interceding, [in our] present life and future assembly before thy very self through Christ our Lord. Amen*

[3] *Whoever devoutly says this salutation every day in honor of Saint Anne, mother of Mary, will assuredly not die a wicked death*

Gaude, felix Anna, the moder of Mari,   *Rejoice, fruitful Anne*
Gaude, thou broghtis forth that borth that al the word con glade,[1]
Gaude, that here Crist Jhesu, heo bere of hur body.
Gaude, heo fed that frelé Food, that Floure that never schal fade!   *noble Nursling*

5   *Gaude, felix Anna*, that bere that blesful floure,
Gaude, that gracious graff that sprong out of Jesse,   *graft; sprung*
Gaude, that blessid brange, hit bere our Saveour;   *branch*
Gaude, he growndid here in grace to graunt us al mercé!   *grounded her*

Gaude, felix Anna, oure blis to us thou broght,
10   *Gaude*, here, that al the word that ladé heo gan lyght;[2]
Gaude, that maiden mercéful, our wele heo hath ewroght;   *weal; brought about*
Gaude, heo savyd al monkynd fore syn to deth was dyght![3]

Gaude, felix Anna, the moder of Messee,   *Messiah*
Gaude, thou consayvyst clene be Joachym, that holé man,   *chastely by*
15   *Gaude*, that long tyme before baren thou hadist be;   *barren you had been*
Gaude, thou broghtist furth that burth was our salvacion!   *birth [that] was our salvation*

Gaude, felix Anna, thou bere of thi body,
Gaude, the moder of Jhesu Crist, that al the word hath wroght,   *world*
Gaude, that fore our love soche a deth wold dye,
20   *Gaude*, with hes pressious blod fro bale to blis us boght!

Gaude, felix Anna, fore us now thou pray,
Gaude, to the quen of even and to here blisful Sun;   *heaven*
Gaude, this salutacion to thee here we say,
Gaude, thou graunt us of thi grace to have remyssioun!

LATIN PROSE PRAYER *DEUS QUI BEATAM ANNAM*   **[W26]**

Ora pro nobis beata Anna quia de fructu ventris tui est nobis gratia data. Oremus collecte.[4]

*Deus qui beatam Annam diu sterilem prole voluisti gloriosa et humano genere salutifera
fecundare, da ut omnes amore filium matrem venerantes in hora mortis utiusque precencia
gaudere mereantur per te, Jhesu Christe, salvatur mundy, rex glorie. Amen.*[5]

---

[1] *Rejoice, you brought forth that birth that did gladden all the world*

[2] *Rejoice, here, so that that lady could illuminate all the world*

[3] *Rejoice, she saved all mankind [for whom] death for sin was prepared*

[4] *Pray for us, blessed Anne, because from the fruit of your womb grace has been given to us. Let us pray together*

[5] *God, who wanted to make fruitful the blessed Anne, long sterile, with a glorious and salvific offspring for
the human race, grant that all venerating in love the son and mother may deserve in the hour of death to rejoice
in the presence of both, through thee, Jesus Christ, savior of the world, king of glory. Amen*

XXXIIII. MEDITATION ON THE HOLY FACE [W27]

LATIN INSTRUCTIONS *QUICUMQUE HANC SALUTACIONEM* [W27]

Quicumque hanc salutacionem in honore Salvatoris per xx dies continuo devote dixerit, Bonefacius papa quartus concessit omnibus vere confessis et contritus plenam remissionem omnium peccatorum et hoc scriptum est apud Romam in ecclesia Sancti Petri coram altare salvatoris.[1]

DRAWING OF THE HOLY FACE ON THE VERNICLE [NOT IN W]

Figure 1: The Holy Face. MS Douce 302, fol. 27v. By permission of the Bodleian Library, University of Oxford.

SALUTATION TO THE HOLY FACE [W27]

Salve, I say, Holé Face of our Saveour,	*Hail*
In the wyche schynth to us an hevenly fygure,	*shines before us a heavenly image*
An graceus on to se!	*One gracious to behold*
Salve, thou settis thi prynt on lynin cloth of witlé coloure,	*imprint; linen; whitish*

---

[1] *Whoever has devoutly said this salutation in honor of the Savior for twenty days in a row, Pope Boniface IV has granted to those who have truly confessed all and are contrite, full remission of all sins, and this has been written at Rome in the church of Saint Peter before the altar of the savior*

5   And betoke hit Veroneca fore love and gret honoure   *gave it [to]*
          Upon here sudoré —   *sudary (i.e., humeral veil)*

      Salve, the fayrnes of this word, a myrrore of holé men,   *word (i.e., sign); mirror for*
          That dissiren fore to se Heven Spirit hen,   *Heaven's Spirit (i.e., God) hence*
          In heven on hie,   *high*
10   *Salve*, delyvers us fro the bond o wyckidnes of syn,   *of*
          And joyns to the compané of tho that holé bene,   *joins [us]; those who are holy*
          Fore thi mercy.

      Salve, our joy here in this lyuf, graunt us of thi grace;   *life*
          Yif we fal throgh frelté, foregif us our trespace,   *If; frailty; forgive*
15   Lord, we thee pray.
      Salve, led us to that cuntré that holé fygure in was,   *lead; country [where]*
          That we may se of Jhesu Crist his clene, pured Face,
          Foreever and fore ay!

      Salve, we now thee beseche, be our helpe in everé place,
20   And be our sokore and refyte and alle our solas,   *succor; refuge; solace*
          Lord Omnipotent,
      Salve, lest he us nuye grimsli, our enmy Satanas,   *horribly harm us*
          And grant us al thi mercé in heven to have a plas,
          Tofore thi Jugement.

Signatum est super nos lumen vultis tui Domine. Dedisti leteciam in corde meo.[1]

LATIN PROSE PRAYER *DEUS QUI NOBIS SIGNATUM VULTIS*   [W27]

Oremus collecte.   *Let us pray together*

Deus qui nobis signatum vultis tui memoreali tuum ad instanciam Veronece ymaginem tuam sudareo impressam relinquere voluisti, per passionem et crusem tuam tribue ut iam nunc in terris per speculum in enigmate ipsam venerare honorare adorare valiamus, ut te tunc, judicem super nos venientem, facie ad faciem se cum videamus Dominum nostrum Jhesum Christum filium tuum. Amen.[2]

---

[1] *The light of thy countenance, O Lord, is signed upon us. Thou hast given gladness in my heart.* Psalm 4:7.

[2] *God, who wished to leave signed for us as a memorial of thy countenance thy likeness stamped on the sudarium at the impetus of Veronica, grant by thy passion and cross that we may now on earth be able to venerate, honor, and worship him (i.e., Christ) through a glass in an obscure manner, just as then we [will see] thee, coming as judge over us, when we see face to face our Lord Jesus Christ thy son. Amen.* Compare 1 Corinthians 13:12: *Videmus nunc per speculum in enigmate tunc autem facie ad faciem,* "We see now through a glass in a dark manner; but then face to face."

 Carols

XXXV. Carol Sequence [W28–W52]

Instructions for Reading 3 [UNNUMBERED IN W]

I pray yow, syrus, boothe moore and las,   *sirs; less*
Syng these caroles in Cristemas.

Carol 1. Ten Commandments [W28]

Hic incipiunt decem precepta in modum cantalene.[1]

    A, mon! Yif thou wold savyd be,
    Foresake thi syn or hit do thee.

And love thi God over al thyng,   [Exodus 20:3–6]
Thi neghbore as thiselfe, I say;   [Matthew 19:19]
Let be your hoth, your false sweryng;   *Forsake; oath* [Exodus 20:7]
In clannes kepe your haleday —   *cleanness; sabbath* [Exodus 20:8–11]
5   Leve ye me.   *Believe*
    A, mon! Yif thou wold savyd be,
    Foresake thi syn or hit do thee.

Thi fader, thi moder, thou worchip ay;   *always* [Exodus 20:12]
Scle no mon fore wordlé thyng;   *Slay; worldly* [Exodus 20:13]
10 Bacbyte no man nyght ne day,   *Slander*
Fore this is Godis est and his bidyng —   *behest; bidding*
      Leve ye me.
    A, mon! Yif thou wold savyd be,
    Foresake thi syn or hit do thee.

15 False witnes loke thou non bere;   *bear* [Exodus 20:16]
Dissayte ne theft, loke thou do non;   *Deceit nor* [Exodus 20:15]

---

[1] *Here begin the Ten Commandments in the form of a song.* Compare Exodus 20:1–17, Matthew 19:18–19. Audelay adds injunctions to avoid backbiting and love one's neighbor, and omits the last two commandments against covetousness.

175

Lechoré thou most foreswere;   [Exodus 20:14]
Here beth comawndmentis, everechon —   *are; every one*
    Leve ye me.
20   A, mon! Yif thou wold savyd be,
    Foresake thi syn or hit do thee.

Thagh thou be kyng and were the croune,   *wear*
Mon, have mynd of thyn endyng;
The wele of Forteune wil tult thee doune,   *wheel; tilt*
25 When thou art cald to thi rekenyng —
    Leve thoue me.
    A, mon! Yif thou wold savyd be,
    Foresake thi syn or hit do thee.

Thou schalt acownt, ful sekyrly,   *account; certainly*
30 Fore al the goodis that God thee send;
Howe thou hast geton hom, in wat degré,   *what*
How thou hast holdyn, hou thou hast spend —
    Leve ye me.
    A, mon! Yif thou wold savyd be,
35   Foresake thi syn or hit do thee.

CAROL 2. SEVEN DEADLY SINS   **[W29]**

De septem peccatis mortalibus.   *Concerning the seven deadly sins*

    In wele beware ore thou be woo;
    Thenke wens thou come, wheder to goo.

Foresake thi Pride and thyn Envy;
Thou schalt fynd hit fore the best,
Covetyse, Wrath, and Lechory,   *Avarice*
Yif thou wilt set thi soule in rest —
5   I say thee so.
    In wele beware ore thou be woo;   *happiness; before*
    Thenke wens thou come, wheder to goo.   *whence; whither*

Glotery, Slouth, al beth acurst;   *Gluttony; accursed*
Thai ben the brondis in hel brenyng;   *brands; firing*
10 Beware betyme or thou be lost;   *in time before*
Thai bryng mon soule to evel endyng —
    I sai thee so.
    In wele beware ore thou be woo;
    Thenke wens thou come, wheder to goo.

15	Agayns Pride, take Buxumnes;	*Obedience*
	Agayns Wrath, take Charité;	
	Agayns Covetys, take Largenes;	*Generosity*
	Agayns Envy, Humeleté —	*Humility*
	I sai thee so.	
20	In wele beware ore thou be woo;	
	Thenke wens thou come, wheder to goo.	
	Agayns Glotore, take Abstenens;	*Abstinence*
	Agayns Lechoré, take Chastité;	
	Agayns Slouthe, take Besenes;	*Busyness*
25	Here is a gracious remedé —	
	I say thee so.	
	In wele beware ore thou be woo;	
	Thenke wens thou come, wheder to goo.	
	Fore his love that youe dere boght,	*dearly*
30	Lerne this lesson, I youe pray;	
	Have this in mynd, foregete hit noght,	
	Fore to heven ther is no nother way —	
	I say thee so.	
	In wele beware ore thou be woo;	
35	Thenke wens thou come, wheder to goo.	

CAROL 3. SEVEN WORKS OF MERCY   [W30]

De septem opera misericordie.[1]

	Wele is him and wele schal be,	
	That doth the Seven Werkis of Mercé.	
	Fede the hungeré; the thirsté gif drenke;	*give*
	Clothe the nakid, as Y youe say;	
	Vesid the pore in presun lyyng;	*Visit*
	Beré the ded, now I thee pray —	*Bury*
5	I cownsel thee.	
	Wele is him and wele schal be,	
	That doth the Seven Werkis of Mercé.	
	Herber the pore that goth be the way;	*Shelter*
	Teche the unwyse of thi conyng;	*wisdom*

---

[1] *Concerning the seven works of mercy.* The subject derives from Matthew 25:31–46, and Audelay treats it elsewhere: *True Living*, lines 173–85 and 238–63, and *God's Address to Sinful Men*, lines 164–71 and 197–220.

10	Do these dedis nyght and day,	*deeds*
	Thi soule to heven hit wil thee bryng —	
	I cownsel thee.	
	Wele is him and wele schal be,	
	That doth the Seven Werkis of Mercé.	

15 And ever have peté on the pore, — *compassion*
And part with him that God thee send; — *share; what*
Thou hast no nother tresoure,
Agayns the Day of Jugement —
I cownsel thee.
20 Wele is him and wele schal be,
That doth the Seven Werkis of Merkis.

The pore schul be mad domusmen — *judges*
Opon the ryche at Domysday; — *rich people*
Let se houe thai con onsware then,
25 Fore al here reverens, here ryal aray — *high office; royal array*
I cownsel thee.
Wele is him and wele schal be,
That doth the Seven Werkis of Mercé.

In hongyr, in thurst, in myschif — wellay! — — *misery; alas*
30 After here almus ay waytyng: — *alms*
"Thay wold noght us vesete nyght ne day."
Thus wil thai playn ham to Heven Kyng —
I cownsel thee.
Wele is him and wele schal be,
35 That doth the Seven Werkis of Mercé.

CAROL 4. FIVE WITS   **[W31]**

De quinque sensus. — *Concerning the five senses*

Thy Fyve Wittis loke that thou wele spende,
And thonke that Lord that ham thee sende.

The furst, hit is thi heryng: — *hearing*
Loke thou turne away thyne ere — *ear*
Fro ydil wordis, untrew talkyng; — *From idle*
The laus of God loke that thou lere — — *laws; learn*
5 Lest thou be chent! — *ruined*
Thy Fyve Wittis loke that thou wele spende,
And thonke that Lord that ham thee sende.

	The second, hit is thi seyng:	*seeing*
	Thou hast fre choys and fre wil	*free choice*
10	To behold al wordlé thyng,	*worldly*
	The good to chese, to leve the ille —	
	Lest thou be chent!	
	Thy Fyve Wittis loke that thou wele spende,	
	And thonke that Lord that ham thee sende.	

15	The third, hit is thi towchyng:	*touching*
	Worche no worke unlawfully;	
	Goveren thi fete in thi walkyng	
	Toward heven, and fle foly —	
	Lest thou be chent!	
20	Thy Fyve Wittis loke that thou wele spende,	
	And thonke that Lord that ham thee sende.	

	The forth, hit is thi smellyng:	
	To saver thi sustinans sote of smelle,	*savor; sustenance (i.e., food) sweet*
	Let resun thee rewle in thyne etyng;	*reason; rule*
25	Beware, fore sorfet hit may thee spille —	*surfeit; harm*
	Lest thou be chent	
	Thy Fyve Wittis loke that thou wele spende,	
	And thonke that Lord that ham thee sende.	

	The fifth, hit is thi tung tastyng:	
30	Thi mete, thi drynke, holsum and clene,	*wholesome*
	Yif hit be lusté to thi lykyng,	*greatly to your liking*
	Then mesuere hit is a mary mene —	*moderation; merry mean*
	Lest thou be chent!	
	Thy Fyve Wittis loke that thou wele spende,	
35	And thonke that Lord that ham thee sende.	

CAROL 5. SEVEN GIFTS OF THE HOLY GHOST   [W32]

	De septem dona Spiritus Sancti.	*Concerning the seven gifts of the Holy Ghost*
	God hath geven of myghtis most	
	The Seven Giftis of the Holé Gost.	
	Mynd, Resun, Vertu, and Grace,	*Reason*
	Humeleté, Chast, and Chareté,	*Chastity*
	These seven giftis God geven has,	
	Be the vertu of the Holé Gost to mon onlé —	
5	Ellis were we lost!	
	God hath geven of myghtis most	*God of most might has given*
	The Seven Giftis of the Holé Gost.	

Mynd makis a mon himselve to know,
And Resun him reulis in his werkis alle,
10   And Vertu makis his goodnes yknow,   *to be known*
And Grace is grownder of hem alle —   *basis*
        Ellis were we lost!
    God hath geven of myghtis most
    The Seven Giftis of the Holé Gost.

15   Humeleté, pride he dothe downe falle;
Chast kepis thee clene in thi levyng;   *pure; living*
Then Chareté is chef of hem alle;   *chief*
Mon soule to blis he dothe hom breng —   *him bring*
        Ellis were we lost!
20   God hath geven of myghtis most
    The Seven Giftis of the Holé Gost.

Have Faythe, Hope, and Chareté;
These be the grownd of thi beleve,
Ellis savyd thou myght not be;
25   Thus Poule in his pistil he doth preve —   *epistle* [1 Corinthians 13:13]
        Ellis were we lost!
    God hath geven of myghtis most
    The Seven Giftis of the Holé Gost.

Thi Faythe is thi beleve of Holé Cherche;   *belief in*
30   Soule, in Hope God hathe hordent thee   *ordained*
Good werkis that thou schuld werche,
And be rewardid in heven on hye —
        Hellis were we lost!
    God hath geven of myghtis most
35   The Seven Giftis of the Holé Gost.

Then Chareté chef callid is he;
He cownselis uche mon that is levyng   *each*
To do as thou woldist me did be thee,   *one; by* [Matthew 7:12]
And kepe Godis est and his bidyng —   *behest; bidding*
40   Ellis were we lost!
    God hath geven of myghtis most
    The Seven Giftis of the Holé Gost.

CAROL 6. DAY OF THE NATIVITY   **[W33]**

In die natalis Domini.   *On the day of the Lord's birth* (December 25)

    Welcum, Yole, in good aray,
    In worchip of the holeday!

Welcum be thou, Heven Kyng,
Welcum, ibore in hon mornyng,   *born; one*
Welcum, to thee now wil we syng —
    Welcum, Yole, forever and ay!
5   Welcum, Yole, in good aray,
    In worchip of the holeday!

Welcum be thou, Maré myld,
Welcum be thou and thi Child,
Welcum, fro the Fynd thou us schilde —   *Fiend; protect*
10   Welcum, Yole, foreever and ay!
    Welcum, Yole, in good aray,
    In worchip of the holeday!

Welcum be ye, Steven and Jone,   *Stephen and John [the Evangelist]*
Welcum, childern everechone,   *children (i.e., Holy Innocents)*
15 Wellcum, Thomas marter, alle on —   *Thomas martyr, all together*
    Welcum, Yole, forever and ay!
    Welcum, Yole, in good aray,
    In worchip of the holeday!

Welcum be thou, good New Yere,
20 Welcum, the twelve days efere,   *together*
    Welcum be ye alle that bene here —
    Welcum, Yole, forever and ay!
    Welcum, Yole, in good aray,
    In worchip of the holeday!

25 Welcum be ye, lord and lady,
    Welcum be ye, al this cumpané,
    Fore Yolis love, now makis meré —   *merry*
    Welcum, Yole, foreever and ay!
    Welcum, Yole, in good aray,
30   In worchip of the holeday!

CAROL 7. DAY OF SAINT STEPHEN   [W34]

In die Sancti Stephani.[1]

    In reverens of oure Lord in heven,
    Worchip this marter, swete Sent Steven.

---

[1] *On the day of Saint Stephen* (December 26). Compare Acts 7:55–59.

Saynt Steven, the first martere,   *martyr*
He ched his blod in herth here;   *shed; earth*
Fore the love of his Lord so dere,
He sofird payn and passion.   *suffered*
5   In reverens of oure Lord in heven,
       Worchip this marter, swete Sent Steven.

He was stonyd with stons ful cruellé,
And sofird his payn ful pasiently: *patiently*
"Lord, of myn enmes thou have mercé,
10   That wot not what thai done."
       In reverens of oure Lord in heven,
       Worchip this marter, swete Sent Steven.

He beheld into heven on he,   *high*
And se Jhesu stonde in his majesté,   *saw*
15   And sayd: "My soule, Lord, take to thee,
And foregif myn enmys everechon."   *every one*
       In reverens of oure Lord in heven,
       Worchip this marter, swete Sent Steven.

Then when that word he had sayd,
20   God therof was wel apayd;   *satisfied*
His hede mekelé to slep he layd;   *meekly*
His sowle was takyn to heven anon.
       In reverens of oure Lord in heven,
       Worchip this marter, swete Sent Steven.

25   Swete Saynt Steven, fore us thou pray
To that Lord that best may;
When our soule schal wynd away,   *pass*
He grawnt us al remyssion.
       In reverens of oure Lord in heven,
30   Worchip this marter, swete Sent Steven.

CAROL 8. DAY OF SAINT JOHN THE EVANGELIST   [W35]

In die Sancti Johannis apopstole et ewangeliste.[1]

I pray youe, breder everechon,   *all brethren*
Worchip this postil, swete Saynt Jon.   *apostle*

---

[1] *On the day of Saint John, apostle and evangelist* (December 27)

Synt Jon is Cristis derlyng dere; *beloved dear*
He lenyd on his brest at his sopere, *leaned; supper [John 13:23]*
And ther he mad hym wonderful chere, *showed; affection*
Tofore his postilis everechon. *Before*
5   I pray youe, breder everechon,
Worchip this postil, swete Saynt Jon.

"Saynt Jon," He said, "my dere derlyng,
Take my moder into thi kepyng; *[see John 19:26–27]*
Heo is my joy, my hert swetyng — *She; heart's darling*
10   Loke thou leve not here anon." *her*
I pray youe, breder everechon,
Worchip this postil, swete Saynt Jon.

"Jon, I pray thee, make here good chere *give her good affection*
With al thi hert and thi pouere; *power*
15   Loke ye to part not in fere *from each other*
In wat cuntré that ever ye goon." *whatever country*
I pray youe, breder everechon,
Worchip this postil, swete Saynt Jon.

"I comawnd youe, my postilis alle,
20   When my moder doth on youe calle,
Anon on kynes that ye down falle, *knees*
And do here worchip therwith anon." *worship her*
I pray youe, breder everechon,
Worchip this postil, swete Saynt Jon.

25   "I pray youe al, on my blessyng,
Kepe ye chareté for oné thyng; *Maintain; any*
Thenke what I said in your waschyng,
Knelyng tofore youe on a stone." *[John 13:14–17]*
I pray youe, breder everechon,
30   Worchip this postil, swete Saynt Jon.

"Farewel, now I wynd youe fro; *depart from you*
To Jerusalem I most goo,
To be betrayd of my fo,
And sofir payn and passiown."
35   I pray youe, breder everechon,
Worchip this postil, swete Saynt Jon."

"A, my Sun! My Heven Kyng!"
Oure lady therwith felle downe, sonyng — *swooning*
This was a dolful departyng!
40   Thai toke here up with gret mon. *moan*

I pray youe, breder everechon,
Worchip this postil, swete Saynt Jon.

"A, my moder! Me dere derlyng!
Let be thi wo and thi wepyng,
45   Fore I most do my Fader bidyng,
Ellis redempcion were ther non."
    I pray youe, breder everechon,
    Worchip this postil, swete Saynt Jon.

"Farewel, my Fader! Farewel, my Chelde!"
50   "Farewel, moder and maid mylde;
Fro the Fynd I wil thee childe,   *shield*
And crowne thee quene in heven trone."
    I pray youe, breder everechon,
    Worchip this postil, swete Saynt Jon.

55   Swete Saynt Jon, to thee we pray,
Beseche that Lord, that best may,
When our soulis schal wynd away,
He grawnt us al remyssion!
    I pray youe, breder everechon,
60   Worchip this postil, swete Saynt Jon.

CAROL 9. DAY OF THE HOLY INNOCENTS   [W36]

In die Sanctorum Innocencium.   *On the day of the Holy Innocents* (December 28)

    With al the reverens that we may,
    Worchip we Childermasday.

Crist crid in cradil, "Moder, ba, ba!"
The childer of Isral cridyn, "Wa, wa!"   *Israel*
Fore here merth hit was aga   *mirth; gone*
When Erod fersly cowth hem fray!   *Herod fiercely did them kill*
5   With al the reverens that we may,
    Worchip we Childermasday.

Al knavechilder with two yere   *male children*
Of age in Bedlem, fere or nere,   *Bethlehem, far* [Matthew 2:16]
Thai chedyn here blod with swerd and spere —   *shed their*
10   Alas, ther was a rewful aray!   *pitiful spectacle*
    With al the reverens that we may,
    Worchip we Childermasday.

	An hunderd and fourté thousand ther were;	[see Apocalypse 14:3 and note]
	Crist ham cristynd, al in fere,	*christened; together*
15	In eor blod, and were martere,	*their; martyred*
	Al clene vergyns — hit is no nay!	
	With al the reverens that we may,	
	Worchip we Childermasday.	

	The crisum-childer to Crist con cry:	*children newly baptized*
20	"We beth slayne fore gret envy!	
	Lord, venge our blod fore thi mercy,	
	And take our soulis to thee, we pray!"	
	With al the reverens that we may,	
	Worchip we Childermasday.	

	An hevenlé voys answerd agayn:	
25	"Abyd awyle, and sofer your payn	*Be patient awhile; suffer*
	Hent the nowmbir be eslayn	*Until the [full] number*
	Of your breder, as I you say."	
	With al the reverens that we may,	
30	Worchip we Childermasday.	

	Fore ye han sofird marterdom	
	For Cristis sake, al and sum,	
	He wil youe crowne in his kyngdam,	
	And folou the Lomb in joy for ay.	[Apocalypse 14:4]
35	With al the reverens that we may,	
	Worchip we Childermasday.	

CAROL 10. SAINT THOMAS ARCHBISHOP OF CANTERBURY   [W37]

De sancto Thome archiepiscopo Cantuarienci.[1]

	I pra you, seris, al in fere,	*pray; together*
	Worchip Seynt Thomas, this holé marter.	*holy martyr*

	For on a Tewsday, Thomas was borne,	
	And on a Tuysday, he was prest schorne,	*tonsured*
	And on a Tuysday, his lyve was lorne,	*lost*
	And sofyrd martyrdam with myld chere.	*composure*
5	I pra you, seris, al in fere,	
	Worchip Seynt Thomas, this holé marter.	

---

[1] *Concerning Saint Thomas, archbishop of Canterbury* (December 29)

Fore Holé Cherche ryght ale hit was —   *[at that time] was all in order*
Ellis we had then songyn "alas!" —
And the child that unborne was   *(i.e., future generations; "us")*
10 Schul have boght his lyve ful dere.
      I pra you, seris, al in fere,
      Worchip Seynt Thomas, this holé marter.

Ther prestis were thral, he mad hem fre,   *Wherever priests were enslaved (oppressed)*
That no clerke hongid schuld be,   *hanged*
15 Bot eretyk, or fore traytré,   *Except heretics, or for treason*
Yif oné seche case fal ther were.   *any such*
      I pra you, seris, al in fere,
      Worchip Seynt Thomas, this holé marter.

Then no child criston schuld be,   *may no child be christened*
20 Ne clerke take ordere in no degré,
Ne mayde mared in no cuntré,   *married*
Without trebeut in the kyng dangere.   *tribute under the king's jurisdiction*
      I pra you, seris, al in fere,
      Worchip Seynt Thomas, this holé marter.

25 Thus Holé Cherche he mad fre;   *free [of secular control]*
Fore fyfté poyntis he dyed, treuly;   *fifty points [of dispute with the king]*
In heven worchipt mot he be,   *worshipped may*
And fader and moder him gete and bere!   *[who] begot and bore him*
      I pra you, seris, al in fere,
30   Worchip Seynt Thomas, this holé marter.

CAROL 11. DAY OF THE LORD'S CIRCUMCISION   **[W38]**

In die circumcicionis Domini.   *On the day of the Lord's circumcision* (January 1)

What tythyngis bryngst us, messangere,   *tidings do you bring; messenger*
Of Cristis borth this New Eris Day?   *birth; Year's*

A Babe is borne of hye natewre,   *high nature*
A Prynce of Pese that ever schal be;   *Peace*
Off heven and erthe he hath the cewre;   *cure*
Hys lordchip is eterneté!   *He is lord of eternity*
5   Seche wonder tythyngis ye may here —   *Such wondrous*
      What tythyngis bryngis thee, messangere? —
        That God and Mon is hon in fere;   *one united*
        Hour syn had mad bot Fyndis pray!   *Our sin has become mere Fiend's prey*
      What tythyngis bryngst us, messangere,
10   Of Cristis borth this New Eris Day?

A semlé selcouth hit is to se —   *seemly wonder*
The burd that had this Barne iborne,   *maiden; Child*
This Child conseyvyd in he degré,   *high*
And maydyn is as was beforne!   *virgin*
15   Seche wonder tydyngus ye mow here
        Of Cristis borth this New Eris Day,
            That maydon and modur ys won yfere,   *one and the same*
            And lady ys of hye aray!
        What tythyngis bryngst us, messangere,
20   Of Cristis borth this New Eris Day?

A wonder thyng is now befall —   *wondrous*
That Lord that mad both se and sun,   *sea*
Heven and erth, and angelis ale,
In monkynde ys now becumme!
25   Whatt tydyngus bryngis us, messangere,
        Of Cristis borth this New Eris Day?
            A faunt that is bot of on yere,   *infant; one*
            Ever as ben and schal be ay!   *as [has] been and shall be ever*
        What tythyngis bryngis thou, messangere,
30   Of Cristis borth this New Eris Day?

Thise lovelé ladé con grete here Chylde: *her*
"Hayle, Sun! Haile, Broder! Haile, Fader dere!"
"Haile, doghter! Haile, suster! Haile, moder myld!" —
This haylsyng was on coynt manere!   *greeting; quaint*
35   Seche wonder tythyngis ye may here
        Of Cristis borth this New Eris Day —
            This gretyng was of so he chere   *such exalted manner*
            That mans pyne, hit turnyd to play!   *mankind's pain*
        What tythyngis bryngst us, messangere,
40   Of Cristis borth this New Eris Day?

That Lord, that al thyng mad of noght,   *from nothing*
Is Mon becum fore mons love;
Fore with his blood, he schul be boght
From bale to blys that is above!
45   Seche wonder tythyngis ye may here
        Of Cristis borth this New Eris Day!
            That Lord us grawnt now our prayoure
            To twel in heven that we may;   *dwell*
        Seche wonder tythyngis ye may here
50   Of Cristis borth this New Eris Day!

CAROL 12. KING HENRY VI   **[W39]**

De rege nostro Henrico Sexto.   *Concerning our king Henry VI*

☞ *A, perles Pryns, to thee we pray,*
    Save our kyng both nyght and day!

Fore he is ful yong, tender of age,
Semelé to se, o bold corage,   *of bold spirit*
Lovelé and lofté of his lenage,   *lineage*
Both perles prince and kyng veray!   *true*
5   A, perles Pryns, to thee we pray,
         Save our kyng both nyght and day!

His gracious granseres and his grawndame,   *grandsires; grandmother*
His fader and moder, of kyngis thay came;
Was never a worthear prynce of name,   *worthier*
10   So exelent in al our day.
         A, perles Pryns, to thee we pray,
         Save our kyng both nyght and day!

His fader fore love of mayd Kateryn,
In Fraunce he wroght turment and tene;   *trouble*
15   His love, hee sayd, hit schuld not ben,   *he (the Dauphin) said*
And send him ballis him with to play.   *sent; [tennis] balls*
         A, perles Pryns, to thee we pray,
         Save our kyng both nyght and day!

Then was he wyse in wars withalle,   *therewith*
20   And taght Franchemen to plai at the balle —
With tenés hold, he ferd ham halle! —   *tennis old; frightened them all*
To castelles and setis thi floyn away.   *At castles and cities they [the balls] flew*
         A, perles Pryns, to thee we pray,
         Save our kyng both nyght and day!

25   To Harflete a sege he layd anon,   *Harfleur*
And cast a bal unto the towne;
The Frenchemen swere be se and sun,   *swore by sea*
Hit was the Fynd that mad that fray.   *attack*
         A, perles Pryns, to thee we pray,
30   Save our kyng both nyght and day!

Anon thai toke ham to cownsele;
Oure gracious kyng thai wold asayle;   *assail*
At Agyncowrt, at that patayle,   *Agincourt; battle*
The floure of Frawnce he fel that day.   *flower (i.e., nobility); defeated*

35   A, perles Pryns, to thee we pray,
            Save our kyng both nyght and day!

            The Kyng of Frawns then was agast —
            Mesagers to him send in hast —
            Fore wele he west hit was bot wast   *knew; wasteful*
40   Hem to witstond in honé way.   *withstand; any*
                A, perles Pryns, to thee we pray,
                Save our kyng both nyght and day!

            And prayd hym to sese of his outrage,   *cease; ferocity*
            And take Kateryn to mareage;
45   Al Frawnce to him schuld do homage,
            And croune him kyng afftyr his day.
                A, perles Pryns, to thee we pray,
                Save our kyng both nyght and day!

            Of Frawnce he mad him anon regent,
50   And wedid Kateren in his present;   *presence*
            Into Englond anon he went,
            And cround our quene in ryal aray.   *royal*
                A, perles Pryns, to thee we pray,
                Save our kyng both nyght and day!

55   Of Quen Kateryn our kyng was borne,
            To save our ryght that was forelorne,   *territorial right*
            Oure faders in Frawns had won beforne;   *[What] our*
            Thai han hit hold moné a day.
                A, perles Pryns, to thee we pray,
60   Save our kyng both nyght and day!

            Thus was his fader a conqueroure,
            And wan his moder with gret onoure;
            Now may the kyng bere the floure   *flower (i.e., prize for excellence)*
            Of kyngis and kyngdams in uche cuntré.   *each country*
65   A, perles Pryns, to thee we pray,
                Save our kyng both nyght and day!

            On him schal fal the prophecé,
            That hath ben sayd of Kyng Herré:
            The holé cros wyn or he dye,   *[That he should] the holy cross win before*
70   That Crist halud on Good Fryday.   *dragged*
                A, perles Pryns, to thee we pray,
                Save our kyng both nyght and day!

            Al wo and werres he schal acese,   *cease*
            And set alle reams in rest and pese,   *realms*

75   And turne to Cristyndam al hethynes —   *all heathens to Christianity*
        Now grawnt him hit so be may!
            A, perles Pryns, to thee we pray,
            Save our kyng both nyght and day!

        Pray we that Lord is Lord of alle
80   To save our kyng his reme ryal,   *royal realm*
        And let never myschip uppon him falle,   *mishap*
        Ne false traytoure him to betray.
            A, perles Pryns, to thee we pray,
            Save our kyng both nyght and day!

85   I pray youe, seris, of your gentré,   *courtesy*
        Syng this carol reverently,
        Fore hit is mad of Kyng Herré —
        Gret ned fore him we han to pray!
            A, perles Pryns, to thee we pray,
90   Save our kyng both nyght and day!

        Yif he fare wele, wele schul we be,
        Or ellis we may be ful soré,
        Fore him schal wepe moné an e —   *many an eye*
        Thus prophecis the Blynd Awdlay.
95   A, perles Pryns, to thee we pray,
            Save our kyng both nyght and day!

CAROL 13. FOUR ESTATES   **[W40]**

        Fac ad quod venisti.   *Do that for which you have come*

            Hit is the best, erelé and late,
            Uche mon kepe his oun estate.

        In wat order or what degré   *whatever [religious] order; rank*
        Holé Cherche hath bownd thee to,
        Kepe hit wele, I cownsel thee;
        Dissire thou never to go therfro.
5   I say, allegate,   *in any case*
            Hit is the best, erelé and late,
            Uche mon kepe his oun estate.

        A hye worchip hit is to thee
        To kepe thi state and thi good name,
10   Leud or lered, werehere hit be,   *Ignorant or learned, whatever*
        Ellis God and mon, thay wol thee blame.
            I say, algate,

Hit is the best, erelé and late,
Uche mon kepe his oun estate.

15   Fore four obisions now schul ye here   *perversions*
      That God hatis hilé in his syght: *hates entirely*
      A hardé prest, a proud frere,   *bold*
      An hold mon lechoure, a couard knyght.   *old; coward*
           I say, algate,
20   Hit is the best, erelé and late,
           Uche mon kepe his oun estate.

      A prest schuld scheu uche mon mekenes,   *show each; meekness*
      And leve in love and charité;
      Throgh his grace and his goodnes,
25   Set al other in unité.   *Set everything in unity*
           I say, algate,
           Hit is the best, erelé and late,
           Uche mon kepe his oun estate.

      A frere schuld love alle holenes,   *holiness*
30   Prayers, penans, and poverté;
      Relegious men, Crist hem ches
      To foresake pride and vaynglory.
           I say, algate,
           Hit is the best, erelé and late,
35   Uche mon kepe his oun estate.

      An hold mon schuld kepe him chast,
      And leve the synne of lechoré;   *forsake*
      Al wedid men schuld be stedfast,   *wedded*
      And foresake the syn of avowtré.   *adultery*
40   I sai, algate,
           Hit is the best, erelé and late,
           Uche mon kepe his oun estate.

      A knyght schuld feght agayns falsnes,
      And schew his monhod and his myght,   *manhood*
45   And mayntene trouth and ryghtwysnes,
      And Holé Cherche and wedowes ryght.   *widows'*
           I say, algate,
           Hit is the best, erelé and late,
           Uche mon kepe his oun estate.

50   Here be al the foure astatis
      In Holé Cherche God hath ordent;   *ordained*
      He bedis you kepe hem wel, alegate —   *bids*
      Wosever he chomys, he wyl be schent!   *Whosoever he (i.e., God) shames; doomed*

55

          I say, algate,
55   Hit is the best, erelé and late,
          Uche mon kepe his oun estate.

CAROL 14. CHILDHOOD   [W41]

Cantalena de puericia.   *A song concerning childhood*

          And God wold graunt me my prayer,   *If*
          A child agene I wold I were!   *wish*

          Fore pride in herte, he hatis alle one;   *he (i.e., a child); entirely*
          Worchip ne reverens kepis he non;   *regard for high rank*
          Ne he is wroth with no mon —
          In chareté is alle his chere!   *manner*
5   And God wold graunt me my prayer,
              A child agene I wold I were!

          He wot never wat is envy;   *knows not what*
          He wol uche mon fard wele him by;   *wishes each man to fare well*
          He covetis noght unlaufully —   *covets*
10   Fore cheré stons is his tresoure.   *cherry pits are*
              And God wold graunt me my prayer,
              A child agene I wold I were!

          In hert he hatis lechori —
          To here therof he is sory! —   *hear; perturbed*
15   He sleth the syn of gloteré,   *slays*
          Nother etis ne drynkis bot fore mystere.   *necessity*
              And God wold graunt me my prayer,
              A child agene I wold I were!

          Slouth he putis away, algate,   *in every case*
20   And wol be besé erlé and late —   *active*
          Al wyckidnes thus he doth hate,
          The seven dedlé synus al in fere.   *together*
              And God wold graunt me my prayer,
              A child agene I wold I were!

25   A gracious lyfe, forsothe, he has —   *life of grace*
          To God ne mon doth no trespas —
          And I in syn fal, alas,
          Everé day in the yere!
              And God wold graunt me my prayer,
30   A child agene I wold I were!

My joy, my myrth is fro me clene —   *[gone] from me entirely*
I turne to care, turment, and tene —   *trouble*
Ded I wold that I had bene   *Dead*
When I was borne, and layd on bere —   *bier*
35   And God wold graunt me my prayer,
     A child agene I wold I were!

Fore better hit were to be unboren,   *unborn*
Then fore my synus to be forelorne,   *damned (utterly lost)*
Nere grace of God that is beforne,   *Were [it] not [for]; came before*
40   Almysdede, and holé prayere!   *Almsdeed*
    And God wold graunt me my prayer,
     A child agene I wold I were!

Now other cumford se I non
Bot schryve me clene with contricion,   *confess*
45   And make here trew satisfaccion,
And do my penans wyle Y am here —
    And God wold graunt me my prayer,
     A child agene I wold I were!

CAROL 15. DAY OF EPIPHANY   [W42]

In die Epephanis &c.   *On the day of Epiphany, etc. (January 6)*

Nowel! Nowel! Nowel!   *Noel*

Ther is a Babe born of a may
   In salvacion of us;
That he be heryd in this day,   *praised*
   Vene, Creatore Spiritus.   *Come, Creator Spirit*
5   Nowel! Nowel! Nowel!

In Bedlem, in that fayre plas,   *place*
   This blessid Barne, borne He was,   *Child*
Him to serve, God grawnt us grace,
   Tu Trinetatis Unitas.   *You the Unity of the Trinity*
10   Nowel! Nowel! Nowel!

The angelis to chepardis songyn and sayd: *shepherds sang*
   "Pes in erth be mon unto!" —
Therwith thai were ful sore afrayd —
   "Glorea in exelsis Deo!"   *"Glory to God in the highest!" (see note)*
15   Nowel! Nowel! Nowel!

The chepardis hard that angel song;   *heard*
  Thai heredon God in Treneté;   *praised*
Moche merth was ham among,   *Much gladness; among*
  Iam lucis ortus sidere.   *Now the star of light having risen*
20   Nowel! Nowel! Nowel!

Thre kyngis thai soght him, herefore,   *therefore*
  Of dyvers lond and fere cuntré,   *diverse; far*
And askidyn were this Barne was bore,   *asked where*
  Hostes Herodes impii.   *Herod, wicked enemy*
25   Nowel! Nowel! Nowel!

He bad ham go seche this Barne: *He (i.e., Herod) bade; seek*
  "Anon this way to me he come,   *they*
That I may do hym worchip beforne,
  Deus Creator omnium."   *God Creator of all things*
30   Nowel! Nowel! Nowel!

The stere apered here face beforne —   *before their faces*
  That gladid here hertes ful graciously! —
Over that plase this Babe was born,
  Jhesu Salvotor seculi.   *Jesus Savior of the world*
35   Nowel! Nowel! Nowel!

Thai knelid adowne with gret reverens;   *kneeled; reverence*
  Gold, sens, and myr, thai offerd him to;   *incense; myrrh*
He blessid ham ale that were present,
  Jhesu nostra Redempcio.   *Jesus our Redemption*
40   Nowel! Nowel! Nowel!

The gold betokens he was a Kyng;
  The sens, a Prest of dyngneté;   *dignity*
The myr betokynth his bereyng,   *burial*
  Magne Deus potencie.   *Great God of power*
45   Nowel! Nowel! Nowel!

The angel hem wernyd in here slepyng
  At Erod the kyng thai schuld not cumme: *To*
"That Babe you bade on his blessyng,
  Christe Redemptore omnium."   *Christ, Redeemer of everyone*
50   Nowel! Nowel! Nowel!

Thai turnyd then another way
  Into kyngdom ful graciously;
Then thai begonon to syng and say,
  "*Salvator mundy Domine.*"   *Savior of the world, Lord*
55   Nowel! Nowel! Nowel!

CAROL 16. SAINT ANNE MOTHER OF MARY   **[W43]**

De Sancta Anna matre Marie.   *Concerning Saint Anne, mother of Mary*

> The moder of Mary, that merceful may,   *maid full of mercy*
> Pray fore us both nyght and day!   *[may] pray*

Swete Saynt Anne, we thee beseche,
Thou pray fore us to oure laday,   *lady (Mary)*
That heo wel be oure soulis leche,   *she; physician*
That day when we schul dey.
5   Herefore we say —
        The moder of Mary, that merceful may,
        Pray fore us both nyght and day!

Throgh thee was gladid alle this word   *gladdened; world*
When Maré of thee borne was,
10   That bere that Barne, that blisful Lord,
That grawntis us al mercé and grace.
        Herefore we say —
        The moder of Mary, that merceful may,
        Pray fore us both nyght and day!

15   Baren thou were ful long before,   *Barren*
Then God he se to thi mekenes,   *determined because of*
That thou schuldist delyver that was forelore,   *what was forlorn*
        Mon soule that lay in the Fyndis distres.
        Herefore we say —
20   The moder of Mary, that merceful may,
        Pray fore us both nyght and day!

Fore Joachym, that holé housbond,
Prayyd to God ful paciently
That he wold send his swete sond,   *gift*
25   Sum froyte betwene you two to be.   *fruit*
        Herefore we say —
        The moder of Mary, that merceful may,
        Pray fore us both nyght and day!

Then God hem grawntid graciously
30   Betwene youe two a floure schul spryng,   *flower should grow*
The rote therof is clepid Jesse,   *root; called [see Isaias 11:1]*
That joye and blis to the word schal beryng.   *world; bring*
        Herefore I say —
        The moder of Mary, that merceful may,
35   Pray fore us both nyght and day!

The blisful branche this floure on greue,   *on which this flower grew*
Out of Jesse, at my wettyng,   *by my understanding*
Was Maré myld that bere Jhesu,   *who bore*
Maydyn and moder to Heven Kyng.
40   Herefore I say —
       The moder of Mary, that merceful may,
       Pray fore us both nyght and day!

Icallid Jhesus of Nazaret,   *Named*
God Sun of hi degré,   *God's; high*
45   As here as Mon that sofyrd deth,   *Was*
And rynyd into Davit dygneté.   *reigned; David's dignity*
             Herefore I say —
       The moder of Mary, that merceful may,
       Pray fore us both nyght and day!

50   In Bedlem, in that blessid place,
Maré myld this Floure hath borne
Betwene an ox and an as,
To save his pepil that was forelorne.
             Herefore I say —
55   The moder of Mary, that merceful may,
       Pray fore us both nyght and day!

Mater, ora Filium,   *Mother, pray to the Son*
That he wyl affter this outleré   *outlawry (i.e., exile in sin)*
Nobis donet gaudium   *[That] he give us joy*
60   *Sine fyne,* fore his mercé.   *Without end*
             Herefore I say —
       The moder of Mary, that merceful may,
       Pray fore us both nyght and day!

CAROL 17. JESUS FLOWER OF JESSE'S TREE   [W44]

Alia cantalena de Sancta Maria.   *Another song concerning Blessed Mary*

       There is a Floure sprung of a tre,   *Flower*
       The rote therof is called Jesse —   *root; [see Isaias 11:1]*
             A Floure of pryce!   *splendor (beauty)*
       Ther is non seche in paradise!   *such*

This Flour is fayre and fresche of heue;   *fresh of hue*
       Hit fadis never, bot ever is new;
The blisful branche this Flour on grew   *on [which] this Flower grew*
       Was Maré myld that bare Jhesu —
5   A Flour of grace!

Agayns al sorow hit is solas!   *solace*
   There is a Floure sprung of a tre,
   The rote therof is called Jesse —
    A Floure of pryce!
10   Ther is non seche in paradise!

The Sede hereof was Godis sond,   *Seed; gift*
   That God himselve sew with his hond;   *sowed*
In Bedlem, in that Holé Lond,   *Bethlehem*
   In medis here herbere ther he hir fond.[1]
15   This blisful Floure
Sprang never bot in Maris boure!   *bower*
   There is a Floure sprung of a tre,
   The rote therof is called Jesse —
    A Floure of pryce!
20   Ther is non seche in paradise!

When Gabrael this mayd met,
   With "*Ave, Maria,*" he here gret;
Betwene hem two this Flour was set,   *implanted*
   And kept was, no mon schul wit,   *conceived; [as] no man shall understand*
25   Hent on a day   *Until*
In Bedlem, hit con spred and spray.   *did spread and sprout*
   There is a Floure sprung of a tre,
   The rote therof is called Jesse —
    A Floure of pryce!
30   Ther is non seche in paradise!

When that Floure began to sprede,
   And his blossum to bede,   *its; bud (i.e., form a bead)*
Ryche and pore of everé sede,   *seed (i.e., kind)*
   Thai marvelt hou this Flour myght sprede!   *marvelled*
35   Til kyngys thre
That blesful Floure come to se.
   There is a Floure sprung of a tre,
   The rote therof is called Jesse —
    A Floure of pryce!
40   Ther is non seche in paradise!

Angelis ther cam out of here toure   *their tower*
   To loke apon this freschelé Floure —   *fresh*
Houe fayre he was in his coloure,
   And hou sote in his savour! —   *sweet; savor*

---

[1] *In grace her shelter there he found for her*, with a punning floral sense: *In meadows her garden then he found in her.* See explanatory note.

45   And to behold
                How soche a Flour myght spryng in golde!   *cold*
                There is a Floure sprung of a tre,
                The rote therof is called Jesse —
                A Floure of pryce!
50   Ther is non seche in paradise!

                Of lillé, of rose of ryse,   *lily; on branch*
                    Of prymrol, and of flour-de-lyse,   *primrose*
                Of al the flours at my devyse,   *I can think of*
                    Thet Floure of Jesse yet bers the prys,   *is supreme*
55   As most of hele   *best remedy*
                To slake oure sorous everedele!   *relieve; sorrows entirely*
                    There is a Floure sprung of a tre,
                    The rote therof is called Jesse —
                    A Floure of pryce!
60   Ther is non seche in paradise!

                I pray youe, flours of this cuntré,   *flowers (i.e., souls)*
                    Whereevere ye go, wereever ye be,
                Hold hup the Flour of good Jesse,   *up*
                    Fore your freschenes and youre beuté,   *Before; freshness; beauty*
65   As fayrist of al,   *fairest*
                And ever was and ever schal!
                    There is a Floure sprung of a tre,
                    The rote therof is called Jesse —
                    A Floure of pryce!
70   Ther is non seche in paradise!

CAROL 18. JOYS OF MARY   [W45]

Et alia de Sancta Maria.   *And another [song] concerning Blessed Mary*

        "Ave, Maria," now say we so,
        Moder and maydon was never non mo!   *any other [like you]*

        Gaude, Maria, Cristis moder,   *Rejoice, Mary*
        Maré, moder of thyn Emne,   *Mate (see note)*
        Thou bare my Lord. Thou bare my Broder.
        Thou bare a cumlé Child and clene.   *comely*
5   Thou stodist ful stil, without wene,   *quietly; doubt*
        When in thyn ere this erand was doo.   *ear; done*
        When gracious God thee lyght within,   *alighted*
                Gabrielis nuncio.   *At Gabriel's announcement*
            "Ave, Maria," now say we so,
10   Moder and maydon was never non mo!   *more [than you]*

      Gaude, Maria, Y gret with grace.   *greet*

      When Jhesu, thi Sun, of thee was bore,

      Fol nygh thi brest thou con him brace.   *Very near; embrace*

      He secud. He soukid. He wept ful sore.   *sighed; sucked*

15   Thou fedist that Flour that never schal fade   *fed*

      With maydns melke, and sang therto: *maiden's milk*

      "Lolay, my Swete! I bare thee, Babe,   *bore*

           Cum peudoris lilleo."   *With the lily of chastity*

      "*Ave, Maria*," now say we so,

20   Moder and maydon was never non mo!

      Gaude, Maria, thi myght was away,   *strength was gone*

      When Crist thi Son on cros con dye,

      Ful dolfully on Good Fryday,

      That moné a moder sone hit se.   *many a mother's son it saw*

25   His blod us boght fro care and strive.   *strife*

      His wateré wondis us waschid fro wo.   *watery wounds*

      The thryd day fro deth to lyve,

           Fulget resureccio!   *The resurrection shines*

      "*Ave, Maria*," now say we so,

30   Moder and maydon was never non mo!

      Gaude, Maria, thou burd so bryght,   *woman*

      Breghter then the blossum that blomyth on the hill, *blooms*

      Ful joyful thou were to se seche a syght,   *see such*

      And al the postilis so swet of wil,   *apostles*

35   Fore, al and sum, thai stod ful stil,   *all together*

      When, fayrst of chap, he swond youe fro[1] —

      Fro erthe to heven he styud ful stil,   *climbed; steadily*

           Motu fertur proprio.   *He moves with his own motion*

      "*Ave, Maria*," now say we so,

40   Moder and maydon was never non mo!

      Gaude, Maria, that Rose on ryse —   *branch (with a pun on arising)*

      Moder and maid, gentil and fre,

      Precious, perrles, princes of pes,   *peerless princess of peace*

      Thi boure is next the Trineté —   *bower; next [to]*

45   Thi Sun as Love al knon of kynd,   *Thy Son known everywhere as Love by nature*

      Thi bodé and soule he toke him to.

      Thou restist with him ther, as we fynd,

           In celi palacio.   *In heaven's palace*

      "*Ave, Maria*," now say we so,

50   Moder and maydon was never non mo!

---

[1] *When, fairest of shape (i.e., Christ), he swooned away from you*

CAROL 19. MARY FLOWER OF WOMEN   [W46]

Et de Sancta Maria.   *And concerning Blessed Mary*

    Heyle, of wymmen flour of alle,
    Thou herst us when we to thee calle!   *hear*

    Blessid mot thou be, thou berd so bryght,   *woman*
    Moder and maidon most of myght,
    Thou art the ster of days lyght,   *star*
    And kepust us when we schul falle.   *support*
5   Heyle, of wymmen flour of alle,
       Thou herst us when we to thee calle!

    Of alle berdis that ever was boren,   *women*
    Blessid mot thou be both even and morn;   *evening*
    Throgh thee were savyd that were forelorne,
10   Moné on beth gret and smale.   *Many a one [who] are*
       Heyle, of wymmen flour of alle,
       Thou herst us when we to thee calle!

    "Hayle" to thee was swettlé sayd   *(i.e., by Gabriel)* [Luke 1:28]
    When Jhesu in thee he was consayved,
15   And throgh thee was the Fende afrayd —   *Fiend [made] afraid*
    Thou madist us fre to make him thralle!   *enslaved*
       Heyle, of wymmen flour of alle,
       Thou herst us when we to thee calle!

    Hayle, chif chosun garbunkul ston,   *choicest carbuncle stone*
20   Of thee was borne both God and Mon;
    When synful mon he makis his mon,
    To him thou art treu as ston in wal.
       Heyle, of wymmen flour of alle,
       Thou herst us when we to thee calle!

25   Haile, be thou quene, emperes of hel,   *empress of hell*
    Of al peté, thou arte the wel.   *fountain*
    We prayn thee, dame and damesel,
    That thou bryng us into thi hal.
       Heyle, of wymmen flour of alle,
30   Thou herst us when we to thee calle!

CAROL 20. CHASTITY FOR MARY'S LOVE   [W47]

De virginitate.   *Concerning virginity*

> *For the love of a maydon fre,*
> *I have me choson to chastité!*

Blessid mot be oure heven quene,
Fore vergyn and maydyn sheo was ful cleene.
Soche another was never yer sene,   *before*
That so wel kept here virgynyté.
5   For the love of a maydon fre,
         I have me choson to chastité!

In word, in will, in dede, in thoght,
Here maydehood defowled sheo noght;   *virginity*
Therfore the Lorde that here hade wroght   *that had created her*
10   Wolde be boron of hyr body.   *born*
         For the love of a maydon fre,
         I have me choson to chastité!

Tofore alle maydenes, to hyr he ches   *chose*
Fore here clannes and here mekenes;
15   Fore mon soule heo schuld reles   *release*
Ever fro the Fynd and his pousté.   *power*
         For the love of a maydon fre,
         I have me choson to chastité!

Seynt Kateryn and Marget and Wynfred,   *Margaret; Winifred*
20   That lovyd ful wel here maydhed,
The sofird to smyte of here hede,   *They suffered the smiting [off] of their heads*
Fore defouled wold thai not be.
         For the love of a maydon fre,
         I have me choson to chastité!

25   Therfore thai be in heven blis,
Where murth and melodé ever ther ys,
And soo shal all maydons, ywys,
That kepon heore worder and here degré.   *vow*
         For the love of a maydon fre,
30   I have me choson to chastité!

Thai foloun our lady with gret reverens,   *follow*
And don here servys in here presens,   *serve her*
Fore agayns the Fynd thai made defense
With the swerd of chastité.

Line numbers: 35 at top, then 5,10,15,20,25,30.

- line 4 "And lese your state, your honesté." → *lose your condition*
- line 7 "An undurmarke Crist con you lene" → *hidden mark; loan*
- line 9 "Yif ye hit tame, hit wil be sene," → *injure*
- line 10 "Do ye never soo prevely." → *privately*
- line 13 "Of that tresour men ben ful fayne," → *treasure (i.e., virginity); eager*
- line 14 "And al here love on youe thai layne," → *their; lay*
- line 15 "And moné a pené fore hit thai payne," → *many a penny for it they [would] pay*
- line 16 "Both selver and gold, lond and fe." → *property*
- line 20 "When hit is knowyn, ye wil have chame —" → *shame*
- line 21 "Oft therfore ye berne gret blame," → *[would] bear*
- line 22 "Never on be other ware wil be." → *[If you] never will beware of another*
- line 25 "Nad that tresoure bene ewroght," → *Had not; made*
- line 26 "To blis we had not bene ebroght;" → *brought (i.e., through Mary)*
- line 27 "Hit faylis never, ne fadis noght;" → *fades*
- line 28 "Ever to mon, hit is redy." → *Always*

#		
35	For the love of a maydon fre,	
	I have me choson to chastité!	

CAROL 21. VIRGINITY OF MAIDS [W 48]

Cantalena de virginibus.   *A song concerning viginity*

#		
	I pray youe, maydys that here be,	
	Kepe your state and your degré.	
	In word, in dede, in wyl, in thoght,	
	Your maydynhede defoule ye noght,	
	Lest to blame that ye ben broght,	
	And lese your state, your honesté.	*lose your condition*
5	I pray youe, maydys that here be,	
	Kepe your state and your degré.	
	An undurmarke Crist con you lene	*hidden mark; loan*
	To marc with — kepe hit clene!	
	Yif ye hit tame, hit wil be sene,	*injure*
10	Do ye never soo prevely.	*privately*
	I pray youe, maydys that here be,	
	Kepe your state and your degré.	
	Of that tresour men ben ful fayne,	*treasure (i.e., virginity); eager*
	And al here love on youe thai layne,	*their; lay*
15	And moné a pené fore hit thai payne,	*many a penny for it they [would] pay*
	Both selver and gold, lond and fe.	*property*
	I pray youe, maydys that here be,	
	Kepe your state and your degré.	
	Yif that tresoure ye don hit tame,	
20	When hit is knowyn, ye wil have chame —	*shame*
	Oft therfore ye berne gret blame,	*[would] bear*
	Never on be other ware wil be.	*[If you] never will beware of another*
	I pray youe, maydys that here be,	
	Kepe your state and your degré.	
25	Nad that tresoure bene ewroght,	*Had not; made*
	To blis we had not bene ebroght;	*brought (i.e., through Mary)*
	Hit faylis never, ne fadis noght;	*fades*
	Ever to mon, hit is redy.	*Always*
	I pray youe, maydys that here be,	
30	Kepe your state and your degré.	

	Yif ye kepyn wele that tresoure,	*preserve*
	Hit schal you bryng to hie honoure;	*high*
	Thagh ye be fayre, of freche coloure,	*fresh*
	Beuté is noght without bonté.	*Beauty; goodness*
35	I pray youe, maydys that here be,	
	Kepe your state and your degré.	

	Trewly, nyer that tresoure were,	*were it not that; were [intact]*
	Of men ye schuld have febul chere;	*feeble favor*
	Avyse you whom ye lene hit here,	*to whom you let have*
40	Yif ye ben begild, that blame not me.	*are beguiled (i.e., seduced)*
	I pray youe, maydys that here be,	
	Kepe your state and your degré.	

	Fore other cownsel nedis youe non,	
	Then doth therafter, everechon,	*So follow [this advice], every one [of you]*
45	Fore this tresoure has holpyn moné hone;	*helped many [a] one*
	Hit marys maydis uche cuntré.	*It allow maids to marry in every land*
	I pray youe, maydys that here be,	
	Kepe your state and your degré.	

CAROL 22. CHASTITY OF WIVES   [W49]

De matrimonio mulierum.	*Concerning the matrimony of women*

	Avyse youe, wemen, wom ye trust,	*whom*
	And beware of "had-I-wyst."	*the regret of "had I known"*

	Hit is ful hevé, chastité,	*heavy*
	With moné maydyns nowoday,	*nowadays*
	That lovyn to have gam and gle —	*sport and mirth*
	That turnes to sorowe, sothly to say! —	*Which turns to sorrow*
5	Alle day thou sist!	*see [that this is true]*
	Avyse youe, wemen, wom ye trust,	
	And beware of "had-I-wyst."	

	Now yif a womon mared schal be,	*if; married*
	Anon heo schal be boght and solde,	
10	Fore no love of hert, truly,	*heart*
	Bot fore covetyse of lond ore gold —	*coveting*
	Al day thou seest!	
	Avyse youe, wemen, wom ye trust,	
	And beware of "had-I-wyst."	

15	Bot thus Godis low and his wil wolde	*law; ordains*
	Even of blod, of good, of ache,	*Equality of birth, of wealth, of age*

Fore love togeder thus com thai schuld,
Fore this makis metlé mareache —   *suitable marriage*
   Ale day thou seest!
20   Avyse youe, wemen, wom ye trust,
   And beware of "had-I-wyst."

And the froyt that coms hom betwene,   *fruit (i.e., offspring)*
Hit schal have grace to thryve and the;   *thrive and prosper*
Ther other schal have turment and tene,   *trouble*
25   Fore covetyse unlaufully —   *avarice*
   Al day thou seest!
   Avyse youe, wemen, wom ye trust,
   And beware of "had-I-wyst."

Ther is no creatuere, as wretyn I fynd,
30   Save onelé mon that doth outtrache,   *only; outrage (i.e., unnatural mating)*
Bot chesyn hom makys of here oune kynd,   *choose for themselves mates; own*
And so thai makyn treu mareache —   *marriage*
   Alle day thou seest!
   Avyse youe, wemen, wom ye trust,
35   And beware of "had-I-wyst."

Bot now a lady wil take a page   *servant*
Fore no love bot fleschelé lust,   *fleshly*
And so here blod is disparage —   *misallied in rank*
Thus lordus and lordchip al day ben lost —   *lords and lordships*
40   Al day thou seest!
   Avyse youe, wemen, wom ye trust,
   And beware of "had-I-wyst."

Lordis and lorchip thus wastyn away
In Englond in moné a place
45   (That makis false ayrs — hit is no nay!)   *heirs*
And lese worchip, honowre, and grace —
   Al day thou seest!
   Avyse youe, wemen, wom ye trust,
   And beware of "had-I-wyst."

CAROL 23. LOVE OF GOD   [W50]

De amore Dei.   *Concerning the love of God*

   I have a Love, is Heven Kyng;
   I love his love foreevermore!

Fore Love is Love and ever schal be,
And Love has bene ore we were bore;   *before; born*
Fore Love, he askys no nother fe   *reward*
Bot love agayn; he kepis no more.
5   I say, herefore,
     I have a Love, is Heven Kyng;
     I love his love foreevermore!

Trew love is tresoure, trust is store,   *wealth*
To a love to Godis plesyng;   *pleasing to God*
10   Bot leude love makis men elore,   *licentious; lost*
To love here lust and here lykyng.   *fleshly pleasure*
          I say, herefore,
     I have a Love, is Heven Kyng;
     I love his love foreevermore!

15   In good love ther is no syn;
Withot love is hevenes;   *Without; distress*
Herefore, to love I nyl not blyn   *cease*
To love my God and his goodnes.
          I say, herefore,
20   I have a Love, is Heven Kyng;
     I love his love foreevermore!

Fore he me lovyd or I him knew;   *before*
Therfore, I love him altherbest,   *best of all*
Ellis my love I myght hit rew;   *regret*
25   I love with him to take my rest.
          I say, herefore,
     I have a Love, is Heven Kyng;
     I love his love foreevermore!

Of al loveres that ever was borne,
30   His love hit passid everechon;
Nad he us lovyd, we were forelorne;   *Had he not*
Without is love, trew love is non.   *his*
          I say, herefore,
     I have a Love, is Heven Kyng;
35   I love his love foreevermore!

CAROL 24. DREAD OF DEATH   [W51]

Timor mortis conturbat me.[1]

> *Ladé, helpe! Jhesu, mercé!*
> *Timor mortis conturbat me.*

Dred of deth, sorow of syn,
Trobils my hert ful grevysly;   *Troubles; grievously*
My soule hit nyth with my lust then —   *harms*
Passio Christi conforta me.[2]
5   Ladé, helpe! Jhesu, mercé!
           Timor mortis conturbat me.   *The fear of death troubles me*

Fore blyndnes is a hevé thyng,   *burdensome*
And to be def therwith only,   *deaf*
To lese my lyght and my herying —   *lose*
10   *Passio Christi conforta me.*   *Passion of Christ, fortify me*
           Ladé, helpe! Jhesu, mercé!
           Timor mortis conturbat me.

And to lese my tast and my smellyng,
And to be seke in my body,
15   Here have I lost al my lykyng —   *pleasure*
      Passio Christi conforta me.
           Ladé, helpe! Jhesu, mercé!
           Timor mortis conturbat me.

Thus God he geves and takys away,
20   And, as he wil, so mot hit be;   *wills; may*
      His name be blessid both nyght and daye —
      Passio Christi conforta me.
           Ladé, helpe! Jhesu, mercé!
           Timor mortis conturbat me.

25   Here is a cause of gret mornyng —   *mourning*
      Of myselfe nothyng I se,
      Save filth, unclennes, vile stynkyng —
      Passio Christi conforta me.
           Ladé, helpe! Jhesu, mercé!
30   *Timor mortis conturbat me.*

---

[1] *The fear of death troubles me.* The phrase is liturgical (see explanatory note).

[2] *Passion of Christ, fortify me.* This is the fifth line of the famous prayer *Anima Christi sanctifica me*, found earlier in MS Douce 302 (fol. 9r). It also appears in *Pope John's Passion of Our Lord*, line 9.

Into this word no more I broght,   *world*
No more I gete with me, trewly,
Save good ded, word, wil, and thoght —
Passio Christi conforta me.
35   Ladé, helpe! Jhesu, mercé!
Timor mortis conturbat me.

The fyve wondis of Jhesu Crist,
My midsyne now mot thai be,   *medicine*
The Fyndis pouere downe to cast —   *Fiend's power*
40 *Passio Christi conforta me.*
Ladé, helpe! Jhesu, mercé!
Timor mortis conturbat me.

As I lay seke in my langure,   *sick; languishing*
With sorow of hert and teere of ye,   *tear of eye*
45 This caral I made with gret doloure —   *sadness*
Passio Christi conforta me.
Ladé, helpe! Jhesu, mercé!
Timor mortis conturbat me.

Oft with these prayere I me blest,   *prayers*
50 *In manus tuas, Domine,*[1]
Thou take my soule into thi rest —
Passio Christi conforta me.
Ladé, helpe! Jhesu, mercé!
Timor mortis conturbat me.

55 Maré moder, merceful may,
Fore the joys thou hadist, lady,
To thi Sun, fore me thou pray —
Passio Christi conforta me.
Ladé, helpe! Jhesu, mercé!
60 *Timor mortis conturbat me.*

Lerne this lesson of Blynd Awdlay:
When bale is hyest, then bot may be,   *misery; highest; remedy may occur*
Yif thou be nyd nyght or day,   *troubled*
Say "*Passio Christi conforta me.*"
65   Ladé, helpe! Jhesu, mercé!
Timor mortis conturbat me.

---

[1] *Into thy hands, Lord.* Luke 23:46. Compare *Seven Words of Christ on the Cross*, lines 74–75.

CAROL 25. SAINT FRANCIS   **[W52]**

De Sancto Fransisco.   *Concerning Saint Francis*

> *Saynt Frances, to thee I say,*
> *Save thi breder both nyght and day!*   *brethren*

A holé confessoure thou were hone,   *one*
And levydist in contemplacion,   *lived*
To thyng on Cristis Passioun,   *think*
That sofyrd deth on Good Fryday.
5   Saynt Frawnces, to thee I pray,
    Save thi breder both nyght and day!

His Passion was in thee so fervent
That he aperd to thi present;   *appeared in your presence*
Upon thi body he set his preynt,   *stigmata*
10 His fyve wondis — hit is no nay!
    Saynt Frances, to thee I say,
    Save thi breder both nyght and day!

Upon thi body thou hem bere,   *you bore them (the wounds)*
Affter that tyme, ful thre yere;
15 To al men syght thai did apere —
No water mygth wasche hem away.
    Saynt Frances, to thee I say,
    Save thi breder both nyght and day.

Weder thou schuldist ete ore drenke,   *Whether*
20 On Cristis Passion thou woldist thynke;
In fyve partys wes thi partyng   *dividing*
Of his sustinans, sothe to say.
    Saynt Frances, to thee I say,
    Save thi breder both nyght and day!

25 Crist he grawnt thee, specialy,
Fore on his Passion thou hadist peté,
To feche thi breder out of purgatori,
That ly in ther in rewful aray.   *pitiful state*
    Saynt Frances, to thee I say,
30   Save thi breder both nyght and day!

Thou thongis Crist of his swete sonde,   *thanked; gift*
And thoghtist to go to the Holé Londe,
Fore dred of deth thou woldist not wond,   *hesitate*
To teche the pepil thi Cristyn fay.   *faith*

35   Saynt Frances, to thee I say,
           Save thi breder both nyght and day!

        Then Crist he knew welle then entent,   *your intent*
        And turned thee out of that talent,   *purpose*
        And bede thee make thi testament,
40   And: "Come to me, fore ens and ay."   *once and always*
           Saynt Frances, to thee I say,
           Save thi breder both nyght and day!

        "A, holé Frawnces, now I se,
        Fore my love that thou woldist dye;
45   Thou schalt have joy perpetualé,
        Thou hast dyssired moné a day."   *[As] you have desired*
           Saynt Frances, to thee I say,
           Save thi breder both nyght and day!

        His holé reule of relegiowne
50   To his breder he wrote anon,
        And prayd ham, fore Cristis Passiowne,
        To kepe hit wel both nyght and day.
           Saynt Frances, to thee I say,
           Save thi breder both nyght and day!

55   A sad ensampil here mow ye se,   *may*
        On Cristis Passioun to have peté,
        And to leve in love and chareté,   *live*
        Then meré in hert be ye may.   *merry*
           Saynt Frances, to thee I say,
60   Save thi breder both nyght and day!

        His last prayer to Crist this was,
        Fore al that sustens this holé place:
        "Gracious God, grawnt ham thi grace,
        Tofore thi Jugement at Domysday."
65   Saynt Frances, to thee I say,
           Save thi breder both nyght and day!

        Pray we to Frawnses, that beth present,   *[you] who are present*
        To save his breder and his covent,   *convent*
        That thai be never chamyd ne chent,   *shamed or disgraced*
70   With wyckid man ne Fyndis fray.   *Fiend's attack*
           Saynt Frances, to thee I say,
           Save thi breder both nyght and day!

        I pray youe, seris, pur charyté,   *for*
        Redis this caral reverently,

75   Fore I mad hit with wepyng eye,
        Your broder Jon the Blynd Awdlay.
            Saynt Frances, to thee I say,
            Save thi breder both nyght and day!

XXXVI. DEVOTIONAL PROSE [NOT IN W]

INSTRUCTIONS FOR READING 4 [UNNUMBERED IN W]

Rede thys offt, butt rede hit sofft,	
And whatt thou redust, forgeete hit noght,	*read*
For here the soth thou maght se	*truth*
What fruyte cometh of thy body.	*fruit*

THE SINS OF THE HEART [NOT IN W]

De peccatis cordis. *The sins of the heart*

These synnys of the hert arne these: evyl thoghtis, evel delytis, ascentyng to syn, dissire of evel, wykkid wyll, evyl suspessions, undevocion (yif thou let thyn hert ené tyme be ydil without ocupacion in the worchipyng of thi God); evol love, erroure, fleschelé afexion to thi fryndis, or to other that thou lovyst, joy in oné mons evel fare
5 (wether thay bene enmyes ore non); dispite of pore men or of synful, to honore ryche men fore her reches, unconabil joy of oné word vanetes, sorow fore the losse of wordis catel, untholomodnes, perplexeté (that is deute what is to do, and wot noght, fore everé mon outh fore to be sekyr what he schal do, whot he schal lefe), obstenacion in evyl, noy to do good, angar to Gode, sorow that he did no more ewol,
10 or that he dud noght that lust or that wyl of his lust-flesche the wyche he myght have done, unstabilnes of thoght, pyne of penance, ypocrecé, love to plese man, dred to plese hom, schame of good dede, joy of evyl dede, synglere wit, covetys of worchyp, of dyngneté, or to be holdyn better then other, ore rysere, or fayrer, or to be more dred, vayngloré of oné goodys of kynd or of happe ore of grace, schame of
15 pore froyndys, pride of ryche kyn ore of gentyl (fore al we are elyche fre before Godys face, bot our dedys makyth ouse better or worse then other), dyspyte of good cownsel and of good techeng.

1 delytis, pleasures; **ascentyng**, assenting. **2 suspessions**, suspicions; **undevocion**, impiety. **4 fleschelé afexion**, carnal affection; **oné**, any. **6 reches**, wealth; **unconabil**, excessive; **word vanetes**, worldly vanities. **7 wordis catel**, worldly possession; **untholomodnes**, intolerance of adversity; **deute**, doubt. **8 sekyr**, decisive; **lefe**, not do. **9 obstenacion**, obstinence; **noy**, annoyance; **angar**, anger; **ewol**, evil. **10 lust**, desire. **11 unstabilnes**, instability; **pyne**, pain; **ypocrecé**, hypocrisy. **12 synglere**, selfish. **13 worchyp**, honor; **rysere**, richer. **14 kynd**, nature; **happe**, chance. **15 froyndys**, friends; **gentyl**, noble [kin]; **elyche fre**, equally free. **16 ouse**, us.

The synys of the mouth aren these: to swere ofsyth, foresweryng, schawnder of Crist ore of oné of his sayntis, to nemne his name without reverens, backbytyng, glosyng, stryvyng, thretyng, sowyng of dyscord, tresown, false wyttenes, evyl cownsel, skornyng, unbuxumnes with worde, to turne good dede to evyl fore to make hom be hold evel that doth hom good (we how to turne our neghtbore dedys into the best, nott in the worst), exityng ené mon to wrath, to reprevyn other of that he doth himselve, veyn speche, mochil speche, to speke way-wordys and ydul or wordys that were ne nede, bostyng, polyschyng of wordys, defendyng of synne, cryyng in laghtur, mowys to make on oné mon, to syng seculer songys and love hom of paromowrs of wordys waneté, to preyse evol dedys, to syng more fore praysyng of men than fore the worchyp of God.

The synys of dede ar these: glotony, lechoré, dronkones, symoné, wychecraft, brekyng of the holé dayse, sacrelege, to resayve Godys body in dedlé synne, wetynglé brekyng of vowys, apostasey, neclegens in Godys servys, to gif evyl ensampyl of evyl dede, to hurte oné mon upon his bodé or on his goodis or in his fame, theft, ravayn, useuré, dyssayte, in sellyng of ryghtwysnes, to herkyn evyl, to gif to harlottis, to withhold nessessaryes fro the bodé or to gif hit outrage, to begyn a thyng that is above oure myght, conscent to syn, fallyng efft in synne, fynyng of more good then we have fore to seme holear or conyngere ore wyser then we are, to holdyn the ofyse that we fulfyl noght to, ore that may noght be holdyn withoutyn syn, to lede karalys, to bryng up a new gyse, to be rebel to his soferens, to defoule hom that has lasse, to synne in syght, in herynge, in smellynge, in towchyng, in handylyng, in giftis, wyghtis wayus, syngnys, bekenyngys, wrytyngys receyve.

The circumstans that ar tyme, stede, maner, nombyr, person, dwellyng, helde (these make on the synne more other lasse), to covet to syn or he be temptid to constrayne him to synne. And other moné: not thynkyng on Godd, ne dredyng, ne lovyng, ne thonkyng him of his good dedys, to do noght alle fore Godys love that he doth, to sorow noght fore his syn as he schuld do, to dysplesen noght to ressayve grace, yef he have ressayvyd grace, to use hit noght as him ought ne kepe hit noght, to turne at the inspyracion of God, to conferme not his wyl to Godys wyl, to gif not his entent to his prayers, bot rabul on and recheth never how thai bene sayd:

18 ofsyth, often; foresweryng, oath-breaking; schawnder, slander. 19 nemne, name; backbytyng, gossiping. 20 glosyng, critiquing; stryvyng, arguing; thretyng, threatening; wyttenes, witness. 21 unbuxumnes, disobedience. 22 hold, considered; how, ought; dedys, deeds. 23 exityng, inciting; wrath, anger; reprevyn, reprove. 24 veyn, vain; mochil, much; speke way-wordys, chatter. 25 polyschyng, rhetorical polishing. 26 mowys to make, mockery; paramowrs, illicit lovers. 27 of wordys waneté, for worldy vanity. 29 symoné, simony. 30 wetynglé, knowingly. 31 apostasey, apostasy (i.e., renunciation of faith); neclegens, negligence; Godys servys, mass; ensampyl, example. 32 ravayn, robbery. 33 useuré, usury; dyssayte, deceit; ryghtwysnes, righteousness. 34 to gif hit outrage, to abuse it (i.e., one's body). 35 efft, again; fynyng, feigning. 36 holear, holier; conyngere, more skillful; ofyse, office. 37 karalys, carols. 38 gyse, fashion; soferens, sovereigns (i.e., betters); lasse, less. 40 wyghtis wayus, devilish ways (see explanatory note); syngnys, signs; receyve, accept. 41 stede, place; helde, age. 42 these make on the synne more other lasse, i.e., these determine the severity of the sin; or, before. 45 dysplesen, to be displeased. 47 turne at, turn away from; conferme, conform. 48 rabul, mutter; recheth, care.

Over-Hippers and Skippers (embedded alliterative stanza)   [not in W]

Over-hippers and skippers, moterers and mumlers —   *Abridgers; mutterers; mumblers*
Tytyvyllis tytild here wordus and takes ham to hys pray;   *Titivillus whispered; prey*
Japers and janglers, haukeers and hunters —   *Jokesters; chatterers; hawkers*
The holé servys of God thai schend when thay say.   *holy service (i.e., mass); destroy*
[5]   Rofyn wyl rede hom ful redely in his rolle anoder day,   *Ruffin; readily; another*
When thay ben called to here cowntis and to here rekenyng —   *accounts; reckoning*
Hou thay han sayde here servys, the Prince of Heven to pay,   *satisfy*
Butt rabulde hit forthe unreverently by caus of hyyng,   *But [rather] mumbled; hurrying*
Without dewocion:
[10]   Fore better hit were stil to be,   *silent*
Then to say Godys servys undewoutly;
Thai scornyn God ful sekyrlé,   *certainly*
And han his maleson.   *curse*

To do neclegens that he is holdyn to do throgh avowe ore comawndment ore is en-
50   joynde in penans, to draw along that is to done sone, havyng no joy of his neghtbore
prophete as him houthe, sorowyng noght of his evol fare, wychestonyng noght
agayns temptaciones, foregifyng noght hom that have done him harme, kepyng
noght trouth to his neghtbors as he wold he dud to him, and yildyng him noght
a good dede fore another yif he may, amenduth not hom that synneth before his
55   ene, peesyng noght strives, techyng hom noght that are unkonyng, comfford hom
noght that are in sorowe ore in sekenes. These synns and other moo makyn men
foule in the syght of God.

Quicumque inspexerit.   *Whosoever will have looked*

An Honest Bed   [not in W]

Whan the chambur of thi soule is clensid fro al syn, thou schalte aray a bedd
therin on this wyse, in the wheche Lorde Jhesu wol haue lykyng to ryst hym. Bot
furst thou most make thi lytter, that schal be made of Mynde-of-al-the-synnys-
that-ever-thou-didyst, gederyng togeder as into a lytter of straw. Then loke thou
5   schake oute of this leter (wyche is in thi mynde) al the dust of Al-syn and of
Foule-thoghtus there wyth the schakeforke of Kyndnes, wyche schal have two
grayns: that one is Wil to amend thee, that other is to pray God of Grace that hit

49 do neclegens that, neglect what; **holdyn,** beholden; **avowe,** oath. **49–50 enjoynde,**
bidden (to do). **50 draw along,** delay. **51 prophete,** profit; **him houthe,** he should;
wychestonyng, resisting. **53 yildyng,** yielding. **54 amenduth,** correct(ing). **55 ene,** eyes;
peesyng noght strives, appeasing not arguments; **unkonyng,** ignorant.

1 aray, adorn. **2 wyse,** way; **ryst hym,** rest himself. **3 lytter,** resting place. **6 schakeforke,**
forked instrument for beating out dust. **7 grayns,** tines.

mow so be. The canves nexte the straue most be an enterelé S<small>OROW</small> fore thi syn,
wyche wyl make thee to watyre the lytter of thi bed with terys of thyn ene, as the
10 prophet sayth Davyth in the Sautere Boke, *Lacremis meis stratum meum rigabo*, that
is to say, "Y have waterd my byd stre alle with terris of myn ene."

The matres of this bede schal be holé M<small>EDYCACIONCE</small>, the wyche wyl put out of
thi soule al foule thoghtis that wil defoule thi soule and enclyne hit to syyn. The two
15 blancketys of thi bed schul be A<small>BSTYNENCE</small> agayns glotoné, and C<small>HASTITÉ</small> agayns
lechoré and lust of fleschelé lykyng.

The nether schete schal be a sekyr B<small>ELEVE</small> without oné doute in oné artekil
therof, fore the beleve is growndytt of ale Cristyn mens relygyone. The over schete
schal be a sekyr H<small>OPE</small> to be savyd throgh good werkys of thi beleve in the grete
mercé of our Lord Jhesu Crist.

20 The keverlet of this bed schul be C<small>HARITÉ</small>, that is, a trew love to God and to thyn
even Cristyn. *Quia caritas operit multitudinem peccatorem*, that is to say, "Charité coverth
the multytude of synne."

The peleus at the hede schul be P<small>ETÉ</small> and P<small>ACIENS</small>. Haue peté of pore pepil
and be paciens in advarceté. The bolstyr that these pylous schul lyne one most be
25 B<small>ESENES</small>-<small>AND</small>-<small>WAKYNG</small> in al good virteuys and werkys, lest hevenes wolde make
thee fal into dyspayre ore slepe long in synne.

The testur at the hede schal be *Lyberum Arbetrium*, that is F<small>RE</small> <small>CHOYS</small>, so that
thou chese no thyng that is agayns the comandment of God or helthe of thi soule.
The curtyns on the ryght syde schal be R<small>YGHT</small>-<small>AND</small>-<small>RESOUNE</small>; on the lyfte syde,
30 U<small>NDERSTONDYNG</small>-<small>AND</small>-<small>WYSDAM</small>. Let thes two curtyns ryn apon the ryngys of T<small>HE</small>
T<small>EN</small> C<small>OMAWNDEMENTIS</small>. Loke fore no thyng that no ryng be brokyn, fore yif thai
be, the curtyns wil sagge downe and then may thyne enmé the Devol loke one into
the bed of Jesu.

The curtene at the fete schal be thi W<small>YL</small>. Let hit ren up on the ryngys of T<small>HE</small>
35 S<small>EVEN</small> W<small>ERKYS</small> O<small>F</small> M<small>ERCÉ</small> so that al thi besenes be evermore alse ferford as thou
may to plese God and help thyn even Cristen. And yif thi fre choys, paraventur,
chese eney thyng at the cownsel of thi wil, loke thou do hit never bot yif resoune
and understondyng be chefe of thi cownsel and acorde wele therto. The seloure
over thi bed schal be S<small>ELENS</small>, that is, kepyng of thi tonge, so that thou slawnder not
40 the nome of God in gret othis sweryng. Kepe thee fro bacbytyng and foule wordys
spekyng. Lat the cordys that the seloure schal be teyd with and that the redel schul
ren upone be made of dowbyl silke or of twyne of P<small>ARCEVERENS</small>, that is, wil to last
stil in good levynge fro the bekynyng of thi lyve to the endyng.

8 canves, canvas; **straue**, straw; **enterelé**, thorough. **9 terys**, tears; **ene**, eyes. **10 Sautere**, Psalter; ***Lacremis . . . rigabo***, *I will water my couch with my tears.* Psalm 6:7. **11 stre**, straw; **terris**, tears. **12 M<small>EDYCACIONCE</small>**, Meditation. **16 nether**, lower; **sekyr**, steadfast; **B<small>ELEVE</small>**, faith; **oné**, any. **17 over**, upper. **20 keverlet**, coverlet. **21 even**, fellow; ***Quia . . . peccatorem***, *For charity covereth a multitude of sins.* 1 Peter 4:8. **23 peleus**, pillows; **P<small>ACIENS</small>**, patience. **24 advarceté**, adversity; **pylous**, pillows; **lyne one**, lie on. **25 B<small>ESENES</small>**, busyness; **virteuys**, virtues; **hevenes**, heavyness. **27 testur**, headboard. **30 ryn**, run. **32 thyne enmé**, your enemy. **35 ferford**, complete. **36 paraventur**, perchance. **37 bot yif**, unless. **38 be chefe of**, guide; **acorde**, agree; **seloure**, canopy. **39 S<small>ELENS</small>**, silence. **40 othis**, oaths; **bacbytyng**, gossip. **41 teyd**, tied; **redel**, curtain. **42 dowbyl**, double; **twyne**, twine; **P<small>ARCEVERENS</small>**, perseverance. **43 bekynyng**, beginning; **lyve**, life.

The hokys that schul be smetyn into the wal to hold the cordys and thes curtens
45   up with, this is a SECUR PURPOS never to turne to thi synne.

Tho most have an amyr that thay schul be smetyn into the wallys in thi schambyr,
with the wyche wallis are thi FOURE AGYS, that is, childehode, youeth, parfite age,
and the last age whan thou art an old mon ore womon. This hamyr schal be COMPAS-
SION of grete payne that our Lorde Jhesu Crist suffyrde on the rode fore our synys.

50   The hede of this hamur schal be made of the hard naylys of yron that the fete
and the handys of our Lorde were naylyd to the crose with.

The chaft therof schal be made of the cros that our Lorde dyed on.

Take hede of the chafte with the charpe poynte of the sperehede that smote
Jhesu to the hert, ere ellys with the charp thornes that thorlet the hede, his brayne
55   panne. Bot yet this bede most be bordyd aboute lest the straw fal oute.

The bordys of this bede schul be THE CARDNALYS VERTUCE. Thou most be
strong in thi beleve agayns temptacions of the Fynd. Thou most be prudent or ellis
slyghe ware and wilé agayne al wordelé sleghtys and soteltys.

Thou most have temperans agayns al fleschelé lustis, and loke that thou be
60   ryghtwyse in al maner levyng, and nayle togeder al tho bordis at the foure cornelnes
with PESE and TROUTH, MEKENES and REWTH. And loke then evermore that al the
clothis of thi bed be quyte, in tokyn of CLANNES, and pouder ham with red rosis,
portreyd with rede blod that our Lord schid in his Passion. This is the bed that our
Lorde speketh of in the Boke of Lawe *Canticorum Primo*: *Lectubus noster iam floridus*
65   *est*, "our bed is ful of flourys." Make CONSIANS thi schawmbyrlyn, fore he can aspy
defautes. And let him lyght up a lamp of love that he may se aboute. Make DREDE
usschere at the dore of thi chambyr, fore he wil let no thyng in at the dorse ne at
the wyndowys that schulde rayse oure Lord Jhesu fro his rest, ne defoule his
chambyr, ne dyssere his bedde.

70   Thus be the bedde that our Lord wil have lykyng to ly in. And when he is in this
bed, angelys wil syng about him this song of prophesé: *Exulta et lauda habitacio Syon,*
quia magnus in medio tui sanctus Israel, "thoue Syon, mon soule, the dwellyng place
of Jhesu, be joyful and glad for the gret Holé God of Israel is now within thee, the
wyche is Jhesus."

44 hokys, hooks; **smetyn**, fastened. **46 Tho**, You; **amyr**, hammer; **schambyr**, chamber.
47 parfite, perfect. **49 suffyrde**, suffered. **50 naylys**, nails. **52 chaft**, shaft. **53 hede**, heed;
smote, struck. **54 ere ellys**, or else; **thorlet**, pierced. **54–55 brayne panne**, skull. **55**
bordyd, boarded. **56 CARDNALYS VERTUCE**, Cardinal Virtues. **58 slyghe ware**, slyly aware;
wordelé, worldly; **sleghtys**, sleights; **soteltys**, subtleties. **59 temperans**, temperance. **60**
ryghtwyse, righteous; **cornelnes**, corners. **61 PESE**, Peace; **TROUTH**, Truth; **MEKENESS**,
Humility; **REWTH**, Compassion. **62 quyte**, white; **pouder**, sprinkle; **rosis**, roses. **63**
portreyd with, depicting; **schid**, shed. **64–65 Lectubus . . . est**, *Our bed is flourishing.*
Canticles 1:15. **65 CONSIANS**, Conscience; **schawmbyrlyn**, chamberlain. **65–66 aspy**
defautes, detect faults. **66 se**, look. **67 usschere**, usher. **68 rayse**, arouse. **69 dyssere**,
disturb. **71–72 Exulta . . . Israel**, *Rejoice, and praise, habitation [of] Sion, for great is he that is*
in the midst of thee, the holy one of Israel. Isaias 12:6.

XXXVII. PATERNOSTER   [W53]

Pater noster qui es in celis.   Our Father who art in heaven [Matthew 6:9]

The Paternoster to expone, · may no man hit pryse,   *expound; appraise it[s full value]*
That of prayers is pris · and most fore to prayse;   *supreme; most [worthy]*
I rede thou rede hit aryght · and out of syn ryse,   *counsel [that]; correctly*
That may restyng in heven · unto thi soule rayse,   *[a] resting [place]; inspire*
5   Fore seven poyntis ther ar sene, · eset in asyse,   *seen, set in position*
The lest ys salve to the synn, · as the Boke sayse.   *least is remedy for sin; Bible*
"Our Fader, the wyche thou hart in heven," · this oresoune yse,   *use*
"Ay ehalouyd be thi name," · in angyr and in ayse.   *Forever hallowed; passion; calm*
           Sanctificetur nomen tuum.   Hallowed be thy name [Matthew 6:9, Luke 11:2]
10   Say whe the same: *we*
     "Oure Fader, the wyche thou art in heven, halouyd be thi name."

The secunde princepal poynt · is of paradyse,   *concerns*
How we schuld pyn us to pray · after that plase,   *exert ourselves; in pursuit of*
Fore uche a herd that is here · mai hold fore hyse
15   The Lord that harouyd hel · wil he in hert hase.[1]
Bot yif thou wyn thee that won, · I hold thee unwyse   *Unless; dwelling*
Fore wele wantyd ther never · non sethyn hit wroght was;[2]
Into that courte fore to cum — · be hit thi covetyse —   *should it be thy desire*
That the kyngdam of heven, · is callid in this case.   *[as it] is called*
20   *Adveniat regnum tuum.*   Thy kingdom come [Matthew 6:10, Luke 11:2]
              "Thi kyngdam us come."
This is the secunde poynt, al and some.   *all and entire*

The thrid poynt to expownd · that is most playne: *quite clear*
Let penans perce thi syn · out of thi soule plane.   *pierce; immediately*
25   The forewart at the fonston · to fulfyl be thou fayne,   *promise; baptismal font; eager*
And not in foundyng to fare · as the wederfane,   *falling [in sin]; go; weathervane*
Bot to abyde at his bone · and at his bidyng bayne,[3]
Both in bale and in blis · abyde at his bane.   *[to] wait for his summons*
Therfore his wil to fulfil · thou wilt thi soule wayne,   *bring*
30   And let thi warlouys werkys · out of thi soule wane.[4]
           Fiat voluntas tua sicut in celo et in terra.[5]
              "Fulfilde be his wil,
     Ryght in erth as in heven," with good and with ylle.

---

[1] Lines 14–15: *For every Christian that is here may claim [paradise] for his [own] / While he has in [his] heart the Lord who harrowed hell*

[2] *There lacks never happiness since it was created*

[3] *But to abide by his command, and to his bidding be inclined*

[4] *And let your fiendish sins depart out of your soul*

[5] *Thy will be done on earth as it is in heaven.* Matthew 6:10.

	The forth poynt is of the flesche · and of the soule fode,	*soul's nourishment*
35	To pray the Fader of Heven · us fore to fede;	
	Thagh thou hadyst hallis of golde, · hit thee behode,[1]	
	And ale we have hit of hym, · that lytyl takyn hede.	*[of] which few take heed*
	Furst bed we the bred · he boght with his blode,	*we pray for; bread*
	Sethyn the blisse above — · his body can foreblede!	*did bleed to exhaustion*
40	As thou art ryghtful Lord, · rent on the rode,	*just; torn*
	Reche us our ochedays bred · this day, as we rede.	*Bring; daily; pray*
	Panem nostrum cotidianum da nobis hodie.[2]	
	"Our ochedays bred,	
	Lord, thou reche us today." Thou art our soulis rede.	*Bring; soul's counsel*

45	When thou hast fraystud the fyrth, · to the fyft fare.	*grasped; fourth [point]; go*
	Thou schalt hit fortheron in thi hert · and ful sone ifere,	*honor; absorb [it]*
	And cri arde upon Crist · to kever us of care,	*hard; shelter; from*
	As he was crownyd on the croyse, · with a voyse clere,	
	And beware of that word · that thou hit wele ware,	*[shall] heed it well*
50	Ellys unborne that thou wore, · better thee were:[3]	
	"And foregef us our det · that doth the soule dare,	*threatens the soul*
	As we our dettyrs foregifth, · fore thi deth dere!"	*debtors; precious death*
	Et dimitte nobis debita nostra, sicut et nos dimittimus debitoribus nostris.[4]	
	"Foregif us our dett,	
55	As we our detturse foregifth." We bid no bet.	*We [can] pray no better*

	The sext poynte of the sevon · that I of syng	*of which I sing*
	Is moste salve to the soule, · in saw and in song,	*healing; proverb*
	That God our Fader ouse lede · into no fowndyng	*temptation (lit. falling)*
	That schulde our forward us let · heven fore to fong,[5]	
60	Ne fore no lykyng ne no lust, · wyle we schulde here lyng;	*pleasure; desire; dwell*
	Mak us to leve that lyve · that last schal so long;	
	Ne fore no want of that wele, · to wepe ne to wryng	
	Where warlawys waltyrne in here wo · fore here mekil wrong.[6]	
	Et ne nos inducas in temptacionem.[7]	
65	"Fore thi Godhede,	*For the sake of*
	Into no fowndyng of synne · that thou us never lede."	

---

[1] *Though you had halls of gold, you were obliged [so to pray]*

[2] *Give us this day our daily bread.* Luke 11:3; compare Matthew 6:11.

[3] *Or else you would be better [off] had you been unborn*

[4] *And forgive us our debst, as we also forgive our debtors.* Matthew 6:12; compare Luke 11:4.

[5] *That should hinder us from our agreement to seize heaven*

[6] Lines 61–63: *[Nor should thou] cause [us] to lose that life that shall last so long; / Nor, for lack of that joy, to weep or to wring [our hands in despair] / Where scoundrels wallow in their woe for their great sin*

[7] *And lead us not into temptation.* Matthew 6:13, Luke 11:4.

Bot delyver us from losse · both erlé and late —
This last poynt fore to lerne · harmus bot lyte —   *[is] but little harm to learn*
Fro al maner of mys · that wold us here mate,   *sin; stymie (lit. checkmate)*
70   That never no males ouse mare · more then a myt.[1]
The bale that is brewyn here · with blys thou abate,   *brewed; [may] thou*
That never the blase of hel · to our soule byte;   *blaze; bite*
And at the day of our deth · that settis no date,   *[for] which no date is set*
The Devyl be doles of us · howso he dyte![2]
75   *Set libera nos a malo. Amen.*   *But deliver us from evil [Matthew 6:13]*
              For dowte of that den,   *fear; cave*
        Lord, "tolyver us from alle evolus." Amen.   *deliver; evils*

XXXVIII. THREE DEAD KINGS   [W54]

De tribus regibus mortuis.   *Concerning three dead kings*

An a byrchyn bonke · ther bous arne bryght,   *birch-covered bank; where boughs are*
I saw a brymlyche bore · to a bay broght;   *ferocious boar brought to bay*
Ronke rachis with rerde · thai ronnon aryght;   *Strong hunting dogs; clamor; speedily*
Of al hore row and hore rest · lytil hom roght.   *their repose; little they cared*
5   Methoght hit ful semelé · to se soche a syght   *It seemed to me very pleasant; such*
How in a syde of a salghe · a sete him he soght;   *beside a willow, he sought a position*
Fro the noyse that hit was new · til hit was ne nyght,
Fro the non bot a napwile · methoght hit bot noght.[3]
            Methoght hit noght bot a throw   *an instant*
10   To se how he throbyt and threw.   *quivered; writhed*
            Hontis with hornes thai kowth blow;   *Huntsmen; could*
            Thai halowyd here howndys with "how!"   *halooed; hounds*
            In holtis herde I never soche hew!   *woods; loud ruckus*

Soche a hew in a holt · were hele to beholde,   *comfort*
15   To se how howndis him hent · and gart him to helde!   *seized; caused him to fall*
Ther come barownce to that bay · with barsletys bolde;   *barons; hunting dogs*
Thai blewyn here bewgulys ful breme · hore brachus to belde.[4]
Thre kyngys ther come, · trewlé itolde.   *numbered*
With tonyng and tryffylyng · and talis thai telde,
20   Uche a wy that ther was · wroght as thai wold.
These wodis and these wastis · thai waltyn al to welde.
            Thai waltyn at here wil to ware

---

[1] *So that malice may never mar us more than a mite*

[2] *[May] the Devil be portionless of us howsoever he prepares*

[3] Lines 7–8: *From the time that the noise [of the hunt] began, at midday, until it was nearly night, / The time seemed to me but nothing, passing as briefly as a nap (lit. from noon but a napwhile)*

[4] *They blew their bugles full clearly, to encourage their dogs*

These wodis and the wastus that ther were.
Herkyns what befel of here fare —
25   Ham lykyd no lorchip in lare! —
The lede that wold, lestyn and lere.[1]

When thai weren of these wodys · went at here wyn,	*had; gone; pleasure*
Thai fondyn wyndys ful wete · and wederys ful wanne.	*wet; storms; dark*
Bot soche a myst upo molde, · with mowth as I youe myn,[2]	
30 Of al here men and here mete · thai mystyn uche mon!	*fellowship; company; missed*
"Al our awnters," quod one, · "that we ar now inne,	*adventures*
I hope fore honor of erth · that anguis be ous on.	*earthly honor; anguish be upon us*
Thagh we be kyngis ful clene · and comen of ryche kyn,	*splendid*
Moche care us is caght; · fore kraft that I can,[3]	
35 Can I no mo cownsel bot chist,	*I predict nothing but trouble*
Bot coverys and cachis sum cest;	*[let us] take cover and concoct some plan*
Be morne may mend this myst;	*amend; fog*
Our Lord may delyver us with lyst,	*joy*
Or lelé our lyvys ar lest."	*truly; lost*

40 Where thai not forth gone · fotis bot a fewe,	*Were; footsteps*
Thai fondon feldus ful fayre · and fogus ful fow;	*fields; pastures of diverse hues*
Schokyn out of a schawe · thre schalkys at schew,	
Schadows unshene · were chapid to chow,[4]	
With lymes long and lene · and leggys ful lew,	*limbs; weak*
45 Hadyn lost the lyp and the lyver · sethyn thai were layd lowe.	*lip; liver; since*
Ther was no beryn that ther was · dorst bec nor bewe,	*man; dared nod nor turn away*
Bot braydyn here brydilys agayne, · hor blongis can blow.[5]	
Here blonkis can blow and abyde;	*horses did pant; halt*
Siche barns thai can hom bede;	*These men [the Living] summoned them*
50 Thai se no sokur hom besyde,	*help*
Bot oche kyng apon Crist cryde,	*each*
With crossyng and karpyng o Crede.	*reciting the Creed*

The furst kyng he had care, · his hert ovrcast,	*overcast*
Fore he knew the cros of the cloth · that coverd the cyst.[6]	

---

[1] Lines 19–26: *With sounding of the hunting horn and jollity and tales [that] they told, / Each man that was there acted as he wished. / All these woods and these wastes they possessed to command. / They governed at will the use / Of these woods and the wastes there. / Hearken what befell of their adventure — / They liked no guidance in learning (i.e., they were heedless)! — / The man who would [be wisely instructed], listen and learn*

[2] *But such a fog [came] on earth, as I relate to you by mouth*

[3] *Much sadness has befallen us; for all that I can do about it*

[4] Lines 42–43: *Having passed from a grove, three men [came] into view, / Horrible phantoms [that] were fated to appear*

[5] *But drew tight their bridles against their horses [that] did pant*

[6] *For he knew the cross on the gravecloth that covered the bodily chest*

55	Forth wold not his fole, · bot fnyrtyd ful fast,	*foal; snorted vigorously*
	His fayre fawkun fore ferd · he fel to his fyst:	*falcon; terror; it fell; fist*
	"Now al my gladchip is gone! · I gre and am agast	*gladness; shudder; aghast*
	Of thre gostis ful grym · that gare me be gryst.	*ghosts; cause me to be afraid*
	Fere of have I walkon · be wodys and be wast,	*Far off*
60	Bot was me never so wo · in word that Y wyst —	*woeful; world; know*
	So wo was me never, I wene;	*think*
	My wit is away other wane;	*insufficient*
	Certis sone hit wil be sene	*Certainly soon*
	Our ronnyng wil turne us to tene;	*running away; trouble*
65	Fore tytle, I trow we bene tane!"	*Despite our rank; believe; are trapped*
	Then bespeke the medil kyng, that mekil was of myght,	*spoke; middle; great*
	Was made as a man schuld · of mayn and of maght:	*should [be]; vigor; prowess*
	"Methenkys, seris, that I se · the selquoth syght,	*strangest*
	That ever segge under sonne · sey and was saght,	*man; sun saw; granted*
70	Of thre ledys ful layth · that lorne hath the lyght —	*creatures; loathly; lost*
	Both the lip and the lyver · his fro the lyme laght!	*is separated from the limb*
	Fore yif we tene to the towne · as we hadyn tyght,	*go; intended*
	Ha ful teneful way, I trow, · that us is taght.	*A; perilous; believe; is pointed out to us*
	Us is taght, as I trow;	
75	I tel you no talis bot trew.	*tales*
	What helpis our hontyng with 'how'?	*What use is*
	Now rayke we to the yonder row,	*[let us] go speedily; row [of dead]*
	Or raddelé our rese mon we rew."	*quickly; rashness we must regret*
	Then speke the henmest kyng — · in the hillis he beholdis;	*hindmost; stares*
80	He lokis under his hondis · and his hed heldis,	*holds his head*
	Bot soche a carful knyl · to his hert coldis,	
	So doth the knyf ore the kye — · that knoc kelddus!¹	
	"Hit bene warlaws thre · that walkyn on this woldis —	*demons; in these woods*
	Oure Lord, wyss us the redé way, · that al the word weldus!	*show; direct; rules*
85	My hert fars fore freght, · as flagge when hit foldus;	*trembles for fright; reed; bends*
	Uche fyngyr of my hond · fore ferdchip hit feldus.	*terror; clenches*
	Fers am I ferd of oure fare;	*Terribly; afraid; adventure*
	Fle we ful fast therfore!	*[Let us] flee*
	Can Y no cownsel bot care —	
90	These dewyls wil do us to dare	*devils; cause; cower in fear*
	Fore drede lest thai duttyn uche a dore!"	*block every escape*
	"Nay, are we no fyndus," quod furst, · "that ye before you fynden;²	
	We wer your faders of fold · that fayre youe have fondon.	

---

¹ Lines 81–82: *But so frightful a knell (shock) chills his heart, / It was like a knife upon cattle — that blow strikes [one] cold*

² *"Nay, we are not fiends," said the first one, "that you find before yourselves"*

Now ye beth lykyr to leve · then levys on the lynden,

95 And lordis of oche towne · fro Loron into Londen.[1]

Those that bene not at your bone · ye beton and byndon;   *who defy your command*

Bot yef ye betun that burst, · in bale be ye bondon.   *make amends for; injury; bound*

Lo, here the wormus in my wome — · thai wallon and wyndon![2]

Lo, here the wrase of the wede · that I was in wondon!   *tie-band; shroud; wrapped in*

100   Herein was I wondon, iwys,

   In word wan that me worthelokyst was.   *world when I was most esteemed*

   My caren was ful cumlé to cysse;   *flesh; comely; kiss*

   Bot we have made youe mastyrs amys   *wrongly*

   That now nyl not mynn us with a mas."   *[You] who will not commemorate; mass*

105 That other body began · a ful brym bere: *[in] a booming voice (lit. clamor)*

"Lokys on my bonus, · that blake bene and bare!   *bones; black*

Fore wyle we wondon in this word, · at worchip we were;[3]

Whe hadon our wyfe at our wil · and well fore to ware.   *We; wealth to expend*

Thenkes ye no ferlé, · bot frayns at me fere: *marvel; learn fear from me*

110 Thagh ye be never so fayre, · thus schul ye fare!

And yif ye leven upon Crist · and on his lore lere,   *If you believe; learn his lore*

Levys lykyng of flesche · and leve not that lare.[4]

   Fore warto schuld ye leve hit? Hit lyus!   *why; believe [in] it; lies*

   His ledys youe be lagmon be leus,   *It leads you astray by falsehoods*

115   When thou art aldyr-hyghtus and hyus;   *proudest and highest of all*

   Away of this word when that thou wryus,   *out of; depart*

   Al thi wild werkys hit wreus."   *reveals*

Then speke laythe upo last, · with lyndys ful lene,   *[the third] loathly one at last; loins*

With eyther leg as a leke · were lapid in lyne: *leek; swathed in linen*

120 "Makis your merour be me! · My myrthus bene mene: *pleasures are poor*

Wyle I was mon apon mold, · morthis thai were myne;   *on earth; deadly sins*

Methoght hit a hede thenke · at husbondus to hene—[5]

Fore that was I hatyd · with heme and with hyne—   *by villagers and household servants*

Bot thoght me ever kyng · of coyntons so clene.[6]

125 Now is ther no knave under Crist · to me wil enclyne,   *there is no peasant; bow*

   To me wil enclyne, to me come,

   Bot yif he be cappid or kyme.   *insane or [a] fool*

---

[1] Lines 93–95: *We were your living (lit. earthly) fathers, who graciously have nurtured you. / At present you are more fit to live than leaves on the linden / And [you are] lords over every town from Lorne (in Scotland) to London*

[2] *Lo, here the worms in my bowels — they swarm and writhe*

[3] *For while we dwelt in this world, we were [held] in esteem*

[4] *Abandon fleshly desire, and rely not on clay*

[5] *I thought it an excellent thing to oppress farmers*

[6] *But considered myself ever a king of splendid acquaintance (i.e., possessing high regard from others)*

	Do so ye dred not the dome —	*judgment*
	To tel youe we have no longyr tome —	*time*
130	Bot turn youe fro tryvyls betyme!"	*trifles soon*

	Now this gostis bene grayth, · to grave thai glyde.	*ready*
	Then began these gomys · graythlé to glade;	*men; promptly; cheer up*
	Thai redyn on the ryght way · and radlé thai ryde;	*agree; forthwith*
	The red rowys of the day · the rynkkys kouthyn rade.	*rays; daylight; men could discern*
135	Holde thai never the pres · be hew ne be hyde,	
	Bot ay the hendyr hert · after thai hade;	
	And thai that weryn at myschip · thai mend ham that myde.[1]	
	And throgh the mercé of God · a mynster thai made.	*minster (i.e., chantry for trentals)*
	A mynster thai made with masse,	*consecrated; a service of mass*
140	Fore metyng the men on the mosse,	*moss (i.e., a public place)*
	And on the woghe wrytyn this was.	*wall; this [poem, or story]*
	To lyte will leve this, allas!	*few [people]; believe*
	Oure Lord delyver us from losse. Amen.	

LATIN POEM *CUR MUNDUS MILITAT SUB VANA GLORIA*   [NOT IN W]

Non honor set honus assumere nomen honoris.[2]

	Cur mundus militat sub vana gloria,	*Why does the world soldier under vainglory's banner*
	Cuius prosperitas est transitoria?	*Whose prosperity is transitory?*
	Tam cito labitur eius potencia	*Its power slips away as quickly*
	Quam vasa figuli que sunt fragilia.	*As the fragile vessels made by a potter.*
5	*Plus crede literis scriptis in glacie*	*Put more trust in letters written on ice*
	Quam mundi fragilis vane fallacie.	*Than in the empty deceit of the fragile world.*
	Fallax in premiis, virtutis specie,	*Deceitful in rewards, in the appearance of virtue,*
	Quis unquam habuit tempus fiducie?	*Who has ever had time for fidelity?*
	Credendum magis est auris fallacibus	*More trust is to be placed in the deceitful breezes*
10	*Te mundi miseri prosperitatibus,*	*[Than] the prosperity of the wretched world.*
	Falcis in sompniis ac vanitatibus,	*False in dreams and vanities,*
	Falcis in studiis et voluptatibus.	*False in endeavors and pleasures.*

---

[1] Lines 135–37: *They never [at all] acted oppressively regarding land or servants, / But ever afterwards they had kinder hearts; / And they who were in sin were mindful of that ultimate reward (i.e., the merit awarded on Doomsday)*

[2] *It is not an honor but a burden to receive the name of honor.* Compare Ovid, *Heroides* 9.31, *non honor est sed onus* (punning on *honor* and *onus*), and see *Marcolf and Solomon*, line 325a.

	Dic ubi Salamon olim tam nobilis,	Say where is Solomon, once so noble
	Vel Sampson ubi est dux invincibilis,	Or where is Samson, invicible leader,
15	Vel pulcher Absolon vultu mirabilis,	Or beautiful Absalom, wondrous in appearance,
	Vel dulcis Jonathas multum amabilis?	Or sweet Jonathan, very lovable?

Dic ubi Salamon olim tam nobilis, — Say where is Solomon, once so noble
Vel Sampson ubi est dux invincibilis, — Or where is Samson, invicible leader,
15 *Vel pulcher Absolon vultu mirabilis,* — Or beautiful Absalom, wondrous in appearance,
Vel dulcis Jonathas multum amabilis? — Or sweet Jonathan, very lovable?

Quo Cesar abiit celsus imperio, — Where has gone Caesar, lofty in power,
Vel Dives splendidus totus in prandio? — Or Dives, all splendid at his banquet?
Dic ubi Tulius clarus eloquio, — Tell me where is Tullius, famous for eloquence,
20 *Vel Aristotiles summus ingenio?* — Or Aristotle, the pinnacle of genius?

Tot clari proceres, tot retro spacia, — So many renowned leaders, so many intervals back,

Tot ora presulum, tot regum forcia, — So many brave faces of officers, so many of kings,

Tot mundi principes, tanta potencia, — So many princes of the world, such great power
In ictu oculi clauduntur omnia. — All are closed [off] in the blink of an eye.

25 *Quam breve spacium hec mundi gloria?* — For how short a time does this glory of the world [last]?

Ut umbra hominis sunt eius gaudia. — Its joys are like the shadow of a human being.
Que tamen subtrahunt eterna premia, — They nevertheless take away eternal rewards,
Et ducunt hominem ad rura devia. — And lead on to the trackless country.

O esca vermium, o massa pulveris, — O food for worms, O pile of dust,
30 *O ros, o vanitas, cur sic extolleris?* — O dew, O vanity, why are you so extolled?
Ignoras penitus, utrum cras vixeris, — You have absolutely no idea whether you will be alive tomorrow,

Fac bonum omnibus quam diu poteris. — [And so] do good to all for as long as you are able.

Hec carnis gloria, que magni penditur, — This glory of the flesh, which is highly valued,
Sacris in literis flos feni dicitur, — In sacred literature is called "the flower of the grass,"
35 *Vel leve folium, quod vento rapitur;* — Or a light leaf which is carried off by the wind;
Sic vita hominis a luce trahitur. — Thus is a person's life dragged from the light [of day].

Nil tuum dixeris quod potes perdere, — Call nothing yours which you can lose,
Quod mundus tribuit intendit rapere, — Whatever the world gives, it intends to snatch away,

Superna cogita, cor sit in ethere, — Think on heavenly things, may your heart be in heaven,
40 *Felix qui poterit mundum contempnere.* — Happy is the one who will be able to despise the world.

AUDELAY'S CONCLUSION   **[W55]**

Sapiencia huius mundi stulticia est apud Deum.[1]

	Here may ye here now hwat ye be.	*hear*
	Here may ye cnow hwat ys this worlde.	*know*
	Here may ye boothe here and se	
	Only in God ys all comforde.	*comfort*
5	For ther nys noon odur Loorde	*is no other*
	That can do as he can.	
	All thyng he made here with a worde,	
	Hwen he had sayde hit was ydon.	*done*
	Herto we were ybore	*born*
10	To serve that Lorde Omnipotent,	
	And kepe wel his comaundement.	
	All thyng here he has us lent	
	To worshyp hym in erthe therfore.	

	Then loke ye hoolde hym forwarde:	*uphold your promise to Him*
15	Forsake your pryde, your veynglory!	
	Sett noght by the joy here of this worlde —	*no stake in*
	Hyt ys butt vayne and vanyté! —	
	But for that your namus wreton thay be	*so that your names may be written*
	In the bok of lyfe in hevun blys,	
20	Ther to have joy perpetualy,	
	Al erthely joy shal sone vanyshe.	*[Because] all*
	Thus may ye se alsoo,	
	How men thay dyon sodenly,	*die*
	And leson here joy and veynglory	*lose*
25	With the twynkelyng of an ye.	*twinkling of an eye*
	Farewel! Thay ben agoo!	*are gone*

Hic vir despiciens mundum.[2]

	Herfore Y have dyspysed this worlde,	*Therefore; despised*
	And have overcomen alle erthely thyng.	
	My ryches in heven with dede and worde	*deed*
30	I have ypurchest in my levyng,	*purchased*
	With good ensampul to odur gefyng.	*By giving good example to others*
	Loke in this book; here may ye se	
	Hwatt ys my wyl and my wrytyng.	

---

[1] *For the wisdom of this world is foolishness with God.* 1 Corinthians 3:19. Compare *Marcolf and Solomon*, line 39a.

[2] *This man despising the world.* The introductory antiphon of the Commemoration of St. Benedict, from his feast in the Roman Breviary (March 21).

	All odur by me war for to be!	*All others beware by my example*
35	Bewarre, brether, Y yow pray,	
	Yowre mysdedes that ye amende	
	Owte of thys worlde or that ye wende,	*before; go*
	For alle ys good that hath good ende.	
	Thus conseles Jon the Blynde Awdelay.	

Cuius finis bonum, ipsum totum bonum. Finito libro. Sit laus et gloria Christo.[1]

40	No mon this book he take away,	
	Ny kutt owte noo leef, Y say forwhy,	*Nor cut out any leaf*
	For hit ys sacrelege, sirus, Y yow say!	*sacrilege*
	Beth acursed in the dede truly!	
	Yef ye wil have any copi,	
45	Askus leeve and ye shul have,	
	To pray for hym specialy	
	That hyt made your soules to save,	
	Jon the Blynde Awdelay.	
	The furst prest to the Lord Strange he was,	*Richard LeStrange*
50	Of thys chauntré, here in this place,	*chantry*
	That made this bok by Goddus grace,	
	Deeff, sick, blynd, as he lay.	

Cuius anime propicietur Deus.[2]

---

[1] *Whose end is good, is himself entirely good. The book is finished. Praise and glory be to Christ.* Compare *Marcolf and Solomon*, line 987a, and the *Finito libro* colophon.

[2] *On whose soul may God be propitious.* Compare the *Finito libro* colophon.

❧ EXPLANATORY NOTES

THE COUNSEL OF CONSCIENCE

[X.] TRUE LIVING   [W1]

True Living expounds the way of the true Christian life. In what remains of the poem, Audelay stresses several basic tenets: the Ten Commandments, the sanctity of celibacy and marriage vows, the seven works of mercy, the five wits, the doctrine of free will, the virtues of Faith, Hope, and Charity, and the Golden Rule. Though not alliterative like *Marcolf and Solomon*, it belongs to the same truth-telling genre, expressing bold criticisms of the clergy while offering a comprehensive verse instruction. (For a survey of the *sothsegger* tradition, see Wawn, "Truth-Telling," pp. 270–87.)

Written in taut 13-line stanzas,the composition of *True Living* probably predates most other works in MS Douce 302 because it seems that Audelay mined it for other compositions. The poem evidently aided the making of seven extant poems: *The Vision of Saint Paul* (one stanza), *God's Address to Sinful Men* (three stanzas), *Chastity of Wives* (six stanzas), *Four Estates* (one stanza), *Ten Commandments* (three stanzas), *Seven Works of Mercy* (five stanzas), and *Seven Gifts of the Holy Ghost* (three stanzas).

The beginning of MS Douce 302 — up to nineteen folios (Fein, "Good Ends," p. 98n3) — is gone, and as a result this first poem in the manuscript lacks its opening. The piece is also incomplete at the end. Pickering, "Make-Up," p. 119, was first to notice that the 4-line marginal verse inserted by Scribe B on fol. 2rb refers the reader to the misplaced ending of the poem. The topic of this conclusion was Doomsday. For an unknown reason it was copied on an earlier leaf, which is now lost.

[Fols. 1ra–2rb (acephalous). *IMEV* *39; *Suppl.*, *NIMEV* *1492.5 (erroneously described as a "treatise on the Deadly Sins and their remedies"). **Hand:** Scribe A in black. **Meter:** Twenty 13-line stanzas, $ababbcbc_4d_{2-3}eee_{3-4}d_{2-3}$, survive, with one stanza extended in length (lines 143–59). This poem begins imperfectly because several leaves have been lost from the opening of the manuscript. **Editions:** Halliwell, pp. 1–10, 82; E. Whiting, pp. 1–10, 225–26.]

13–25   Audelay reuses this stanza (adapting its meter) in *The Vision of Saint Paul*, lines 340–52.

20   This line inspires the work's modern title.

23   *what deth that ever he dy.* See explanatory note to *Marcolf and Solomon*, line 682.

55   *spase ham to repent.* Whiting, p. 225, notes that this phrase derives from the mass. The formula appears frequently in Audelay's verse, e.g., *True Living*, line 125;

Audelay's Epilogue to The Counsel of Conscience, lines 26 and 74; and *Song of the Magnificat,* line 45.

65–115   These four stanzas on marriage may be compared to Mirk's sermon on marriage in *Festial* (Erbe, *Mirk's Festial,* pp. 289–93). On correspondences between Mirk and Audelay, see Powell, "John Audelay and John Mirk." See also *Marcolf and Solomon,* lines 709–13.

78–103   These two stanzas are the basis for Audelay's *Chastity of Wives* carol. Six of the carol's seven stanzas (that is, twenty-four lines) are crafted directly from these twenty-six lines.

108   *schenchypus.* The verb *shendshipen,* "disgrace, embarrass, confound," appears rarely in Middle English. The *MED* records it only twice, and Audelay's use is the earlier one.

109   *lotoby.* See *MED lote-bi,* n.(a), "lover, paramour, concubine," from *loten* v.(1), "to lie concealed, lie low."

119   *kynde.* Audelay uses this word often to assert the basis for right human action. It is particularly prominent in this poem and *Marcolf and Solomon.* Simpson, "Saving Satire," pp. 402–03, discusses how both Audelay and Langland advocate "a theology of communal practice inspired both by conscience and by natural (i.e. 'kyndly') sympathy."

120   *nother.* The usual term in MS Douce 302 is *no nother,* while variations of this particular line recur several times in Audelay's verse with that phrase, leading Halliwell and Whiting to emend here (unnecessarily) to *no nother.* Compare *The Remedy of Nine Virtues,* line 55; *God's Address to Sinful Men,* line 111; *Audelay's Epilogue to* The Counsel of Conscience, line 414; and *Seven Deadly Sins,* line 32.

127   *Yeff ye wyl mend that ye do mysse.* As E. Whiting notes, p. 225, this phrase is ubiquitous in Audelay's verse. Here he links it with a favorite biblical phrase, in which God declares he does not wish the death of a sinner (Ezechiel 33:11, and also Ezechiel 18:23, 18:32). Compare the use of this passage elsewhere in Audelay's works: *Marcolf and Solomon,* lines 790–92; *Our Lord's Epistle on Sunday,* line 115; *The Vision of Saint Paul,* lines 365a–b; and *God's Address to Sinful Men* (where it is the refrain). The biblical verse is also invoked in a Suffolk priest's 1429 confession of Lollardy (Shinners and Dohar, *Pastors and the Care of Souls,* p. 280).

130–33   These lines are repeated in Audelay's *Four Estates,* lines 1–4. Audelay advocates a social philosophy that each person must maintain the estate that falls to him. He frequently repeats this idea as an injunction. It informs the burden of two other carols (*Four Estates* and *Virginity of Maids* — "Kepe your state and your degré"). See also *True Living,* line 62; *Visiting the Sick and Consoling the Needy,* lines 48–49; *Pope John's Passion of Our Lord,* line 110; *Song of the Magnificat,* line 37; and *Chastity for Mary's Love,* line 28.

143–59   The length of this stanza is extended by four lines. While it might seem that Scribe A omitted five final lines of one stanza and four first lines of another, the uninterrupted enumeration of the Ten Commandments and Audelay's use elsewhere of the lines found in this stanza (see next two explanatory notes) argue for its being original.

143–54   These lines supply three stanzas of Audelay's *Ten Commandments*: lines 143–46 = carol lines 1–4; lines 147–49 = carol lines 8–10; and lines 151–54 = carol lines 15–18. As in the carol Audelay adds backbiting (lines 149–50) and leaves out covetousness.

156–59   These lines are something of a formula for Audelay. Compare *The Remedy of Nine Virtues*, lines 73–75, and *Audelay's Epilogue to The Counsel of Conscience*, lines 244–46, and it is interesting to note the correspondence of line 158 with *Ten Commandments*, line 23, showing further how Audelay reworked *True Living* for his carols.

173–79   These lines enumerating the seven works of mercy are repeated in *Seven Works of Mercy*, lines 1–4, 8–10, and see also *God's Address to Sinful Men*, lines 164–73, where lines 170–71 = *True Living*, lines 175–76. Audelay used other lines to construct more of this carol (see below, explanatory notes to *True Living*, lines 238–43, 251–58).

186–93   In topic, though not in wording, compare Audelay's *Five Wits*.

203–07   On the doctrine of free will, compare *The Vision of Saint Paul*, lines 216–22, and also references in *The Remedy of Nine Virtues*, lines 32, 69; *Five Wits*, line 9; and *Audelay's Epilogue to The Counsel of Conscience*, lines 219–21, 397–99.

212–33   Several of these lines are repeated in three stanzas of Audelay's *Seven Gifts of the Holy Ghost*: lines 212–15 = carol lines 22–25, lines 225–28 = carol lines 29–32, and lines 229–31 = carol lines 36–38.

231   Audelay cites the Golden Rule often; compare *Marcolf and Solomon*, lines 12, 543; *The Remedy of Nine Virtues*, line 60; and *Seven Gifts of the Holy Ghost*, line 38.

238–43   These lines are repeated by Audelay in *God's Address to Sinful Men*, lines 197–202. Lines 238–41 match his *Seven Works of Mercy*, lines 15–18.

251–58   These lines are repeated as a whole stanza in *God's Address to Sinful Men*, lines 213–20, and they form two stanzas of *Seven Works of Mercy*, lines 22–25, 29–32.

263   Pickering, "Make-Up," p. 119, proposes that the marginal verse following *True Living* (*Instructions for Reading 1*) indicates that this poem lacks its ending, that is, a description of Doomsday. The ending is indeed abrupt, and the discourse has progressed to a Judgment Day scenario.

INSTRUCTIONS FOR READING 1   [NOT IN W]

These verses are written partially in the margin by Scribe B, indicating a sequence for the reader and demonstrating that at least thirteen folios are absent from the front of MS Douce 302. Whiting prints the instructional rubric in her introduction but omits it from the main text of poems. Halliwell, pp. 82–83, comments: "These four verses were probably dictated by Audelay, and go far to prove that the MS. was the first copy made. The leaf referred to is lost with the commencement."

[Fol. 2rb. *NIMEV* 3324.55. **Hand:** Scribe B in red (squeezed between other items); a large blue paraph has been inserted beside these lines. **Meter:** Two tetrameter couplets. **Editions:** Coxe, p. 50; Halliwell, pp. 10, 82–83; E. Whiting, p. vii.]

1   *come in here.* These words support Pickering's idea that Scribe B is referring the
           reader to a misplaced ending of *True Living*, which by scribal error ("the defawte
           of the wrytere") was copied earlier in the manuscript ("Make-Up," p. 119).
           Compare Scribe B's use of the phrase "here cum in" to insert a Latin heading
           in *Marcolf and Solomon* (see textual notes for *Marcolf and Solomon*, lines 345–46).

2   *wrytere.* This word seems to refer to the scribe, but it could refer to Audelay as
           author and compiler of the anthology.

XI. MARCOLF AND SOLOMON   [W2]
     Marcolf and Solomon is the lengthiest poem in MS Douce 302, and in recent years it has
become the one most intensely studied, i.e., by Green, "Marcolf the Fool"; Simpson, "Saving
Satire"; Pearsall, "Audelay's *Marcolf and Solomon*"; Green, "Langland and Audelay"; and
others. John the Blind Audelay here presses a case for social complaint, admonishing each
of the religious orders — monks, friars, and secular clergy — and exhorting them to honor
their holy vows and duties. Its narrative veil is that Marcolf (or Marcol) the fool speaks truth
to the king (Solomon), pointing out society's irrational ills so that the state (through its
ecclesiastical officers) may recover harmony and good sense. Readers have set it in the truth-
telling tradition of *Mum and the Sothsegger* (e.g., Wawn, "Truth-Telling," especially p. 281).
Its date has been much discussed, and a degree of consensus has arisen that it was written
after Arundel's *Constitutions* of 1409, and perhaps near the time of Oldcastle's rising (1414;
for a brief history, see Goldberg, *Medieval England*, pp. 233–37, especially p. 234).
Regarding *Marcolf and Solomon*'s politics and theology, Simpson locates it in the "gray area"
between Lollard protest and orthodox reform, though, unquestionably, Audelay sees himself
making complaint within the bounds of conservative moral teaching and the Church's long-
standing institutions. Despite the poem's litany of complaints, Citrome identifies its "real
message" to be "that priests are absolutely indispensible to the pursuit of salvation, and their
authority is unimpeachable" (*Surgeon*, p. 90).
     Alliterative in style and fervid in its spiritual call, this poem is often compared to *Piers
Plowman*, an analogy that originated from Pearsall's assertion that Langland's poem "pro-
foundly influenced" Audelay's (*Old English and Middle English Poetry*, p. 249). Pearsall has
now modified his stance, proposing instead that *Marcolf and Solomon* is the product of a gen-
eral climate of religious ferment and dissent ("Audelay's *Marcolf and Solomon*," pp. 147–49).
Meanwhile, Green and Simpson argue that even as *Marcolf and Solomon* reflects the religious
controversies of Lancastrian England, the work itself remains deeply evocative of Langland's
poem. The two texts share alliterative style, apocalyptic manner, and even some verbal mark-
ings, while they differ in general outlook: Langland is more openly a social reformer while
Audelay asks for correction to occur within the established institutions and hierarchies of
the Church, as, at the same time, he urges the laity to speak out about dangerous abuses.
He prods the orders to uphold their vows to God, abandon their internal squabbles, and
unite in their common work to save souls. In the explanatory notes below, I list several of
the passages in *Piers Plowman* (ed. Schmidt) that critics have compared to passages in
Audelay's *Marcolf and Solomon*.

Marcolf and Solomon is written in an alliterative 13-line stanza, a form that bridges, on one hand, the nonalliterative 13-line type that Audelay uses for *True Living*, *The Remedy of Nine Virtues*, *Visiting the Sick and Consoling the Needy*, *Our Lord's Epistle on Sunday*, *The Vision of Saint Paul*, *Audelay's Epilogue to The Counsel of Conscience*, and *Audelay's Conclusion*, and, on the other, the dense alliterative strophes (11- and 13-line) found in *Paternoster* and *Three Dead Kings*. Having a style that resides somewhere between these poles, *Marcolf and Solomon* is most allied in metrical terms to the single interpolated stanza *Over-Hippers and Skippers* found in the extract of prose at the end of the manuscript, and to the salutations in 9-line alliterative stanzas to Saint Bridget and Saint Winifred, in which the 13-line form is reduced by one quatrain.

Another important stylistic feature of *Marcolf and Solomon* is the heading of most stanzas with an epigram in Latin. More often than not, these passages are biblical in origin, and they provide keys to understanding Audelay's professional credo as he asserts his feelings about the roles of the ecclesiastical orders. Often they quote Scripture in an abbreviated fashion. In such cases, I provide the Douay-Rheims Bible verse in full in the footnotes because it frequently offers the poet's complete register of meaning.

Despite *Marcolf and Solomon*'s satisfying ending (closure by Marcolf and then a signature stanza from Audelay), readers need to keep in mind that the poem may not have its full conclusion. This fact puts something of a check on Stanley's suggestion that the poem's length could be numerologically significant: "exactly one thousand [lines] (in seventy-seven stanzas), followed by an autobiographical stanza" ("Verse Forms," p. 118n49). While Stanley's argument is intriguing, especially in light of evidence elsewhere of numerological structure (see explanatory notes to *Visiting the Sick and Consoling the Needy*), there is a good possibility that *Marcolf and Solomon* suffers loss at the end: its last line is written as the catchphrase to the next quire, which is missing (see explanatory note to line 1013). What we have stops at the base of the last column of a verso, without an explicit (and technically without even the last line of the stanza). The next item, *The Remedy of Nine Virtues*, begins *in medias res*, with many intervening works missing. Therefore, because four folios are lost after fol. 7v, one cannot be at all certain that *Marcolf and Solomon* is complete.

In this edition I have divided *Marcolf and Solomon* into sections, with headings appearing in boldface, in order to highlight the movements and shifts in Audelay's sometimes rambling argument. The headings derive from the analysis of Pearsall, "Audelay's *Marcolf and Solomon*," pp. 142–43. Major themes covered by Audelay include: spiritual naturalness and unnaturalness (the theological concept of *kynd*, also invoked by Langland); the inherent goodness of societal estates and religious orders; the individual and spiritual corruption of those who live in *covetyse*; the humility of the righteous; the imperative to speak truth; the nature of wisdom and folly (with frequent allusion to Ecclesiastes); the sacred keys given to the clergy — originally to Saint Peter — to loose and bind; the establishment of clerical peace and harmony, which Audelay terms a *loveday*; the ecclesiastical duty to save souls and call people away from error (sometimes labeled "Lollard"); and the necessity of maintaining a clean, shriven conscience.

[Fols. 2rb–7vb (ends imperfectly). *IMEV, NIMEV* 947. *MWME* 9:2981 [61]. **Hands:** Scribe A, poem (black) and the majority of the Latin stanza headings (red); Scribe B, in red, incipit, eight Latin stanza headings (three on fol. 4rb, three on fol. 5va, and two on fol. 6va), explicit, and drawings and marginal indicators to point out specific passages (lines 350–51, 532–33, 697–701). **Ordinatio:** Scribal signals for colored initials (which were not inserted) appear at lines 92, 118, and 170; an ambiguous notation appears at line 378; and Scribe B inserts "Nota" before his inserted heading for line 780. **Audelay Signature:** Line 1008 (Scribe A); compare line 503. **Initial:** Large *G* in blue with red filigree (three lines high). **Meter:** Seventy-eight alliterative 13-line stanzas, ababbcbc$_4$d$_{2-3}$eee$_{3-4}$d$_{2-3}$, survive. Putter, "Language and Metre," p. 517, and Green, "Langland and Audelay," pp. 157–58, comment on the poem's alliterative metrics; Stanley, "Verse Forms," p. 118n49, proposes a numerological length. **Editions:** Halliwell, pp. 10–51, 83–87; E. Whiting, pp. 10–46, 226–33.]

Incipit	The translation of the first heading (Scribe B's incipit) follows Pearsall, "Audelay's *Marcolf and Solomon*," p. 141, who identifies the theme of the poem as "the desire that friars (*rectores fratres*) and secular priests (*rectores ecclesie*) should work together harmoniously for the benefit of those laymen who are in their care." Pearsall challenges Simpson's view ("Saving Satire," p. 397) that the poem addresses the relationship between clergy and laity. For the translation of *concordia* as "loveday," compare *Marcolf and Solomon*, explanatory note to line 390, and lines 392–93, 622, 973–74.
1–9	On hearing God's counsel by reading the Bible, compare *Marcolf and Solomon*, lines 211–12, and *Audelay's Epilogue to The Counsel of Conscience*, lines 352–55. Simpson argues that Audelay's opening "defence of scriptural truth" runs "parallel with Lollard positions" ("Saving Satire," p. 395).
12	On Audelay's frequent citation of the Golden Rule, see the explanatory note to *True Living*, line 231.
13	*kynde*. For Simpson, "Saving Satire," pp. 402–03, Audelay's "theological emphasis on kindliness" offers an "essential connection" to Langland; compare Pearsall, "Audelay's *Marcolf and Solomon*," p. 144. The term is also prominent in *True Living* (see explanatory note to line 119).
13a	The stanza heading is drawn from the Athanasian Creed. For a translation of the creed from the *Sarum Breviary*, see Shinners and Dohar, *Pastors and the Care of Souls*, pp. 151–52.
19	*crysum*. The reference is to one's christening service.
26–27	The stanzas are linked here by concatenation, a stylistic feature normally reserved for more ornate alliterative stanzaic verse, such as *Three Dead Kings*.
32	*obey obedyans*. Audelay repeats or varies this phrasing at *Marcolf and Solomon*, lines 176, 288, and *Salutation to Saint Bridget*, line 182; in each of those instances, obeying "obedyans" refers to keeping one's sworn monastic vows.
40	On the Marcolf and Solomon tradition of the cunning fool with license to speak harsh yet truthful sayings to the king in power, see explanatory note to *Marcolf and Solomon*, lines 66–69.
42–43	The proverb "In wele beware ore thou be woo" appears in *Audelay's Epilogue to The Counsel of Conscience*, line 218, and as the burden for Audelay's *Seven Deadly Sins* (see explanatory note). There is an echo of it in *Marcolf and Solomon*, line 949, too. On the currency of the phrase, see Pearsall, "Audelay's *Marcolf and Solomon*," pp. 147 and 151n29.

53   *take good eme*. This phrase is one of Audelay's clerical tags for issuing a moral
          warning; compare *Marcolf and Solomon*, lines 679, 997, *The Remedy of Nine Virtues*,
          line 90, and *Visiting the Sick and Consoling the Needy*, line 391. See *MED yeme*, n.(b).

55   Compare *Three Dead Kings*, lines 111–13. A recurring alliteration on the letter *l* in
          lines 53, 55, 57, and 80, with semantic prominence given to the like-sounding
          words *leve*, *love*, and *lyve*, gives this stanza a musical effect that approximates the
          thematic alliteration found in *The Four Leaves of the Truelove* (Fein, *Moral Love
          Songs*, pp. 180–96), another moral poem in 13-line stanzas.

58   *Soferayns*. E. Whiting defines this word as "betters," but it is a synonym for God,
          as in *Marcolf and Solomon*, line 199.

59   *kyndlé know . . . treu as ané ston*. The proverbial simile appears in *Mary Flower of
          Women*, line 22. On "kyndely" knowing, compare *Piers Plowman* B.1.142 (Simp-
          son, "Saving Satire," p. 403), and see explanatory note to *Marcolf and Solomon*,
          line 13.

66–69   On Audelay's use of the dialogic tradition of Marcolf (a rustic, truth-telling fool)
          and Solomon (a wise king in want of counsel), see E. Whiting, p. 226; Green,
          "Marcolf the Fool"; Simpson, "Saving Satire," pp. 399–401, especially p.
          400n40; and Pearsall, "Audelay's *Marcolf and Solomon*," pp. 139–40. On the Latin
          tradition itself, see Bradbury, "Rival Wisdom." Here the trope works more as a
          framing device (it concludes at lines 988–89) than as a sustained fiction (it
          revives only at lines 92, 391, and 417). Green, p. 575n47, observes that the poem
          embeds other references to fools, folly, and kings as equals to knaves (lines 81,
          465–68, 562, and 849). He also speculates about who Audelay had in mind as the
          addressee: "we might naturally wonder whom Audelay envisages as playing
          Solomon to his Marcolf. Surely Henry V, who was only twenty-four at his
          accession is a doubtful candidate, and his son, the infant Henry VI, even more
          so. By far the best bet (and another reason for believing that Audelay composed
          his Marcolf poem sometime between 1410 and 1413) would seem to be Henry
          IV" (Green, p. 567). Simpson, p. 402, points out a likeness to the "lunatyk" in
          Piers Plowman B.Prol.123–24 and C.9.107–14, but Pearsall, p. 146, refutes the
          comparison, noting that Audelay's Marcolf is merely a "flimsy mask."

70   Simpson, "Saving Satire," p. 400, notes how the speaker Marcolf shifts the burden
          of public truth-telling to Solomon, here and at lines 94, 392–94, and 421–22,
          with the whole text ultimately attributed to Solomon, saying what he was exhorted
          to say by Marcolf (lines 988–89). See explanatory note to *Marcolf and Solomon*,
          line 430–42.

71   *lanternys of lyf*. Simpson, "Saving Satire," p. 394, suggests that this line may evoke
          the title of the Lollard tract *The Lanterne of Light* (c. 1409–15); compare also *Mar-
          colf and Solomon*, lines 104 and 630, the idea always being directed critically at
          parish priests, whose light should burn brightly for the laity. See too Pearsall,
          "Audelay's *Marcolf and Solomon*," pp. 142–43. Citrome detects in this passage
          Audelay's concern "with his own troubled conscience" (*Surgeon*, pp. 84–85).

78   *Here horne is eblaw*. Proverbial, meaning "exposed publicly." Compare Chaucer's *Legend of Good Women*, line 1383, "Have at thee, Jason! Now thyn horn is blowe!" See B. Whiting and Whiting, *Proverbs*, H485.

81   *foly*. See explanatory note to *Marcolf and Solomon*, lines 66–69.

85   *unkynd*. Compare *Piers Plowman* B.5.269, where Coveitise is called an "unkynde creature" (Simpson, "Saving Satire," p. 403).

89   *secatour*. For other warnings by Audelay not to entrust one's affairs to an executor, see *Marcolf and Solomon*, line 258; *Visiting the Sick and Consoling the Needy*, lines 71–73, 89, 99, 345–47; and *On the World's Folly*, lines 58–60. Executors were proverbially untrustworthy and thievish. Halliwell, p. 84, quotes the saying "Two *secaturs* and an overseer make three thieves." The commonplace occurs in *Piers Plowman* C.2.192 and C.6.143 (Pearsall, "Audelay's *Marcolf and Solomon*," p. 146). For more instances, see E. Whiting, pp. 227 and 229, and *MED secutour*, n.

92   On the Marcolf and Solomon frame, see explanatory note to *Marcolf and Solomon*, lines 66–69.

94   On Solomon as the public satiric speaker, see explanatory note to *Marcolf and Solomon*, line 70.

95   Forrest, *Detection of Heresy*, p. 165, points to this line on proud priests as evidence of a widespread belief that "heresy would be manifested and revealed." Audelay repeats the line elsewhere to refer to corrupt friars and heretics; see explanatory note to *Marcolf and Solomon*, lines 678–88.

101–04   Audelay asserts that were the priesthood to do its duty with parishioners, and avoid all avarice, then the laity would return home to religious truths, and turn away from (by implication) heretical views. On the anti-Lollard resonance in Audelay's metaphor of light, see explanatory note to *Marcolf and Solomon*, line 71.

105–08   On the natural goodness of animals, compare *True Living*, lines 91–93, and see the citations provided by E. Whiting, p. 227.

109   Compare *Piers Plowman* B.18.204 (Simpson, "Saving Satire," p. 403).

123   *Bayard for bryd ne fore brend*. Bayard is a horse's name (*MED baiard*, n.[1]; see also Chaucer's *Troilus and Criseyde*, 1.218–24). Elsewhere, Audelay invokes a proverb about blind Bayard (*Marcolf and Solomon*, lines 952 [explanatory note], 993, and *Audelay's Epilogue to The Counsel of Conscience*, line 381). The expression *for bryd ne fore brend* is a crux with little useful commentary. To make sense of the expression (which feels proverbial), I take *bryd* to be *MED breid*, n.(1)1(b), "rashness," and *brend* as the past participle as noun of *MED brennen*, v.5a(c), "passion." E. Whiting's definition of *brend* as "brent-goose" does not seem to fit the context, through there may be an obscure proverb evoked here: "for bird nor for brent-goose." See also the suggestion for *brend* in the *MED* under *brend*, ppl. as n.(a) "brindled or brown color; a horse of this color," with a citation of Audelay's line. How this definition makes sense of the line is unclear, and the *MED* does not offer any help as to the meaning of *bryd*.

131–43   *pore prest . . . unkynde*. Audelay describes a humble and genuinely good priest whose very virtue is maligned by those who "smelle a Lollere in the wynd," as Chaucer puts it in the Epilogue to the Man of Law's Tale (*CT* II[B₁]1173). Many have commented on this passage: see, e.g., Green, "Marcolf the Fool," p. 568; Simpson, "Saving Satire," pp. 398, 401; Bennett, "John Audelay: Life Records," pp. 42–43; Powell, "John Audelay and John Mirk," p. 90; Pickering, "Make-Up," p. 118; and Pearsall, "Audelay's *Marcolf and Solomon*," pp. 143–44. Forrest, *Detection of Heresy*, pp. 167–68, points to lines 131–33 to illustrate the difficulties inherent in the detection of heresy in Audelay's time. Catto, "Religious Change under Henry V," p. 105, observes how the "refutation of Lollardy was an important part of the agenda of contemporary theologians." On Audelay's anti-Lollardism, see also the explanatory notes to *Marcolf and Solomon*, lines 669–88, 678–88, and *Audelay's Epilogue to The Counsel of Conscience*, lines 248–60.

144–52   Audelay displays considerable skill as a satirist in this portrait of the corrupt yet richly companionable cleric Sir John. Commentaries on this passage include: Halliwell, p. 84; E. Whiting, p. 227; Simpson, "Saving Satire," pp. 398 (a "brilliant and sustained example of Chaucerian ironic satire"), 401; Bennett, "John Audelay: Life Records," pp. 31, 42–43 (perhaps Audelay draws here a self-portrait of his life with the Lestranges in London); and Pearsall, "Audelay's *Marcolf and Solomon*," p. 142 (a "wonderfully comic stanza" exhibiting "an unexpected gift for traditional anticlerical satire").

146   *orglus*. See *MED orgel*, n.(2), "A kind of musical instrument," with a possible pun on *orgel*, n.(1), "Pride, haughtiness, presumption."

148–49   *ner a parsun or a vecory*. E. Whiting, p. 227, captures the socially pretentious idiom embedded in this passage, translating it as: "you would never take this fine fellow for a parson or a vicar; he is a gentleman!"

150   *baslard*. See *MED baselard*, n.(1), "A kind of (fashionable) dagger, curved or straight, worn in an (ornamental) sheath at the girdle." On priests wearing forbidden baselards, see citations provided by E. Whiting, pp. 227–28. Compare also *Piers Plowman* B.15.121, 124 (Pearsall, "Audelay's *Marcolf and Solomon*," p. 146; Green, "Langland and Audelay," p. 156).

151   *pautener*. See *MED pautener(e*, n.(2), "A purse, bag, pouch." E. Whiting, p. 228, translates this line as "from his open purse, everyone is paid, or satisfied."

172–82   E. Whiting's note, p. 228, identifies these lines as regulations drawn from the rule of Saint Benedict.

176   *obey obedyans*. See explanatory note to *Marcolf and Solomon*, line 32. One may also observe how the vocalic alliteration of line 174, on *a(-b)*, finely parallels the alliteration on *o(-b)* in line 176.

183–87   Simpson, "Saving Satire," pp. 401, notes the successive, unmarked changes in third- and second-person address that occur here and "across the whole poem," arguing that "the strategy of rapid, unannounced changes of address is clear: formally Marcol creates a sense of both potential inclusion and present fragmentation, which is a formal response to the state of the Church as he sees it."

190   *hold up youre houshold and youre housyng.* This line exhorts monks to maintain
           their monasteries, monastic standards, and familial structures; see *MED houshold*,
           n.1b. The command is paralleled in later passages that (1) exhort alms to sup-
           port the households of friars (*Marcolf and Solomon* line 458); and (2) request that
           livings and "households" be granted only to secular clergy who are suitably edu-
           cated (*Marcolf and Solomon*, line 567). Compare also *Marcolf and Solomon*, line
           583, where Audelay asks that secular clergy reside and openly maintain a house-
           hold in their parishes.

196–98   On this complaint over how poorly some monks sing psalms and recite prayers
           on behalf of souls, compare the 13-line stanza *Over-Hippers and Skippers* appear-
           ing at the end of MS Douce 302. The metrics of *Over-Hippers and Skippers*
           matches *Marcolf and Solomon*, and it could even be a stanza now lost from the
           longer poem (Fein, "Thirteen-Line Alliterative Stanza," p. 64). See also
           explanatory note to *Cur mundus*, line 40.

203   *no lykyng ne no lust.* Compare *Piers Plowman* B.16.32, C.11.82, C.13.152, C.16.211
           (Pearsall, "Audelay's *Marcolf and Solomon*," p. 151n26).

210–11   On God speaking through Holy Writ, compare *Marcolf and Solomon*, lines 1–9
           (explanatory note), and *Audelay's Epilogue to The Counsel of Conscience*, lines
           352–55.

215   *mese.* The meaning wanted here and at line 809 is "dispute, make division," a
           figurative usage for a verb meaning "divide up (into portions)," usually in refer-
           ence to food (see *OED mess*, v.; *MED messen*, v.[2]). The *MED* assigns Audelay's
           mese to *mesen*, v., "to soothe, placate, relieve of grief," but the lexicographers
           query Audelay's term as a mistake for *masen*, v., "to be confused or bewildered."
           E. Whiting follows the first meaning in glossing it as "moderate," but this
           meaning ill suits the context.

235–43   Green, "Langland and Audelay," p. 157, offers a scansion of these lines, noting
           that "Audelay . . . has a number of defective lines with only three lifts, a situation
           that is very rare in Langland."

236   Simpson, "Saving Satire," p. 400, notes the boldness of this line, and Green,
           "Marcolf the Fool," p. 568, comments that Audelay "evidently found the guise
           of the plain-speaking churl a useful cover."

237–40   Pearsall, *Old English and Middle English Poetry*, pp. 249–50, cited this passage in
           his early argument for a profound influence of *Piers Plowman* upon Audelay's
           poem. He has now modified that stance, seeing in Audelay's verse the "more
           widespread and resonant tradition" of complaint, satire, and prophecy with
           apocalyptic overtones, as found in *The Simonie, Piers Plowman*, and numerous
           religious-didactic poems (Pearsall, "Audelay's *Marcolf and Solomon*," p. 148).
           Compare too *Marcolf and Solomon*, lines 990–91.

238   *beryn Cristis kay.* Compare *Marcolf and Solomon*, lines 805a (explanatory note),
           869, 961a, and *Visiting the Sick and Consoling the Needy*, line 199.

242   Simpson, "Saving Satire," p. 391, notes that this "trenchant criticism" of both temporal and spiritual laws makes it likely that *Marcolf and Solomon* was composed later than Arundel's *Constitutions* of 1409; he goes on to propose that the poem was written "in the ambience of the Oldcastle Rising of 1414." See also explanatory notes to lines 501 and 503.

250   A line similar to this one appears at *Marcolf and Solomon*, line 289.

255   Pearsall, "Audelay's *Marcolf and Solomon*," pp. 145–46, notes that this exhortation — to continue to endow the Church as one's fathers did (found also at *Marcolf and Solomon*, line 274) — contrasts directly to Langland's position (which leans toward the later Lollard position) not to break up estates to give to wealthy clergy (*Piers Plowman* C.5.163, C.17.56–58).

258–59   Compare *Visiting the Sick and Consoling the Needy*, line 73, and *On the World's Folly*, lines 58–59. For Audelay's opinion that one should take care of one's own soul before death and not entrust it to others, see explanatory note to *Marcolf and Solomon*, line 89.

274–86   In this critique of disendowment, Green, "Marcolf the Fool," p. 575n42, sees Audelay underscoring his orthodoxy. See also explanatory note to *Marcolf and Solomon*, line 255.

279   Stanley, "*True Counsel of Conscience*," p. 155, compares the collocation of *counsel* and *care* to *Three Dead Kings*, lines 35, 89.

280   This line resembles *Marcolf and Solomon*, line 316, and *Salutation to Saint Bridget*, line 22.

281   *cheré fayre*. The proverbial phrase denotes transient joys. See *MED cheri*, n.2(a), the citations given there, and others provided by Halliwell, p. 85, and E. Whiting, p. 229.

287   *covens*. For the meaning "fellows," only in Audelay, see *MED covine*, n.1(b).

287–91   Green, "Marcolf the Fool," compares these lines to John Ball's letters, noting in particular a phrase found there: "knoweth your freende fro your foo" (pp. 570, 575n43, 575n45).

288   *obey obedyens*. See explanatory note to *Marcolf and Solomon*, line 32.

289   A similar version of this line appears at *Marcolf and Solomon*, line 250.

290   Compare *Piers Plowman* B.18.204 (Simpson, "Saving Satire," p. 403).

291   *kyndlé*. See explanatory note to *Marcolf and Solomon*, line 13.

315   *ground*. Simpson, "Saving Satire," p. 394, detects in this word, repeated at lines 330, 355, 651, and 785, a Lollard resonance.

316   This line resembles *Marcolf and Solomon*, line 280, and *Salutation to Saint Bridget*, line 22.

330   *grounde*. See explanatory note to *Marcolf and Solomon*, line 315.

330–31   Green, "Langland and Audelay," pp. 158–59, notes the directness of address ("Then loke thou"), as if from a pulpit, and compares this tendency to Langland's rhetorical style, e.g., in *Piers Plowman* B.10.207–08.

342   *Saynt Thomas*. Thomas Becket, martyred archbishop of Canterbury, was revered for his strong stance on behalf of the Church against pressure from secular powers. Compare Audelay's *Saint Thomas Archbishop of Canterbury* (and see explanatory notes). Pearsall, "Audelay's *Marcolf and Solomon*," p. 146, notes this line as another instance of Audelay's strict orthodoxy.

344   E. Whiting, p. 230, notes that "This line must refer to the boldness of lords and lewd men who interfere in the secret business of the chapters." The verb *mon* is the auxiliary "must, shall," as asserted by Stanley, "Alliteratitive *Three Dead Kings*," pp. 269–70, but disputed by Putter, "Language and Metre," p. 505, who reads it as Middle English *mannen*, "take charge" or "to people, occupy." See also the explanatory note to *Three Dead Kings*, line 78.

355   *ungroundid*. See explanatory note to *Marcolf and Solomon*, line 315.

369   Compare *Piers Plowman* B.7.183 (Green, "Langland and Audelay," pp. 158, 167), and C.1.166, C.3.159, C.9.333 (Pearsall, "Audelay's *Marcolf and Solomon*," p. 151n26).

390   *loveday*. The term refers to a day appointed for a meeting between enemies, set for the purpose of striking a reconciliation. See *MED lovedai*, n., and compare *Marcolf and Solomon*, burden (explanatory note), and lines 393, 974, and *Our Lord's Epistle on Sunday*, line 46. Pearsall, "Audelay's *Marcolf and Solomon*," pp. 146–47, contrasts Audelay's sincere plea for harmony to the more cynical uses of the term found in Chaucer (General Prologue, *CT* I[A]258) and Langland (*Piers Plowman* C.3.196, C.5.158, C.11.17). See also Chaucer's *House of Fame*, line 695; and Kathleen Kennedy, "Maintaining Love through Accord," pp. 166, 174n4.

391–94   On the Marcolf and Solomon frame, see explanatory notes to *Marcolf and Solomon*, lines 66–69 and 70.

393   Detecting "Audelay's legitimation of satire," Simpson, "Saving Satire," p. 403, compares this line to *Piers Plowman* B.11.101–02. On the term *loveday*, see explanatory notes to *Marcolf and Solomon*, incipit and line 390.

394   *favele*. See *MED favel*, n., "Flattery, insincerity; duplicity, guile, intrigue," with this note: "The figure of Favel, with these characteristics, was created by Langland in *Piers Plowman*. All other uses of the figure and the term seem to be derived from this source." Compare *Marcolf and Solomon*, line 1005, and *Piers Plowman* A.2.23, A.2.114, B.2.42, and B.2.166. For other comments, see Halliwell, pp. 86–87; E. Whiting, pp. 230 (the idiom *curry favel*) and 233; Barney, "Allegorical Visions," p. 128 (the term in *Piers Plowman*); and Green, "Langland and Audelay," p. 155.

408   This line is similar to *Marcolf and Solomon*, line 612.

409   *cumberment.* See *MED combrement*, n.(c), "sinning, sinfulness," for which this line by Audelay is cited.

410   *clene kalender.* Compare *Marcolf and Solomon*, line 614.

417   On the Marcolf and Solomon frame, see explanatory note to *Marcolf and Solomon*, lines 66–69.

420   *clergé.* Audelay or the scribe evidently intends one to understand by this word the meaning of Old French *clergise*: "Learning, knowledge, scholarship" (*MED*, n.1).

421–22   On Solomon as the public satiric speaker, see explanatory note to *Marcolf and Solomon*, line 70.

426–30   Although speaking in the voice of the rustic Marcolf, who exhorts the powerful king to speak the truth, Audelay seems here to declare his own poetics of truth-telling: blurt it out and do not lie, because God is the ultimate knower of Truth and one's ultimate audience. He adds that if you cover up the truth, you will appear ignorant and illiterate. If you do tell the truth, it is possible that you will offend people, so you should ask them, both politely and piously, to excuse you, because, presumably, they too wish truthful things to be openly exposed. As is typical, Audelay shows more fear of God's judgment than of man's. Compare these lines to *Marcolf and Solomon*, lines 443–46 (cited by Wawn, "Truth-Telling," p. 281, who sets Audelay's poem in the truth-telling tradition of *Mum and the Sothsegger*).

430   *four oordyrs.* The four medicant orders are the Augustinians, the Carmelites, the Dominicans, and the Franciscans. The phrase is standard; see *MED ordre*, n.9(b).

430–42   This stanza offers praise of the fraternal founders. Compare Audelay's *Saint Francis*. Since Solomon is supposed, at line 988, to have been speaking the poem, line 430 may be the beginning of Solomon's speech (Pickering, "Make-Up," p. 133n17).

443–44   Pearsall, "Audelay's *Marcolf and Solomon*," p. 147, comments that Audelay's "[g]nomic and proverbial-sounding expressions have sometimes a Langlandian ring," and he cites for comparison *Piers Plowman* C.3.424, C.4.88–89.

443–55   On this fervent advocacy of truth-telling, see explanatory note to lines 426–30. Green "Marcolf the Fool," p. 570, hears "a particular kind of political potency" in this whole stanza, especially if it is to come from the mouth of "the anarchic Marcolf," but, in fact, it may not (see explanatory note to lines 430–42). Simpson, "Saving Satire," pp. 400–01, believes that in lines 440–46 Marcolf "brilliantly capitalizes on an account of mendicancy to justify his own satire of the friars" as his exhortations become "simultaneously a direction to friars and to the satirist of friars." For Pearsall's refutation of Simpson, see explanatory note to lines 456–68.

452   *Asay thi frynd or thou have nede.* See E. Whiting, p. 231, for other instances of this proverbial expression.

456–68 This stanza on friars projects, for Pearsall, "Audelay's *Marcolf and Solomon*," p. 143, a tone of "enigmatic irony." According to Simpson, "Saving Satire," p. 402, "Both Langland and Audelay are . . . orthodox critics of ecclesiastical covetousness, whose principal target is the friars, and whose principal solution to the problem of medicancy is a 'fyndyng' [compare *Piers Plowman* B.20.384]." Countering Simpson's argument, Pearsall, "Audelay's *Marcolf and Solomon*," pp. 141–45, finds Audelay's treatment of friars to be distinctly unlike Langland's: "Where for Langland the friars' systematic practice of begging is what inevitably leads to scandalous abuse, for Audelay it is the proper traditional basis of their livelihood" (p. 145).

458 On Audelay's concern that each ecclesiastical order properly maintain its household, see the explanatory note to *Marcolf and Solomon*, line 190.

465–68 On how these lines relate to the Marcolf frame, see explanatory note to *Marcolf and Solomon*, lines 66–69.

469–81 Audelay's attack is upon covetous abuses committed by individual friars, who are therefore like Judas because for monetary gain they pervert the fraternal traditions. See Pearsall, "Audelay's *Marcolf and Solomon*," pp. 142, 143, 145; and Simpson, "Saving Satire," p. 396.

473 On Judas's treason, compare *Marcolf and Solomon*, lines 753a and 758; *Prayer on Christ's Passion*, lines 4–5; *O Deus qui voluisti*, lines 4–5 and 18; *Virtues of the Mass*, lines 103–08; *Seven Hours of the Cross*, lines 13–18; and *The Vision of Saint Paul*, line 234.

485 Compare *Piers Plowman* C.13.8, C.21.67 (Pearsall, "Audelay's *Marcolf and Solomon*," p. 151n26).

490–95 These lines may allude directly to *Piers Plowman*. If so, Audelay seems here to respond to antifraternal satirists such as Langland (with his figure of the plowman) by offering a gentler counterargument: that society should support with its charity the institution of fraternal mendicancy while condemning those individual friars who commit covetous acts.

495–503 Forrest, *Detection of Heresy*, p. 144, reads these lines as pertaining to a "latent suspicion of mendicants" as heretics: "Audelay's desire that his readers beware of false prophets, both mendicant and Lollard, is indicative of the early fifteenth-century atmosphere in which anti-heresy legislation could be misinterpreted as pertaining to the friars." There is an ominous and secretive quality to this stanza. Audelay appears to feel liable to attack for speaking against covetous clergy. Scribe B sharpens this sense when he emends Scribe A's *wold*, line 499, to *hold*.

501 *to stond at a stake*. Green, "Marcolf the Fool," p. 566, sees this direct reference to the burning of heretics (compare line 676) as an indicator of the poem's date: "The specificity . . . suggests that it was composed after the promulgation of the statute *De Heretico Comburendo* and the death of the Lollard William Sawtry in 1401, and quite possibly after John Badby's gruesome death in 1410, but its references to the dangers of Lollardy and its dark hints that clerical venality and discord might offer an occasion for popular rebellion would surely have been

rendered less urgent by Oldcastle's abortive rising at St Giles' Fields on January 10, 1414." See also explanatory notes to lines 242 and 503.

503   *Blynd as Y am.* Audelay drops the mask here. The present tense verb *am* leads Green to conclude that Audelay was blind in the period to which he dates the poem, 1410–13. It is possible, however, that references to Audelay's blindness (as well as some of the signature stanzas) were edited into poems during the compiling of MS Douce 302. On the dating of *Marcolf and Solomon*, see explanatory notes to lines 242 and 501, and discussions by Green, "Marcolf the Fool," pp. 566–67; Simpson, "Saving Satire," p. 391; Meyer-Lee, "Vatic Penitent," pp. 65–66; Pickering, "Make-Up," pp. 118–19; and Pearsall, "Audelay's *Marcolf and Solomon*," p. 140. Compare also Audelay's second signature at the end of the poem (line 1008).

504–06   These lines recur in *Audelay's Epilogue to The Counsel of Conscience*, lines 374–76.

507   On this insertion of a mixed Latin-French line, see E. Whiting's note, p. 231, and compare *Marcolf and Solomon*, line 701 (explanatory note).

526   *soulehele.* Compare *Marcolf and Solomon*, line 798. *Soulehele* is the stated purpose for Audelay's *The Counsel of Conscience*, the larger "book" to which this poem apparently belongs. See explanatory notes to *Audelay's Epilogue to The Counsel of Conscience*, lines 105 and 248–60.

533   Scribe B inserts here in red ink a marginal illustration of a pointing hand, hence emphasizing Audelay's edict against hypocrites preaching. The idea that a person will be judged by his deeds is a commonplace in Audelay, though Forrest, *Detection of Heresy*, p. 165, points to line 533 as directed at the detection of heresy; see explanatory note to *Marcolf and Solomon*, lines 678–88.

534   E. Whiting, p. 231, notes that this line provides "an awkward paraphrase" of the Latin heading.

543   On Audelay's frequent citation of the Golden Rule, which appears in the first stanza of *Marcolf and Solomon*, see the explanatory note to *True Living*, line 231.

549   *bescherewd. MED bishreuen*, v.2(a): "To make wicked, deprave, corrupt."

560   *to Oxford to scole.* Halliwell, pp. 85–86, adds this note: "These curious lines have already been quoted by Mr. James Heywood in his edition of the Merton College Statutes."

562   On how these lines relate to the Marcolf frame, see explanatory note to *Marcolf and Solomon*, lines 66–69.

566   *personache.* See *MED personage*, n.(2), "A benefice or maintenance granted to a parson; property or residence associated with a parson's benefice; parsonage." On Audelay's concern that households be properly maintained by the ecclesiastical orders, see the explanatory note to *Marcolf and Solomon*, line 190.

583   *houshold.* See explanatory note to *Marcolf and Solomon*, line 190.

612   This line is similar to *Marcolf and Solomon*, line 408.

614   *clene calender.* Compare *Marcolf and Solomon*, line 410.

622   *Thai schuld never be at dyscord.* See explanatory notes to *Marcolf and Solomon*, incipit
           and line 390.

630   *lanterns lyght.* See explanatory note to *Marcolf and Solomon*, line 71.

644   *the treuth of here toung.* The phrase *true of [one's] tongue* occurs frequently in *Piers
           Plowman* (Green, "Langland and Audelay," pp. 158, 166).

651   *ground of al goodnes.* See explanatory note to *Marcolf and Solomon*, line 315.

664   Compare *Piers Plowman* C.9.107–14 (Simpson, "Saving Satire," p. 402).

669–88   On Audelay's anti-Lollardism, see explanatory notes to *Marcolf and Solomon*, lines
           131–43, and *Audelay's Epilogue to The Counsel of Conscience*, lines 248–60. For
           comments specifically on lines 669–76, see Green, "Marcolf the Fool," p. 568;
           Simpson, "Saving Satire," pp. 399, 401 (the "stanza is unquestionably an attack
           on the broad brush and draconian punishment of anyone who dares to criticize
           the Church"); and Pearsall, "Audelay's *Marcolf and Solomon*," p. 144 ("Audelay
           warns of the dangers faced by laymen who speak out and tell the truth").

676   On this reference to the burning of heretics, see explanatory note to *Marcolf and
           Solomon*, line 501.

678–88   This interesting stanza describes the deeds that mark a Lollard, with Audelay
           also declaring that heretics will be judged — principally by God — by their own
           actions and words. He notes how unmistakably Lollardy may be detected, be-
           cause the heretic "refuses his obligations to the Church, to worship the Cross, or
           to attend services" (Pearsall, "Audelay's *Marcolf and Solomon*," p. 144). Simpson,
           "Saving Satire," p. 401, observes that "the stanza is, plausibly, less an attack on
           Lollardy than on those who would persecute Lollards." Forrest sees here the
           reconfiguration of an existing debate, that is, the "latent suspicion of mendicants"
           as heretics: "Audelay's desire that his readers beware false prophets, both mendi-
           cant and lollard, is indicative of the early fifteenth-century atmosphere in which
           anti-heresy legislation could be misinterpreted as pertaining to the friars" (p.
           144). It is noteworthy that Audelay elsewhere applies the wording of line 678 to
           wicked priests and friars (see *Marcolf and Solomon*, lines 95, 533), thus showing
           that, as Forrest puts it, "heresy would be manifested and revealed" for persons
           of any office or profession (p. 165). Hudson, *Premature Reformation*, notes, though,
           that Audelay's attitude seems relatively tolerant — "Audelay's only response to
           these crimes is to forbid his flock to pray for their perpetrators" (p. 435); she
           compares Audelay's statement to the behavioral latitude granted to someone like
           Margery Kempe. The stanza itself is short by one line, and Stanley, "Verse Forms,"
           p. 118n49, proposes a numerological reason. His explanation may, however, be
           flawed because it is possible that the poem lacks its full ending; one cannot know
           for certain how many lines it originally possessed (see explanatory note to
           Marcolf and Solomon, line 1013).

679   *take good eme.* See explanatory note to *Marcolf and Solomon*, line 53.

682 *on what deth he dye*. The word *deth* (MS *deþ*) may be a mistake for *dey* ("day"); compare *Visiting the Sick and Consoling the Needy*, line 355, but see also *True Living*, line 23.

693 *Slus* is a plural form for the monetary unit shilling (*MED shilling*, n.1[a]). *Schof* is the preterite of the verb *shouven* and means "reject, refuse." See E. Whiting's note, p. 231.

695 *sorche*. This verb, unattested elsewhere in Middle English, is queried in the *MED* under *sorchen* and is supposed to be either derived from Old French *sorchëoir*, v., "to fall on, attack," or an error for Middle English *serchen*, v.2(a), "to seek out." The meaning given by the lexicographers for Audelay's word is "to inflict (excommunication on sb.)."

701 The French of this line is similar to the mixed Latin-French of line 507; both seem whispered conspiratorially, as if simultaneously hiding and betraying a secret. Marcolf/Audelay may be alluding to a specific scandal involving illicit sexual behavior. Lechery, which is personified at the end of the stanza, can buy its way out of punishment from the consistory courts.

705 *Mede the maydyn*. Lady Mede is an allegorical figure who represents the seductive corruption of money and reward in society; she appears in Passus 2 and 3 of Langland's *Piers Plowman*, e.g., B.2.20 (Hudson, "Legacy of *Piers Plowman*," p. 262; Simpson, "Saving Satire," p. 403). Her appearance twice in Audelay's works (here and *On the World's Folly*, line 17) may derive from a common cultural usage or from Audelay's direct knowledge of Langland's work. For differing opinions on this question, see Green, "Langland and Audelay," and Pearsall, "Audelay's *Marcolf and Solomon*."

709–13 Audelay deplores the fact that priests will sanction divorce, against God's law, for the sake of money. For Audelay's views on marriage, see also *True Living*, lines 65–115, *Virginity of Maids*, and *Chastity of Wives*.

718 Compare *Piers Plowman* B.6.39–40 (Green, "Langland and Audelay," p. 154).

728 *castun in the new fayre*. The phrase *new fayre* seems to denote a place of corrupt modern practice; see *MED feire*, n.1(b), where the instances, one from *Piers Plowman* and one from a Lollard text, refer to the "new fair," perhaps an event in London, as a site of immoral diversion. E. Whiting, p. 232, discusses the term as an idiom referring to bartering, seeing in the passage a condemnation of curates who make deals for multiple benefices. Compare *Piers Plowman* B.5.321 (Green, "Langland and Audelay," pp. 154–55) and C.6.377 (Pearsall, "Audelay's *Marcolf and Solomon*," p. 146).

730 *permetacion*. The *MED* defines Audelay's word as "the exchange of offices or benefices." See *permutacioun*, n.(b). The next line makes it clear that he condemns a contemporary practice of holding multiple benefices. Compare *Piers Plowman* B.Prol.29 (Simpson, "Saving Satire," p. 403) and C.3.33 (Pearsall, "Audelay's *Marcolf and Solomon*," p. 146).

731   *pluralytis*. The *MED* defines *pluralite*, n.(c), as follows: "the simultaneous tenure
         by one cleric of more than one benefice; especially ones in which he has spiritual
         charge of people in a district." Audelay even blames the pope for permitting this
         abuse. Pollard, *Late Medieval England*, p. 209, provides a succinct description of
         the practice.

753a   This Latin heading is written by Scribe B. On Judas's treason, compare *Marcolf
         and Solomon*, lines 473, 753a, and 758; *Prayer on Christ's Passion*, lines 4–5; *O Deus
         qui voluisti*, lines 4–5 and 18; *Virtues of the Mass*, lines 103–08; *Seven Hours of the
         Cross*, lines 13–18; and *The Vision of Saint Paul*, line 234.

779a   Scribe B inserts what seems to be a marker of topic ("confession and the sacra-
         ment of the altar") beside Scribe A's typical liturgical/biblical heading.

780–805 In arguing for the poem's "para-Lollardy," Simpson, "Saving Satire," p. 395,
         notes here how the fictional voice of the poem "sometimes encourages lay diso-
         bedience of sorts: after one stanza (beginning at line 780) encouraging obedi-
         ence, Marcol changes his tack rather in the next: do as the curates command, he
         directs his lay readers, but 'do not as þei don', unless they practice what they
         preach." See also Green, "Marcolf the Fool," p. 575n42; Pearsall, "Audelay's
         Marcolf and Solomon," p. 140.

785   *grownd of al goodnes*. See explanatory note to *Marcolf and Solomon*, line 315.

790–92   These lines echo one of Audelay's recurrent biblical allusions (from Ezechiel
         18:23, 18:32, 33:11), one which may have had a special resonance in regard to
         the correction of Lollards. See explanatory note to *True Living*, line 127.

798   *soulehele*. Compare *Marcolf and Solomon*, line 526, and see explanatory notes to
         Audelay's Epilogue to The Counsel of Conscience, lines 105, 248–60.

805a   This heading invokes the biblical passage (Matthew 16:19) traditionally under-
         stood to sanctify papal and priestly authority as granted directly from Christ.
         Compare *Marcolf and Solomon*, lines 238, 869, 961a, and *Visiting the Sick and Con-
         soling the Needy*, line 199. See also Simpson, "Saving Satire," pp. 396–97, and
         Pearsall, "Audelay's *Marcolf and Solomon*," pp. 140–41.

809   *mese*. See explanatory note to *Marcolf and Solomon*, line 215.

820   Audelay's dictum to the laity to be shriven at least once a year adheres to ortho-
         dox practice (see Pearsall, "Audelay's *Marcolf and Solomon*," p. 146).

828–31   The sense of these lines is: They (i.e., the curates) must answer, by law, for your
         soul if you are confessed; however, if you don't confess, you will have to answer
         for yourself, and be doomed.

832–96   These stanzas expound orthodox doctrine. Audelay "defends the efficacy of the
         mass, even when celebrated by a sinful priest, and gives an orthodox account of
         transsubstantiation" (Green, "Marcolf the Fool," p. 575n42; see also Simpson,
         "Saving Satire," p. 393; Pearsall, "Audelay's *Marcolf and Solomon*," p. 141). Com-
         pare Audelay's *Devotions at the Levation of Christ's Body* and *Virtues of the Mass*.

848   *defouteryng.* For this word meaning "faltering, failure," related to either *defauten*
          or *falteren* and found only in Audelay, see *MED defoutering*, ger.

849   On how these lines relate to the Marcolf frame, see explanatory note to *Marcolf
          and Solomon*, lines 66–69.

858–83   On Audelay's exposition of the Trinity in terms of the sun, compare *Piers Plow-
          man* B.17.204–44 (Simpson, "Saving Satire," p. 403; Green, "Langland and
          Audelay," pp. 160–61). One should also compare Audelay's metaphorical simili-
          tude to that in another 13-line alliterative poem, that is, the exposition of the
          Trinity and Mary by means of a botanical conceit, in *The Four Leaves of the True-
          love* (Fein, *Moral Love Songs*, p. 180–96).

869   *louse and bynde.* See explanatory note to *Marcolf and Solomon*, lines 805a.

897–922   Citrome offers a penetrating analysis of the medical metaphor elaborated in
          these two stanzas, noting how the medieval distinction between surgeon and
          physician is played out theologically. The stanzas compare "the urgency of
          confession to that of surgical treatment, and the total authority of the priest over
          matters of the soul to the surgeon's over those of the body. . . . While the
          'surgeon' of the first stanza is clearly the priest, the implied physician of the
          second is none other than Jesus Christ, or *Christus Medicus*" (*Surgeon*, pp. 90–92).

902   *penetawnsere.* Compare *Piers Plowman* C.22.320 (Pearsall, "Audelay's *Marcolf and
          Solomon*," p. 146). See also E. Whiting, p. 232; Simpson, "Saving Satire," p. 393.

917   *know kyndlé.* See explanatory note to *Marcolf and Solomon*, line 13.

923–44   These lines were reworked by Audelay when he composed *God's Address to Sinful
          Men*, lines 137–59 (Pickering, "Make-Up," p. 130).

923   *wayt.* "Take heed, consider." See *MED waiten*, v.1b(b) and 2b(a).

925   *yeesy penans.* Compare *God's Address to Sinful Men*, lines 113, 139.

927–28   Audelay's belief in the salvific effect of the Paternoster is enacted by its actual
          presence (*Paternoster*, an alliterative English exposition of the prayer's seven
          points) towards the end of MS Douce 302.

937–43   This brief allegory of the Four Daughters of God (Psalm 84:11), which is devel-
          oped further in lines 974a–80, comprises the climactic moment of Audelay's
          poem — itself being a general call for harmony (i.e., a *loveday*; see explanatory
          notes to *Marcolf and Solomon*, incipit and line 390) among the ecclesiastical
          orders so that they may direct full energy toward their sacred joint purpose, the
          saving of souls. Audelay repeats the trope in *God's Address to Sinful Men*, lines
          144a–51 (bor-rowing from *Marcolf and Solomon*). The figure holds importance
          in *Piers Plowman* (Passus B.18 and C.20), where it delivers the climax of the
          Harrowing of Hell scene (Alford, "Design of the Poem," pp. 56–58). E. Whiting,
          p. 232, provides more citations on the Four Daughters of God.

938–39   Audelay's treatment of the allegory is not without problems, which may be prob-
          lems of scribal transmission. In line 938, Audelay seems to render the Daughter
          Mercy (*Misericordia*) as a doublet: "Mercy *and grace*"; in line 939, the sense would

be better if *rest* were *cest*, i.e., "kissed" (compare Psalm 84:11). Similar problems exist, however, in *God's Address to Sinful Men*, lines 147–48, which is apparently a direct reworking of this passage: there Grace, not Peace, appears with Mercy as one of the Daughters. Faced with these discrepancies, I have let the manuscript readings stand without emendation. The rendering of the biblical text is much more precise at *Marcolf and Solomon*, lines 975–82.

949   For the proverb resonating in this line, see explanatory note to *Marcolf and Solomon*, lines 42–43.

952   *blustyrne . . . Bayard*. Here and at *Marcolf and Solomon*, line 993, and *Audelay's Epilogue to The Counsel of Conscience*, line 381, Audelay uses a proverb about blind Bayard, a horse, "blustering forth" as a figure for blind recklessness (s.v. *MED baiard*, n.(1)(c), and *blusteren*, v.2). The proverb may have held a special resonance for Blind Audelay. References to blind Bayard as a "blusterer" also occur in *Piers Plowman* B.5.514 and *Cleanness*, line 886. Compare *Marcolf and Solomon*, line 123 (another reference to Bayard).

952–56   *Audelay's Epilogue to The Counsel of Conscience*, lines 381–85, appears to be a reworking of these lines.

961a   On this invocation of Matthew 16:19, see explanatory note to *Marcolf and Solomon*, line 805a.

963–65   Of this passage, Simpson, "Saving Satire," p. 401, comments: "The whole poem announces itself as requiring interpretive skill."

974   *loveday*. See explanatory note to *Marcolf and Solomon*, line 390.

975–87   Compare *Piers Plowman* B.18.418–23a (Simpson, "Saving Satire," p. 403; Pearsall, "Audelay's *Marcolf and Solomon*," p. 142). On the Four Daughters of God in Audelay's poem, see explanatory note to *Marcolf and Solomon*, lines 937–43.

987a   This proverb is also appears in *Audelay's Conclusion*, line 39a (explanatory note), at the end of MS Douce 302.

988–89   On Solomon as the ultimate speaker of this poem, see explanatory notes to *Marcolf and Solomon*, lines 66–69, 70, 430–42.

990–91   On Audelay's prophetic and apocalyptic tone, see explanatory note to *Marcolf and Solomon*, lines 237–40.

993   *Bayard the blynd*. See explanatory note to *Marcolf and Solomon*, line 952.

997–99   These lines resemble *The Remedy of Nine Virtues*, lines 90–93, and *Visiting the Sick and Consoling the Needy*, lines 391–94. On the phrase *take good eme* in line 997, see explanatory note to *Marcolf and Solomon*, line 53.

1001   Of this line, Green, "Marcolf the Fool," pp. 570–71, comments: "Though [Audelay] is quick to boast of the risks he is taking . . . I think it highly unlikely that he really believed he was putting his life in danger by criticizing the ecclesiastical hierarchy; nor can he really have imagined that Marcolf's persona could have offered him much protection even if he had been. Though the persona is maintained with reasonable consistency, he is quite ready to drop it on occasion (i.e., at l. 503) and he signs off the poem with a version of his usual signature." See also Simpson, "Saving Satire," pp. 392, 400; and Citrome, *Surgeon*, pp. 92–93.

1003   *parté*. Simpson, "Saving Satire," p. 395, comments: "Marcol . . . implies that each 'party', including the lay party, has a legitimate voice and deserves to be heard."

1005   *Favel*. See explanatory note to *Marcolf and Solomon*, line 394.

1008–13   On Audelay's self-naming here and at line 503, see Meyer-Lee, "Vatic Penitent," pp. 65–66, who proposes that "all mention of Audelay's blindness represents material added during the compilation of the codex" and that "virtually all acts of self-naming were also included during this process." See also explanatory note to *Marcolf and Solomon*, line 503.

1013   The last line is written as the catchphrase (and thus it is formally lacking from the stanza). The next folio (the beginning of a new quire) is missing. If the poem is complete, then the missing next recto would have contained only its last line. That the scribe would have deliberately ended his copy of the poem in this manner is unlikely.

[XV.] THE REMEDY OF NINE VIRTUES   [W3]

Audelay crafts this poem from a Latin source, *Novum virtutes*, a text loosely associated with Richard Rolle (Horstmann, *Yorkshire Writers*, 2:455). The poem purports to reveal nine chief virtues handed down by Christ himself, and thus, like *Our Lord's Epistle on Sunday* and *God's Address to Sinful Men*, it is couched as an address by God to humanity. E. Whiting, p. 233, estimates that at least five stanzas are missing at the beginning, where it seems that four leaves are gone from the manuscript. The text here begins with the sixth virtue. The nine virtues are: (1) to give alms, (2) to weep for Christ's Passion, (3) to suffer a word for Christ, (4) to break sleep to say orisons, (5) to have compassion, (6) to say no word of backbiting, (7) to give good counsel, (8) to pray, and (9) to love God. Because the poem as we have it opens with the detail of going barefoot in the street in penance (a detail also found in the source and analogues), Bennett, "John Audelay: Life Records," suspects that the missing folios had a political resonance recalling the outrage of 1417, which may account for their removal (pp. 41–41, 47; see also Bennett, "John Audley: Some New Evidence").

[Fol. 8ra–b (acephalous). *IMEV* *71; *Suppl.*, *NIMEV* *3780.5. *MWME* 7:2537–38 [157]. **Hands:** Scribe A, poem in black; Scribe B, explicit in red. **Audelay Signature:** Line 102 (Scribe A). **Meter:** The poem has eight 13-line stanzas, $ababbcbc_4d_2eee_{3-4}d_2$. **Latin Source:** *Novum virtutes*, extant in MS Caius College 140, fol. 132r. **Middle English Verse Analogues:** "Nine Points" (Horstmann, *Yorkshire Writers*, 2:455–56; *NIMEV* 1188); "A Good Lesson of IX Vertewis" (Bowers, "Middle English Poem"; *NIMEV* 212). **Middle English Prose Analogues:** "Points Best Pleasing to God" (Horstmann, *Yorkshire Writers*, 1:110–12, from MSS Vernon, Rawlinson C.285, and Harley 1704). **Editions:** Halliwell, pp. 51–54, 87–88; E. Whiting, pp. 46–49, 233.]

14   On Audelay's special interest in the sin of slander and backbiting, which he habitually adds to the Ten Commandments, see the explanatory note introducing *Ten Commandments*.

17   *stydest*. For the sense "strive toward a higher or more perfect spiritual, moral, or intellectual state," see *MED stien*, v.6(a).

32   *fre choyse*. On the doctrine of free will in Audelay's works, see the explanatory note to *True Living*, lines 203–07.

43   E. Whiting, p. 233, notes that "The reference is to the pillar hermits of whom St. Simeon Stylites was the most famous."

44   *rayssors*. *MED rasour(e*, n.(c), "an instrument of torture."

51–102   E. Whiting, p. 233, notes that this portion of the poem does not appear in the analogues. Much of it does appear, however, in other Audelay poems (see explanatory notes below). For example, most of the last two stanzas resurface in *Visiting the Sick and Consoling the Needy*.

60   On Audelay's frequent citation of the Golden Rule, see the explanatory note to *True Living*, line 231.

73–76   These lines are formulaic; compare *True Living*, lines 156–59, and *Audelay's Epilogue to The Counsel of Conscience*, lines 244–46.

77–89   This is Audelay's typical signature stanza. Compare *Visiting the Sick and Consoling the Needy*, lines 378–90; *Our Lord's Epistle on Sunday*, lines 196–208; *The Vision of Saint Paul*, lines 353–65; and *Audelay's Epilogue to The Counsel of Conscience*, lines 495–507. The closest match to lines 85–89 is to be found in *Audelay's Epilogue to The Counsel of Conscience*, lines 490–94.

80   *salutary*. The *MED* cites this line as the only known instance of the noun *salutari*, "remedy."

90–97   These lines are repeated in *Visiting the Sick and Consoling the Needy*, lines 391–98. Lines 90–92 are similar, too, to *Marcolf and Solomon*, lines 997–99. On the phrase *take good eme* in line 90, see explanatory note to *Marcolf and Solomon*, line 53.

99–102   Compare *On the World's Folly*, lines 61–66; *Our Lord's Epistle on Sunday*, lines 202–08; and *Audelay's Epilogue to The Counsel of Conscience*, lines 504–07. Line 99 also appears in *Salutation to Saint Bridget*, line 204. On the word *laust* in line 99, see *MED losen*, v.3(1a), "to free, untie, let loose," with Audelay's line cited among the examples.

XVI. SEVEN BLEEDINGS OF CHRIST   [W4]
      This piece is an indulgence prayer on the name of Jesus, comprised of three introductory stanzas, fifteen stanzas in address to Jesus, and five instructional stanzas. Its purpose is to bring "remedy" for the seven deadly sins by means of reciting the seven bleedings of Christ, methodically matched to the sins and then to seven tokens of the Crucifixion. Woolf, *English Religious Lyric*, pp. 222–23, notes the confused history of this theme and others "firmly rooted in the emotive meditation on the Passion." Hirsh, *Boundaries of Faith*, pp. 91–110, especially pp. 99–100, describes the ways the theme was featured in indulgences. One of the venerated tokens is the Veronica cloth (lines 67–72) so prominently hailed later in MS Douce 302 (fol. 27va) by a drawing, a salutation, and a prayer (all of which also carry

an indulgence). The worshiper is to follow a reading of *Seven Bleedings of Christ* with a recitation of fifteen Paternosters and fifteen Aves. Moreover, one should recite it every day; and — to "be sekyr" of salvation — one should teach it to "another mon" (lines 134–35). The structural likeness between this lyric and the popular indulgence prayer the Fifteen Oes — sometimes associated with St. Bridget, sometimes with Rolle — is striking. As in the prose prayer, there are fifteen addresses to Jesus (each prefixed "O") with a prescribed recitation of fifteen Paternosters and fifteen Aves to achieve a specific outcome. On the Fifteen Oes, see Duffy, *Stripping of the Altars*, pp. 218, 249–56. On devotion to the Holy Blood elsewhere in Audelay, also carrying an indulgence, see *Pope John's Passion of Our Lord*, lines 89–120.

The analogous poem printed by Brown, *Religious Lyrics of the XVth Century*, consists of eight stanzas with stanzas 1–6 matching *Seven Bleedings of Christ*, stanzas 4–10. The wording is often quite similar and the meter is the same. Wrath and Envy have been reversed, as in the fourteenth-century poem printed by Brown, *Religious Lyrics of the XIVth Century* (see explanatory note to lines 19–60). The evidence suggests that there was a common Latin original for this prayer.

[Fols. 8rb–9ra. *IMEV* ("An orison of the Wounds and the 'Arms of Christ' by Audelay"), *NIMEV* 292. **Hands:** Scribe A, poem in black; Scribe B, incipit and explicit in red. **Initials:** Large *A* in blue with red filigree (three lines high). In many stanzas beginning "O Jhesu," the initial black *O* is marked in red (stanzas 4–16); the *O* of line 58 is so marked by accident. **Meter:** Twenty-three 6-line stanzas, aa₄b₃cc₄b₃. **Middle English Analogue (stanzas 4–10 only):** "A Prayer by the Wounds against the Deadly Sins" (Brown, *Religious Lyrics of the XVth Century*, pp. 95–97 [no. 62]). **Editions:** Halliwell, pp. 55–60, 88; E. Whiting, pp. 50–54, 233–34.]

19–60   This petition for deliverance from the seven sins in a meditation upon seven holy occurrences parallels the petition in *Seven Words of Christ on the Cross*, lines 5–12. To these seven stanzas on the seven deadly sins, compare "A Prayer to be delivered from the Deadly Sins" (Brown, *Religious Lyrics of the XIVth Century*, pp. 218–19 [no. 123]), an indulgence prayer that appears to be translated from the same source. The verse form is the same, but the wording is different. A Paternoster and an Ave are to be said between each stanza. The second petition is for deliverance from Wrath, while in Audelay it is for deliverance from Envy. The last petition is for Charity; in Audelay it is for deliverance from Wrath. For other variants on what was probably a widespread indulgence, see Brown, *Religious Lyrics of the XVth Century*, pp. 283–84, and E. Whiting, pp. 233–34. On Audelay's treatment of the seven deadly sins elsewhere in MS Douce 302, see *Seven Words of Christ on the Cross*, lines 5–12; *Prayer of General Confession*, lines 5–8; *Seven Deadly Sins*, lines 1–24; and *Childhood*, lines 1–15.

67–72   Compare *Salutation to the Holy Face*, lines 1–7, the drawing next to it, and the prose prayer that follows it, *Deus qui nobis*. That salutation and image also appear to function as an indulgence.

93   The tradition of the blind "knyght" Longinus tells of his piercing the side of Christ during the Crucifixion and regaining eyesight when touched by drops of Christ's blood. The story is based on John 19:24 and the apocryphal Gospel of Nicodemus, and it influenced the Holy Grail legend of Arthurian romance. For Blind Audelay, the story may carry a personal resonance. Compare *Prayer on*

Christ's Passion, line 24; *O Deus qui voluisti*, line 30; *Pope John's Passion of Our Lord*, line 68; and *Seven Hours of the Cross*, line 48.

103–09   This stanza contains an extra line.

110–17   The saying of a specified number of Paternosters and Aves, along with daily recitation, indicates the status of this piece as carrying an indulgence. Compare the Passion poem printed by Bühler, "Middle English Prayer Roll," pp. 558–61, where each stanza is punctuated with "Pater noster ave Maria," as well as similar forms described by Hirsh, *Boundaries of Faith*, pp. 96–100. Audelay emphasizes the spiritual efficacy of the poem: it is a tool for salvation. Compare too the indulgence prayers on the instruments of the Passion printed by R. Morris, *Legends of the Holy Rood*, pp. 170–96. On the *arma Christi* tradition, see Robbins, "'Arma Christi' Rolls"; Gray, "Middle English Illustrated Poem," pp. 187; Hirsh, *Boundaries of Faith*, pp. 124–49, especially pp. 129–36; and A. Nichols, "O Vernicle."

XVII. PRAYER ON CHRIST'S PASSION   [W5]

The first half of this poem (lines 1–24) translates loosely the Latin verse prayer *O Deus qui voluisti*, which is soon to follow (on fol. 9rb).

[Fol. 9ra–b. *IMEV, NIMEV* 2452. **Hands:** Scribe A, poem in black; Scribe B, incipit in red. **Initials:** Small *O* in red and blue (one and a half lines high). The black initial letters of stanzas are marked in red, with one error: the *D* of line 29 is marked instead of the *A* of line 31. **Meter:** Seven 6-line stanzas, aa$_4$b$_3$cc$_4$b$_3$. **Editions:** Halliwell, pp. 60–61, 88; E. Whiting, pp. 54–56, 234.]

4–5   On Judas's treason elsewhere in MS Douce 302, see *Marcolf and Solomon*, lines 473, 753a, and 758; *O Deus qui voluisti*, lines 4–5 and 18; *Virtues of the Mass*, lines 103–08; *Seven Hours of the Cross*, lines 13–18; and *The Vision of Saint Paul*, line 234.

16–17   Compare *O Deus qui voluisti*, line 25, and *Seven Hours of the Cross*, lines 21–22.

23   Compare *O Deus qui voluisti*, line 29; *Seven Words of Christ on the Cross*, lines 61–62; *Pope John's Passion of Our Lord*, line 51; and *Seven Hours of the Cross*, line 39.

24   By tradition Longinus thrust the spear into Christ's side. On the tradition of blind Longinus in Blind Audelay's works, see the explanatory note to *Seven Bleedings of Christ*, line 92, and compare *O Deus qui voluisti*, line 30; *Pope John's Passion of Our Lord*, line 68; and *Seven Hours of the Cross*, line 48.

31–35   Audelay alludes elsewhere in this section of the manuscript to the thief redeemed by Christ; see *Tu Domine* and *Seven Words of Christ on the Cross*, lines 25–30.

37–38   This is a mnemonic formula. Compare *Instructions for Prayer 1*, *Seven Words of Christ on the Cross*, line 109, and *Instructions for Prayer 8*.

XVIII. THE PSALTER OF THE PASSION   [W6]

The seven items under this numeral and heading together form a devotional prayer sequence designed to bring remission of sin to the petitioner. It mixes prayers with instructions, building up to and then focusing on the details of Christ's persecution and suffering. Its seven parts are:

(1)   English instructions for prayer (four lines);

(2)   A well-known Latin hymn and prayer, *Anima Christi sanctifica me*;

(3)   More English instructions for prayer (two lines);

(4)   A short Latin verse prayer (four lines), petitioning Christ naked on the cross for mercy (to be substituted for the Paternoster and Ave);

(5)   More English instructions for prayer with a rosary (along with the hours of the Virgin and saying the Creed);

(6)   A Latin prayer in remembrance of the Passion, seemingly to be recited with a rosary (the scribe denotes its mnemonic repetition by copying it twice);

(7)   A final prayer in Latin prose petitioning for deliverance from the pains of hell, in the name of Christ's pains on the cross.

INSTRUCTIONS FOR PRAYER 1 [W6]

[Fol. 9rb. *IMEV, NIMEV* 3888. **Hands:** Scribe A, poem in black; Scribe B, incipit (for everything under the numeral XVIII.) in red. **Ornament:** These four lines are underlined in red and marked with a blue paraph in the left margin. I have kept the underlining, though not in red. **Meter:** Two tetrameter couplets. **Edition:** E. Whiting, p. 56.]

1   *Wele is him that wele can* is a formula used by Audelay at the beginning or end of a devotion that leads to remission of sin. Compare *Prayer on Christ's Passion*, line 37; *Seven Words of Christ on the Cross*, line 109; and *Instructions for Prayer 8*.

LATIN VERSE PRAYER *ANIMA CHRISTI SANCTIFICA ME* [W6]

Audelay opens the devotion with a familiar Catholic hymn (Daniel, *Thesaurus Hymnologicus*, 1:345). He omits the seventh line and changes the eleventh line. The fifth line, "*Passio Christi conforta me*," resurfaces elsewhere in Audelay's poetry, becoming the refrain for *Dread of Death* and appearing in *Pope John's Passion of Our Lord*, line 9. On the prayer's use in medieval English devotions, see Duffy, *Marking the Hours*, p. 28.

[Fol. 9rb. **Hands:** Scribe A, poem in black; Scribe B, initial letter of each line marked in red. **Edition:** E. Whiting, pp. 56 (lines 5–16), 234.]

INSTRUCTIONS FOR PRAYER 2 [W6]

[Fol. 9rb. Not in *IMEV, NIMEV*. **Hands:** Scribe A, poem in black; Scribe B, red mark on *I* (initial made by Scribe A). **Meter:** One tetrameter couplet. **Edition:** E. Whiting, p. 56 (lines 17–18).]

LATIN VERSE PRAYER *O PENDENS DUDUM* [W6]

[Fol. 9rb. **Hands:** Scribe A, poem in black; Scribe B, red mark on *O* (initial made by Scribe A). **Edition:** E. Whiting, p. 56 (lines 19–22).]

INSTRUCTIONS FOR PRAYER 3 [W6]

[Fol. 9rb. Not in *IMEV, NIMEV*. **Hand:** Scribe A, poem in black. **Meter:** Three tetrameter couplets. **Edition:** E. Whiting, p. 57 (lines 23–28).]

LATIN VERSE PRAYER *O DEUS QUI VOLUISTI* [W6]

Audelay translates this Latin prayer loosely in his *Prayer on Christ's Passion*, which appears earlier on fol. 9ra–b. It is a memorized recitation, in which lines 15–26 replicate, roughly, lines 1–14. The initials of lines 6 and 13 are not tipped in red because Scribe A did not begin these lines with capital letters.

[Fol. 9rb–va. **Hands:** Scribe A, poem in black; Scribe B, half of the initial letters marked in red (i.e., lines 1–5, 7–12, 14–17); red paraphs mark lines 1 and 15. **Edition:** E. Whiting, pp. 57–58 (lines 29–58), 234.]

1–26   Compare *Prayer on Christ's Passion*, lines 1–20.

4–5   On Judas's treason, repeated at line 18, compare *Marcolf and Solomon*, lines 473, 753a, 758; *Prayer on Christ's Passion*, lines 4–5; *Virtues of the Mass*, lines 103–08; *Seven Hours of the Cross*, lines 13–18; and *The Vision of Saint Paul*, line 234.

27–30   Compare *Prayer on Christ's Passion*, lines 21–24.

LATIN PROSE PRAYER *TU DOMINE PER HAS SANCTISSIMAS PENAS TUAS*   **[W6]**
[Fol. 9va. **Hands:** Scribe A, in black; Scribe B, red marks on *T* and *Q* (in *Qui*) (initials made by Scribe A). **Edition:** E. Whiting, p. 58.]

XIX. SEVEN WORDS OF CHRIST ON THE CROSS   **[W7]**
     Woolf, *English Religious Lyric*, p. 222, praises the genuine meditative spirit expressed in this poem: "Audelay's style has a tender lucidity that catches excellently the force of so much love, whilst gently relating it to the meditator's prayer." She also summarizes the Latin devotional tradition of Seven Words in works attributed to Bede, Arnold of Bonneval, and Bonaventure. See also Barratt, "Prymer and Its Influence," pp. 276–78; and Duffy, *Stripping of the Altars*, pp. 248–49. In the poem the number seven mystically and mnemonically guides the devotion, a template that occurs elsewhere in *The Counsel of Conscience*, i.e., in *Seven Bleedings of Christ* and *Seven Hours of the Cross*. Most stanzas have an anaphoric first line — "O, Jhesu" — as a salutation evocative of fifteenth-century cults of the Holy Name. The instruction to adorn the poem by saying seven Paternosters and seven Aves (lines 97–101) indicates that it is to carry an indulgence.
     The stanzas are composed in pairs:

          1–2. Introduction, with a pairing of the seven words to the seven sins (i.e., the sins to be remitted);
          3–4. Luke 23:34, and a petition for God to forgive the petitioner's enemies;
          5–6. Luke 23:42–43, and a petition for grace as was received by the two thieves;
          7–8. John 19:26–27, and a petition for compassion;
          9–10. Matthew 27:46/Mark 15:34, and a petition for mercy;
          11–12. John 19:28–29, and a petition for contrition through weeping and a thirst for everlasting life;
          13–14. Luke 23:46, and a petition for one's spirit to be commended into God's hands;
          15–16. John 19:30, and a petition for gaining heaven upon death;
          17–18. A reminder to say seven Paternosters and seven Aves, and to seek confession, contrition, and satisfaction;
          19. Conclusion, reminding the reader that worship of these words will bring remission of sin.

[Fol. 9va–10ra. *IMEV, NIMEV* 2468. **Hands:** Scribe A, poem in black; Scribe B, incipit and explicit in red. **Initial:** Large *O* in blue with red filigree (three lines high). **Meter:** Nineteen 6-line stanzas, aa₄b₃cc₄b₃. **Latin Source:** "*De septem verbis Christi in cruce*," attributed to Bede (*PL* 94.562) and standard in books of hours (Woolf, *English Religious Lyric*, pp. 220–22). **Middle English Analogues:** "A Prayer on the Words of Christ on the Cross" (Person, *Cambridge Middle English Lyrics*, pp. 6–8 [no. 4]); "The Seven Words from the Cross" (Brown, *Religious Lyrics of the XVth Century*, pp. 142–44 [no. 96]). **Editions:** Halliwell, pp. 62–66, 88; E. Whiting, pp. 58–62, 234–35.]

5–12   This petition for deliverance from the seven deadly sins in a meditation on seven things parallels the petition in *Seven Bleedings of Christ*, lines 19–60 (see explanatory note).

25–30   Audelay alludes elsewhere in this section of the manuscript to the thief redeemed by Christ; see *Prayer on Christ's Passion*, lines 31–35, and the Latin prayer *Tu Domine*.

40–42   Compare *Seven Hours of the Cross*, lines 42–44, and *Day of Saint John the Evangelist*, lines 7–16.

45   *dere derlyng*. Compare *Day of Saint John the Evangelist*, line 7.

50–54   Compare *Seven Hours of the Cross*, line 47.

62–63   Compare *Prayer on Christ's Passion*, line 23; *O Deus qui voluisti*, line 29; *Pope John's Passion of Our Lord*, line 51; and *Seven Hours of the Cross*, line 39.

74–75   Compare *Dread of Death*, line 50.

85   Compare *Pope John's Passion of Our Lord*, line 54.

109–10   These lines are a mnemonic tag. Compare *Prayer on Christ's Passion*, lines 37–38, *Instructions for Prayer 1*, and *Instructions for Prayer 8*.

XX. Devotions at the Levation of Christ's Body   [W8]

The entire sequence is called a "salutation" in Scribe B's incipit (fol. 10ra) and explicit (fol. 10va), and he assigns it the numeral XX. Halliwell omits this sequence from his edition, but Ella Keats Whiting felt it to be "of interest because of the instruction it gives for the celebration of the sacrament" (p. 235). This mostly vernacular, liturgically based exercise seems designed for a layperson's instruction. It consists of:

(1)   Instructions to the layperson on how to prepare oneself in mind and gesture (kneeling);
(2)   A salutation to Christ's body (to be said or read during the Levation itself);
(3)   Further instructions on how one's utterance of the next prayer will bring remission of sin;
(4)   A prayer for pardon (to be said after the Levation);
(5)   A prayer of adoration (in Latin prose);
(6)   A prayer of praise and benediction (in Latin verse).

The sequence progresses through the sacrament, spiritually advancing the participant in prayer and wonder, from English to Latin. One may compare the service depicted here to an explication of the Levation during mass found in *The Lay Folks Mass* (Simmons, *Lay Folks*

Mass Book, pp. 38–60). The prayers found there do not resemble those recorded here by Audelay, who seems to lead this devotion in his capacity as chaplain. The whole sequence is very like those dedicated to Christ and the saints found in the salutations section of MS Douce 302. It is evidently positioned here as a preface to the next poem, *Virtues of the Mass*. One may also compare this sequence to Audelay's exposition of the mass in *Marcolf and Solomon*, lines 832–96. On salutations and prayers conjoined with didactic instructions for following the mass — a subject also worked by Lydgate — see Rubin, *Corpus Christi*, pp. 155–63, especially p. 160, and on the Levation specifically, pp. 63–82.

INSTRUCTIONS FOR PRAYER 4   **[W8]**
[Fol. 10ra. *IMEV*, *NIMEV* 4052 (both indexes combine this item with the next three items). **Hands:** Scribe A, poem in black; Scribe B, incipit in red (referring to entire sequence XX) and underlining of poem in red. **Initial:** Large *W* in blue with red filigree (three lines high). **Meter:** One 6-line stanza, $aa_4b_3cc_4b_3$. **Edition:** E. Whiting, p. 62 (lines 1–6).]

SALUTATION TO CHRIST'S BODY   **[W8]**
     Called a salutation by Scribe B's incipit for section XX, this poem may be compared to the series of salutary poems later in the manuscript (fols. 22v–27v). It is metrically unlike any other poem in the Audelay manuscript. A shift to septenary a-lines occurs in stanzas 3–5, where the articles of belief are affirmed. Compare *Visiting the Sick and Consoling the Needy*, lines 300–20, a paraphrase of the Apostles' Creed.

[Fol. 10ra–b. Not in *IMEV*, *NIMEV* as a separate item (see 4052). *MWME* 7:2559–61 [204]. **Hand:** Scribe A, poem in black. **Initials:** Scribe A's black initials *T* and *A* in lines 14–15 are marked in red. **Meter:** Seven 8-line stanzas, $aaa_{4-7}b_3ccc_4b_3$, with "Haile" anaphora in many a- and c-lines. **Middle English Analogues:** Verse prayers on the Levation are numerous; see *IMEV*, p. 763, s.v. "Levacion prayers." Many are gathered in Robbins, "Levation Prayers," pp. 131–46. One occurs in the Vernon MS (Horstmann, *Minor Poems of the Vernon MS*, p. 25). **Edition:** E. Whiting, pp. 62–64 (lines 7–62).]

7   *Halnere*. See *MED aumener*, n. (1), "One who distributes alms for another; an official distributor of alms; a servant at a meal who distributes food," with this line cited among the examples.

26   An early reader (whose style is unlike that of either of the scribes) highlights the word *assencion* (or perhaps all of lines 25–28) by drawing a sleeved hand pointing upward at it, in the right margin. This drawing seems to point to the sacred moment of Levation, a point that marks the center of the poem as well. The drawing is the best-formed of several small, crude figures made by the same hand on fols. 3rb, 5rb, 6rb, 7rb (a flower?), 9rb, 10rb, 11rb, 13rb (a vertical line), 18rb (marking the climax of *Vision of Saint Paul*, lines 236–40), 27vb, and 28va. On the nonscribal hands in the manuscript, see the textual notes.

36   *gloryouse face*. Compare *Salutation to the Holy Face*, which dramatically expresses this idea accompanied by a drawing.

INSTRUCTIONS FOR PRAYER 5   **[W8]**
[Fol. 10rb. *IMEV* unnumbered (p. 186); not in *NIMEV* as a separate item (see 4052). **Hand:** Scribe A, poem in black. **Meter:** One 8-line stanza, $aaa_4b_3ccc_4b_3$. **Edition:** E. Whiting, p. 64 (lines 63–70).]

PRAYER FOR PARDON AFTER THE LEVATION   **[W8]**
[Fol. 10rb–va. Not in *IMEV*, *NIMEV* as a separate item (see *NIMEV* 4052). **Hand:** Scribe A, poem in black. **Meter:** Three 6-line stanzas, aa$_{4-7}$b$_3$cc$_4$b$_3$. **Edition:** E. Whiting, pp. 64–65 (lines 71–88).]

1–5   *O Lord Jhesu Crist . . . Hongyng on cros.* These words open *Prayer for Forgiveness* in
             the sequence that follows *Virtues of the Mass.* Audelay's *Prayer for Forgiveness* is the
             only piece listed in the *IMEV* and *NIMEV* with the first words "O Lord Jhesu
             Crist," suggesting that this prayer opening is an Audelay mannerism.

LATIN PROSE PRAYER *ADORAMUS TE CHRISTE ET BENEDICIMUS*   **[W8]**
[Fol. 10va. **Hand:** Scribe A, prayer in black. **Initials:** The black initials *A* (*Adoramus*) and *E* (*Ecce*) are
marked in red. **Edition:** E. Whiting, p. 65.]

LATIN VERSE PRAYER *LAUDES DEO DICAM PER SECULA*   **[W8]**
[Fol. 10va. **Hands:** Scribe A, prayer in black; Scribe B, explicit (referring to the entire sequence XX)
in red. **Initials:** The black initial *Q* (*Qui*) is marked in red, as are the *A*, *M*, and *N* of *A. M. [E.] N.*
Edition: E. Whiting, p. 65 (printed as prose).]

XXI. VIRTUES OF THE MASS   **[W9]**
     Audelay's *Virtues of the Mass* is a verse sermon that expounds the utility of the mass if
properly observed. Rubin calls it a "religious poem and a manual in one." She notes how
Audelay "gives the participant in communion an active role, reciting the *Pater noster* and the
Ave Maria; he also surveys the rudiments of knowledge codified by Pecham in the Lambeth
Council of 1281" (*Corpus Christi*, p. 108). Audelay's emphasis upon lay participation may be
compared to similar instructions promulgated in verse and prose by orthodox churchmen
of the early fifteenth century — e.g., Lydgate, Mirk, and the compilers of the Vernon Manu-
script and the *Lay Folks Mass Book*; for more sentiments of this type, see the "Schematic
Approach to the Mass" (late 1470s) found in "A York Priest's Notebook" (Shinners and
Dohar, *Pastors and the Care of Souls*, pp. 154–55; compare pp. 165–70). Audelay's beliefs
about the mass, also expressed in *Marcolf and Solomon*, lines 832–96, are thus informed by
traditional Church doctrine. The concern for propriety exhibited by him and other writers
existed in a contemporary context of rituals growing more elaborate: "the mass was becoming
more and more of a spectacle and less and less of a communion" (Beckwith, *Christ's Body*,
p. 36; see also Catto, "Religious Change under Henry V," especially p. 109; and Duffy, *Strip-
ping of the Altars*, pp. 91–130). On social conflict over the mass in late medieval society, amid
Wycliffite disputes about transubstantiation, see Beckwith, especially pp. 33–37.
     As sermon, Audelay's poem contains an oft-told, amusing exemplum about a man of
great piety (here Augustine of Canterbury, not bishop of Hippo) who is able to see a devil
record the sinful words of gossips during mass. Because there is so very much to record, the
devil quickly runs out of parchment. Seeing the frustrated devil's slapstick antics (he tugs
at the parchment with his teeth and bangs his head against the wall), the great man laughs
aloud — a scandalous thing to do during mass. The devil is here named Ruffin, as in Harley
3954; the same devil-name surfaces in the alliterative stanza *Over-Hippers and Skippers* cop-
ied later in Audelay's manuscript. In other sources the recording demon is usually Tutivillis.
While the Vernon poem cites numerous authorities on the virtues of the mass, e.g.,
Ambrose, Augustine, Bede, Bernard, Gregory, and Jerome, the primary figure in Audelay's
version is Augustine (Bede and Bernard are just mentioned), with Gregory granting the

final pardon enacted by one's hearing the poem (lines 410–11). In Audelay's telling of the exemplum, Gregory, who sent Augustine to England to convert the English (lines 274-82) is also Augustine's questioner. One may also note that Haughmond was an Augustinian house, and that Augustine seems to be designated a member of the order.

Audelay's *Virtues of the Mass* contains many 12-line stanzas derived from a source shared with the West Midland Vernon analogue (c. 1390), but the passages not corresponding to the Vernon poem are generally composed in 6-line stanzas. (On the 12-line stanza of the Vernon "How to Hear Mass," see Fein, "Twelve-Line Stanza Forms," p. 394.) The Audelay passages not found in the Vernon poem are: lines 31–36, 67–86, 91–168, 205–10, 223–52, and 352–414. The late fifteenth-century version found in MS Harley 3954, in East Midland dialect with some Northernisms, is closer to Audelay's *Virtues of the Mass* than to Vernon. Putter, "Language and Metre," pp. 505–06, 510, suggests that Audelay and Harley derive from a common antecedent. There is, nonetheless, much variation between them. The Harley version consists of fifty-three 6-line stanzas. In that version stanzas 30–44 deliver the exemplum, which is formally marked off with an incipit (*Narracio seint augustinum*) and explicit (*finis*).

[Fols. 10va–12rb. *IMEV, NIMEV* 1986 (mistakenly counts "fifty-three 6 line st."); compare *IMEV* 1988, 4276. *MWME* 7:2557 [197], 9:3265. **Hands:** Scribe A, poem in black; Scribe B, incipit and explicit in red. **Initials:** Large *L* in blue with red filigree (three lines high). Black *O* (*Or*) of line 30 is marked in red. **Meter:** Sixty-nine 6-line stanzas, aa₄b₃cc₄b₃, with thirty-six stanzas combinable as 12-line stanzas, aa₄b₃cc₄b₃dd₄b₃ee₄b₃, indicating the form of Audelay's model. **Analogues:** "How to Hear Mass," in fifty-seven 12-line stanzas (aa₄b₃cc₄b₃dd₄b₃ee₄b₃), Vernon MS, fols. 302va–303vc (Simmons, *Lay Folks Mass Book*, pp. 128–47; Furnivall, *Minor Poems of the Vernon MS*, pp. 493–511); London, BL MS Harley 3954, fols. 74r–76r (unedited, except for an extract corresponding to lines 271–348; see Wright and Halliwell, *Reliquiae Antiquae*, 1.59–60). **Editions:** Halliwell, pp. 66–81, 88; E. Whiting, pp. 65–79 (lines 50–414 misnumbered), 235–37.]

1–12   Compare "How to Hear Mass," stanza 2 (lines 13–24).

3   *helth.* The references here and in line 10 to the healing powers of the mass reinforce Audelay's stated purpose for his book *The Counsel of Conscience*, that is, *soulehele* (see explanatory notes to Audelay's Epilogue to *The Counsel of Conscience*, lines 105, 248–60).

13–24   Compare "How to Hear Mass," stanza 3 (lines 25–36).

25–30   Compare "How to Hear Mass," half of stanza 4 (lines 37–42).

37–42   Compare "How to Hear Mass," half of stanza 7 (lines 33–84).

41   For another admonition on how to say mass, compare the alliterative stanza *Over-Hippers and Skippers* that appears later in the Audelay manuscript, and also *Marcolf and Solomon*, lines 196–98, and *The Vision of Saint Paul*, lines 83–88 (explanatory note).

43–54   Compare "How to Hear Mass," stanza 9 (lines 97–108).

43–65   Rubin, *Corpus Christi*, p. 108, summarizes the "stock of benefits accruing from the mass" that Audelay lists here: "the company of angels all day, freedom from the threat of being struck blind on that day or suffering death, and from the need for food or drink." E. Whiting, p. 236, calls the image of line 47, of angels painting the faces of mass-goers, a "meaningless line," but it is like a tale in *Handlyng Synne* in which a priest knows the worthiness of those receiving the sacrament when God transforms their faces to pure brightness, or black, or red, or swollen, etc. This exemplum appears in the Vernon Manuscript (Horstmann, *Minor Poems of the Vernon MS*, pp. 206–07) and in *Speculum Sacerdotale* (Weatherly, pp. 123–25).

55–66   Compare "How to Hear Mass," stanza 10 (lines 69–73).

67   The emphasis upon Augustine's authority is a feature of this poem; lines 66–86 do not appear in the Vernon text.

79–84   Rubin, *Corpus Christi*, p. 108, summarizes these lines: "Belief in the sacrament is stressed, as well as proper kneeling at the sacring with clasped hands and with thoughts intent on Christ."

87–90   Compare "How to Hear Mass," part of stanza 6 (lines 69–72).

103–08   "Here, the reader is reminded that the eucharist was founded at the Last Supper by Christ and that Judas had received it unworthily" (Rubin, *Corpus Christi*, p. 108). On Judas's treason, compare *Marcolf and Solomon*, lines 473, 753a, 758; *Prayer on Christ's Passion*, lines 4–5; *O Deus qui voluisti*, lines 4–5, 18; *Seven Hours of the Cross*, lines 13–18; and *The Vision of Saint Paul*, line 234.

124   Compare the exposition of these seven points in *Paternoster*.

138–43   Audelay enumerates the Ten Commandments in *True Living*, lines 143–54, as well as in *Ten Commandments*.

160–62   Audelay repeats these verses at lines 364–66.

169–80   Compare "How to Hear Mass," stanza 12 (lines 133–44).

181–92   Compare "How to Hear Mass," stanza 13 (lines 145–56). Compare, too, line 181 to Vernon's "Of Austin, Ambrose, Bernard, and Bede" (line 91).

193–204   Compare "How to Hear Mass," stanza 22 (lines 253–64).

211–16   Compare "How to Hear Mass," second half of stanza 14 (lines 163–68).

217–22   Compare "How to Hear Mass," first half of stanza 14 (lines 157–62). In line 217 Saint Augustine is substituted for the Vernon text's Saint Jerome. E. Whiting offers this translation: "St. Austin says that for a thousand souls, if thou wouldst here (on earth) sing a single mass, it counts for neither more nor less than a mass for every soul." Compare *Visiting the Sick and Consoling the Needy*, lines 92–93.

253–64   Compare "How to Hear Mass," stanza 11 (lines 121–32).

265–76   Compare "How to Hear Mass," stanza 24 (lines 277–88). The reason for Saint Augustine's order of silence during the mass will be illustrated by the upcoming exemplum, which demonstrates how devils record every word said. On the pastoral tradition of the recording demon, see Jennings, "Tutivillus"; Lee, "'This is no fable,'" pp. 743–60; and Rubin, *Corpus Christi*, p. 154.

275   *gyn.* See *MED ging(e,* n.1(b), "a body of retainers or followers, a retinue, house-
                 hold." E. Whiting glosses the word as "kin," a less likely derivation and meaning.

277–88   Compare "How to Hear Mass," stanza 25 (lines 289–300).

283   The word *the* is used as an article in the phrase *the Austyn,* not as a second-person
                 pronoun, as Whiting's punctuation indicates. Compare line 311. Audelay refers
                 to Augustine as a monk, that is, "the Austin," and thus as one who shares the
                 name of the order of monks residing in Haughmond Abbey.

289–300   Compare "How to Hear Mass," stanza 26 (lines 301–12).

298–342   Augustine and Gregory appear in the Vernon version as well, but the actors
                 differ in the analogues; see E. Whiting, p. 237. Analogues appear in Robert of
                 Brunne's *Handlyng Synne* (Furnivall, pp. 290–93, lines 9261–9314) and *The Book
                 of the Knight of La Tour-Landry* (Wright, pp. 41–42, amidst several more exem-
                 plary tales about the mass's virtues). For further commentary, see Fein, "Thir-
                 teen-Line Alliterative Stanza," p. 72n14–15; and Greene, *Early English Carols,* p.
                 443, note to no. 372, stanza 3.

301–12   Compare "How to Hear Mass," stanza 27 (lines 313–24).

309   *grone.* The manuscript reading *grame* does not rhyme and anticipates the same
                 word in the next line. The Vernon reading is adopted here.

311   *the Austyn.* See explanatory note to line 283.

313–24   Compare "How to Hear Mass," stanza 28 (lines 325–36).

325–36   Compare "How to Hear Mass," stanza 30 (lines 349–60).

337–48   Compare "How to Hear Mass," stanza 31 (lines 385–96).

349   Compare "How to Hear Mass," line 370.

364–66   These lines repeat *Virtues of the Mass,* lines 160–62.

411   This statement that Saint Gregory has established a pardon for those who hear
                 "this sermon" prepares for the next item in MS Douce 302, *Saint Gregory's
                 Indulgence.*

XXII. FOR REMISSION OF SINS   **[W10]**

     This sequenced item, which follows directly from the ending of *Virtues of the Mass,* is
identified as carrying an indulgence sanctioned by Saint Gregory the Great, pope from 590
to 604. Numbered XXII by Scribe B, it is a soul-cleansing devotional exercise designed to
lessen one's time in purgatory. The sequence is composed entirely in English couplets. Its
sections are differentiated by underlining, paraphs for stanzas or divisions, Latin rubrics,
and three large initials. The first twenty-two lines are underlined in red, and paraphs mark
Saint Gregory's Indulgence as two 10-line stanzas, followed by a couplet of instruction. In all,
there are five sections:

(1)   An introduction (underlined in red), explaining how what follows carries
        an indulgence established by Saint Gregory when Christ's figure appeared
        before him;
(2)   An instructional couplet (also underlined in red) asking the participant
        to pray the next item with sincerity;
(3)   A standard prayer of confession;
(4)   A second instruction to pray devoutly;
(5)   A prayer for forgiveness.

SAINT GREGORY'S INDULGENCE   [W10]

In the left margin Scribe B has written in red: *here within for / . . . eye* [or *eyd*] *a fygur*[*e*].
This partially cut-off fragment appears to be the remnant of an instruction directed to the
reader; it may refer the reader to the drawing on fol. 22va, or to some other image now lost.
It is an indication that Audelay had an image in mind to accompany this sequence.

[Fol. 12va. *IMEV, NIMEV* 3834. **Hands:** Scribe A, poem in black; Scribe B, all lines underlined in red,
and incipit in red. **Initial:** Large *A* in blue with red filigree (three lines high). **Meter:** Ten tetrameter
couplets, marked by blue paraphs as two 10-line stanzas. **Edition:** E. Whiting, pp. 79–80 (lines 1–20).]

incipit   The word *papa* is written in red after *Gregorio* and deleted in black ink. Because
             there is no evidence elsewhere in the book of a later hand with a reformist
             agenda, I take this deletion to be by Scribe B. Compare textual note to *Latin
             Instructions Quicumque hanc salutacionem*, line 2.

1–4   "According to the legend, Pope Gregory, while celebrating Mass in the church
             of Santa Croce in Gerusaleme in Rome, had experienced a vision of Christ,
             seated on or standing in his tomb, displaying his Wounds and surrounded by the
             Implements of the Passion. The legend almost certainly derives from an early
             medieval Byzantine icon displayed in the church of Santa Croce, which had a
             chapel dedicated to St Gregory" (Duffy, *Stripping of the Altars*, p. 238; compare
             pp. 108–09). The story developed into the image of Christ as the Man of Sorrows,
             "appearing naked on the altar bleeding into the chalice" (Rubin, *Corpus Christi*,
             p. 310). It also developed as a devotion (often illustrated), offering promises of
             indulgence and effectively popularized in primers (Barratt, "Prymer and Its
             Influence," pp. 268–71). For specimens of the image, see Duffy, *Marking the
             Hours*, pp. 27, 39, 43, 72.

INSTRUCTIONS FOR PRAYER 6   [W10]
[Fol. 12va. Not in *IMEV, NIMEV* as a separate item (see 3834). **Hands:** Scribe A, poem in black;
Scribe B, both lines underlined in red and marked by a red paraph. **Meter:** One tetrameter couplet.
Edition: E. Whiting, p. 80 (lines 21–22).]

PRAYER OF GENERAL CONFESSION   [W10]

This Middle English prayer survives in many variants and copies. For another version
in seven manuscripts, see *NIMEV* 3231; a copy of this variant appears in the Vernon
Manuscript (Horstmann, *Minor Poems of the Vernon MS*, pp. 19–20; Patterson, *Middle English
Penitential Lyric*, pp. 50–53, 162–63), where it opens (in twenty-two couplets) a longer poem

of confession. There is a good degree of minor verbal variation among the manuscripts, but the rhymes tend to be consistent.

[Fol. 12va–b. *IMEV*, *Suppl.*, *NIMEV* 3233. Brown, *Register of Middle English Religious and Didactic Verse*, 1:114. **Hands:** Scribe A, poem in black; Scribe B, incipit in red. **Initial:** Medium *S* in blue with red filigree (two lines high). **Meter:** Nineteen tetrameter couplets. **Other MSS:** Cambridge, CUL Ii.6.43, fols. 90v–91v (twenty couplets; Brown, *Religious Lyrics of the XIVth Century*, pp. 109–10, 271–72 [no. 87]); London, BL MS Addit. 47663 (L), fol. 84r (eighteen couplets; Furnivall, *Minor Poems of the Vernon MS*, pp. 785–86); *olim* Fellowes, fol. 166v (sold Sotheby's, July 6, 1964, lot 231). **Edition:** E. Whiting, pp. 80–81 (lines 23–60), 237–38.]

2   *Coubabil.* Brown, *Religious Lyrics of the XIVth Century*, pp. 271–72, notes that surviving copies of the *Prayer of General Confession* divide into two groups: those with the word *copable* at this point, and those with the word *gulti*. The Vernon version belongs to the latter group. The three manuscripts listed above belong, with MS Douce 302, to the *copable* group.

5–8   The Vernon text arranges the sins differently: "In Pruide, in Envye, In lecherye, / In Sleuþe, In Wraþþe, In Glotenye, / In al þis worldus Couetyse" (Horstmann, *Minor Poems of the Vernon MS*, p. 19, lines 5–7). On Audelay's treatment of the seven deadly sins elsewhere, see explanatory note to *Seven Bleedings of Christ*, lines 19–60.

6   The poem printed by Brown, *Religious Lyrics of the XIVth Century* (based on the Cambridge and London manuscripts), has the order of sins reversed: "yn glotonye, yn lecherye" (p. 109, line 6).

10–16   On sinning with the five wits, Patterson notes a parallel passage in a prose confession from an Office of the Visitation of the Sick: "I knowleche to god and to owre lady seynte marie and to alle þe halwen of heuene, that I have senned, with mowth spoken, with feet goon, with eyen seyen, with eren hered, with nose smelled, with herte þowht, and with al myn senful body myswrowth" (Littlehales, *English Fragments*, p. 8, qtd. Patterson, *Middle English Penitential Lyrics*, p. 162). Compare Audelay's *Five Wits*, and see also E. Whiting's note, p. 238.

24   Audelay uses this line elsewhere, in contexts of sincere petition, in *Seven Words of Christ on the Cross*, line 20, and *Saint Winifred Carol*, line 164.

30   The poem printed by Brown, *Religious Lyrics of the XIVth Century*, inserts a couplet after this line: "For sennes þat ich habbe <do> / yn al my lyue hider-<to>" (p. 110, lines 31–32).

INSTRUCTIONS FOR PRAYER 7   **[W10]**
[Fol. 12vb. Not in *IMEV*, *NIMEV*. **Hand:** Scribe A, poem in black. **Meter:** One tetrameter couplet. **Edition:** E. Whiting, p. 81 (lines 61–62).]

PRAYER FOR FORGIVENESS   **[W10]**
   Audelay concludes the sequence for remission of sins with this prayer for forgiveness, written in a "stanza" of five couplets, as was *Saint Gregory's Indulgence* (see above). The scribe inserts a blue paraph to the left of the initial *O*, as he did earlier for *Saint Gregory's Indulgence*

and *Instructions for Prayer 6*. The entire sequence is fitted onto one page (fol. 12va–b), and the final *Amen* (written by Scribe A) closes the devotion.

[Fol. 12vb. *IMEV, NIMEV* 2489. Brown, *Register of Middle English Religious and Didactic Verse*, 1:114. **Hands:** Scribe A, poem in black; Scribe B, incipit in red. **Initials:** Medium *O* in red (two lines high). Black *A* (*Amen*) after line 10 is marked in red. **Meter:** Five tetrameter couplets. **Edition:** E. Whiting, p. 81 (lines 63–72).]

XXIII. Visiting the Sick and Consoling the Needy   [W11]

In this poem the concept of "visiting" involves both a pastoral consolation of the "needy" and the metaphysical afflictions God rains upon the sinful soul. The inspiration from Anselm, mentioned often (lines 1, 105, 119, 380), seems to be his office for visiting the dying, *Admonitio morienti et de peccatis suis nimium formidanti* (*PL* 158.685–88). Several stanzas appear to be borrowed from other poems by Audelay (as indicated below). Citrome, *Surgeon*, pp. 93–94, notes how "This poem conflates two common genres, the *consolatio* (consolation) and the visitation of the sick, both of which presented physical affliction as issuing directly from God."

In structure this work displays symmetry: stanzas 1–15, upon the hardship yet value of being afflicted in this life, as a means to expiate one's sinfulness, with Peter, Mary Magdalene, and Thomas made the exemplars of God's mercy extended to sinners; stanza 16 (the center), on Peter exalted as heaven's gatekeeper and on the establishment of Holy Church and her priests; and stanzas 17–31, on the tenets and sacraments of Holy Church as the way to salvation. The basic message is to be prepared for "soden deth" (line 395) and to trust the Church's teachings and servants, not leaving the welfare of one's soul to one's executors. Audelay's use of a symmetrical structure, however fleeting in effect, in a poem of thirty-one 13-line stanzas shows him to be working consciously within a tradition reserved primarily for 13-line alliterative poems (see explanatory note to lines 196–204). This fact offers some insight on Audelay's thoughtful metrics, and particularly on his craftsmanlike knowledge of verse styles matched to content.

[Fols. 12vb–14va. *IMEV, NIMEV* 2853. *MWME* 7:2568 [219]. **Hands:** Scribe A, poem in black; Scribe B, incipit and explicit in red. Marginal symbols (possibly misplaced paraphs) appear at lines 202 and 229. **Initials:** Large *S* in blue with red filigree (three lines high). Black *A* (*Amen*) in line 403 is marked in red. **Audelay Signature:** Line 390 (Scribe A). **Meter:** Thirty-one 13-line stanzas, ababbcbc$_4$d$_3$eee$_{3-4}$d$_3$. **Edition:** E. Whiting, pp. 82–94, 238–39.]

9–13   Audelay repeats these lines in *Our Lord's Epistle on Sunday*, lines 178–82, and *The Vision of Saint Paul*, lines 258–61.

29–34   These lines are virtually identical to *Audelay's Conclusion*, lines 16–21.

48–49   On Audelay's attitude about social rank, see the explanatory note to *True Living*, lines 130–33.

71–73   For the sentiment of this passage, that one should take care of one's own soul and not trust others to care for it after one's death, see explanatory note to *Marcolf and Solomon*, line 89.

87–91   See explanatory note to *Marcolf and Solomon*, line 89.

89   For other warnings by Audelay not to trust one's affairs to an executor, see *Visiting the Sick and Consoling the Needy*, lines 99, 345–47, and *Marcolf and Solomon*, line 89 (explanatory note).

92–94   A single mass during one's lifetime is more effective than a thousand after one's death. Compare *Virtues of the Mass*, lines 217–22, which may refer to the same tenet, though the wording is somewhat different.

99   On executors, see explanatory note to *Marcolf and Solomon*, line 89.

106–13   Citrome notes in these lines echoes of Audelay's many autobiographical references to his own afflictions, as well as signs of the "uneasy interdependence" that connects spiritual sin to bodily illness (*Surgeon*, p. 94).

145   For this reference to Mary Magdalene being forgiven, E. Whiting, p. 239, cites Luke 7:47, which occurs in the story of the sinful woman anointing Jesus' feet (Luke 7:37–50); this unnamed woman was often associated with Mary Magdalene (mentioned later, at Luke 8:2). Compare *The Vision of Saint Paul*, explicit (and explanatory note).

156–64   These lines and the sense of the whole stanza recur in *God's Address to Sinful Men*, lines 33–39, where the reference to Luke 15:7 is explicit.

161   Four score is eighty men, but Luke 15:7 references ninety-nine men.

170–78   These lines repeat a stanza in *Audelay's Epilogue to The Counsel of Conscience*, lines 157–65. Line 171 is a formula that recurs in other contexts; compare *Visiting the Sick and Consoling the Needy*, line 207; *Pope John's Passion of Our Lord*, line 102; and *The Vision of Saint Paul*, line 332.

196–204   Audelay designs this poem so as to create this central stanza — on the foundation of Holy Church and its priesthood — flanked by fifteen stanzas on either side. It is quite interesting to note Audelay's deployment of an older tradition in Middle English 13-line stanzaic verse: the opening of a portal at the center of the poem. In *The Four Leaves of the Truelove*, the event is the Harrowing of Hell. In *The Dispute between Mary and the Cross*, it is the rebirth of mankind through Mary during the Harrowing. Here, Christ opens the gate of heaven, with Peter made porter. See my discussion in Fein, "Form and Continuity in the Alliterative Tradition," and in my editions of *The Four Leaves of the Truelove* and *The Dispute between Mary and the Cross* (Fein, *Moral Love Songs*).

199   *louce and bynd*. The words evoke the biblical passage seen to sanctify priestly authority as granted directly from Christ. Compare *Marcolf and Solomon*, lines 238, 805a, 961a.

202   A scribal symbol in the margin, resembling a paraph, is inserted to the left of this line, which occurs at the exact center of the poem. The same symbol appears next to line 229.

209–11   With the Church established and heaven's gates opened, the joy expressed in these lines follows the tradition described above (explanatory note to lines 196–204). In keeping with this sacred joy, Audelay evokes the cross in line 211:

"Est and west, north and south." This line recalls one like it at the exact center of Thomas of Hales' *Love Rune* (Fein, *Moral Love Songs*, p. 35, line 100; Fein, "Roll or Codex?" p. 18).

218   *he token.* The idea that God plants sacred signs in nature to betoken his impending judgment recurs in Audelay's *The Counsel of Conscience*; compare *On the World's Folly*, lines 31–42, and *Audelay's Epilogue to The Counsel of Conscience*, lines 57–58.

229   A scribal symbol resembling a paraph marks this line in the left margin. The same symbol appears next to line 202.

287–94   On these lines, Hirsh, *Boundaries of Faith*, p. 100n20, comments: "Audelay's linking of Christ's blood with the Eucharist and with redemption is graceful and conventional, insisting upon the salvational nature of the Passion, as well as the biblical linking of sacrifice and salvation." Compare, too, Audelay's *Seven Bleedings of Christ*.

295–96   *And beware. . . that uncriston be.* Forrest, *Detection of Heresy*, p. 72, detects in these lines an echo of Chancery proceedings against heresy, which prodded the reporting of heretics to the authorities.

345–47   On executors, see explanatory note to *Marcolf and Solomon*, line 89.

355   *that day when ye schul dee.* See explanatory note to *Marcolf and Solomon*, line 682.

378–90   This is Audelay's typical signature stanza. Compare *The Remedy of Nine Virtues*, lines 77–89; *Our Lord's Epistle on Sunday*, lines 196–208; *The Vision of Saint Paul*, lines 353–65; and *Audelay's Epilogue to The Counsel of Conscience*, lines 495–507. The last two stanzas of *Visiting the Sick and Consoling the Needy* borrow closely from the last two stanzas of *The Remedy of Nine Virtues*.

391–98   Compare *The Remedy of Nine Virtues*, lines 90–97. Lines 391–93 are similar, too, to *Marcolf and Solomon*, lines 997–99. On the phrase *take good eme* in line 391, see explanatory note to *Marcolf and Solomon*, line 53.

BLIND AUDELAY'S ENGLISH PASSION   [W12–W14]

Blind Audelay's English Passion carries an indulgence much like the other devotional sequences in *The Counsel of Conscience*. It consists of:

(1)   Instructions (underlined in red) readying the reader for the whole sequence;
(2)   A meditation on the vanity of the world;
(3)   A meditation on the Passion according to the Gospel of John, closing with worship of the five wounds of Christ, to be followed by a recitation of five Paternosters, five Aves, and the Creed (this poem is said to carry an indulgence granted by Pope John XXII of Avignon);
(4)   A prayer explicit;
(5)   A meditation on the Seven Hours of the Cross.

Audelay provides the title for this section in *Audelay's Prayer Explicit to Pope John's Passion*. At this point in the manuscript, Scribe B's guideposts do not entirely agree with the program set out by Scribe A. Scribe B underlines instructions in red, but he does not insert a new numeral, as would be expected by internal signs that Audelay here introduces a devotional sequence honoring the Passion and bringing remission of sins. Instead, Scribe B's numeral heads *Pope John's Passion of Our Lord*, the longest item in the sequence.

Audelay uses a generic term to name the sequence — it is a "Passion" (*Instructions for Reading 2*, line 3) — and later he will repeat the term and call the sequence his own composition in English (*Audelay's Prayer Explicit to Pope John's Passion*, lines 2–3). It is unusual for Scribe B not to follow the program evidently in place when Scribe A began his work. The error seems the result either of inadvertency or of a confusing layout. Scribe B assigns a numeral to *Pope John's Passion of Our Lord* because of its visual prominence; it possesses the only large blue-and-red initial in the series. Thus, by layout, *Instructions for Reading 2* and *On the World's Folly* join as a preface (on fol. 14va–b, with only a red initial *I* squeezed into a margin) to *Pope John's Passion of Our Lord* (opening on fol. 15ra), and the two subsequent red initials on fol. 15v ("*O* Jhesu" and "*Crist*") aid one's meditative progress to *Seven Hours of the Cross*.

INSTRUCTIONS FOR READING 2   [W12]
The instructions preface the rest of the sequence, referring to its parts.

[Fol. 14va–b. *IMEV* unnumbered (p. 213); not in *NIMEV*. Brown, *Register of Middle English Religious and Didactic Verse*, 1:114. **Hands:** Scribe A, poem in black; Scribe B, all lines underlined in red. **Initial:** Large *I* in black (three lines high, set in the margin at the base of fol. 14va). **Meter:** Three tetrameter couplets, with red paraphs marking lines 1 and 5. The rhymes may borrow from those of the next item. **Edition:** E. Whiting, p. 94 (these lines are not numbered).]

3   *this Passion*. The phrase refers to the whole sequence and most particularly to *Pope John's Passion of Our Lord*.

4   This line advertises *Seven Hours of the Cross* by citing its eighth line.

6   This line summarizes *On the World's Folly*, lines 7–15.

ON THE WORLD'S FOLLY   [W12]
Despite E. Whiting's presentation of this poem in 3-line stanzas, Scribe B's red paraphs and flourishes, and the syntactical breaks, indicate strophes of 6 lines. Stanza 1 is in Latin, and stanza 2 translates the Latin. Most of the English stanzas employ similar rhyme-sounds, that is, a-rhymes on *-e* or *-ay*; b-rhymes on *-on*, *-yn*, or *-ent*. This poem opens the meditation by asking the meditant to reject worldly desires because God's laws are "turnyd up-so-doun" (line 13). Later the poet refers to "Mede, that swet maydyn" (line 17), a phrase that suggests Audelay's familiarity with *Piers Plowman*.

[Fol. 14vb–15ra. *IMEV*, *NIMEV* 1211 (both indexes list line 5 as the first line). **Hands:** Scribe A, poem in black; Scribe B, line 3 in red. **Initials:** The black initial letters of all lines except lines 1 and 3 (which is all in red) are marked in red. **Audelay Signature:** Line 72 (Scribe A). **Meter:** Twelve 6-line stanzas, $aa_4b_3aa_4b_3$. **Edition:** E. Whiting, pp. 94–97 (the Latin lines are not numbered), 239.]

17   *Mede, that swet maydyn*. Lady Mede is an allegorical figure that may derive from
            a common cultural usage or from direct knowledge of Langland's work. See
            explanatory note to *Marcolf and Solomon*, line 705.

25–27   Variants of these lines also occur in *Audelay's Epilogue to The Counsel of Conscience*,
            lines 110–12, and *Ten Commandments*, lines 29–32.

31   *he*. E. Whiting notes that "several illegible letters [are] interlined after *he*," but
            the letters here are legible: *he token* is corrected by Scribe B to *hede ȝe tokyn*. This
            appears to be a rare instance in which Scribe A's copy is better. Scribe B may
            have intended to write *þe* for *ȝe* and expects *an* to be read as *and*: "Here may you
            see and heed the token." I have retained the copy of Scribe A, as did Whiting.

31–42   Natural portents of God's judgment (*he tokyn* and *trew tokyn*) are a recurrent
            element in Audelay's works; compare *Visiting the Sick and Consoling the Needy*, line
            218, and *Audelay's Epilogue to The Counsel of Conscience*, lines 57–58.

58–60   For Audelay's opinion that one should take care of one's own soul before death
            and not entrust it to others, see explanatory note to *Marcolf and Solomon*, line 89.

67–72   This stanza is a condensed variant of Audelay's signature stanza. Compare lines
            67, 71–72, to *Our Lord's Epistle on Sunday*, lines 205, 207–08, and *Audelay's Epi-
            logue to The Counsel of Conscience*, lines 504, 506–07, and see also *The Remedy of
            Nine Virtues*, lines 101–02.

XXIIII. POPE JOHN'S PASSION OF OUR LORD   [W13]

Pope John's Passion of Our Lord is to become part of one's daily spiritual discipline. It is
a meditative exercise focused upon the Passion as told in the Gospel of John, the "central
text of the Good Friday liturgy" (Duffy, *Stripping of the Altars*, p. 237), with a few standard
details from the other Gospels. It ends by turning the worshiper's thoughts to the five
wounds, and it is to be concluded by a saying of five Paternosters, five Aves, and the Creed
(lines 105–20). He or she is also to pair it with the next poem, *Seven Hours of the Cross*, an-
other mental renactment of the Passion, for the two are linked in Scribe B's incipit, in Scribe
A's *Instructions for Reading 2*, and by the numeral given to both pieces. *Seven Hours of the
Cross* ends, likewise, as a means for "ful remyssion" (line 85). As further evidence of the con-
nection, the Vernon analogue to *Seven Hours of the Cross* ends by referring to an indulgence
granted by Pope John (see explanatory note to *Seven Hours of the Cross*, lines 82–90).

[Fol. 15ra–va. *IMEV, NIMEV* 2764 (both indexes combine this item with *Audelay's Prayer Explicit to
Pope John's Passion*). *MWME* 7:2571–73 [227]. **Hands:** Scribe A, poem in black; Scribe B, first stanza
(lines 1–8) underlined in red, and incipit in red. **Initials:** Large *P* in blue with red filigree (three lines
high), and medium *O* in red (two lines high), with face drawn in it (line 89). **Meter:** Fifteen 8-line
stanzas, ababbcbC$_4$, with two refrains interchanged: "al hit was for love of thee" and "on thi Passion
to have peté." The last stanza does not have either refrain. **Edition:** E. Whiting, pp. 97–101, 239–40.]

incipit   The incipit, written by Scribe B, sets this item in sequence with the next item.

1   *XXII*. The MS reading, *xij*, is erroneous and has here been emended (though the
             error may be Audelay's). The reference is to John XXII, pope at Avignon from
             1316 to 1334. On this indulgence, see Duffy, *Stripping of the Altars*, pp. 237–38.

9   Compare *Anima Christi sanctifica me*, line 5, and *Dread of Death*.

16   Used here as a refrain, this line occurs in *God's Address to Sinful Men*, line 45, and
                   it is echoed in several Middle English lyrics that voice Christ's emotional appeal
                   to humankind from the cross. See, for example, Brown, *Religious Lyrics of the
                   XIVth Century*, pp. 2 (no. 3, line 5), 67 (no. 51, line 4), and 227 (no. 127, line 28).

17   *Gospel of Jon.* The order of events follows the Passion as told in John 19, with ex-
                   ceptions at lines 30, 57–63, which come from the other Gospels.

41–46   This gruesome detail is common in medieval Passion plays, though it is not
                   found in the Gospels.

50–52   Compare *Prayer on Christ's Passion*, line 23; *O Deus qui voluisti*, line 29; *Seven
                   Words of Christ on the Cross*, line 40–42; and *Seven Hours of the Cross*, line 39.

65–66   Compare *Seven Hours of the Cross*, lines 50–51.

67   On the tradition of blind Longinus in Blind Audelay's works, see the explanatory
                   note to *Seven Bleedings of Christ*, line 92, and compare *Prayer on Christ's Passion*,
                   line 24; *O Deus qui voluisti*, line 30; and *Seven Hours of the Cross*, line 48.

89   The red initial *O* has a face drawn inside it, as elsewhere when a prayer opens
                   with an address to God. Compare *Salutation to Jesus for Mary's Love*, line 91, and
                   Deus qui beatam Annam, line 1. The poem turns at this point to a consideration of
                   the five wounds (compare Audelay's *Seven Bleedings of Christ*) and the indulgence
                   created when they are addressed by five Paternosters, five Aves, and the Creed.

110   On Audelay's conservative attitude on upholding one's station, see the explan-
                   atory note to *True Living*, lines 130–33.

AUDELAY'S PRAYER EXPLICIT TO *POPE JOHN'S PASSION*   [W13]
[Fol. 15va. Not in *IMEV*, *NIMEV* as a separate item (see 2764). **Hand:** Scribe A, poem in black.
Audelay Signature: Line 2 (Scribe A). **Meter:** Two tetrameter couplets. **Edition:** E. Whiting, p. 101.]

SEVEN HOURS OF THE CROSS   [W14]
     This poem follows the canonical division of the seven stages of the Passion, an ancient
Christian trope appearing frequently in medieval English literature (Woolf, *English Religious
Lyric*, pp. 234–37; Barratt, "Prymer and Its Influence," pp. 272–76; Duffy, *Stripping of the
Altars*, pp. 225, 237). The first and last stanzas are Audelay's original compositions; the
second through ninth stanzas are based on Latin originals, which Audelay translates into
English verse. Audelay has used the first lines of Latin stanzas for his headings. In addition
to the Vernon poem, which bears persistent though loose verbal similarities to Audelay's
poem, other Middle English treatments of the topic can be found in Brown, *Religious Lyrics
of the XIVth Century*, pp. 39–44 (no. 30), 50–51 (no. 34; see also R. Morris, *Legends of the Holy
Rood*, pp. 222–24), and 69–70 (no. 55). *Seven Hours of the Cross* represents the second time
in *The Counsel of Conscience* that Audelay positions a seven-part mnemonic meditation at the
end of a long devotional Passion sequence; earlier in MS Douce 302, *Seven Words of Christ
on the Cross* followed *The Psalter of the Passion*. Compare also *Seven Bleedings of Christ*.

[Fols. 15va–16ra. *IMEV*, *NIMEV* 623. **Hand:** Scribe A, poem and incipit in black, and Latin stanza headings in red. **Initial:** Medium *C* in red (two lines high), with quatrefoil drawn in it. **Meter:** Ten 9-line stanzas, aaaa$_7$b$_3$ccc$_4$b$_3$. **Latin Source:** Simmons, *Lay Folks Mass Book*, pp. 83, 85, and 87. **Middle English Analogues:** Vernon MS "The Hours of the Cross," in fourteen 8-line stanzas, aaaa$_7$b$_3$b$_7$cc$_4$ (Horstmann, *Minor Poems of the Vernon MS*, pp. 37–42); "York Hours of the Cross" (Simmons, *Lay Folks Mass Book*, pp. 82, 84, 86). **Edition:** E. Whiting, pp. 101–04, 240.]

1	Red initial *C* has a quatrefoil drawn inside it. With the *O* of *Pope John's Passion of Our Lord*, line 89, this ornament brings meditational focus to fol. 15v.
8	This line is cited in the fourth line of *Instructions for Reading 2*.
9a–14	The heading alludes to an anonymous fourteenth-century Latin hymn: "*Patris sapiencia, veritas diuina, / Deus homo captas est hora matutina, / A notis discipulis cito derelictus, / A iudeis traditus, venditus, afflictus*" (Simmons, *Lay Folks Mass Book*, p. 83, lines 8–11). Lines 10–14 paraphrase the hymn itself, which was well known by English readers because books of hours incorporated it into the Office of the Virgin and from there it was adapted to vernacular primers (Woolf, *English Religious Lyric*, p. 235; Barratt, "Prymer and Its Influence," pp. 272–76). Littlehales, *Prymer or Lay Folks' Prayer Book*, p. 15, prints a specimen: "The wisdom of þe fadir, / þe treuþe of þe hiȝ king, / God and man was takun / In þe morenyng. / Of hise knowun disciplis / Soone he was forsak; / Sold & put to peyne, / Mankynde saaf to make." For another Middle English version, see Simmons, p. 82, lines 12–17.
13–18	On Judas's treason, compare *Marcolf and Solomon*, lines 473, 753a, 757; *Prayer on Christ's Passion*, lines 4–5; *O Deus qui voluisti*, lines 4–5, 18; *Virtues of the Mass*, lines 103–08; and *The Vision of Saint Paul*, line 234.
39	Compare *Prayer on Christ's Passion*, line 23; *O Deus qui voluisti*, line 29; *Seven Words of Christ on the Cross*, lines 61–62; and *Pope John's Passion of Our Lord*, line 50.
42–44	Compare *Seven Words of Christ on the Cross*, lines 40–42, and *Day of Saint John the Evangelist*, lines 7–16.
47	Compare *Seven Words of Christ on the Cross*, lines 50–54.
48	On the tradition of blind Longinus in Blind Audelay's works, see the explanatory note to *Seven Bleedings of Christ*, lines 92, and compare *Prayer on Christ's Passion*, line 24; *O Deus qui voluisti*, line 30; and *Pope John's Passion of Our Lord*, line 68.
50–51	Compare *Pope John's Passion of Our Lord*, lines 65–66.
57	Cited by Woolf, *English Religious Lyric*, p. 236.
82–90	The pronoun shifts from *he/him* to *ye* in this stanza (line 88). The Vernon analogue provides a concluding stanza (in a shortened 6-line form) that connects the piece to an indulgence granted by Pope John: "Þe Pope Ion haþ graunted: A ful feir pardoun / To alle þat siggen þis Matyns: Wiþ good deuocioun: / A ȝer in purgatorie: Of Remissioun, / So þat heo ben clene i-schriuen: Wiþ verrey Contricioun, / Þorwh Grace. / God send us lyues fode: And in heuene a place. AMEN" (Horstmann, *Minor Poems of the Vernon MS*, p. 43, lines 113–18). On this indulgence, see Duffy, *Stripping of the Altars*, pp. 237–38.

XXV. OUR LORD'S EPISTLE ON SUNDAY   **[W15]**

The archetype of this poem had a widespread distribution in the Middle Ages, according to Priebsch, ranging from Latin, Welsh, Old English, Old French, and Old Czech. Thirteenth-century English chronicles record its use by Abbot Eustace of Flay, a religious reformer and preacher of the crusade, as an eccentric instrument of popular devotionalism (W. R. Jones, "Heavenly Letter," pp. 166–75). The only verse version in Middle English is this one by Audelay, though the tradition does appear in an anonymous sermon edited from Durham University Library MS Cosin V.IV.2 by V. M. O'Mara (*Study and Edition of Selected Middle English Sermons*, pp. 115–40). Priebsch prints a Latin text from an English MS (Royal 8.F.vi) that must be closely related to Audelay's own source text. Only a few points in Audelay's poem do not correspond to material in this Latin copy, and some of these gaps were probably supplied by his actual source. The tradition is that the letter descended from Christ's own hand directly to Saint Peter named bishop, sometimes of Antioch, sometimes of Nimes, sometimes of Gaza. Audelay's version derives from the Gaza tradition. *Our Lord's Epistle on Sunday* explains the importance of Sunday in God's own stern voice. Many manuscripts pair this text with *The Vision of Saint Paul*, as does Audelay. Latin texts of these two works appear side by side in MS Royal 8.F.vi, with the *Visio* (fols. 23r–24r) preceding the *Epistle* (fol. 24r–v). This fifteenth-century manuscript was copied by an English scribe who signs himself Thomas Brewse. It contains sermons, miracles, tales, and homilies (some set in England) chiefly in Latin with some English notes.

Two other works in *The Counsel of Conscience* adopt the speaking voice of God: *The Remedy of Nine Virtues* and *God's Address to Sinful Men* (the work that follows *The Vision of Saint Paul*).

[Fols. 16ra–17ra. *IMEV, NIMEV* 2324. **Hands:** Scribe A, poem in black, and long incipit (fol. 16ra, base) in red; Scribe B, short incipit (fol. 16rb, top) in red. **Initial:** Large *N* in blue with red filigree (three lines high). **Audelay Signature:** Line 208 (Scribe A). **Meter:** Sixteen 13-line stanzas, ababbcbc$_4$d$_3$eee$_4$d$_3$. **Latin Source:** "Second Redaction of the Epistle," as found in London, BL MS Royal 8.F.vi, fol. 24r (Priebsch, "John Audelay's Poem," pp. 400–06). **Editions:** Priebsch, "John Audelay's Poem," pp. 397–407; E. Whiting, pp. 104–11, 240–41.]

incipits   The order of incipits is reversed because the one by Scribe B provides the topical "title" for the piece, while Scribe A's incipit provides an introduction spoken by "Peter of Gaza." One can compare the double incipit for the *Salutation to Jesus for Mary's Love* and the long incipit and explicit for *The Vision of Saint Paul*.

1–13   These lines paraphrase and expand Scribe A's incipit. They do not appear in the Latin text of MS Royal 8.F.vi, which opens with a phrase similar to Scribe B's incipit: "*Incipit epistola de Cristo filio dei et de sancto die dominico.*"

46   *loveday.* See explanatory note to *Marcolf and Solomon*, line 390.

86–91   This passage does not appear in the Latin text of MS Royal 8.F.vi.

99   *word of wordis.* "forever and ever, to all eternity." The *MED* provides many examples of this Middle English phrase deriving from translation of the Vulgate phrases "*in saeculum*," "*in saeculum saeculi*," "*in saecula saeculorum*"; see *world*, n. 6. (b). Audelay uses the phrase elsewhere in *Our Lord's Epistle on Sunday*, line 142; *God's Address to Sinful Men*, line 259; and *Song of the Magnificat*, line 91.

114–17　This is a difficult passage, but the emendation of Priebsch and Whiting (*for* for *fro* in line 114) does not help it significantly. The idea expressed comes from one of Audelay's favorite biblical phrases, in which God declares he does not wish the death of a sinner (Ezechiel 33:11, and also Ezechiel 18:23, 18:32). Compare the *Nolo mortem peccatoris* refrain in *God's Address to Sinful Men*, the parallel use of this biblical passage in the *The Vision of Saint Paul*, explicit, as well as its occurrences in *True Living*, line 128, and *Marcolf and Solomon*, line 790. Interestingly, the passage is cited in a Suffolk priest's 1429 confession of Lollardy (Shinners and Dohar, *Pastors and the Care of Souls*, p. 280).

142　*word of wordis*. See explanatory note to *Our Lord's Epistle on Sunday*, line 99.

144–48　These lines do not appear in the Latin text of MS Royal 8.F.vi. Priebsch locates a corresponding passage in "the corrupt Todi MS" ("John Audelay's Poem," p. 405), which he does not further identify.

170–205　These three stanzas do not correspond to anything in the Latin text.

170–82　This stanza on the joys of heaven contains elements found in other Audelay 13-lines poems. The closest corresponding stanza is *The Vision of Saint Paul*, lines 249–61. Compare lines 174–75 to *The Vision of Saint Paul*, lines 253–54, and *God's Address to Sinful Men*, lines 253–54; and lines 178–82 to *The Vision of Saint Paul*, lines 258–61, and *Visiting the Sick and Consoling the Needy*, lines 9–13.

196–208　This is Audelay's signature stanza. Compare *The Remedy of Nine Virtues*, lines 77–89; *Visiting the Sick and Consoling the Needy*, lines 378–90; *The Vision of Saint Paul*, lines 353–65; and *Audelay's Epilogue to The Counsel of Conscience*, lines 495–507.

XXVI. The Vision of Saint Paul   [W16]

The Vision of Saint Paul is Audelay's translation from Latin of "the most influential of all the medieval accounts of journeys to the otherworld" (Easting, "'Choose yourselves,'" p. 170; see also Silverstein, *Visio Sancti Pauli*). Many other Middle English writers also translated this popular narrative, including one poet whose work appears in the Vernon Manuscript (see below). Amid many warnings in *The Counsel of Conscience* about the pains of hell, this piece makes them visually real, as gazed upon by an astonished Paul, a figure to whom Audelay gives prominence elsewhere. The apostle is invoked in the first poem that survives in MS Douce 302, *True Living*, line 215, for his letter on faith, hope, and charity (as safeguards against Doomsday), and again in the last item of *The Counsel of Conscience*, *Audelay's Epilogue to The Counsel of Conscience*, line 16, where Paul's visitation of blindness seems a model for Audelay's own condition. Paul's journey through hell is led by the archangel Michael. One may note that a feather-winged effigy of Michael stands between the outside arches of the chapter house in the remains of Haughmond Abbey. There he is depicted holding a shield and a cross-staff, with which he pierces a dragon at his feet.

　　The poem possesses an unusually long incipit and explicit, both written by Scribe A, and there is no opening initial. These departures from normal layout may be part of the way in which Audelay formally joins this piece to *Our Lord's Epistle on Sunday*. The linkage was traditional: with both pieces moralizing upon the value of the Sabbath, their Latin texts appear side by side in other manuscripts. The long incipit of the *Our Lord's Epistle on Sunday* along with the long incipit and explicit for *The Vision of Saint Paul* may also suggest a shared exemplar. While Audelay's Latin original can be speculatively reconstructed, no known manuscript has been shown to match all its features (Easting, pp. 170–71). Audelay also adds many lines of his own — 155 out of 365 by Easting's estimate. His general method is "to start a new stanza with a new movement in the Latin, but then to elaborate in the later part of the stanza, perhaps when the demands of the rhyme scheme make it easier to invent freely than to translate faithfully" (Easting, p. 177).

As with *Seven Hours of the Cross*, *The Vision of Saint Paul* has an analogue in the Vernon MS, a 346-line poem in tetrameter couplets (fols. 230rc–231ra; R. Morris, *Old English Miscellany*, pp. 223–32), but in this case verbal correspondences are negligible. Seven Audelay stanzas — including his signature stanza and another borrowed from *True Living* — have no parallel in the Vernon text. The narrative affinities may be charted as follows:

Audelay Stanza	Vernon Lines	Audelay Stanza	Vernon Lines
1 (1–13)	V 1–12	15 (184–96)	V 201–14
2 (14–26)	V 13–20	16 (197–209)	V 215–30
3 (27–39)	V 21–36	17 (210–22)	V 231–54
4 (40–52)	V 37–54	18 (223–35)	***
5 (53–66)	V 55–86	19 (236–48)	V 255–72
6 (67–79)	V 87–102	20 (249–61)	***
7 (80–92)	V 103–14	21 (262–74)	V 273–90
8 (93–105)	***	22 (275–87)	V 291–314
9 (106–18)	V 115–28	23 (288–300)	V 315–30
10 (119–31)	V 129–50	24 (301–13)	V 331–40
11 (132–44)	V 151–62	25 (314–26)	***
12 (145–57)	V 163–72	26 (327–39)	***
13 (158–70)	V 173–88	27 (340–52)	***
14 (171–83)	V 189–200	28 (353–65)	***

[Fols. 17ra–18vb. *IMEV, NIMEV* 3481. *MWME* 2:646 [320d]. **Hand:** Scribe A, poem in black, long incipit and long explicit in red. **Audelay Signature:** Line 365 (Scribe A). **Meter:** Twenty-eight 13-line stanzas, ababbcbc₄d₃eee₄d₃. A nonrhyming Latin line is inserted in the fifth stanza, breaking the pattern. **Latin Prose Source:** "Vision of Saint Paul Latin Redaction IV," as found, e.g., in London, BL MS Harley 2851 (Brandes, "Über die Quellen," pp. 44–47; Perman, "Henri d'Arci," pp. 316–19; for a translation, see Barber and Bate, *Templars*, pp. 111–15). Gardiner, *Medieval Visions of Heaven and Hell*, pp. 179–94, surveys scholarship on the tradition, which appeared in many cultures and languages. **Other Versions in Middle English:** Three in verse, two in prose (Easting, *Annotated Bibliographies*, pp. 31–42). **Editions:** R. Morris, *Old English Miscellany*, pp. 210–22; E. Whiting, pp. 111–23, 241–42.]

21–26   Easting notes that these lines are added by Audelay: "Presumably, Audelay is being sufficiently careful here that we should also match up heads and tongues with gluttony, and hands and feet with sloth" ("'Choose yourselves,'" p. 173).

30   *stod on a lye.* See *MED lei(e*, n.2(g), "on fire, ablaze, alight," for which Audelay's line is cited.

36–51   Audelay here converts a Latin narrative passage into the archangel Michael's direct speech.

37	*monslers*. This word, meaning "manslayers," is added by Audelay, and "one might claim it is a significant (uncensored?) moment, given Audelay's involvement in his patron's fatal fracas in St. Dunstan's in the East on Easter Sunday 1417" (Easting, "'Choose yourselves,'" p. 173).
39	*deseredyn*. See *MED disheriten*, v.1(a). "To dispossess (sb.) of an inheritance." E. Whiting's gloss of the word — "desired" — is incorrect.
43	*broudun*. See *MED brouden*, v.1(b), "to writhe, twist." The *MED* provides only three instances of the verb's appearance, one being this one and another by Lydgate.
49	Audelay speeds up the revolutions of the whirling, burning wheel from one thousand per day, in the source, to one thousand per hour (Easting, "'Choose yourselves,'" p. 174; Barber and Bate, *Templars*, p. 112).
54–56	"This demonic scene of sheep-eating fish is less surreal when the Latin shows that Audelay may have missed a crucial link" (Easting, "'Choose yourselves,'" p. 174): in the Latin the fish are likened by simile to wolves that devour sheep (Barber and Bate, *Templars*, p. 112). Compare Vernon: "Of hem tok I no more kep, / But as a lyun doth of a schep" (lines 63–64). While the word *chep* seems best explained as a translation of *oves*, one might perhaps construe Audelay's sense to be "as if it were a bargain (i.e., cheap)." The difficulty with this solution is that in Audelay's day *chep* was a noun only (*MED chep*, n.1(a), "bargaining, dickering"), and it generally had to appear in a phrase such as *to god chepe* to denote "at low cost."
83–88	Easting notes that there is much elaboration by Audelay throughout this section, and especially here on "the unneighborly prevention of others from hearing Mass by chattering" ("'Choose yourselves,'" p. 175). On Audelay's concern for the problem of disrespect shown for God's service, compare *Marcolf and Solomon*, lines 196–98; *Virtues of the Mass*, lines 40–42; *Over-Hippers and Skippers*, lines 1–13; and the explanatory note to *Cur mundus*, line 40.
139–44	Here Audelay elaborates on "unchaste girls who slew their infants" (Easting, "'Choose yourselves,'" p. 177), and he is somewhat less harsh than the Latin writer. Audelay portrays such girls as victims whom the devil blinds with despair. This softens somewhat the Latin original, rendered in lines 135–38, where they abjure penance and throw their infants to both hounds and pigs (Barber and Bate, *Templars*, p. 113).
146	*kamels*. The tantalized fast-breakers ride camels in Audelay and also in some Latin versions. The mistranslation of "*super canalia amnis*" (above channels of water) was therefore something that Audelay inherited and did not invent. See Easting, "'Choose yourselves,'" p. 177; Barber and Bate, *Templars*, p. 113.
165	*neclygent mon*. Easting, "'Choose yourselves,'" explains that many texts indicate that the man was a negligent bishop; Audelay may be changing this detail, or he may have had a exemplar that lacked the word *episcopus* (p. 178).
173	*gret payn*. The phrase needs to be construed as superlative: "greatest pains." See Easting, "'Choose yourselves,'" p. 179.

209   The emphasis on the Church's necessary sacraments is added by Audelay.

216–35   This passage is Audelay's longest addition within the body of the narrative (Easting, "'Choose yourselves,'" pp. 180–81). In the original, Michael speaks a 1-line sentence. On the doctrine of free will (line 218) in Audelay's works, see the explanatory note to *True Living*, lines 203–07.

234   On Judas's treason, compare *Marcolf and Solomon*, lines 473, 753a, 757; *Prayer on Christ's Passion*, lines 4–5; *O Deus qui voluisti*, lines 4–5, 18; *Virtues of the Mass*, lines 103–08; and *Seven Hours of the Cross*, lines 13–18.

236–40   An early reader, probably the same one who noted the climax of Audelay's Levation sequence, has marked this passage with two large *x*s in the left margin. See explanatory note to *Salutation to Christ's Body*, line 26.

249–61   This stanza on the rejoicing of those in heaven is Audelay's addition, and he builds it from units used in other 13-line poems in *The Counsel of Conscience*, especially the companion poem *Our Lord's Epistle on Sunday*. Compare *Visiting the Sick and Consoling the Needy*, lines 10–13; *Our Lord's Epistle on Sunday*, lines 174–75, 179–83; and *God's Address to Sinful Men*, lines 253–54.

275–87   Lines 277 and 282 are Audelay's own additions. He is elaborating on the depth of Christ's sacrifice for humankind and God's own appeal for human repentance. By filling out this stanza with God's direct address to people, Audelay appears to be preparing for the content of the next poem in the *The Counsel of Conscience* series: *God's Address to Sinful Men*. He is also borrowing from a lyric tradition of Christ's appeal from the cross; in Middle English, see, for example, Brown, *Religious Lyrics of the XIVth Century*, pp. 2 (no. 3, line 5), 67 (no. 51, line 4), 227 (no. 127, line 28), and *In a Valley of This Restless Mind* (Fein, *Moral Love Songs*, pp. 57–86). Compare also *Pope John's Passion of Our Lord*, lines 49–56.

293–300   On the Sunday respite, see Silverstein, *Visio Sancti Pauli*, pp. 79–81.

314–26   E. Whiting, p. 241, claims that this passage is not found in the Latin, but Easting, "'Choose yourselves,'" pp. 171, 182, shows that it is.

317   The number 4,140 is a corruption of 144,000 (Apocalypse 7:4). Easting, "'Choose yourselves,'" p. 182, discusses how this number was often garbled in transmission. Compare the number of slain innocents in Audelay's *Day of the Holy Innocents*, line 13 (and explanatory note).

340–52   This stanza corresponds to *True Living*, line 13–25.

353–65   This is another variation of Audelay's usual signature stanza. Compare *The Remedy of Nine Virtues*, lines 77–89; *Visiting the Sick and Consoling the Needy*, lines 378–90; *Our Lord's Epistle on Sunday*, lines 196–208; and *Audelay's Epilogue to The Counsel of Conscience*, lines 495–507. Lines 361–65 also occur in *Audelay's Conclusion*, lines 35–39.

explicit   This item, written by Scribe A, appears at the base of fol. 18vb. I therefore include it with *The Vision of Saint Paul*, varying from E. Whiting, who made it the incipit for *God's Address to Sinful Men*. It serves usefully as a bridge between the two works, concluding the vision of hell's pains with God's promise that sinners can be saved. It also has God speak in direct address, using the words from Ezechiel 33:11 ("I do not wish the death of a sinner, but rather that he turn and live") that will be the refrain of the next poem. Note too that God speaks in direct address in *The Vision of Saint Paul*, lines 275–87. Audelay uses the Ezechiel passage frequently (see explanatory note to *Our Lord's Epistle on Sunday*, lines 114–17). The poet here references numerous other biblical passages. Compare Isias 45:22: "Return to me, for I have redeemed thee"; Mark 3:18: "For he called the Cananaean and the publican to repentance"; and Psalms 33:12: "And so you also, unbelievers, come and hear, because I will teach you the fear of the Lord." The reference to "the one who wept for [her] sin" alludes to Mary Magdalene (compare *Visiting the Sick and Consoling the Needy*, line 145, and explanatory note). The final sentence of this long explicit readies the reader for the next item: "And so you also, unbelievers, come and hear."

XXVII. THE LORD'S MERCY   [W17–W18]

Scribe B's incipit and numeral at the top of fol. 19ra seem intended to embrace the final three works of *The Counsel of Conscience* and provide a topical name for this closing movement:

    (1)   *God's Address to Sinful Men*;
    (2)   *Audelay's Epilogue to The Counsel of Conscience*; and
    (3)   *Finito libro* colophon.

With the spectacles witnessed in *The Vision of Saint Paul* creating a point of emotional climax, the rest of *The Counsel of Conscience* reminds the reader of God's mercy — first, as granted to sinners in general, and then, more directly, as will be delivered to Audelay and to users of his book. The lack of a distinguishing large initial to signal the beginning of *Audelay's Epilogue to The Counsel of Conscience* connects it visually to *God's Address to Sinful Men*, though the two poems are metrically different.

GOD'S ADDRESS TO SINFUL MEN   [W17]

Combined with *Our Lord's Epistle on Sunday*, this piece frames *The Vision of Saint Paul* with God's direct injunctions and appeals. (For another piece adopting God's voice, see *The Remedy of Nine Virtues*.) It also prefaces *Audelay's Epilogue to The Counsel of Conscience*, highlighting the broad final movement of *The Counsel of Conscience* in which Audelay's exhortations for penance merge with a personal belief that his own physical afflictions betoken God's mercy. Lacking about forty percent of its original length (because of a missing folio), this poem contains many phrases and passages found elsewhere in Audelay's works. While the sequence of composition cannot be fully ascertained, it does seems likely that this work borrows from *True Living* (as do several carols), the apparently earlier work (see Pickering, "Make-Up," pp. 129–30). There are also many interesting correspondences with *Marcolf and Solomon*.

[Fols. 19ra–20rb. *IMEV, NIMEV* 171. **Hands:** Scribe A, poem in black and Latin stanza headings in red; Scribe B, incipit (for everything under the numeral XXVII) and one stanza heading (on fol. 19rb) in red. **Initial:** Large *A* in blue with red filigree (three lines high). **Meter:** Thirty-three 8-line stanzas (with several missing; see explanatory note to line 189), ababbcbC$_4$, with a Latin refrain: "*Nolo mortem* *peccatoris.*" One irregular 12-line stanza (lines 221–32) rhymes ababababbabA₄ with all b-lines in Latin. **Edition:** E. Whiting, pp. 123–33, 242–43.]

8   On Audelay's frequent use of this biblical passage, compare *True Living*, line 128; *Marcolf and Solomon*, line 790; *Our Lord's Epistle on Sunday*, line 115; and the explicit to *The Vision of Saint Paul*. It may hold a contemporary resonance in regard to correction of Lollards; it occurs in a confession of heresy made by a Suffolk priest in 1429 (Shinners and Dohar, *Pastors and the Care of Souls*, p. 280).

33–39   These lines also appear in *Visiting the Sick and Consoling the Needy*, lines 157–64.

45   Audelay uses a variant of this line elsewhere as a refrain; see explanatory note to *Pope John's Passion of Our Lord*, line 16. Compare also *The Vision of Saint Paul*, lines 275–87.

52   The importance of Sunday as God's own day is the central topic of *Our Lord's Epistle on Sunday* and an important subsidiary topic in *The Vision of Saint Paul*, where the souls in hell receive a Sunday reprieve from torment.

84–87   Citrome notes the tension inherent in these lines on God's vengeance upon the unrepentant, written by the chaplain whose ailments remain unabated (*Surgeon*, p. 95).

98   Noting "the cultural primacy of the rhetoric of confession" pervasive in Audelay's works, Citrome cites this symbolic action of kneeling before the priest as enjoined by manuals of confession (*Surgeon*, p. 87).

113   *esy penans.* Compare *Marcolf and Solomon*, line 925; the proper administration of penance is further developed in *God's Address to Sinful Men*, lines 137–44, a passage borrowed from *Marcolf and Solomon*.

137–59   These three stanzas derive from two stanzas of *Marcolf and Solomon*. Lines 137–43 correspond to *Marcolf and Solomon*, lines 923–28; lines 145–51 to *Marcolf and Solomon*, lines 936–44; and lines 153–59 to *Marcolf and Solomon*, lines 931–35.

145–51   On the trope of the Four Daughters of God (Psalm 84:11), which is a bit confused here (Peace, not Grace, should be one of the Daughters), see the explanatory notes to *Marcolf and Solomon*, lines 937–43, 938–39.

170–71   These lines correspond to *True Living*, lines 175–76. On the seven works of mercy theme, compare, more broadly, *True Living*, lines 173–79, and *Seven Works of Mercy*, lines 1–4, 8–10.

189   The loss of a folio after line 189 indicates that an estimated twenty-two stanzas are missing.

197–220   Here Audelay borrows quite directly from *True Living*, lines 238–58; compare also *Seven Works of Mercy*, lines 15–32.

213–20   Audelay borrows these lines from *True Living*, lines 251–58, and they also appear as two stanzas of *Seven Works of Mercy* (lines 22–25, 29–32).

233–39   For the legend of Saint Martin, bishop of Tours, see Jacobus de Voragine, *The Golden Legend*, trans. Ryan, 2:292–300. The story alluded to here tells of Martin cutting his cloak in two in order to share it with a poor stranger, whom he learns later by a vision was Christ himself (2:292). On this story as a reinforcement to the seven works of mercy, see Goldberg, *Medieval England*, p. 230.

253–54   Compare *Our Lord's Epistle on Sunday*, lines 174–75, and *The Vision of Saint Paul*, lines 253–54.

259   *word of wordis*. "forever and ever, to all eternity." The *MED* provides many examples of this Middle English phrase deriving from translation of the Vulgate phrases "*in saeculum*," "*in saeculum saeculi*," "*in saecula saeculorum*"; see *world*, n. 6. (b). Audelay uses the phrase elsewhere in *Our Lord's Epistle on Sunday*, lines 99, 142, and *Song of the Magnificat*, line 91.

AUDELAY'S EPILOGUE TO THE COUNSEL OF CONSCIENCE   [W18]

This poem possesses a rudimentary *chanson d'aventure* framing device at lines 27 and 482, and this frame draws attention to what may be Audelay's plan for structural elegance: an introduction (two stanzas), a main body (thirty-five stanzas), a conclusion (two stanzas). He uses symmetry by stanza count in at least one other 13-line poem, *Visiting the Sick and Consoling the Needy* (see explanatory notes for that poem). In the central stanza of *Audelay's Epilogue to The Counsel of Conscience* (lines 248–60), Audelay defends himself from charges of Lollardy, feeling himself besieged by "Godis enmys" (line 249). The *chanson d'aventure* opening is a feature of *Three Dead Kings* (appearing later in MS Douce 302) and other Middle English poems in the 13-line stanzaic tradition (e.g., *The Four Leaves of the Truelove*, *Summer Soneday*, *Awntyrs off Arthure*). It is also, of course, the opening mode for *Piers Plowman*, *Pearl*, and many short lyrics (catalogued by Sandison).

The poem is important both for the presence of many autobiographical details — matched in the manuscript only by the *Finito libro* colophon and *Audelay's Conclusion* — and for its naming of the manuscript to this point: *The Counsel of Conscience* or *The Ladder of Heaven* (lines 417–48). The poem serves as an encouragement to those who seek "soulehele" (line 105), the same term used, interestingly, by the compiler of the Vernon Manuscript to characterize its contents.

[Fols. 20rb–22vb. *IMEV*, *NIMEV* 1200. **Hands:** Scribe A, poem in black; Scribe B, Latin stanza headings in red. **Initials:** None, but see explanatory note to line 27. **Audelay Signatures:** Lines 6, 507 (both by Scribe A). **Meter:** Thirty-nine 13-line stanzas, $ababbcbc_4d_3eeed_{3-4}$. **Edition:** E. Whiting, pp. 133–49, 243.]

1   This poem begins with no capital or break from the preceding poem, except for the change in meter, which is marked in red at lines 10 and 12 here and in the succeeding stanzas (as are all 13-line stanzas in the manuscript). There is an indicator for a break at line 27. Citrome reads this opening line as marking a transition from the last poem, with Audelay framing himself as "interced[ing] with God on behalf of his sinful race to prevent an impending onslaught of divine vengeance. . . . [The line] suggests not only an author bringing an extended project to a close but a man at the end of life settling his affairs" (*Surgeon*, p. 95).

14–26   Citrome comments: "In this single passage Audelay rationalizes his illness in three distinct ways: as an example to others to reform their lives, as a manifestation of Christ's mercy, and as an early purgatory here in the world" (*Surgeon*, p. 96). On the idea of illness as an earthly purgatory, compare *Audelay's Epilogue to The Counsel of Conscience*, lines 478–79, and the explanatory note to *Childhood*, lines 43–46.

27   This line reads as the opening of a *chanson d'aventure*, and line 482 indicates the frame's closure. That Audelay depicts himself supine upon a bed, visited by a divine messenger with a prophetic warning, evokes the feel of a dream vision. A marginal mark indicates that a large initial was to appear at the head of this stanza. The same mark appears beside completed initials on fols. 15r and 16r.

57   *hye tokenyng*. The idea that God plants sacred signs in nature to betoken his impending judgment recurs elsewhere in Audelay's *The Counsel of Conscience*; compare *Visiting the Sick and Consoling the Needy*, line 218, and *On the World's Folly*, lines 25–36. Later in *Audelay's Epilogue to The Counsel of Conscience* these signs are taken as the signs of Doomsday foretold in Luke 17:24–30 (see lines 185–208).

105   *soulehele*. This term (also given in Latin, *Salus anime*) is the title applied to the Vernon Manuscript by its compiler (Doyle, "Shaping," p. 3). Pearsall, *Old English and Middle English Poetry*, takes its sense there to be "a comprehensive library of religious reading for every use" (p. 140), which is much like the aim of Audelay's *The Counsel of Conscience*. The term was widespread in devotional and literary use; see *MED soule-heil*, n., and *soule-hele*, n. Compare *Marcolf and Solomon*, lines 526, 798; *Virtues of the Mass*, line 3 (explanatory note); and *Audelay's Epilogue to The Counsel of Conscience*, lines 248–60 (explanatory note).

110–12   Variants of these lines also occur in *On the World's Folly*, lines 25–27, and *Ten Commandments*, lines 29–32.

115   Audelay reiterates this grouping of "word, will, deed, and thought" — the four "treasures" that we take with us when we die — two more times in *Audelay's Epilogue to The Counsel of Conscience*, at lines 146 and 281; twice in *Salutation to Saint Bridget*, at lines 35 and 38; *Chastity for Mary's Love*, line 7; *Virginity of Maids*, line 1; and *Dread of Death*, line 32.

146   On "word, will, deed, and thought," see the explanatory note to *Audelay's Epilogue to The Counsel of Conscience*, line 115.

154   Falling into sin through "frailty" is a formulaic thought for Audelay. Compare *Audelay's Epilogue to The Counsel of Conscience*, line 300; *Salutation to Jesus for Mary's Love*, line 71; *Song of the Magnificat*, line 77; and *Salutation to the Holy Face*, line 13.

155   *gren*. See *MED grin(e*, n.(b), "a trick, stratagem, deceit; temptation."

157–65   These lines repeat a stanza in *Visiting the Sick and Consoling the Needy*, lines 170–78. Line 158 is a formula that occurs in other contexts; compare *Visiting the Sick and Consoling the Needy*, line 207; *Pope John's Passion of Our Lord*, line 102; and *The Vision of Saint Paul*, line 332.

185–208   See explanatory note to *Audelay's Epilogue to The Counsel of Conscience*, line 57.

202–03   The incompleteness of these lines is peculiar. E. Whiting notes that they cannot be read because of an "imperfection in the parchment" (p. 139). The absent words would occupy the space where there is a sewn hole. Scribe A avoided the patched hole entirely when he wrote text on fol. 21va. However, when he had earlier arrived at this point on fol. 21rb, it appears that he left the lines incomplete. The lacuna may itself enact the terror of beholding the signs of Doomsday. Scribe B does not add any corrections, and there are signs of erasure to the right of the sewn hole.

218   This proverb is the burden for Audelay's *Seven Deadly Sins* (see explanatory note), and it also underlies *Marcolf and Solomon*, lines 42–43.

220–21   "Heaven or hell — it's your choice." Audelay repeats this idea later in the poem, at lines 398–99. On Audelay's discussions of free will elsewhere, see explanatory note to *True Living*, lines 203–07.

244–46   Audelay uses this formula in *True Living*, lines 156–59, and *The Remedy of Nine Virtues*, lines 73–75.

248–60   This stanza is the central one of *Audelay's Epilogue to The Counsel of Conscience*. It points to the orthodoxy that Audelay claims for himself and his writings (and especially, here, for the works contained in *The Counsel of Conscience*). It is intriguing that Audelay has used the concept of seeking *soulehele* (see explanatory note to line 105) to describe his endeavor, because that earlier vast compendium of "Sawlehele," the Vernon Manuscript, seems to have been likewise an effort to affirm the Church's true teachings against a rising Lollard threat (Blake, "Vernon Manuscript," pp. 58–59; Heffernan, "Orthodoxies' *Redux*," pp. 79–80). Audelay speaks elsewhere, especially in *Marcolf and Solomon*, lines 131–43, 669–88, of how different true belief is from Lollardy, and how dangerous it has become to speak out fervently in defense of authorized Church teachings. Hudson, *Premature Reformation*, characterizes Audelay's position here — that "enthusiasm for virtue" might be taken for Lollardy — as an "extreme" stance among early fifteenth-century clerical writers (pp. 22–23).

281   On "word, will, deed, and thought," see explanatory note to *Audelay's Epilogue to The Counsel of Conscience*, line 115.

300   On the formula of falling into sin through frailty, see explanatory note to *Audelay's Epilogue to The Counsel of Conscience*, line 154.

321   Jean Beleth, a twelfth-century Parisian doctor of divinity, was the author of *Rationale divinorum officiorum* (*PL* 202.1–166; see also Douteil, *Iohannis Beleth*). Orthodox English preachers of the fifteenth century frequently cited Beleth as an authority on Church ritual and liturgical observance; see, for example, *Speculum Sacerdotale* (Weatherly, pp. xxvii–xxx); and Wenzel, *Latin Sermon Collections*, pp. 61, 320.

352–55   On God speaking through Holy Writ, compare *Marcolf and Solomon*, lines 1–9 (explanatory note), 210–11. Audelay's rhetorical style, amply salted with Scripture, exemplifies this belief.

374–76   These lines occur in *Marcolf and Solomon*, lines 504–06.

381   Audelay uses the proverb about blind Bayard (a horse) "blustering forth" as a sign of someone's recklessness. The comparison here is to Audelay himself as blind prophetic poet. The proverb also occurs in *Marcolf and Solomon*, lines 952 (explanatory note) and 993.

381–85   These lines occur in *Marcolf and Solomon*, lines 952–56.

398–99   See explanatory note to *Audelay's Epilogue to The Counsel of Conscience*, lines 220–21.

417–18   *The Cownsel of Conseans . . . The Ladder of Heven*. Audelay names his "book" here. The makeup of MS Douce 302 indicates that this dual title refers to all the preceding matter, apparently, that is, everything contained on fols. 1r–22v, the first section of the manuscript. The colophon repeats this dual title.

478–79   On Audelay's notion that his illness constitutes an early purgatory, see the explanatory note to *Audelay's Epilogue to The Counsel of Conscience*, lines 14–26.

482–85   Lines 482–83 close the *chanson d'aventure* frame initiated at line 27, and they also refer directly to Audelay's daily existence in an abbey "here be west," that is, Haughmond Abbey, as identified in the *Finito libro* colophon. Audelay portrays himself as a sick man who, although bedridden, is often wakeful and stricken in conscience (i.e., lacking in "rest"). In this state he diligently and dolorously "makes" his book. Compare *Audelay's Conclusion*, lines 40–52. Line 484 appears in *Dread of Death*, line 43. Haberly uses these four lines to preface an illustrated woodcut edition (*Alia Cantalena de Sancta Maria by John Awdlay*) of Audelay's *Jesus Flower of Jesse's Tree*. Haberly's accompanying woodcut depicts the poet supine in his bed with a monk-scribe seated next to him, writing at a desk.

489–90   Citrome sees an emphasis on Christ's righteous vengeance (rather than mercy) in this passage; he also reads the passage as highly personalized to Audelay's situation as an ill old man (*Surgeon*, p. 97).

495–507   This stanza is another variant of Audelay's signature stanza. Compare *The Remedy of Nine Virtues*, lines 77–89; *Visiting the Sick and Consoling the Needy*, lines 378–90; *Our Lord's Epistle on Sunday*, lines 196–208; and *The Vision of Saint Paul*, lines 353–65.

499   *quoth*. It is possible that the word and meaning intended here is *cowth*, "am able to do"; compare the similar wordings of *The Remedy of Nine Virtues*, line 81; *Visiting the Sick and Consoling the Needy*, line 382; *Our Lord's Epistle on Sunday*, line 200; and *The Vision of Saint Paul*, line 357.

LATIN PROSE COLOPHON *FINITO LIBRO*   [W18]
[Fol. 22vb. **Hand:** Scribe B, in red. **Ornament:** The final word "Amen" is written on a banner, which is drawn around it. **Audelay Signature:** Written by Scribe B. **Edition:** Coxe, pp. 50–51; Halliwell, p. vi; E. Whiting, p. 149.]

Finito libro. Sit laus et gloria Christo. These words are a tag frequently written by scribes when the copying is done (Schaff, *Middle Ages*, p. 550); compare *Audelay's Conclusion*, line 39a.

Cuius anime propicietur Deus. Compare *Audelay's Conclusion*, explicit.

SALUTATIONS

XXVIII. DEVOTIONS TO JESUS AND MARY HIS MOTHER   [W19]
This four-part devotion consists of:

(1) An innovative salutation in honor of Mary, the five joys, and Christ's Incarnation;
(2) A prayer benediction recalling Doomsday;
(3) A prayer on the five joys;
(4) An instructional couplet advocating daily remembrance of the five joys.

The sequence opens with Mary's punning invitation to say "ave" and be without woe. After Scribe A copies the salutation, Scribe B copies the prayers and instructions that follow. Both prayers recall topics emphasized in the salutation, in layered form: Jesus and judgment at its nucleus; Mary and her joys in its frame. Anticipation of Doomsday and the longed-for sight of God's face unite this devotion with the closing salutation sequence to the Holy Face.

incipits   The two incipits are written in red by Scribe B on three lines. The first is a general opening and instruction to say "Ave." The second one (which occupies its own line) conveys Mary's words directly to the reader or spectator of her effigy. The salutation thus opens as a dialogue with Mary, who speaks first and actually requests the poem. Mary's words, moreover, contain a pun: "May they always be without woe (*sine ave*) who to me say 'Hail'" (*ave* = *a ve*, "without woe"); compare *Prayer on the Joys of the Virgin*, lines 11–12. I am indebted to Radd Ehrman for detecting the pun.

SALUTATION TO JESUS FOR MARY'S LOVE   [W19]
This opening salutation initially addresses Mary as Virgin Mother, and then it addresses Jesus as Redeemer. Direct access to Jesus is achieved gradually by means of worship of Mary and a contemplation of her five joys (lines 81–88). The poem itself mimics human mother-and-child form by embedding the anaphoric salutation to Jesus ("O Jhesu," lines 91–153) inside an anaphoric salutation to Mary ("Hayle," lines 1–90, 154–59). There are two different 2-line refrains: one for the Mary section and another for the Jesus section. Joined by meter — and by having one salutation nestled inside the other — the two parts of this poem operate as a single unit, the child enfolded in the mother. Citation of the five joys seems to cue a spiritual advance from Mary to her Son directly. Audelay's *Salutation to Jesus for Mary's Love* illustrates how fifteenth-century orthodox religion held that access to God was best achieved through the saints, a view challenged by Lollardy (Richmond, "Religion," pp. 188–90; Hudson, *Premature Reformation*, pp. 311–13).

[Fols. 22vb–23va. *IMEV*, *NIMEV* 1068 (listing this item as joined to the next three items). **Hands:** Scribe A, poem in black; Scribe B, incipits in red (see above). **Initials:** Large *H* in blue with red filigree (three lines high) and medium *O* in red (two lines high), with face drawn in it (at line 91). **Meter:** Sixteen 10-line stanzas, ababbcbcDD$_4$, with stanza 15 lacking its tenth line (see explanatory note to line 149). **Edition:** E. Whiting, pp. 149–54, 244.]

5–8	The salutation begins, appropriately, upon ideas of Jesus' miraculous conception in the womb.
18	*sowke.* The word puns subtly with *socur* in line 14 above, underscoring Mary's nurturing support. The idea of the sinner receiving divine succor, or grace, runs through the poem. Jesus will later be called "both solans and socour" (line 107) and one who can "sokore" the petitioner's soul (line 128).
24	*styyng.* For the sense "growing," see *MED stiing(e*, ger., where the usual sense is "ascending," but compare *stien*, v. 6(c), "increase."
33–34	The petitioner trembles as a sinner before Christ as Judge, the role of God that emerges forcefully in lines 141–54. There is also here a sense of approaching the mother to ask her to assuage the wrath of the Father.
54	*Maré Mawdlen.* An example of the saved sinner, which Audelay uses several times in *The Counsel of Conscience*. Compare *Visiting the Sick and Consoling the Needy*, line 145; *Seven Hours of the Cross*, line 35; and the Latin prose incipit *His dicit Dominus Deus* that concludes *The Vision of Saint Paul*.
56	*he me.* A verb may be left out; compare line 64, "He me save."
61	Compare *Salutation to Mary*, line 74.
62	*medicyn of al our syne.* See Citrome's discussion of Mary as female healer, where he cites this line and *Salutation to Mary*, line 101 (*Surgeon*, pp. 100–02, at 102).
71	On the formula of falling into sin through frailty, see explanatory note to *Audelay's Epilogue to The Counsel of Conscience*, line 154.
81–88	This stanza recounts the five joys of the Virgin, a subject repeated in the prayer-poem that follows. The subject provides the penitent's admittance to Jesus in line 91, "fore these joys v." For a survey discussion of Middle English lyrics to the Virgin and her joys, see Woolf, *English Religious Lyric*, pp. 274–308.
91	The embedded salutation to Jesus, with new refrain, begins here. The enlarged initial *O* is drawn in red and contains a face (denoting direct address to God; compare *Pope John's Passion of Our Lord*, line 89, and *Deus qui beatam Annam*, line 1). The salutation to Jesus is composed in lines that are tauter than the surrounding lines in address to Mary.
91–94	The syntax must be read as if the anaphoras — "O Jhesu" — are emotive exclamations interrupting the sentence, from which they are separate. The meaning here is: "For these Five Joys, which thy mother had of thee — she who was both virgin and wife — thus was none more honored than she."

98   The allusion to "thi tabernakil in heven toure" suggests Jesus being addressed in the womb. Such allusions continue in the next stanza.

107   On Jesus as *socour*, see explanatory notes to lines 18 and 128.

114   *Rewere*. The *MED* confirms that the meaning is "Merciful One" in reference to God (*reuer(e*, n.[a]), not "river," as glossed by E. Whiting.

128   *sokore*. This word culminates an intense appeal for mercy (lines 112–20), and then intense hope for salvation (lines 121–28), suggesting, with a play on the previous pun (line 18), that Jesus through his mother will be the penitent's own maternal nurturer. Bodily metaphors for spiritual transformation emerge in the next stanza (lines 134–38), and they culminate in the penitent's hoped-for re-"birth," which is termed a release from "secounde deth" (line 146).

131–34   Audelay understands the mystical tradition of inverted bodily metaphor: to cleanse his heart, he must both receive Christ within it and enter Christ's heart. Such metaphors of enclosing and being enclosed exploit and mix physical signs of gender, sexuality, pregnancy, and wounds, here in a poem that mimics in its very form the Incarnation in Mary's womb. For background on the tradition in Middle English, see my edition of *In a Valley of This Restless Mind* (Fein, *Moral Love Songs*, pp. 57–86) and McInerney's article on Julian of Norwich ("*In the Meydens Womb*").

146   *secounde deth*. See explanatory note to line 128.

149   The second refrain line, "O Jhesu, fore thi moder love, mayde Mary," is expected after this line, but the copyist (Scribe A) omits it. In compensation for the absent line, however, the c- and d-rhymes match, and the a-rhyme of the next stanza is also the same. Thus the omission of the final line about Mary may be meant to partake in a crescendoed approach toward Jesus, just before the salutation to Mary returns at lines 154–59.

150   The professed hope is for sight of God's Holy Face, as enacted at the climax of the salutation section of the Audelay manuscript (see *Salutation to the Holy Face*, and also *Seven Bleedings of Christ*, lines 67–72). In this line the penitent anticipates his own resurrection / rebirth, ascending from the earthly filth of sin (line 147) via Jesus and Virgin, who reemerges now as Queen of Heaven, Lady of the World, and Empress of Hell (lines 154–56).

151   *Domysday*. Doomsday provides a thematic frame that joins the poems on Christ in Audelay's salutations section. Compare *Salutation to the Holy Face*, line 24.

PRAYER RUBRIC   [W19]

This piece recalls the climactic scene of "dredful Domyday" in *Salutation to Jesus for Mary's Love*, line 151, in its prayer for mercy. Its second line anticipates the exact words that close the salutations section (*Salutation to the Holy Face*, line 24), thus pointing to Audelay's artistic construction of this whole section.

[Fol. 23va. Not in *IMEV*, *NIMEV* as a separate item (see 1068). **Hand:** Scribe B, poem in red. **Meter:** Two tetrameter couplets. E. Whiting mistakenly combines this item and the next two with the *Salutation to Jesus for Mary's Love*. **Edition:** E. Whiting, p. 154.]

2   *Graunt mercy tofore thy Jugement.* This phrase is common in Audelay's poetry. Compare *Our Lord's Epistle on Sunday*, lines 194–95, and *Salutation to the Holy Face*, lines 23–24 (the final English lines in the salutations section).

PRAYER ON THE JOYS OF THE VIRGIN   **[W19]**

This piece recalls the five joys of Mary (Nativity, Resurrection, Ascension, Assumption, Coronation), which *Salutation to Jesus for Mary's Love* has demonstrated to be an access point to direct contemplation of Jesus' divinity in incarnate form.

[Fol. 23va. Not in *IMEV*, *NIMEV* as a separate item (see 1068). **Hand:** Scribe B, poem in black with red initial. **Initial:** Medium *O* in red (two lines high). **Meter:** One 12-line stanza, ababbabaacac$_4$. **Edition:** E. Whiting, pp. 154–55.]

1   *O.* Whiting mistakenly attaches this capital to the preceding line. Because hand and meter change and a capital is inserted, it is altogether surprising that she mistook this prayer as part of *Salutation to Jesus for Mary's Love*. For other treatments of the five joys in MS Douce 302, see *Salutation to Jesus for Mary's Love*, lines 81–88, and (less overtly) *Joys of Mary*.

11–12   On deliverance from sorrow through Mary's five joys, compare Mary's words to the penitent at the opening of this sequence: "May they always be without woe who to me say 'ave.'"

INSTRUCTIONS FOR PRAYER 8   **[W19]**

This instructional couplet is a mnemonic tag found in various forms elsewhere in MS Douce 302. Compare *Instructions for Prayer 1*; *Prayer on Christ's Passion*, line 37; and *Seven Words of Christ on the Cross*, line 109.

[Fol. 23va. Not in *IMEV*, *NIMEV* as a separate item (see 1068). **Hand:** Scribe B, poem in red (as one cramped line). **Meter:** One tetrameter couplet. **Edition:** E. Whiting, p. 155.]

XXIX. OTHER DEVOTIONS TO MARY   **[W20–W21]**

Two salutations separated by E. Whiting are actually placed in sequence by the scribes. Both laud Mary in 12-line stanzas, though metrically they are quite distinct from each other. The first one, with "Haile" anaphora, has the medieval petitioner praise the Virgin as a way, ultimately, to petition her to be his "mayn-paroure" (line 118), that is, legal surety, on the Day of Judgment. The second one is a beautiful hymn of the Annunciation, in which Gabriel as proto-saluter addresses the Virgin with "Haile!"

SALUTATION TO MARY   **[W20]**

This Marian lyric reiterates the subject of the last salutation, but with more direct and sustained attention to the Virgin herself. Again, Audelay emphasizes Mary as virgin and mother. Employing a refrain and ornamental alliteration, the stanza form matches that of *Pearl* and many Vernon lyrics (Fein, "Twelve-Line Stanza Forms," pp. 382–97, especially p. 385). Moreover, the 12-line stanza was a frequently chosen medium for poems to the Virgin. Two other copies of this salutation are extant; Audelay's version is the oldest and longest. A 12-line Vernon lyric in eleven stanzas, with the refrain "Þow prey for vs to þi sone so fre" (Horstmann, *Minor Poems of the Vernon MS*, pp. 134–37), is similar in form, alliteration, and "Hail" anaphora, but not in phrasing or content. Similar phrases may, however, be found in Audelay's *Salutation to Jesus for Mary's Love*. On Middle English lyrics with anaphoric "haile," see Driver, "John Audelay and the Bridgettines," pp. 192–95, 209–10n4. Woolf, *English Religious Lyric*, pp. 274–308, discusses the Middle English tradition of lyrics to the Virgin (with little mention, however, of Audelay).

[Fols. 23va–24rb. *IMEV, Suppl., NIMEV* 1083 (compare *IMEV, NIMEV* 1041). **Hands:** Scribe A, poem in black; Scribe B, incipit and explicit in red. **Initial:** Medium *H* in blue with red filigree (two lines high). **Meter:** Ten 12-line anaphoric stanzas with a refrain, ababababbcbC$_4$ (i.e., the meter of *Pearl*), often with ornamental alliteration. **Seven-Stanza Variant:** Cambridge, CUL Ff.2.38, fols. 31v–32r (Person, *Cambridge Middle English Lyrics*, pp. 11–13 [no. 10]); Cambridge, Magdalene College MS Pepys 1584, fols. 102v–104r. **Edition:** E. Whiting, pp. 155–59, 244–45.]

1		*fond.* This word means "created, made"; see *MED founden*, v.(2) 4). E. Whiting glosses it mistakenly as the preterite of the verb *finden*, i.e., "found."

4		Compare the carols that associate Mary with the Tree of Jesse: *Saint Anne Mother of Mary*, lines 36–39, and *Jesus Flower of Jesse's Tree*.

23		The "haile" anaphora usually addresses Mary, but a few lines are directed to Christ, as here.

33		*norcheles.* See *MED norcheles*, n., where the only citation is this line from MS Douce 302: "one without a nurse or protector."

37–39		Compare *Salutation to Jesus for Mary's Love*, line 21.

46		*silour.* See *MED celure*, n., "canopy," where this line is the only example of a figurative usage, "shelter." Compare *An Honest Bed*, line 38.

50		*a, waiful wyght!* The punctuation is to make sense of the sudden shift to a singular noun after naming the guilty heretics.

78		This line refers to the sword of sorrow that pierced Mary's heart at the Crucifixion, derived from Luke 2:35 (Simeon's prophecy). It is a common feature of Marian piety.

80		*thi Breder.* I.e, Christ in his humanity. This line twists the usual formula that views the Virgin, paradoxically, as mother to her Father and spouse to her Son. Here she is Joseph's wife and spouse, and sister in flesh to Jesus.

89–95		These lines allude to the Harrowing of Hell, the freeing of the patriarchs in hell made possible by Christ's Incarnation in Mary's body. The stanza plays on a metaphor of jewels and their light (embodied in Mary, engendered in her) bringing about an illumination through Christ of the dark regions of hell.

98   Compare *Salutation to Jesus for Mary's Love*, line 2.

101   *medycyne that ale may mend*. See Citrome's discussion of Mary as female healer, where he cites this line and *Salutation to Jesus for Mary's Love*, line 62 (*Surgeon*, pp. 100–02, at p. 102).

106   Compare *Salutation to Jesus for Mary's Love*, line 98.

115–19   Like *Salutation to Jesus for Mary's Love* and *Salutation to the Holy Face*, this poem ends with contemplation of Doomsday.

118   *mayne-paroure*. The *MED* defines *main-pernour*, n.: "One who offers himself as surety that another (especially a prisoner to be released on bail) will fulfill his legal obligation to appear in a court when required." The spelling found in MS CUL Ff.2.38 is *maynpurnoure* (line 82; see Person, *Cambridge Middle English Lyrics*, p. 13).

GABRIEL'S SALUTATION TO THE VIRGIN   [W21]
Stevens, "*Angelus ad virginem*," analyzes Audelay's poem in relation to the Latin hymn. He notes how Audelay "omits the whole of Stanza 3 of the standard Latin version," taking instead a stanza unique to Oxford, Bodleian Library MS Digby 147 (p. 310).

Said to be composed by Gabriel, Audelay's poem begins in dramatic suspense, the reader made privy to the Annunciation in terms that speak delicately, almost erotically, of Mary. "Quakyng" upon Gabriel's entry, she is destined to become the gate of heaven (line 11). After Gabriel's salutation "Haile!" stanzas 1 and 2 portray the biblical dialogue (Luke 1:34–35). In stanza 3 Mary's womb increases for nine months, and, as soon as the Son emerges, he punishes "oure dedly foo" (line 36) in manly fashion, the Passion occurring virtually at once. Stanza 4 celebrates the central miracle — "A maydon to ber a barne!" (line 48). The final stanza conveys the sense of that joy to mankind, praying Mary to intercede for us, allowing us to be included "afftur thys owtlary" (line 60), thus realizing her maternal destiny as the gate of heaven for all mankind.

[Fol. 24rb–va. *IMEV, Suppl., NIMEV* 3305. **Hands:** Scribe A, first portion of poem in black (most of stanzas 1–3); Scribe B, remainder of poem in black (lines 36–60), and incipit and explicit in red. (The scribes rarely divide the task of redaction in this manner, but compare *Day of the Lord's Circumcision* and *Chastity for Mary's Love*.) **Initial:** Medium *T* in blue with red filigree (two lines high). **Meter:** An exquisite Annunciation hymn composed in five 12-line stanzas in an intricately modulated pattern, $a_4b_3a_4b_3cc_4dde_2f_{3-4}e_4f_3$, with occasional unevenness. The a-rhyme matches the f-rhyme in the third stanza. The meter is modeled on the Latin original, and was surely fitted to the same music (see Stevens, *Music and Poetry*, pp. 40–43, who sets stanzas 1, 3, and 5 to the tune). **Latin Source:** *Angelus ad Virginem* (Dearmer et al., *Oxford Book of Carols*, pp. 106–08 [no. 52]; compare Mone, *Lateinische Hymnen*, 2:55). **Middle English Analogue:** Brown, *English Lyrics of the XIIIth Century*, pp. 75–76 (no. 44). **Editions:** E. Whiting, pp. 159–60, 245–46; Saupe, pp. 47–48, 174–76. Both previous editors have combined lines 7–9 of each 12-line stanza (following the manuscript).]

1   In setting this line to the medieval music for *Angelus ad virginem*, Stevens, *Music and Poetry*, p. 40, elides a syllable: "Th'angel."

4–5   Compare *Mary Flower of Women*, line 13.

11   Rendering the poem in its musical setting, Stevens, *Music and Poetry*, p. 40,
            shortens the phrase *thee the* to *the* (= "thee").

21   In the manuscript this line is written alone, which E. Whiting calls a mistake, but
            it is an indication of the actual 12-line meter.

25   According to Stevens, *Music and Poetry*, p. 40, the musical meter elides a syllable:
            "Th'angel."

31   *outyed*. See *MED outyede*, v.(a), "went out, departed," though the examples
            provided there do not include instances of childbirth.

35   *knok*. Here indeed is a vigorous image of Christ's birth. The moment is fully
            conflated with the Passion. Emerging from the womb in battle mode, Jesus bears
            the cross on his bruised shoulders and delivers the Devil a sound blow. The
            energy of this startling conceit is somewhat like the violently compressed
            religious metaphors in *The Dispute between Mary and the Cross* (see Fein, *Moral
            Love Songs*, pp. 87–160, especially lines 1–13, 290, 508–15).

36   Scribe B copies this line and the final two stanzas.

41   *sydus sere*. For the definition "womb affording safety," see Putter, "Language and
            Metre," p. 509n51. Though the context confirms that Christ is blessing Mary's
            literal sides, the phrase suggests the idiom *on sydes sere*; see *MED ser(e*, adj.(2)(d),
            "entirely, all around, in all ways."

60   Compare *Saint Anne Mother of Mary*, line 58: "That he wyl affter this outleré,"
            and the analogous Latin burden of a carol found in MS Balliol 354: "*Mater, ora
            Filium / Vt post hoc exilium / Nobis donet gaudium / Beatorum omnium*" (Greene, *Early
            English Carols*, p. 119 [no. 178]).

XXX. Song of the Magnificat   [W22]

   This poem, a biblical paraphrase, is Mary's salutation to her Son and Lord. Its place-
ment by Audelay after Gabriel's salutation continues the narration of events from Luke 1.
Moreover, as a salutation voiced by the Virgin herself, it completes a laudatory "conversation"
on Mary in this sequence of praise-poems initiated at Mary's own request (see incipit to
Salutation to Jesus for Mary's Love). Other Middle English paraphrases of the *Song of the
Magnificat* are by James Ryman (Greene, *Early English Carols*, p. 162 [no. 257]) and John
Lydgate (in *Life of Our Lady*, though sometimes copied separately; see *IMEV, NIMEV* 2574).

[Fols. 24va–25ra. *IMEV, Suppl., NIMEV* 2271 (erroneously listed as eight 13-line stanzas). **Hands:**
Scribe A, poem in black; Scribe B, incipit and explicit in red. **Initial:** Medium *M* in blue with red
filigree (two lines high). **Meter:** Thirteen 8-line stanzas with a Latin refrain, ababbcbC$_4$. **Edition:** E.
Whiting, pp. 161–64, 246.]

19   *you*. Compare Luke 1:48: "Because he hath regarded the humility of his
            handmaid; for behold from henceforth all generations shall call *me* blessed"
            (italics added). The text changes the pronoun from *me* to *you*, which may be
            scribal error. I have left the reading and punctuated so that Mary utters the

phrase as God's own regard and discourse, which seems the only way to interpret the pronoun *you*.

37   *here stat and here degré*. See the explanatory note to *True Living*, lines 130–33.

42   *sparpil*. See *MED sparplen*, v. "scatter, disperse."

49–56   This medieval exemplum is set anachronistically within Mary's speech, where it illustrates the biblical line on the mighty being cast down from their thrones; see Powell, "John Audelay and John Mirk," p. 101. On Robert of Sicily, the subject of a Middle English romance, see Hornstein, "*King Robert of Sicily*," especially p. 13n2; *MWME* 1:171–72 [115]; and E. Whiting, p. 246. Audelay seems to know the romance, or at least its legend of Robert's hearing the *Magnificat* sung and then questioning that God can put down the mighty and exalt the humble (Luke 1:52).

77   On the formula of falling into sin through frailty, see explanatory note to *Audelay's Epilogue to The Counsel of Conscience*, line 154.

91   *word of wordis*. "forever and ever, to all eternity." The *MED* provides many examples of this Middle English phrase deriving from translation of the Vulgate phrases "*in saeculum*," "*in saeculum saeculi*," "*in saecula saeculorum*"; see *world*, n.6(b). Audelay uses the phrase elsewhere in *Our Lord's Epistle on Sunday*, lines 99, 142, and *God's Address to Sinful Men*, line 259.

XXXI. SALUTATION TO SAINT BRIDGET   [W23]

A married mother of eight, Bridget of Sweden (c. 1303–73) was canonized as saint in 1391. Characterizing Audelay's salutation to her as "simultaneously heartfelt, eccentric in form, and full of obscure historical reference," Driver notes how it also provides "important witness" to the historical founding of the Bridgettine order in England ("John Audelay and the Bridgettines," p. 191). This establishment of the order at Syon Abbey was by royal decree of Henry V in 1415, and its founding built political as well as spiritual capital for the Lancastrian dynasty (Warren, *Spiritual Economies*, pp. 118–30; Catto, "Religious Change under Henry V," pp. 110–11; B. Morris, *St. Birgitta of Sweden*, p. 171). Audelay formally compliments "[o]ur gracious Kyng Herré the V" for this deed (lines 136–48). On the unusual metrics of this piece, see the explanatory note to *Salutation to Saint Winifred*. Audelay composed these two salutations in the same verse form.

[Fols. 25ra–26rb. *IMEV, Suppl., NIMEV* 1058. *MWME* 9:3123. **Hands:** Scribe A, poem in black; Scribe B, incipit in red. **Initial:** Large *H* in blue with red filigree (three lines high). **Audelay Signature:** Line 202 (Scribe A). **Meter:** Twenty-three alliterative 9-line stanzas, abab$_{4\text{-}5}$c$_{2\text{-}3}$ddd$_{3\text{-}4}$c$_{2\text{-}3}$ (compare *Salutation to Saint Winifred* and *Marcolf and Solomon*). **Middle English Prose Life of Bridget:** "The Lyfe of Seynt Birgette" (Blunt, *Myroure of Oure Ladye*, pp. xlvii–lix). **Editions:** Cumming, pp. xxxi–xxxvii; E. Whiting, pp. 164–71, 246–47.]

10–18   Bridget's status as "wedow, wyfe, and may" elevates her to a state similar to Mary's triune mystical essence (mother, wife, and maiden). The reference here to Mary's appearance before Bridget stems from *The Revelations of Saint Birgitta* (see, e.g., Cumming, pp. 106–07). Mary's early appearance in Audelay's poem offers transition from the preceding group of salutations and prayers featuring praise of the Virgin. On the curiosity of Bridget's postmaternal virginity, see Driver, "John Audelay and the Bridgettines," pp. 191, 195–99.

22   This line resembles *Marcolf and Solomon*, lines 280 and 316.

35   On "word, will, deed, and thought," repeated in line 38, see explanatory note to *Audelay's Epilogue to The Counsel of Conscience*, line 115.

57   *Pope Urban.* "Pope Urban V confirmed the Rule of St. Bridget's congregation in 1370" (E. Whiting, p. 246). See also Cumming, p. xxvi.

63   *playn remyssion.* A theological term for complete remission of sin, though Audelay seems to use the adj. *plein* for Anglo-French *plener.* See *MED plenere*, adj.(b), and *remissioun*, n. 2. *plenere* ∼, "full forgiveness of sin; also, remission of punishment (by an indulgence)."

74   *mendist.* This is the verb *minden*, "to mention" (*MED minden*, v.), not *menden*, "to amend, improve," as emended by Whiting.

84   *gemfulli. MED* glosses "gemfulli" here to mean "in a caring manner."

136   *Chene.* "Sheen (Richmond), in Surrey, the royal manor at which Queen Anne of Bohemia died. After her death Richard [II] destroyed the house but Henry V rebuilt it and founded there the Carthusian house of Sheen" (E. Whiting, p. 246). On the influence of Saint Bridget in England, see Cumming, pp. xxix–xxxix.

136–49   This passage on the founding of Syon Abbey in 1415 honors Henry V for his piety and military prowess on behalf of the nation and reminds Audelay's readers to pray for the soul of the king who founded the convent within his manor of Isleworth on the Thames, opposite Sheen. On the political importance of Henry V's foundation of Syon, see Warren, *Spiritual Economies*, pp. 111–33. Compare, too, lines 195–97 on Henry VI. For a possible Syon connection elsewhere in MS Douce 302, see the explanatory note for *An Honest Bed*.

140–43   The Vincula Indulgence (in commemoration of Saint Peter's freedom from prison) was given on Lammas Day (August 1), a festival associated with harvest and the collection of rents. Driver notes the interesting connection between this detail and the book of Margery Kempe: "The Lammas Day pardon given by the Bridgettines to pilgrims to Syon is known to modern scholars mainly because Margery Kempe famously visited Sheen in about 1434, 'three days before Lammas Day to purchase her pardon through the mercy of the Lord'" ("John Audelay and the Bridgettines," p. 206).

145   *ihold.* This reading agrees with E. Whiting; alternatively, one might read, as does Cumming, *I hold*, "I maintain."

154–71   These stanzas recount some regulations of the rule of Saint Bridget (modified from the Augustinian rule). See further Aungier, *History and Antiquities of Syon Monastery*, pp. 249–409.

163   See *MED unethes*, adv.2a.

182   *obey obedyans.* See explanatory note to *Marcolf and Solomon*, line 32.

195–97   These three lines invoke a communal prayer for young King Henry VI's safety.

XXXII. DEVOTIONS TO SAINT WINIFRED   [W24–W25]

This sequence is part of a broad series of salutations that venerate female saints (Mary, Bridget, Winifred, Anne, and Veronica) for their virginity or chastity, and the miraculous healing powers associated with their sanctity.

The sequence of devotions to Winifred consists of:

(1)   A salutation to Winifred in carol form (the only carol outside the carols section of the manuscript);

(2)   A second salutation, in an alliterative meter that matches *Salutation to Saint Bridget*;

(3)   A Latin verse prayer;

(4)   A Latin prose prayer.

The seventh-century Welsh Saint Winifred was, for Audelay, a local saint, her relics having been transferred from Wales to Shrewsbury (four miles north of Haughmond Abbey) in 1138. Holywell was the site of her miraculous spring and a popular destination for pilgrims. It is interesting to note that Saint Winifred's effigy stands among those carved in the outside arches of the chapter house at Haughmond Abbey. She is there depicted with her foot upon the head of Prince Caradoc, the king's son who attacked her for her chastity. On the presence of an extended devotion to this saint in MS Douce 302, Melissa Jones, "Swete May, Soulis Leche," p. 3, notes that "Audelay, consistently fervid about matters of faith throughout his poetry, expresses an authentic appreciation for Winifred's chastity and healing powers, and the double treatment of her legend indicates the intensity of his devotion." Winifred's status and popularity were heightened in 1415 when her feast day was made binding throughout England (Duffy, *Stripping of the Altars*, p. 44; compare p. 163).

SAINT WINIFRED CAROL   [W24]

The way the scribes share the copying of this carol is different from the pattern found in the carol sequence. There Scribe A always copies the burden, and Scribe B later inserts a title. The *Saint Winifred Carol* does not receive a title, but Audelay does name its genre, and it does have carol form. Its length may suggest that it was not meant to be sung; Audelay refers to it as being read (line 176).

Audelay's hagiographic carol combines all three types of the genre: *vita*, *passio*, and *miraculum*. It recounts how the young virgin fled from Prince Caradoc, who, catching hold of her, violently decapitated her. This murderous attempt (for it was ultimately unsuccessful) initiated a host of miracles at the crime scene when a well sprang up from dry land. Several miracles are enumerated, including how Winifred's life was preserved: her uncle Saint Beuno reset her head on her neck so that only an attractive pearl-like necklace of white skin remained (lines 23–28); henceforth, according to tradition, her name changed from Brewafour to Winifred, "white thread." For other treatments of Winifred in MS Douce 302, see *Salutation to Saint Winifred* and *Chastity for Mary's Love*, line 19.

[Fol. 26rb–vb. *IMEV*, *NIMEV* 413. *MWME* 6:1992 [317]. **Hands:** Scribe A, poem in black; Scribe B, burden in red. **Initial:** Small *A* in red (1.5 lines high). **Audelay Signature:** Line 120 (Scribe A). **Meter:** Thirty 6-line stanzas, aaab₃₋₄BB₄, with 2-line tetrameter burden. The same 6-line stanza form appears frequently in Audelay's carol sequence, though none of his carols there matches this one in length. **Other English Lives of Winifred:** John Mirk, *Festial*, "De Solempnitate Sancte Wenefrede" (Erbe, pp. 177–82); William Caxton, *The Golden Legend* (Ellis, 6:127–32). **Editions:** E. Whiting, pp. 171–75, 247–48; Greene, *Early English Carols*, pp. 191–93, 420–21 (no. 314).]

16   *dry valay.* The dryness of the valley precedes the coming of the miraculous spring. Greene cites a parallel passage in prior Robert of Shrewsbury's Latin legend of Winifred: "*Locus vero ubi sanguis illius effusus est primitus sicca vallis dicebatur*" (*Early English Carols*, p. 421). See Robert of Shrewsbury, *Admirable Life*, pp. 58–59.

23–28 The name Winifred means "white thread,'" a reference to this visible sign of her passion. The 1635 translation of Robert of Shrewsbury's legend by recusant I. F. recounts the story thus: "And when the people had cryed with great deuotion, *Amen* vnto [Beuno's] prayer, the Virgin as newly wakened from sleep, wiped her eyes & face, besmeared with sweat and dust before, as hauing tumbled on the ground, filling all present, and her Parents there amongst them, with joy and admiration; observing also, as they more fixedly beheld her, a pure white circle, no bigger then a small threed, to remayne in her faire Necke, shewing the place where it had ben cut off before, and was miraculously then to her body conioyned; which because it euer afterwards remayned conspicuously seene after the same manner, *Brewa*, her name before, is said to haue ben changed by the peoples great veneration, and loue towards her, into *Wenefride* by *Wen*, which doth signify *white* in the old British tongue" (Robert of Shrewsbury, *Admirable Life*, pp. 56–57).

49–60 The first miracle described by Audelay is of a child swept away in a river who wondrously escapes harm from the millwheel. This account is the first record of a local Holywell tradition associated with Winifred. A similar miracle was recorded in 1608. There a joiner's four-year-old daughter escaped injury after dangerously falling into the river flowing from the well and being swept under the millwheel. Her mother and Thomas the miller served as witnesses, and Thomas further affirmed that "he knew five other children, that in the same manner had been violently carried under the sayd wheele and had no harme at all thereby" (De Smedt, "Documenta de S. Wenefreda," p. 318). E. Whiting, pp. 247–48, notes that an analogous story appears in the life of Thomas à Becket.

61–66 The second miracle is somewhat sketchy. Melissa Jones, "Swete May, Soulis Leche," p. 3, offers this understanding: "a man drops a groat down Winifred's well and recovers it later, apparently in a different well." As Greene, *Early English Carols*, p. 420, notes, some miracles recounted by Audelay are otherwise unknown and probably based "on tradition local to Shrewsbury rather than on a particular written source."

67–96 Melissa Jones, "Swete May, Soulis Leche," p. 3, explains the third miracle as follows: "Winifred's well suddenly and mysteriously ceases to flow when a quantity of wine is stored in her chapel. The water begins to flow again when the wine, which turns out to be poisoned, is cast into the street, and a man taken ill by drinking it is miraculously cured." Like the incident of the lost groat, this story survives only in Audelay's narrative.

93   *plumys*. Greene, *Early English Carols*, and E. Whiting both gloss this word "pumps,"
            but that meaning seems contrary to the workings of a natural well. The meaning
            is "plumes," with an image of the well waters shooting up as feathery spray.
            Winifred's well is a metonym for her head; she communicates by means of its
            miraculous waters. *Hedus bere* means, therefore, "head's gesture." See *MED bere*,
            n.(9)(b), "bearing, gesture, manner."

157–60   Greene, *Early English Carols*, p. 421, observes that "There may be a reference
            here to the natural gratification of Shrewsbury people at the order of 1391 for
            the feast of St. Winifred to be observed throughout the province of Canterbury."

165   *soulis leche*. Melissa Jones, "Swete May, Soulis Leche," p. 5, suggests that
            Audelay's devotion to Winifred may be, in part, a personal appeal from the
            afflicted chaplain to her miraculous healing capacities

169–74   This stanza is adapted and repeated in *Saint Francis*, lines 67–70.

172   *pray*. E. Whiting's emendation to *fray* is unnecessary and changes the sense
            (Greene, *Early English Carols*, p. 421). The phrase *Fyndis pray* occurs in Audelay's
            Day of the Lord's Circumcision, line 8. For *Fyndis fray*, see *Salutation to Jesus for
            Mary's Love*, line 68, and *Saint Francis*, line 51.

176   *Redis this carol*. Greene, *Early English Carols*, p. 420, comments: "The use of
            'Redis' instead of 'Singis' in the last stanza might be taken to show recognition
            by Audelay that he was in this case writing a literary narrative instead of a lyric
            to be sung. But the word is similarly used in [Audelay's *Saint Francis*], and the
            rhyming of the fourth line of each stanza with the burden leaves no doubt that
            the piece is intended as a true carol"; see also Copley, "John Audelay's Carols
            and Music," pp. 211–12. Compare *Saint Francis*, lines 73–78.

SALUTATION TO SAINT WINIFRED   [W25]

As a salutation to Winifred, this piece is a companion to the preceding carol. Metrically,
however, it belongs with *Salutation to Saint Bridget*. Both employ heteromorphic alliterative
meter in the long lines and a "Haile" anaphora. The alliteration is sometimes irregular, with
aa/bb alliterative patterns permitted, as in much stanzaic alliterative verse (see, e.g., *The Four
Leaves of the Truelove* [Fein, *Moral Love Songs*, pp. 171–73]). The stanza is a 9-line variant of
that used (in thirteen lines) by Audelay in *Marcolf and Solomon* and *Over-Hippers and Skippers*.
The chief differences rest in the absence of one long-line quatrain and the presence of the
anaphora. The chaplain may have been familiar with a late fourteenth-century practice of
composing saints' hymns in 14-line alliterative stanzas (compare the hymns to Saints
Katherine, John the Evangelist, and John the Baptist [Ruth Kennedy, ed., *Three Alliterative
Saints' Hymns*]; two of these hymns employ anaphora).

[Fol. 26vb–27rb. *IMEV, NIMEV* 1084. **Hands:** Scribe A, poem in black; Scribe B, incipit and explicit
in red. **Initial:** Medium *H* in blue with red filigree (two lines high). **Meter:** Seven alliterative 9-line
stanzas, abab$_{4\text{-}5}$c$_{2\text{-}3}$ddd$_{3\text{-}4}$c$_{2\text{-}3}$ (compare *Salutation to Saint Bridget* and *Marcolf and Solomon*). **Edition:** E.
Whiting, pp. 175–78, 248.]

30   *chere*. E. Whiting notes that this verb is a preterite with final *d* omitted.

33   *servys*. E. Whiting notes the use here of the present tense for the preterite (and provides other manuscript examples).

56   *Grownder*. This word recurs in a similar context in *Seven Gifts of the Holy Ghost*, line 11, and the *MED* cites Audelay for its earliest known usage. See *grounder*, n., "originator; basis, origin."

LATIN VERSE PRAYER *VIRGO PIA WYNFRYDA*   [W25]

[Fol. 27rb. **Hands:** Scribe A, poem in black; Scribe B, incipit in red. **Initials:** Black initial letters of each line marked in red. **Edition:** E. Whiting, p. 178.]

LATIN PROSE PRAYER *DEUS QUI BEATUM VIRGINEM TUAM WENFRYDAM*   [W25]

This prayer emphasizes the saint's miraculous restoration to bodily wholeness, which pertains to her power to heal others.

[Fol. 27rb. **Hands:** Scribe A, incipit (*Oremus*) and poem in black; Scribe B, incipit (*collecte*) in red. There is a blue paraph before the word *Oremus*. **Initial:** Medium *D* in red (two lines high), with quatrefoil drawn inside it. Each letter of the final *A. M. E. N.* is marked in red. **Edition:** E. Whiting, p. 178.]

XXXIII. DEVOTIONS TO SAINT ANNE   [W26]

This sequence consists of an English verse salutation and a Latin prose prayer. Audelay emphasizes in both parts the miracle of Saint Anne's fruitful womb, which gave birth to Mary after a long period of barrenness. As with Saint Winifred, Audelay composed both a salutation and a carol in honor of Saint Anne, mother of Mary; see *Saint Anne Mother of Mary* in the next section.

SALUTATION TO SAINT ANNE   [W26]

Woolf, *English Religious Lyric*, p. 296, calls Audelay's style in this *gaude* poem "a pleasing example of how well limpid simplicity of style can carry complexities of story or thought." In its use of the imagery of the Tree of Jesse, it links with Audelay's two carols that play upon that theme, *Saint Anne Mother of Mary* and *Jesus Flower of Jesse's Tree*. The wondrous quality of Saint Anne's unexpected fertility, leading to the birth of Mary and later the Messiah, contributes to a conceptual thread of miraculous healing that runs through the salutations. For references to other Middle English treatments of Saint Anne, see Parker, *Middle English Stanzaic Versions*, pp. x–xi. On the legend of Saint Anne, see Jacobus de Voragine, *The Golden Legend* (trans. Ryan, 2:149–58). Useful modern studies of the cult of Saint Anne include Duffy, *Stripping of the Altars*, pp. 181–83; Ronan, *S. Anne*; Ashley and Sheingorn, *Interpreting Cultural Symbols*; and Nixon, *Mary's Mother*.

[Fol. 27rb. *IMEV, NIMEV* 894. **Hands:** Scribe A, poem in black; Scribe B, incipit in red. **Initial:** Medium *G* in blue with red filigree (two lines high). **Meter:** Six septenary 4-line stanzas, abab$_7$, with Latin anaphoras "*Gaude, felix Anna*" (line 1) and "*Gaude*" (lines 2–4). **Edition:** E. Whiting, pp. 178–79, 248.]

4   *frelé Food*. A common phrase for a noble child or baby. See *MED freli*, adj.1(a), and *fode*, n.(2) 1. (a). Many examples refer to the Christ Child.

5–8   Compare *Saint Anne Mother of Mary*, lines 36–38, and *Jesus Flower of Jesse's Tree*, lines 3–4. The development of Mary as a branch of Jesse features in those two carols and in *Salutation to Mary*, line 4. On Anne's iconographic place in this tradition, see Sheingorn, "Appropriating the Holy Kinship," pp. 170–71, and Sautman, "Saint Anne in Folk Tradition," p. 85. On the Tree of Jesse tradition in general, see Watson, *Early Iconography of the Tree of Jesse*.

9–12   The consonance of the rhyme words in these lines resembles the style found in *Paternoster* and *Three Dead Kings*. According to Putter, "Language and Metre," p. 514, Audelay's effort here — compared to the pyrotechnics of those poems — is "mere child's play."

13–16   On Anne's long period of barrenness, compare *Saint Anne Mother of Mary*, lines 15–18.

14   *clene*. Woolf, *Early English Lyric*, p. 296, comments: "The precise meaning of 'clene' is not plain: it could refer either to the legend that St. Anne miraculously conceived at the moment when she and Joachim embraced at the Golden Gate or, more probably, to the less fanciful belief, that Mary, being begotten at God's command in the passionless quiet of old age, was born without any taint of lust. Whatever the interpretation, the verse shows the purity of the Virgin reflected in the chaste circumstances of her conception and her pre-eminence emphasized by supernatural intervention in the natural course of procreation."

LATIN PROSE PRAYER *DEUS QUI BEATAM ANNAM*   **[W26]**
[Fol. 27rb–va. **Hands:** Scribe A, long incipit and prayer in black; Scribe B, word *collecte*, in red. **Initials:** Medium *D* in red (two spaces high), with face drawn inside it. In the long incipit the black letters *O* (*Ore*), *q* (*quia*), and *O* (*Oremus*) are marked in red. **Edition:** E. Whiting, p. 179.]

1   Red initial *D* has a face drawn inside it, as elsewhere when a prayer opens with an address to God. Compare *Pope John's Passion of Our Lord*, line 89, and *Salutation to Jesus for Mary's Love*, line 91.

XXXIIII. MEDITATION ON THE HOLY FACE   **[W27]**
This sequence consists of:

(1)   Latin prose instructions, which identify the salutation as carrying an indulgence from Rome, granted by Pope Boniface IV and designed to be said twenty days in a row;
(2)   A drawing of Christ's Face on the Veronica Shroud, a visual meditative site to accompany the verbal exercise;
(3)   A salutation to the Holy Face;
(4)   A closing prayer in Latin prose.

The sequence of salutations brings one to this point of climax, as if rehearsing the much-anticipated sight of God's holy face on Doomsday itself. The overarching devotional logic possesses an aesthetic wholeness: from God incarnate in Mary's womb (*Salutation to Jesus for Mary's Love*) to God upon the sudary of Veronica. In each, God is imaged in human form and made accessible by the mediation of female sanctity. Thus God's miraculous Incarnation is experienced as real and translatable into spiritual grace for the sinner. In a climate of Lollard challenges regarding prayer to saints, a greater turn toward Christocentric piety led orthodox believers to use figures of the body of Christ — the Veronica, for example — as a means to approach God (Richmond, "Religion," pp. 188–90; Hudson, *Premature Reformation*, pp. 311–13; Pollard, *Late Medieval England*, pp. 218–19).

LATIN INSTRUCTIONS *QUICUMQUE HANC SALUTACIONEM* [W27]
[Fol. 27va. **Hands:** Scribe B, in red. **Edition:** E. Whiting, p. 179.]

incipit   *Bonefacia papa.* The incipit explains that the salutation carries an indulgence authorized by Boniface IV, pope from 608 to 615.

SALUTATION TO THE HOLY FACE [W27]
The drawing resembles one of a series commonly found on indulgence rolls, with lyrics to go with each illustration (the *Arma Christi*; *NIMEV* 2577), as reproduced in R. Morris, *Legends of the Holy Rood*, pp. 170–93, especially pp. 170–71. Sometimes the lyrics migrated into manuscripts, but their primary medium was probably the pocket-size velum roll; compare London, BL MSS Addit. 22029 and Addit. 32006 (both rolls) with London, BL MS Royal 17 A.27, fol. 80r–v, and MS Addit. 11748, fols. 144v–157r (both manuscripts, the latter one lacking the illustrations). A poem often appended to the *Arma Christi* explains that viewing this image of the Vernicle will grant pardon (*NIMEV* 1370; R. Morris, pp. 194–96, lines 216–18; see also the alternate ending printed on p. 192). On the *Arma Christi* rolls, see Robbins, "'Arma Christi' Rolls"; Gray, "Middle English Illustrated Poem," pp. 187–89; and A. Nichols, "O Vernicle." For a provocative essay on the tradition in general, see Hirsh, *Boundaries of Faith*, pp. 124–49, especially pp. 129–36. Elsewhere, Audelay uses the tradition in *Seven Bleedings of Christ*, an indulgence prayer-poem.

[**Drawing:** Fol. 27va. **Hand:** The drawing, in black ink, with mouth colored red, was probably made by Scribe B. The red ink matches the Latin instructions copied immediately above. This drawing does not appear in E. Whiting's edition. **Salutation:** Fol. 27va. *IMEV, NIMEV* 3073. **Hand:** Scribe A, in black. **Initial:** A black *D* in the explicit (*Dedisti*) is marked in red. **Meter:** Four 6-line stanzas, aa₇b₃aa₇b₃, with Latin anaphora "*Salve*" marking the first and fourth lines. Even though the scribe has marked every three lines with paraphs, the rhymes indicate 6-line stanzas. **Edition:** E. Whiting, pp. 179–80, 248 (poem printed in 3-line stanzas).]

5   *Veroneca.* On the legend of Veronica, which stresses the healing power of the cloth and its image, see Jacobus de Voragine, *The Golden Legend* (trans. Ryan, 1:212). Compare too Audelay's *Seven Bleedings of Christ*, lines 67–72 (another prayer indulgence). Citrome discusses the perceived healing power of Veronica's veil, which features in *The Siege of Jerusalem* and many charms (*Surgeon*, pp. 64–65). On the popularity of the Vernicle in English medieval devotions, see Duffy, *Marking the Hours*, pp. 14–15, 28, 54. A bas-de-page scene of Veronica receiving the image of Christ on her veil (perhaps the earliest example in England) appears in the Carew-Poynz Hours (Fitzwilliam Museum MS 48, fol. 75; reproduced by Binski and Panayotova, *Cambridge Illuminations*, p. 195). I am indebted to Ann Nichols for this reference.

13   On the formula of falling into sin through frailty, see explanatory note to
            Audelay's Epilogue to The Counsel of Conscience, line 154.

22   *nuye grimsli*. "Harm grimly." See *MED grimsli*, adv., where this line is the only
            passage cited.

LATIN PROSE PRAYER *DEUS QUI NOBIS SIGNATUM VULTIS* [W27]

[Fol. 27va. **Hands:** Scribe A, incipit (*Oremus*) and prayer in black; Scribe B, incipit (*collecte*), in red.
Initials: Medium initial *D* in red (two lines high), with quatrefoil drawn inside it. The black *O* in the
incipit is marked in red. **Other MS:** Boulogne-sur-Mer, Bibliothèque Municipale MS 93, fol. 6v (Scott,
Later Gothic Manuscripts, vol. 1, fig. 24). **Edition:** E. Whiting, p. 180.]

CAROLS

XXXV. CAROL SEQUENCE [W28–W52]

Audelay's carol sequence possesses an apparent order by number (twenty-five) and
arrangement by topic: the articles of faith; the feasts of the Church; support of king (Henry
VI) and the social order; veneration of the Holy Family (Anne, Mary, Christ, all of whom
branch from the Tree of Jesse); and then a celebration of virginity, chastity, and love of
God; a holy fear of death; and, lastly, honor to Saint Francis, the promoter of vernacular
Christian song. Although the manuscript does not contain music, the carols were likely
meant to be sung, with the possible exception of the longer ones, such as *King Henry VI* and
Saint Francis (Copley, "John Audelay's Carols and Music," pp. 211–12). The sequence has
received recent critical treatment by Boffey, "Audelay's Carol Collection," and Reichl,
"Middle English Carol," pp. 152–56, both of whom compare it to other collections in
manuscripts. Audelay's is the earliest such collection. The carol sequence may be a principal
reason that the manuscript migrated into the hands of a minstrel (Taylor, "Myth of the
Minstrel Manuscript," pp. 65–66).

INSTRUCTIONS FOR READING 3 [UNNUMBERED IN W]

[Fol. 27vb, upper margin. Not in *IMEV*, *NIMEV*. **Hand:** Scribe B, poem in red. **Meter:** One
tetrameter couplet. **Editions:** Coxe, p. 51; E. Whiting, p. 180.]

CAROL 1. TEN COMMANDMENTS [W28]

It is noteworthy that Carols 1–5 form a group centered on basic articles of faith (Ten
Commandments, Seven Deadly Sins, Seven Works of Mercy, Five Wits, and Seven Gifts of
the Holy Ghost). These carols are all composed in a 7-line stanza, and they are similar in
length: Carols 1–4 have five stanzas, and Carol 5 has six.

On Audelay's treatment of the Ten Commandments, Greene, *Early English Carols*, p.
428, was first to note that the chaplain "takes some liberties with the Commandments as
they were prescribed to be taught by the Synod of Lambeth (1281). . . . He introduces
Christ's injunction from Matthew xix.19. . . . He also omits the Ninth and Tenth Com-
mandments against covetousness and adds one of his own against backbiting." Audelay
repeats this formulation in *True Living*, lines 143–54, which is probably the earlier work,
especially as its verses also were also reused in Carols 3, 5, 13, and 22. On this subject of the
commandments, compare, too, *Virtues of the Mass*, lines 138–43. An unrelated Middle
English lyric on the Ten Commandments appears in the Vernon Manuscript; it has thirteen

8-line stanzas and the refrain "And kepe wel Cristes Comaundement" (Brown, *Religious Lyrics of the XIVth Century*, pp. 148–51 [no. 102], 278).

[Fol. 27vb. *IMEV, NIMEV* 304. *MWME* 6:1994 [327]. **Hands:** Scribe A, carol and burden in black; Scribe B, incipit in red. **Initial:** Medium *A* in blue with red filigree (2 lines high). **Meter:** Five 7-line stanzas, abab$_4$C$_2$CC$_4$, with 2-line tetrameter burden, introduced by tag-refrain "Leve ye me." **Editions:** Chambers and Sidgwick 1910, p. 479; E. Whiting, pp. 181, 249; Greene, *Early English Carols*, pp. 197–98, 428–29 (no. 324).]

burden	The saying is proverbial and homiletic. Compare Chaucer's Physician's Tale ("Forsaketh synne, er synne yow forsake" [*CT* VI(C) 286]) and Parson's Tale ("And therfore repentant folk, that stynte for to synne and forlete synne er that synne forlete hem, hooly chirche holdeth hem siker of hire savacioun" [*CT* X(I) 93]). For the proverb, see B. Whiting and Whiting, *Proverbs*, pp. 520–21 [S335].
1	*And.* This word, connected syntactically to the burden, tells us that the burden was sung first.
1–4	These lines are taken from *True Living*, lines 143–46.
2	Compare Matthew 19:19, where Jesus adds: "Thou shalt love thy neighbour as thyself." The Vernon lyric "Keep Well Christ's Commandments" also instructs: "And let þi neiȝhebor, frend and fo, / Riht frely of þi frendshupe fele" (Brown, *Religious Lyrics of the XIVth Century*, p. 149, lines 17–18).
8–10	These lines are taken from *True Living*, lines 147–49.
10	*Bacbyte.* The injunction against slander is added by Audelay. Bennett, "John Audelay: Life Records," p. 41, suggests that it comes in part from Audelay's personal experience, including his part in Lord LeStrange's public scandal. Backbiting is also added to the commandments in *True Living*, lines 149–50.
15–18	These lines are taken from *True Living*, lines 151–54.
22	A parallel to this line exists in a carol from MS Sloane 2593. See Greene, *Early English Carols*, p. 213 (no. 356, stanza 1, line 2).
29–32	Variants of these lines also occur in *On the World's Folly*, lines 25–27, and *Audelay's Epilogue to The Counsel of Conscience*, lines 110–12.

CAROL 2. SEVEN DEADLY SINS   **[W29]**

On Audelay's treatment elsewhere of the theme of the seven deadly sins, see *Seven Bleedings of Christ*, lines 19–60 (explanatory note); *Seven Words of Christ on the Cross*, lines 5–12; *Prayer of General Confession*, lines 5–8; and *Childhood*, lines 1–15. This carol is part of an internal series (Carols 1–5) on articles of the faith.

[Fols. 27vb–28ra. *IMEV, NIMEV* 858. *MWME* 6:1994 [328]. **Hands:** Scribe A, carol and burden in black; Scribe B, incipit in red. **Initial:** Large *I* in blue with red filigree (eight lines high, in margin). **Meter:** Five 7-line stanzas, abab$_4$C$_2$CC$_4$, with 2-line tetrameter burden, introduced by tag-refrain "I say thee so." (*NIMEV* mistakenly lists the meter as "five 4-line st. and 2-line burden.") **Other MS:**

Aberystwyth, NLW 334A, endleaf. **Editions:** Chambers and Sidgwick 1910, p. 480; E. Whiting, pp. 182, 249; Greene, *Early English Carols*, pp. 198, 429 (no. 325).]

burden   *In wele beware ore thou be woo.* This proverb is also found in Audelay's *Marcolf and Solomon*, lines 42–43 (with an echo of it also at line 949), and in *Audelay's Epilogue to The Counsel of Conscience*, line 218. A Middle English lyric in fourteen 8-line stanzas uses this proverb as its refrain ("Eche man be war, er hym be wo"). It appears in Oxford, Bodl. Lib. MS Digby 102, fols. 113r–114r (Kail, *Twenty-Six Political and Other Poems*, pp. 60–64). See Greene, *Early English Carols*, p. 429, for other literary occurrences of the proverb.

CAROL 3. SEVEN WORKS OF MERCY   [W30]

   Seven Works of Mercy reveals Audelay's method of recasting earlier compositions in different meters and for different contexts. Nearly the entire carol is crafted from *True Living*, lines 173–85, 238–63, and (less directly) *God's Address to Sinful Men*, lines 164–71, 197–220. Audelay also mined material from *True Living* when he composed Carols 1, 5, 13, and 22. On the poet's treatment of the seven works of mercy, Greene, *Early English Carols*, p. 429, comments: "Audelay is again somewhat original . . . and deviates slightly from the list formulated by the Synod of Lambeth. He seems to have in mind the seven 'corporal' works, but of these he omits to mention the ransoming of the captive and the visiting of the sick. The injunction to 'teach the unwise' he takes over from the list of 'spiritual' works."

   Scribe B seems to have wanted to delete the tag-refrain line 5 of each stanza, but he missed line 26. With the fifth line retained (as here), the meter conforms to that found in many Audelay carols, and it matches, in particular, the others on the articles of belief (Carols 1–5). If the fifth line were deleted, the stanza would be unique among Audelay's carols.

   On the importance of the seven works of mercy as a codified teaching for pious behavior in late medieval England, see Goldberg, *Medieval England*, pp. 230–31. Poems on the seven works of mercy have been printed from MS Lambeth 491 (Bülbring, pp. 388–89) and the Vernon Manuscript (Horstman, *Minor Poems of the Vernon MS*, pp. 34–35). Many more lyrics on the topic survive in manuscripts and remain unprinted (*IMEV*, p. 767, s.v. "Mercy, works of").

[Fol. 28ra. *IMEV, NIMEV* 792. *MWME* 6:1994 [329]. **Hands:** Scribe A, carol and burden in black; Scribe B, incipit in red. **Initial:** Medium *W* in red (two lines high). **Meter:** Five 7-line stanzas, abab$_4$C$_2$CC$_4$, with 2-line tetrameter burden, introduced by tag-refrain "I cownsel thee." **Editions:** Chambers and Sidgwick 1910, pp. 480–81; E. Whiting, pp. 183, 249; Greene, *Early English Carols*, pp. 198, 429 (no. 326).]

1–4   These lines appear in *True Living*, lines 173–76, and *God's Address to Sinful Men*, lines 164–66, 169–70.

8–11   A version of these lines appears in *True Living*, lines 177–79, and *God's Address to Sinful Men*, lines 167, 171, 173–74. The parallel for line 11 is found only in *God's Address to Sinful Men*.

15–18   See *True Living*, lines 238–41, and *God's Address to Sinful Men*, lines 197–200.

22–25   See *True Living*, lines 251–54, and *God's Address to Sinful Men*, lines 213–16.

24   *Let se.* The MS is difficult to read due to rubbing and fading. The reading here is supported by Audelay's identical lines at *True Living*, line 253, and *God's Address to Sinful Men*, line 215. Other editors' variants are therefore probably incorrect: *Loke* (Chambers and Sidgwick 1910, followed by Whiting) and *Loo, se* (Greene, *Early English Carols*).

29–32   See *True Living*, lines 255–58, and *God's Address to Sinful Men*, lines 217–20.

29   *wellay.* Greene's *well ay* gives a different interpretation of the same MS reading, but it is not supported by the parallel reading *weleway* in *True Living*, line 255; compare *God's Address to Sinful Men*, line 217.

31   This line voices the complaint of the poor against the rich, as will be uttered on Doomsday. Greene, *Early English Carols*, punctuates line 29 as the beginning of the quote, but he neglects to punctuate the end of the quote. Whiting does not indicate a speech here by means of quotation marks.

CAROL 4. FIVE WITS   [W31]

This subject is addressed elsewhere in MS Douce 302 at *Prayer of General Confession*, lines 10–16 (explanatory note). A poem on the five wits appears in MS Lambeth 491 (Bülbring, "Handscrift Nr. 491," p. 388) and also speaks in the imperative, but it bears no further likeness to Audelay's carol (Greene, *Early English Carols*, p. 429). Another lyric survives in the Vernon Manuscript (Horstmann, *Minor Poems of the Vernon MS*, p. 35). For a few others that remain unprinted, see *IMEV*, p. 784, s.v. "Wits, five bodily."

[Fol. 28ra–b. *IMEV*, *NIMEV* 3346. *MWME* 6:1995 [331]. **Hands:** Scribe A, carol and burden in black; Scribe B, incipit in red. **Initial:** Medium *T* in red (two lines high). **Meter:** Five 7-line stanzas, abab₄C₂CC₄, with 2-line tetrameter burden, introduced by tag-refrain "Lest thou be chent." **Editions:** Chambers and Sidgwick 1910, pp. 481–82; E. Whiting, pp. 184, 249; Greene, *Early English Carols*, pp. 199, 429–30 (no. 328).]

9   *fre choys and fre wil.* On the topic of free will in Audelay's works, see the explanatory note to *True Living*, lines 203–07.

32   This line is a proverb; see B. Whiting and Whiting, *Proverbs*, pp. 395–96 [M454]; and Greene, *Early English Carols*, pp. 429–30.

CAROL 5. SEVEN GIFTS OF THE HOLY GHOST   [W32]

Three stanzas of this carol are borrowed directly from Audelay's *True Living*, a poem in 13-line stanzas. The chaplain also mined material from this apparently earlier work for Carols 1, 3, 13, and 22. Greene, *Early English Carols*, p. 429, comments: "Audelay's formulation of the Seven Gifts differs from that of other literature on the subject. The traditional gifts are those enumerated in Isaiah xi. 2, 3. . . . Audelay's 'mind' can be identified with 'intellectus' and 'resun' with 'consilium', but the others he has taken from the Cardinal Virtues. . . . He has certainly confused his theology." A poem on the same subject appears in the Vernon Manuscript (Horstmann, *Minor Poems of the Vernon MS*, p. 34; Patterson, *Middle English Penitential Lyrics*, p. 128 [no. 51]).

[Fol. 28rb. *IMEV, NIMEV* 2173. *MWME* 6:1995 [330]. **Hands:** Scribe A, carol and burden in black; Scribe B, incipit in red. **Initial:** Medium *G* in red (two lines high). **Meter:** Six 7-line stanzas, abab₄C₂CC₄, with 2-line tetrameter burden, introduced by tag-refrain "Ellis were we lost." **Editions:** Chambers and Sidgwick 1910, pp. 482–83; E. Whiting, pp. 185–86, 249–50; Greene, *Early English Carols*, pp. 198–99, 429 (no. 327).]

burden   Compare the opening of the Vernon lyric, "God þat art of mihtes most, / Þe seuen ʒiftus of the holigost / I preye þat þou ʒiue me" (Horstmann, *Minor Poems of the Vernon MS*, p. 34, lines 1–3).

11   *grownder*. Compare *Salutation to Saint Winifred*, line 56, and the explanatory note to that line.

22–25   These lines derive from *True Living*, lines 212–15.

29–32   These lines derive from *True Living*, lines 225–28.

30   *Soule*. The emendation of MS *oule* to *Soule* is based on *True Living*, line 226. Previous editors read *onle*.

36–38   These lines derive from *True Living*, lines 229–31.

38   On Audelay's frequent citation of the Golden Rule, see the explanatory note to *True Living*, line 231.

CAROL 6. DAY OF THE NATIVITY   [W33]
      This carol of convivial Yuletide joy and welcome begins a new internal group of five carols (Carols 6–10) that follows the Church calendar of observance for December 25 to December 29. The same sequence occurs for sermons in Mirk's *Festial* (Erbe, pp. 21–44) and *Speculum sacerdotale* (Weatherly, pp. 5–18), where the next topics are Circumcision and Epiphany (compare Carols 11 and 15). The existence of a closely related carol in Sloane 2593 causes Greene, *Early English Carols*, p. 344, to posit a prototype carol behind both and to deduce that "Audelay's original authorship of the carol is doubtful." Carols 6–10 are all written in 6-line stanzas. Of these, only this one (probably known from a familiar model) has a refrain at the fourth line.

[Fol. 28rb–va. *IMEV, Suppl., NIMEV* 3877. *MWME* 6:1945-46 [6]. **Hands:** Scribe A, carol and burden in black; Scribe B, incipit in red. **Initial:** Medium *W* in red (2 lines high). **Meter:** Five 6-line stanzas, aaaBBB₄, with 2-line tetrameter burden and introductory refrain line "Welcum, Yole, forever and ay." **Other MS:** London, BL MS Sloane 2593, fol. 32r (15th cent.): five 6-line stanzas, aaa₄B₂BB₄ (Greene, *Early English Carols*, pp. 4, 343–44 [no. 7B]). **Editions:** Sandys, *Christmastide*, pp. 218–19; Chambers and Sidgwick 1910, p. 483; E. Whiting, pp. 186–87, 250; Greene, *Selection of English Carols*, pp. 55–56, 187 (no. 2); Greene, *Early English Carols*, pp. 3–4, 343–44 (no. 7A).]

7–9   These lines are not present in the Sloane carol.

13–15   By naming these saints, Audelay invokes the sequence of feast days that immediately follow Christmas Day: Saint Stephen's Day (December 26); Saint John's Day (December 27); Holy Innocents Day (December 28) and Saint Thomas of Canterbury's Day (December 29). This sequence also marks the subject matter of Carols 6–10. Compare the second stanza of the related carol in MS Sloane 2593.

20   Greene provides a useful note on the "alternative ways of regarding the Christmas season" embodied in this carol and the one in MS Sloane 2593 (*Early English Carols*, p. 344). Audelay's poem celebrates the twelve days to Epiphany (January 6; see Carol 15), while the Sloane poem celebrates the forty days to the Purification, extending the welcome to Candlemas.

CAROL 7. DAY OF SAINT STEPHEN [W34]

In the sequence of Carols 6–10, this one celebrates the Day of Saint Stephen, December 26. The grouping of the martyrdoms of Stephen, John the Evangelist, and the Holy Innocents follows Church tradition. In *The Golden Legend*, it is explained that these three exemplify "all the different classes of martyrs, associating them closely with the birth of Christ, which was the cause of their martyrdom. For there are three kinds of martyrdom: the first is willed and endured, the second willed but not endured, the third endured without being willed. Saint Stephen is an example of the first, Saint John of the second, the Holy Innocents of the third" (Jacobus de Voragine, trans. Ryan, 1:49–50).

[Fol. 28va. *IMEV, NIMEV* 3057. *MWME* 6:1959 [95]. **Hands:** Scribe A, carol and burden in black; Scribe B, incipit in red. **Initial:** Medium *I* in red (two lines high). **Meter:** Five 6-line stanzas, aaabBB₄, with 2-line tetrameter burden. **Editions:** Chambers and Sidgwick 1910, pp. 483–84; E. Whiting, pp. 187, 250; Greene, *Early English Carols*, pp. 52, 364 (no. 97).]

1–21   The events follow the biblical account in Acts of Apostles 7:55–60. The story of Saint Stephen's martyrdom is also recounted by Jacobus de Voragine in *The Golden Legend* (trans. Ryan, 1:45–50), along with further legends about finding Stephen's relics and the miracles that attended that event (trans. Ryan, 2:40–44). Caxton's English *Golden Legend* contains these accounts as well (Ellis, 2:152–61, 4:165–72).

CAROL 8. DAY OF SAINT JOHN THE EVANGELIST [W35]

Saint John the Evangelist was the patron saint of Haughmond Abbey. His statue appears among others in the columns outside the chapter house, where he is depicted holding a palm branch and scroll and standing upon an eagle (his emblem). In the sequence of Carols 6–10, this one celebrates the Day of Saint John the Evangelist, December 27. Greene, *Early English Carols*, prints other carols dedicated to Saint John (nos. 103–06).

[Fol. 28va–b. *IMEV, NIMEV* 2929. *MWME* 6:1960 [100]. **Hands:** Scribe A, carol and burden in black; Scribe B, incipit in red. **Initial:** Large *I* in red (five lines high, in margin). **Meter:** Ten 6-line stanzas, aaabBB₄, with 2-line tetrameter burden. **Editions:** Chambers and Sidgwick 1910, pp. 484–85; E. Whiting, pp. 188–89, 250; Greene, *Early English Carols*, pp. 55, 365 (no. 102).]

1–4   From the account of the Last Supper, John 13:23: "Now there was leaning on Jesus' bosom one of his disciples, whom Jesus loved." On John as Jesus' most beloved disciple, see too Jacobus de Voragine, *The Golden Legend* (trans. Ryan, 1:50–55, especially p. 50; for Caxton's version, see Ellis, 2:161–76). On the martyrological significance of John the Evangelist, see the explanatory note to Carol 7.

7   *dere derling*. Compare *Seven Words of Christ on the Cross*, line 45.

7–16   These stanzas allude to and imaginatively expand on John 19:26–27, a passage
            frequently cited in Middle English narratives of the Passion; compare *Seven
            Words of Christ on the Cross*, lines 40–42, and *Seven Hours of the Cross*, lines 42–44.

46   The logic of human redemption gained through Christ's suffering — and
            enacted painfully and emotionally in Mary as well — is a feature of many
            dialogic lyrics between Mary and Christ, framed usually as lullabies or *planctus
            Mariae*. See, e.g., "Dialogue between Our Lady and Jesus on the Cross" (Brown,
            English Lyrics of the XIIIth Century, pp. 87–88 [no. 49]; and my discussion in
            MWME 11:4192–93 [20]).

CAROL 9. DAY OF THE HOLY INNOCENTS   **[W36]**
      In the sequence of Carols 6–10, this one celebrates the Day of the Holy Innocents,
December 28. Greene, *Selection of English Carols*, prints three other carols on this theme (nos.
109–12). On the martyrological grouping of Carols 7–9, see the explanatory note to *Day of
Saint Stephen*. The legend of the Holy Innocents is recounted in Jacobus de Voragine, *The
Golden Legend* (trans. Ryan, 1:56–59; for Caxton's version, see Ellis, 2:176–82). On the
literary and visual tradition of the Massacre of the Innocents, see Oosterwijk, "Long lullynge
haue I lorn!" especially p. 3.

[Fols. 28vb–29ra. *IMEV, Suppl., NIMEV* 601 (mistakenly called "nativity carol"). *MWME* 6:1961 [106].
Hands: Scribe A, carol and burden in black; Scribe B, incipit in red. **Initial:** Medium *W* in red (two
lines high). **Meter**: Six 6-line stanzas, aaabBB$_4$, with 2-line tetrameter burden. **Editions**: Chambers
and Sidgwick 1910, pp. 485–86; E. Whiting, pp. 189–90, 250; Greene, *Selection of English Carols*, pp.
79–80, 200 (no. 22); Greene, *Early English Carols*, pp. 58, 367–68 (no. 108).]

1–2   These lines appear in a carol fragment from Cambridge, Gonville and Caius
            College MS 383 (fifteenth century), printed by Greene, *Early English Carols*, p.
            292 (App., no. ii); variants appear in another carol (Greene, p. 73 [no. 125A,
            stanza 16]).

7   This passage is based on Matthew 2:16. According to Greene, *Early English
            Carols*, p. 367, "The tradition was that Herod was called to Rome directly after
            his interview with the Magi and was a year on the road each way. Hence, when
            he returned, he ordered the killing of all male children of two years and under."
            Compare Mirk's *Festial* (Erbe, p. 36).

13   "Audelay's figure of 140,000 as the number slain is not quite the customary one.
            The number was generally put in the Middle Ages at 144,000, in defiance of all
            historical possibility, by identifying the Innocents with the white-clad host of
            Revelation [Apocalypse] xiv. 3" (Greene, *Early English Carols*, pp. 367–68).
            Compare, too, the numbers of pains in hell in Audelay's *The Vision of Saint Paul*,
            line 317 (explanatory note).

34   Compare Apocalypse 14:4, of the redeemed on the Day of Judgment: "These are
            they who were not defiled with women: for they are virgins. These follow the

Lamb whithersoever he goeth. These were purchased from among men, the first fruits to God and to the Lamb."

Carol 10. Saint Thomas Archbishop of Canterbury [W37]

An effigy of Saint Thomas of Canterbury, with mitre and archbishop's cross-staff, stands between the arches of the chapter house in the remains of Haughmond Abbey. In the sequence of Carols 6–10, this one celebrates Saint Thomas's Day, December 29. For other carols on this theme, see Greene, *Early English Carols*, nos. 114, 115, 115.1, 116. Of Audelay's carol, he comments: "Audelay, as is natural for one so solicitous for the rights of the clerical orders, exaggerates somewhat the services of Thomas to the Church, and his exposition of the points at issue is hardly the historical one" (p. 369). Jacobus de Voragine's *Golden Legend* also places Thomas in liturgical sequence after Stephen, John the Evangelist, and the Holy Innocents (trans. Ryan, 1:59–62; for Caxton, see Ellis, *Golden Legend*, 2:182–97). For the liturgical office of Saint Thomas, see Reames, "Liturgical Offices." For mentions of Saint Thomas elsewhere in MS Douce 302, see *Marcolf and Solomon*, line 342 (explanatory note), and *Day of the Nativity*, line 15.

[Fol. 29ra. *IMEV, NIMEV* 838. *MWME* 6:1961–62 [110]. **Hands:** Scribe A, carol and burden in black; Scribe B, incipit in red. **Initial:** Large *I* in red (eight lines high, in margin). **Meter:** Five 6-line stanzas, aaabBB₄, with 2-line tetrameter burden. **Editions**: Chambers and Sidgwick 1910, pp. 486–87; E. Whiting, pp. 190–91, 251; Greene, *Early English Carols*, pp. 60, 368–69 (no. 113).]

burden   The MS reading *sers* is emended to *seris*, Audelay's usual two-syllable form, to maintain tetrameter.

1–3   The opening of this carol commemorates a blessed birth and martyrdom, connecting it to the openings of the preceding and succeeding carols, *Day of the Holy Innocents* and *Day of the Lord's Circumcision*. For the traditional significance of Tuesdays in Saint Thomas's life, see Greene, *Early English Carols*, pp. 368–69; and Reames, "Liturgical Offices," p. 592n34. In line 2 Audelay goes beyond tradition and fact: Thomas was ordained on a Saturday.

13–22   For historical background, see Greene, *Early English Carols*, p. 369.

26   *fyfté poyntis*. Though the number varies in the records, the received tradition on Thomas Becket was that he suffered martyrdom because he disputed numerous points decreed in a royal charter. Greene, *Early English Carols*, pp. 369–70, provides a full and helpful explanation of this crux (note to no. 114, stanza 9).

28   Compare a carol on Thomas found in Oxford, Bodl. Lib. MS. Eng. poet. e.1 (fifteenth century): "Hys moder be blyssyd that hym bar, / And also hys fader that hym begat" (Greene, *Early English Carols*, p. 61 [no. 115, stanza 2]).

Carol 11. Day of the Lord's Circumcision [W38]

This carol honors the Day of the Circumcision, January 1, so it carries forward the chronology of an internal group (Carols 6–10) that mark holy days December 25 to 29. One may compare the exposition of the Lord's Circumcision in *The Golden Legend* (trans. Ryan, 1:71–78), Mirk's *Festial* (Erbe, pp. 44–47), and *Speculum sacerdotale* (Weatherly, pp. 16–18).

Audelay's carol is the longest of the three versions of it that survive; the others possess
musical settings and four stanzas, each in different arrangements. The fifth stanza is unique
to MS Douce 302.

This lovely, innovative carol embeds the burden at lines 5–6 and then repeats it at lines
9–10. The repetitions at lines 5–6 are indicated by the words *ut supra*, or the first words of
the burden, or both (see textual notes). Three stanzas (2, 4, 5) vary the burden wording in
the fifth line, "Seche wonder tythyngis ye may here." E. Whiting prints the manuscript
version diplomatically and thus shows how the five stanzas there are uneven in length (8,
7, 8, 7, 8 lines) and vary in providing indications of where and how to repeat the burden.
Greene, *Early English Carols*, deduces a 9-line stanza, but to create this he must omit Scribe
A's line 6 (see also Copley, "Popular Fifteenth-Century Carol," pp. 387–89). Following the
indications of Scribes A and B, I am led to believe that the carol has 10-line stanzas (fifty
lines in total). It is evident that Scribe A's copy was defective, particularly for the third
stanza, and that Scribe B has made extensive correction. In this regard, one may compare
the shared scribal labor evident in *Gabriel's Salutation to the Virgin* and *Chastity for Mary's Love*.

Extrapolating from the musical settings in the other manuscripts, it seems probable that
stanzas were sung by a soloist, burden-refrains by a chorus, so that a joyous dialogue emerged
between a company and a "messenger"; see Greene's interesting note on the question of per-
formance (*Early English Carols*, p. 372), and see also Copley, "John Audelay's Carols and
Music," p. 209. Although Audelay's version is the most fully preserved text, Greene doubts
(perhaps unfairly) that Audelay composed this carol: "The spirited rhythm is so much
superior to Audelay's usual metres that his original authorship must be regarded as doubtful"
(*Early English Carols*, p. 372). This carol under the title "What Tidings?" — with lyrics
ascribed to Audelay — has been adapted for modern choral performance and recordings.

[Fol. 29ra–b. *IMEV, Suppl., NIMEV* 21 ("New Year carol"). *MWME* 3:843-44 [10], 6:1962 [115].
Hands: Scribe A, carol and burden in black; Scribe B, incipit in red. The carol has been heavily
corrected by Scribe B. **Initial:** Medium *W* in red (two lines high). **Meter:** Five 10-line stanzas,
ababCDcdCD$_4$. (*NIMEV* mistakenly lists the meter as "four 7-line st. and 2-line burden.") **Other MSS:**
Cambridge, TCC MS O.3.58, recto (fifteenth century): burden and stanzas 1, 3, 2, 4 (Greene, *Early
English Carols*, p. 63 [no. 117b]); Oxford, Bodl. Lib. MS Arch. Selden B.26, fols. 15v–16r (fifteenth
century): burden and stanzas 1, 2, 4, 3 (Dearmer et al., *Oxford Book of Carols*, pp. 78–79 [no. 40];
Greene, *Early English Carols*, p. 63 [no. 117c]). **Modern Choral Adaptations:** Stevens,"What Tidings
Bringest Thou?" *Mediaeval Carols*, pp. 8–9 (no. 11), 20 (no. 27); Hoddinott, "What Tidings?" **Sound
Recordings:** The Elizabethan Singers 1966; New York Pro Musica Antiqua 1978; Oxford Camerata
1993. **Editions:** Chambers and Sidgwick 1910, pp. 487–88; E. Whiting, pp. 191–93, 251; Greene,
Selection of English Carols, pp. 83–84, 204–05 (no. 25); Greene, *Early English Carols*, pp. 62–63, 372 (no.
117a). **Modernized Edition**: Sisam and Sisam, *Oxford Book of Medieval English Verse*, pp. 386–87 (no.
117a).]

6   Sense, meter, and the wording of other stanzas indicate that the original line at
           this point may have been "Of Cristis borth this New Eris Day." Greene, *Early
           English Carols*, omits this line (and lines 16, 26, 36, 46) to achieve a uniform 9-
           line meter of ababCcdCD$_4$.

8   This line appears to signify that the Devil may now attempt only to prey on
           sinning humans, but not assume they are damned. With the coming of Christ,
           mankind is now redeemable.

CAROL 12. KING HENRY VI [W39]

This carol comes twelfth of twenty-five, a position treated as the center of the sequence. A prominent and distinctive leaf-point in the foliage of the ornamental initial *A* seems designed to highlight the carol and signify Henry's sovereignty as important to Audelay's carol collection. Henry V died in France on August 31, 1422, when his son was yet an infant (born on December 6, 1421). Henry VI was crowned king of England at Westminster on November 6, 1429 (at age eight), and king of France in Paris, on December 16, 1431 (at age ten). Greene, *Early English Carols*, p. 475, suggests that "this circumstance excuses Audelay's devoting most of the carol to the exploits of the new king's father rather than to the virtues of the boy himself." Audelay's patriotic loyalty to the monarch emerges elsewhere, most notably in *Salutation to Saint Bridget*. In the *Chastity of Wives* carol, he laments a decline in England's noble bloodlines caused by female inconstancy. Useful discussion of this carol, with comparison to *The Agincourt Carol* (Robbins, *Historical Poems*, pp. 91–92 [no. 32]) and a Lydgate poem, appears in the essay by Hirsh, "Wo and werres"; see, too, McKenna, "Henry VI," pp. 154–55. On celebrations of Henry V's monarchy in fifteenth-century literature, see Dockray, *Henry V*, pp. 13–32, and Allmand, *Henry V*, especially p. 427. For accounts of Henry VI's years of minority (1422–37), see Pollard, *Late Medieval England*, pp. 92–115, and Wolffe, *Henry VI*, pp. 25–47. Griffiths, "Sense of Dynasty," details the vigorous sense of dynasty motivating regnal ambitions during this era.

[Fol. 29rb–va. *IMEV, Suppl., NIMEV* 822. *MWME* 6:2011 [437]. **Hands:** Scribe A, carol and burden in black; Scribe B, incipit in red. **Initial:** Medium *A* in red (two lines high), with trailing foliage that curves into a leaf pointing back at lines 1–4 of the poem. **Meter:** Sixteen 6-line stanzas, aaabBB$_4$, with 2-line tetrameter burden. **Editions:** Halliwell, pp. viii–x; Chambers and Sidgwick 1910, pp. 488–90; E. Whiting, pp. 193–95, 251–52; Robbins, *Historical Poems*, pp. 108–10 (no. 41); Greene, *Early English Carols*, pp. 258–59, 475–76 (no. 428); Hirsh, *Medieval Lyric*, pp. 195–99 (no. B9).]

13–15   Audelay's sequence of events is inaccurate. Henry V's marriage to Catherine of Valois (on June 2, 1420) was not an issue before his defeat of the French in 1419. The tennis ball incident occurred in 1415. See E. Whiting, p. 252, and Greene, *Early English Carols*, p. 476.

15   *hee*. As E. Whiting notes, p. 251, there is no antecedent for this pronoun, but it must be the Dauphin: "The Dauphin said that Henry's love for Katharine should not be."

19–22   Greene, *Early English Carols*, p. 476, comments: "The tennis-ball incident and its sequel of 'teaching the French the game' caught Audelay's imagination as it later did Shakespeare's." See also Dockray, *Henry V*, p. 53, and Allmand, *Henry V*, p. 427.

25   *Harflete*. The reference is to the town of Harfleur, taken by siege September 22, 1415, upon Henry V's landing in France in the summer. Compare *The Agincourt Carol*: "He sette a sege, þe sothe for to say, / To harflu tovne with ryal a-ray; / Þat tovne he wan & made a-fray" (Robbins, *Historical Poems*, p. 91).

33   *Agyncowrt*. I.e., the battle of Agincourt, on October 25, 1415 (on which, see Curry, *Agincourt*). Robbins, *Historical Poems*, provides a succinct summary of the events leading to this victory for the English (pp. 285–86) as well as a description

of the elaborate pageants that followed Henry V's triumphant return to London (pp. 296–97).

63–64   McKenna, "Henry VI," pp. 154–55, cites these lines as an instance of "congratulatory stanzas" evocative of domestic propaganda in celebration of Henry VI's dual coronation as king of England and of France. If this is so, it would date Audelay's carol sequence and the MS to after 1431. Robbins, *Historical Poems*, p. 108, dates Audelay's *King Henry VI* "1429."

73–76   Greene, *Early English Carols*, p. 476, comments: "Audelay's prophecy is given a tragic irony by the events of Henry VI's reign. The last stanza, however, shows that the poet recognized the possibilities of disaster facing the new sovereign."

CAROL 13. FOUR ESTATES   [W40]

The opening stanza of this carol borrows directly from Audelay's *True Living*, a poem in 13-line stanzas. Audelay also mined material from this apparently earlier work for Carols 1, 3, 5, and 22.

[Fol. 29va–b. *IMEV, Suppl., NIMEV* 1588. *MWME* 6:1997 [350]. **Hands:** Scribe A, carol and burden in black; Scribe B, incipit in red. **Initial:** Medium *H* in red (two lines high). **Meter:** Eight 7-line stanzas, abab$_4$C$_2$CC$_4$, with 2-line tetrameter burden, introduced by tag-refrain "I say, algate." **Editions:** Chambers and Sidgwick 1911, pp. 68–69; E. Whiting, pp. 195–97; Kaiser, *Medieval English*, p. 295; Greene, *Early English Carols*, pp. 209–10, 435–36 (no. 347). **Modernized Edition:** Davies, *Medieval English Lyrics*, pp. 171–73.]

1–4   On Audelay's staunch attitude on upholding one's station, see *True Living*, lines 130–33 (and explanatory note).

CAROL 14. CHILDHOOD   [W41]

Salter, *Fourteenth-Century English Poetry*, p. 17, praises this carol for its "warmth of feeling for the innocence of a child — an emotion more unusual in [Audelay's] age than we might think possible," and she astutely notes how that emotion is not "indulged," but rather "turned to useful account in his numerous Nativity lyrics" (compare *Jesus Flower of Jesse's Tree*, lines 42–44). Greene's praise is more muted: "The attitude of reverence for childhood expressed by Audelay in this carol is unusual . . . and has been deservedly praised. Nevertheless, the expression of it is rather stiff and conventional with its systematic introduction of the Deadly Sins and is more probably inspired by the words of Jesus . . . than by sympathetic association with real children" (*Early English Carols*, p. 459). The biblical passages referenced by Greene are Matthew 18:3 ("Amen I say to you, unless you be converted, and become as little children, you shall not enter into the kingdom of heaven") and Mark 10:15, Luke 18:17 ("Amen, I say to you: Whosoever shall not receive the kingdom of God as a child, shall not enter into it").

[Fols 29vb, 31ra. *IMEV, NIMEV* 840. *MWME* 6:2007 [417]. **Hands:** Scribe A, carol and burden in black; Scribe B, incipit in red. **Initial:** Medium *A* in red (two lines high). **Meter:** Eight 6-line stanzas, aaabBB$_4$, with 2-line tetrameter burden. **Editions:** Chambers and Sidgwick 1911, pp. 69–70; E. Whiting, pp. 197–98; Greene, *Early English Carols*, pp. 245, 459 (no. 412).]

1–15   On Audelay's treatment of the seven deadly sins, see explanatory note to *Seven Bleedings of Christ*, lines 19–60.

1–6   For a psychoanalytical reading of these lines, see Citrome, *Surgeon*, pp. 103–05, who comments that "metaphors [of childhood] act in concert with . . . supremely ambivalent experiences of parental power to strengthen the authority of the clergy" (p. 104).

10   *cheré stons.* Playing with cherry stones is here a sign of childish innocence, but John Lydgate's *Testament* portrays the same activity as a youthful waste of time and a turning from God: "My wyttes fyve in wast I did alle vse, / Redier cheristones for to telle / Than gon to chirche, or here the sacryng belle" (MacCracken, *Minor Poems of John Lydgate*, p. 353, lines 646–48). Greene, *Early English Carols*, p. 459, calls Audelay's detail "a pleasant touch."

16   *mystere.* "Necessity." See *MED mister*, n.5(a).

43–46   Citrome reads this passage as another instance of Audelay viewing his afflictions as an early purgatory (*Surgeon*, p. 103); compare the explanatory note to *Audelay's Epilogue to The Counsel of Conscience*, lines 14–26.

CAROL 15. DAY OF EPIPHANY [W42]

With a burden of "Nowel!" and evocations of the Christmas season, this lovely carol is composed for the Day of Epiphany, January 6. There survive two variant versions of Audelay's carol, both much shorter and possessing different 2-line burdens. In Audelay's poem the fourth line of each stanza is the opening of a different Latin hymn; several of these hymns are specific to Epiphany (lines 24, 29, 44) or to Christmas (lines 14, 49). These Latin lines are tabulated with their hymnal uses and their other carol occurrences by Greene, *Early English Carols*, pp. lxxxvi–lxxxviii. Appropriately, Audelay's version develops the story of the Three Magi; compare Jacobus de Voragine, *The Golden Legend* (trans. Ryan, 1:78–84) and *Speculum Sacerdotale* (Weatherly, pp. 18–21). The Sloane version treats the Magi story in only one stanza, and the even shorter Balliol version omits it.

[Fol. 31ra–b. *IMEV, Suppl., NIMEV* 3526 (compare *IMEV, NIMEV* 20). *MWME* 6:1963 [120]. **Hands:** Scribe A, carol and burden in black; Scribe B, incipit in red. **Initial:** Medium *N* in red (two lines high). **Meter:** Eleven 5-line macaronic stanzas, abab$_4$C$_3$, with a nonrhyming 1-line burden (a form unique among Audelay's carols). **Variants:** five stanzas, London, BL MS Sloane 2593, fol. 27v–28r (fifteenth century; Greene, *Early English Carols*, pp. 67–68 [no. 122B]); four stanzas, Balliol College Oxford MS 354, fol. 221v (sixteenth century; Greene, *Early English Carols*, p. 68 [no. 122C]). **Editions:** Chambers and Sidgwick 1911, pp. 70–71; E. Whiting, pp. 198–200, 252–53; Kaiser, *Medieval English*, p. 295 (stanzas 6, 10 omitted); Greene, *Early English Carols*, pp. 67, 376 (no. 122A).]

4   *Vene, Creatore Spiritus.* Hymn used for Whitsunday, Terce, and also the first words of the ordinary of the mass (Greene, *Early English Carols*, p. lxxxviii). For editions and commentary, see Daniel, *Thesaurus Hymnologicus*, 1:213–15; Dreves and Blume, *Analecta Hymnica Medii Aevi*, 2:93; Mone, *Lateinische Hymnen*, 1:241–42; Trench, *Sacred Latin Poetry*, pp. 186–88; and Walpole, *Early Latin Hymns*, pp. 373–76.

9   *Tu Trinetatis Unitas.* Hymn used for the Friday after Octave of Epiphany, Matins
            (Greene, *Early English Carols*, p. lxxxviii). For editions and commentary, see
            Daniel, *Thesaurus Hymnologicus*, 1:35–36; Dreves and Blume, *Analecta Hymnica
            Medii Aevi*, 2:33; Mone, *Lateinische Hymnen*, 1:379–80; and Walpole, *Early Latin
            Hymns*, pp. 272–73.

14   *Glorea in exelsis Deo.* This line derives from the biblical Nativity story (Luke 2:14)
            and is omitted from Greene's chart; see Daniel, *Thesaurus Hymnologicus*,
            2:267–75. Vulgate Luke 2:14 reads *gloria in altissimis Deo*; *exelsis* precedes the
            Vulgate in Greek liturgical forms of the *Gloria*. In music, it is the preferred form
            because of its rhythmical scansion.

19   *Iam lucis ortus sidere.* Hymn used for Advent, First Sunday, Prime (Greene, *Early
            English Carols*, p. lxxxvii). See Daniel, *Thesaurus Hymnologicus*, 1:56–57; Dreves
            and Blume, *Analecta Hymnica Medii Aevi*, 4:238; Mone, *Lateinische Hymnen*,
            1:177–78; and Walpole, *Early Latin Hymns*, pp. 293–94.

24   *Hostes Herodes impii.* Hymn used for Vigil of Epiphany, Vespers (Greene, *Early
            English Carols*, p. lxxxvii). See Daniel, *Thesaurus Hymnologicus*, 1:147–49.

29   *Deus Creator omnium.* Hymn used for First Sunday after Octave of Epiphany, I
            Vespers (Greene, *Early English Carols*, p. lxxxvi). See Daniel, *Thesaurus
            Hymnologicus*, 1:17–18; Mone, *Lateinische Hymnen*, 1:381–82; and Walpole, *Early
            Latin Hymns*, pp. 44–49. For the hymn translated to English, see Van Buren,
            Latin Hymns in English Verse, pp. 28–31.

34   *Jhesu Salvotor seculi.* Hymn used for (a) First Sunday after Easter, Compline, and
            (b) All Saints, I Vespers (Greene, *Early English Carols*, p. lxxxvii). See Daniel,
            Thesaurus Hymnologicus, 1:297–98, and compare Mone, *Lateinische Hymnen*,
            1:399–400, "*Jesu redemptor saeculi.*"

39   *Jhesu nostra Redempcio.* Hymn used for Vigil of Ascension, Compline (Greene,
            Early English Carols, p. lxxxvii). See Daniel, *Thesaurus Hymnologicus*, 1:63–64;
            Dreves and Blume, *Analecta Hymnica Medii Aevi*, 2:49; Mone, *Lateinische Hymnen*,
            1:230–31; and Walpole, *Early Latin Hymns*, pp. 364–65.

42   *Prest.* On this liturgical interpretation of the incense, and the word *prest* applied
            to Christ, see an analogous carol cited by Greene, *Early English Carols*, p. 354
            (no. 47), and his note on its fifth stanza: "The doctrine of Christ's priesthood
            concerns itself with the sacrificial aspect of His life and death and would be a
            natural reference for a writer who wished to emphasize . . . the human qualities
            of the Saviour."

44   *Magne Deus potencie.* Hymn used for Thursday after Octave of Epiphany, Vespers
            (Greene, *Early English Carols*, p. lxxxvii). See Daniel, *Thesaurus Hymnologicus*,
            1:61, and Dreves and Blume, *Analecta Hymnica Medii Aevi*, 2:32.

49   *Christe Redemptore omnium.* Hymn used for Christmas, Matins (Greene, *Early
            English Carols*, p. lxxxvi). See Dreves and Blume, *Thesaurus Hymnologicus*, 51:49,
            and Walpole, *Early Latin Hymns*, pp. 306–08. Compare Mone, *Lateinische Hymnen*,
            3:27, 3:496, and Daniel, *Thesaurus Hymnologicus*, 1:78–79, "*Iesu redemptor omnium.*"

54   *Salvator mundy Domine*. Hymn used for Advent, First Sunday (Greene, *Early
          English Carols*, p. lxxxviii). See Daniel, *Thesaurus Hymnologicus*, 4:209, and Mone,
          Lateinische Hymnen, 1:47–48.

CAROL 16. SAINT ANNE MOTHER OF MARY   [W43]

This carol may have been intended for singing on the day of Saint Anne (July 26) or at
Christmas. Audelay also composed a *gaude* poem to Anne, copied in the salutations section
of MS Douce 302. Woolf, *English Religious Lyric*, p. 297, praises this carol as "a Marian
variation of the Tree of Jesse," noting that "though the reference of the imagery is doctrinal,
it retains in Audelay's style some of the associations of natural imagery, the beauty of flowers
and perhaps even of the joy in their growth." She finds "a sense of delight in the poem" that
"the more formal and ornate style of Lydgate" lacks. In their shared Tree of Jesse theme, this
carol and the next are explicitly paired. Warren, *Spiritual Economies*, pp. 111–33 (especially
pp. 123–24), details the use of this image in nationalist discourse, called upon to serve
Henry V's "incarnational politics" (p. 123).

On Saint Anne in general, Greene, *Early English Carols*, p. 418, comments: "The fashion
of devotion to St. Anne and the formation of guilds in her honour was growing rapidly in
England at the time this carol was written down, her day having been made a feast of
obligation in 1382. The diocese of Hereford, which included southern Shropshire, though
not Haughmond itself, was particularly zealous in this devotion." For references to other
Middle English treatments of Saint Anne, see Parker, *Middle English Stanzaic Versions*, pp.
x–xi. On the legend of Saint Anne, see Jacobus de Voragine, *The Golden Legend* (trans. Ryan,
2:149–58). Useful modern studies of the cult of Saint Anne include Ronan, *S. Anne* (listing
sites of devotion in Hereford); Ashley and Sheingorn, *Interpreting Cultural Symbols*; and
Nixon, *Mary's Mother*.

[Fol. 31rb–va. *IMEV, NIMEV* 3244. *MWME* 6:1991 [313]. **Hands:** Scribe A, carol and burden in black;
Scribe B, incipit in red. **Initial:** Medium *T* in red (two lines high). **Meter:** Nine 7-line stanzas,
abab$_4$C$_2$CC$_4$, with 2-line tetrameter burden, introduced by tag-refrain "Herefore we/I say." **Editions:**
Chambers and Sidgwick 1911, pp. 71–73; E. Whiting, pp. 200–01, 253; Greene, *Early English Carols*,
pp. 189–90, 418 (no. 311).]

3   *oure soulis leche*. According to Citrome, an intensely personalized petition
          develops in Audelay's sequencing of material, which culminates in this plea to
          Mary's mother: "we can glimpse Audelay's despair at the unraveling of his illness
          narrative — his failure to find relief from his afflictions through either the
          healing properties of confession or the intercessory powers of Mary — in the
          pattern of spiraling pleas for mediation that have occurred throughout the
          anthology. Indeed, he has prayed for Christ to intercede with God, Mary to
          intercede with Christ, and then . . . for St. Anne to intercede with Mary"
          (*Surgeon*, p. 110).

15–18   On Saint Anne's long period of barrenness, compare *Salutation to Saint Anne*
          lines 13–16. The narrative of Mary's conception is "coloured by echoes of the
          Annunciation" (Woolf, *English Religious Lyric*, p. 297). Sautman describes the folk
          tradition of Saint Anne: "ancient figure of motherhood, . . . first mother in the

family of Christ, protector of women in childbed, the sterile tree who bore fruit in the autumn of her age" ("Saint Anne in Folk Tradition," p. 85).

24   For this wording, compare *Chastity of Wives*, line 22.

30–31   Compare *Jesus Flower of Jesse's Tree*, lines 7–8.

36–38   Compare *Jesus Flower of Jesse's Tree*, lines 3–4. The development of Mary as a branch of Jesse links this carol to the next one (as do lines 30–31). On Anne's iconographical place in this tradition, see Sheingorn, "Appropriating the Holy Kinship," pp. 170–71; and on the Tree of Jesse tradition in general, see Watson, *Early Iconography of the Tree of Jesse*. The dual exposition on Christ's human lineage and birth underscores what must be an intentional grouping of these carols. Compare also *Salutation to Saint Anne*, lines 5–8.

43–46   Analogous lines appear in an Annunciation poem: "Call him Jesu of Nazareth, / God and mon in on degree. / Right as mon schall suffur dethe / And regne in David dignite" (Chambers and Sidgwick, *Early English Lyrics*, p. 113, lines 33–36; see also Breul, "Zwei Mittelenglische Christmas Carols," pp. 401–02).

58   Compare *Gabriel's Salutation to the Virgin*, line 60: "Afftur thys owtlary." Greene, *Early English Carols*, p. 418, notes that this stanza translates, in part, the Latin burden of a carol found in MS Balliol 354: "*Mater, ora Filium / Vt post hoc exilium / Nobis donet gaudium / Beatorum omnium*" (no. 178 in his edition; and compare the burden of no. 195).

Carol 17. Jesus Flower of Jesse's Tree   [W44]

Despite the incipit, the central focus of this carol is Jesus, Mary's fruit. On Audelay's tendency to blend Marian and Christ-Child piety, compare *Salutation to Jesus for Mary's Love*, the first piece in the salutation section, which is also labeled (by Scribe B) a poem to the Virgin, but it addresses the Virgin and her joys in order to access Jesus. In both these poems one approaches Christ devotionally via his natural kinship to Mary. The Tree of Jesse motif describes Mary's conception in the preceding *Saint Anne Mother of Mary*, and now the image is in full bloom: the branch is Mary, the flower Christ. Woolf, *English Religious Lyric*, p. 287, cites this carol as a "charming" elaboration of "the standard tradition." Of the two surviving versions, Greene, *Early English Carols*, p. 394, comments that Audelay's is "better" and "seems to be the earlier." On the Tree of Jesse tradition in general, see Watson, *Early Iconography of the Tree of Jesse*. On its political use for the making of Lancastrian dynastic claims, see McKenna, "Henry VI," pp. 160–61, and Warren, *Spiritual Economies*, pp. 123–24. On the unknown musical setting of this carol, see Copley, "John Audelay's Carols and Music," pp. 210–11.

Of special note is Haberly's 1926 edition, a hand-produced art-volume limited to 450 copies and illustrated with seventeen woodcuts executed by Haberly in the style of William Morris. Haberly's art develops a visual theme of Mary and Jesus as the conjoined flower of salvation progressively unfurled in Christian narrative. The edition casts Audelay's carol as a devotional poem rather than a song.

[Fol. 31va–b. *IMEV, Suppl., NIMEV* 3603 (mistakenly called "carol to the Virgin Mary"). *MWME* 6:1974 [172]. **Hands:** Scribe A, carol and burden in black; Scribe B, incipit in red. **Initial:** Medium

T in red (two lines high). **Meter:** Seven 10-line stanzas, aaaa$_4$b$_2$bCC$_4$D$_2$D$_4$. **Other MS:** Balliol College, Oxford MS 354, fol. 220v (sixteenth century; Dyboski, *Songs, Carols*, p. 6; Flügel, "Liedersammlungen des XVI. Jahrhunderts," pp. 230–31; Greene, *Early English Carols*, pp. 115 [no. 172b]). **Editions:** Chambers and Sidgwick 1911, pp. 73–74; E. Whiting, pp. 202–03, 253; Greene, *Early English Carols*, pp. 115, 394 (no. 172a). **Modernized Editions:** Chambers and Sidgwick 1907, pp. 110–11, 350 (no. LVII); Rickert, *Ancient English Christmas Carols*, pp. 160–61; Haberly, *Alia Cantalena de Sancta Maria by John Awdlay*, pp. 3–17; Sitwell, *Atlantic Book of British and American Poetry*, pp. 8–9; Sisam and Sisam, *Oxford Book of Medieval English Verse*, pp. 388–89 (no. 158).]

burden   Compare *Saint Anne Mother of Mary*, lines 30–31.

3–4   Compare *Saint Anne Mother of Mary*, lines 36–38.

14   *medis*. Whiting's gloss of *medis* as "midst" is unlikely to be correct. From evidence in the *MED*, the word is probably *mede*, n.(4)2(b), "gift, reward," or, in this context, "in grace," with a light pun, suited to the carol's floral trope, on *mede*, n.(2)(a), i.e., "in Bethlehem meadows."

33   *sede* appears in the manuscript and corrects the reading *lede* given by all previous editors. See *MED sed*, n.3(b), "a race, line, stock; species, kind."

42–44   Salter, *Fourteenth-Century English Poetry*, p. 17, cites these lines to illustrate how Audelay's feelings for a child's innocence, which he expresses in *Childhood*, are "not indulged" but rather are "turned to useful account in his numerous Nativity lyrics."

46   *golde*. The word means "cold," although E. Whiting translates it "gold." The reference is to Christ's birth in winter, deploying the vegetative metaphor.

CAROL 18. JOYS OF MARY   [W45]
This carol can be compared to Audelay's treatment of the five joys of Mary in *Salutation to Jesus for Mary's Love*, lines 81–88, 91, and *Prayer on the Joys of the Virgin*. Woolf, *English Religious Lyric*, p. 297, asserts that "Audelay is the only fifteenth-century writer on the five joys, who, encouraged by the theme, is able to break through ornateness and formality" such as one finds in Lydgate, to reach true "affective meditation." Although Greene, *Early English Carols*, p. 403, considers original authorship by Audelay to be "doubtful," noting how the meter is unique among his carols, Woolf praises this carol for its "sweetness and gentle feeling typical of Audelay's poetry" and declares it the only "poetically pleasing" carol on the five joys theme (*English Religious Lyric*, p. 297). Numerous Middle English carols addressed to Mary are conveniently gathered in Greene's 1977 edition, with three others there that enumerate Mary's five joys (nos. 231, 232, 233). There is also a fine Harley lyric on the subject (Brook, *Harley Lyrics*, pp. 65–66; *MWME* 11:4200 [27]).

[Fols 31vb, 30ra. *IMEV, NIMEV* 895 (mistakenly listed as six stanzas). *MWME* 6:1981–82 [232]. **Hands:** Scribe A, carol and burden in black; Scribe B, incipit in red. **Initial:** Medium *A* in red (two lines high). **Meter:** Five 10-line macaronic stanzas, ababbcbcCC$_4$. Each stanza opens with the anaphora "*Gaude Maria*"; each has a Latin eighth line, drawn from a single Marian hymn (see explanatory note to line 8). **Other MS:** Balliol College, Oxford MS 354, fol. 219a (sixteenth century; Greene, *Early English Carols*, pp. 144–45, 403 [no. 230]). **Editions:** Chambers and Sidgwick 1911, pp. 74–75; E. Whiting, pp. 203–04, 253–54.]

2   *moder of thyn Emne*. The curiosity of Mary's kinship to God is the focus here.
           Mary is mother of her own Father, Husband, and Brother; compare *Salutation
           to Mary*, line 80: "Haile, thi Breder thou hast eborene." The manuscript word
           emne is strange, however, and editors have found it hard to construe. E. Whiting,
           p. 254, glosses *emne* as "equal," but the sense is poor, and the word *even* is not
           a noun, according to the *MED*. Greene, *Early English Carols*, p. 403, thinks that
           the word is "probably a scribal blunder which escaped the corrector's eye"; the
           rhyme calls for the word to end in *-ene*, and the parallel line in Balliol reads
           "Mary myld, of the I mene," a phrase that Greene adopts. The manuscript
           reading might be an error for *emane / emene*, from OE *gemana*; see *MED imone*,
           n.(1)(c), "a companion, mate." The word is not, however, recorded later than the
           fourteenth century.

8   E. Whiting, p. 254, first detected the hymnal source for the Latin eighth line of
           each stanza (Dreves and Blume, *Analecta Hymnica Medii Aevi*, 31:176; Mone,
           Lateinische Hymnen, 2:172). The English lines do not, however, translate this
           hymn on the five joys (Greene, *Early English Carols*, p. 403).

11–18   Woolf, *English Religious Lyric*, p. 297, cites this stanza and freely emends it, as
           follows: "Gaude Maria, yglent with grace, / Whan Jhesus thi Son on the was bore,
           / Full nygh thy brest thou gan him brace; / He sowked, he sighhed, he wepte full
           sore. / Thou fedest the flowr that never shall fade / With maydons mylke and
           songe therto, / 'Lulley, my swet, I bare the, babe, / Cum pudoris lilio.'"

45   The translation follows E. Whiting, p. 254.

CAROL 19. MARY FLOWER OF WOMEN   [W46]

   Many epithets for Mary in this carol may also be found in Audelay's *Salutation to Mary*,
which has the refrain "Hail, Blessed Fruit! Hail, Sweet Flower!"

[Fol. 30ra. *IMEV, NIMEV* 536 ("carol of the Virgin Mary"). *MWME* 6:1975–76 [177]. **Hands:** Scribe
A, carol and burden in black; Scribe B, incipit in red. **Initial:** Medium *H* in red (two lines high).
Meter: Five 6-line stanzas, aaabBB$_4$, with 2-line tetrameter burden. **Editions:** Chambers and Sidgwick
1911, pp. 75–76; E. Whiting, pp. 205, 254; Greene, *Early English Carols*, pp. 118, 395 (no. 177).]

13   Compare Audelay's *Gabriel's Salutation to the Virgin*, lines 4–36, dramatizing how
           the event of God's Incarnation and birth moves rapidly to an offensive strike
           against the Devil.

22   *treu as ston*. Audelay uses this proverbial simile in *Marcolf and Solomon*, line 59.

28   *hal*. MS: *bal*. I agree with Greene that the emendation is needed; he argues that
           E. Whiting's gloss of *bal*, "world, sphere," is not an attested medieval term for
           heaven (p. 395), and the evidence in the *MED* supports this position.

CAROL 20. CHASTITY FOR MARY'S LOVE   [W47]

   It is evident that a compiler (presumably Audelay) wanted this carol to appear at this
point in the manuscript, but he did not immediately have it at hand or in memory. Scribe
A inserted a portion of it (omitting the burden), and left lines blank (more than needed) to

accommodate the rest of its verses. Scribe B completed the job and inserted corrections (see textual notes). A similar division of labor in the body of a text occurs in *Gabriel's Salutation to the Virgin* and *Day of the Lord's Circumcision*. The carol is composed in Audelay's standard 6-line carol stanza. Despite the category assigned it by *NIMEV*, "carol of women," the chastity celebrated in the poem could be that of male religious — secular clergy and/or cloistered monks. The female martyr saints named in line 19 were venerated at Haughmond (see explanatory note), and line 27 seems more a generalization about female virgins than an injunction pointed towards real women.

[Fol. 30ra–b. *IMEV, Suppl., NIMEV* 535 ("carol of women"). *MWME* 6:2004 [401]. **Hands:** Scribe A, parts of the carol in black; Scribe B, incipit in red, burden and much of the carol in black. **Initial:** Medium *B* in red (two lines high), marking the first line instead of the burden. **Meter:** Six 6-line stanzas, aaabBB₄, with 2-line tetrameter burden. **Editions:** Chambers and Sidgwick, pp. 76–77; E. Whiting, pp. 206–07, 254; Greene, *Early English Carols*, pp. 234, 450–51 (no. 397).]

7   On "word, will, deed, and thought," see the explanatory note to *Audelay's Epilogue to The Counsel of Conscience*, line 115.

19   *Kateryn and Marget and Wynfred.* These female martyrs were all beheaded upon refusal to give up their virginity. They are honored in the architecture of Haughmond Abbey: their effigies stand among those still surviving between the outside archways to the chapter house. Catherine holds a wheel and sword, standing on the crown of the head of the Emperor Maxentius, who had her martyred; Margaret of Antioch stands on a dragon and pierces it with her cross; and Winifred (a local saint) stands on the head of her would-be murderer Caradoc. On the lives of Saints Katherine and Margaret, see Jacobus de Voragine, *The Golden Legend* (trans. Ryan, 2:334–41 and 2:232–33). Audelay honors Winifred in the salutations section of the manuscript, where she receives a *vita* in carol stanzas and a salutation-poem (*Saint Winifred Carol* and *Salutation to Saint Winifred*).

28   Compare this line to *Four Estates*, line 1, "In wat order or what degré," and see the explanatory note to *True Living*, lines 130–33.

Carol 21. Virginity of Maids   [W48]
Unlike the last carol, which treats the virtue of chastity in saintly and vocational terms, this carol points its message directly at secular unmarried women, preaching that they have a moral duty to preserve virginity before marriage. As Greene, *Early English Carols*, p. 451, comments of the pragmatic message in the last stanza: "Audelay's praise of the worldly value of chastity is consonant with his prudential attitude throughout." The carol belongs to a tradition of clerical counsel to women to maintain their virginity; see, e.g., Thomas of Hales' *Love Rune* (Fein, *Moral Love Songs*, pp. 11–56, with a bibliography of Middle English works on pp. 27–28).

[Fol. 30rb–va. *IMEV, Suppl., NIMEV* 1595 ("carol of women"). *MWME* 6:2004 [402]. **Hands:** Scribe A, carol and burden in black; Scribe B, incipit in red. **Initial:** Large *I* in red (seven lines high, in margin). **Meter:** Eight 6-line stanzas, aaabBB₄, with 2-line tetrameter burden. **Editions:** Chambers and Sidgwick 1911, pp. 77–78; E. Whiting, pp. 207–08, 254; Greene, *Early English Carols*, pp. 235, 451 (no. 398).]

burden   On Audelay's conservative attitude on upholding one's station, see the explanatory note to *True Living*, lines 130–33.

1   On "word, will, deed, and thought," see the explanatory note to *Audelay's Epilogue to The Counsel of Conscience*, line 115.

CAROL 22. CHASTITY OF WIVES [W49]

Greene, *Early English Carols*, entitles this carol *On the Decadence of Marriage*, noting how it and the preceding carol demonstrate Audelay's adherence to social rank and class-based mores. The sixth stanza expresses disgust for ladies who "wil take a page" for fleshly lust and courtly fashion, and the seventh sees England in decline as a result. For Audelay, such behavior by gentlewomen disgraces the upper classes and creates unlawful heirs, causing English nobility to waste away. Six of the seven stanzas of this carol borrow directly from two consecutive stanzas of Audelay's *True Living*. Audelay also revised material from this earlier work for Carols 1, 3, 5, and 13.

[Fol. 30va. *IMEV, Suppl., NIMEV* 1630 ("carol of marriage"). *MWME* 6:2007 [416]. **Hands:** Scribe A, carol and burden in black; Scribe B, incipit in red. **Initial:** Medium *A* in red (two lines high, with tail trailing down margin). **Meter:** Seven 7-line stanzas, abab$_4$C$_2$CC$_4$, with 2-line tetrameter burden, introduced by tag-refrain "All day thou seest." **Editions:** Chambers and Sidgwick 1911, pp. 78–79; E. Whiting, pp. 208–09, 254; Greene, *Early English Carols*, pp. 244–45, 459 (no. 411).]

burden   The phrase is proverbial. See Greene, *Early English Carols*, p. 459; E. Whiting, p. 254; Chambers and Sidgwick, 1911, p. 84; and *MED had-I-wist(e*, n.: "Regret for something done in heedlessness or ignorance; vain regret."

1–4   Stanza 1 is the only stanza of this carol not also found in *True Living*.

8–11   Stanza 2; compare *True Living*, lines 78–81.

15–18   Stanza 3; compare *True Living*, lines 82–85.

22–25   Stanza 4; compare *True Living*, lines 87–90. For line 25, Audelay has filled out a short line in a different meter by simply adding the word *unlaufully*.

29–32   Stanza 5; compare *True Living*, lines 91–94.

30   Compare *True Living*, line 92, and textual note.

31   Compare *True Living*, line 93, and textual note.

36–39   Stanza 6; compare *True Living*, lines 95–98.

43–46   Stanza 7; compare *True Living*, lines 99–103. The reference to "Englond" is an addition.

CAROL 23. LOVE OF GOD [W50]

In this carol Audelay displays something fairly rare in his verse, that is, a capacity for compressed wordplay of the type best known in the gnomic *Earth upon Earth* and its variants (*MWME* 11:4172 [1]). Here, the term *love* suffuses every line, where its meanings — religious and profane — are devotionally intertwined and meditated upon, to create, in the words of Hirsh, *Medieval Lyric*, p. 193, a "gentle reflection . . . upon what [Audelay] and many of his contemporaries would have regarded as the greatest of medieval themes, the love which exists between God and all of humankind." Salter, *Fourteenth-Century English Poetry*, p. 17, calls this carol "reminiscent of Herbert in balanced moods of reconciliation and praise," and uses it to note Audelay's finest trait: "The stability of his best verse, perfectly shaping emotion to the celebrative language of the Church, is, in its modest way, impressive." This carol about the love of God forms the logical culmination of an internal group of carols on chastity, virginity, and marriage (Carols 20–23).

[Fol. 30va–b. *IMEV, NIMEV* 831. *MWME* 6:1987 [272]. **Hands:** Scribe A, carol and burden in black; Scribe B, incipit in red. **Initial:** Large *I* in red (eight lines high, in margin). **Meter:** Five 7-line stanzas, $abab_4C_2CC_4$, with 2-line tetrameter burden, introduced by tag-refrain "I say, herefore." **Editions:** Chambers and Sidgwick 1911, p. 79; E. Whiting, p. 210; Greene, *Early English Carols*, pp. 170–71, 412 (no. 272); Hirsh, *Medieval Lyric*, pp. 193–94 (no. B8). **Modernized Edition:** Sisam and Sisam, *Oxford Book of Medieval English Verse*, pp. 390–91 (no. 159).]

CAROL 24. DREAD OF DEATH   [W51]

Dread of Death is the best-known carol of Audelay's collection — and the most praised. Greene, *Early English Carols*, p. 442, rates it "one of the most personal of all the carols [in Middle English]," with "its directness and apparent sincerity, as well as its tale of personal affliction," which sets "it apart from the more conventional laments on the 'Timor mortis' theme." Salter, *Fourteenth-Century English Poetry*, p. 17, lauds its fusion of personal and communal experience: "[Audelay's] personal situation — he was blind, deaf and ailing — is put at the service of the community: 'timor mortis' is, for him, a pressing theme . . . [b]ut it is made to yield consolation." Woolf ranks it with George Herbert's verse (*English Religious Lyric*, p. 7), naming it "[o]f the many *Timor mortis* poems by far the most moving. . . . In this, for perhaps the first time in an English lyric poem, the poet truly speaks in his own voice" (*English Religious Lyric*, p. 335; see also pp. 387–88). Comparing this carol to Lydgate's "A Prayer in Old Age" (MacCracken, *Minor Poems of John Lydgate*, pp. 20–21), Tristram, *Figures of Life and Death*, p. 222n12, finds both poets capable of a rare meditative tone of "present and personal experience." This carol belongs with *Audelay's Epilogue to The Counsel of Conscience* and *Audelay's Conclusion* as important clues in our understanding of Audelay's individuality and personality, as committed to verse. It contains lines shared with *Audelay's Epilogue to The Counsel of Conscience*, and like *Saint Francis*, it bears Audelay's name.

[Fols 30vb, 32ra. *IMEV, Suppl., NIMEV* 693. *MWME* 6:2000 [372]. **Hands:** Scribe A, carol and burden in black; Scribe B, incipit in red. **Initials:** Medium *L* in red (two lines high). On fol. 32ra (the last full column of the carols section), the first letter of every line is marked in red; in this carol the marked initials occur in lines 40, 43–46, 49–52, 55–58, 61–64. **Audelay Signature:** Line 43 (Scribe A). **Meter:** Eleven 6-line macaronic stanzas, $aaaBBB_4$, with 2-line tetrameter burden and introductory Latin refrain *"Passio Christi conforta me."* **Editions:** Chambers and Sidgwick 1911, pp. 80–81; E. Whiting, pp. 211–12, 255; Silverstein, *English Lyrics*, pp. 105–06 (no. 84); Greene, *Early English Carols*, pp. 219–20, 442 (no. 369). **Modernized Editions:** Sisam and Sisam, *Oxford Book of Medieval English Verse*, pp. 391–93 (no. 160); Davies, *Medieval English Lyrics*, pp. 170–71, 339 (no. 81).]

burden   *Timor mortis conturbat me.* The source of this line is liturgical. Compare the
            seventh *leccio* in the Office of the Dead (Job 17:1–3, 11–15), as found in *The
            Prymer or Lay Folks' Prayer Book*: "Þe drede of deeþ trubliþ me euery dai, þe while

y synne & repente me not, for in helle is no redempcion" (Littlehales, *Prymer or Lay Folks' Prayer Book*, p. 68). On the Middle English *Timor mortis* tradition, see Patterson, *Middle English Penitential Lyric*, pp. 100–08, 180–84 (nos. 34–39), and compare the fifteenth-century paraphrase of the Office of the Dead in *Pety Job* (Fein, *Moral Love Songs*, pp. 289–359, especially pp. 324–27). Gillespie, "Moral and Penitential Lyrics," pp. 80–85, discusses how feelingly some penitential lyrics express the personal anguish of inward suffering.

4   *Passio Christi conforta me.* Audelay draws this line from the prayer *Anima Christi sanctifica me*, copied earlier in MS Douce 302, and he also uses it in *Pope John's Passion of Our Lord*, line 9.

25–38   Citrome notes how, with its "excremental rhetoric" of pastoral literature, this passage offers "a startling admission of penitential self-loathing," and also how Audelay's continuous "illness narrative" in MS Douce 302 returns here to the restorative medicine of Christ's five wounds (*Surgeon*, pp. 109–10).

32   On "deed, will, and thought," see the explanatory note to *Audelay's Epilogue to The Counsel of Conscience*, line 115.

43–45   Compare *Audelay's Epilogue to The Counsel of Conscience*, lines 482–84.

50   Compare *Seven Words of Christ on the Cross*, lines 74–75.

56   On Audelay's reverence for the five joys of the Virgin, see *Salutation to Jesus for Mary's Love*, *Prayer on the Joys of the Virgin*, and *Joys of Mary*.

62   This is a proverbial phrase. See Greene, *Early English Carols*, p. 442.

CAROL 25. SAINT FRANCIS   [W52]

Audelay's motive for composing a carol in honor of Saint Francis cannot be known. Given that Haughmond Abbey was Augustinian, E. Whiting, p. 255, finds it "unusual that Audelay should glorify St. Francis, the founder of one of the rival orders." But Greene, *Early English Carols*, p. 418, points out how, in *Marcolf and Solomon*, Audelay shows himself to be "no enemy of the friars as such, but only of those who gave way to avarice or other sins," and that Audelay expresses there his admiration for the founders of the orders (*Marcolf and Solomon*, lines 430–31). Melissa Jones, "Swete May, Soulis Leche," p. 2, suggests that the reason for Audelay's giving honor and place of prominence to Saint Francis is both religious and literary: "The final carol is dedicated to St Francis of Assisi, creator of the vernacular Christian song, in whom the carol-composing Audelay must have held particular esteem." That Audelay signed the carol suggests that he held Saint Francis in special reverence (the signature in the preceding carol seems to signify such a personal meaning), but it may also indicate, more simply, that Audelay wanted his name noted at the end of the carol sequence, where it was to be "read."

[Fol. 32ra–b. *IMEV, Suppl.*, *NIMEV* 44. *MWME* 6:1991 [312]. **Hands:** Scribe A, carol and burden in black; Scribe B, incipit in red. **Initial:** Medium *S* in red (two lines high). On fol. 32ra (the last full column of the carols section), the first letter of every line is marked in red; in this carol the marked initials occur in the burden and in lines 1–4, 7–10, 13–16, 19–22, 25–28, 31–34, 37–40. **Audelay Signature:** Line 55 (Scribe A). **Meter:** Thirteen 6-line stanzas, aaabBB₄, with 2-line tetrameter burden.

Editions: Chambers and Sidgwick 1911, pp. 81–82; E. Whiting, pp. 212–14, 255; Greene, *Selection of English Carols*, pp. 122–23 (no. 61); Greene, *Early English Carols*, pp. 188–89, 417–18 (no. 310).]

burden	*breder*. According to Greene, *Early English Carols*, p. 418, the term is "probably meant to designate not only the friars of Francis's own order but his 'brothers' in the wider sense of all Christians."
3–4	"St. Francis had a particular devotion to the Passion of Christ" (Greene, *Early English Carols*, p. 417).
5	Where the burden has the word *say*, this line substitutes the word *pray*.
9	*preynt*. For the story, see Jacobus de Voragine, *The Golden Legend* (trans. Ryan, 2:220–30; for Caxton's version, see Ellis, *Golden Legend*, 5:215–34).
14	*thre*. Greene, *Early English Carols*, p. 417, notes that the actual number of years during which Francis bore the stigmata was two and not three.
21	Greene, *Early English Carols*, p. 417, understands this line as meaning that out of piety Francis would divide his food in five parts in memory of Christ's wounds, but the source is obscure. Similar practices are well attested in the fifteenth century. See, e.g., Pantin, "Instruction for a Devout and Literate Layman," pp. 398–422.
31	*thongis*. "thankedst." E. Whiting notes that this verb is a present tense used for the preterite; compare *Salutation to Saint Winifred*, line 30.
31–34	Greene, *Early English Carols*, p. 418: "St. Francis set out in 1212 on a mission to the heathen in Palestine, but his ship was wrecked, and he was forced to return. In 1219 he actually went to the Near East and attempted the conversion of some Mohammedans, but soon returned to Italy."
39	*testament*. That is, "the Testament of St. Francis containing his last instructions to his brethren, dictated by him shortly before his death" (Greene, *Early English Carols*, p. 418).
40, 43–46	These lines are Christ's words to Saint Francis.
49–52	Greene, *Early English Carols*, p. 418: "The first Rule was given out by St. Francis and orally approved by Pope Innocent III in 1210, not, as the carol implies, later than the Testament. The latter enjoins obedience to the Rule as it had been revised in the saint's lifetime."
67–72	This stanza is adapted and repeated in *Saint Winifred Carol*, lines 169–74.
73–78	These lines, especially 73–74, formally close the carol sequence, joining with the opening couplet to frame the collection. While the opening couplet — "I pray you, syrus, boothe moore and las, / Syng these caroles in Cristemas" (written by Scribe B) — references the carols as songs, these closing lines refer to reading. Overall, the frame signals an intent already evident in the work of Scribe A to present the carols as a series. On the reference to reading rather than singing this carol, compare *Saint Winifred Carol*, lines 175–80, and see Copley, "John Audelay's Carols and Music," pp. 211–12.

MEDITATIVE CLOSE

XXXVI. DEVOTIONAL PROSE   [NOT IN W]

INSTRUCTIONS FOR READING 4   [NOT IN W]
    These couplets provide a rubric instruction for reading the two prose meditations that
come next in the manuscript. They also denote the opening of the last section, which, after
the carols, contemplates one's preparation for death. The verses ask a meditative reader to
peruse this section frequently and attentively as a way to think upon the spiritual rewards
("fruyte") that may follow one's bodily life. Haberly closes his 1926 illustrated woodcut
edition of *Jesus Flower of Jesse's Tree* with this verse.

[Fol. 32rb. *IMEV, Suppl., NIMEV* 2795. **Hand:** Scribe B, in red. **Meter:** Two tetrameter couplets.
Editions: Coxe, p. 51; E. Whiting, p. x; Fein, "Thirteen-Line Alliterative Stanza," p. 66. **Modernized
Edition:** Haberly, *Alia Cantalena de Sancta Maria by John Awdlay*, p. 19.]

THE SINS OF THE HEART   [NOT IN W]
    The Form of Living was the Yorkshire hermit Richard Rolle's last work, written in
1348–49 for the instruction of Margaret Kirkby, a young recluse. Drawn from this popular
treatise's sixth chapter, Audelay's extract catalogues sins according to a threefold scheme
of bodily origin: sins of the heart, sins of the mouth, and sins of the hand (i.e., deed). In MS
Douce 302 the extract is not attributed to Rolle. For comparison of this text to versions
found in other Rolle manuscripts, see Fein, "Thirteen-Line Alliterative Stanza."

[Fol. 32rb–vb. **Hands:** Scribe A, text in black; Scribe B, incipit (in margin) and explicit in red.
Initials: The text opens with a medium *T* in blue with red filigree (two lines high), and there are three
more medium initial *T*s in red (two lines high), marking the opening of sections. **Other MSS:** There
are twenty-nine manuscripts of Richard Rolle's *The Form of Living*, and fourteen others, excluding MS
Douce 302, that preserve extracts. For a list of manuscripts, see Ogilvie-Thomson, *Richard Rolle*, pp.
xvi–xvii, xxxvi–xliv. **Edition:** Fein, "Thirteen-Line Alliterative Stanza," pp. 61–74.]

37   *karalys.* Rolle's condemnation of singing carols strikes an incongruous note in
            the context of MS Douce 302 and its strong collection of carols. See Fein,
            "Thirteen-Line Alliterative Stanza," p. 74n35.

40   *wyghtis.* The word means literally "of the devil"; see *MED wight*, n.1(c). The
            meaning of the final phrase seems to be: "to accept devilish ways in the form of
            gifts, signs, beckonings, and writings."

41   The red initial *T* indicates a new section here, at a point not in agreement with
            other manuscripts. See Fein, "Thirteen-Line Alliterative Stanza," p. 66.

explicit   *Quicumque inspexerit.* Doyle, "'Lectulus noster floridus,'" p. 182n15, observes that
            Scribe B writes here in a more formal bastard anglicana, which he employs later
            for the Latin poem *Cur mundus.* This script also appears in the Latin biblical
            passages written in red by Scribe B in *An Honest Bed.*

OVER-HIPPERS AND SKIPPERS [NOT IN W]

Audelay demonstrates here his readiness to appropriate and alter borrowed texts. The word *rabul* in the Rolle passage (line 49) causes him to digress in verse upon an abuse and spiritual danger — the poor saying of prayers by inattentive priests during mass. On this theme, compare *Marcolf and Solomon*, lines 196–98 (explanatory note); *Virtues of the Mass*, lines 40–42; and *The Vision of Saint Paul*, lines 83–88 (explanatory note). This matter was also a grave concern for Langland and later Lollard reformers. But Audelay, who speaks from a position of orthodoxy, denounces the abuse so that churchmen themselves might correct it rather than face God's "maleson." The alliterative stanza — which turns craftily upon a pun (prayer and Fiend's prey) and paints a lively vernacular image of comic devils at work — may be Audelay's own composition (perhaps originally from *Marcolf and Solomon*), or it could be remembered as a preaching tag from elsewhere. If borrowed, its appearance in Audelay's favorite 13-line stanza form argues for his "translation" of it to his own idiom.

[Fol. 32vb. *NIMEV* 2736.11. **Hand:** Scribe A, poem in black, with lines 1–8 written as prose; Scribe B, many corrections in black. **Meter:** One alliterative 13-line stanza, ababbcbc₄d₃eee₄d₃ (compare *Marcolf and Solomon*). **Edition:** Fein "Thirteen-Line Alliterative Stanza," pp. 61–74.]

[1]–[3] This colorful list of epithets for those who commit a variety of verbal infractions against prayer develops out of a longstanding vernacular tradition in sermon exempla (see Jennings, "Tutivillus," pp. 11–20; and Fein, "Thirteen-Line Alliterative Stanza," pp. 64–65). It may be significant that a specimen of the tradition occurs in MS Sloane 1584 appended to the Latin poem *Cur mundus*, which also appears in MS Douce 302. See explanatory note to *Cur mundus*, line 40.

[5] *Rofyn.* Compare the occurrence of the same devil-name in Audelay's *Virtues of the Mass*, line 299, within the amusing story of Saint Augustine, who witnesses the antics of the recording demon and then shocks Saint Gregory by laughing aloud during mass. For variants of this tale, see the explanatory note to *Virtues of the Mass*, lines 265–76, 298–342. For the tradition of the recording devil, see Jennings, "Tutivillus," and Lee, "'This is no fable,'" pp. 743–60.

AN HONEST BED [NOT IN W]

Comparable in manner to the *Abbey of the Holy Ghost* (Blake, *Middle English Religious Prose*, pp. 82–102), this prose meditation deserves to be better known. It allegorizes the penitent soul as a bed made ready for Christ. The piece first came to modern light when Doyle edited one of its several copies in 1994. The MS Douce 302 text, one of the earliest, has not previously been printed. The scriptural bases for the allegory are Psalm 6:7 ("I have laboured in my groanings, every night I will wash my bed: I will water my couch with tears"), Canticles 1:15 ("Behold thou art fair, my beloved, and comely. Our bed is flourishing"), and Isaias 12:6 ("Rejoice, and praise, O thou habitation of Sion: for great is he that is in the midst of thee, the holy one of Israel"). Later manuscripts incorporate the allegory into large clerical compendia, and one of them, the Jesus College manuscript, is tied by an early ownership mark to Syon Abbey. (Compare Audelay's *Salutation to Saint Bridget*.) Audelay uses the allegory in tandem with the Rolle extract to enact a meditative process of penance and calm devotional readiness for death and union with Christ.

[Fols. 32vb–33va. **Hands:** Scribe A, text in black; Scribe B, Latin passages in red. **Initials:** Medium *W* in red (two lines high). Small *Q* (*Quia*) in red (1 line high). Fifteen initial letters are marked in red: *T* (*The matres*), *T* (*The nether schete*), *T* (*The keverlet*), *T* (*The peleus*, also marked with a red paraph), *T* (*The testur*), *T* (*The curtene*), *T* (*The hokys*), *T* (*Tho most*), *T* (*The hede*), *T* (*The chafte*), *T* (*The bordys*), *T* (*Thou most*), *O* (*Our bed*), *T* (*Thus be*), *T* (*Thoue Syon*). **Other MSS:** Oxford, University College MS 123, fols. 74v–75v (early fifteenth century); Cambridge, Saint John's College MS G.8, fols. 49v–52r (c. 1425–50); Oxford, Bodleian Library MS Laud misc. 19, fols. 22v–30v (early sixteenth century); Oxford, Jesus College MS 39, pp. 560–62 (late fifteenth century; incorporated into *Disce mori*); Oxford, Bodleian Library MS Laud misc. 99, fols. 123r–124r (c. 1490–1525; incorporated into *Disce mori*); Oxford, Bodeian Library MS Eng. th. c. 57, fols. 131v–132v (c. 1442–50; incorporated into *Ignorancia sacerdotum*). **Edition:** None from MS Douce 302, but see Doyle, "'Lectulus noster floridus,'" pp. 179–90 (edited from Oxford, University College MS 123).]

XXXVII. Paternoster   [W53]

This verse exposition of the Lord's Prayer in English belongs with a general impetus to instruct the laity in the tenets of faith. Many other poems in MS Douce 302 indisputably by Audelay fall into this pastoral category, for example, the first five carols and *True Living*. The seven petitions of the Paternoster are mentioned in *The Virtues of the Mass*, line 124, and the prayer's salvific effect is stated in *Marcolf and Solomon*, line 927–28. Other examples of the Paternoster in English verse are printed by Patterson, *Middle English Penitential Lyric*, pp. 108–10. Of related interest are the didactic *Paternoster* diagram appearing in the Vernon MS, fol. 231v (Henry, "'Pater Noster in a table ypeynted'") and other treatments in late medieval English culture (Hussey, "Petitions of the Paternoster"). Although the exposition seems entirely orthodox, it does invite, as a vernacular rendering, comparison with the controversies about biblical translation and about prayer versus preaching (see especially Aston, *Lollards and Reformers*, pp. 212–13, 216–17; Hudson, *Premature Reformation*, pp. 310–11, 424–25). Nonetheless, the alliterative poem belongs with an official movement, originating at least a generation earlier, to disseminate instruction on the Paternoster in English: "Mirk had urged parish clergy to encourage their parishioners to say their prayers in English, for 'hit ys moch more spedfull and meritabull to you to say your Pater Noster yn Englysche then yn suche Lateyn, as ye doth. For when ye speketh yn Englysche, then ye knowen and understondyn wele what ye sayn'" (Duffy, *Stripping of the Altars*, p. 80, citing Erbe, *Mirk's Festial*, p. 262; see also Woolf, *English Religious Lyric*, p. 377). In this regard, one might also compare the supreme place accorded the Paternoster by Chaucer's Parson (*CT* X(I)1038–46).

As a specimen of fourteenth-century high alliterative style, this poem bears formal affinities — and almost certainly a shared exemplar — with the next item, *Three Dead Kings*. Though Audelay's authorship of these two poems remains dubious, he is likely responsible for the creative use made of them here at the end of his manuscript, where they produce a sobering devotional effect. The much-corrected redactions of these poems show that the scribes found their language and metrical exactitude to be challenging and foreign. Yet the scribes handle both poems with care, indeed reverence. I am indebted to Dr. Ruth Kennedy (Royal Holloway, University of London) for sharing her views of the metrical and lexical features of this intricate piece. Although we have not always agreed, my editorial labor has been much enriched by her comments.

[Fols. 33va–34ra. *IMEV, NIMEV* 3445. **Hands:** Scribe A, poem in black; Scribe B, incipit and Latin ninth line of each stanza in red. **Initial:** Medium *T* in blue with red filigree (two lines high). **Meter:** Seven alliterative 11-line stanzas, $ababababc_4d_2d_4$, with a- and b-lines that alliterate in line-pairs and

observe near-exact consonance; caesuras in the long lines; and the ninth line of each stanza in Latin.
Edition: E. Whiting, pp. 214–17, 255–56.]

1   *pryse*. On expanding the abbreviation for *ri* to *ry* for visual rhyme, see Putter,
            "Language and Metre," p. 513n71.

4   This line may lack an original *r*-word.

5   *ther ar sene*. The first half-line in the manuscript lacks an original *s*-word. One
            may posit that for MS *ther bene in*, the poet wrote something like *ther ar sene*, "For
            seven points are seen there, set in position." The word *bene* is probably a
            corruption of *sene*, a word consonant with *synn* in line 6. Putter, "Language and
            Metre," p. 506, discusses how the occurrences of *ar* and *bene* differ between the
            Paternoster and *Three Dead Kings*, on one hand, and the other texts of MS Douce
            302, on the other. On this difference, see also the explanatory note to *Three Dead
            Kings*, line 94.

6   There are two scribal readings of this line, both flawed. Scribe A's line reads: *The
            lest salve hyt is to synn as the boke sayse*. Scribe B made corrections but failed to
            delete Scribe A's *is*: *The lest ys salve is to the synn as the boke sayse*. I have retained
            Scribe B's corrected line (omitting *is*). Stanley, "Verse Forms," p. 112n38, argues
            that the manuscript reading *lest* is problematic because it implies "that the seven
            points to be expounded are of differing significance, so that one of them is the
            least; such a differential evaluation seems unlikely for The Lord's Prayer."
            Putter, "Language and Metre," p. 513n73, suggests emending *lest* to *surest*. I
            retain *lest* because the poet's invoking of the phrase "the least of these" would
            seem to be a normal, idiomatic way to begin enumerating a series of items (as
            will occur here), and the preceding line has just stated that there are seven
            points to expound.

7   *yse*. The manuscript word *thou* is unnecessary for sense (the verb is imperative)
            and extends the line unmetrically. On the spelling *yse* (in rhyme) for *use*, see E.
            Whiting's note, p. 255. See also Stanley, "Verse Forms," p. 112n38: "probably
            present subjunctive singular of *usen*, 'observe (as a rite)'"; and Putter, "Language
            and Metre," p. 509n52.

14   *herd*. "Christian." See *MED hired*, n.1(c) and 2(c), usually in a collective sense,
            i.e., "household, familia, disciples, courtiers, etc." Putter, "Language and
            Metre," p. 518, translates it as "man."

18   *thi*. The pronoun refers to the reader. It could refer to God, but in that context
            the noun *covetyse* is an odd synonym for *will*.

24   *plane*. From the manuscript reading (*playne* with *y* dotted for deletion), one can see
            that at least one of the scribes rechecked the poem for visual rhymes. The word
            itself has merely shifted from adjective to adverb (see *MED plain(e*, adj. and *plain(e*,
            adv.).

25   *to fulfyl be thou fayne*. This half-line combines the work of both scribes, Scribe B
            correcting Scribe A. Scribe B inserts the a-verse, beginning in the margin and
            writing over some erased words. The b-verse, "[*wil* marked for deletion] *to fulfyl*

thou schuldist be ful fayne," is hypermetric and must still contain error. Dropping the words *schuldist* and *ful*, as I have done, does not change the meaning. The full line originally written by Scribe A reads "[erasure] *wil to fulfyl thou schuldist be ful fayne.*" It appears that the caesura in Scribe A's line occurred before the word *thou.*

26   *fare.* The original *f*-word missing from this line is obviously *fare.* The manuscript reading is *be.*

       wederfane. The simile for falling (*foundyng*) into sin is the shifting of a weathervane, which follows the changing wind. Sinning is depicted as a passive act of no resistance to worldly, wicked external forces. Putter, "Language and Metre," p. 518, thinks that the adjective *fikel* may have preceded *wederfane.*

27   *bayne.* Scribe B inserts the word *be* before *bayne.* Elsewhere in this line, Scribe B also inserts the words *& at* over an erased *to* (by Scribe A). Putter, "Language and Metre," p. 518, points out that *to his bidyng bayne* is better metrically. See *MED bain*, adj.1.(a), "be inclined, willing, eager."

29   *wilt.* The line lacks at least one original *w*-word, which the emendation adopted here provides (*schalt* to *wilt*). The line reiterates the English gloss of the Latin, repeating the verb *fulfil* found in lines 25 and 31. The verb *fulfil* may thus be a mistake (drawn in because of the Latin) for *awayte*, which would yield the precise sense that flows from line 28.

29–30 *thi soule wayne . . . thi soule wane.* Ruth Kennedy (in private correspondence) suggests that the similar endings of these lines are likely to represent dittography on the part of a scribe.

30   *warlouys.* This word also occurs in *Three Dead Kings*, line 83, and in *Patience*, line 258, and *Cleanness*, line 1560.

36   *behode.* The emendation of MS *behouyd* to *behode* is suggested by Dickins, "Rhymes," p. 517, and supported by Putter, "Language and Metre," p. 505. The form is Northern; see *MED bihoven*, v.

38   *bed we.* Alliteration indicates that *aske* is a substitution for its synonym *bede*, "pray, ask for." The emendation restores metrical regularity and consonance with *bred* and *blode.* The substitution and word reversal (*bed we* to MS *we aske*) appears to have occurred via simple scribal error: a misreading of anglicana *bed* for *wea*, and *w* for *sk.*

       blode. On this spelling instead of MS *blood*, see Putter, "Language and Metre," p. 501.

41   *ochedays.* "Daily." See *MED ech*, pron. 3(b), often in a Paternoster context.

50   *wore.* Putter, "Language and Metre," p. 525n101, notes that the poet reached outside his dialect in using this predominantly East Midlands form.

54   *dett.* This word in the manuscript is followed by the phrase *debitoribus nostris* (in Scribe B's hand and red ink), which E. Whiting prints here. As Dickins, "Rhymes," p. 517, notes, this phrase correctly belongs with line 53, where it

completes the citation of Matthew 6:12 from the Vulgate. The full Paternoster "point" was too long to fit into the single manuscript line left blank by Scribe A. It is surprising that Whiting did not notice how, by misplacing the phrase, she disrupted the poet's meter.

56–66   The negative constructions of this stanza form a stylistic feature inspired by the Latin petition *not* to be led into temptation.

57   *salve*. The manuscript reads *helpe*, but the alliteration on *s* indicates the original word, which scribal error (misreading *salue* in an anglicana hand) might account for.

58   *lede*. The line may lack an *f*-word here, but the word *lede* may also be ruled by the traditional translation "lead us not into temptation." It is interesting to note how the metrically aberrant *lede* in this line and *let* in line 59 anticipate the *l*-alliteration of lines 60–61.

59   *fong*. Emendation of MS *fyng* to *fong* is indicated by the rhyme. See *MED fongen*, v., "grasp or seize."

61   *Mak us*. As Putter, "Language and Metre," p. 520, notes, "*Makust to* is the scribe's auditory impression of *make us to*. The infinitive *make*, parallel with *let*, is dependent on *schulde*."

62   *of that*. Scribe B corrects Scribe A's *es no*, which, if left to stand, alters the meaning to "Nor, for no want is (there) no happiness . . ." Though I retain the correction, A's reading may in fact be better given the poet's stylistic feature here of negative syntax, which runs through the sixth stanza in imitation of this particular Paternoster "point." See my explanatory note to lines 56–66, and compare the construction of line 58.

65   This line lacks alliteration because it is ruled by the need to offer a traditional translation of the Latin line, but it does set up the alliteration on *l* used in lines 66–67.

67   *losse*. See explanatory note to *Three Dead Kings*, line 143.

72   This line may lack an original *b*-word.

77   *Amen*. This word is written in black by Scribe A and completes the last rhyme. In *Three Dead Kings* the final *Amen* is also written by Scribe A, but there it does not provide a rhyme.

XXXVIII. THREE DEAD KINGS   [W54]

Three Dead Kings narrates the classic ghost-story motif of the Three Living and Three Dead in a *tour de force* of densely alliterative stanzas. This popular *memento mori* theme enacts a moment in which three noblemen (often, kings) come face to face with uncanny mirror-images of themselves as they will be in death (often, their actual dead fathers walking abroad as animated corpses). Images and stories of this iconic encounter seem to have migrated to England from France in the thirteenth century, and expressions of it, more often visual than verbal, are found dispersed throughout the Continent. In medieval England its typical media were pictorial, that is, wall paintings in numerous parish churches (c. 1300 to c. 1550) and just a few manuscript illuminations (c. 1290 to c. 1335). The most interesting illuminations appear in the De Lisle Psalter, the Taymouth Hours, and the Smithfield Decretals. In two of these manuscripts rudimentary, rhyming speeches — in English and in order of age — accompany the six figures:

First (Youngest) Living:	Ich am afert.
Second (Middle) Living:	Lo whet ich se.
Third (Eldest) Living:	Methinketh hit beth develes thre.
First (Youngest) Dead:	Ich wes wel fair.
Second (Middle) Dead:	Such sheltou be.
Third (Eldest) Dead:	For Godes love, be wer by me.

The most ornate presentation in an English manuscript, the De Lisle Psalter, has these lines inscribed above the six elegantly drawn and painted figures. A formal Anglo-Norman poem is laid out in the space below the image.

As a product of the alliterative verse tradition, *Three Dead Kings* holds literary distinction and richly rewards close study. Middle English scholars have sometimes compared its dexterous wordplay and consonance to *Sir Gawain and the Green Knight* and the other poems of MS Cotton Nero A.x. Like *Gawain*, *Three Dead Kings* utilizes the motif of a hunt as foreboding preface to a mortal encounter. In this regard, it also resembles such other alliterative poems as *The Parlement of the Thre Ages*, *The Awntyrs off Arthure*, and *Somer Soneday* (Turville-Petre, "'Summer Sunday,'" p. 3). At the same time, its metrics seem to relate it to some Harley lyrics and the other verse written in an intricate 13-line alliterative stanza, such as *The Pistel of Swete Susan* and *The Four Leaves of the Truelove* (Fein, "Early Thirteen-Line Stanza"; Lawton, "Diversity of Middle English Alliterative Poetry," pp. 162–64). Any effort to locate the place of *Three Dead Kings* in the Middle English corpus must recall, moreover, that it has an alliterative companion in the *same* manuscript, that is, *Paternoster*, a poem that seems certain to derive from the same exemplar and probably the same poet (if not Audelay). In addition, *Three Dead Kings* must be seen for its survival in the full context of a planned verse anthology, that is, amidst Audelay's own oeuvre and book project, which includes many poems composed in Audelay's signature 13-line stanza. And for two of these, *Marcolf and Solomon* and *Over-Hippers and Skippers*, Audelay crafts an *alliterative* stanza with its own distinctive, and quite different, style.

Paternoster and *Three Dead Kings* do depart formally from other poetical works found in MS Douce 302. Their precious metrics and arcane vocabularies constitute obvious distinctions. The ever-scrupulous scribes take special care with these works, as they may be seen to do elsewhere when poems possess exceptional styles (see, e.g., the explanatory notes to *Gabriel's Salutation to the Virgin* and *Day of the Lord's Circumcision*). Under these circumstances, the scribes tend to produce a greater number of detectible errors than occur when they copy poems voicing Audelay's standard tones of didactic moral warning. Although the question of Audelay's authorship of *Three Dead Kings* and *Paternoster* remains unanswered, a chorus of scholarly consensus has echoed E. Whiting's assessment, pp. xxiv–xxviii, that Audelay cannot have been the author of either poem. Putter directly addresses the authorship question in his metrical and linguistic examination of the two works, and he concludes that because they both betray an original Northern dialect, they could not therefore have been composed by John the Blind Audelay.

A vigorous voice of dissent has arisen, however, in a series of three articles. Stanley, "*The True Counsel of Conscience*," "Verse Forms," and "Alliterative *Three Dead Kings*," has argued that the astonishing degree of variety in metrical experimentation and genre that occurs in the whole of MS Douce 302, along with a good number of verbal correspondences between *Paternoster* and *Three Dead Kings*, on one hand, and the rest of the contents, on the other, suggest that we should not take the separate authorship of these two works to be a settled matter. Stanley demonstrates, moreover, how poets may readily reach outside their dialects for rhymes and special terms, and he thinks it possible that Audelay did so in composing these alliterative poems. While no one goes so far as Stanley in defending Audelay's talents as a versatile poet, there are reasons to be cautious about dismissing his place in the authorship of these poems. First of all, whoever may be responsible for their creation, we can safely credit Audelay for their placement in his book, and in this sense *Paternoster* and *Three Dead Kings* join many other compositions in MS Douce 302 that may be traced to earlier sources or are translations from Latin texts (*Virtues of the Mass* and *The Vision of Saint Paul*, for example), but yet are transmuted through Audelay's particular vision and thoroughly worked into his *compilatio*. Such a perspective demands, in the second place, an assessment of *why* Audelay preserves this poem and places it at the end of his book. It is clear that it is meant to call forth a remembrance of last things as the book ends, becoming a moral mirror for the reader and doing so, intriguingly, just before Audelay holds himself up as such a mirror in *Audelay's Conclusion* (Fein, "Death and the Colophon").

There are also pivotal, para-authorial questions to be asked about Audelay's engagement with *Three Dead Kings*. His book, MS Douce 302, demonstrates his close knowledge of alliterative verse styles and motifs belonging to an earlier generation, no doubt experienced when he was a young man. He had absorbed traditions that ranged from the popular Langlandian idiom to the tighter *Gawain*-type stanzas with bob and wheel. From *Marcolf and Solomon* to *Three Dead Kings*, we can confidently perceive the range of his models, and observe how a feel for this range is expressed in poems that are indisputably his. By the early fifteenth century verse fashions had changed, but Audelay gives us much to ponder about how alliterative narrative and moralizing in its late fourteenth-century heyday led a youthful enthusiast to preserve its contours as his own career as a pious writer matured as he aged (Fein, "Thirteen-Line Alliterative Stanza"; Bennett, "John Audelay: Life Records," p. 44; Pickering, "Make-Up," p. 119). Thus one can never know for certain that these two alliterative poems are not works Audelay created when he was younger and working perhaps within a more literary milieu — one prizing invention and ingenuity — for a different sort of audience. Or, by the same token (and more in line with current opinion), whether he took them from some old source, hung onto them as inspirational models, and transplanted them to his book when and where he needed them. Meyer-Lee, "Vatic Penitent," p. 59, notes that *Three Dead Kings* is unusual in MS Douce 302 because it is such a strongly narrative poem. Other than *The Vision of Saint Paul*, Audelay rarely delves into narrative, though, like Langland in his *Piers Plowman*, the chaplain creates an implicit narrative throughout his book: it is of a conscience well counseled and a life reaching its good end. One may note, in this regard, that *Paternoster* and *Three Dead Kings* participate wholly in the meta-narrative of Audelay's book.

A final note about the poem's history of commentary and criticism is in order. With its verbal complexity and exacting form, *Three Dead Kings* has intrigued many readers. There has been a century's worth of philological attempts to use the poet's own constricted rules of alliteration and consonance to restore garbled rhymes and correct scribal errors. Beyond the four editions listed above (Storck and Jordan, "John Awdelays Gedicht"; E. Whiting; Fein, "Middle English Alliterative Tradition"; and Turville-Petre, *Alliterative Poetry*), four lexical commentaries have been compiled. These are by Dickins ("Rhymes," 1932); McIntosh ("Some Notes," 1977); Putter ("Language and Metre," 2004); and Stanley ("Alliterative *Three Dead Kings*," 2009). Sifting through these scholars' cumulative insights and drawing upon the *MED*, I have found that many old cruxes now have reasonable solutions, often with a fair degree of consensus, though, of course, not all problems *are* resolvable without some lingering dispute. In addition, the body of criticism, which dates back about forty years, has grown steadily, offering useful explications of *Three Dead Kings* in its pictorial and literary contexts. For these treatments, see Woolf, *English Religious Lyric*, p. 346; Turville-Petre, "'Summer Sunday,'" pp. 7–9; Tristram, *Figures of Life and Death*, pp. 164–66; Pearsall, *Old English and Middle English Poetry*, pp. 185, 250; Fein, "Early Thirteen-Line Stanza," pp. 115–18, and "Life and Death," pp. 87–92; Chism, *Alliterative Revivals*, pp. 241–51; and, most recently, Kinch, "Image, Ideology, and Form."

[Fol. 34ra–vb. *IMEV, NIMEV* 2677. *MWME* 9:3261 [199]. **Hands:** Scribe A, poem and final *Amen* in black; Scribe B, incipit in red. **Initial:** Medium *A* in blue with red filigree (two lines high). **Meter:** Eleven alliterative 13-line stanzas, $abababab_4cdccd_3$, with concatenation at the eighth and ninth lines, alliteration in line-pairs, near-exact consonance, and caesuras in the long lines. Alliteration extends over two or more lines, in the pattern aabbccddddeff (except for stanza 1, which has one more alliterating unit: aabbccddeefgg). **Middle English Analogue:** "Ich am afert," a 6-line poem accompanying pictorial depictions of the Three Dead and Three Living in two manuscripts, the De Lisle Psalter and the Taymouth Hours (see text below, and Fein, "Life and Death," pp. 84–85). **Editions:** Storck and Jordan, "John Awdelays Gedicht"; E. Whiting, pp. 217–23, 256–59; Fein, "Middle English Alliterative Tradition," pp. 20–36, 147–65; Turville-Petre, *Alliterative Poetry*, pp. 148–57.]

1   *byrchyn . . . bous.* Stanley, "Alliterative *Three Dead Kings*," p. 258, compares this alliterative collocation to a similar one in the Scottish poem *Golagros and Gawane*, line 31.

          arne. "Are." This rare form also appears in Audelay's *Gabriel's Salutation to the Virgin*, line 46. The word is discussed by E. Whiting, p. xxxvii; Putter, "Language and Metre," p. 506; and Stanley, "Alliterative *Three Dead Kings*," p. 257.

3   *rerde.* "Noise, clamor." Stanley, "Alliterative *Three Dead Kings*," p. 271, notes that this word is common in the works of the *Gawain*-poet but does not appear in *Piers Plowman*.

4   *row . . . rest.* This collocation occurs also in Audelay's *The Vision of Saint Paul*, line 300.

7–8   These lines image "a creature's lifetime as a 'new noyse' lasting till 'ny3t,' going from its apex to its endpoint in what seems a mere instant ('bot a napwile'), which the narrator considers 'bot no3t', two final chilling words in this alliterative string that cast doubt upon life's presumed worth" (Fein, "Early Thirteen-Line Stanza," p. 118). The compressed brilliance of this image — life seen as a symbolic day, and passing as if in a dreamlike flash of noise and excitement — seems somewhat diminished by a recently proposed emendation by Putter, "Language and Metre," p. 521. He suggests that *bot a napwile* should be *unto napwile*, with *napwile* defined as "the time for sleeping, bedtime" rather than as "the length of a nap" (the meaning found in the *MED nap*, n.(2), and accepted by editors). Putter argues that the emendation would lessen the "clumsy" word order and improve the sense as it flows from line 7; line 8 would then mean: "From noon until bedtime, the time seemed to me but nothing."

10   *throbyt and threw*. The first of these verbs is rare in Middle English (*MED throbben*, v., "twist violently, shudder"). The second is common, but not in this sense (*MED throuen*, v.(1)7, "writhe"). According to Stanley, "Alliterative *Three Dead Kings*," p. 273, they appear for sound as much as meaning: "If, as seems likely, phonaesthesis involves these verbs, exactitude of sense is not to be expected: the sound helps to convey the meaning."

16   *barsletys*. This term, from Anglo-French *bercelet*, refers to hunting dogs trained to follow wounded game.

19   *tonyng*. The manuscript reads *donyng*. On this plausible error, see Turville-Petre, *Alliterative Poetry*, p. 151, and *MED tonen*, v.(a), "producing musical sounds." Stanley, "Alliterative *Three Dead Kings*," p. 261, argues, however, that some poets may have considered *d* and *t* close enough for alliteration. He defines MS *donyng* as "din, confused noise" (*MED dinen*, v.[1]) and cites possible examples of *d/t* alliteration in *Marcolf and Solomon*, lines 342, 937–38. Turville-Petre emends line 64 in a similar way (not adopted here).

25   *lykyd*. Turville-Petre, *Alliterative Poetry*, p. 152, emends this word to *lakyd*, a change that Stanley, "Alliterative *Three Dead Kings*," p. 266, sensibly refutes as unnecessary. Turville-Petre's change is based on a dubious reading of *lare* as "earth" (*MED leir*, n.[2]) rather than its more natural meaning in this context: "teaching, wisdom" (*MED lor(e*, n.[2]2b[a], "that which is learned, spiritual wisdom"). Putter, "Language and Metre," p. 522, also refutes Turville-Petre's interpretation, but his own rendition of lines 24–26 (taking *Ham* in line 25 as referring to the poet's audience) is implausible. Line 25 needs to be read as an aside and warning: "*They* (i.e., the kings) were quite reckless in not heeding wise and spiritual counsel (which is why this dire thing happened to them)." Compare explanatory note to line 112.

28   *wanne*. The different spellings of the rhyme words of lines 28, 30, 32, and 34 do not affect the rhymes. According to Stanley, "Alliterative *Three Dead Kings*," p. 274, emendation is therefore unnecessary "unless to make them look more exactly rhyming. . . . In this text <on> has merged with <an> in sound, and <nne> is pronounced as if written <n>."

34   *fore kraft that I can*. Putter, "Language and Metre," p. 515n76, observes that this phrase is idiomatic: "for all that I can do about it." See also Stanley, "Alliterative *Three Dead Kings*," pp. 260–61, and *MED craft*, n.(1)1, "strength, force, power."

35   *no mo*. Manuscript *mo no* may be explained as an erroneous insertion by Scribe B, who interlined *no* after rather than before the word *mo*. *Counsel* and *care* are also collocated in line 89 and *Marcolf and Solomon*, line 279.

        chist. This emendation of MS *care*, first suggested by McIntosh, "Some Notes," p. 387, is strongly supported by Stanley, "Alliterative *Three Dead Kings*," pp.

258–59. The noun *chist*, "trouble, tribulation, suffering," derives from OE *ceast* (see *MED chest*, n.2). Putter, "Language and Metre," pp. 515–16, offers a speculative emendation of this line based on his sense that the initial alliteration should be on *r*.

36   *cest*. The manuscript reads *rest*, but the word wanted is *cest*, "plan, scheme, strategem," derived from Old Norse. Compare Old Icelandic *kast*; *kest* in *Gawain*, line 2413, and *Cleanness*, line 1070; and *MED cast*, n.1(h). It is possible to explain the confusion between *c* and *r*; the two letters are very similar in Scribe A's hand. Compare explanatory note to *Three Dead Kings*, line 64.

41   *fogus ful fow*. "Very brightly colored meadows." For good explanations of this phrase, see Dickins, "Rhymes," p. 517; McIntosh, "Some Notes," p. 387; and Stanley, "Alliterative *Three Dead Kings*," p. 262. E. Whiting, p. 280, mistakenly glosses the phrase as "very few fogs," but *fogge* is a rare word meaning "grass" (*MED fogge*, n.); compare *Cleanness*, line 1683.

42   *at schew*. On this emendation and the rhyme words of this stanza, see Putter, "Language and Metre," p. 523n93, and Stanley, "Alliterative *Three Dead Kings*," p. 283n34.

43   *chapid to chow*. Putter, "Language and Metre," p. 523, proposes the translation given here, "were fated to appear," rather than "were shaped to show." The encounter is, he notes, "an appointment with destiny." Compare explanatory notes to *Three Dead Kings*, lines 69 and 137.

46   *nor*. Putter, "Language and Metre," p. 520, suggests emending this word to *nother* so that the b-verse follows metrical rules deduced by Hoyt Duggan (see Putter, "Language and Metre," p. 519n83), but he acknowledges that the "error is commonplace" in Middle English alliterative verse. The a-verse appears to have lost a word beginning with *b*.

        bewe. See Stanley, "Alliterative *Three Dead Kings*," p. 258, "bend, change direction," and *MED bouen*, v.(1)5b.

49   The translation given for this line follows that of Turville-Petre, *Alliterative Poetry*, p. 153, "These men (the Dead) summoned them (the Kings)," which Stanley, "Alliterative *Three Dead Kings*," p. 257, supports. The verb *bede* (MS *byde*) is not likely to mean "took thought," an action assigned to the Living, as proposed by McIntosh, "Some Notes," p. 388.

52   *crossyng and karpyng o Crede*. With the sign of the cross and frenzied assertions of faith, this moment in the poem marks the point of encounter between Living and Dead. In the traditional visual iconography, the division point for the mirrorlike image is frequently a staked high cross, which this line invokes as a sign of the encounter (Fein, "Life and Death," p. 88).

56–57   The first king, holding a falcon and expressing fear, accords with the visual and verbal tradition of the Three Living and Three Dead; he is the youngest Living (Fein, "Life and Death," pp. 83–88).

57   *gre*. For the meaning "to shudder," see *MED grien*, v., and *Gawain*, line 2370. The word is discussed by McIntosh, "Some Notes," p. 388, and Stanley, "Alliterative *Three Dead Kings*," p. 263, and it does not need to be emended.

58   *gare me be gryst*. Stanley, "Alliterative *Three Dead Kings*," p. 259, provides a useful note on this phrase, which in the manuscript is *care me be cryst*. It was a crux until solved by McIntosh, "Some Notes," p. 388.

59   *Fere of.* "Far off." Emendation of this phrase is unnecessary. Previous editors have read *Fore of* and emended to *Fore oft*.

60   *word*. Scribe B inserts the word *this* before *word*. Its insertion causes the b-verse to deviate from metrical rules for alliterative verse deduced by Hoyt Duggan (see Putter, "Language and Metre," pp. 519n83, 520); it is here omitted.

64   *ronnyng*. MS *ronnyg* has been misread as *connyg* by all editors except Fein, "Middle English Alliterative Tradition," p. 30 (who emended the manuscript reading to *romyng*). The correct emended reading is, however, *ronnyng* (*MED rennen*, v.(1), especially 4, "run away, flee, attempt an escape"), which entirely fits the context (compare lines 72–73). The Living are caught and may not escape. Emendation to *connyng* is made by Storck and Jordan, "John Awdelays Gedicht," p. 184 ("jagdkunst," sportsmanship), and by E. Whiting, pp. 257–58 ("knowledge, skill"). Turville-Petre, *Alliterative Poetry*, p. 154, emends to *tounyng*, "horn-blowing," in support of the line's alliteration on *t* (compare line 19). Stanley, "Alliterative *Three Dead Kings*," p. 261, disputes Turville-Petre's change and defines *connyg* as "expertise (of hunting)" (see too Stanley, "Verse Forms," p. 112n37).

65   *tytle*. See *MED title*, n.3, "An appellation attaching to an individual or family by virtue of rank, social position, or office." Putter, "Language and Metre," p. 508, suggests that *tytle* is a form of the adverb *titly*, "soon," which Stanley, "Alliterative *Three Dead Kings*," p. 273, disputes. Stanley forwards the meaning given by Turville-Petre, *Alliterative Poetry*, p. 154, "as of right, with due claim." The sense, however, is that the kings find themselves entrapped, dismayingly, despite their high rank; on the motif of paralyzing entrapment in the poem, enacted metrically as well as narratively, see Fein, "Early Thirteen-Line Stanza," pp. 117–18.

66   *bespeke*. The manuscript reading is *besepke*, not *besopke*, as other editors have thought; I have emended it to *bespeke*, "spoke out" (*MED bispeken*, v.). Other editions have printed *bespoke*. The word could well be a scribal substitute for a synonym beginning with *m*. The likeliest word, *meled*, was suggested by McIntosh, "Some Notes," p. 388; it would add to the consonance of *medil* and *mekil* later in the line.

      medil. This word is doubtless the original of MS *ii.*, as suggested by McIntosh, p. 388, but not adopted by other editors. Not only does its consonance with *mekil* prove persuasive; it is also the term commonly applied to the "middle" age of life, which the second Living traditionally represents. See *MED middel*, adj.2(a), and numerous examples cited there, including *The Parlement of the Thre Ages*, lines 151 and 649, in which the second of the Three Ages is named "Medill Elde."

68–69   The second Living points out what he sees, and this feature accords with the verbal tradition of the Three Living and the Three Dead (Fein, "Life and Death," pp. 83–88).

69   *was saght*. This phrase, apparently correct, is difficult to translate. E. Whiting, p. 258, glosses the line: "that ever a man saw and was reconciled to it [so that he could keep his senses]." McIntosh's version, "Some Notes," pp. 388–89, is: that ever a man saw "and accepted, faced up to." Neither interpretation fits well with the normal meaning of *saght* ("desired, sought after"). Turville-Petre, *Alliterative Poetry*, p. 154, defines it as "'afflicted by' (ppl. of *seek*); cf. *Somer Soneday* 109, *sout*." Stanley, "Alliterative *Three Dead Kings*," p. 272, proposes the meaning "felt at peace." Putter, "Language and Metre," p. 518n82, gives the definition "was encountered," citing a line from *Awntyrs off Arthure* and *MED sechen*, 9(c). Putter's solution nears the mark. The best definition, "was granted," may be found in an analogous line in *Pearl*: "So watȝ al samen her answar soȝt" (line 518), for which Gordon glosses *soȝt* (see *sech*) as "found, given" (*Pearl*, p. 152). This meaning, apparently rare, is not recorded in the *OED*, but compare *MED sechen*, v.9(d), *ben sought*, "to be found, be." On how the apparition of the Dead is to be understood as a granted "gift," compare explanatory notes to lines 43 and 137.

70   *layth*. This adjective (*leyth*) appears in Audelay's *Marcolf and Solomon*, line 536, to describe the beggar Lazarus. See *MED loth*, adj.2(a) and 2(b). Compare *Three Dead Kings*, line 118, and *The Parlement of the Thre Ages*, line 152.

78   *raddelé*. Stanley, "Alliterative *Three Dead Kings*," p. 271, notes that this adverb, meaning "quickly, readily, immediately," appears frequently in the contents of MS Douce 302.

          mon. "Must, shall." The appearance of this auxiliary verb in *Three Dead Kings* and only once elsewhere in MS Douce 302 (see explanatory note to *Marcolf and Solomon*, line 344) is used by Putter, "Language and Metre," p. 505, to argue for the Northern provenance of the poem. Stanley, "Alliterative *Three Dead Kings*," pp. 269–70, refutes Putter's argument: "One swallow does not make a summer, and one use of *mon* does not make a northern text."

79–80   Putter notes that the b-verse of line 79 is unmetrical according to the rules deduced by Hoyt Duggan ("Language and Metre," p. 519n83), and he suggests emending it to *i-hillid he beholdis* or *in hillyng he beholdis* ("hiding his head he looks").

79–91   In expressing his sensations of the chill of death and declaring that the Dead are "dewyls," the third king fits the verbal and visual iconography of the third and oldest Living (Fein, "Life and Death," pp. 83–88). On the spellings of the rhyme words in this stanza and the next one, Dickins, "Rhymes," p. 51, notes that "The variations between -*en* and -*on*, -*is* and -*us*, in final inflexional syllables are merely scribal and of no significance for the rhyme scheme of the poem."

81–82   My translation of lines 81–82 differs from that of previous commentators (for lexical details, see the next three explanatory notes). The simile here likens the figurative blow to the living king's courage to the literal deathblow of a knife upon a slaughtered animal. The repetition of *coldis* / *kelddus* is grimly ironic as its meaning too progresses from figurative to literal. These lines participate in a carefully calibrated animal imagery, which, as I have described previously, denotes a progressive "decline in human dominance (a boar brutally hunted, but then the manned horses rearing and snorting in terror and the pet falcon fainting) leading to a total inversion" of power, which first appears in this simile of slaughtered cattle; "finally there are worms graphically wallowing in the corpses of the Dead" (Fein, "Early Thirteen-Line Stanza," p. 118n44).

81   *knyl.* The *MED* (*knil*, n.) cites only this passage as evidence for the sense "blow, shock," but surely the primary meaning "tolling for the dead" also affects the image. Turville-Petre, *Alliterative Poetry*, p. 154, emends with uncertainty: "MS. *kynl* may be read as either *knyl*, 'knell', hence 'shock', or *kyl*, 'blow' (*MED cul*, n.[2])." See also E. Whiting, p. 258, and McIntosh, "Some Notes," p. 389.

82   *ore the kye.* A misinterpretation of the phrase *ore the kye*, "over the kyne (i.e., cattle)," has created confusion among editors and commentators. The spellings *ki* and *kie* are well attested for the plural of *cou*, n., "cattle" (see *MED*), particularly in Northern texts. Nonetheless, Storck and Jordan, "John Awdelays Gedicht"; E. Whiting; McIntosh, "Some Notes"; Turville-Petre, *Alliterative Poetry*; and Putter, "Language and Metre," have all taken this phrase to mean "or the key" (*MED keie*, n.[1]) and render the line (as stated by McIntosh, "Some Notes," p. 389): "and then the kind of grim chill strikes at his heart that the back of the hand feels when a knife or a key freezingly touches it." Compare especially Turville-Petre, p. 154, and Putter, p. 519n85–86.

    knoc. Turville-Petre, *Alliterative Poetry*, p. 154, emends to *the knoc*, "the knuckle," to improve sense, and Putter, "Language and Metre," p. 519, approves this change on metrical grounds because it corrects the b-verse, but he also acknowledges that the sense "knuckle" is "insecurely attested" (he translates it "bruise": see his note 86, and compare McIntosh, "Some Notes," p. 389). Attestations are indeed scant (*MED knoke*, n., and *knokel*, n.). As for meter, good poets are licensed to alter theirs to achieve special effects, and the sharp break in normal b-verse rhythm — *that knoc kelddus!* — transfers a portion of the shock to the reader. E. Whiting, p. 258, translates *knoc* as "shock." The *MED* (s.v. *knok(ke*, n.) defines the word here as "figurative blow" and cites analogous usages in *Piers Plowman* and in Audelay's *Gabriel's Salutation to the Virgin*, lines 34–36: "Beryng on his chulderis bloo / The holé cros that kene a knok / Unto oure dedly Foo."

83   *warlaws.* This word also occurs in *Paternoster*, line 30, and in *Patience*, line 258, and *Cleanness*, line 1560.

89   The collocation of *cownsel* and *care* also occurs in *Three Dead Kings*, line 35, and *Marcolf and Solomon*, line 279.

92   *fyndus.* Putter, "Language and Metre," p. 504n25, proposes that the poet's word was *fenden*, "fiends."

93–98   When the first Dead (the one who died most recently) recalls his fairness and points to the worms in his "womb," he adheres to the time-honored iconography of the Three Living and Three Dead (Fein, "Life and Death," pp. 83–88).

93   *of fold*. Literally "of earth," with *fold* in its normal Middle English meaning. See Stanley, "Alliterative *Three Dead Kings*," p. 270, for a philological discussion. This definition is more likely than the proposed alternative: "of old" (E. Whiting, p. 258: "*old* is spelled *fold* for the sake of the alliteration").

94   *beth*. Putter, "Language and Metre," p. 507, discusses the distribution of *bene* and *ar* in the poems of MS Douce 302, finding a distinction between *Paternoster* and *Three Dead Kings*, taken together, and the other contents. See also explanatory note to *Paternoster*, line 5.

          lykyr. *Lykyr* is the comparative adjective "more suited"; see *MED lik*, adj.1(d), and examples cited. Glossing *lykyr* as the adjective "more likely," E. Whiting's translation seems overly influenced by the verb *liken*: "You are more fond of living than leaves on the linden and than lords from Lorne to London" (p. 258). McIntosh, "Some Notes," p. 389, corrected this reading by pointing out that line 94 is parallel in import to line 95, but he too mistranslated the adjective by supplying the verbal sense: "you have more lust for life . . ." The evidence cited in the *MED* points to the usual meaning for *lykyr*. By emending *lykyr* to *lytyr*, Turville-Petre, *Alliterative Poetry*, p. 155, translates line 94 as: "Now you take more delight in living than leaves on the linden tree." Stanley, "Alliterative *Three Dead Kings*," p. 267, offers this translation: "now you are more likely to leave." This interpretation would render *leve* as "leave" rather than "life."

          lynden. The rhyme necessitates this emendation of MS *lynde*, the normal Middle English name for the tree. *Lynden* (or *lyndon*) was originally an adjectival form, which in modern English has become the noun. The word here represents an early unrecorded use of the adjective as a substantive. According to the *OED*, the noun *linden* may have gained currency through translations of German romance, as an adoption of the German plural *linden*, or as the first element in *linden-baum*. The first record of the noun is dated 1577. The linden, with its delicate leaves easily set in rapid motion by the wind, symbolized lightheartedness, and also carelessness. See *MED lind(e)*, n.1b. Because the form is not attested in the fifteenth century, Stanley, "Alliterative *Three Dead Kings*," p. 267, opposes this emendation, taken by all editors, and finds preferable a removal of all *-en* and *-on* endings in the rhyme words of this stanza.

95   *Loron*. Stanley, "Alliterative *Three Dead Kings*," pp. 267–68, provides a note on this place-name: "It seems odd that Lorne in Argyllshire should have been singled out for a comment, unless it were for some topical allusion involving the nobles of the Campbell family in the early fifteenth century."

96–97   Stanley, "Alliterative *Three Dead Kings*," p. 257, elucidates the sense of just reward in the wordplay here: "as you beat and bind those who disobey you, so you will be bound in torment unless you atone for that wrong."

98	*wyndon.* "Writhe, twist." E. Whiting, p. 322, glosses the verb as "wind, go, twist," and for the phrase *walwen and winden*, see *MED winden*, v.(1)2(b). Stanley, "Alliterative *Three Dead Kings*," p. 274, translates this word as "enshroud" (*MED winden*, v.[1]4), seeing a hyperbolic nonce-use: "worms so numerous, they enshroud the corpse."
99	*wrase.* See *MED wrase*, n.(a), where this line is quoted, and Stanley, "Alliterative *Three Dead Kings*," p. 275: "band (for tying a winding-sheet)."
104	*mynn.* Trentals for the dead would have been among the chantry priest Audelay's professional interests. On the state of the Three Dead, who are doomed without the salvific masses for their souls, see Fein, "Early Thirteen-Line Stanza," pp. 117–18. Stanley, "Alliterative *Three Dead Kings*," p. 269, notes that while the collocation *mynn . . . mas* is not common in Middle English, it does occur in Audelay's *Virtues of the Mass*, line 198, and (less closely) lines 165–66, 338–39.
108	*well fore to ware.* "Wealth to spend or dispose of." Putter, "Language and Metre," p. 523, proposes the translation given here, which is more plausible than the usual interpretation: "We had our wife at our will and well to possess (or enjoy)." See *MED waren*, v.(2), where sense (a) is "spend, expend"; and this line (as well as line 22) is cited under the less-well-attested sense (d), "possess." Compare also Stanley, "Alliterative *Three Dead Kings*," pp. 274–75.
109	*frayns at me fere.* The phrase means "learn fear from me (by my example)." The meaning of *frayns* is "learn, find out by inquiring" (*MED frainen*, v.6; compare Stanley, "Alliterative *Three Dead Kings*," p. 263). *Fere*, "fear" (MS *ferys* emended for rhyme), is incorrectly defined by E. Whiting, p. 279, Dickins, "Rhymes," p. 518, and Stanley, p. 262, as "companionship, group of companions."
110	*thus schul ye fare.* The second Dead typically issues this kind of warning to the Living about their inevitable future conditions: "as I am now, so shall you be." On the tradition, see Fein, "Life and Death," pp. 83–88.
112	*lare.* This word may pun on two meanings: "teaching" (*MED lor(e*, n.[2]) and "earth, filth" (*MED leir*, n.[2]). For this interpretation, see Stanley, "Alliterative *Three Dead Kings*," pp. 265–66, who offers the definition "the teaching of the flesh." Compare explanatory note to line 25.
114	*lagmon.* This word occurs only here and in *Gawain*, line 1729, where the construction is the same (*leden bi lagmon*). Commentators agree on the meaning "lead (one) astray," but the exact derivation and meaning of *lagmon* is uncertain. For discussion and conjectural etymologies, see Menner, "Middle English 'Lagmon'"; Matthews, "*bi lag mon*"; and McIntosh, "Some Notes," pp. 390–92. Stanley, "Alliterative *Three Dead Kings*," p. 265, notes that "Nothing has more intensely led to connecting *Three Dead Kings* with *Sir Gawain and the Green Knight* than the coincident occurrence of this word in these two poems and nowhere else."
	leus. "Falsehoods." See Stanley, "Alliterative *Three Dead Kings*," p. 267, who supports the interpretation of E. Whiting, p. 258, which is followed here. Turville-Petre, *Alliterative Poetry*, p. 156, offers an alternate but dubious meaning

for MS *lyus*, emended to *leus* for rhyme: "'over the fields,' hence 'hither and thither'; *MED lie(e*, n.(3)? Or possibly a form of *MED lie*, n.(1), 'falsehood.'"

115   *aldyr-hyghtus and hyus*. "Proudest and highest of all." The prefix *aldyr-* applies to both superlative adjectives, as does *over-* in the opening words of Audelay's interpolated alliterative stanza *Over-Hippers and Skippers*. Reading *hyghtus* and *hyus* as adjectives accords with previous editors and commentators except for Stanley, "Alliterative *Three Dead Kings*," pp. 264–65. He believes that the loss of final *-t* in the superlative *-hyghtus* could be scribal and that *hyus* is the verb meaning "hurry," with the full clause running into the next line: "and you hasten away from this world." Putter, "Language and Metre," p. 507 and n40, argues that the superlative ending without final *-t* is a feature of the poem's original Northern dialect, an argument that Stanley questions.

116   *wryus*. "Turn, depart, reject" (*MED wrien*, v.[2]5[b]). Compare Audelay's similar uses of the verb in *Marcolf and Solomon*, lines 202, 564, 916, and 995.

117   *wreus*. "Reveals, makes known" (*MED wreien*, v.1, and Stanley, "Alliterative *Three Dead Kings*," pp. 275–76). The *MED* cites the word under a rarer meaning (v.3[c], "denounce"), but that definition seems less appropriate in this context.

118   *laythe upo last*. On *laythe*, see the explanatory note to line 70; here the adjective serves as a substantive: "loathly one." Stanley, "Alliterative *Three Dead Kings*," pp. 273–74, provides a note upon the unusual construction *upo last*.

120–30 The third (and oldest) Dead's speech reminds the Living to read the Dead as a reflected image of themselves — "Makis your merour be me!" — and, didactically, to "turn youe from tryvyls betyme!" On how this speech accords with the iconography, see Fein, "Life and Death," pp. 83–88. Compare, too, Elde's identical warning in *The Parlement of the Thre Ages*: "Makes youre mirrours bi me" (Ginsberg, p. 52, line 290).

122   *at . . . hene*. According to the *MED*, this is the last occurrence of this verb, derived from OE *hynan*, "treat with contempt," and its construction with *at* is not recorded elsewhere (Stanley, "Alliterative *Three Dead Kings*," p. 264). McIntosh, "Some Notes," p. 390, suggests plausibly that *at* is an error for *al*.

123   *with heme and with hyne*. This collocation occurs in *The Owl and the Nightingale*, line 1115; see a discussion by Cartlidge, *Owl and the Nightingale*, pp. 127–28.

124   Stanley, "Alliterative *Three Dead Kings*," p. 260, offers a well-reasoned alternate translation: "but never did a king with his entourage seem to me so faultless (as I am)."

134   *kouthyn rade*. "Could discern," but it might mean "recognize immediately," if *rade* is to be understood as an adverb rather than a verb. Stanley, "Alliterative *Three Dead Kings*," pp. 260, 271, lays out the competing interpretations and the editors' explanations. See also Putter, "Language and Metre," p. 524. On the meaning of the action, see Fein, "Early Thirteen-Line Stanza," p. 118 ("the figure of life as a symbolic day returns as the three kings ride home against the red rays of dawn"), and Fein, "Life and Death," pp. 88–89.

135 *Holde thai never the pres be hew ne be hyde.* For the idiom *holden presse*, see *MED presse*, n.5(a), "to act oppressively," and compare 6(a), "to keep something subject to pressure." In the b-verse there is a pun upon the alliterating words. The common expression *hew and hyde* (literally "skin and complexion") meant idiomatically "entirely, in every way"; hence, here it means "not at all" (see *MED heu*, n.2[b], where this line is cited). But the words can also mean "servant and land." For this second sense the *MED* cites the line again; see *hide*, n.(2)1a. A *hew* is specifically a household servant; a *hide* is a varying measurement of land, originally the amount needed to support a family with its dependents and servants. Both Whiting and McIntosh missed the pun. E. Whiting, p. 259, discovered the appropriate sense "servant and land"; McIntosh, "Some Notes," p. 390, "corrected" her reading in favor of the idiomatic expression. Turville-Petre, *Alliterative Poetry*, p. 157, follows McIntosh's reading, as have subsequent commentators. Putter, "Language and Metre," pp. 525–26, has recently offered a drastic reinterpretation of the line, taking the idiom to its literal level. He would read MS *p's* as *pris* not *pres* and he translates the line as follows: "They never attached pre-eminent value to complexion or skin, / But ever afterwards they had humbler hearts." He comments: "after the encounter with the three decaying corpses, the kings no longer set their store by outer appearances but are cured of their pride." Stanley, "Alliterative *Three Dead Kings*," p. 264, finds Putter's interpretation "persuasive," because the phrase *holden prise* is well-attested, though he prefers that *hender* be translated "kindlier." It seems more natural, however, that the lesson learned be expressed through improved actions (less tyranny over lands and people and more piety in sponsoring trentals) than through private perceptions.

137 *myschip.* Stanley, "Alliterative *Three Dead Kings*," p. 269, points out that this non-etymological spelling of a word derived from Old French *meschief* also occurs in Audelay's *King Henry VI*, line 81.

     myde. Previous editors (other than Fein, "Middle English Alliterative Tradition," p. 36) have not emended MS *tyde*, which yields a ready sense ("they amended themselves at that time," taking the verb as *menden*), but this is not a *better* sense than the word required by the line's alliteration on *m* (Dickins, "Rhymes," p. 518). The correct reading continues the idea that even though this wondrous encounter with a *ferly* has frightened the kings out of their wits, it also brings them a chastening sense of God's grace. See explanatory notes to lines 43 and 69; *MED mede*, n.(4)2(a), "moral consequences or spiritual reward; requital, retribution, just deserts; the ultimate reward of vice or virtue"; and *minden*, v., in its usual reflexive construction, "remember, call to mind."

141 *woghe.* "Wall" (*MED wough*, n.[1]). On the curious effect of "embalming" the poem as a wall inscription in the very process of its being read, see Fein, "Life and Death," pp. 88–89. On the frequency of the Three Living and Three Dead as a motif painted on English parish church walls, see Storck, "Aspects of Life and Death: I," "Aspects of Life and Death: II"; Williams, "Mural Wall Paintings"; Tristram, *Figures of Life and Death*, pp. 164–65; Fein, "Early Thirteen-Line

Stanza," p. 117 and n43; Fein, "Life and Death," pp. 73–74; and Oosterwijk, "Of Corpses, Constables and Kings."

143   *losse*. Stanley, "Alliterative *Three Dead Kings*," p. 268, notes that when this word means "perdition, damnation," as here, it shares more with Wycliffite texts than with *Piers Plowman* or the *Pearl*-poet's poems of MS Cotton Nero A.x. This meaning for *losse / lost* is common, however, in MS Douce 302. Compare especially *Paternoster*, line 67, "Bot delyver us from losse both erlé and late"; *Prayer on Christ's Passion*, lines 29–30, "Delyver my soule, Lord, fro losse, / Fro the payns of helle"; *Marcolf and Solomon*, line 380, "Leve thou me that his love schal not turne to losse"; *The Remedy of Nine Virtues*, lines 88–89, "Ellus were ye lyke to be lost, / And better unbore"; and the refrain line in *Seven Gifts of the Holy Ghost*, line 5, "Ellis were we lost!"

         Amen. See explanatory note to *Paternoster*, line 77.

LATIN POEM *CUR MUNDUS MILITAT SUB VANA GLORIA*   [NOT IN W]

The Audelay manuscript version of this well-dispersed Latin moral poem, dating to at least the thirteenth century, has not been previously printed. Earlier editors cite various traditions of authorship: Bernard of Clairvaux, Robert Grosseteste, or Jacopone da Todi (whose works are too late for consideration). Rigg's history of Anglo-Latin literature, p. 303, attests to the extreme popularity of this lyric rumination upon the vanity of worldly attachments. It appears often in English and Continental anthologies. A Middle English translation survives in a dozen manuscripts. A second medieval English rendering (*IMEV, NIMEV* 3475) is extant; and a Tudor version appeared in 1576 (Raby, *History of Christian-Latin Poetry*, p. 436). The translation provided here (the only modern one to my knowledge) has been produced by Prof. Radd Ehrman (Kent State University), for whose generosity I am grateful.

Scribe A's hand disappears from the manuscript with the copying of this poem by Scribe B. On how MS Douce 302 ends in three successive phases, see Fein, "Death and the Colophon."

[Fol. 34vb. **Hand:** Scribe B in red and black. **Initials:** Opening medium *C* in red (two lines high), followed by a small red initial (one line high) at the opening of each stanza. **Other MSS:** The poem appears in numerous manuscripts (see Wright, *Latin Poems*, p. 147). **Editions:** Wright, *Latin Poems*, pp. 147–48; Raby, *Oxford Book of Medieval Latin Verse*, pp. 433–34, 501 (no. 284), where the stanzas are ordered 1–2–3–7–8–9–10–4–5–6 (see also Raby, *History of Christian-Latin Poetry*, pp. 435–36). **Middle English Translation:** Brown, *Religious Lyrics of the XIVth Century*, pp. 237–39, 287 (no. 134) (*IMEV, NIMEV* 4160).]

33   *Hec*. The initial *H* was originally a red *I*, which the scribe later altered into an *H* in black ink.

40   The copy of this poem in MS Sloane 1584, fols. 13v–14r, adds the following, metrically distinct lines after line 40: *Sabbata nostra colo, de stercore surgere nolo, / Sabbata nostra quidem, Salomon, celebris ibidem. / Hii sunt psalmos corrumpunt nequiter almos, / Momler, forscypper, stumler, scaterer, overhipper.* "I worship on our Sabbaths, [but] I am unwilling to rise from the dung; / You indeed worship on our Sabbaths in the same place, Solomon. / These are [the ones who] villainously

corrupt the nurturing psalms: / [Syllable-]mumblers, skippers, stumblers, scatterers, leap-froggers." These lines belong to the same sermon tradition that inspires the list of verbal infractions found in *Over-Hippers and Skippers* (Fein, "Thirteen-Line Alliterative Stanza," pp. 64–65), and they seem also to be set within a dialogue of Marcolf and Solomon. The lines in the Sloane Manuscript are noted by Wright, *Latin Poems*, p. 148.

AUDELAY'S CONCLUSION   [W55]

These four concluding stanzas are much like *Audelay's Epilogue to The Counsel of Conscience* in their autobiographical manner, and the Latin surrounding the final stanza possesses the precise phrasing of the *Finito libro* colophon. Audelay here closes with a bold flourish of retrospective finality, proclaiming his purpose consummated. He also invokes, by means of the physical manuscript, the heavenly book recording the names of the saved. Following this image comes another vigorous assertion of authorship: the claim that this book displays Audelay's own "wyl" and "wrytyng." Then the poet signs off by making a penitential, pious appeal for prayers for "Jon the Blynde Awdelay," situated visually and spatially in an abbey, placed there to serve as chantry priest for Lord Lestrange but now lying gravely ill upon his deathbed.

[Fol. 34ra–b. *IMEV, NIMEV* 1210. *MWME* 9:3020 [272]. **Hand:** Scribe B, poem in black with Latin stanza headings in red. **Initial:** Small *S* (one line high) in red. **Ornament:** The final line is written as if on a banner, which is drawn under it in red. **Audelay Signatures:** Lines 39, 48 (both written by Scribe B). **Meter:** Four 13-line stanzas, ababbcbc$_4$d$_3$eee$_4$d$_3$. **Edition:** E. Whiting, pp. 223–24, 259.]

16–21   These lines are virtually identical to *Visiting the Sick and Consoling the Needy*, lines 29–34.

27–31   On Audelay's presentation of himself in this passage as an exemplum for the reader, see Fein, "Good Ends," p. 108, and Citrome, *Surgeon*, p. 110.

39a   The Latin heading paraphrases a common proverb: *Si finis bonus est, totum bonum erit*, or *Cuius finis bonus est, ipsum quoque bonus est*: "If the end is good, everything will be good," or "All's well that ends well." It may have been coined by Boethius, to whom it is attributed by Peter Lombard (see footnote for *Marcolf and Solomon*, line 987a). The rest of the Latin heading, as well as the explicit (*Cuius anime propicietur Deus*), repeats portions of the *Finito libro* colophon found at the end of *The Counsel of Conscience*. The phrase *Finito libro; sit laus et gloria Christo* is a common tag used by scribes (Schaff, *Middle Ages*, p. 550).

40–43   These lines borrow from the tradition of the book curse, that is, asking readers not to deface the book, of which Chaucer's poem to Adam his scribe is an example. See Olson, "Author, Scribe, and Curse."

46–52   These lines give the last signature of John the Blind Audelay at the manuscript endpoint, a spot designed to be noticed. Recorded here are also the name of the poet's patron (Richard Lestrange of Knockin), as well as Audelay's residence ("this place," that is, Haughmond Abbey), his occupation (chantry priest), and his condition (deaf, sick, and blind). The avowed aims of this passage are to petition for personal prayers for Audelay's soul from future readers and to advertise the pious salvific purpose of the book's contents (Fein, "Good Ends," pp. 109–10). The gesture of petitioning prayers from a reader may be compared to the conclusion of John Mirk's *Instructions for Parish Priests*: "Now, dere prest, .I. pray þe, / For goddes loue þow pray for me; / More .I. pray þat þow me mynge, / In þy masse when thow dost synge" (Peacock, p. 59, lines 1913–16).

⚜ TEXTUAL NOTES

The following notes record readings of the manuscript at those points where other editors have made different assessments of the textual evidence, as well as at points of important physical detail.

In general, Scribe A copied texts, and Scribe B later added incipits and explicits and acted as proofreader. Wherever Scribe B played a significant, uncharacteristic role in the textual copying, the affected lines are noted. Not noted, however, are the many correcting marks made by the scribes. Wherever final readings are determinate, those readings are adopted without comment. On how the scribes divided their work on particular items, see the explanatory notes.

Modernized editions with altered spellings and wordings (Chambers and Sidgwick 1907, Davies, Haberly, Sisam and Sisam, and Sitwell) are not recorded in the textual notes. Hands that date later than those of the two scribes are also not recorded. In MS Douce 302 there are two significant early hands, both probably medieval:

> (1) An inexperienced writer who copies stray phrases in the margin (fols. 16rb, 16va, 29ra, 34rb, and 35ra).

> (2) A doodler, whose simple drawings and occasional crosses appear most frequently on upper recto pages, b-column, perhaps to record his reading progress (fols. 3rb, 5rb, 6rb, 7rb, 9rb [two marks], 10rb, 11rb, 13rb, 18rb [the climax of *The Vision of Saint Paul*], 27vb, and 28va). The involvement of this reader is evident in his drawing of a sleeved hand pointing to the word "assencion" in *Salutation to Christ's Body*, line 26 (fol. 10rb), a line that marks the raising of the host in the Levation.

There are also two modern readers whose hands appear on the pages of MS Douce 302:

> (1) A reader who notes the correspondence of *True Living*, line 78, and *Chastity of Wives*, line 8, by inserting in fine-line black ink the cross-reference in the margins of fols. 1rb and 30va. This may be the same hand that numbers the folios in the upper right-hand corners. It may also be the hand that "corrects" the reading *Hontis* in *Three Dead Kings*, line 11.

> (2) A reader who marks texts in pencil, using left-hand marginal crosses and long vertical squiggles to highlight passages of interest. This reader was perhaps an early cataloguer. He is especially interested in political comments and in Audelay's self-identifications in signatures and autobiographical moments. His hand pervades the book, appearing beside the texts of *True Living, Marcolf and Solomon, Visiting the Sick and Consoling the Needy, Instructions for Reading 2, Audelay's Prayer Explicit to Pope John's Passion, Our Lord's Epistle on Sunday, The Vision of Saint Paul, Audelay's Epilogue to The*

Counsel of Conscience, Song of the Magnificat, Salutation to Saint Bridget, Saint Winifred Carol, King Henry VI, Joys of Mary, Virginity of Maids, Chastity of Wives, Dread of Death, Saint Francis, Over-Hippers and Skippers, An Honest Bed, Paternoster, Three Dead Kings, and *Audelay's Conclusion.*

In addition to these extraneous hands, the book contains a few marks of early ownership. Erased notes on fol. 35rb (visible by ultraviolet light) record that a Coventry minstrel named William Wyatt once possessed the book, and that he passed it on to an Augustinian canon named John Barker in Launde, Leicestershire. These transactions likely took place in the fifteenth century. On fol. 35v, which looks like an original outside cover of the book, the name "John" appears many times amid doodles and verse jottings unrelated to the contents of MS Douce 302. A much later owner was late eighteenth-century bibliophile Richard Farmer, master of Emmanuel College, Cambridge, whose handwritten sheet catalogue was bound with the book in 1803 by Francis Douce, its next owner. Douce contributed the woodcut pasted into the back inside cover of the bound book, which makes reference to *Three Dead Kings* (Fein, "Life and Death," pp. 90–91; Fein, "John Audelay and His Book," pp. 5, 24n13). Later, in 1834, Douce's vast collection of manuscripts, charters, books, and antiquarian holdings transferred to the Bodleian Library, Oxford. A detailed history of ownership and printed descriptions of MS Douce 302 is provided in Fein, "John Audelay and His Book," pp. 4–15.

ABBREVIATIONS: C: Cumming; **CS¹**: Chambers and Sidgwick 1910; **CS²**: Chambers and Sidgwick 1911; **Di**: Dickins (lexical comments); **Do**: Doyle; **F¹**: Fein 1985; **F²**: Fein 1994; **G¹**: Greene 1962; **G²**: Greene 1977; **Ha**: Halliwell; **Hi**: Hirsh 2005; **K**: Kaiser; **M**: McIntosh (lexical comments); **Mo**: R. Morris 1872; **MS**: Douce 302; **P**: Priebsch; **Pu**: Putter; **R**: Robbins 1959; **S**: Sandys; **Sa**: Saupe; **Si**: Silverstein 1971; **SJ**: Storck and Jordan; **St**: Stanley 2009 (lexical comments); **T**: Turville-Petre 1989; **W**: Whiting.

THE COUNSEL OF CONSCIENCE

[X.] TRUE LIVING [W1]

9	*comaundment.* So MS, Ha. W: *comanndment.*
13	*mon.* MS: *me.* Ha, W: *men.*
19	*Ther.* So MS, Ha. W: *þe.*
23	*deth.* So MS, W. Ha: *dey.*
26	*sodom, into.* So MS, W. Ha: *sodomi to.*
53	*sacrement.* So Ha, W. MS: *sacremet.*
61	*choson.* So MS, W. Ha: *chosen.*
68	*womon.* So MS, W. Ha: *wemon.*
83	*Evan . . . evan . . . evan.* So Ha, W. MS: *euran . . . euran . . . euran (ra* abbreviation written above *eun*).
87	*ayres.* So MS (*ayrs* corrected to *ayres* by Scribe B). Ha, W: *ayrs.*
93	*houne.* So MS, W. Ha: *honne.*
96	*fleschely.* So Ha, W. MS: *flschely.*
120	*nother.* So MS. Ha, W: *no other.*
135	*ressayvd.* So MS. Ha, W: *ressayued.*
	sacrement. So Ha, W. MS: *sarcement.*

167	*brennyng.* So Ha, W. MS: *brennyg.*
178	*cunnyng.* So Ha, W. MS: *cunnyg.*
195	*wittis.* So MS. Ha, W: *wyttis.*
	bynn welle. So MS (interlined by Scribe B). Ha: *hym well.* W: *byn well.*
201	*Bott.* So MS, W. Ha: *Better.*
218	*chif.* So MS (erasure before word), W. Ha: *the chif.*
241	*the.* So Ha, W. MS: *de.*
255	*weleway.* So MS (letter *a* after second *e* has been erased). Ha, W: *weleaway.* Compare *God's Address to Sinful Men,* line 217, and *Seven Works of Mercy,* line 29.

INSTRUCTIONS FOR READING 1 [NOT IN W]

3	*thirtenth.* MS: *xiii.*

XI. MARCOLF AND SOLOMON [W2]

1	*lernyng.* So Ha, W. MS: *lernyg.*
2	*fyndon.* So MS, Ha. W: *fynden*
	Holé. So Ha, W. MS: *hele.*
17	*Criston.* So MS. Ha, W: *Cristen.*
19	*crysum.* So W. MS: *criysum* (*ri* and *m* abbreviated). Ha: *crysun.*
29	*schuln.* So MS. Ha, W: *schulun.*
30	*schale.* So MS (*e* abbreviated). Ha, W: *schal.*
37	*grauntud.* So MS, W. Ha: *grauntid.*
43	*wo.* So MS, W. Ha: *won.*
50	*forwarde.* So Ha, W. MS: *fowarde.*
52a	*meum.* So Ha. MS, W: *meam.*
58	*Soferayns.* So MS, Ha. W: *soferayn.*
64	*rewarde.* So MS. Ha, W: *reward.*
70	*Do.* The initial *D* is marked with red.
81	*foluyn.* So MS (*u* written by Scribe B). Ha: *fowyn.* W: *foloyn.*
91a	*Averte.* So MS (*er* abbreviated), W. Ha: *Ante.*
92	A marginal indicator for a large initial appears at the opening of this line.
97	*reume.* So Ha, W. MS: *reuerme* (*er* abbreviated).
110	*comaundmentis.* So MS, Ha. W: *comanndmentis.*
111	*ale.* So MS (*e* abbreviated). Ha, W: *al.*
	Hwere. So MS (*h* inserted by Scribe B). Ha, W: *were.*
114	*your.* So Ha, W. MS: *ȝoȝ.*
118	A marginal indicator for a large initial appears at the opening of this line.
125	*prest.* So MS (*re* abbreviated), W. Ha: *prist.*
129	*ale.* So MS. Ha, W: *al.*
133	*lekon.* So MS. Ha, W: *likon.*
143	*beth.* So Ha, W. MS: *boþ.*
143a	*declinant a mandatis tuis.* So W. MS: *declinat amantis.* Ha: *declinant amantis.*
147	*spend.* So MS (*e* abbreviated), W. Ha: *spund* (Ha, W read the same abbreviation as *e* at line 146; compare textual note to line 748).
150	*selver.* So MS. Ha, W: *silver.*
153	*schale.* So MS (*e* abbreviated). Ha, W: *schal.*

156	*Y pray.* So MS, Ha. W: *Y-pray.*
157	*vanité.* So MS (*i* dotted), Ha. W: *vanete.*
165	*fulfyle.* So MS (*e* abbreviated), W. Ha: *fulfyl.*
169a	*Relegio.* So MS, W. Ha: *Religio.*
170	A marginal indicator (*I*) for a large initial appears at the opening of this line.
173	*penawns.* So W. MS, Ha: *penaws.*
181	*lest.* So Ha, W. MS: *leost* (*o* interlined).
197	*hom.* So MS. Ha, W: *ham.*
199	*Sovereyns.* So MS, Ha. W: *souereyn.*
200	*praysy.* So MS, Ha. W: *prayse.*
208a	A Latin heading inserted in the left margin is trimmed away and mostly lost; only the fragmentary phrase remains.
211	*redon.* So MS. Ha, W: *reden.*
	speke. So MS, Ha. W: *spekes.*
219	*comawndoun.* So MS (final *n* abbreviated); Ha, W: *comawndon.*
221a	*intellegit.* So MS, W. Ha: *intelligit.*
223	*sokeron.* So MS. Ha: *sokere.* W: *sokeren.*
226	*yclunggun.* So W. MS, Ha: *ycluggun.*
228	*ale.* So MS (*e* abbreviated). Ha, W: *al.*
240	*Y dred.* So MS, W. Ha: *That did.*
	reeme. So MS (*e* interlined). Ha, W: *reme.*
244	*ye.* So Ha, W. MS: *ȝef.*
246	*farewelle.* So MS (final *e* abbreviated). Ha, W: *farewell.*
258	*mon.* So Ha, W. MS: *mom* (extra minim).
265	*ale.* So MS, W. Ha: word omitted.
266	*sayd.* So MS (*y* inserted by Scribe B). Ha, W: *sad.*
273a	Scribe A writes this heading before line 248, and then indicates that it should be moved to this location. Ha, W do not detect this scribal correction.
280	*ale.* So MS (*e* abbreviated). Ha, W: *al.*
289	*bodys.* So W. MS: *bodyius.* Ha: *bodyms.*
293	*is.* So MS, Ha. W: *his.*
301	*visis ale.* So MS, W. Ha: *visibal.*
302–12	*you leede . . . sodenly.* Lines written by Scribe B.
303	*vanygloré.* So MS. Ha, W: *vaynglorie.*
319	*fore.* So MS, W. Ha: *for.*
321	*lytyl.* So W. MS, Ha: *lyty.* Lines 320–21 are written around a hole in the parchment.
325	*Anon gurd.* So MS, W. Ha: *and gud.*
329	*covernour.* So Ha, W. MS: *coverour.*
332	*devour.* So Ha, W. MS: *dedevour.*
338	Line written by Scribe B.
342	*Thomas.* So Ha, W. MS: *Thomans* (*n* abbreviated).
345–46	Scribe B writes these lines vertically in the margin, adding in red *here com in.*
346	*thrale.* So MS (*e* abbreviated). Ha, W: *thral.*
350–51	Marginal drawing of hand with pointing finger highlights these lines.

358	*gestlé*. So MS, Ha. W: *gostle*.
	holénes. Scribe A's *a* is corrected to *o* by Scribe B in red ink.
384	*myry*. So Ha, W. MS: *myrþ*.
388	*ey ever encresse*. MS, Ha: *eȝever encresese*. W: *ȝever encrese*.
405	*covetyse*. MS, Ha, W: *govetyse*. Emended for alliteration.
431	*four bernes*. So Ha, W. MS: *iiii. be...nes* (erasure).
447	*unkynd*. So Ha, W. MS: *unnkynd* (second *n* abbreviated).
449	*have, Y thee*. So MS. Ha: *Have I the*. W: *haue þe*.
450	*ale*. So MS. Ha, W: *al*.
452	*Asay*. So MS, Ha. W: *Assay*.
457	*say*. So MS (first letter is uncertain), Ha. W: *lay*.
462	*prayes*. So MS, Ha. W: *prayers*.
463	*governyng*. So Ha, W. MS: *goveryng*.
468a	*Dingnus*. So MS. Ha, W: *Dignus*.
476	*Redelé*. So W. MS, Ha: *Rededele*.
488	*wyttlé*. MS, Ha: *wytle and wyttle*. W: *wytle*.
489	*Here mys and here*. So MS, W. Ha: *Her mys and her*.
499	*agayns*. So Ha, W. MS: *aȝang*.
	hold. So MS (*w* corrected to *h*). Ha, W: *wold*.
506	*han*. So MS (*n* abbreviated), Ha. W: *ham*.
507	*sonn gelo cuiuscam*. So MS, W. Ha: *songe locum acam*.
512	*ye*. So MS, Ha. W: *wen ȝe*.
532–33	The scribe inserts here a marginal illustration of a pointing hand.
533a	*Nulli*. MS, Ha, W: *nullum* (*m* abbreviated).
534	*wyle*. So MS (*e* abbreviated). Ha, W: *wyl*.
535	*Wyle*. So MS (*e* abbreviated). Ha, W: *Wyl*.
538	*ale*. So MS, Ha. W: *al*.
543	*Do*. So Ha, W. MS: *Doer* (*er* abbreviated).
549–55	These lines are heavily corrected by Scribe B.
550	*daunse*. So MS, W. Ha: *daunce*.
551	*Fore*. So MS, Ha. W: *For*.
554	*att*. MS: *at att* (*att* is in Scribe B's hand). Ha: *and att*. W: *al att*.
559a	*neclegere*. So MS. Ha: *non legere*. W: *nec legere*.
573	A black marginal mark by Scribe A seems to indicate that the heading is to be inserted; it was later supplied by Scribe B.
577	*ye*. So MS (*ȝe*), Ha. W: *þe*.
579	*gef*. So MS. Ha. W: *ȝif*.
580	*soulys*. So Ha, W. MS: *souly*.
586	A black marginal mark by Scribe A seems to indicate that the heading is to be inserted; it was later supplied by Scribe B.
598a	*irascatur*. So MS. Ha, W: *nascatur*.
599	A black marginal mark by Scribe A seems to indicate that the heading is to be inserted; it was later supplied by Scribe B.
624a	*Erant*. So Ha. MS, W: *Erat*.
628	*ale*. So MS (*e* abbreviated). Ha, W: *al*.
642	*tak*. So MS. Ha: *toke*. W: *tok*.
652	*ale*. So MS. Ha, W: *al*.

654	*dystory*. So MS. Ha: *dystroy*. W: *dystry*.
676a	*Ve vobis*. So MS, W. Ha: *De vobis*.
686	One scribe marks the position of the omitted line, but it is not supplied.
688a	*intelligere*. So Ha, W. MS: *intellere*.
691	*ale*. So MS, W. Ha: *al*.
	reprevyng. So Ha, W. MS: *repreuyg*.
697–701	Scribe B inserts here a large marginal drawing of a horn to signal the passage.
701a	*Christianas*. So Ha, W. MS: *Christiani*.
706	*neyre*. So Ha. MS: *neyȝe*. W: *next*.
714a	*vult*. So Ha, W. MS: *vlt*.
739	*take*. So MS. Ha, W: *tak*.
	mo. So W. MS, Ha: *more*.
747	*Yit*. So MS, Ha. W: *ȝif*.
748	*ben*. So MS (*e* abbreviated), Ha. W: *bun* (Ha, W read the same abbreviation as *e* at line 146; compare textual note to line 147).
	rekynyng. MS: *rekynyg*. Ha: *rekenys*. W: *rekenyng*.
753a	This Latin heading is written by Scribe B on eight lines that were left blank by Scribe A; the final words are squeezed in.
753a	*meum*. So MS (second *m* abbreviated). Ha, W: *mei*.
753b	*temperale*. So MS (*er* abbreviated). Ha, W: *temporale*.
	simulis. So MS. Ha, W: *similis*.
754	*I fynd*. These words are inserted by Scribe B.
756	*Yef*. So MS. Ha, W: *ȝif*.
773	*ressayve*. So MS, Ha. W: *reassayue*.
779a	Scribe B inserts what seems to be a marker of topic ("confession and the sacrament of the altar") beside Scribe A's typical liturgical/biblical heading.
779a	*Nota*. So MS (written in margin). Ha, W: omitted.
779b	*Dominum*. So MS (abbreviated *dm*), W. Ha: *suum*.
780	*ale*. So MS. Ha, W: *al*.
795	*sauus*. So MS (*us* abbreviated). Ha, W: *saus*.
797	*doun*. So MS (*n* abbreviated), Ha. W: *don*.
808	*sacrementte*. So MS. Ha, W: *sacremente*.
813	*telle*. So MS, Ha. W: *tell*.
818a	*constitucionis*. So W. MS: *constituconis* (both *n*s abbreviated). H: *constitutiones*.
828	*fore youe*. MS, W: *fre ȝoue*. Ha: *fre ȝeve*.
834	*his owne*. So MS (*i* dotted). Ha, W: *hes owne*.
	ressayvs. So MS (*ressayus*), W. Ha: *ressayns*.
838	*auuctoreté*. So MS. Ha: *auctoreté*. W: *aunctorete*.
860	*Bohold*. So MS. Ha, W: *Behold*.
864	*Ho*. So MS, Ha. W: *He*.
882	*have*. So MS, Ha. W: *hane*.
925	*Engeyne*. So MS, Ha. W: *Engoyne*.
933	*qwensche*. So MS. Ha: *quench*. W: *quenche*.
938	*dele and tok*. So MS (written by Scribe B over an erasure, *&* interlined). Ha: *ale tok*. W: *dele to* (reading *deletok*).
943	*turrne Treth*. So MS. Ha: *turne treuth*. W: *turrnes treuþ*.

954	*Frerys.* Ha, W; MS: *F...erys.* (*r* under an erasure).
964	*have.* So MS, Ha. W: *hane.*
993	*Blust.* So MS. Ha, W: *Bluster.*
1000b	*quia.* MS (*ui* abbreviated), Ha, W: *qui.*
1001	*trouth.* So MS, Ha. W: *treuþ.*
1003	*heere.* So MS (*re* interlined). Ha, W: *here.*
1004	*ne lykyng.* So MS. Ha, W: *no lykyng.*
1012	*ma.* So MS, Ha. W: *may.*
1013	The last line is written as the catchphrase. The next folio (the beginning of a new quire) is missing.

[XV.] THE REMEDY OF NINE VIRTUES   [W3]

11	*curst truly.* MS: *cursetrly.* Ha: *cursed trly.* W: *cursed truly.*
45	*my.* MS, Ha, W: *me.*
67	*body.* So Ha, W. MS: *bedy.*

XVI. SEVEN BLEEDINGS OF CHRIST   [W4]

2	*seven.* So Ha, W. MS: *seue.*
48	*seyled.* So MS, Ha. W: *soyled.*
61	*strong.* So Ha, W. MS: *storng.*
91	*Spere.* So MS, W. Ha: *spore.*
94	*contricion.* So Ha, W. MS: *cotricion.*

XVII. PRAYER ON CHRIST'S PASSION   [W5]

incipit	Scribe B inserted the wrong incipit ("*De salutacione corporis Christi*"; see *Salutation to Christ's Body*), crossed it out, and then wrote the correct one.

LATIN VERSE PRAYER *O DEUS QUI VOLUISTI*   [W6]

16	*redemcionem.* So W. MS: *redemconem.*
20	*Anni.* So MS. W: *Ann.*
30	*vulnerare.* So W. MS: *vilnerare.*

LATIN PROSE PRAYER *TU DOMINE PER HAS SANCTISSIMAS PENAS TUAS*   [W6]

1	*indignis.* So MS. W: *indignus.*
3	*latronem.* So W. MS: *latrone.*
	vivis. So W. MS: *vivi.*
	regnas. So W. MS: *regnans.*

XIX. SEVEN WORDS OF CHRIST ON THE CROSS   [W7]

1	*cros.* So MS, Ha. W: *croys.*
4	*tho.* So MS, Ha. W: *þe.*
8	*Glotony.* So W. MS, Ha: *glotonry.*
14	*elé.* So MS, W. Ha: *els.*
61	*thou.* So Ha, W. MS: omitted.
	Citio. So W. MS, Ha: *cicio.*
62	*drynke.* So MS, Ha. W: *drynk.*
73	*spiritualy.* So MS, W. Ha: *specialy.*

75	*Comendo.* So MS, W. Ha: *Commendo.*
80	*antwyn.* So MS, W. Ha: *entwyn.*
93	*oure.* So MS, Ha. W: *houre.*
104	*very.* So MS, W. Ha: *every.*
107	*my.* So W. MS, Ha: *may.*
108	*schenchip.* So MS, W. Ha: *scenchip.*
114	*remyssion.* So MS, W. Ha: *remyssioun.*

XX. DEVOTIONS AT THE LEVATION OF CHRIST'S BODY   [W8]

incipit   *Christi Jhesu.* So MS. W: *Ihesu Christi.*

INSTRUCTIONS FOR PRAYER 4   [W8]

1   *seyst.* MS, W: *scyst.*

SALUTATION TO CHRIST'S BODY   [W8]

16	*Carnacion.* So W. MS: *carnacon.*
17	*lady.* So MS, W (reads *lidy*).
26	*assencion.* So W. MS: *þou assencion.*
29	*everé.* So W. MS: *euer* (*er* abbreviated).
49	*ai.* So MS. W: *ay.*
	Governowre. MS, W: *couernowre.* Emended for alliteration.
51	*seke.* So MS. W: *sek.*

INSTRUCTIONS FOR PRAYER 5   [W8]

7   *fynd ewretyn.* So MS. W: *fynde wretyn.*

LATIN PROSE PRAYER *ADORAMUS TE CHRISTE ET BENEDICIMUS*

incipit	*benedecimus.* So MS. W: *benedicimus.*
2	*vivorum et.* So W. MS: *vivorum &e &.*
5	*benignissime.* So W. MS: *bengnissime.*

LATIN VERSE PRAYER *LAUDES DEO DICAM PER SECULA*

7   *A. M. E. N.* So W. MS: *A. M. N.*

XXI. VIRTUES OF THE MASS   [W9]

33	*synys.* So MS, W. Ha: *synnys.*
40	*mon.* So MS. Ha, W: *men.*
49	*lest.* So MS, W. Ha: *lost.*
51	W misnumbers this line as 50 and continues the error until the end of the poem.
	In thi. So MS (*in* interlined). Ha, W: *Thi.*
54	*Sothlé.* So MS, W. Ha: *Soyle.*
55	*yeve.* So MS, W. Ha: *yene.*
56	*schreve.* So MS, W. Ha: *schrene.*
58	*day.* So W. MS, Ha: *eday.*
90	*discipilis.* So MS (second *i* interlined). Ha, W: *disipilis.*
92	*prestis.* So MS (*re* abbreviated), W. Ha: *pristis.*

117	*spesialy*. So MS, W. Ha: *specialy*.
127	*worchipis*. So Ha, W. MS: *wo ...chipis* (a dark blot obscures the *r*).
141	*Crist*. So Ha, W. MS: *cristis* (final *s* erased).
142	*ham*. So MS, W. Ha: *tham*.
146	*schew*. So Ha, W. MS: *sechew*.
184	*he*. So MS (interlined), W. Ha: *be*.
	wold. So MS (*w* interlined), W. Ha: *hold*.
187	*expone hit opres*. So MS, W. Ha: *exponere habit opus*.
193	*yo*. So MS, W. Ha: *you*.
210	*en*. So MS (*n* abbreviated), Ha. W: *in*.
223	*herst*. So MS, W. Ha: *herist*.
232	*ye*. So MS, W. Ha: *he*.
239	*masse*. So MS, W. Ha: *mass*.
245	*syngyng*. So W. MS, Ha: *synyng*.
246	*ever*. So Ha, W. MS: *eu* (lacks *er* abbreviation).
252	*bryng*. So MS, W. Ha: *bring*.
258	*be*. So Ha, W. MS: *b*.
260	*Lese*. So MS (written in left margin by Scribe B), W. Ha: omitted.
261	*Half*. So MS, W. Ha: *Lese*.
265	*bedth*. So MS (*bedþ*). W: *bed* (reads *bedn*); Ha: *bede*.
266	*ye*. So W. MS, Ha: *he*.
280	*dernes*. So MS, W. Ha: *dirnes*.
285	*Cospel*. So MS, W. Ha: *gospel*.
286	*red*. So MS, W. Ha: *rod*.
292	*witin*. So MS. Ha, W: *within*.
295	*that he ded*. So MS (written over an erasure; *ded* is difficult to read). Ha: *ther he did*; W: *þat he dyd*.
297	*speke*. So MS, W. Ha: *speek*.
298	*teth*. So MS, W. Ha: *tethe*.
299	*as*. So MS (corrected from *aice*), W. Ha: *alfe*.
300	*began*. So MS, W. Ha: *bigan*.
303	*marbys stone*. So MS, W. Ha: *marbystone*.
309	*grone*. MS: *grame*, Ha, W. See explanatory note.
311	*the*. So MS, Ha. W: *þen*.
312	*myldelé*. So MS, W. Ha: *mysdele*.
314	*wytles*. So W. MS, Ha: *wytytles*.
325	*adevyd*. So MS, W. Ha: *adenyd*.
326	*stoned*. So W. MS, Ha: *stonede*.
332	*wyndow*. So Ha, W. MS: *wydow*.
334	*Tho*. So MS, W. Ha: *The*.
338	*everé masse*. So MS, W. Ha: *evenmasse*.
355	*hard*. So MS, W. Ha: *hand*.
356	*proferbe*. So MS (*ro* abbreviated), W. Ha: *prefende*.
	prove. So Ha. MS: *preve* (*re* abbreviated); W: *preue*.
359	*to*. So MS, W. Ha: *for to*.
368	*wemen*. So MS, W. Ha: *women*.

369	*Cristyndam*. So MS, W. Ha: *Crystyndam*.
	an han. So MS (*han* interlined), W. Ha: *an* omitted.
379	*seven to*. So MS (*vii to*), W. Ha: *unto*.
404	*parfyte*. So MS (*ar* abbreviated), W. Ha: *perfyte*.
412	*schal*. So Ha, W. MS: *sch*.
413	*Jhesu*. So MS, W. Ha: *Jeshu*.
414	*bryng*. So MS, W. Ha: *bring*.

SAINT GREGORY'S INDULGENCE   [W10]

incipit	*Gregorio in tale*. So W. MS: *Gregorio in papa in tale* (*papa* marked for deletion, probably by Scribe B; see explanatory note).
9	*nowmbur*. So W. MS: *nowbur*.
10	*Twenty thousand*. So MS (abbreviated *Xx Ml*). W: *Xx.iij*. Compare *The Vision of Saint Paul*, line 317.

INSTRUCTIONS FOR PRAYER 6   [W10]

2	*confession*. So W. MS: *confessicion*.

PRAYER OF GENERAL CONFESSION   [W10]

5	*Pride*. So W. MS: *pridy* (*ri* abbreviated, *d* interlined).
29	*hereof*. So MS. W: *here oft*.

PRAYER FOR FORGIVENESS   [W10]

1	*O Lord*. So W. MS: *O ord* (Scribe B inserts a capital *O* instead of an *L*).

XXIII. VISITING THE SICK AND CONSOLING THE NEEDY   [W11]

40	*boonys*. So MS (first *o* interlined). W: *bonys*.
41	*What*. So W. MS: *wkat*.
	boone. So MS (first *o* interlined). W: *bone*.
59	*payn*. So W. MS: *pan.y* (*n.* interlined).
89	*cecatoure*. So MS. W: *cekatoure*.
91	*When*. So W. MS: *werhen* (*er* abbreviated).
106	*agayns*. So W. MS: *aȝayng*.
148	*Thomas*. MS: *tohnaias*. W: *Tohmas*.
153	*With watere*. MS: *Wt atere*. W: *Watere*.
164	*Bot*. MS, W: *Boþ*.
171	*his*. So W. MS: *hisis*.
214	*dight*. So W. MS: *diþȝt*.
219	*lyght*. MS: *layȝt* or *lgyȝt* (*a* or *g* interlined). W: *lygȝt*.
224	*penans*. So W. MS: *penas*.
225	*wil*. So W. MS: *and wil*.
230	*Jugement*. So W. MS: *in jugement*.
241	*And to*. So MS (*& to* written in left margin by Scribe B). W: *To*.
298	*not borne*. So MS. W: *borne*.
299	*redemcion*. So W. MS: *redemcon*.
301	*thorghe*. So W. MS: *þoȝȝe*.
315	*Sone*. So MS. W: *Son*.

321	*conclucion*. So W. MS: *coclucion*.
361	*prayers*. So MS. W reads *praye...* but the letters *ers* are visible in the manuscript.
376	*grete cause*. So MS. W: *cause grete*.
398	*amend it*. So MS. W: *amend*.

INSTRUCTIONS FOR READING 2 [W12]
| 1–6 | W does not number these lines. |
| 4 | *mon*. MS, W: *men*. |

ON THE WORLD'S FOLLY [W12]
1–6	W does not number the Latin lines and prints the poem in 3-line stanzas, but the scribe's paraphs indicate 6-line stanzas.
3	*Videte*. Written in red in the right margin by Scribe B.
15	*And*. Written by Scribe B; the black *F* of *Fore* is marked in red.
31	*he tokyn*. So W. MS: *hede ʒe tokyn*. See explanatory note.
36	*hathe be*. Written by Scribe B.

XXIIII. POPE JOHN'S PASSION OF OUR LORD [W13]
1	A marginal indicator for a large initial appears at the opening of this line. *XXII*. MS: *xij*, W. See explanatory note.
18	*entent*. So W. MS: *enten*.
31	*a rodde*. So MS (*de* interlined). W: *rodds*.
33	*hed*. So MS. W: *had*.
67	*knyght*. So W. MS: *kynʒt*.

SEVEN HOURS OF THE CROSS [W14]
3	*synus*. So MS. W: *synnus*.
12	*dyspilis*. So MS. W: *dysiplis*.
36a	*conclavatus*. So W. MS: *conclauatis*.
41	*Hongyng*. So W. MS: *Honyng*.
48	*knight*. So W. MS: *knʒt*.
	throst. So W. MS: *thrast*.
50	*senterio*. So MS. W: *sentorio*.
66	*prophcy*. So MS. W: *prophecy*.
67	*mynyng*. So MS, W (reads *mynyg*).
84	*contricion*. So W. MS: *contricon* (*ri* abbreviated).

XXV. OUR LORD'S EPISTLE ON SUNDAY [W15]
incipits	The two incipits appear in reverse order in the manuscript. See explanatory note.
	sivitatem. So MS (first *i* written over a *c*), W. P: *scivitate*.
1	A marginal indicator for a large initial appears at the opening of this line.
13	*perdecion*. So MS, W. P: *perdicon*.
16	*syrus*. So MS, W. P: *Syris*.
33	*That the*. So W. MS: *þat þat þe*.
	swolewd. So MS. P, W: *swolewed*.
40	*seris*. So MS, W. P: *Siris*.

47	*bryng mon.* So MS, W. P: *bring men.*
61	*serys.* So MS, W. P: *Sierys.*
68	*alle.* So MS, W. P: *all.*
71	*generacions.* So MS, W. P: *generacons.*
80	*ale.* So MS, W. P: *al.*
88	*alle.* So MS, W. P: *all.*
90	*schale.* So MS, W. P: *schal.*
102	*lobors.* So MS. P, W: *labors.*
114	*fro.* So MS. P, W: *for.*
122	*knouth.* So MS, W. P: *knov.*
134	*the.* So MS, W. P: *þus.*
144	*then.* So MS (interlined by Scribe B). P, W: omitted.
150	*honlé.* So MS, W. P: *houle.*
153	*prophetus.* So W. MS: *prohetus.*
	postlius. So MS. P: *postlis*; W: *postilus.*
155	*holy.* So MS, P. W: *hole.*
	ther. So MS, W. P: *þat.*
160	*wike.* So MS. P, W: *wik.*
162	*in.* So W. MS, P: *of in.*
164	*toke.* So MS (*ke* interlined by Scribe B), W. P: *tok.*
190	*Sounonday.* So W. MS: *sounoday.* P: *Suneday.*
202	*thonke.* So MS. P, W: *thonk.*

XXVI. The Vision of Saint Paul   [W16]

16	*wemen.* So MS. Mo, W: *women.*
22	*then.* So MS, W. Mo: *þon.*
25	*lechory.* So MS, W. Mo: *lechery.*
59	*mancion.* So MS. Mo, W: *moncion.*
	ordent ther. So MS, W. Mo: *þer ordent.*
79	*lyvus.* So MS, W. Mo: *lyues.*
80	*armus.* So MS, W. Mo: *armes.*
99	*them.* So MS (*m* abbreviated), Mo. W: *þe.*
121	*blake.* So MS. Mo, W: *blak.*
157	*thrust.* So MS, Mo. W: *þurst.*
179	*quod.* So MS (abbreviation), Mo. W: *quoþ.*
182	*payns.* So MS, W. Mo: *payne.*
216	*Quod.* So MS (abbreviation), Mo. W: *Quoþ.*
224	*wrat.* So MS, W. Mo: *wrath.*
227	*disperacion.* So MS (*er* abbreviated), W. Mo: *disparacion.*
230	*synnud.* So Mo, W. MS: *synund* (second *n* abbreviated).
241	*anglis.* So MS, W. Mo: *angelis.*
253	*hert.* So MS, W. Mo: *ne hert.*
268	*Loke.* So MS, Mo. W: omitted.
305	*worthenes.* So MS, W. Mo: *worthines.*
309	*thonke.* So MS. Mo, W: *thonk.*
311	*worchipful.* So MS, W. Mo: *worch it ful.*
313	*schale.* So MS. Mo, W: *schal.*

317	*Four thousand a hundred.* So MS (*Iiii. Ml. a C.*), Mo, W.
318	*hunder.* So MS, Mo. W: *hunderd.*
319	*bekynyng.* So Mo, W. MS: *bekynyg.*
334	*have.* So MS, Mo. W: *hane.*
341	*fore.* So MS, Mo. W: *for.*
explicit	Whiting prints this explicit (in the hand of Scribe A) with the next item.

GOD'S ADDRESS TO SINFUL MEN [W17]

1	*Alle.* So MS. W: *All.*
36	*four score and twenty.* MS: *iiij score and xxy* (*y* may be deleted). W: *iiij score.*
37	*nedis.* So MS. W: *þer is.*
57	*with.* So W. MS: *we.*
101	*Hwen.* So W. MS: *Hwom.*
114	*injoyns.* MS, W: *inyoyns.*
120b	*secundum Augustinum.* So MS (*inum* abbreviated). W: omitted.
123	*confusion.* So W. MS: *cofusion.*
125	*yf.* So MS (*ʒf*). W: *ʒif.*
	levyng. So MS. W: *leuying.*
137	*curatours.* So MS. W: *curateours.*
144a	This Latin heading is mistakenly written by Scribe A at the base of the stanza, as noted by W. Compare line 152a.
148	*Ryghwysnes.* So MS. W: *ryghtwysnes.*
151	*mo.* So MS. W: *mot.*
152a	This Latin heading is mistakenly written by Scribe A at the base of the stanza, as noted by W. Compare line 144a.
182	*your.* So W. MS: *ʒour ʒour.*
189	A folio is missing at this point in the manuscript.
202	*cowntys.* So W. MS: *cowtys* (*tys* interlined).
220	*playn.* So W. MS: *plany* (*n* interlined).
225	*Querite.* So MS (*e* corrected to *i*). W: *Querete.*
231	*sene.* So MS. W: *sone.*
238	*clothyd.* So W. MS: *cloþy.*
	iwys. So MS. W: *i-wis.*
242	*lying.* So W. MS: *ly.*

AUDELAY'S EPILOGUE TO THE COUNSEL OF CONSCIENCE [W18]

1	A change in meter marks the beginning of this poem, but there is no enlarged initial.
27	A marginal mark indicates that a large initial was to appear at the head of this stanza.
30	*nyght.* So MS, W (reads *n …t*).
34	*overe.* So MS. W: *ouer.*
38	*covetyse.* So W. MS: *couese.*
41	*fryght.* So W. MS: *fyʒt.*
78	*soche.* So MS. W: *seche.*
92	*spirytualy.* MS: *spiytualy.* W: *sprytualy.*
104	*forth.* So W. MS: *foreþ.*

106	*ston.* So MS. W: *stond.*
109	*pra.* So MS. W: *pray.*
144	*loke.* So MS. W: *lok.*
146	*thoght.* So W. MS: *oþoʒt.*
147	*whent.* So MS. W: *when.*
156	*covetys.* So W. MS: *covety.*
166	*wil not.* So W. MS: *wil.*
	twice. MS: *ii.*
172	*deth.* So MS. W: *doþ.*
199	*amende.* So MS. W: *amend.*
200	*takyns.* So MS. W: *tokyns.*
202–03	These verses are incomplete, apparently because of a sewn hole in the parchment.
312	*don.* So W. MS: *dn.*
340	*levyng.* So W. MS: *leyng.*
366	*lebors.* So MS. W: *labors.*
407	*wold.* So W. MS: *wol.*
491	*lordis.* So W. MS: *lordist.*
505	*reverens.* So W. MS: *reuers.*

SALUTATIONS

XXVIII. DEVOTIONS TO JESUS AND MARY HIS MOTHER   [W19]

incipits	Written by Scribe B on three lines.

SALUTATION TO JESUS FOR MARY'S LOVE   [W19]

3	*Hale.* So MS. W: *Hayle.*
8	*swet.* So W. MS: *swe.*
25	*Hayle.* So MS (*Haly,* with *e* interlined above the *a* and *l*). W: *Hayl.*
	synnys. So W. MS: *synnyis* (*i* interlined).
41	*hert.* So MS. W: *hort.*
	myn. So W. MS: *mynt.*
44	*ale.* So MS. W: *al.*
	moner. So W. MS: *noner.*
45	*grace.* So W. MS: *gra.*
81	*lady.* So W. MS: *lad.*
121	*stidfast.* So W. MS: *sidfast.*
124	*these.* So W. MS: *þe.*
128	*ye.* MS, W: *He.*
141	*I.* So W. MS: omitted.
143	*make.* So MS (*e* abbreviated). W: *mak.*

SALUTATION TO MARY   [W20]

28	*vergyns.* So W. MS: *vergyng* (*er* abbreviated).
50	*wyght.* MS: *iyʒt.* W: *wiyʒt.*
51	*to.* So W. MS: *ton* (*n* abbreviated).

| 68 | *Too.* So MS. W: *To.* |
| 82 | *us.* So MS. W: *ys.* |

GABRIEL'S SALUTATION TO THE VIRGIN   [W21]

7	*schal.* MS, W, Sa: *schalt.* Emended for rhyme.
11	*thee the.* MS, W: *þe þe.* Sa: *the thee.*
16	*stedfast.* So W, Sa. MS: *sedfast.*
21	This line is written alone, which W calls a mistake, but it is an indication of the actual 12-line meter.
25	*this.* So MS. W, Sa: *thie.*
33	*the.* So W, Sa. MS: *þ.*
	floke. So MS (*e* abbreviated). W, Sa: *flok.*
35	*holé.* So W, Sa. MS: *hohole.*
36–60	Scribe B copies this line and the final two stanzas.
42	*ded.* So MS. W, Sa: *did.*
43	*ber.* So MS, W. Sa: *ther.*
52	*leene.* So MS. W, Sa: *leane.*

XXX. SONG OF THE MAGNIFICAT   [W22]

4	*vergyn and.* So MS (*&* interlined). W: *vergyn* (reads *vergyng*).
16	*mea.* So W. MS: *mead.*
17	*makenes.* So MS. W: *mekenes.*
23	*mangefygat.* So MS. W: *mangnefygat.*
31	*the.* So MS (*þe*). W: *ye.*
50	*be.* So MS. W: *he.*
57	*pittis.* So MS. W: *putis.*
69	*hor.* So MS. W: *her.*
76	*is.* So MS. W: *His.*
80	*mea.* So W. MS: omitted.

XXXI. SALUTATION TO SAINT BRIDGET   [W23]

incipit	*illi suam.* So C, W. MS: *illa suam.*
	benedictionem. So W. MS, C: *benedictionem suam.*
3	*thi.* So MS, W. C: *þu.*
15	*tere.* So W. MS, C: *chere.*
18	*and.* So MS (*&*), W. C: *ond.*
22	*Hayle.* So C, W. MS: *Hay.*
28	*tresour.* So W. MS, C: *tesouur.*
30	*never.* So MS, W. C: omitted.
31	*faythfullé.* So MS, W. C: *fayþfully.*
36	*schuld.* So MS, C. W: *chuld.*
38	*wil.* So MS, W. C: *will.*
43	*dystré.* So MS, W. C: *distre.*
50	*he.* So MS, W. C: omitted.
51	*grace.* So C. MS, W: *crace.* Emended for alliteration.
52	*plase.* So MS, W. C: *place.*
56	*fere.* So MS, W. C: *fore.*

60	*Peters.* So C, W. MS: *Petrs.*
65	*becawse.* So MS, W. C: *be-cause.*
69	*schal.* So MS, W. C: *schall.*
76	*worthelé.* So W, C. MS: *wo...þele.*
84	*gemfulli.* So MS, W. C: *gracfulli.*
88	*chryven.* So MS, W. C: *chryve.*
94	*reverens.* So W. MS: *reuerent.* C: *reuerenc.*
104	*pardoun.* So MS (*ar* abbreviated), W. C: *perdon.*
106	*vesityn.* So MS, W. C: *veset yn.*
108	*everechon.* So MS (*er* abbreviated), W. C: *euerchon.*
110	*Governoure.* So C. MS, W: *couernoure.* Emended for alliteration.
116	*Treneté.* So MS, W. C: *trenite.*
	recomend. So MS, W. C: *recommend.*
123	*Thus.* So MS (*us* abbreviated), W. C: *Þer.*
127	*prelat.* So MS (*re* abbreviated), W. C: *prelet.*
132	*werchip.* So MS, C. W: *worchip.*
134	*joi.* So W, C. MS: *oi.*
143	*pardon.* So MS (*ar* abbreviated), W. C: *perdon.*
144	*part.* So MS (*ar* abbreviated), W. C: *a pert.*
151	*pardon.* So MS (*ar* abbreviated), W. C: *perdon.*
156	*no.* So MS, W. C: omitted.
158	*the.* So C, W. MS: *he.*
161	*the.* So W. MS, C: *þer.*
163	*onethus.* So W. MS: *oneþtus* (*us* abbreviated). C: *oneþtes.*
166	*prevé.* So MS (*re* abbreviated), W. C: *prive.*
	Prynce. So W. MS, C: *Priynce* (*ri* abbreviated).
167	*nyght.* So MS, W. C: *niȝt.*
172	*gostelé.* So MS, W. C: *gotele.*
173	*part.* So MS (*ar* abbreviated), W. C: *pert.*
175	*part.* So MS (*ar* abbreviated), W. C: *pert.*
179	*lasce.* So MS, C. W: *lasse.*
180	*Bot.* So C, W. MS: *Bo.*
192	*worthé.* MS, W, C: *worþ.*
195	*Kyng.* So W. MS: *knyg.*
196	*nyght.* So MS, W. C: *niȝt.*
201	*hom.* So MS, W. C: *hem.*
205	*reverens.* So C, W. MS: *reuers.*

SAINT WINIFRED CAROL   [W24]

1	*As.* So W, G². MS: *Aas* with capital *A* written in blue in the margin.
19	*Then.* So W, G². MS: *Þe.*
31	*han.* So MS, G². W: *had.*
46	*numerus.* So MS, G². W: *immens.*
50	*a myl-wele.* So MS (*wele* interlined), G². W: *myl.*
52	*might.* So MS (*i* interlined), W. G²: *meght.*
93	*plumys.* So W, G². MS: *pulmys.*
124	*vestementus.* So MS, G². W: *vestementis.*

130	*then.* So W, G². MS: *þe.*
172	*pray.* So MS, G². W: *fray.*

SALUTATION TO SAINT WINIFRED [W25]

7	*mervell.* So MS. W: *mervelle.*
10	*charité.* So MS. W: *charete.*
38	*Haile.* So MS (written in margin). W: omitted.
42	*eswem.* So W. MS: *yeswem.*
49	*Haile, him to love.* So W. MS: phrase written twice.
56	*Governour.* MS, W: *Covernour.* Emended for alliteration.

LATIN VERSE PRAYER *VIRGO PIA WYNFRYDA* [W25]

5	*Quia per te.* Written in the left margin. The *e* of *est* is marked in red.

LATIN PROSE PRAYER *DEUS QUI BEATUM VIRGINEM TUAM WENFRYDAM* [W25]

1	*vergenem.* So MS (*er* abbreviated). W: *virgenem.*
2	*interveneente.* So MS. W: *interveniente.*
	conveneente. So MS. W: *conveneante.*
3	*ipsissem.* So W. MS: *ipisse.*

SALUTATION TO SAINT ANNE [W26]

5	*bere.* So W. MS: *here.*
	blesful. So W. MS: *besful.*
18	*Gaude.* So W. MS: *Gauede.*

LATIN PROSE PRAYER *DEUS QUI BEATUM ANNAM* [W26]

incipit	*collecte.* So W. MS: *collecta.*
2	*venerantes in hora mortis.* So W. MS: *venerantes in hore morte in hora mortis.*
3	*salvatur.* So MS (*ur* abbreviated). W: *salvator.*

LATIN INSTRUCTIONS *QUICUMQUE HANC SALUTACIONEM* [W27]

2	*papa.* MS: word seems to have been crossed out and then restored. W: omitted.

SALUTATION TO THE HOLY FACE [W27]

2	*schynth.* So W. MS: *schynþt.*
10	*us.* So MS. W: omitted.
23	*grant.* So MS. W: *graunt.*
explicit	*in corde.* So W. MS: phrase written twice.

LATIN PROSE PRAYER *DEUS QUI NOBIS SIGNATUM VULTIS* [W27]

1	*instanciam.* So MS. W: *infanciam.*
2	*nunc.* So W. MS: *nuc.*

CAROLS

CAROL 1. TEN COMMANDMENTS [W28]
9   *Scle*. So MS (letter *c* interlined), G^2. CS^1, W: *Sle*.
17   *Lechoré*. So MS, W, G^2. CS^1: *lechere*.
24   *tult*. So MS, W, G^2. CS^1: *cust*.
31   *geton hom*. So MS, W, G^2. CS^1: *geten hem*.
32   *holdyn*. So MS, W, G^2. CS^1: *heldyn*.

CAROL 2. SEVEN DEADLY SINS [W29]
22   *Glotoré*. So MS, W, G^2. CS^1: *glotory*.
24   *Slouthe*. So MS, W, G^2. CS^1: *slouth*.

CAROL 3. SEVEN WORKS OF MERCY [W30]
2   *Clothe*. So MS, W, G^2. CS^1: *Cloþ*.
3   *presun*. So MS (*re* abbreviated), W. CS^1, G^2: *prisun*.
5   Line erased by Scribe B; faintly visible.
12   Line erased by Scribe B; faintly visible.
16   *part*. So MS (*ar* abbreviated), CS^1, W. G^2: *pert*.
19   Line erased by Scribe B; faintly visible.
23   *Opon*. So MS, W. CS^1: *Vpon*. G^2: *Apon*.
24   *Let se*. MS reading uncertain. CS^1, W: *Loke*. G^2: *Loo, se*. See explanatory note.
       onsware. So MS, G^2. CS^1, W: *onswere*.
29   *wellay*. So MS, W, CS^1. G^2: *well ay*. See explanatory note.
33   Line erased by Scribe B; faintly visible.

CAROL 4. FIVE WITS [W31]
burden   *wele*. So MS, G^2. CS^1, W: *wel*.
4   *laus*. So MS, followed by W, G^2. CS^1: *love*.
10   *wordlé*. So MS, W, G^2. CS^1: *wonder*.
25   *sorfet*. So CS^1, W, G^2. MS: *forfet*.
32   *mary*. So MS, CS^1, G^2. W: *mery*.
33   Line omitted in MS, CS^1, W. G^2 prints the line.

CAROL 5. SEVEN GIFTS OF THE HOLY GHOST [W32]
8   *makis*. So MS, W, G^2. CS^1: *make*.
9   *werkis*. So MS, W, G^2. CS^1: *workis*.
11   *grownder*. So MS (*er* abbreviated). CS^1, G^2, W: *grownde*.
15   *dothe*. So MS, W, G^2. CS^1: *doþ*.
18   *hom*. So MS, W, G^2. CS^1: *hem*.
30   *Soule*. MS: *oule*. CS^1, W, G^2: *Onle*. See explanatory note.

CAROL 6. DAY OF THE NATIVITY [W33]
burden   *Welcum*. So W, G^1, G^2. MS, S, CS^1: *Wwelcum*.
       good. So MS (first *o* interlined), S, W. CS^1: *glad*. G^1, G^2: *glod*.
       aray. So MS, W, G^1, G^2. S, CS^1: *array*.
       holeday. So MS, W, G^1, G^2. S, CS^1: *holiday*.

2   *ibore*. So MS, W, G^1, G^2. S: *þu born*. CS^1: *bore*.
9   *us*. So MS, CS^1, W, G^1, G^2. S: *as*.
10   *foreever*. So MS, CS^1, W, G^2. S, G^1: *for ever*.
14   *childern*. So MS, CS^1, W, G^1, G^2. S: *childrn*.
15   *alle on*. So MS, CS^1, W. S: *all on*. G^1, G^2: *allon*.

CAROL 7. DAY OF SAINT STEPHEN   [W34]
2   *He*. So CS^1, W, G^2. MS: *Hit* (*H* with interlined *t*).
13   *heven*. So MS, W, G^2. CS^1: *hoven*.
27   *When*. So MS, W. CS^1, G^2: *Whan*.
28   *grawnt us*. So MS (*us* abbreviated), G^2. CS^1, W: *grawntus*.

CAROL 8. DAY OF SAINT JOHN THE EVANGELIST   [W35]
burden   *breder*. So MS, W, G^2. CS^1: *broder*.
14   *pouere*. So MS, W, G^2. CS^1: *powere*.
15   *part*. So MS (*ar* abbreviated), CS^1, W. G^2: *pert*.
21   *kynes*. So MS, CS^1. W: *kneys*. G^2: *knyes*.
31   *wynd*. So MS (*away* deleted after *wynd*), CS^1, W. G^2: *wynd away*.
39   *departyng*. So MS (*ar* abbreviated), CS^1, W. G^2: *depertyng*.
49   *Chelde*. So MS. CS^1: *chylde*. W, G^2: *childe*.

CAROL 9. DAY OF THE HOLY INNOCENTS   [W36]
burden   *reverens*. So CS^1, W, G^1, G^2. MS: *reuers*.
2   *Isral*. So G^1, G^2. MS, CS^1, W: *Iral*.
15   *eor*. So MS, CS^1, G^1, G^2. W: *hor*.
16   *vergyns*. So MS (*er* abbreviated), W, G^1, G^2. CS^1: *virgyns*.
26   *Abyd*. So W. MS, G^1, G^2: *Abyds*. CS^1: *Abyde*.

CAROL 10. SAINT THOMAS ARCHBISHOP OF CANTERBURY   [W37]
burden   *pra*. So MS, CS^1, G^2. W: *pray*.
        seris. MS, CS^1, W, G^2: *sers*. See explanatory note.
        this. So MS, W, G^2. CS^1: *þe*.
7   *ale*. So MS. CS^1, W, G^2: *al*.
16   *seche*. So MS. CS^1, W, G^2: *soche*.
        fal. So MS, W. CS^1, G^2: *fel*.
19   *Then*. So CS^1, W, G^2. MS: *The*.
21   *Ne*. So MS (capital *N* is formed as in *Childhood*, line 3), CS^1, W, G^2 (who all read MS *þe*).

CAROL 11. DAY OF THE LORD'S CIRCUMCISION   [W38]
incipit   *circumcicionis*. So CS^1, W, G^2. MS: *circucicionis*. G^1: omitted.
burden   *What*. So CS^1, W, G^1, G^2. MS: *Hwhat* (Scribe B's ornamental initial in red is *H*, Scribe A's *what*).
1   *of hye natewre*. Written by Scribe B.
3   *the*. Interlined by Scribe B.
4   *Hys*. So MS, W, G^1, G^2. CS^1: *His*.
12   *Barne*. So MS (written by Scribe B), W, G^1, G^2. CS^1: *berne*.

15	Line written by Scribe B.
16	Line omitted in MS. In the next stanza Scribe B writes *ut supra* at this stanza point (line 26), and Scribe A writes *ut supra* at later places where the burden is to be repeated (lines 29, 35, 45, 49).
17–18	Lines written by Scribe B. The next four lines (at the base of fol. 29ra) are erased and left blank.
17	*yfere.* So MS, W, G¹, G². CS¹: *yn fere.*
23	*ale.* So MS (*e* abbreviated). CS¹, W, G¹, G²: *al.*
25	*Whatt.* So MS (Scribe B), G¹, G². CS¹, W: *What.*
	bryngis. So CS¹, W. MS: *bryngi...* (last letter cut off). G¹, G²: *bryngu[st].* This line, with *ut supra*, is written in the right margin by Scribe B.
31	*Thise.* So CS¹, W. MS: *iese.* G¹, G²: *These.*
	con grete here Chylde. Written by Scribe B.
	here. So MS, CS¹. W, G¹, G²: *her.*
34	*haylsyng.* So MS, W, G¹, G². CS¹: *haylsing.*
35	*wonder.* So CS¹, W, G¹, G². MS: *woder.*
37	*so he.* So MS, G¹, G². CS¹, W: *soche.*
44	*From.* So MS, W, G¹, G². CS¹: *fro.*

CAROL 12. KING HENRY VI   [W39]

burden	The initial *A* is decorated with foliage pointing to the opening lines. It is drawn over a small *a* written by Scribe A.
	Pryns. So Ha, CS¹, W, R, G², Hi. MS: *Peryns* (*er* abbreviated).
4	*prince.* Word interlined by Scribe B.
8	*moder.* So R, G². MS, Ha, CS¹, W, Hi: *moderis.*
9	*worthear.* So MS (*a* interlined), CS¹, W, R, G², Ha. Hi: *worthier.*
19	*withalle.* So MS (*e* abbreviated), Ha, CS¹, W, Hi. R, G²: *withall.*
20	*balle.* So MS (*e* abbreviated), CS¹, W, Hi. Ha, R, G²: *ball.*
21	*halle.* So MS (*e* abbreviated), Ha, CS¹, W, Hi. R, G²: *hall.*
22	*thi.* So MS, CS¹, W. Ha, R, G²: *thei.* Hi: *thai.*
33	*Agyncowrt.* So MS, CS¹, W, R, G², Hi. Ha: *Agyncourt.*
	patayle. So MS, CS¹, W, R, G². Ha, Hi: *batayle.*
37	*Frawns.* So MS, CS¹, W, R, G², Hi. Ha: *Frawnce.*
43	*sese.* So MS, Ha, CS¹, W, G², Hi. R: *ses.*
57	*beforne.* So Ha, CS¹, W, R, Hi. MS, G²: *before.*
67	*On.* So MS, Ha, CS¹, W, R, G². Hi: *Of.*
70	*halud.* So MS, W, R, Hi. Ha, CS¹, G²: *habud.* The MS reading is ambiguous; see W's note (p. 252).
74	*alle reams.* So Ha, W, Hi. MS, CS¹: *alle al reams.* R, G²: *all reams.*
75	*hethynes.* So MS, CS¹, W, R, G², Hi. Ha: *hevyness.*
79	*alle.* So MS (*e* abbreviated), Ha, CS¹, W, Hi. R, G²: *all.*
81	*falle.* So MS (*e* abbreviated), Ha, CS¹, W, R. G², Hi: *fall.*
91	*schul.* So MS, Ha, CS¹, W, G², Hi. R: *schuld.*
94	*Thus.* So MS, Ha, CS¹, W, G², Hi. R: *This.*

CAROL 13. FOUR ESTATES   [W40]

burden	*oun estate.* So MS. CS², W, K, G²: *oune state.*

5	*allegate*. So MS. CS², W, K, G²: *allgate*. Scribe A writes *ut supra* after the fifth line of every stanza.
15	*obisions*. So MS, K, G². CS², W: *abusions*.
30	*poverté*. So CS², W, K, G². MS: *pouert*.
36	*chast*. So MS, W, K, G². CS²: *chaste*.
52	*alegate*. So MS. CS², W, K, G²: *algate*.
53	*Wosever*. So MS, CS². W, K, G²: *Wosoever*.
	chomys. So MS, W, K, G². CS²: *chamys*.

CAROL 14. CHILDHOOD   [W41]

1	*alle one*. So MS (*e* in *alle* abbreviated), CS². W: *all one*. G²: *allone*.
12	After this line at the bottom of fol. 29v, one must turn to fol. 31r, because fols. 30 and 31 are interposed.
22	*synus*. So MS, G². CS², W: *synns*.
31	*myrth*. So MS, W, G². CS²: *myry*.
38	*synus*. So MS (*us* abbreviated), W, G². CS²: *synes*.

CAROL 15. DAY OF EPIPHANY   [W42]

9	*Trinetatis*. So MS, W, K, G². CS²: *trinitatis*.
11	*chepardis*. So MS (*ar* abbreviated), CS², W, K. G²: *cheperdis*.
14	*exelsis*. So MS, CS², K, G². W: *excelsis*.
16	*chepardis*. So MS (*ar* abbreviated), CS², W, K. G²: *cheperdis*.
17	*heredon*. So MS, W, K, G². CS²: *hered on*.
18	*merth*. So MS, W, K, G². CS²: *mery*.
26	*bad*. So CS², W. G²: *bed*. This line is repeated in the manuscript, occurring at the base of a column and the head of the next. G² selects *bed* from the line at the base of fol. 31ra.
36	*reverens*. So CS², W, K, G². MS: *reueres*.
38	*ale*. So MS (*e* abbreviated), W, G². CS², K: *al*.
46	*wernyd*. So MS, W. CS², G²: *warnyd*.
53	*begonon*. So MS, W, K, G². CS²: *be gonen*.

CAROL 16. SAINT ANNE MOTHER OF MARY   [W43]

1	*Anne*. So G². MS, CS², W: *Tanne*.
8	*alle*. So MS (*e* abbreviated), CS², W. G²: *all*.
10	*blisful*. So MS, CS², W. G²: *blissful*.
29	*hem*. So CS², W, G². MS: *he*.
46	*rynyd*. So MS, CS², G². W: *reynyd*.

CAROL 17. JESUS FLOWER OF JESSE'S TREE   [W44]

burden	*sprung*. So CS², W, G². MS: *sprng*.
	called. So MS, CS², G². W: *callid*.
14	*In medis*. So CS², W, G². MS: word *In* is obscure.
21	*Gabrael*. So MS, CS², W. G²: *Gabreel*.
25	*Hent*. So MS, W, G². CS²: *houe*.
31	*sprede*. So MS (*e* abbreviation), CS², W. G²: *spred*.
32	*his*. So W, G². MS, CS²: *his his*.

33	*sede.* So MS. CS^2, W, G^2: *lede.*
35	*Til.* So MS (word is barely legible), G^2. CS^2, W: *And.*
	kyngys. So W, G^2. MS: *kyngnys.* CS^2: *kyngnge.*
51	*lillé.* So CS^2, W, G^2. MS: letter *i* is rubbed out.
54	*Thet.* MS, CS^2, W: *ȝet.* G^2: *That.*
	prys. So CS^2, W, G^2. MS: *preys* (*re* abbreviated).
67	*There is a Floure.* The scribe copies this portion of the burden here.

CAROL 18. JOYS OF MARY   [W45]

2	*of thyn Emne.* So MS, CS^2, W. The parallel line in Balliol reads: "Mary myld, of the I mene."
8–9	These lines are reversed in the manuscript (*Ave maria ut supra / Gabrielis nuncio*). CS^2 and W arrange them as here.
26	*wo.* So CS^2, W. MS: *w.*
27	*lyve.* So MS, W. CS^2: *liue.*
33	This line occurs at the top of fol. 30ra.
37	*styud.* So MS, W. CS^2: *stynd.*
45	*Love al.* So MS, W. CS^2: *soueal.*

CAROL 19. MARY FLOWER OF WOMEN   [W46]

burden	*alle.* So MS (*e* abbreviated), CS^2, W. G^2: *all.*
	calle. So MS (*e* abbreviated), CS^2, W. G^2: *call.*
4	*falle.* So MS (*e* abbreviated), CS^2, W. G^2: *fall.*
7	*alle.* So MS (*e* abbreviated), CS^2, W. G^2: *all.*
	berdis. So MS (the *e* is legible), G^2, W. CS^2: *lordis.*
14	*consayved.* So MS (*e* interlined), CS^2, W. G^2: *consauyd.*
16	*thralle.* So MS (*e* abbreviated), CS^2, W. G^2: *thrall.*
19	*chosun.* So MS, W, G^2. CS^2: *chosen.*
28	*hal.* So G^2. MS, CS^2, W: *bal.*

CAROL 20. CHASTITY FOR MARY'S LOVE   [W47]

incipit	*virginitate.* So CS^2, W, G^2. MS: *virgintate.*
burden	Written by Scribe B on one manuscript line.
1	*Blessid.* So W, G^2. MS, CS^2: *BBlessid* (first *B* is the ornamental initial).
	be. So MS (*he* deleted before *be*), W, G^2. CS^2: *he be.*
	oure. Written by Scribe B.
2	*vergyn.* So MS, W, G^2. CS^2: *virgyn.*
	sheo was ful cleene. Written by Scribe B.
3	*Soche.* Written by Scribe B.
	yer sene. Written by Scribe B.
4	*here.* So MS, CS^2, W. G^2: *her.* This line, except for the first two words (*That so*), is written by Scribe B.
7–10	These lines, except for the first two words (*In word*), are written by Scribe B.
8	*sheo.* So MS, W, G^2. CS^2: *shee.*
13	This line is written by Scribe B, followed by two blank lines.
16	*Ever.* So MS (written by Scribe B in the margin), G^2. CS^2: *&.* W: *Euen.*
19	*Seynt.* So MS, G^2. CS^2, W: *Saynt.* Written by Scribe B in the margin.

21	*The.* So MS, CS², W. G²: *Thei.*
22	*defouled wold.* So MS, W, G². CS²: *defouled isold.* The word *defouled* is written by Scribe B. A blank line follows this line.
26	*ever ther ys.* Written by Scribe B.
28	*worder and.* So MS, W, G². CS²: *wordes in.* Lines 27–28 are written by Scribe B.

CAROL 21. VIRGINITY OF MAIDS   [W48]

burden	*I.* So W. MS, CS²: *II* (the first *I* is the ornamental initial).
14	*layne.* So CS², W, G². MS: *lay.*
15	*payne.* So CS², W, G². MS: *pay.*
21	*Oft.* So G². MS, CS², W: *Of.*
25	*ewroght.* So MS, W, G². CS²: *iwroȝt.*
39	*lene.* So MS, W, G². CS²: *loue.*

CAROL 22. CHASTITY OF WIVES   [W49]

15	*thus.* So CS², W. G². MS: *þaus.*
17	*com.* So MS, CS², W. G²: *come.*
18	*metlé.* So MS, W, G². CS²: *mecle.*
19	*Ale.* So MS (*e* abbreviated), W, G². CS²: *Al.*
	seest. So CS², W. MS, G²: *sees.*
25	*unlaufully.* So MS, W, G². CS²: *unlawfully.*
26	*Al.* So MS, CS², W. G²: *All.*
30	*doth.* So W, G². MS, CS²: omitted.
31	*chesyn.* So W, G. MS: *þesyn.* CS²: *þe syn.*
32	*treu.* So MS, CS², W. G: *triu.*
33	*Alle.* So MS (*e* abbreviated), W. CS², G²: *All.*
38	*disparage.* So MS (*ar* abbreviated), CS², W. G²: *disperage.*
40	*day.* So MS (*a* deleted before *day*), W, G². CS²: *a day.*
43	*lorchip.* So MS, W, G². CS²: *lordchip.*

CAROL 23. LOVE OF GOD   [W50]

burden	Written by Scribe A on one manuscript line.
	foreevermore. So MS (*er* abbreviated, final *e* visible under red ink of a paraph), CS², W, Hi. G²: *fore euermor.*
10	*elore.* So MS, W, G², Hi. CS²: *a lore.*
16	*Withot.* So MS, CS². W, G², Hi: *Without.*
17	*blyn.* So CS², W, G², Hi. MS: *bly.*
24	*rew.* So MS, W, G², Hi. CS²: *new.*
31	*lovyd.* So CS², W, G². MS: *lovy.*
32	*Without.* So CS², W, G², Hi. MS: *With* (abbreviated *wᵗ*).
	is. So MS, CS², G². W, Hi: *his.*

CAROL 24. DREAD OF DEATH   [W51]

4	*conforta.* So W, G². MS, CS²: *confarte.*
21	*both.* So MS, W, G². CS²: *beth.*
44	*and teere of ye.* Written by Scribe B.
57	*To.* So MS (written over an erasure), G². CS², W: *Of.*

CAROL 25. SAINT FRANCIS   [W52]

incipit   *Fransisco.* So MS, G². CS²: *francisco.* G¹: omitted.

5   *pray.* So MS, CS², W. G¹, G² : line omitted. Although the burden has *say*, this
               line (written by Scribe A) substitutes *pray.*

9   *preynt.* So MS (*re* abbreviated), G¹, G². CS², W: *prynt.*

14   *yere.* So CS², W, G¹, G². MS: *ye.*

21   *partys.* So MS (*ar* abbreviated), CS², W. G¹, G²: *pertys.*
               partyng. So MS (*ar* abbreviated), CS², W. G¹, G²: *pertyng.*

28   *ly in.* So MS. CS², W, G¹, G²: *lyin.*

40   *ens.* So MS, W, G¹, G². CS²: *ever.*

45   *perpetualé.* So W, G¹, G². MS: *perpetual.* CS²: *perpetually.*

63   *Gracious.* So CS², W, G¹, G². MS: *Grcious.*

73   *pur.* So MS (*ur* abbreviated), W, G¹, G². CS²: *par.*

MEDITATIVE CLOSE

THE SINS OF THE HEART   [NOT IN W]

incipit   *cordis.* So F². MS: *cord.*

9   *angar.* So MS. F²: *angur.*
               ewol. So F². MS: *wol.*

10   *noght.* So F². MS: *no...t* (letters are obscure).

11   *penance.* So F². MS: *pena...ce* (letters are obscure).

15   *froyndys.* So MS. F²: *fryndys.*

18   *schawnder.* So MS (*er* abbreviated). F: *schawnd.*

31   *brekyng.* So F². MS: *brelyng.*

40   *bekenyngys.* So F². MS: *bekenygys.*

44   *alle.* So MS. F²: *all.*

51   *wychestonyng.* So MS (*wyche* copied in margin). F²: *wyche-stondyng.*

explicit   *Quicumque.* So F². MS: *uicumque* (red initial omitted).

AN HONEST BED   [NOT IN W]

10   *prophet.* MS: *prohet* (*ro* abbreviated).

12   *MEDYCACIONCE.* MS: *medy medycacionce.*

13   *enclyne.* MS: *enolyne.*

29   *The curtyns.* MS: *Te curtyns.*

33   *of Jesu.* MS: *of.* Reading supplied by University College, Oxford, MS 123 (see
               Do, p. 188).

36   *choys.* MS: *ioys.*

44   *The hokys.* MS: *Te hokys.*

56   *The bordys.* MS: *Te bordys.*

70   *in this.* MS: *in þis in þis.*

XXXVII. PATERNOSTER   [W53]

1   *pryse.* MS: *prise* (*ri* abbreviated), W.

5   *ther ar sene.* MS: *ther bene in* (*in* interlined by Scribe B), W.

6   *The lest ys salve to the synn.* MS has two readings: *þe lest salue hyt is to synn* (Scribe A); *þe lest ys salue is to þe synn* (Scribe B). W: *Þe lest salue hyt is to þe synn*. See explanatory note.

7   *yse.* MS, W: *þou yse.*

11   *Fader.* This word is inserted by Scribe B.

12   *The.* MS, W: *Te.*

13   *plase.* MS: *...ace.* W: *place.*

24   *plane.* So MS (*playne* with *y* dotted for deletion). W: *playne.*

25   *forewart.* So MS. W: *foreward.* Scribe B writes the first half of line 25 partly in the margin and over an erasure, deleting the word *wil* before *to.*
     to fulfyl þe thou fayne. MS, W: *to fulfyl þou schuldist be ful fayne.* See explanatory note.

26   *fare.* MS, W: *be.*

27   *bayne.* MS: *be bayne* (*be* interlined by Scribe B), W.

29   *wilt.* MS, W: *schalt.* See explanatory note.

36   *behode.* MS, W: *behouyd.* See explanatory note.

38   *bed we.* MS, W: *we aske.* See explanatory note.
     blode. MS, W: *blood.*

52   *dettyrs.* MS, W: *dettys.*

54   *dett.* After this word Scribe B writes *debitoribus nostris* in red ink. W: *dett debitoribus nostris.* See explanatory note.

57   *salve.* MS, W: *helpe.*

59   *fong.* MS, W: *fyng.*

61   *Mak us.* MS, W: *Makust.* See explanatory note.

62   *of that.* Written by Scribe B, who deletes Scribe A's *es no.*

77   *evolus.* So MS. W: *euelus.*

XXXVIII. THREE DEAD KINGS   [W54]

4   *roght.* So F[1], T (suggested by Di, M, supported by St). MS, SJ, W: *þoȝt.*

5   *syght.* So F[1], T (and supported by P). MS, SJ: *seȝt.* W: *siȝt.*

8   *bot a.* So MS, SJ, W, F[1], T. Recommended by P: *unto.*

10   *threw.* So SJ, W, F[1], T. MS: *þrow.*

11   *Hontis.* So MS (a later hand has deleted the *i* and interlined *er*), T. SJ, W, F[1]: *Honters.*

15   *how.* So F[1] (recommended by M). MS, SJ, W, T: *þe.*
     gart. So MS, F[1], T. SJ, W: *gar.*

17   *belde.* So W, F[1], T (and recommended by Di). MS: *bild* (squeezed into the margin), SJ.

18   *kyngys.* MS *g* interlined by Scribe B.
     itolde. So T. MS, SJ, W, F[1]: *I tolde.*

19   *tonyng.* So T. MS, SJ, W, F[1]: *donyng.*

21   *welde.* So W, F[1], T (and supported by Di, St). MS, SJ: *wylde.*

25   *Ham.* So MS (*m* abbreviated), W, F[1], T. SJ: *hem.*
     lykyd. So MS, SJ, W, F[1]. T: *lakyd.*

27   *went.* So T. MS, SJ, W, F[1]: *gone.*
     wyn. So SJ, W, F[1], T. MS: *wyle.*

28   *wanne.* So MS, SJ, F[1] (and recommended by St). W: *won.* T: *wane.*

29	*with mowth as.* So MS, SJ, W, T. F¹: *that mowþ not.*
	I youe. So T. MS, SJ, W, F¹: *youe.*
	myn. So T (and supported by P). MS: *men.* SJ, W, F¹: *min.*
30	*mete.* So MS, W, F¹, T. SJ: *mates.*
	mon. So MS, SJ, W, F¹ (and recommended by St). T: *man* (and supported by P).
31	*quod.* So MS (abbreviation), T. SJ: *þer saide.* W, F¹: *quoþ.*
	ar. So T (and supported by P). MS, SJ, W, F¹: *beþ.*
32	*honor.* So MS, W, F¹, T. SJ: *he nor.*
	on. So MS, SJ, W, F¹ (and recommended by St). T: *an.*
34	*that I can.* So MS (*I* interlined by Scribe B and indistinct), F¹, T. SJ, W: *that can.*
35	*no mo.* Recommended by St. MS *no* interlined by Scribe B. SJ, W, F¹, T: *mo no.*
	bot chist. So F¹ (recommended by M, St). MS, SJ, W: *bot care.* T: *be Cryst* (recommended by Di). P suggests emending the whole line to *Can I no craft til sonne-rist.*
36	*cest.* So F¹. MS, SJ, W, T: *rest.*
39	*lest.* So W, F¹, T (and supported by St). MS, SJ: *lost.*
40	*Where.* So MS, W, F¹, T. SJ: *Were.*
42	*a schawe.* MS *a* interlined, *s* inserted by Scribe B.
	schalkys. So SJ, W, F¹, T. MS: *schalys.*
	at schew. So F¹ (recommended by Di, M, P). MS: *at ens.* SJ, W: *at ene.* T: *ischeue.* St recommends: *at on scheue,* "in one showing."
43–48	An erasure has damaged the first letters of these lines; ultraviolet light confirms the readings (M).
43	*unshene.* So MS, SJ, W, T. F¹: *unschene.*
	chapid. So MS, W, T. SJ, F¹: *shapid.*
	chow. So W, T. MS: *chew.* SJ: *show.* F¹: *schow.*
45	*lowe.* MS, SJ, W, F¹, T: *loue.*
47	*blongis.* So MS, W, F¹, T. SJ: *blonkis.*
	blow. So SJ, W, F¹, T. MS: letters cut off by binding after *bl.*
49	*Siche.* So MS, T. SJ, W, F¹: *Seche.*
	bede. So F¹, T (recommended by Di, M). MS, SJ, W: *byde.*
52	*o.* So MS, W, F¹, T. SJ: *of.*
55	*fnyrted.* MS *n* interlined by Scribe B.
56	*fyst.* So SJ, W, F¹, T (and supported by P). MS: *fest.*
57	*gre.* So MS, F¹. SJ, W: *grede.* T: *grue* (recommended by M).
58	*gare.* So F¹, T (recommended by M). MS: *care.* SJ: *chace.* W: *cace.* Di suggests *gars.*
	be gryst. So F¹, T (recommended by M). MS, SJ, W: *be cryst.* Di: *to grist.*
59	*Fere of.* So MS, F¹. SJ, W, T: *Fore oft* (reading MS *Fore* instead of *Fere* and emending MS *of* to *oft*).
60	*word.* MS: *þis word* (*þis* interlined by Scribe B), SJ, W, F¹, T. See explanatory note.
64	*ronnyng.* MS: *ronnyg.* SJ, W: *connyng.* F¹: *romyng.* T: *tounyng.*
66	*bespeke.* So F¹. MS: *besepke.* SJ, W, T: *bespoke* (incorrectly reading MS *besopke*). M suggests that the original word was a synonym beginning with *m*: *meled* or *melte.*

	medil. Recommended by M. MS, SJ, W, F¹: *ij*. T: *secund*.
67	*maght*. So W, F¹, T (and supported by St). MS, SJ: *myȝt*.
68	*seris*. So MS (*er* abbreviated), W, F¹, T. SJ: *this*.
	selquoth. So MS, W, F¹, T. SJ: *selquoþest*.
71	*and the lyver*. So SJ, W, F¹, T. MS: the words *& þe* are indistinct and partially obscured by a blot; the ampersand is visible by ultraviolet light (M).
	his. So MS, W, F¹, T. SJ: *is*.
72	*we tene*. So MS (the word *we* is indistinct), W, F¹, T. SJ: *we tende*.
73	*Ha*. So MS, W, F¹, T. SJ: *a*.
74–75	These two lines are written as one line in the manuscript.
81	*knyl*. So SJ, W, F¹, T. MS: *kynl*.
82	*kye*. So MS, W, F¹, T. SJ: *key*.
	that. So MS, SJ, W, F¹. T: *þat þe*.
84	*weldus*. So SJ, W, F¹, T (and supported by St). MS: *wildus* (*us* abbreviated).
85	*fars*. So MS, T. SJ, W, F¹: *fares* (incorrectly reading MS *fare*).
	foldus. So SJ, W, F¹, T (and supported by St). MS: *feldus* (*us* abbreviated).
87	*Fers*. So MS, W, F¹, T. SJ: *fore*.
87–88	These two lines are written as one line in the manuscript.
92	*quod*. So MS (abbreviation), T. SJ: *sayde the*. W, F¹: *quoþ*.
93	*of fold*. So MS, W, F¹, T. SJ: *of old*.
94	*lykyr*. So MS, SJ, W, F¹. T: *lytyr*.
	lynden. So W, F¹, T. MS: *lynde*, SJ (and supported by St).
96	*byndon*. So SJ, W, F¹, T (and supported by St). MS: *bedon* (*n* abbreviated).
97	*burst*. So MS, SJ, F¹, T. W: *brust*.
100	*Herein was I wondon*. So MS, W, F¹, T. SJ: *Herein I was Iwondon*.
101	*word*. So MS, W, F¹, T. SJ: *ward*.
102	*cysse*. So F¹ (recommended by Di). MS, SJ, W: *cusse*. T: *kysse*.
106	*bene*. So MS, W, F¹, T. SJ: *ben*.
107	*wyle we*. So F¹, T (recommended by M). MS, SJ, W: *wyle*.
108	*Whe*. So MS, W, F¹, T. SJ: *we*.
	and well. MS (*& well* interlined by Scribe B), T. SJ, W, F¹: *well*.
109	*fere*. So F¹, T (recommended by Di, supported by St). MS, SJ, W: *ferys*.
111	*lere*. So F¹, T (recommended by Di, supported by St). MS, SJ, W: *lerys*.
114	*leus*. So T (supported by St). MS, SJ, W, F¹: *lyus*.
115	*aldyr-hyghtus*. So MS, F¹, T. SJ, W: *aldyr hyȝtust* (recommended by M).
	hyus. So F¹, T. MS, SJ, W: *hyust*.
116	*wryus*. So F¹, T. MS, SJ, W: *wryust*.
118	*lyndys*. So MS, W, F¹, T. SJ: *lendys*.
121	*morthis*. So MS (preceded by *my* deleted), SJ, F¹, T. W: *merthis*.
122	*at*. So MS, SJ, W, T. F¹: *al* (suggested by M).
124	*ever*. Recommended by T. MS, SJ, W, F¹, T: *neuer*.
125	*is ther no*. So SJ, W, F¹. MS: *is þer*. T: *nis þer*. St suggests: *nis þer no*, or *nis þer neuer*.
	under. So MS, W, F¹, T. SJ: *onder*.
127	*he*. So MS, W, F¹, T. SJ: *ye*.
	kyme. So F¹, T (recommended by Di, M, St). MS, SJ, W: *kymyd*.
129	*longyr*. MS: *r* interlined.

131	*glyde.* So F^1, T (recommended by Di, St). MS, SJ, W: *glydyn.*
132	*gomys.* So F^1, T (recommended by M). MS, SJ, W: *comys.*
133	*ryde.* So F^1, T (recommended by Di, St). MS, SJ, W: *rydyn.*
136	*hendyr.* So SJ, W, F^1, T. MS: *hengyr.*
137	*myde.* So F^1. MS, SJ, W, T: *tyde.*
140	*the men.* So SJ, W, F^1, T. MS: *then* (with the *n* abbreviated, and a deleted thorn) *men.*
	mosse. So F^1, T (recommended by Di, St). MS, SJ, W: *masse.*
141	*woghe.* MS: written over an erasure.
142	*will.* MS (written over another word), W, F^1, T. SJ: *we.*

LATIN POEM *CUR MUNDUS MILITAT SUB VANA GLORIA*   [NOT IN W]

11	*sompniis.* MS: *sompnic.*
14	*invincibilis.* MS: *ivincibilis.*
15	*vultu.* MS: *wltu.*
17	*imperio.* MS: *inperio.*
27	*tamen.* MS: *tantum* (*m* abbreviated).
29	*pulveris.* MS: *puluerie.*
33	*magni penditur.* MS: *magna panditur.*
35	*leve.* MS: *leui.*
37	*potes.* MS: *potest.*

AUDELAY'S CONCLUSION   [W55]

11	*comaundement.* So MS. W: *comanndement.*
19	*hevun.* So MS. W: *heuen.*
39a	*finis bonum.* MS, W: *bonus.* Compare *Marcolf and Solomon*, line 987a.
44	*wil.* So W. MS: *wl.*

N.B. The letter "a" attached to line numbers indicates the heading written after the line. The letter "b" indicates a second heading.

Prayer on Christ's Passion (23), *O Deus qui voluisti* (29), *Seven Words of Christ on the Cross* (62), *Pope John's Passion of Our Lord* (51–52), *The Vision of Saint Paul* (281); 19:30: *Seven Words of Christ on the Cross* (85), *Pope John's Passion of Our Lord* (54–56); 19:34: *Seven Bleedings of Christ* (92), *Prayer on Christ's Passion* (24), *Pope John's Passion of Our Lord* (69), *Seven Hours of the Cross* (48); 19:38–42: *Seven Bleedings of Christ* (103–05), *Seven Hours of the Cross* (60–64); 20:11–18: *Visiting the Sick and Consoling the Needy* (185–86); 20:25: *Visiting the Sick and Consoling the Needy* (148, 187–88); 20:29: *Visiting the Sick and Consoling the Needy* (191–95)

Acts of Apostles: 4:32: *Marcolf and Solomon* (624a); 7:55–59: *Day of Saint Stephen* (2–22)

Romans: 1:13: *Marcolf and Solomon* (494a); 2:5–6: *God's Address to Sinful Men* (8a); 11:25: *Marcolf and Solomon* (494a); 12:17: *Marcolf and Solomon* (533a)

1 Corinthians: 3:19: *Marcolf and Solomon* (39a), *Audelay's Conclusion* (incipit); 10:1: *Marcolf and Solomon* (494a); 11:24–29: *Marcolf and Solomon* (753a); 11:27: *Marcolf and Solomon* (831a); 12:1: *Marcolf and Solomon* (494a); 13:1: *Marcolf and Solomon* (416a); 13:12: *Deus qui nobis signatum vultis*; 13:13: *True Living* (212–33), *Marcolf and Solomon* (11), *Seven Gifts of the Holy Ghost* (22–25)

2 Corinthians: 1:8: *Marcolf and Solomon* (494a)

Galatians: 6:5: *Marcolf and Solomon* (117a)

1 Thessalonians: 4:9: *Marcolf and Solomon* (169a, 268); 4:12: *Marcolf and Solomon* (494a); 5:14: *Marcolf and Solomon* (688a); 5:15: *Marcolf and Solomon* (533a)

1 Timothy: 3:2: *Marcolf and Solomon* (714a); 5:18: *Marcolf and Solomon* (468a)

Titus: 1:7: *Marcolf and Solomon* (714a)

Hebrews: 9:7: *Marcolf and Solomon* (546a); 11:34: *Marcolf and Solomon* (896a); 12:6: *Visiting the Sick and Consoling the Needy* (111)

James: 1:27: *Marcolf and Solomon* (169a)

1 Peter: 2:13: *Marcolf and Solomon* (779b); 3:9: *Marcolf and Solomon* (533a); 4:8: *An Honest Bed* (21–22)

Apocalypse: 7:4: *The Vision of Saint Paul* (317); 14:3: *Day of the Holy Innocents* (13); 14:4: *Day of the Holy Innocents* (34)

 # LINE INDICES

INDEX OF ENGLISH VERSE BY FIRST LINE

(N.B. Burdens for carols are in italics.)

INDEX OF ENGLISH PROSE BY FIRST WORDS

INDEX OF LATIN VERSE BY FIRST LINE

INDEX OF LATIN PROSE BY FIRST WORDS

(N.B. Excluded are Latin stanza headings and rubrics to English poems.)

 # BIBLIOGRAPHY

Alford, John A. "The Design of the Poem." In *A Companion to Piers Plowman*. Ed. John A. Alford. Berkeley: University of California Press, 1988. Pp. 29–65.

Allmand, Christopher. *Henry V*. Berkeley: University of California Press, 1992.

Aston, Margaret. *Lollards and Reformers: Images and Literacy in Late Medieval Religion*. London: Hambledon Press, 1984.

Audelay, John. "What Tidings?" Adapted by Jaqueline Froom. Music by Alun Hoddinott. London: Oxford University Press, 1965.

Aungier, George James. *The History and Antiquities of Syon Monastery, the Parish of Isleworth, and the Chapelry of Hounslow*. London: J. B. Nichols and Son, 1840.

Barber, Malcolm, and Keith Bate, trans. *The Templars: Selected Sources*. Manchester: Manchester University Press, 2003.

Barney, Stephen A. "Allegorical Visions." In *A Companion to Piers Plowman*. Ed. John A. Alford. Berkeley: University of California Press, 1988. Pp. 117–33.

Barratt, Alexandra. "The Prymer and Its Influence on Fifteenth-Century English Passion Lyrics." *Medium Ævum* 44 (1975), 264–79.

Beckwith, Sarah. *Christ's Body: Identity, Culture and Society in Late Medieval Writings*. London: Routledge, 1993.

Bede. *Bede's Ecclesiastical History of the English People*. Ed. Bertram Colgrave and R. A. B. Mynors. Oxford: Oxford University Press, 1979.

Bennett, Michael. "John Audley: Some New Evidence on His Life and Work." *Chaucer Review* 16 (1982), 344–55.

——. "John Audelay: Life Records and Heaven's Ladder." In Fein, *My Wyl and My Wrytyng*. Pp. 30–53.

Binski, Paul, and Stella Panayotova, eds. *The Cambridge Illuminations: Ten Centuries of Book Production in the Medieval West*. London: Harvey Miller, 2005.

Blake, N. F., ed. *Middle English Religious Prose*. London: E. Arnold, 1972.

——. "Vernon Manuscript: Contents and Organisation." In *Studies in the Vernon Manuscript*. Ed. Derek Pearsall. Cambridge: D. S. Brewer, 1990. Pp. 45–59.

Blunt, John Henry, ed. *The Myroure of Oure Ladye*. EETS e.s. 19. London: N. Trübner, 1873; rpt. Millwood, NY: Kraus Reprint, 1975.

Boffey, Julia. "Audelay's Carol Collection." In Fein, *My Wyl and My Wrytyng*. Pp. 218–29.

Boffey, Julia, and A. S. G. Edwards. *A New Index of Middle English Verse*. London: British Library, 2005.

Bowers, Robert H. "A Middle English Poem on the Nine Virtues." *Southern Folklore Quarterly* 31 (1967), 37–47.

Bradbury, Nancy Mason. "Rival Wisdom in the Latin *Dialogue of Solomon and Marcolf*." *Speculum* 83 (2008): 331–65.

Brandes, Hermann. "Über die Quellen der mittelenglischen Versionen der Paulus-Vision." *Englische Studien* 7 (1884), 34–65.

Braswell, Laurel. *The Index of Middle English Prose, Handlist IV: A Handlist of Douce Manuscripts Containing Middle English Prose in the Bodleian Library, Oxford*. Cambridge: D. S. Brewer, 1987. Pp. 70–71.

Breul, Karl. "Zwei mittelenglische Christmas Carols." *Englische Studien* 14 (1890), 401–08.

Brook, G. L., ed. *The Harley Lyrics: The Middle English Lyrics of MS. Harley 2253*. Fourth ed. Manchester: Manchester University Press, 1968.

Brown, Carleton. *A Register of Middle English Religious and Didactic Verse*. 2 vols. Oxford: Oxford University Press, 1916, 1920.

———, ed. *English Lyrics of the XIIIth Century*. Oxford: Clarendon Press, 1932.

———, ed. *Religious Lyrics of the XVth Century*. Oxford: Clarendon Press, 1939.

———, ed. *Religious Lyrics of the XIVth Century*. Second ed. rev. G. V. Smithers. Oxford: Clarendon Press, 1957.

Brown, Carleton, and Rossell Hope Robbins. *The Index of Middle English Verse*. New York: Columbia University Press, 1943.

Bühler, Curt F. "A Middle English Prayer Roll." *Modern Language Notes* 52 (1937), 555–62.

Bülbring, K. D. "Handscrift Nr. 491 der Lambeth-Bibliothek." *Archiv für das Studien der neueren Sprachen und Literaturen* 86 (1891), 383–92.

Burrow, John A., ed. "The Poet as Petitioner." In *Essays on Medieval Literature*. Oxford: Clarendon Press, 1986. Pp. 161–76.

Cannon, Christopher. "Monastic Productions." In *The Cambridge History of Medieval English Literature*. Ed. David Wallace. Cambridge: Cambridge University Press, 1999. Pp. 316–48.

Cartlidge, Neil, ed. *The Owl and the Nightingale: Text and Translation*. Exeter: University of Exeter Press, 2001.

Catto, Jeremy. "Religious Change under Henry V." In *Henry V: The Practice of Kingship*. Ed. G. L. Harriss. Oxford: Oxford University Press, 1985. Pp. 97–115.

Chambers, E. K., and F. Sidgwick, eds. *Early English Lyrics: Amorous, Divine, Moral and Trivial*. 1907. Rpt. New York: October House, 1967.

———, eds. "Fifteenth Century Carols by John Audelay." *Modern Language Review* 5 (1910), 473–91.

———, eds. "Fifteenth Century Carols by John Audelay." *Modern Language Review* 6 (1911), 68–84.

Chism, Christine. *Alliterative Revivals*. Philadelphia: University of Pennsylvania Press, 2002.

Citrome, Jeremy J. *The Surgeon in Medieval English Literature*. New York: Palgrave Macmillan, 2006.

Copley, J. "John Audelay's Carols and Music." *English Studies* 39 (1958), 207–12.

———. "A Popular Fifteenth-Century Carol." *Notes and Queries* 204 (1959), 387–89.

Coxe, H. O. *Catalogue of the Printed Books and Manuscripts Bequeathed by Francis Douce, Esq., to the Bodleian Library*. Oxford: Oxford University Press, 1840. Pp. 50–52.

Cumming, William Patterson. *The Revelations of Saint Birgitta*. EETS o.s. 178. London: Oxford University Press, 1928; rpt. Millwood, NY: Kraus Reprint,1971.

Curry, Anne. *Agincourt: A New History*. Stroud: Tempus, 2005.

Daniel, Hermann Adalbert. *Thesaurus Hymnologicus sive Hymnorum Canticorum Sequentiarum Circa Annum MD Usitatarum Collectio Amplissima*. 5 vols. Leipzig: J. T. Loeschke, 1855–56.

Davies, R. T., ed. *Medieval English Lyrics: A Critical Anthology*. London: Faber and Faber, 1963.

Dean, James M., ed. *Richard the Redeless and Mum and the Sothsegger*. Kalamazoo, MI: Medieval Institute Publications, 2000.

Dearmer, Percy, R. Vaughan Williams, and Martin Shaw, eds. *The Oxford Book of Carols*. Second ed. London: Oxford University Press, 1964. [Music edition.]

De Smedt, Charles, ed. "Documenta de S. Wenefreda." *Analecta Bollandiana* 6 (1887): 305–52.

Dickins, Bruce. "The Rhymes in MS. Douce 302, 53 and 54." *Proceedings of the Leeds Philosophical and Literary Society (Literary and Historical Section)* 2 (1932), 516–18.

Dockray, Keith. *Henry V*. Stroud: Tempus Publishing, 2004.

Douteil, Heriberto, ed. *Iohannis Beleth: Summa de ecclesiasticis officiis*. 2 vols. Turnholt: Brepols, 1976.

Doyle, A. I. "The Shaping of the Vernon and Simeon Manuscripts." In *Studies in the Vernon Manuscript*. Ed. Derek Pearsall. Cambridge: D. S. Brewer, 1990. Pp. 1–13.

———. "'Lectulus noster floridus': An Allegory of the Penitent Soul." In *Literature and Religion in the Later Middle Ages: Philological Studies in Honor of Siegfried Wenzel*. Ed. Richard G. Newhauser and John A. Alford. Binghamton, NY: Medieval and Renaissance Texts and Studies, 1994. Pp. 179–90.

Dreves, Guido Maria, and Clemens Blume, eds. *Analecta Hymnica Medii Aevi*. 55 vols. 1886–1922. Rpt. New York: Johnson Reprint, 1961.

Driver, Martha W. "John Audelay and the Bridgettines." In Fein, *My Wyl and My Wrytyng*. Pp. 191–217.

Duffy, Eamon. *The Stripping of the Altars: Traditional Religion in England 1400–1580*. New Haven, CT: Yale University Press, 1992.

———. *Marking the Hours: English People and Their Prayers 1240–1570*. New Haven, CT: Yale University Press, 2006.

Dyboski, Roman, ed. *Songs, Carols, and Other Miscellaneous Poems from the Balliol MS. 354, Richard Hill's Commonplace Book*. EETS e.s. 101. London: Oxford University Press, 1908; rpt. 1937.

Easting, Robert. *Annotated Bibliographies of Old and Middle English: III. Visions of the Other World in Middle English*. Cambridge: D. S. Brewer, 1997.

———. "'Choose yourselves whither to go': John Audelay's *Vision of Saint Paul*." In Fein, *My Wyl and My Wrytyng*. Pp. 170–90.

Edwards, A. S. G. "Fifteenth-Century Middle English Verse Author Collections." In *The English Medieval Book: Studies in Memory of Jeremy Griffiths*. Ed. A. S. G. Edwards, Vincent Gillespie, and Ralph Hanna. London: British Library, 2000. Pp. 101–12.

Elizabethan Singers, The. *Carols of Today*. London: Argo, 1966. [Sound recording]

Ellis, F. S., ed. *The Golden Legend, or, Lives of the Saints as Englished by William Caxton*. 7 vols. London: J. M. Dent, 1900.

Embree, Dan, and Elizabeth Urquhart, eds. *The Simonie: A Parallel-Text Edition Edited from MSS Advocates 19.2.1, Bodley 48, and Peterhouse College 104*. Heidelberg: Carl Winter Universitätsverlag, 1991.

Erbe, Theodor, ed. *Mirk's Festial: A Collection of Homilies by Johannes Mirkus (John Mirk)*. EETS e.s. 96. London: Kegan Paul, Trench, Trübner, 1905; rpt. Millwood, NY: Kraus Reprint, 1975.

Fein, Susanna. "The Middle English Alliterative Tradition of the Allegorical *Chanson d'Aventure*: A Critical Edition of *De tribus regibus mortuis*, *Somer Soneday*, *The Foure Leues of the Trewlufe*, and *Death and Liffe*." Ph.D. diss., Harvard University, 1985.

———. "Form and Continuity in the Alliterative Tradition: Cruciform Design and Double Birth in Two Stanzaic Poems." *Modern Language Quarterly* 53 (1992), 100–25.

———. "A Thirteen-Line Alliterative Stanza on the Abuse of Prayer from the Audelay MS." *Medium Ævum* 63 (1994), 61–74.

———. "Twelve-Line Stanza Forms in Middle English and the Date of *Pearl*." *Speculum* 72 (1997), 367–98.

———, ed. *Moral Love Songs and Laments*. Kalamazoo, MI: Medieval Institute Publications, 1998.

———. "Roll or Codex? The Diptych Layout of Thomas of Hales's 'Love Rune.'" *Trivium* 31 (1999), 13–23.

———. "The Early Thirteen-Line Stanza: Style and Metrics Reconsidered." *Parergon* 18 (2000), 97–126.

———, ed. *Studies in the Harley Manuscript: The Scribes, Contents, and Social Contexts of British Library MS Harley 2253*. Kalamazoo, MI: Medieval Institute Publications, 2000.

———. "Life and Death, Reader and Page: Mirrors of Mortality in English Manuscripts." *Mosaic* 35 (2002), 69–94.

———. "Good Ends in the Audelay Manuscript." *Yearbook of English Studies* 33 (2003), 97–119.

———. "Death and the Colophon in the Audelay Manuscript." In Fein, *My Wyl and My Wrytyng*. Pp. 294–306.

———. "John Audelay and His Book: Critical Overview and Major Issues." In Fein, *My Wyl and My Wrytyng*. Pp. 3–29.

———, ed. *My Wyl and My Wrytyng: Essays on John the Blind Audelay*. Kalamazoo, MI: Medieval Institute Publications, 2009.

Flügel, Ewald. "Liedersammlungen des XVI. Jahrhunderts, Besonders aus der Zeit Heinrichs VIII." *Anglia* 26 (1903), 94–285.

Forrest, Ian. *The Detection of Heresy in Late Medieval England*. Oxford: Clarendon Press, 2005.

Furnivall, F. J., ed. *The Minor Poems of the Vernon MS. Part II.* EETS o.s. 117. London: Kegan Paul, Trench, Trübner, 1901; rpt. Millwood, NY: Kraus Reprint, 1987.

———, ed. *Robert of Brunne's Handlyng Synne.* EETS o.s. 119, 123. London: Kegan Paul, Trench, Trübner, 1901, 1903; rpt. as one vol. Millwood, NY: Kraus Reprint, 1975.

Gardiner, Eileen. *Medieval Visions of Heaven and Hell: A Sourcebook.* New York: Garland, 1993.

Gillespie, Vincent. "Moral and Penitential Lyrics." In *A Companion to the Middle English Lyric.* Ed. Thomas G. Duncan. Cambridge: D. S. Brewer, 2005. Pp. 68–95.

Ginsberg, Warren. *Wynnere and Wastoure and The Parlement of the Thre Ages.* Kalamazoo, MI: Medieval Institute Publications, 1992.

Goldberg, P. J. P. *Medieval England: A Social History 1250–1550.* London: Hodder Arnold, 2004.

Gordon, E. V., ed. *Pearl.* Oxford: Clarendon Press, 1953.

"The Gospel of Nicodemus, or Acts of Pilate." In *The Apocryphal New Testament.* Ed. and trans. Montague Rhodes James. Oxford: Oxford University Press, 1989. Pp. 94–165.

Gray, Douglas. "A Middle English Illustrated Poem." In *Medieval Studies for J. A. W. Bennett.* Ed. P. L. Heyworth. Oxford: Clarendon Press, 1981. Pp. 185–205.

———. "Fifteenth-Century Lyrics and Carols." In *Nation, Court and Culture: New Essays on Fifteenth-Century English Poetry.* Ed. Helen Cooney. Dublin: Four Courts Press, 2001. Pp. 168–83.

Green, Richard Firth. "Marcolf the Fool and Blind John Audelay." In *Speaking Images: Essays in Honor of V. A. Kolve.* Ed. Robert F. Yeager and Charlotte C. Morse. Asheville, NC: Pegasus Press, 2001. Pp. 559–76.

———. "Langland and Audelay." In Fein, *My Wyl and My Wrytyng.* Pp. 153–69.

Greene, Richard Leighton, ed. *A Selection of English Carols.* Oxford: Clarendon Press, 1962.

———, ed. *The Early English Carols.* Second ed. Oxford: Clarendon Press, 1977.

Griffiths, R. A. "The Sense of Dynasty in the Reign of Henry VI." In *Patronage, Pedigree and Power in Later Medieval England.* Ed. Charles Ross. Gloucester: Alan Sutton, 1979. Pp. 13–36.

Haberly, Loyd, ed. *Alia Cantalena de Sancta Maria by John Awdlay.* Long Crendon: The Seven Acres Press, 1926.

Halliwell, James Orchard, ed. *The Poems of John Audelay: A Specimen of the Shropshire Dialect in the Fifteenth Century.* Percy Society 47. London: T. Richards, 1844.

Hanna, Ralph. *Pursuing History: Middle English Manuscripts and Their Texts.* Stanford: Stanford University Press, 1996.

———. "Augustinian Canons and Middle English Literature." In *The English Medieval Book: Studies in Memory of Jeremy Griffiths.* Ed. A. S. G. Edwards, Vincent Gillespie, and Ralph Hanna. London: British Library, 2000. Pp. 27–42.

Heffernan, Thomas J. "Orthodoxies' *Redux*: The *Northern Homily Cycle* in the Vernon Manuscript and Its Textual Affiliations." In *Studies in the Vernon Manuscript.* Ed. Derek Pearsall. Cambridge: D. S. Brewer, 1990. Pp. 75–88.

Henry, Avril. "'The Pater Noster in a table ypeynted' and Some Other Presentations of Doctrine in the Vernon Manuscript." In *Studies in the Vernon Manuscript.* Ed. Derek Pearsall. Cambridge: D. S. Brewer, 1990. Pp. 89–113.

Hirsh, John C. *The Boundaries of Faith: The Development and Transmission of Medieval Spirituality.* Leiden: E. J. Brill, 1996.

———, ed. *Medieval Lyric: Middle English Lyrics, Ballads, and Carols.* Oxford: Blackwell, 2005.

———. "'Wo and werres . . . rest and pese': John Audelay's Politics of Peace." In Fein, *My Wyl and My Wrytyng.* Pp. 230–48.

Hoddinott, Alun. See Audelay.

Hornstein, Lillian Herlands. "*King Robert of Sicily*: Analogues and Origins." *PMLA* 79 (1964), 13–21.

Horstmann, Carl, ed. *The Minor Poems of the Vernon MS. Part I.* EETS o.s. 98. London: Kegan Paul, Trench, Trübner, 1892; rpt. Millwood, NY: Kraus Reprint, 1987.

———, ed. *Yorkshire Writers: Richard Rolle of Hampole and His Followers.* 2 vols. London: Swan Sonnenschein, 1895–96.

Hudson, Anne. *The Premature Reformation: Wycliffite Texts and Lollard Heresy*. Oxford: Clarendon Press, 1988.

———. "The Legacy of *Piers Plowman*." In *A Companion to Piers Plowman*. Ed. John A. Alford. Berkeley: University of California Press, 1988. Pp. 251–66.

Hussey, Maurice. "The Petitions of the Paternoster in Medieval English Literature." *Medium Ævum* 27 (1958), 8–16.

Jacobus de Voragine. *The Golden Legend: Readings on the Saints*. 2 vols. Trans. William Granger Ryan. Princeton, NJ: Princeton University Press, 1993.

Jennings, Margaret. "Tutivillus: the Literary Career of the Recording Demon." *Studies in Philology* 74 (1977), 1–95.

Jones, Melissa. "'Swete May, Soulis Leche': The Winifred Carol of John Audelay." *Essays in Medieval Studies* 14 (1997), 1–7.

Jones, W. R. "The Heavenly Letter in Medieval England." *Medievalia et Humanistica* 6 (1975), 163–78.

Kail, J., ed. *Twenty-Six Political and Other Poems*. EETS o.s. 124. London: Kegan Paul, Trench, Trübner, 1904.

Kaiser, Rolf, ed. *Medieval English: An Old English and Middle English Anthology*. Third ed. Berlin: Markobrunner, 1958.

Kane, George, E. Talbot Donaldson, and George Russell, eds. *Piers Plowman: The Three Versions*. Second ed., rev. George Kane. Berkeley: University of California Press, 1988.

Kennedy, Kathleen E. "Maintaining Love through Accord in the *Tale of Melibee*." *Chaucer Review* 39 (2004), 165–76.

Kennedy, Ruth, ed. *Three Alliterative Saints' Hymns: Late Middle English Stanziac Poems*. EETS o.s. 321. Oxford: Oxford University Press, 2003.

Ker, N. R. *Facsimile of British Museum MS. Harley 2253*. EETS o.s. 255. London: Oxford University Press, 1965.

Kinch, Ashby. "Image, Ideology, and Form: The Middle English *Three Dead Kings* in Its Iconographic Context." *Chaucer Review* 43 (2008): 48–81.

Langland, William. *Piers Plowman: A Parallel-Text Edition of the A, B, C and Z Versions*. Ed. A. V. C. Schmidt. London: Longman, 1995.

Lawton, David A. "The Diversity of Middle English Alliterative Poetry." *Leeds Studies in English* 20 (1989), 143–72.

Lee, Brian S. "'This is no fable': Historical Residues in Two Medieval Exempla." *Speculum* 56 (1981), 728–60.

Lerer, Seth. "Medieval English Literature and the Idea of the Anthology." *PMLA* 118 (2003), 1251–67.

Littlehales, Henry, ed. *The Prymer or Lay Folks' Prayer Book*. EETS o.s. 105, 109. London: Kegan Paul, Trench, Trübner, 1895, 1897; rpt. as one vol., 1975.

———, ed. *English Fragments from Latin Medieval Service-Books*. EETS e.s. 90. London: Kegan Paul, Trench, Trübner, 1903; rpt. 1975.

Lloyd, Richard. "The Fairest Flower: Carol for Unaccompanied Mixed Voices." Hildenborough: Encore Publications, 1995.

MacCracken, Henry Noble, ed. *The Minor Poems of John Lydgate, Part I*. EETS e.s. 107. London: Oxford University Press, 1911; rpt. 1961.

———, ed. *The Minor Poems of John Lydgate, Part II*. EETS o.s. 192. London: Oxford University Press, 1934; rpt. 1961.

Machan, Tim William. *Textual Criticism and Middle English Texts*. Charlottesville: University Press of Virginia, 1994.

Madan, Falconer. *A Summary Catalogue of Western Manuscripts in the Bodleian Library at Oxford*. 7 vols. Oxford, Oxford University Press, 1895. 4:585–86.

Matthews, William. "*bi lag mon*: A Crux in *Sir Gawayn and the Grene Knyȝt*." *Medievalia et Humanistica*, n.s. 6 (1975), 151–55.

McInerney, Maud Burnett. "*In the Meydens Womb*: Julian of Norwich and the Poetics of Enclosure." In *Medieval Mothering*. Ed. John Carmi Parsons and Bonnie Wheeler. New York: Garland, 1996. Pp. 157–82.

McIntosh, Angus. "Some Notes on the Text of the Middle English Poem *De tribus regibus mortuis*." *RES*, n.s. 28 (1977), 385–92.

McKenna, J. W. "Henry VI of England and the Dual Monarchy: Aspects of Royal Political Propaganda, 1422–1432." *Journal of the Warburg and Courtauld Institutes* 28 (1965), 145–62.

Menner, Robert J. "Middle English 'Lagmon' (*Gawain* 1729) and Modern English 'Lag.'" *Philological Quarterly* 10 (1931), 163–68.

Meyer-Lee, Robert J. "The Vatic Penitent: John Audelay's Self-Representation." In Fein, *My Wyl and My Wrytyng*. Pp. 54–85.

Migne, J.-P., ed. *Patrologiae cursos completus . . . series latina*. Paris, 1844–64.

Minnis, A. J. *Medieval Theory of Authorship: Scholastic Literary Attitudes in the Later Middle Ages*. Philadelphia: University of Pennsylvania, 1988.

Mone, Franz Joseph, ed. *Lateinische Hymnen des Mittelalters*. 3 vols. 1853–55. Rpt. Aalen: Scientia Verlag, 1964.

Mooney, Linne R. "Chaucer's Scribe." *Speculum* 81 (2006), 97–138.

Morris, Bridget. *St Birgitta of Sweden*. Woodbridge: Boydell Press, 1999.

Morris, Richard, ed. *An Old English Miscellany*. EETS o.s. 49. London: N. Trübner, 1872; rpt. London: Oxford University Press, 1969.

———, ed. *Legends of the Holy Rood; Symbols of the Passion and Cross-Poems*. EETS o.s. 46. London: N. Trübner, 1881; rpt. New York: Greenwood Press, 1969.

Mum and the Sothsegger. See Dean.

New York Pro Musica Antiqua. *English Medieval Carols and Christmas Music*. Los Angeles: Everest Records, 1978. [Sound recording on 12–inch disc.]

Nichols, Ann Eljenholm. "'O Vernicle': Illustrations of an Arma Christi Poem." In *Tributes to Kathleen L. Scott: English Medieval Manuscripts and Their Readers*. Ed. Marlene Villalobos Hennessy. Turnhout: Harvey Miller/Brepols, 2009.

Nichols, Stephen G., and Siegfried Wenzel, eds. *The Whole Book: Cultural Perspectives on the Medieval Miscellany*. Ann Arbor: University of Michigan Press, 1996.

Nixon, Virginia. *Mary's Mother: Saint Anne in Late Medieval Europe*. University Park: Pennsylvania State University Press, 2004.

Ogilvie–Thomson, S. J., ed. *Richard Rolle: Prose and Verse, Edited from MS Longleat 29 and Related Manuscripts*. EETS o.s. 293. Oxford: Oxford University Press, 1988.

Oldroyd, George. "The Flower of Jesse: A Carol Set for Unaccompanied Singing." London: Oxford University Press, 1948.

Olson, Glending. "Author, Scribe, and Curse: The Genre of *Adam Scriveyn*." *Chaucer Review* 42 (2008): 283–97.

O'Mara, V. M., ed. *A Study and Edition of Selected Middle English Sermons*. Leeds: University of Leeds, 1994.

Oosterwijk, Sophie. "'Long lullynge haue I lorn!': The Massacre of the Innocents in Word and Image." *Medieval English Theatre* 25 (2003): 3–53.

———. "Of Corpses, Constables and Kings: The *Dance Macabre* in Late Medieval and Renaissance Culture." *Journal of the British Archaeological Association* 157 (2004): 61–90.

Oxford Camerata. *Medieval Carols*. Jeremy Summerly. NAXOS 8.550751. [Sound recording]

Pantin, W. A. "Instruction for a Devout and Literate Layman." In *Medieval Learning and Literature: Essays Presented to Richard William Hunt*. Ed. J. J. G. Alexander and M. T. Gibson. Oxford: Clarendon Press, 1976. Pp. 398–422.

Parker, Roscoe E., ed. *The Middle English Stanzaic Versions of the Life of Saint Anne*. EETS o.s. 174. London: Oxford University Press, 1928; rpt. Millford, NY: Kraus Reprint, 1971.

Patterson, Frank Allen, ed. *The Middle English Penitential Lyric*. New York: Columbia University Press, 1911; rpt. New York: AMS, 1966.

Peacock, Edward, ed. *Instructions for Parish Priests by John Myrc*. EETS o.s. 31. London: Kegan Paul, Trench, Trübner, 1902; rpt. New York: Greenwood Press, 1969.

Pearsall, Derek. *Old English and Middle English Poetry*. London: Routledge, 1977.

———. "Audelay's *Marcolf and Solomon* and the Langlandian Tradition." In Fein, *My Wyl and My Wrytyng*. Pp. 138–52.

Perman, R. C. D. "Henri d'Arci: The Shorter Works." In *Studies in Medieval French Presented to Alfred Ewert in Honour of His Seventieth Birthday*. Ed. E. A. Francis. Oxford: Clarendon Press, 1961. Pp. 279–321.

Person, Henry A., ed. *Cambridge Middle English Lyrics*. Second ed. Seattle: University of Washington Press, 1962.

Pickering, Oliver. "The Make-Up of John Audelay's *Counsel of Conscience*." In Fein, *My Wyl and My Wrytyng*. Pp. 112–37.

Pollard, A. J. *Late Medieval England 1399–1509*. Harlow: Longman, 2000.

Powell, Susan. "John Audelay and John Mirk: Comparisons and Contrasts." In Fein, *My Wyl and My Wrytyng*. Pp. 86–111.

Priebsch, R. "John Audelay's Poem on the Observance of Sunday and Its Source." In *An English Miscellany Presented to Dr. Furnivall in Honour of His Seventy-Fifth Birthday*. Ed. W. P. Ker, A. S. Napier, and W. W. Skeat. 1901. Rpt. New York: Benjamin Blom, 1969. Pp. 397–407.

Putter, Ad. "The Language and Metre of *Pater Noster* and *Three Dead Kings*." *Review of English Studies*, n.s. 55 (2004), 498–526.

Raby, F. J. E. *A History of Christian-Latin Poetry from the Beginnings to the Close of the Middle Ages*. Second ed. Oxford: Clarendon Press, 1953.

———, ed. *The Oxford Book of Medieval Latin Verse*. Oxford: Clarendon Press, 1959; rpt. 1970.

Rasmussen, J. K. *Die Sprache John Audelay's (Laut- und Flexionslehre)*. Bonn: C. Geordi, 1914.

Reames, Sherry. "Liturgical Offices for the Cult of St. Thomas Becket." In *Medieval Hagiography: An Anthology*. Ed. Thomas Head. New York: Routledge, 2001. Pp. 561–93.

Reichl, Karl. "The Middle English Carol." In *A Companion to the Middle English Lyric*. Ed. Thomas G. Duncan. Cambridge: D. S. Brewer, 2005. Pp. 150–70.

Richmond, Colin. "Religion." In *Fifteenth-Century Attitudes: Perceptions of Society in Late Medieval England*. Ed. Rosemary Horrox. Cambridge: Cambridge University Press, 1994. Pp. 183–201.

Rickert, Edith, ed. *Ancient English Christmas Carols 1400–1700*. New York: Duffield, 1915.

Rigg, A. G. *A History of Anglo-Latin Literature 1066–1422*. Cambridge: Cambridge University Press, 1992.

Robbins, Rossell Hope. "The 'Arma Christi' Rolls." *Modern Language Review* 34 (1939), 415–21.

———. "Levation Prayers in Middle English Verse." *Modern Philology* 40 (1942), 131–46.

———, ed. *Historical Poems of the XIVth and XVth Centuries*. New York: Columbia University Press, 1959.

Robbins, Rossell Hope, and John L. Cutler. *Supplement to the Index of Middle English Verse*. Lexington: University of Kentucky Press, 1955.

Robert, Prior of Shrewsbury. *The Admirable Life of Saint Wenefride: 1635*. Trans. I. F. of the Society of Jesus. Ed. D. M. Rogers. London: Scholar Press, 1976.

Ronan, Myles V. *S. Anne: Her Cult and Her Shrines*. London: Sands & Co., 1927.

Rubin, Miri. *Corpus Christi: The Eucharist in Late Medieval Culture*. Cambridge: Cambridge University Press, 1991.

Rutter, John. "There is a Flower." Oxford: Oxford University Press, 1986.

Salter, Elizabeth. *Fourteenth-Century English Poetry: Contexts and Readings*. Oxford: Clarendon Press, 1983.

Sandison, Helen Estabrook. *The "Chanson d'Aventure" in Middle English*. Bryn Mawr, PA: Bryn Mawr College, 1913.

Sandys, William. *Christmastide: Its History, Festivities and Carols*. London: John Russell Smith, 1852.

Saupe, Karen, ed. *Middle English Marian Lyrics*. Kalamazoo, MI: Medieval Institute Publications, 1998.

Sautman, Francesca. "Saint Anne in Folk Tradition: Late Medieval France." In *Interpreting Cultural Symbols: Saint Anne in Late Medieval Society*. Ed. Kathleen Ashley and Pamela Sheingorn. Athens: University of Georgia Press, 1990. Pp. 69–94.

Schaff, David S. *The Middle Ages from Gregory VII, 1049, to Boniface VIII, 1294.* History of the Christian Church, V. Gen. ed. Philip Schaff. 1907. Rpt. Grand Rapids, MI: Wm. B. Eerdmans, 1960.

Scott, Kathleen L. *Later Gothic Manuscripts 1390–1490.* 2 vols. London: Harvey Miller, 1996.

Severs, J. Burke, Albert E. Hartung, and Peter G. Beidler, eds. *A Manual of the Writings in Middle English, 1050–1500.* 11 vols. New Haven, CT: Connecticut Academy of Arts and Sciences, 1967–2005.

Sheingorn, Pamela. "Appropriating the Holy Kinship: Gender and Family History." In *Interpreting Cultural Symbols: Saint Anne in Late Medieval Society.* Ed. Kathleen Ashley and Pamela Sheingorn. Athens: University of Georgia Press, 1990. Pp. 169–98.

Shinners, John, and William J. Dohar, eds. *Pastors and the Care of Souls in Medieval England.* Notre Dame, IN: University of Notre Dame Press, 1998.

Silverstein, Theodore. *Visio Sancti Pauli: The History of the Apocalypse in Latin Together with Nine Texts.* London: Christophers, 1935.

——, ed. *English Lyrics before 1500.* Evanston, IL: Northwestern University Press, 1971.

Simmons, Thomas Frederick, ed. *The Lay Folks Mass Book or the Manner of Hearing Mass.* EETS o.s. 71. London: Oxford University Press, 1879; rpt. 1968.

The Simonie. See Embree and Urquhart.

Simpson, James. "Saving Satire after Arundel's *Constitutions*: John Audelay's 'Marcol and Solomon.'" In *Text and Controversy from Wyclif to Bale: Essays in Honour of Anne Hudson.* Ed. Helen Barr and Ann M. Hutchinson. Turnhout: Brepols, 2005. Pp. 387–404.

Sisam, Celia, and Kenneth [Sisam], eds. *The Oxford Book of Medieval English Verse.* Oxford: Clarendon Press, 1970.

Sitwell, Edith, ed. *The Atlantic Book of British and American Poetry.* Boston: Little, Brown, 1958.

Stanley, Eric. "*The True Counsel of Conscience* or *The Ladder of Heaven*: In Defense of John Audelay's Unlyrical Lyrics." In *Expedition nach der Wahrheit: Poems, Essays, and Papers in Honour of Theo Stemmler.* Ed. Stefan Horlacher and Marion Islinger. Heidelberg: Winter, 1996. Pp. 131–59.

——. "The Verse Forms of Jon the Blynde Awdelay." In *The Long Fifteenth Century.* Ed. Helen Cooper and Sally Mapstone. Oxford: Clarendon Press, 1997. Pp. 99–121.

——. "The Alliterative *Three Dead Kings* in John Audelay's MS Douce 302." In Fein, *My Wyl and My Wrytyng.* Pp. 249–93.

Stevens, John. "*Angelus ad virginem*: The History of a Medieval Song." In *Medieval Studies for J. A. W. Bennett.* Ed. P. L. Heyworth. Oxford: Clarendon Press, 1981. Pp. 297–328.

——, ed. *Mediaeval Carols.* Second ed. London: Stainer and Bell, 1970.

——. *Music and Poetry in the Early Tudor Court.* London: Methuen, 1961.

Storck, Willy F. "Aspects of Life and Death in English Art and Poetry I." *Burlington Magazine* 21 (1912), 249–56.

——, "Aspects of Life and Death in English Art and Poetry II: Catalogue Raisonné of Representations." *Burlington Magazine* 21 (1912), 314–19.

Storck, Willy F., and Richard Jordan, eds. "John Awdelays Gedicht 'De tribus regibus mortuis': Eine englische Fassung der Legende von den drei Lebenden und den drei Toten." *Englische Studien* 43 (1910–11), 177–88.

Taylor, Andrew. "The Myth of the Minstrel Manuscript." *Speculum* 66 (1991), 43–73.

Trench, Richard Chenevix, ed. *Sacred Latin Poetry, Chiefly Lyrical, Selected and Arrayed for Use.* Third ed. London: Kegan Paul, Trench, 1886.

Tristram, Philippa. *Figures of Life and Death in Medieval English Literature.* New York: New York University Press, 1976.

Turville-Petre, Thorlac. "'Summer Sunday,' 'De tribus regibus mortuis,' and 'The Awntyrs off Arthure': Three Poems in the Thirteen-Line Stanza." *Review of English Studies*, n.s. 25 (1974), 1–14.

——, ed. *Alliterative Poetry of the Later Middle Ages: An Anthology.* Washington, D.C.: The Catholic University of America Press, 1989.

Van Buren, J. H., trans. *Latin Hymns in English Verse.* Boston: Old Corner Book Store, 1904.

Walpole, A. S., ed. *Early Latin Hymns.* 1922. Rpt. Hildesheim: Georg Olms, 1966.

Warren, Nancy Bradley. *Spiritual Economies: Female Monasticism in Later Medieval England*. Philadelphia: University of Pennsylvania Press, 2001.

Watson, Arthur. *The Early Iconography of the Tree of Jesse*. London: Oxford University Press, 1934.

Wawn, Andrew. "Truth-Telling and the Tradition of *Mum and the Sothsegger*." *Yearbook of English Studies* 13 (1983), 270–87.

Weatherly, Edward H., ed. *Speculum Sacerdotale*. EETS o.s. 200. London: Oxford University Press, 1936.

Wenzel, Siegfried. *Latin Sermon Collections from Later Medieval England: Orthodox Preaching in the Age of Wyclif*. Cambridge: Cambridge University Press, 2005.

Whiting, Bartlett Jere, with the collaboration of Helen Wescott Whiting. *Proverbs, Sentences, and Proverbial Phrases from English Writings Mainly before 1500*. Cambridge, MA: The Belknap Press of Harvard University Press, 1968.

Whiting, Ella Keats, ed. *The Poems of John Audelay*. EETS o.s. 184. London: Oxford University Press, 1931; rpt. Millwood, NY: Kraus Reprint, 1971.

Williams, E. Carleton. "Mural Wall Paintings of the Three Living and the Three Dead in England." *Journal of the British Archaeological Association*, Third ser., 7 (1942), 31–40.

Wolffe, Bertram. *Henry VI*. London: Eyre Methuen, 1981. Rpt. New Haven, CT: Yale University Press, 2001.

Woolf, Rosemary. *The English Religious Lyric in the Middle Ages*. Oxford: Clarendon Press, 1968.

Wright, Thomas, ed. *The Latin Poems Commonly Attributed to Walter Mapes*. Camden Society 16. London: Printed for the Camden Society by J. B. Nichols and Son, 1841; rpt. New York: AMS, 1968.

———, ed. *The Book of the Knight of La Tour-Landry*. EETS o.s. 33. Second ed. London: Kegan Paul, Trench, Trübner, 1906; rpt. New York: Greenwood Press, 1963.

Wright, Thomas, and James Orchard Halliwell, eds. *Reliquiae Antiquae*. 2 vols. London: William Pickering, 1841, 1843.

Wülfing, J. Ernst. "Der Dichter John Audelay und Sein Werk." *Anglia* 18 (1896), 173–217.

GLOSSARY

abstenans *abstinence*
acorde *agree*
adevyd *deafened*
advarceté *adversity*
aga *gone*
aleans *strangers*
altherbest *best of all*
amende *amend*
amenduth *correcting*
amyr *hammer*
angur *anger*
apostasey *apostasy, renunciation of faith*
aray *adorn*
arteklus *articles*
ascentyng *assenting*
aschelere *ashlar*
asyoyle *absolve*; **asoylis** *absolves*
atheamond *adamant, diamond*
avowe *oath*
avowtere, avowtre *adultery*
ayrus *heirs*
aysel *vinegar*

bakbyte *gossip, slander*; **backbytyng** *gossiping*
bale *misery, sorrow*
barne *child*
barownce *barons*
Bayard *proverbial blind horse*
bec *nod*
bedis, beedis *prayers*
bekynyng *beginning*
belde *encourage*
beleve *faith*
benyngneté *mildness*
berdis *women*
besenes *busyness*

bewe *turn away*
blongis, blonkis *horses*
blynd *blind*
bofet *buffet*
bolstyr *bolster*
bordyd *boarded*
boron *born*
borth *birth*
boure *bower*
brange *branch*
brayne panne *skull*
breder *brother*
breme *clearly*
brewyn *brewed*
brymluche *ferocious*
buxumnes *obedience*
byd *ask*
byrchyn *birch*

canves *canvas*
caral *carol*
Carnacione *Incarnation [of Christ]*
cetis *cities*
cewre *cure*
chaft *shaft*
chalouyd *hallowed*
chamyd *shamed*
charbokil *carbuncle*
charnel *burial place*
chast *chaste*
chauntre *chantry*
chent *ruined, shamed*
chepardis *shepherds*
cherche *church*
chere *composure*
chist *trouble, care*
chornay *journey*

chryve *shrive*
chylde *child*
clannes *cleanness*
clanse *cleanse*
cnow *know*
Comor *Gomorrah*
conseles *counsels*
consians *conscience*
conyng *wisdom*
conyngere *more skillful*
corage *spirit, courage*
cornelnes *corners*
corns *grains*
cos *kiss*
couard *coward*
coubabil *culpable*
couchid *placed*
covent *convent*
covetyse *avarice*
coyntons *acquaintance*
crace *grace*
croyse *cross*
curtyns *curtains*
cysse *kiss*
cyst *bodily chest*

dampnacion *damnation*
dampnen *accuse, judge*; **dampnyd** *accused, judged*
dedys *deeds*
deeff *deaf*
defowled *polluted*
degré *position, social place*
delytis *pleasures*
derkens *darkness*
derlyng *darling*
deseredyn *disinherited*
dettyrs *debtors*
deute *doubt*
deynteth *think*
deystere *daystar*
disparage *misallied in rank*
doloure *sadness*
dome *doom*
domysman *judges*
doole *portion*
dowbyl *double*

dred *awe*
dyngneté *reverence*
dyssayte *deceit*
dyssere *disturb*

efft *again*
ego *having gone*
ehandild *having handled*
elevyde *left*
elore *lost*
elyche fre *equally free*
ene *eyes*
enjoynde *bid to do*
enmys *enemies*
ensampil *example*
enterele *thorough*
eor *their*
eretyk *heretic*; **ertekes** *heretics*
even *fellow*
everechon *everyone*
ewol *evil*
ewroght *having misdone*
exityng *inciting*
extorcioners *extortionists*
eyrus *heirs*

Fader *father*
fadis *fades*
faunt *infant*
favele *duplicity*
faylis *fails*
fedist *feel*
ferford *complete*
fersly *fiercely*
ffynyng *feigning*
fleschele *fleshly*; **fleschele afexion** *carnal affection*
floure *flower*
fnyrtyd *snorted*
fold *old*
folis *fool's*
foluyn *follow*
fonston, fontston *baptismal font*
forehete *contracted*
foresweryng *oath-breaking*
forlorne *utterly lost*
fray *kill*

frere *friar*
froyndes *friends*
froyt, fruyte *fruit*
fuyrus *fires*
Fynd *Fiend*

gal *gall*
garbunkul *carbuncle*
Gason *Gaza*
gefyng *giving*
gentoreo *centurion*
gentyl *noble (kin)*
glosyng *critiquing*
glyde *glide*
Goddis *God's*
gomys *men*
gostlé *spiritual*
graff *graft*
grayns *tines*
grayth *ready*
graythlé *promptly*
gre *shudder*
grevysly *grievously*
grouned *crowned*
grow025 grownder *basis*
gyrdis *dashes, throws*
gyse *fashion*

haloue *hallow*; **halouyd** *hallowed*
halowyd *hallooed*
halud *dragged*
happe *chance*
harde *bold*
harouyd *harrowed*
hede *heed*
hee *eye*
heerus *hair*
helde *age*; (v.) *fall*
henmest *hindmost*
hent *seized*
herber, herbere *shelter*
heredon *praised*
hestis *commandments*
hethynese *heathens*
hevenes *distress, heavyness*
hew *ruckus*
hokys *hooks*

hold *old; considered*
holdyn *beholden*
holear *holier*
holeday *holy day*
holtis *woods*
hongyng *hanging*
hontis *hunters*
hordent *ordained*
hosbondusmen *husbandmen, farmers*
how *ought*
howndys *hounds*
huyrus *payments*
hwat *what*
hwosoever *whosoever*

in fere *together*
infyrmety *infirmity*

kamel *camel*
karalys *carols*
kerke *kirk, church*
keverlet *coverlet*
knoulache *knowledge*
knyl *knell*
knyle *kneel*
kovenande *covenant, employment*
kowth *could*
kutt *cut*
kynd *nature*
kyndlé *natural*
kyth *people*

lasse *less*
laudabeleté *praiseworthiness*
layte, leytis *lightening*
leef *leaf*
leeve *permission*
lefe *not do*
leggys *legs*
lele *lily*
lenage *lineage*
lene *loan, lend*
leud *lewd, unlearned*
Loller *Lollard*; **Lollere** *Lollardry*
lorn *lost*
loveday *day for settling differences*
lust *desire*

lyght *alight*
lyghtyng *shining*
lykyng *pleasure*
lymes *limbs*
lyng *dwell*
lyp *lip*
lytter *resting place*
lyve *life*
lyver *liver*

males *malice*
mare *ruin*
mareache *marriage*
mared *married*
matres *mattress*
may, maydyn *maiden or virgin*
maydehood *maidenhood, virginity*
maydhed *maidenhead*
maydyn *maiden or virgin*
mede *reward, benefit*
medycacionce *meditation*
mekeness *humility*
mendist *mentioned*
merakil *miracle*; **meraclys** *miracles*
mercé *mercy*
merour, myrrore *mirror*
merth, murth, myrth *mirth*
merwesly *miraculously*
mesache *message*
metlé *suitable*
mochil *much*
moder *mother*
mold *earth*
monheed *manhead*
monkynd *mankind*
monslers *manslayers*
mon soul *man's soul*
morotyde *morning*
morthis *deadly sins*
mowys *makes mockery*
mynster *minister*
myschifusly *miserably*
mysdede *misdeed*; **mysdedus** *misdeeds*

napwile *timespan of a nap*
naylus, naylys *nails*
neclegens *negligence*

nemne *name*
nether *lower*
noght *not*
noryschid *nourished*
noy *annoyance*
nyd *troubled*

obisions *perversions*
obstenacion *obstinance*
odur *other*
ofsyth *often*
ofyse *office*
one *any*
orebbil, orebil *horrible*
othis *oaths*
ottrache *outrage*
ouse *us*
over *upper (bedding)*
owtlary *outlawry, outside God's law*

paciens *patience*
paramowrs *illicit lovers*
paraventur *perchance*
parceverens *perseverance*
parchemen *parchment*
parel *peril*
patrearkis *patriarchs*
peleus *pillows*
pepul *people*
perre *jewel*
pese *peace*
pesis *pieces*
peté, pité *compassion*
pistil *epistle*
polyschyng *rhetorical polishing*
postillis *apostles*
pouder *sprinkle*
pousté *power*
poverté *poverty*
presun *prison*
preynt *print, impression, stigmata*
pris *supreme*
prophete *profit*
pylous *pillows*
pyne *pain*

quene *queen*
quyte *white*

rabul *mutter*
radlé *quickly, promptly*
rakkis *paths*
rase *tear*
raveners *robbers*
ravyn *ravine*
rayse *arouse*
rebé *ruby*
receyve *accept*
reches *wealth*
recheth *care*
rede *read*
redel *curtain*
renegatis *renegades*
reprevyn *reprove*
reverens *reverence*
rewere *dispenser of mercy*
rewful *pitiful*
rewme *realm*
rewth *compassion*
rob *plunder*
robbid *robbed*
rode, rod *cross*
rod-tre *cross*
rogud *pulled*
rosis *roses*
rou *peace, repose*
rowys *rays*
rug *pull*
ryful *riffle*
ryghtwysnes *righteousness*
ryn *run*
rynkkys *men, warriors*
rysere *richer*

sacrelege *sacrilege*
sacreyng *consecration*
salghe *willow*
Satanas *Satan*
sauter *psalter*
saw *proverb, saying*
schakeforke *forked instrument for beating out dust*
schambyr *chamber*

schawnd *slander*
schend *destroyed*
schid *shed*
schorne *shorn, tonsured*
schreud *wicked*
schryft *confession*
schryve *confess*
scorgis *scourges*
se *throne*
secud *sighed*
secur *assured*
sees *cease*
segge *man*
seke *sick*
sekyr *decisive, steadfast*
sekyrlé *certainly*
selcouth *wonder*
selens *silence*
selid *sealed*
seloure *canopy*
selquoth *strangest*
selys *seals*
sene *seen*
sesud *ended*
silour *shelter*
sleghtys *sleights*
smetyn *fastened*
smote *struck*
sodom *sodomy*
soferens *sovereigns, betters*
soferest *suffered*
sokyr *succor*
song *tale, story*
soreue *sorrow, contrition*
sorous *sorrows*
soteltys *subtleties*
soth *truth*
sowke *suck, nurse*
soyle *absolve*
sparpild *spattered*
speke way-wordys *chatter*
spillid *killed*
stede *place*
stekyng *protruding*
steven *voice*
stoned *astonished*
stont *stupefied*

store *wealth*
strakid *flowed*
straue, stre *straw*
stryvyng *arguing*
styedust *ascended*
stynche *stench*
sudoré *sudary, sweat-cloth, shroud*
suffyrde *suffered*
sun *son*
suspessions *suspicions*
swerd *sword, war*
swolewd *swallowed*
symony *simony, ecclesiastical bribery*
synglere *selfish*
syngnys *signs*
synnes *sins*

tabernakil, tabirnakil *tabernacle*
talis *tales*
temperans *temperance*
tene *physical suffering*
terantis *tyrants*
terris, terys *tears*
testur *tester*
tethis *tithes*
teyd *tied*
thorlet *pierced*
thretyng *threatening*
throbyt *quivered*
throw *an instant; writhed*
tounus *towns*
traytre *treason*
tren *trees*
trouth *truth*
tryffylyng *trifling*
turment *bring to ruin, oppress*
turne *convert*
twyght *torn*
twyne *twine*
twynkelyng *twinkling*
tythyngis *tidings*

unbuxumnes *disobedience*
unconabil *excessive*
underde *hundred*
undevocion *impiety*
undurmarke *hidden mark*

unkonyng *ignorant*
unkynde *discourteous*
unstabilnes *instability*
untholomodnes *intolerance of adversity*
useuré *usury*
usschere *usher*

vanyshe *vanish*
vayle *veil*
veker *vicar*
verament *truly*
veray *true*
vergyn *virgin*
vesid *visit*
veyn *vain*
veynglory *vainglory*
virteuys *virtues*
voys *voice*

wallon *swarm*
waltyn *chose*
warlaws *demons, scoundrels*
warlouys *fiendish*
wasche *wash*
wastus *wastes*
wede *shroud*
wedow *widow*
wend *go*
wene *doubt*
wercheng *making*
wesitacion *visitation*
wetyngle *knowingly*
wike *week*
wodis *woods*
wold *old*
wome *stomach, bowels*
wondon *wrapped*
worchip, worchyp *worship, honor*
wordelé *worldly*
wordis catel *worldly possession*
word vanetes *worldly vanities*
worthelokyst *most esteemed*
woundis *wounds*
wrase *tie band*
wrath *anger*
wychestonyng *resisting*
wyfis *women*

wyghtis wayus *devilish ways*
wynd *depart*
wyndon *writhe*
wyse *way*
wyt *wit, wisdom*
wyttenes *witness*

Y *I*
yclunggun *withered*

ydyght *ordained*
yevyn *given*
yildyng *yielding*
yod *swam*
yong *young*
ypocrecé *hypocrisy*
ypurchest *purchased*

William Dunbar, *The Complete Works*, edited by John Conlee (2004)

Chaucerian Dream Visions and Complaints, edited by Dana M. Symons (2004)

Stanzaic Guy of Warwick, edited by Alison Wiggins (2004)

Saints' Lives in Middle English Collections, edited by E. Gordon Whatley, with Anne B. Thompson and Robert K. Upchurch (2004)

Siege of Jerusalem, edited by Michael Livingston (2004)

The Kingis Quair and Other Prison Poems, edited by Linne R. Mooney and Mary-Jo Arn (2005)

The Chaucerian Apocrypha: A Selection, edited by Kathleen Forni (2005)

John Gower, *The Minor Latin Works*, edited and translated by R. F. Yeager, with *In Praise of Peace*, edited by Michael Livingston (2005)

Sentimental and Humorous Romances: Floris and Blancheflour, Sir Degrevant, The Squire of Low Degree, The Tournament of Tottenham, and The Feast of Tottenham, edited by Erik Kooper (2006)

The Dicts and Sayings of the Philosophers, edited by John William Sutton (2006)

"Everyman" and Its Dutch Original, "Elckerlijc," edited by Clifford Davidson, Martin W. Walsh, and Ton J. Broos (2007)

The N-Town Plays, edited by Douglas Sugano, with assistance by Victor I. Scherb (2007)

The Book of John Mandeville, edited by Tamarah Kohanski and C. David Benson (2007)

John Lydgate, *The Temple of Glas*, edited by J. Allan Mitchell (2007)

The Northern Homily Cycle, edited by Anne B. Thompson (2008)

Codex Ashmole 61: A Compilation of Popular Middle English Verse, edited by George Shuffelton (2008)

Chaucer and the Poems of "Ch", edited by James I. Wimsatt (revised edition 2009)

William Caxton, *The Game and Playe of the Chesse*, edited by Jenny Adams (2009)

🍂 COMMENTARY SERIES

Haimo of Auxerre, *Commentary on the Book of Jonah*, translated with an introduction and notes by Deborah Everhart (1993)

Medieval Exegesis in Translation: Commentaries on the Book of Ruth, translated with an introduction and notes by Lesley Smith (1996)

Nicholas of Lyra's Apocalypse Commentary, translated with an introduction and notes by Philip D. W. Krey (1997)

Rabbi Ezra Ben Solomon of Gerona, *Commentary on the Song of Songs and Other Kabbalistic Commentaries*, selected, translated, and annotated by Seth Brody (1999)

John Wyclif, *On the Truth of Holy Scripture*, translated with an introduction and notes by Ian Christopher Levy (2001)

Second Thessalonians: Two Early Medieval Apocalyptic Commentaries, introduced and translated by Steven R. Cartwright and Kevin L. Hughes (2001)

The "Glossa Ordinaria" on the Song of Songs, translated with an introduction and notes by Mary Dove (2004)

🍂 DOCUMENTS OF PRACTICE SERIES

Love and Marriage in Late Medieval London, selected, translated, and introduced by Shannon McSheffrey (1995)

Sources for the History of Medicine in Late Medieval England, selected, introduced, and translated by Carole Rawcliffe (1995)

A Slice of Life: Selected Documents of Medieval English Peasant Experience, edited, translated, and with an introduction by Edwin Brezette DeWindt (1996)

Regular Life: Monastic, Canonical, and Mendicant "Rules," selected and introduced by Douglas J. McMillan and Kathryn Smith Fladenmuller (1997); second edition, selected and introduced by Daniel Marcel La Corte and Douglas J. McMillan (2004)

Women and Monasticism in Medieval Europe: Sisters and Patrons of the Cistercian Reform, selected, translated, and with an introduction by Constance H. Berman (2002)

Medieval Notaries and Their Acts: The 1327–1328 Register of Jean Holanie, introduced, edited, and translated by Kathryn L. Reyerson and Debra A. Salata (2004)

MEDIEVAL GERMAN TEXTS IN BILINGUAL EDITIONS SERIES

Sovereignty and Salvation in the Vernacular, 1050–1150, introduction, translations, and notes by James A. Schultz (2000)

Ava's New Testament Narratives: "When the Old Law Passed Away," introduction, translation, and notes by James A. Rushing, Jr. (2003)

History as Literature: German World Chronicles of the Thirteenth Century in Verse, introduction, translation, and notes by R. Graeme Dunphy (2003)

VARIA

The Study of Chivalry: Resources and Approaches, edited by Howell Chickering and Thomas H. Seiler (1988)

Studies in the Harley Manuscript: The Scribes, Contents, and Social Contexts of British Library MS Harley 2253, edited by Susanna Fein (2000)

The Liturgy of the Medieval Church, edited by Thomas J. Heffernan and E. Ann Matter (2001; second edition 2005)

TO ORDER PLEASE CONTACT:

Medieval Institute Publications
Western Michigan University
Kalamazoo, MI 49008-5432
Phone (269) 387-8755
FAX (269) 387-8750
http://www.wmich.edu/medieval/mip/index.html

Typeset in 10/13 New Baskerville
and Golden Cockerel Ornaments display
Designed by Linda K. Judy
Manufactured by McNaughton & Gunn, Inc.

Medieval Institute Publications
College of Arts and Sciences
Western Michigan University
1903 W. Michigan Avenue
Kalamazoo, MI 49008-5432
http://www.wmich.edu/medieval/mip

 WESTERN MICHIGAN UNIVERSITY